D0217922

CLOVIS CACHES

CLOVIS CACHES

RECENT DISCOVERIES & NEW RESEARCH

Edited by **BRUCE B. HUCKELL** and **J. DAVID KILBY**

UNIVERSITY OF NEW MEXICO PRESS ≈ ALBUQUERQUE

Printed in the United States of America
19 18 17 16 15 14 1 2 3 4 5 6

Library of Congress Cataloging-in-Publication Data

Clovis caches : recent discoveries and new research / edited by Bruce B. Huckell and J. David Kilby.
pages cm
Includes bibliographical references and index.
ISBN 978-0-8263-5482-2 (cloth : alk. paper) — ISBN 978-0-8263-5483-9 (electronic)
1. Clovis points—West (U.S.) 2. Clovis culture—West (U.S.) 3. Paleo-Indians—West (U.S.)—Antiquities. 4. Tools, Prehistoric—West (U.S.) 5. Antiquities, Prehistoric—West (U.S.) 6. West (U.S.)—Antiquities. I. Huckell, Bruce B., editor, author. II. Kilby, J. David. (James David), editor, author.
E99.C832C59 2014
978'.01—dc23
2013045093

JACKET COVER PHOTOGRAPHS: Courtesy of the collections of Bruce B. Huckell and J. David Kilby
BOOK DESIGN: Catherine Leonardo
Composed in 10.25/13.5 Minion Pro Regular
Display type is Vendetta Medium and Cronos Pro

Contents

≈

Illustrations

FIGURES

TABLES

Chapter 1

Clovis Caches

DISCOVERIES, IDENTIFICATION, LITHIC TECHNOLOGY, AND LAND USE

Bruce B. Huckell and J. David Kilby

≈

A man walks into your office with a box of flaked stone artifacts under his arm; as he unpacks them and spreads them out across your desk, he says that he found them all together 30 years ago, eroding out of a plowed field. That field, he mentions, is within an area of rolling prairie, not near any obvious landmarks. There are two dozen artifacts—none are finished projectile points. Half of them are bifaces, a few small ones plus a couple very large ones that all appear unfinished; the rest are flakes or blade-like flakes. They are made of high-quality lithic materials that are from at least three sources that you can recognize, two of which are more than 150 km away from where the artifacts were found. As you're handling them, he asks exactly the questions you're pondering: Who made them? How old are they? Why were they left out on the landscape in a pile? What does their presence "in the middle of nowhere" signify about the lifeways of the people who left them?

CACHES IN ANTHROPOLOGICAL PERSPECTIVE

Answering these questions begins with considering that this particular collection of artifacts represents a distinctive class of archaeological site—a cache. Caches differ from other kinds of sites in that they consist of artifacts or materials in useful condition and forms that appear to have been set aside for later use, rather than objects that were used, broken, or discarded at the place of their use (such as a camp site). The caching of flaked stone artifacts, other materials, or foodstuffs is a tactic that has been employed by hunter-gatherer groups for tens of thousands of years. At the most basic level, caches are typically viewed by archaeologists as the placement ("hiding") of various resources in anticipation of future need. Beyond this general definition, caches may in fact be made for a variety of reasons, ranging from utilitarian/secular to ceremonial or mortuary, with the latter suggesting that the "future need" may be in the next world. The tactic is most likely linked to environmental conditions, diet breadth/patch-choice decisions, lithic tool design requirements, lithic material source distribution, the nature and frequency of group movements across a landscape, and probably other factors less obvious (at least to us in the present), including ritual observances.

There have been attempts to systematize the study of caches using ethnological and archaeological data. Binford (1979, 1980), on the basis of his Eskimo ethnoarchaeological research, suggested two types of caching of materials in anticipation of future use. The first—passive gear caches—related to the storage of objects used in seasonally specific subsistence pursuits at particular locales near which they would be used in the future. A second type—insurance gear caches—consisted of more general objects that could be manipulated or modified to fit a range of possible needs but that were not specific to a season. Thomas (1985:29–38) expanded on Binford's treatment and considered variation in hunter-gatherer caching with an eye on prehistoric and recent Great Basin groups. He offered a suite of four cache types: the resource cache (foodstuffs, raw materials); the tool cache (personal gear or insurance gear, after Binford's terms); the communal cache (bulky, site-specific objects that "go with" a place); and the afterlife cache (grave goods). It is tempting to use these typologies when dealing with all prehistoric caches. However, Thomas (1985:30) made a valuable summary observation: "The intact cache has a high degree of archaeological visibility; its positioning and contents are directly conditioned by the role it played in the settlement strategy that created it." Thus, while we may be able to assign intact caches to particular types, it is important to bear in mind that caches reflect time- and place-specific decisions. Understanding and interpreting caches thus requires some different approaches than those typically employed for habitation sites, and this volume is a collection of papers that present a number of approaches to investigating and interpreting caches left by Clovis groups inhabiting western North America at the close of the Pleistocene.

DISCOVERING CLOVIS CACHES

Whether or not they ultimately prove to be the initial colonizers of North America, Clovis hunter-gatherers left in their wake a remarkable archaeological record, extending from the Atlantic to the Pacific and from southern Canada to the Isthmus of Panama (Haynes 1964). A consistently similar lithic tool assemblage and distinctive techniques for stone-tool manufacture are evident across this range, and it has been suggested that these are one key to their successful spread over North America south of the ice sheets (Kelly and Todd 1988). Remarkably, the time that it took Clovis people to spread across this area may have been as little as three centuries (Waters and Stafford 2007; but see G. Haynes et al. 2007). The record of their passing ranges from isolated projectile points to mammoth, mastodon, and bison kills, short-term camps and quarries, and isolated caches of flaked stone and bone artifacts that may contain from as few as 5 to more than 100 specimens. The first caches were reported in 1963, one in southern Idaho and one in eastern New Mexico. In the last two or three decades, it is likely true that caches left by Clovis hunter-gatherers across the central part of North America have achieved greater public and professional archaeological attention than caches from anywhere else in the world. Figure 1.1 presents the locations of those caches that have been reported, and Table 1.1 summarizes their contents. The caches presented in the various chapters of this volume are shown in bold on Figure 1.1.

The first recognized Clovis cache came to light 50 years ago (although it was initially interpreted as a camp), with the discovery and publication of the Simon cache in south central Idaho (Butler 1963; Butler and Fitzwater 1965; Woods and Titmus 1985). It is, as Butler (1963:22) described it, "an extraordinary collection of chipped stone artifacts," which is an apt description for most Clovis caches. In many ways Simon set the model for Clovis caches—five Clovis fluted points, including three very long, slender ones; 20 bifaces ("points" or "knives" of varying kinds, as they were termed by Butler); and four other items, including a side scraper, convex-end scraper, spokeshave, and unworked spall fragment. Later refitting of the side scraper, spokeshave, and one flake knife into a single artifact reduced the total to 27 (Butler and Fitzwater 1965).

This same year was also when a second Clovis cache was reported from Blackwater Draw by Green (1963); it consisted of 17 complete and partial prismatic blades. Although lacking diagnostic Clovis points, the cache was convincingly attributed to Clovis by Green's detailed stratigraphic study and identification of sediment adhering to the blades as "gray sand," the unit known at the time to contain only Clovis artifacts (Green 1963); this unit is now designated the "speckled sand" (Unit B of Holliday 1997:Figure 3.11; Units B_1-B_3 of Haynes 1995).

Interestingly, these two caches established something of a pattern, whereby subsequently discovered caches dominated by bifaces were more common on the central and northern Plains/Columbia Plateau and those dominated by blades were more common on the southern Plains. Also, both the Green and Simon caches were exposed and scattered by heavy equipment during the course of sand and gravel quarrying at Blackwater Draw and the construction of a road at Simon. The frequency with which caches are brought to light by earth moving has been, regrettably, another repeated pattern.

Since the 1960s, caches compositionally similar to Simon have been found on the central and northern Plains, including Anzick, south central Montana (Lahren 2001; Owsley and Hunt 2001; Wilke et al. 1991); Drake, northeastern Colorado (Stanford and Jodry 1988); East Wenatchee (also known as the Richey or Richey-Roberts cache) in central Washington (Gramly 1993; Mehringer 1988; Mehringer and Foit 1990); Fenn, probably from the Wyoming-Idaho-Utah border region (Frison and Bradley 1999); de Graffenried, from the southeastern part of Texas (Collins et al. 2007); and Crook County, in northeastern Wyoming (Tankersley 1998, 2002:104–134). To the list can be added Rummells-Maske (Anderson and Tiffany 1972; Morrow and Morrow 2002), which was recovered in eastern Iowa. Like Simon, these were easily attributable to Clovis because they included Clovis fluted points.

Since the Blackwater Draw Green cache was brought to professional attention, other caches consisting largely of Upper Paleolithic–type prismatic blades and in some cases flakes were discovered, including the Franey cache in northwestern Nebraska (Grange 1964) and Pelland in northern Minnesota (Stoltman 1971). Both of these caches have been interpreted as Clovis, although it has been stated that the Pelland site would have been under the waters of glacial Lake Agassiz during Clovis time (Pettipas 2011:114). More recently discovered blade caches include Keven Davis in east central Texas (Collins 1999b:75–144) and the Dickenson cache (also known as the 1990 Blackwater Draw blade or West Bank cache) from Blackwater Draw (Montgomery and Dickenson 1992a). Lacking associated projectile points, these caches proved more challenging to attribute to Clovis or any other particular culture-historical entity, although Green used the properties of sediments adhering to the blades in his Blackwater Draw cache to argue that they were derived from the Clovis-bearing gray sand stratum. Michael Collins and his colleagues (Bradley et al. 2010:10–55; Collins 1999a, b; Collins and Lohse 2004; Collins et al. 2003)—working with the Keven Davis cache and the Clovis assemblages from the Pavo Real and Gault quarry/camp/workshop sites—have demonstrated that prismatic blades are a common feature of the Clovis technological repertoire on the southern High Plains/Llano Estacado and elsewhere in the western United States (Huckell 2007) but are absent in Folsom and younger Paleoindian cultural complexes. Collins has shown that Clovis blade manufacture was technologically consistent and produced distinctive features of core morphology, preparation, and rejuvenation as well as striking platform construction, curvature, and technological details such as the preparation and straightening of exterior ridges (Collins 1999b:51–71; also see Bradley et al. 2010:10–55). Blades have come to be strongly associated with Clovis, and although occasionally blades are found in younger cultural contexts they tend to differ in technological details (Kilby 2008:38).

Over the past four decades additional caches of flaked stone artifacts have come to light that are more challenging to assign to a particular culture or time period. These consist of bifaces, blades and/or blade-like flakes, unifacially retouched tools, and occasionally cores, but no Clovis points. Examples include Anadarko, in southwestern Oklahoma (Hammatt 1970); Busse, in northwestern Kansas (Hofman 1995; Kilby 2008:75–78); and Sailor-Helton, in southwestern Kansas (Mallouf 1994), all of which were originally discovered in the 1950s or 1960s. Kilby (2008) has studied these collections in the last few years and finds them credible as Clovis caches. If blades or bifaces are present, it is possible to make technological assessments of possible age and cultural affinity of these caches, but often these caches are challenging to interpret.

Another challenge is that caches are rarely recovered from their original stratigraphic contexts by archaeologists. Commonly caches are wrested from the earth by heavy equipment operators, stunned landscapers using Bobcats, ecstatic collectors, or curious ranchers and farmers with shovels, trowels, or bayonets. The result is that stratigraphic information is typically poor or lacking. Further, caches may have been discovered decades ago, and the person(s) involved in the discovery may no longer be available to interview. An extreme example is the Fenn cache (Frison and Bradley 1999), which was perhaps found near the beginning of the twentieth century and can only be approximately placed in the area where Utah, Idaho, and Wyoming meet. Additionally, in the absence of clearly diagnostic artifacts, and with the knowledge that later hunter-gatherers also used the tactic of lithic artifact caching, we are faced with trying to determine whether a given cache lacking fluted points is or is not Clovis. The importance of this challenge goes significantly further, directly to reconstructing Clovis lithic technological organization, including strategies of raw material procurement, transport, and reduction; patterns of mobility and land use; and ultimately questions about the process by which the New World was peopled.

ISSUES IN THE STUDY OF CLOVIS CACHES

It seems that almost every year for the past decade or so at least one new cache of definite or possible Clovis origin has come to the attention of archaeologists. As they do, it is increasingly apparent that caching of stone and bone artifacts was a common practice of these earliest successful colonizers of the New World and that the contents of caches offer archaeologists an unparalleled source of information to complement the assemblages from kill and camp sites. In 2010 we organized a session at the Society for American Archaeology meetings in St. Louis to bring together researchers to discuss Clovis caches. The symposium had three principal goals: (1) to share information about recently discovered or recently recognized caches; (2) to investigate ways in which caches, particularly those without diagnostic Clovis fluted points, could be reliably identified as Clovis; and (3) to consider the role(s) of caches within Clovis technology, mobility, and land use. This volume contains papers presented at that symposium along with additional invited papers from those who were unable to attend it. In publishing these papers, we hope not only to provide new descriptions and interpretations of Clovis caching but to stimulate thinking about the challenges we face in making interpretive sense of this phenomenon.

The chapters making up the volume contribute to the study of Clovis caches in three general realms, and most chapters address two or more of them. First, new caches are presented for which descriptions have not been previously published or have been published only in part. These include seven from places as far apart as Texas (the Hogeye cache, Lohse et al., Chapter 9), Oklahoma (the JS cache, Bement, Chapter 5), New Mexico (the Dickenson cache, Condon et al., Chapter 3), Iowa (the Carlisle cache, Hill et al., Chapter 6), Colorado (the Mahaffy cache, Bamforth, Chapter 4, and the CW cache, Muñiz, Chapter 7), and North Dakota (the Beach cache, Huckell, Chapter 8). In addition, another look at the contents of the cache that started it all, Simon, is provided (Santarone, Chapter 2). These chapters expand information about the range of variation in cache contents, thus enhancing knowledge of the kinds of products that Clovis hunter-gatherers chose to manufacture, transport, and ultimately place in the ground as part of a wide-ranging pattern of population movement and land use. Further, several authors address the critical question of how a cache assemblage that lacks fluted points or other diagnostic artifacts can be reliably assigned to Clovis. Two chapters are focused primarily on issues of land use and lithic material exploitation and transport. In addition to Bamforth's consideration of the Mahaffy cache in Chapter 4, Holen (Chapter 10) and Kilby (Chapter 11) look more broadly at the value of caches as a means of understanding Clovis mobility strategies. The next few paragraphs address these themes in greater detail.

NEWLY DISCOVERED AND RECENTLY RECOGNIZED CACHES

Figure 1.1 shows the locations of Clovis caches, with the names of those discussed in this volume set in boldface. Three—the Mahaffy (Bamforth, Chapter 4), JS (Bement, Chapter 5) and CW (Muñiz, Chapter 7) caches—were discovered in the past few years and are good representatives of numerically large caches that lack Clovis points. Two more are caches that were unearthed in the 1970s but went unrecognized as Clovis until the first decade of the twenty-first century: the Carlisle (Hill et al., Chapter 6) and Beach (Huckell, Chapter 8) caches. Like Mahaffy, JS, and CW, no Clovis points were present with either of these. Another cache found in the past few years, in southern Texas, the Hogeye cache (Lohse et al., Chapter 9), contains both generalized bifaces and nearly completed Clovis points. These caches expand the geographical distribution of caches to the north and east and suggest that Colorado is something of an epicenter for Clovis caches. The Dickenson blade cache has been described briefly in prior publications but receives expanded treatment here (Condon et al., Chapter 3). Finally, new artifacts are reported from the granddaddy of them all, the Simon cache (Santarone, Chapter 2). Chapter 2 provides a new perspective on the range of artifacts that were originally present in the cache as well as offering a cautionary tale about whether all artifacts pertaining to the cache were completely recovered by the discoverer or fully shared between discoverer and researcher.

These caches also reflect the various ways—both direct and circuitous—by which caches come to professional attention. All but two of the caches (the Dickenson and Carlisle caches) were found by members of the public, who usually accomplished recovery of the caches themselves. Ones that came to light recently, such as the Mahaffy, JS, and CW caches, happened to reach archaeologists who were aware of the Clovis caching phenomenon and could take quick action to examine them and document the circumstances of their contexts. However, it is important to note that caches discovered prior to 1975 or 1980 had a much lower probability of being recognized or even considered as possible Clovis caches if they lacked points. The Carlisle and Beach caches are good examples; the former was recovered during a contract archaeological

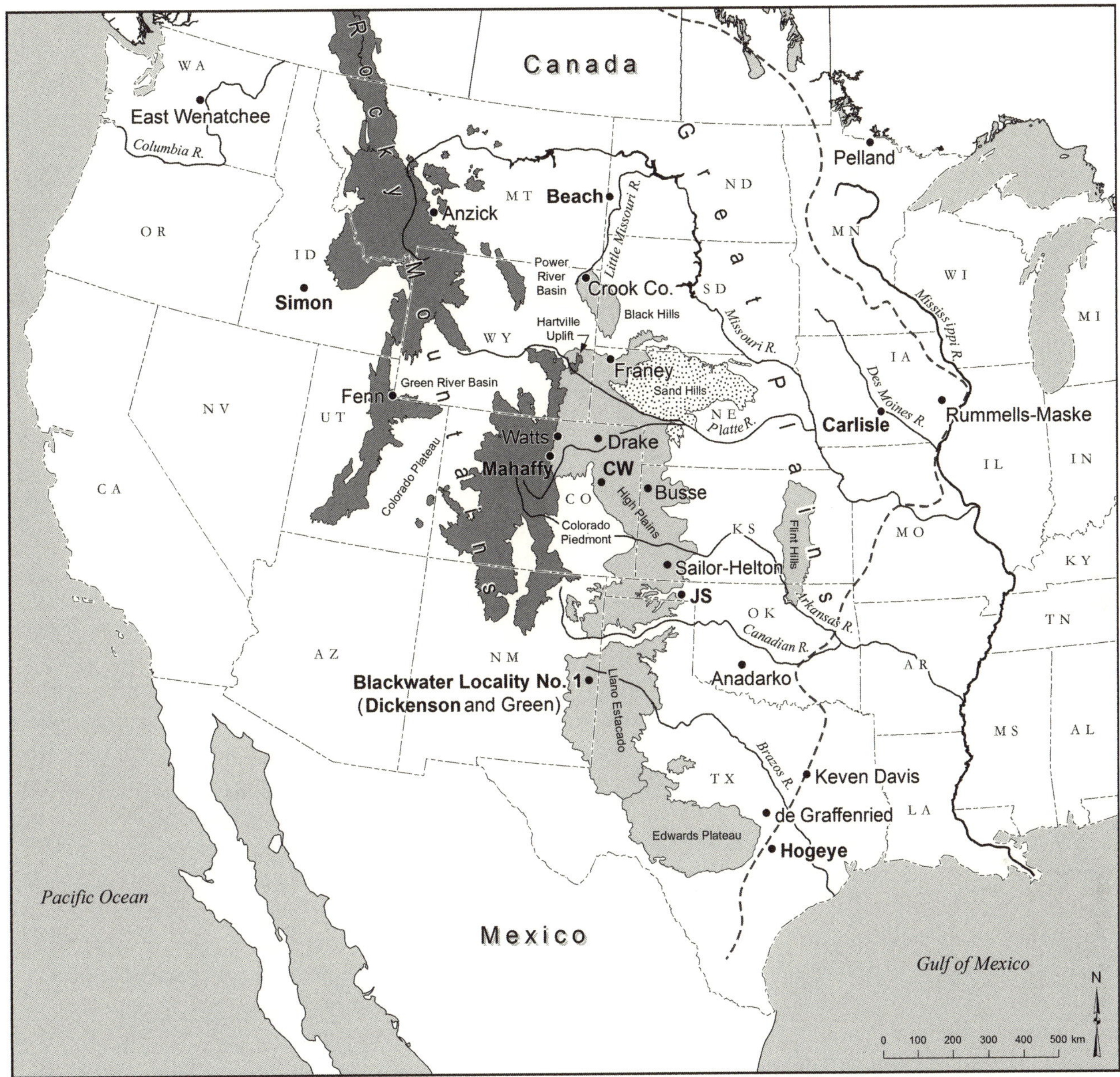

Figure 1.1 The distribution of Clovis caches in the western United States. Names in bold are caches treated in this volume. The dashed line marks the eastern limit of the Great Plains (map created by Matthew G. Hill).

project investigating a much younger site while the latter was exposed by cultivation. Even though specimens from the Beach cache were sent to major western universities or examined by professional archaeologists, they were not thought to be Clovis. The Carlisle cache came to light during cultural resource–management investigations at a late prehistoric site in 1968, and although its discovery was noteworthy from the perspective of investigators, it was presumed to be part of the late prehistoric occupation. From the benefit of knowledge developed since 1980 about the distinctive aspects of Clovis technology, such as blade manufacture and overshot flaking of bifaces, it is now more likely that a cache will be recognized quickly as Clovis. Further, Clovis caches are now more likely to achieve public exposure through various media, including the Internet. A small handful of potentially Clovis caches have been publicized on the web.

Nevertheless, it is highly probable that both museums and private individuals have unrecognized caches of potential Clovis origin in their collections or households and that these will continue to come to the attention of professional archaeologists. At the same time, it is worth recalling that there can be instances in which a putative Clovis cache is presented to an institution or a collector, as with the infamous "Woody's Dream" cache (Preston 1999). In that case, the artifacts were manufactured by a talented contemporary knapper, artificially aged, and packaged with a fictitious historical pedigree. We can take some comfort from the ultimate failure of the cache to pass the professional vetting process, but it was accepted as genuine for a time. Such instances are reasons to retain a healthy skepticism about caches that show up on one's doorstep.

CLOVIS LITHIC TECHNOLOGY

One of the consistent threads that runs through the chapters in this book is a focus on the importance of understanding how cached artifact assemblages fit into the larger patterns of Clovis lithic technology. Whether a chapter is centered on a single cache assemblage or takes a comparative perspective through the use of multiple caches, the role of technology is highlighted. At the most basic level, technology forms a critical, and in some cases the only, means to determine whether a given cache can be confidently attributed to Clovis, particularly in cases where fluted points or other diagnostic artifacts are absent. Several publications (Bradley 2010; Bradley et al. 2010; Collins 1999a, 1999b; Huckell 2007; and Waters, Pevny, and Carlson 2011, among them) on Clovis lithic technology are available, and they form a solid foundation upon which to base initial assessments of the age and affiliation of cache artifacts. However, it is also the case that cached assemblages that are demonstrably Clovis can contribute much to resolving questions about Clovis technology that remain unapproachable from assemblages that are derived from kill or camp sites. This is because cached assemblages are more likely to consist of objects that were removed from the technological system early in the manufacturing process and that retain much of their potential utility for performing a variety of tasks. Kill and particularly camp sites typically contain artifacts that were lost or intentionally discarded at more advanced stages in their trajectory of use, breakage, and resharpening. Caches therefore are more likely to contain objects manufactured at quarry sites and then transported, possibly used to a degree during transport, and then placed into what was, in most cases, likely viewed by their makers/users as temporary storage (Kilby 2008).

Several of the chapters in this volume devote attention to technological matters, first as a means of evaluating the age and possible attribution of a cache to Clovis, and second as a means of developing further insights into Clovis technology. For those caches where stratigraphic context and radiometric dating are not options, technological analysis is often the only means to determine whether or not they are Clovis. Chapters discussing the Dickenson cache at Blackwater Draw (Condon et al., Chapter 3), the Mahaffy cache (Bamforth, Chapter 4), the JS cache (Bement, Chapter 5), the Carlisle cache (Hill et al., Chapter 6), the CW cache (Muñiz, Chapter 7), and the Beach cache (Huckell, Chapter 8) highlight this approach. The importance of overshot flaking as a Clovis technological signature receives attention, as do matters of biface morphology and size, the presence of fluting or end thinning, and aspects of blade-manufacturing technology and morphology. At the same time, caution is urged against assuming too much about the unique association of certain aspects of artifact manufacturing technology and morphology with Clovis. Do we know with sufficient certainty that overshot flaking is unique to Clovis or, more to the point, that in its absence we can reliably say that a biface is/isn't Clovis? The same holds for blades, and in that case there is clear evidence that at least some later groups also manufactured blades. How can we isolate and use distinctive features of Clovis blade manufacture to separate Clovis blades from the products of later blade-making groups? Traveling a bit further down this increasingly murky path, what (if anything) can be said of the culturally/temporally diagnostic technological aspects of caches that are dominated by flakes and blade-like flakes? There are no simple answers, and the authors in these chapters present cautious objective analyses of the artifacts as a means of assigning particular caches to the Clovis technological tradition.

The use of technological analysis can be greatly aided in those rare situations in which it is possible to put a Clovis cache back into its original stratigraphic context, as related for the Dickenson cache (Condon et al., Chapter 3), the Mahaffy cache (Bamforth, Chapter 4), the JS cache (Bement, Chapter 5), the Carlisle cache (Hill et al., Chapter 6), and the Beach cache (Huckell, Chapter 8). In some of these cases the stratigraphic setting of the original cache was clarified by new fieldwork or careful study of exposed sediments shortly after the discovery or excavation of the cache. An appropriate cautionary case in which stratigraphic context was key goes back to the geological studies of Sheldon Judson in the vicinity of the San Jon site in the 1940s. Judson discovered a cache eroding out of an arroyo wall that consisted of 44 artifacts, including five large bifaces ("blades," in his terms) and an assortment of what were identified as end scrapers, side scrapers, and flake knives (Roberts 1942:22–23). Photographs of a sample of the artifacts were also provided by Roberts (1942:Plates 8 and 9), and from those one gains an initial impression that the cache might well be Clovis. The five large bifaces range from 18 cm to 24.5 cm in length and from 10 cm to 13 cm in width (as measured to the nearest 5 mm using the scale in Roberts's Plate 8). Twenty tools presented in Roberts's Plate 9 are all made on what appear to be blades or blade-like flakes. If this cache were to be presented to an archaeologist today, without any depositional context, he or she could have a challenging time determining its age from artifact technology and morphology alone. However, Judson discovered this cache in very young sediments, some 2 ft (0.61 m) below the former land surface, and was able to assign the deposit to his third period of alluviation, which he dated to no older than the late A.D. 1400s. A fire pit adjacent to the cache produced charred pronghorn bones and charcoal, and a second, "nearby" pit yielded modern bison bones (Roberts 1942:23). The bifaces are likely preforms for large knives of the late prehistoric period. As a concluding observation, detailed technological analysis of cache assemblages such as this one can be quite important and help isolate the cultural/temporal diagnostic value of particular technological features of late prehistoric versus Clovis caches. To the best of our knowledge, this cache has never been reanalyzed since its discovery 60 years ago.

Other aspects of Clovis technological organization may also be reflected by caches, and one of these is the organization of lithic artifact production—who made these technically challenging bifaces and other artifacts, and were there flint-knapping specialists during Clovis times? Lohse and colleagues (Chapter 9) take up this question using the Hogeye, de Graffenried, and Fenn caches. In their estimation, part-time specialists were most likely the ones responsible for the manufacture of the most technologically sophisticated bifacial artifacts represented in the caches, as reflected by patterns of flake removal and standardization of products. Thus the work of these skilled knappers is disproportionately represented in caches, although multiple knappers may have contributed to a given cache.

CLOVIS LAND USE

The value of these caches for understanding Clovis land-use strategies as well as technological organization is difficult to overstate. First, the caches reveal directly what Clovis foragers identified as the most important forms of lithic artifacts to transport. As such they provide insights into the sorts of products created at lithic quarry sites and the forms in which they were transported. They thus afford a sense of Clovis decision making and planning as the products were selected and carried away from quarries into the biotic foraging environment, where the opportunities for easy resupply of lithic material might be infrequent or lacking altogether. Several of the caches discussed in this volume speak to the diversity of lithic artifact forms that were transported and cached. It appears to be the case that bifaces are the most frequently represented artifacts across the present sample of caches, showing up in all but one of the caches treated herein (Table 1.1). The importance of bifacially flaked artifacts in the Clovis technological system has been stressed by several previous workers (Bamforth 2002; Bradley et al. 2010; Wilke et al. 1991), a fact reflected not just by caches but also by assemblages of debitage from kill/camp sites such as the Sheaman site on the Wyoming–South Dakota border (Frison 1982c) and the Murray Springs site in southeastern Arizona (Huckell 2007). Larger bifaces may have served as cores for flake production and, through a process of parsimonious reduction over an extended period of time, as knives and ultimately as projectile points. Finished projectile points can be included in this general category as well, as shown at the Drake (Stanford and Jodry 1988) and Rummells-Maske (Anderson and Tiffany 1972; Morrow and Morrow 2002) caches. Blades also appear to have been frequently transported, as suggested by caches such as the Green and Dickenson caches at Blackwater Draw (Condon et al., Chapter 3) and the Keven Davis cache in Texas (Collins 1999b) and by blades as elements in such other caches as East Wenatchee (Gramly 1993), Beach (Huckell et al. 2011), Pelland (Stoltman 1971), Franey (Grange 1964), and Anadarko (Hammatt 1970). However, simple flakes and blade-like flakes are also present in several caches, as noted above and as described herein for the Mahaffy (Bamforth, Chapter 4), JS (Bement, Chapter 5), and Carlisle (Hill et al., Chapter 6) caches. Other lithic forms less commonly observed in caches are cores for the production of flakes or blades, hammerstones, and small pieces of debitage. Bone or proboscidean ivory rods (Bradley 1996) were also present in the Anzick (Lahren and Bonnichsen 1974) and East Wenatchee (Gramly 1993:52–60) caches and possibly in the Drake cache (Stanford and Jodry 1988). It is certainly possible that other organic materials—perhaps including leather or fiber bags that contained cached artifacts—were originally included in caches but have left no trace. In summary, it appears that virtually everything that could conceivably be needed in material-poor foraging environments could be and was transported and cached. Whether there is any patterned variation in the nature of products carried and cached across particular portions of the Clovis range is open to discussion; present evidence suggests that caches with blades are more common on the southern Plains than on the northern Plains, but it remains to be determined whether this is more apparent than real, perhaps a product of the current sample of cached assemblages.

The other critical aspect of Clovis land use that can be approached using caches is the distance, direction, and nature of group movements, as discussed by Bamforth in Chapter 4, Kilby in Chapter 11, and Holen in Chapter 10. It has been proposed (Meltzer 2004) that caches are related to the initial colonization of the North American continent and reflect the landscape learning process as opposed to a strategy associated with the patterned seasonal movements of groups who already had command of the distribution of both lithic and biotic resources. Kilby suggests that the latter is a more likely explanation for most, but perhaps not all, caches, a conclusion reached by Bamforth as well (Chapter 4). Kilby documents a recurrent pattern of the movement of flaked stone products northward and eastward from known source areas, prior to their deposition in caches. In some situations these movements reflect

TABLE 1.1. Clovis Caches And Their Contents

CACHE	ARTIFACT CLASS							TOTAL
	Points	Bifaces	Cores	Blades	Flakes	Bone Rods	Other	
Anadarko		2	4	26				32
Anzick	8	62		1	9	6		86
Beach[a]		99		2				101
Busse		13	1	33	30		1	78
Carlisle[a]		25			18			43
Crook County	1	8						9
CW[a]		11			3			14
de Graffenried		5						5
Dickenson[a]				4	1			5
Drake	13						1	14
East Wenatchee	14	20		4	8	12		58
Fenn	20	35		1				56
Franey		1	1	35	36		1	74
Green				17				17
Hogeye[a]	13	39						52
JS[a]		13		30	69			112
Keven Davis				14				14
Mahaffy[a]		11		7	62		1	82
Pelland				9				9
Rummells-Maske	22				1			23
Sailor-Helton			10	40	115			165
Simon[a]	8	40			14		1	63
Watts		6						6

Source: Modified from Kilby (2008:Table 11) and updated as of 2013.
[a]*Caches presented in this volume.*

scales of hundreds of kilometers (such as the Drake cache) but in others the distance of transport may be less than 20 km (Huckell et al. 2011). Holen (Chapter 10) emphasizes that the nature of the grassland ecosystem in the central Plains features localized sources of knappable stone separated by large areas devoid of lithic resources. He suggests that caching is intimately related to mobility structured by mobile prey resources, including bison, as well as the end-Pleistocene megafaunal extinction.

Finally, as shown in Figure 1.1, caches are found only within a limited portion of the known Clovis range, largely corresponding with the Great Plains biome. Despite the fact that fluted points (Clovis and later types) reach their greatest densities in the eastern United States, Clovis caches are not known from that portion of the country, with two possible exceptions in the central eastern Great Lakes region: a group of 33 artifacts found together at the Sugarloaf site (a habitation site) in Massachusetts (Gramly 1998:33–35, Plate 10) and a possible cache of 17 artifacts (8 of them finished Vail/Debert fluted points; Bradley et al. 2008:130–136) scattered by cultivation from one locus of the Lamb site (also a habitation site) in far western New York (Gramly 1999). Both sites may be either coeval with or slightly later than Clovis. The Thedford II site in southwestern Ontario produced a disturbed but probable cache of at least 8 and possibly 13 artifacts, all either finished ("mint") Barnes (post-Clovis) points or point preforms (Deller and Ellis 1992:99–100). There are, in addition, probable mortuary offerings that accompany a cremation at the post-Clovis Crowfield site in southwestern Ontario (Deller and Ellis 1984; Deller et al. 2009). One feature that distinguishes these Great Lakes–area caches is that they are associated with residential sites rather than being isolated, as are nearly all caches from the western United States. This absence or paucity of eastern Clovis caches, if not the product of sample bias, may be a reflection of differing subsistence/settlement systems or mobility organization, or perhaps a consequence of lithic material distribution and accessibility in the region. Further, if caches (either ritual or utilitarian) were placed at residential sites in the eastern United States, a different organizational system may be reflected, one that was predicated on the return to specific habitable places rather than larger patches or regions, as seems to be the case in the West. Given the discovery of large numbers of fluted points from plowed fields, lack of exposure probably cannot explain the lack of caches.

Clovis caches are a critical source of information in continuing efforts to understand the ways in which these ancient hunter-gatherers exploited the late Pleistocene landscape. The chapters in this volume are designed to augment knowledge of the phenomenon by bringing new caches to the attention of archaeological researchers, exploring ways to use lithic technological signatures to identify caches that are potentially Clovis, using cache assemblages to understand Clovis organization and production of technology, and considering what caches may tell us about patterns of movement in the course of subsistence. We hope that the individual contributions will stimulate thinking about Clovis and provide some investigative pathways forward as new Clovis caches come to light.

ACKNOWLEDGMENTS

First and foremost, thanks to our collaborators for the excellent studies they have contributed to this volume. It is always challenging to keep current in research environments as dynamic and diverse as those concerning caches, Clovis, and the peopling of North America. Both of us have learned a great deal from them, and we are honored to include their work in this volume. Thanks as well to Fred Sellet and one anonymous colleague who reviewed the draft volume and offered many helpful suggestions for its improvement. We are very grateful to John Byram and the staff of the University of New Mexico Press for all their hard work in bringing this volume to completion.

Chapter 2

New Insights into the Simon Clovis Cache

Paul Santarone

When I began my research on the Simon Clovis cache in 2005, I thought that I was undertaking a straightforward project. However, while reading the published reports on the cache I was struck by discrepancies in the information reported. Careful examination showed that artifact inventories and descriptions did not agree between publications. As a result I undertook to determine how and why these discrepancies came about and to attempt to create a complete inventory of the documentable artifact assemblage. This chapter reports what I discovered about the history of the Simon site and the artifact inventory of the Simon cache. I also discuss how "changes" to the assemblage call into question popular inferences concerning the contents and nature of Clovis mixed biface caches. I use the term cache throughout this chapter, consistent with established practice. The use of this term is not intended to imply any particular function.

Since some readers may not be familiar with the Simon cache, I begin by providing contextual background on the site and the assemblage. Following the contextual information I discuss what I have called "assemblage drift"—unreported changes in an archaeological assemblage since initial recovery (Santarone 2007). I next present the methods I used to document that previously unreported artifacts were part of the Simon cache assemblage, and then I describe the known cache assemblage. Finally, I discuss how the addition of previously unknown (and/or unreported) artifacts changes which inferences about the cache can be supported. Clearly my research provides a cautionary tale, but it also adds further insights into the roles of caches in Clovis lifeways.

DISCOVERY OF THE CACHE

The Simon cache site is located several kilometers east of the rural town of Fairfield in Camas County, south central Idaho. The larger landform on which the site lies is known as the Big Camas Prairie. The Snake River Plain is situated to the south of the Big Camas Prairie and the Soldier, Smoky, and Sawtooth Mountains are to the north. The Big Camas Prairie is separated from the Snake River Plain by inhospitable lava flows and rugged hills.

Although specific details vary between witnesses, it is clear that heavy-equipment disturbance of the surface of a cultivated field led to the initial discovery of cache artifacts. Heavy equipment may have also been used in the recovery of artifacts (Bill Simon, personal communication 2008). Although the artifacts were discovered in the late summer or early fall of 1961, the collection was not brought to the attention of archaeologists until later that year (Butler 1963). The first archaeologists to visit the site arrived in early August 1962. During this visit it was determined that "nothing of archaeological value remained at the site" (Butler 1963:22).

Butler (1963:23) reported the find as a collection of "29 chipped stone implements and an unworked spall fragment." Butler noted that a large portion of the artifacts was broken prior to his examination. However, he attributed essentially all the breakage to contact with the heavy equipment that exposed the cache. Butler described 23 of the artifacts as points, although from his usage it is clear that he does not mean projectile points; this is likely a source of some confusion. Six of these 23 points were described as edge-ground lanceolate points with fluting or basal thinning. The remaining 17 are bifaces of various shapes and sizes with pointed distal ends. The six remaining artifacts were described as a pair of discoid knives, a large flake knife, a spokeshave, a unifacial side scraper, and a bifacial end scraper. Two years later Butler and Fitzwater (1965) reported that three artifacts described by Butler (1963) conjoin into a single artifact. Using Butler's (1963) illustrations and descriptions it is possible to document which artifacts were present when the cache was initially reported. Table 2.1 presents a summary of Butler's descriptions and correlates his figure numbers with the current accession numbers of the artifacts.

Thus far, what I have described substantially agrees with the published information on the discovery of the cache. But after the initial publication of the find neither the site nor the assemblage remained static. Few archaeologists realize that professional archaeological investigations at the site have been conducted at intervals since 1963. Further, additional artifacts have been recovered and artifacts have been separated into multiple collections. For clarity the history of the artifacts is discussed separately from the history of investigations at the site.

FIELDWORK

The most extensive work conducted at the site are professional excavations performed in 1967, 1968, and 1969 under the direction of Dr. Earl Swanson. A manuscript concerning this work was drafted for publication; however, it was never published. Excavations consisted of hand-dug trenches near the find site and a series of backhoe trenches for stratigraphic analysis (Swanson et al. n.d.). The 1967–1969 fieldwork did result in the recovery of additional Clovis artifacts. Artifacts recovered during Swanson's fieldwork are curated at the Idaho Museum of Natural History (IMNH) in Pocatello. Since 1969 the site has been visited by archaeologists and some additional fieldwork has been conducted (Bill Simon, personal communication 2008). Recent fieldwork was conducted by the Archaeo-Imaging Lab and Idaho State University, under the sponsorship of the Idaho Heritage Trust. This fieldwork was conducted in 2008 and included extensive remote-sensing investigations. The testing of geophysical anomalies identified by remote sensing was conducted in 2008 and 2010. Remote-sensing investigations and site testing have helped to clarify previous work conducted at the site but no additional Clovis materials have been recovered from subsurface deposits. A report on this research is in preparation (E. S. Lohse, personal communication 2010).

ARTIFACTS

Division of the Simon cache assemblage had begun by the time the 1969 excavations were complete. The artifacts recovered by Idaho State University archaeologists at the site from 1967 to 1969 are curated at the IMNH. There are eight formal Simon cache artifacts in the collections of the IMNH. This collection includes some artifacts from the initial cache discovery that apparently were donated by the Simon family to the IMNH. Specifically, the Simon family donated the artifacts that make up the large conjoinable biface (Figure 2.1) discussed by Butler and Fitzwater (1965). Based on archival photographs of the artifacts in the possession of the Simon family at the time, it appears that this donation occurred prior to 1969. The remaining artifacts originally reported by Butler (1963) were kept by the Simon family. It is now apparent that family members (and quite possibly others) occasionally recovered additional artifacts from the area of the find in the years following the initial discovery. The 32 cache artifacts possessed by the Simon family were donated to the Herrett Center in 1997 (Phyllis Oppenheim, personal communication 2008). To complicate matters further, two biface fragments have been recovered since 1997. The first was recovered in 2007 by Steve Kohntopp during a site visit to arrange future fieldwork. The second was recovered in 2008 by Dr. Ken Kvamme during remote-sensing research on the site. Both biface fragments were subsequently donated to the Herrett Center by the Simon family.

TABLE 2.1. Inventory of Butler (1963) Cache Artifacts and Descriptions

LOCATION	ACCESSION NUMBER	BUTLER FIGURE NUMBER	BUTLER DESCRIPTION
Herrett	97-1-25	3a	Edge-ground lanceolate point
Herrett	97-1-26	3b	Edge-ground lanceolate point
Herrett	97-1-27	3c	Edge-ground lanceolate point
Herrett	97-1-28	3d	Edge-ground lanceolate point
Herrett	97-1-29	3e	Edge-ground lanceolate point
Herrett	97-1-18	3f	Oval point
Herrett	97-1-19	3g	Oval point
Herrett	97-1-22	3h	Oval point
Herrett	97-1-21	3i	Oval point
Herrett	97-1-10	4a	Oval point
Herrett	97-1-8	4b	Oval point
Herrett	97-1-1	4c	Oval point
Herrett	97-1-2	5a	Oval point
Herrett	97-1-7	5b	Oval point
Herrett	97-1-4	5c	Lanceolate point
Herrett	97-1-17	5d	Oval point
Herrett	97-1-15	5e	Oval point
Herrett	97-1-5	5f	Lanceolate point
Herrett	97-1-9	6a	Discoid knife
Herrett	97-1-11	6b	Discoid knife
Herrett	97-1-14	6c	Lanceolate point
IMNH	18-A-21	6d	Side scraper
IMNH	1529-25[a]	6e	End scraper
IMNH	1529-25[a]	6f	Unworked spall
Herrett	97-1-3	7a	Shouldered point
Herrett	97-1-12	7b	Oval point
IMNH	18-A-21	7c	Spokeshave
IMNH	18-A-21	7d	Flake knife
Herrett	97-1-16[b]	Not shown	Edge-ground lanceolate point
Herrett	97-1-23[b]	Not shown	Oval point

Note: Herrett = Herrett Center for Arts and Science, College of Southern Idaho, Twin Falls; IMNH = Idaho Museum of Natural History, Idaho State University, Pocatello.

[a] *The location of the artifact is unknown; the accession number refers to an archival photograph.*

[b] *The artifact listed is the most likely candidate for being the one that Butler (1963) describes, based on form, material description, and dimensions.*

METHOD

Creating a timeline marking the major events in the history of the Simon cache since discovery illustrates the opportunities that were present for assemblage drift (Figure 2.2). There are five major potential sources for assemblage drift: first, the length of time that has elapsed since the initial discovery; second, a history of changing investigators and institutions; third, the assemblage being shown, moved, donated, and so on; fourth, continued observation and investigation of the site locale; and finally, differential curation of artifacts.

These are the factors that have contributed to the addition and subtraction of artifacts from the known cache assemblage since its discovery in 1961.

An examination of the discrepancies in the published descriptions made it clear that the entire known assemblage had never been documented or discussed. This presented me with a problem. It is clearly possible that the additional artifacts may have come into the collection from outside the cache context. There are two potential possibilities for introducing noncache artifacts into the cache assemblage. The first is a mixing of collections from a variety of sites in uncontrolled curation. The second is a mixing of artifacts from different site components present at the cache location. The first possibility was eliminated by communication with the Simon family. Even though they retained the cache of artifacts for many years, members of the Simon family are not artifact collectors. Also, archaeologists had made the importance of the cache very clear to the Simons, so they took care not to add any artifacts that they encountered while farming to the collection unless they were discovered near the original find spot. Therefore, admixture from outside sources is very unlikely. The second potential source of admixture was evaluated by visiting the site to verify the absence of unrelated archaeological materials in the area of the find. I found that the site area does contain *minimal* archaeological materials that appear unrelated to the Clovis component. This archaeological material consists of a sparse (less than 10 pieces per 100 m^2) scatter of small volcanic glass flakes. The source of this volcanic glass is likely the small (less than 5 cm) volcanic glass nodules native to the location. Because of this I accepted any technologically compatible artifacts recovered from the site area as part of the cache assemblage. Artifacts that could be inspected directly were also verified as part of the cache by the presence of red ochre on the artifact.

Figure 2.1 Conjoined biface (IMNH 18-A-21) (288 mm long)

How could I establish whether or not a particular artifact should be included in the cache assemblage? The histories of the individual artifacts determined how they were verified. The artifacts that were simplest to verify were those that appeared in the Butler (1963) and Butler and Fitzwater (1965) publications. These artifacts are clearly associated with the discovery of the cache. What about artifacts added in the approximately 50 years since? Artifacts from the 1967–1969 site investigations were easy to verify since these were documented to have been recovered from the site by professional archaeologists. Additional artifacts described in Woods and Titmus (1985) are technologically consistent with Clovis and show traces of red ochre, as do the previously undocumented artifacts included in the donation by the Simon family in 1997. The recoveries of two artifacts at the site since 1997 were both witnessed by archaeologists, and both artifacts are technologically consistent with the other cache materials. I conclude that all the artifacts now in the collections of the IMNH and the Herrett Center attributed to the Simon Clovis cache are indeed part of the cache.

Finding that additional artifacts belong to the assemblage raises the question of whether artifacts have also gone missing. To determine whether this had occurred, I used a series of photographs that were taken circa 1969 as part of investigations at the site. These photos are curated in the site archives of the IMNH. The photographs document the artifacts that were in the possession of the Simon family at the time (Figure 2.3). By comparing archival photographs with the artifacts present in IMNH and Herrett Center collections I was able to document additional artifacts from the cache present with the collection around 1969. Initially I discovered six artifacts that are now known only in photographs. Using photos of the missing artifacts as verification, one has since been rediscovered in the collections of the Herrett Center.

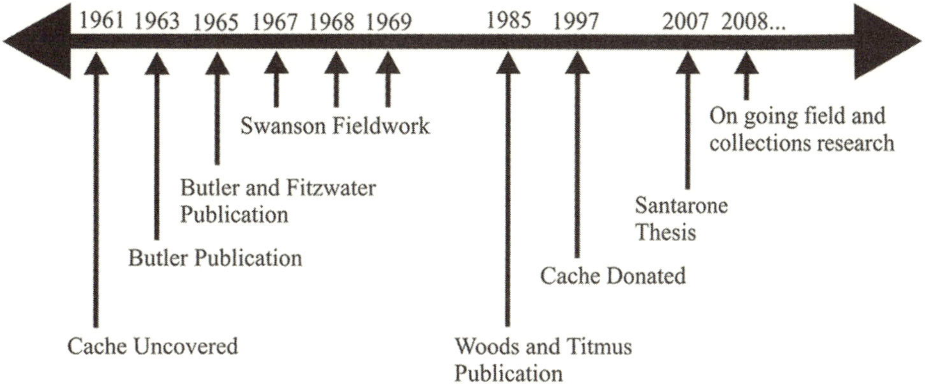

Figure 2.2. Timeline of important events in the history of the Simon cache

DISCUSSION

Using the documents and resources available, I was able to establish the known cache assemblage at five different points of time (Figure 2.4): 1963, circa 1969, 1985, 1997, and post-1997. When the artifacts are aligned in terms of time two important points can be noted. First, it appears that generally the size of the artifacts recovered from the site diminished through time. This suggests that the majority of any large artifacts or artifact fragments have likely been recovered. Any artifacts that remain at the site are likely to be small and more difficult to locate. Second, based on the attributes of the artifacts that have "dropped out" of the collection, it appears that the most complete artifacts were preferentially curated. That is, the artifacts that were kept together and have been published are generally those artifacts that are most complete and visually impressive. This select sample of the assemblage came to be identified as the Simon cache, and it is this not fully representative sample that contributed to inferences concerning the nature of Clovis caches. This raises the question of how we can make valid comparisons between caches if the samples of the assemblages we are using are potentially not representative and if the composition of

Figure 2.3. Archival photograph (IMNH 1529-25) showing artifacts currently missing from the Simon cache

the actual assemblage is unknown. Documenting additional artifacts provides an opportunity to examine how the inclusion of these artifacts changes the assemblage character and the interpretation of the cache as a whole.

Unchanged by the addition of artifacts are the cultural-historical designation of the cache and the basic technological description. In categories such as raw material diversity, tool class inventory and diversity, character of workmanship, and evidence of use, the changes are dramatic. I describe these changes below.

INVENTORY

One problem with compiling an inventory of artifacts present in the Simon cache is the extensive breakage and fragmentation of the artifacts. Clearly some of the breakage is the result of contact with agricultural equipment (as evidenced by metallic marks). Equally clearly, some of the breakage was present prior to the deposition of the cache. For this inventory I took a conservative approach. Only those conjoinable artifacts that were definitively fragmented prior to deposition were counted as multiple artifacts. Predepositional breakage was definitively established by the presence of reworking on conjoinable artifact surfaces. All other conjoinable artifact fragments were counted as single artifacts. It should be noted that since most conjoinable artifacts have been glued back together inspection of break surfaces was often impossible. This adds to the conservative nature of this inventory. Using this approach the Simon cache consists of at least 63 artifacts, including 48 bifaces or biface fragments, 5 flake tools, 9 pieces of debitage, and 1 nodule of red ochre. Of this inventory, 58 are currently in museum collections and 5 are known only from photographs (whereabouts are unknown). Table 2.2 provides an inventory of bifaces with artifact and raw material classifications. The order of artifacts in this table reflects Figure 2.4.

RAW MATERIAL

I created two schemes for categorizing the raw materials used in the cache. One scheme was very general and the other specific. The general scheme consisted of broad material categories. In the most general division three categories of raw material occur in the cache—cryptocrystalline silicates, quartz crystal, and quartzite. All but one artifact fell into either the cryptocrystalline silicate or quartz-crystal category. The remaining artifact was classified as quartzite because of its fine granular appearance and matte surface luster. The absence of volcanic glass is curious given that at least three high-quality volcanic glass sources (Bear Gulch, Browns Bench, and Malad) exist within approximately 150 to 375 km of the site. All three of these volcanic glass sources are known to have been used by Clovis peoples (E. S. Lohse, personal communication 2009).

To establish the raw material categories for my more specific categorization, I used a version of the minimum analytical nodule analysis technique (Andrefsky 2005; Larson 1994; Larson and Kornfeld 1997). For the designation of individual raw materials, I focused on primary and secondary coloration. I also used the color, shape, and texture of any inclusions as part of my classification. I paid attention to gradients in color that could indicate the range of variation within a raw material and therefore help to unify some raw material types. I did not use exposure to ultraviolet light. Other researchers have used different methods and come up with slightly differing results (i.e., Kilby 2008). To my mind the differences in designations can be accounted for by the classic lumper vs. splitter dichotomy on the part of individual analysts. While on the subject of raw material, it should be noted that there is evidence in the collection for the use of heat treatment (Kilby 2008; Santarone 2007). This evidence includes greasy surface luster, pot-lidding, crazing, and differences in color and texture between interior and exterior portions of artifacts. Because of this, changes in material appearance that resulted from heat treatment could also be operating to increase the number of material categories (although I think that this is unlikely).

The investigation of the raw materials present in the Simon cache was not designed to attempt to identify actual raw material sources. Instead my categories were constructed to more closely identify nodules of raw material (similar to Hall 2004). There are two reasons for this approach. First, crypto- or microcrystalline silicate toolstone sources in the region are both extensive and poorly documented. The other reason to focus on nodules is that a single source area may display a range of material colors and inclusions. Although investigators have attributed some artifacts to particular raw material sources (Kilby 2008; Kohntopp 2010), these investigators have tended to come

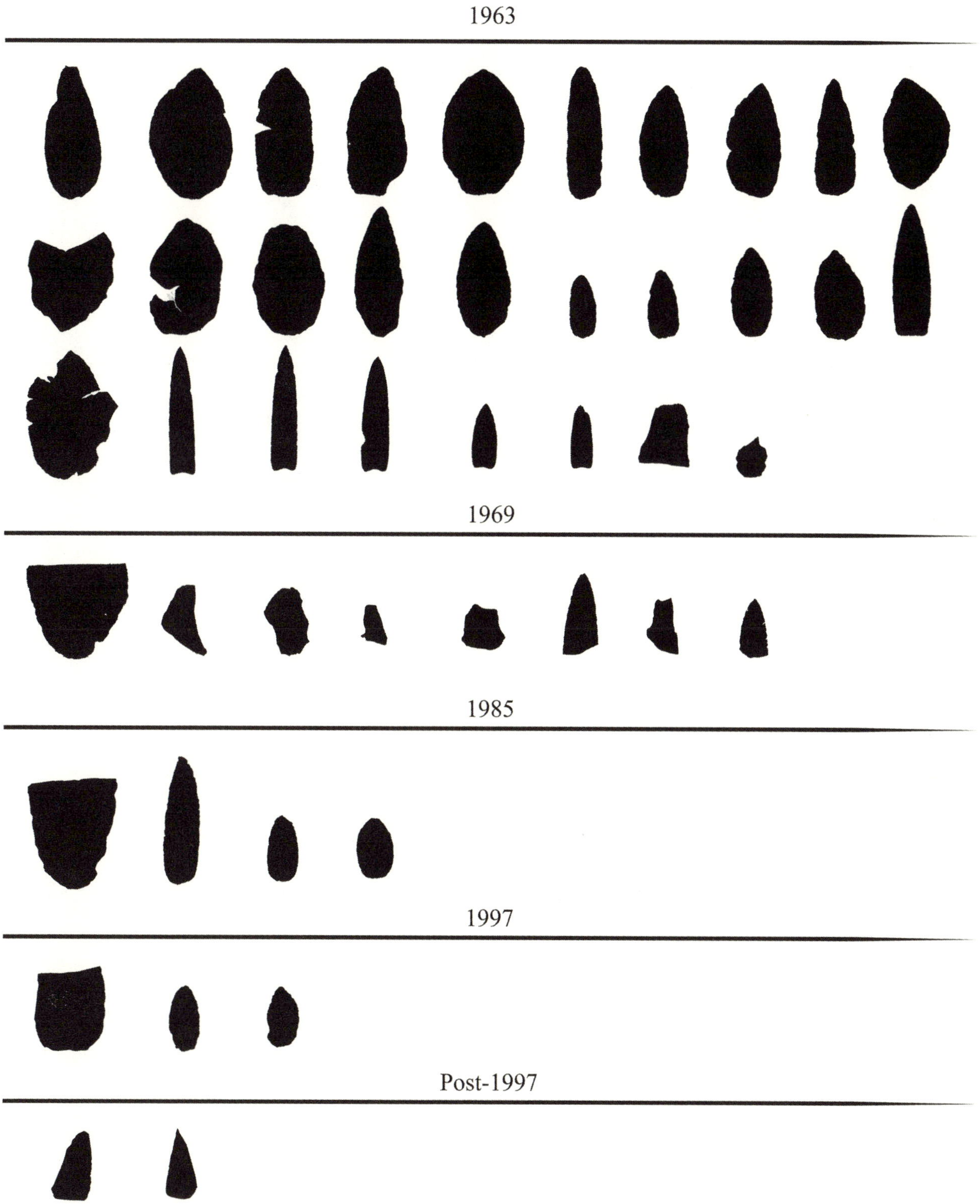

Figure 2.4. Visual representation of Simon cache assemblage changes through time

TABLE 2.2. Inventory of Cache Bifaces with Artifact and Raw Material Categories

LOCATION	ACCESSION NUMBER	DESCRIPTION	RAW MATERIAL
		1963	
Herrett	97-1-2	Middle stage biface	Blue-white CCS
Herrett	97-1-1	Late stage biface	Blue-white CCS
Herrett	97-1-4	Early stage biface	Blue-white CCS
Herrett	97-1-5	Early stage biface	White/tan CCS
Herrett	97-1-3	Early stage biface	Quartz crystal
Herrett	97-1-14	Middle stage biface	Red with black band CCS
Herrett	97-1-7	Middle stage biface	Blue-white CCS
Herrett	97-1-8	Middle stage biface	Brown/green CCS
Herrett	97-1-15	Middle stage biface	White/tan CCS
Herrett	97-1-10	Early stage biface	Greenish-gray quartzite
Herrett	97-1-12	Middle stage biface	Quartz crystal
Herrett	97-1-9	Early stage biface	Brown/green CCS
Herrett	97-1-11	Early stage biface	Brown/tan mottled CCS
Herrett	97-1-17	Knife	White/brownish
Herrett	97-1-18	Knife	Yellow CCS
Herrett	97-1-19	Late stage biface	Green CCS
Herrett	97-1-21	Middle stage biface	Yellow/green with red CCS
Herrett	97-1-22	Knife	Red/brown with light inclusions CCS
Herrett	97-1-23	Middle stage biface	Flesh-colored CCS
Herrett	97-1-16	Preform	White translucent CCS
IMNH	18-A-21 (LC)	Conjoined biface[d]	Light blue/gray CCS
Herrett	97-1-26	Projectile point	Striped light tan CCS
Herrett	97-1-25	Projectile point	Tan/brownish CCS
Herrett	97-1-27	Projectile point	Tan/brownish CCS
Herrett	97-1-29	Projectile point	White/tan CCS
Herrett	97-1-28	Projectile point	Brown translucent CCS
Unknown	1529-25-1[a]	Indeterminate stage biface	Yellow/red CCS
Unknown	1529-25-3[a]	Indeterminate stage biface	Yellow/red CCS
		1969	
IMNH	1651-2	Early stage biface	Black CCS
Unknown	1529-25-2[a]	Indeterminate stage biface	Red and flesh-colored CCS
IMNH	18-A-21 (PB1)	Indeterminate stage biface	Flesh-colored CCS
IMNH	5462	Graver	Light gray/white CCS
Unknown	N/A[b]	Spokeshave?	Unknown
IMNH	152917	Projectile point	Light brown/gray with stripes CCS
IMNH	1529-33-1	Projectile point	Tan/yellow with black CCS
Herrett	Unknown[c]	Projectile point	Brown translucent CCS

LOCATION	ACCESSION NUMBER	DESCRIPTION	RAW MATERIAL
		1985	
Herrett	97-1-6	Middle stage biface	Yellow mottled CCS
Herrett	97-1-13	Late stage biface	Blue-white CCS
Herrett	97-1-20	Middle stage biface	Tan mottled CCS
Herrett	97-1-24	Middle stage biface	Quartz crystal
		1997	
Herrett	97-1-31	Indeterminate stage biface	Blue-white CCS
Herrett	97-1-32	Indeterminate stage biface	Yellow/green with red CCS
Herrett	97-1-30	Indeterminate stage biface	Quartz crystal
		Post-1997	
Herrett	09-3-1	Late stage biface	White translucent CCS
Herrett	09-3-2	Preform	White translucent CCS

Note: Herrett = Herrett Center for Arts and Science, College of Southern Idaho, Twin Falls; IMNH = Idaho Museum of Natural History, Idaho State University, Pocatello; CCS = cryptocrystalline silicate.

[a]The location of the artifact is unknown; the accession number listed refers to an archival photograph at the IMNH.

[b]The location of the artifact is unknown, as is the accession number; last seen as part of accession number IMNH 18-A-21.

[c]This artifact was missing but was recently rediscovered; no accession number is available.

[d]This artifact is accessioned as one piece; however, it is actually four artifacts. In the analysis, it is treated as two early-stage bifaces and two scrapers.

from beyond the region and therefore lacked any regional context for their identifications. At best such identifications should be considered in terms of a "compares favorably" observation rather than a definitive identification of a material source.

Artifacts appearing only in photographs presented a difficult challenge since they could only be assigned to raw material categories based on the available photos. Such designations have some inherent limitations, since detail is limited and coloration is dependent on camera settings, proper film developing, and the stability of color film over time. To arrive at reasonable raw material designations, I digitized the archival photos. The images used were selected based on the presence of reported artifacts in the frame with previously unreported artifacts.

I adjusted the digital photos with Photoshop 13.0 and/or Corel Photo-Paint to match the appearance of the known artifacts in the photo with their physical appearance. I made these adjustments in the presence of the actual known artifacts. I assumed that when the colors of known artifacts looked correct to me, the unknown artifacts would also be approximately true to their original color. The outcome may not be ideal, but it is superior to removing the previously unknown artifacts from the analysis.

At the nodule scale the inclusion of the additional artifacts increased the raw material diversity dramatically. Table 2.3 lists all specific raw material categories used in this analysis and illustrates the changes in raw material diversity over time. This result is particularly interesting because the Simon cache has already been identified as the Clovis cache showing the greatest amount of raw material diversity (Kilby 2008). Also of interest and more in line with the point of this chapter, the relative frequencies of raw materials show significant changes over time since the initial discovery and reporting of the cache. For example, quartz crystal has doubled in abundance, moving from a secondary type to one of the dominant raw material types. Further, the relative frequencies of raw materials have not stabilized. The last two artifact recoveries from the site have doubled the frequency of "white translucent CCS."

TOOL CLASSES

Over the past few decades it has become fashionable to view Clovis mixed biface caches as models of a single reduction trajectory (see Wilke 2002; Wilke et al. 1991; Woods and Titmus 1985). The object or final product of

TABLE 2.3. Raw Material Category Abundance by Year

Raw Material Description	1963	1969	1985	1997	POST-1997	TOTAL
Blue-white CCS	4		1	1		6
Light blue/gray CCS	4					4
Quartz crystal	2		1	1		4
White/tan CCS	3					3
White translucent CCS	1				2	3
Red with black band CCS	2					2
Tan/brownish CCS	2					2
Yellow/red CCS	2					2
Brown translucent CCS	1	1				2
Yellow/green with red CCS	1			1		2
Brown/green CCS	1					1
Greenish-gray quartzite	1					1
Brown/tan mottled CCS	1					1
White/brownish CCS	1					1
Yellow CCS	1					1
Green CCS	1					1
Red/brown with light inclusions CCS	1					1
Flesh-colored CCS	1					1
Light tan striped CCS	1					1
Black CCS		1				1
Red and flesh-colored CCS		1				1
Tan/yellow with black CCS		1				1
Light gray/white CCS		1				1
Light brown/gray with striped CCS		1				1
Yellow mottled CCS			1			1
Tan mottled CCS			1			1

Note: CCS = cryptocrystalline silicate.

this reduction trajectory is argued to be projectile points (Wilke et al. 1991). Certainly this approach has its uses and is a valid analytical scheme. However, viewing mixed biface caches exclusively in terms of a set reduction trajectory also has several inherent problems. First, the approach ignores tool forms that exist within the trajectory leading to projectile points. For example, bifaces in various forms make good tools in their own right; they are useful for butchery, woodworking, digging, and other tasks (Huckell 2007:189–191). Thinking of bifaces only as transitional forms between blanks and projectile points limits the perception of these forms as tools. Second, a reduction trajectory approach focused on projectile points ignores tool forms that fall wholly outside of the projectile point trajectory. This is especially true when such forms are also based in bifacial reduction. Several bifaces in the Simon cache are clearly not intended for reduction into projectile points. The best example is an asymmetrical, heavily pot-lidded bifacial knife (Herrett No. 97-1-17). Finally, and most importantly in this research, the reduction-trajectory approach imposes an artificially low upper limit on tool class diversity. In other words, the only artifact designations available for use are whatever "stages" the analyst is content to "identify." While some imposition of categories on a reduction continuum may be necessary, the impacts of such schemes on the analysis should be appreciated.

As an alternative I chose to look at the Simon cache in terms of generic morphological categories (i.e., scraper, knife, graver, etc.) in addition to classifying bifaces in terms of reduction "stage." Since this chapter does not include a detailed discussion of use-wear studies (which will appear in another publication), no actual function is implied. It is well known that actual uses often deviate from morphological type (Odell 1981). I decided to use only one category per artifact. There are valid alternatives to this method (such as that of Knudson 1983) that would probably supply different results. Biface categories were retained for artifacts that were not assigned an alternative label. See Table 2.4 for a list of the artifact categories used. The result of this analysis is that artifact-class diversity nearly doubles from previous studies (Table 2.4). The relative frequency of artifact classes also changes with the addition of previously unreported artifacts.

PERCEPTIONS OF CLOVIS CACHES

There are a variety of perceptions (ideas or beliefs) concerning Clovis mixed biface caches that the previously reported Simon cache assemblage has helped to support. Below I discuss how these popular assertions fare when the previously unreported Simon cache artifacts are considered. In some cases the assertions were already undermined by the existing evidence, and I discuss from both perspectives.

Mixed biface caches have been argued to consist of "oversize" artifacts that were unsuitable for everyday use (Bonnichsen 1977; Gramly 1993; Wilke et al. 1991; Woods and Titmus 1985). At the time of their discovery the Simon cache projectile points were the largest examples ever reported. The large bifaces and projectile points from East Wenatchee (Gramly 1993) and Anzick (Wilke et al. 1991) have been used as examples of oversize artifacts as well. The previously unreported artifacts from the Simon cache provide evidence that cache artifacts that appear unused nonetheless may have been intended for use. One example is a projectile point fragment (IMNH No. 152917) that compares favorably in terms of size and shape to the large complete points in the collection that possesses evidence of use. This evidence of use includes the type of breakage, tip fracture, and microscopic striations parallel to the longitudinal

TABLE 2.4. Artifact Category Abundance by Year

Artifact Category	1963	1969	1985	1997	POST-1997	TOTAL
Middle stage biface	8		3			11
Early stage biface	8	1				9
Debitage		9				9
Projectile point	5	3				8
Indeterminate stage biface	2	2		3		7
Flake tool		5				5
Late stage biface	2		1		1	4
Knife	3	3				3
Scraper	2					2
Preform	1				1	2
Graver		1				1
Spokeshave		1				1
Ochre nodule		1				1

axis of the point (Santarone 2006). Another projectile point fragment from the Simon cache documented in archival photographs (IMNH No. 1529) and recently rediscovered in museum collections shows clear evidence of a reworked impact fracture and partially completed reworking of a midpoint break as well (Figure 2.5). The assertion that Clovis cache artifacts are "oversize" is also called into question because flaked stone tool technologies are inherently reductive. To borrow Shott and Ballenger's (2007:153) analogy—picking pencil stubs out of the garbage is not a good way to determine the attributes of pencils prior to use. Mixed biface caches do not consist of tools abandoned due to exhaustion of their utility and therefore should be expected to differ from tools that archaeologists recover that were abandoned due to their lack of remaining use-life (Kilby 2008). Additionally, evidence has been reported recently that, at least at the Gault site, Clovis knappers were routinely producing very large bifaces and projectile point preforms (Bradley et al. 2010). This suggests that the bifaces and projectile points from Clovis caches may not have been unusual in their systemic context. The pristine appearance and relatively large size of the five well-known Simon cache projectile points contributed to the idea that such projectiles were not intended for use. The presence in the cache of used projectile points (and, indeed, other tools) demonstrates that an apparent lack of practical utility in the eyes of modern viewers was not necessarily shared by the Clovis people who chose artifacts for inclusion in the cache.

Another popular perception is that Clovis mixed biface caches are made up of artifacts that display an exceptional level of knapping mastery. Also part of this assertion is the knapping of extremely exotic raw material types (for example, quartz crystal). In part this perception is driven by the preferential curation of the largest and most complete artifacts, and also by the practice of choosing particular (aesthetically pleasing) artifacts to highlight in publication text and illustrations. Admittedly, this perception is also accurate at least in part as shown by the presence of some truly exceptional examples of the knapper's art. However, concentrating attention on the exceptionally high-quality examples of knapping in mixed biface caches is missing the forest for the trees. To step back and look at the Simon assemblage as a whole, especially with the addition of the previously unreported artifacts—which consist mainly of fragments, recycled tools, and expedient tool forms—a clearer picture develops. The artifacts in the Simon cache display a range of knapping skill (and/or effort). In addition to examples of extremely skilled knapping, there are examples of average and even poor or haphazard knapping.

I have shown that the artifacts cached at the Simon site were more varied in form, life history, and material than published sources indicate. Rather than merely consisting of complete bifaces and pristine projectile points, the cache includes heavily used formal tools, expedient flake tools, and debitage. This suggests that future utility may not have been a necessary attribute for inclusion in the cache. The Simon cache includes a wide diversity of raw material. Clearly, the people who left this cache were in possession of a broad array of raw materials likely acquired from at least several sources. Unfortunately, the lithic sources in both the local area and the broader region are typically not well known or documented, making the interpretation of raw material diversity problematic. Although large, apparently unused, and very finely made artifacts are part of the Simon cache assemblage, the general statement that the cache consists of oversize, pristine artifacts demonstrating extreme knapping mastery cannot be supported.

The known inventory of the Simon Clovis cache has fluctuated over time since the discovery of the cache in 1961. Additional artifacts have come into the cache through archaeological fieldwork and causal encounter. Artifacts from the assemblage have also been lost. Through historical research, I have been able to document the most complete inventory for the Simon cache that has ever been compiled and to document the known assemblages at different points in time. One result of this research has been to show how the inferences drawn from the cache have been compromised by the use of an incomplete and not fully representative inventory. The changes in the assemblage of the Simon cache over time

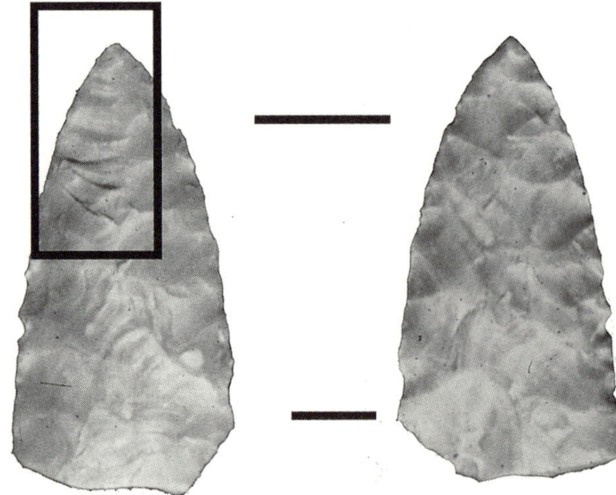

Figure 2.5. Projectile point fragment showing reworking (74 mm long)

provide a cautionary tale for archaeologists working with similar assemblages.

Mixed biface caches provide attractive opportunities for archaeologists to study the technological organization and mobility patterns of Clovis peoples. However, archaeologists need to use these assemblages with caution. Clovis mixed biface caches represent a trifecta of potential interpretive problems: (1) a rare site type, (2) uncontrolled recovery and curation, and (3) comparatively small inventories. Rarity of encounter makes it difficult to develop reasonable expectations of what should be present. Uncontrolled recovery and curation create a potential for assemblage drift—for the addition or subtraction of artifacts from the assemblage. Finally, the comparatively small inventories cause a magnification of the impacts of any assemblage drift on the interpretation of the assemblage. Because of these factors, using mixed biface cache assemblages requires a commitment to understanding the assemblage as a sample. Using a historical approach to understanding the cache assemblage allows for the detection of assemblage drift. Being aware of the potential for problems allows researchers to develop methods for addressing research questions that are robust to the factors likely influencing the documented assemblage, resulting in securely grounded interpretations.

Chapter 3

A Contextual and Technological Reevaluation of the Dickenson Blade Cache, Blackwater Locality No. 1, Roosevelt County, New Mexico

Peter C. Condon, George Crawford, Vance T. Holliday, C. Vance Haynes Jr., and Jill Onken

INTRODUCTION

In 1962 Blackwater Locality No. 1, the Clovis type site, yielded the first documented cached assemblage of 17 blades (i.e., the Green cache) associated with late Pleistocene deposits in North America (Green 1963; Stanford 1991; Collins 1999b) (Figure 3.1). This discovery significantly contributed to the recognition of a regionally related Clovis blade technology, a critical milestone in the study of early Paleoindian adaptive strategies on the southern High Plains (Green 1963; Kilby and Huckell 2003; Kilby 2008). Equally important, the 1962 Green cache provided a type assemblage that could be placed in stratigraphic context and chronologically correlated, establishing a standard by which other early Paleoindian blades and blade caches could be compared.

Twenty-eight years later, a cache of five blades (i.e., the Dickenson cache) was recovered within a section of collapsed wall along the western boundary of the Clovis type site, approximately 260 m north of the Green cache location (Montgomery and Dickenson 1992a) (Figure 3.2). The collapse, caused by a combination of seasonal rainfall and drainage from the irrigation system associated with the adjacent dairy farm, occurred south of the Mitchell Folsom Locality and removed a large portion of the west bank wall, including the buried arroyo channel documented by Hester in 1972.

An initial examination of the slump pile revealed two unbroken blades and one blade fragment. Over the next several months, two additional blades were collected from the same locale. Following the second discovery, the conjoining piece to the previously collected fragment was recovered a short distance from the initial discovery spot. Comparable to the blades in the Green cache, the Dickenson blades were made from a lightly speckled/mottled-gray Edwards Formation chert (Montgomery and Dickenson 1992a:32). A subsequent excavation of the slump pile by Eastern New Mexico University failed to yield additional artifacts (Montgomery and Dickenson 1992a).

Continued stratigraphic and archaeological investigations along the West Bank provided a stratigraphic context for the Dickenson cache along with additional archaeological data. In 1991 C. V. Haynes mapped the entire West Bank stratigraphic sequence. In 2000, as part of a stabilization project, Eastern New Mexico University excavated a trench across the buried arroyo, revealing the microstratigraphy and artifacts, both treated in this paper. In 2010 V. T. Holliday conducted soil coring across the paleo-arroyo and in the adjacent Mitchell Folsom Locality.

Field characteristics from the arroyo fill helped reveal the depositional history of the channel and provided the geologic context for the Dickenson cache. The recovery of an in situ blade tool during the 2000 excavation pointed toward a possible spatial connection to the 1990 cache and offered direction toward investigating its provenience.

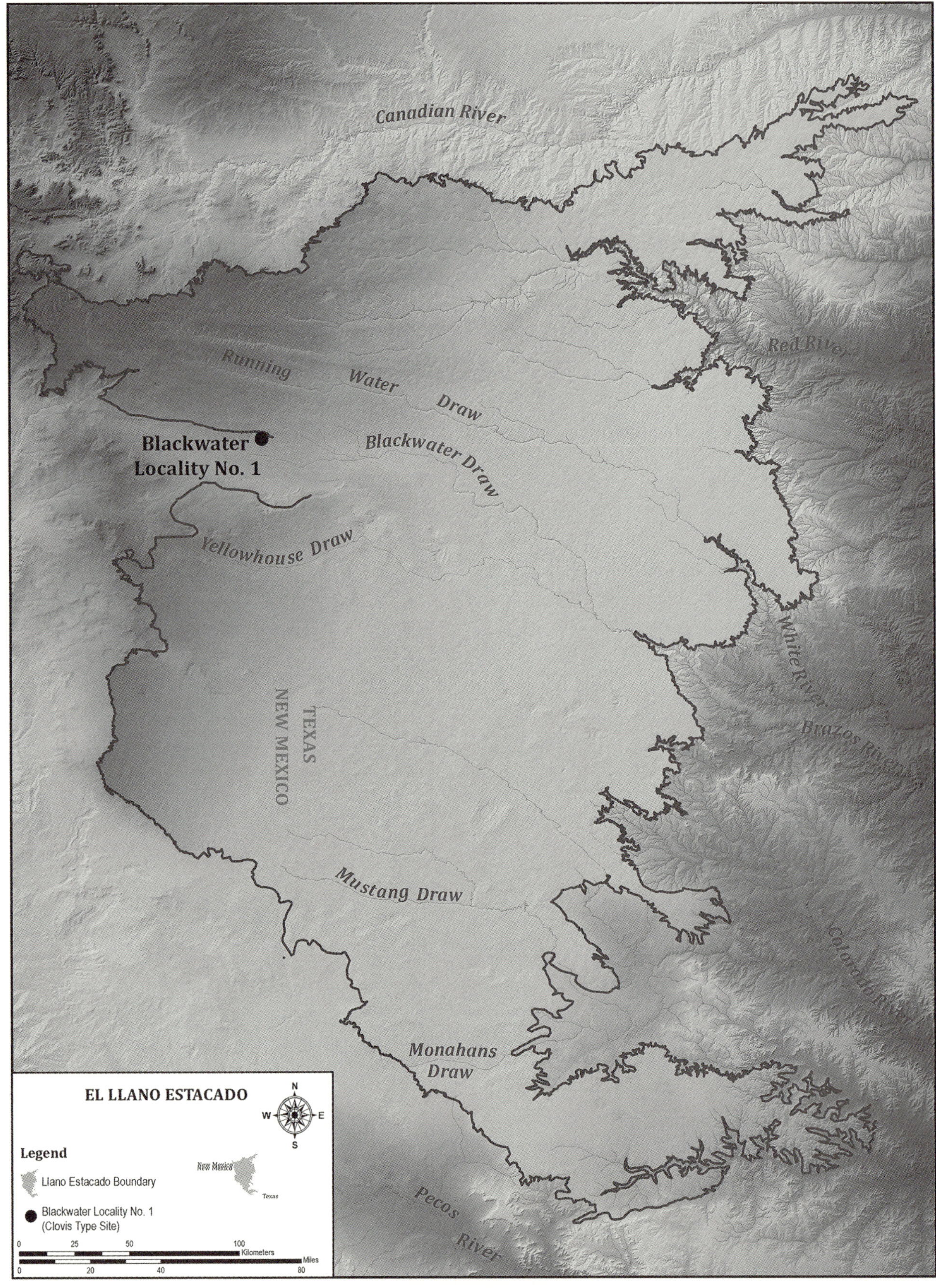

Figure 3.1. Map showing the location of Blackwater Draw Locality No. 1 on the Llano Estacado (modified from Holliday 1997:3)

These data tentatively provide a synthesis from which a technological comparison between the Green and Dickenson blade caches can be conducted. The resulting data sets allowed for a bridging of the contextual and technological aspects of the cache, establishing a depositional framework prior to examining the suite of characteristics attributed to Clovis blade manufacture.

FIELD AND LABORATORY ANALYSIS

Most of the stratigraphic data was gathered from a 1 m by 5 m north–south trench excavated to a depth of 2.5 m in 2000. Additional information came from dating the arroyo fill (C. Vance Haynes Jr., personal communication 2011) and from Giddings Core 10–9, recovered northwest of the 2000 excavations by Holliday in 2010. Coring continued for another 2 m below the floor of the excavations, resulting in a partial cross section of the buried arroyo channel. Field methods included the documentation and sampling of five strata (I, II, III, IV, IVa) exposed in profile during the West Bank excavation. A sixth stratum (IVb) was identified in soil cores below the base of excavation.

Following the depositional interpretations, metric and nonmetric analyses were applied to the 1990 blade assemblage. Using Collins's (1999b:85–88) series of measurements, the range of variability between the Green ($n = 17$) and Dickenson caches ($n = 5$) was evaluated, allowing for a quantitative comparison of these two assemblages (Green 1963; Montgomery and Dickenson 1992a; Collins 1999b; Condon 2000).

THE DICKENSON CACHE

The following discussion presents the visual elements and diagnostic characteristics identified for each of the five Dickenson blades (Figure 3.3). Form and condition are evaluated for each blade, highlighting distinctive characteristics and establishing technological associations that will assist in the comparative process.

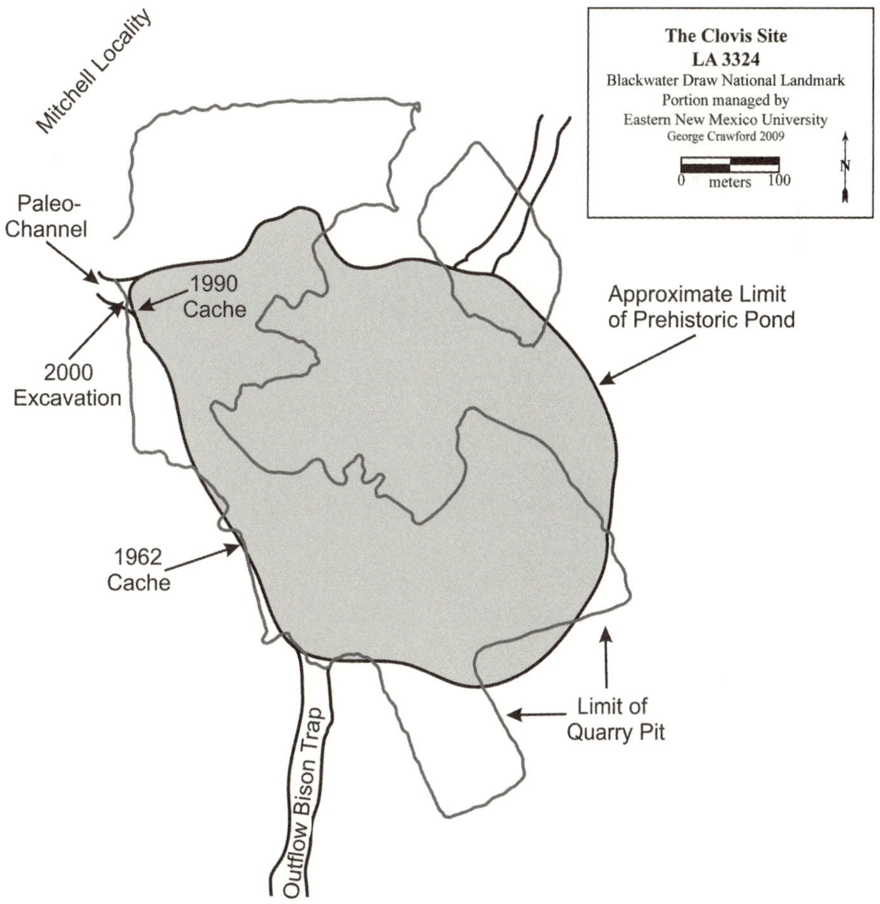

Figure 3.2. Location of Green (1962) and Dickenson (1990) caches at Blackwater Draw Locality No. 1

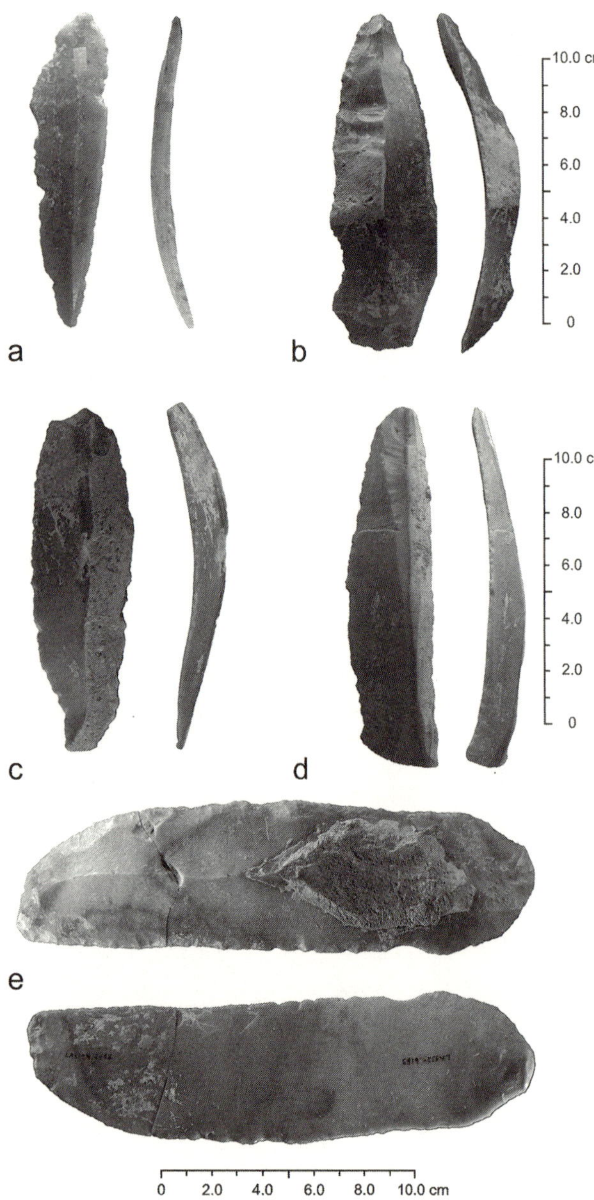

Figure 3.3. Dickenson blade cache: (a) 1.1990.1.6184, (b) 1.1990.1.6185, (c) 1.1990.1.6186, (d) 1.1990.1.6187, and (e) 1.1990.1.6183/6188 (photographs modified from ENMU Archives)

1.1990.1.6183/6188

Blade 1.1990.1.6183/6188 consists of two pieces that conjoin to form the largest of the five blades in the Dickenson cache (Figure 3.3e). Cortex is clearly visible on the dorsal surface. The removal of two blades earlier in the reduction process produced a prominent longitudinal arris that divides the lower half of 1.1990.1.6183/6188. These earlier blade detachments initiated in the opposite direction of the existing platform and failed to remove the cortex remaining on the exterior of the blade. Overlapping retouch scars along the distal margin removed evidence of this earlier platform. The proximal end of the blade reveals multiple scars extending from the left lateral and upper-right lateral margins, possibly isolating the present platform. Linear retouch and smaller informal flake scars form a consistent bimarginal pattern the length of the blade.

The platform displays multiple facets, possible grinding, a lenticular outline, and a pronounced lip at the ventral surface/platform juncture. The bulb of force is diffuse, while in contrast, the eraillure scar is relatively deep and well defined. Flake scars on both the dorsal and ventral surfaces obscure the termination and form a bifacial edge at the distal margin. Unlike the remaining four blades, 1.1990.1.6183/6188 reveals a shallow longitudinal curve suggestive of early removal in the reduction sequence. The transverse break separating the blade into two segments most likely occurred during the wall collapse, suggesting that this blade was originally intact.

1.1990.1.6184

Blade 1.1990.1.6184 (Figure 3.3a) is the smallest of the five blades in both length and width. One primary arris runs the length of the blade; a second parallels the right margin. A third, minor scar intersects with the first just below the proximal end. No cortex is present. Calcareous sediment adheres to the left side of the dorsal surface and to a lesser extent along the right. Both lateral margins exhibit linear retouch, with deep flake detachments resulting in an irregular left margin. The flake pattern along the right edge is more continuous and consistent.

The platform of 1.1990.1.6184 is multifaceted, isolated, and oval in outline. The bulb of force is more salient, yet still relatively flat. A minor lip is present at the ventral surface/platform juncture; the absence of an eraillure scar is noted. Several flake scars are intrusive into the ventral surface; however, these scars are infrequent, often singular, occurring primarily on the right ventral margin. Ripple marks are noted near the distal end. Sediment is present along the upper portion of the ventral surface. This blade is moderately curved, indicating a removal farther along in the reduction process, an interpretation tentatively supported by the lack of cortex.

1.1990.1.6185

This cortical blade is asymmetrical in outline and distinguished by a primary longitudinal arris that nearly extends the length of the dorsal surface (Figure 3.3b). A complete blade, 1.1990.1.6185 retains evidence of two prior blade detachments to the right of the central arris (Montgomery and Dickenson 1992a). These two previous removals overlap one another, creating a second arris paralleling the right lateral margin. Four perpendicular scars extend from the left lateral margin across the dorsal surface of the blade. These scars were partially removed by the previously mentioned blade detachments that produced the central arris present on 1.1990.1.6185. Cortex separates the perpendicular scars from one another. Cemented calcareous sediments are visible on the dorsal surface. Linear retouch and smaller use-wear scars form a consistent pattern along both the right and left lateral margins. A cluster of scars obscures the distal margin.

The platform is isolated and multifaceted, with a small width and thickness. The bulb of force is defined; a marginal platform lip was noted, as was the absence of an eraillure scar. The interior surface is smooth with undulations present on the lower third of the blade (Montgomery and Dickenson 1992a). Inconsistent flake scars occur along the left ventral edge of the blade. A small patch of sediment adheres to the ventral surface. The scar pattern, presence of cortex, and high degree of curvature indicate that this blade was removed early in the reduction sequence.

1.1990.1.6186

This intact blade has two parallel, longitudinal flake scars that extend the length of the dorsal surface (Figure 3.3c). A partial third arris parallels the left lateral margin. Three minor detachments removed sections of the left and right central arris prior to blade removal. All scars noted on the dorsal surface are unidirectional, initiating from the current platform. Although uncertain, the termination of the blade appears to have removed a portion of the core (Montgomery and Dickenson 1992a). Calcareous sediment is observed along the right-side exterior of the blade. No cortex is present. Linear flake scars are present on the right and left lateral edges and minimally along the distal margin.

The platform is isolated, multifaceted, and narrow in width. The small flake removed from the upper dorsal surface reduced the platform thickness, resulting in a measurement well below the other four blades. A lip is present at the ventral surface/platform juncture. An absence of an eraillure is noted. The partial bulb of force is easily defined. Sediment is minimally present on the interior of the blade. A curvature index of 9.1 assigned to this blade suggests that the reduction sequence was more advanced when 1.1990.1.6186 was removed from the core.

1.1990.1.6187

This cortical blade is intact with a single central arris that extends the entirety of the dorsal surface (Figure 3.3d). The arris was formed by the prior removal of a single blade initiating from the current platform, which removed the cortex from the left half of the blade. A small chip or fissure offset from the arris is visible in the midsection of the dorsal surface. The distal margin exhibits a cortical termination. Cortex covers the majority of the right exterior of the blade. Calcareous sediment adheres to the upper-left portion of the blade. At least three minor scars have impacted the proximal end of the blade. Edge modification consists of linear scars along the left lateral margin. The right lateral margin shows inconsistent flake scars impacting the distal half of the blade edge.

A well-defined eraillure scar has impacted the platform and removed a portion of the bulb of force. Despite the damage, the platform still retains several facets, suggesting striking platform preparation and possible grinding. The remnant bulb of force is clearly defined. The interior surface shows undulations as well as a series of small flake scars intrusive into the ventral surface from the right lateral margin. Sediment adheres to the right ventral surface of the blade. The high percentage of cortex combined with a moderately high curvature index points toward removal during the early stages of core reduction.

STRATIGRAPHIC SEQUENCE

The paleo-arroyo on the West Bank has been known to researchers at Blackwater Draw since at least the time of F. E. Green's work in the early 1960s. Hester (1972:12, Figure 15) indicates a buried "arroyo" in the same area. The research reported here is the first attempt at synthesizing what is known about the drainage. In addition, archaeological and stratigraphic work at the Mitchell Folsom Locality, approximately 25 m north of the West Bank excavations (Boldurian 1990; Haynes 2011; Holliday 1995), provides further geoarchaeological context.

Hester (1972:12, Figure 15) shows the West Bank paleo-channel entering from the northwest. Holliday's Core 10-9, located northwest of both the 2000 excavations and the paleo-arroyo mapped on the West Bank, encountered a stratigraphic sequence very similar to that documented during the 2000 excavations, suggesting that the buried channel did flow from northwest to southeast.

The ancient arroyo is entrenched into the Blackwater Draw Formation (BD Fm) and associated lake beds. The BD Fm is a Pleistocene eolian deposit that accumulated episodically across the High Plains surface (Holliday 1989, 1997). In the area of the Blackwater Draw site the BD Fm interfingers with carbonate-rich lake-bed deposits that accumulated on the floor of the drainage basin (Holliday 1995). The BD Fm and the carbonates are part of Unit A, as defined and described by Haynes (1975, 1995) (Table 3.1). The youngest carbonate layer and the Gomez soil of Green (Stratum B of Holliday 1995; Haynes and Warnica 2012) rests on top of the youngest soil of the BD Fm and forms a distinct marker bed around the Blackwater Draw site. An organic-rich mud at the base of Holliday's (1995) Stratum B yielded late Pleistocene radiocarbon dates (~22,900 B.P. on the West Bank, Haynes 1995; ~21,140 B.P. on the North Bank, Holliday 1995). Locally, between the BD Fm and Stratum B is a thin layer of alluvial sand and gravel (Stratum A of Holliday 1995). Above the Stratum B carbonate along the West Bank is an eolian sheet sand with a moderately well-expressed Bt horizon (Stratum C). The Folsom occupation at the Mitchell site is associated with Stratum C (Stratum II of Boldurian 1990).

The upper half of the fill in the paleo-arroyo was exposed during the 2000 excavations (Figure 3.4). Additional stratigraphic data were recovered from a series of hand-auger cores taken down from the base of the excavations after the digging was completed. Six strata were identified, numbered from the top down: I, II, III, IV, IVa, IVb. Stratum IVb is a calcareous gravel and sand. The full depth of the channel fill was not penetrated by the auger coring but it is estimated to be at least 90 cm thick. The core data show that Stratum IVb slopes down to the north. The top of the layer was encountered approximately 280 cm below surface at the south end of the excavations. It is unclear what the depth is to the north. A similar layer was also exposed elsewhere on the West Bank and is likely Holliday's Stratum A at the Mitchell Folsom Locality. As exposed along the West Bank, Stratum A is flat-lying across the top of the BD Fm south of the paleo-arroyo and is redeposited down the channel as Stratum IVb. This aspect of IVb indicates that the sand and gravel at the base of the channel is likely reworked from the layer on top of the BD Fm. As noted above, the sand and gravel is dated approximately 22,000 RCYBP where it rests on the BD Fm (Holliday 1989). In the paleo-channel, charcoal recovered from fill that postdates the sand and gravel was dated between 12,100 and 13,400 RCYBP (Table 3.2) (Haynes 2011).

Stratum IVa is calcareous sand with distinct iron oxide–rich laminae and common, minute freshwater *Planorbidae* sp. shells (Emerson and Jacobson 1976). A steeply retouched blade tool was found in the upper portion of Stratum IVa. This tool was made from Edwards Plateau chert visually similar to that of the cached blades (Figure 3.5). The laminations and the shell suggest that the unit was water-lain. Stratum IV is a more massive calcareous sand, though weak bedding is apparent, with lithic artifacts, including a reworked Midland point (Figure 3.6). Midland points, which are possibly contemporaneous

TABLE 3.1. Correlation of Stratigraphic Designations

HOLLIDAY 1997	HAYNES 1995
C (upland sand sheet)	Not recognized
B	A_9
A (alluvial sand/gravel)	Not recognized
Blackwater Draw Formation	A^3–A^8

TABLE 3.2. Chronometric Data for West Bank Arroyo Channel (Haynes 2011)

AA NO.	SAMPLE NO.	MATERIAL	D13C	F	14C AGE B.P.
AA94994	23BWD91A3	Organic sand	-18.2	0.1942±0.00016	13,167±65
AA94995	23BWD91B	Humates	-17.0	0.1896±0.00016	13,357±65
AA94996	25BWD91A3	Organic sand	-17.3	0.2213±0.00017	12,115±60
AA94997	25BWD91B	Humates	-17.5	0.2636±0.00018	10,711±54

with Folsom, generally date between 10,490 and 10,170 B.P. at the Clovis type site (Haynes and Warnica 2012; Hester 1972; LeTourneau 2000; Taylor et al. 1996).

Stratum III is 50 to 80 cm thick, brown, consolidated sandy loam. The weathering characteristics (brown coloration and structure) are indicative of a soil B horizon. These characteristics and the archaeological stratigraphy suggest that Stratum III may be a facies of the sandy soil (Stratum C) associated with the Folsom occupation in the Mitchell Locality. Strata I and II are minimally weathered layers of sand. They are part of the late Holocene (and possibly Historic) eolian sand sheet (Unit G of Haynes 1975, 1995) that blankets the area. One complete Agate Basin point made from Alibates silicified dolomite was recovered from Stratum III (see Figure 3.6). Agate Basin artifacts were found above and at times intermingled with the Folsom deposits along the north bank of the Clovis type site by Haynes and Agogino (1966), suggesting a possible late temporal overlap at this site (Agogino and Rovner 1969; Green 1963; Haynes and Warnica 2012; Hester 1972; Holliday 2005). However, Haynes and Warnica (2012) found no stratigraphic overlap between the Folsom strata and the Agate Basin strata in their more recent study.

EVALUATING TECHNOLOGY: BLADE MORPHOLOGY AND ATTRIBUTE SELECTION

The Clovis blade is defined as a specialized flake, derived primarily from a unidirectional core (Bradley et al. 2010; Collins 1999b). The blade is long, relatively narrow, and curved in longitudinal section with single or double dorsal flake scars that run parallel or subparallel to the lateral

West Bank Arroyo Excavation

ENMU Archives_Crawford 2000

Test Unit Plan View / Auger Cores

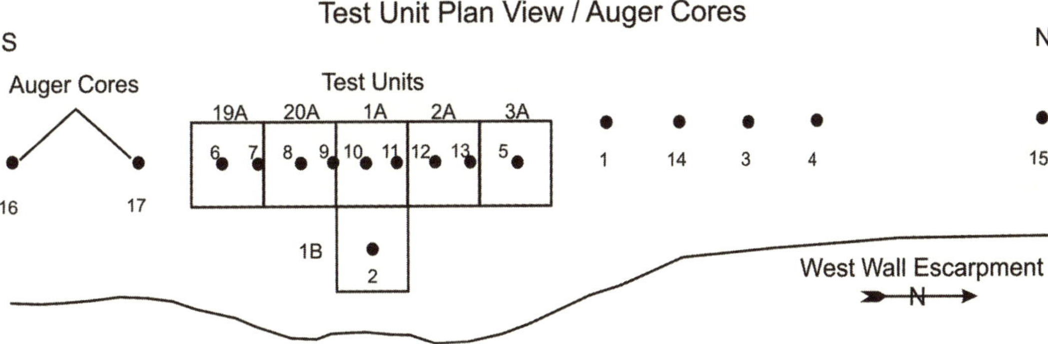

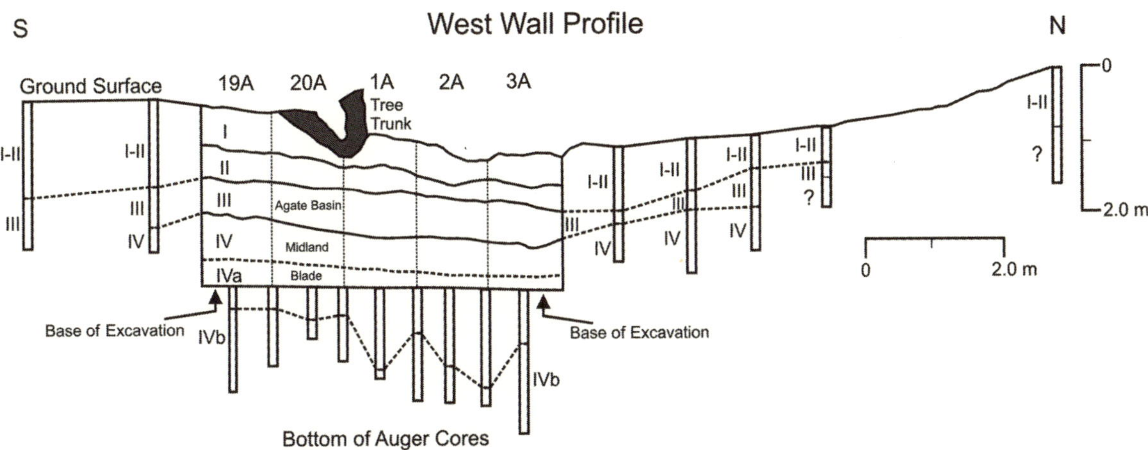

Figure 3.4. West Bank Arroyo excavation and west wall cross section

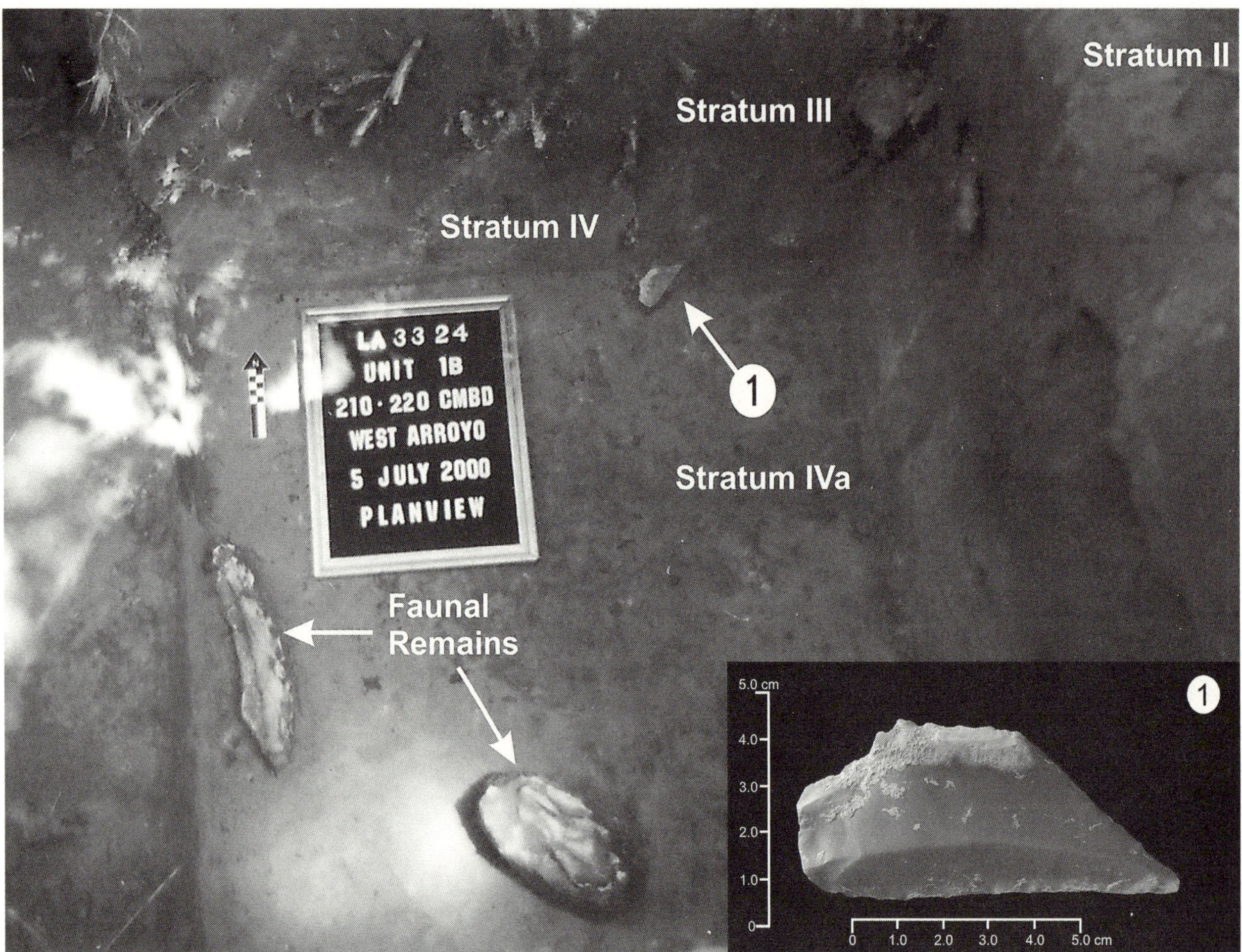

Figure 3.5. Blade tool recovered from upper portion of Stratum IVa, West Bank Arroyo excavation (inset photograph courtesy of ENMU Archives)

margins (Collins 1999b). Length and curvature are maximized, while overall thickness is minimized. Blade transverse cross sections are plano-convex, triangulate, subtriangulate, rectangular, or trapezoidal (Collins 1999b; Crabtree 1982). Platform remnants are prepared and faceted, with a restricted width and thickness. Ventral surfaces are often devoid of compression rings, with a diffuse bulb of force (Collins 1999b; Crabtree 1982; Green 1963).

Based on research by Collins (1999b) and Bradley et al. (2010), seven statistically measurable attributes and three nonmetric attributes were selected for analysis on the Green and Dickenson blades caches (Figure 3.7). The metric analyses focused on morphological and technological attributes that would quantify the range of blade variability between the two caches. Maximum length measures the long axis of a blade from proximal end to distal margin. Length was measured for unbroken specimens ($n = 9$), consisting of 62-120-01, 62-120-02, 62-120-03, and 62-120-04 from the Green cache and all five of the Dickenson cache blades. Maximum width measured the widest section of the blade ($n = 22$) and included all specimens. Maximum thickness ($n = 22$) was measured for the thickest portion of the blade away from the bulb of force on unbroken blades and blade fragments (Figure 3.7).

Platform width measures the maximum distance between the two platform-remnant and lateral-margin junctures ($n = 12$). Platform depth measures the maximum distance between the interior and exterior margins of the platform remnant. Platform measurements were carried out on both complete and proximal blade fragments. Blade curvature index was determined using the formula *b / a x 100*, where *a* is the maximum length of the blade and *b* is the maximum distance between the ventral surface of the blade and the perpendicular measurement between the proximal and distal margins of the blade. The greater the curvature of the blade, the higher the index value (Collins 1999b:86). Thirteen blades and blade fragments were selected for curvature analysis.

Three nonmetric indices were selected for this study and informed on reduction sequence and technique: (1) estimated percentage of cortex addressed stage of reduction; (2) dorsal flake-scar count, which was also used to evaluate reduction sequence (n = 22); and (3) bulbar definition subjectively described the bulb of force as either diffuse or salient and evaluated applied force and reduction technique (n = 12).

All data were recorded in metric units of measure using Mitutoyo digital calipers (accurate to 0.01 mm). Mean values and standard deviations were calculated for applicable attributes. Platform remnant analysis was conducted with the aid of a 10.5x–45x Bausch and Lomb stereoscope. Box plots were generated to evaluate length, width, and thickness measurements as well as platform-remnant width and depth variables. Due to the small sample size, the nonparametric Mann-Whitney U Test was calculated for maximum length, width, and thickness, platform-remnant width and depth, and curvature.

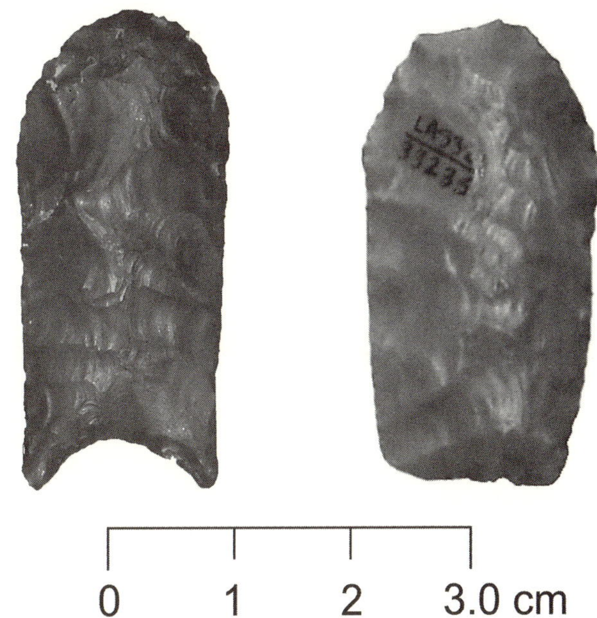

Figure 3.6. Midland point recovered from Stratum IV (*left*); Agate Basin recovered from Stratum III (*right*) (images courtesy of ENMU Archives)

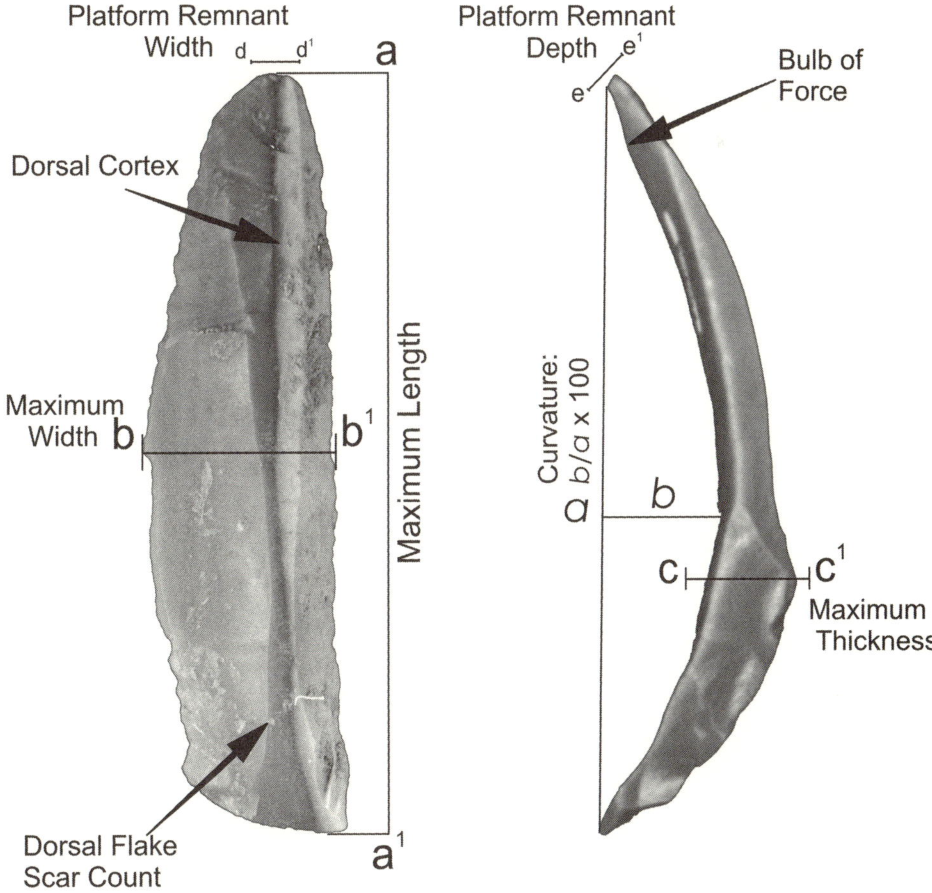

Figure 3.7. Metric and nonmetric variables selected for analysis (different blades shown for effect)

BLADE ANALYSIS RESULTS

The blade analysis was structured using Collins's (1999) recording methods, which allowed for data compatibility. Summary statistics are presented in Table 3.3 and Table 3.4. The statistical analysis suggests that the two blade assemblages are similar in maximum length and thickness as well as platform-remnant width and depth. In each case, the resulting Mann-Whitney p value exceeded the .05 significance level, suggesting that the two samples were not significantly different at the 95 percent confidence level. Differences are noted regarding maximum width with a p value of .004, well below the .05 threshold. A difference was also noted for the curvature index, which yielded a p value of .003, indicating a significant difference in the mean curvature of the two sample groups. In both comparisons, the Green blades are wider and more strongly curved than the 1990 blades.

The relative frequencies for cortex percentage revealed that nine of the Green cache blades retained no cortex (52.94 percent). The remaining eight specimens (47.06 percent) exhibited dorsal cortex, of which only two (11.76 percent) had greater than 50 percent remaining on the dorsal surface. The Dickenson cache yielded slightly higher frequencies, with 60 percent (n = 3) of the blades retaining cortex. These blades (n = 3) contained less than 50 percent cortex on their dorsal surface.

The flake-scar counts for the Green cache showed one blade (5.88 percent) with no dorsal scars, while seven had two scars (41.17 percent), three (23.52 percent) had three scars, and five (29.41 percent) displayed a single scar. Flake counts for the Dickenson cache revealed that

TABLE 3.3. Comparative Blade Attribute Analysis for the Green and Dickenson Caches

ARTIFACT NO.	MAX. L	MAX. W	MAX. TH	PLT. W	PLT. TH	BULB DEF.	FLK SCARS	INDEX CURVE	CORTEX PERCENTAGE
GREEN cache									
1. 62-120-01	136.5	33.6	11.70	4.2	1.9	Salient	3	10.98	5%
2. 62-120-02	152.8	31.7	10.90	6.2	2.1	Salient	3	112.43	0%
3. 62-120-03	138.4	29.4	17.60	7.9	3.7	Salient	2	115.89	0%
4. 62-120-04	138.9	29.6	13.30	3.1	1.2	Salient	2	117.27	30%
5. 62-120-05	97.1	29.5	9.20	8.7	2.9	Salient	2	112.35	2%
6. 62-120-06	101.7	28.8	11.70	8.3	3.0	Salient	2	113.76	0%
7. 62-120-07	127.3	34.7	16.80	na	na	na	4	116.49	30%
8. 62-120-08	98.7	33.8	11.20	na	na	na	2	112.15	0%
9. 62-120-09	70.8	27.89	18.36	na	na	na	2	na	5%
10. 62-120-10	74.8	22.39	10.81	7.9	2.1	Salient	3	na	0%
11. 62-120-11	54.9	31.87	9.78	na	na	na	0	na	95%
12. 62-120-12	63.9	28.34	13.82	na	na	na	1	na	40%
13. 62-120-13	86.64	32.8	13.80	na	na	na	1	na	70%
14. 62-120-14	66.43	26.99	12.73	na	na	na	3	na	0%
15. 62-120-15	67.86	29.44	9.89	na	na	na	1	na	0%
16. 62-120-16	93.84	34.02	18.57	na	na	na	1	na	0%
17a. 62-120-17	69.47	33.6	11.50	na	na	na	2	na	0%
17b. 62-120-17	58.64	30.93	11.27	na	na	na	1	na	0%
DICKENSON cache									
1. 1.1990.1.6183/88	229.2	109.1	33.20	17.8	5.4	Diffuse	1	15.76	20%
2. 1.1990.1.6184	120.2	30.9	7.20	5.8	2.7	Salient	2	17.5	0%
3. 1.1990.1.6185	131.0	48.1	14.60	7.4	3.7	Salient	2	112.1	40%
4. 1.1990.1.6186	127.0	38.9	14.0	7.2	4.9	Salient	1	19.1	50%
5. 1.1990.1.6187	138.6	35.0	11.70	8.1	1.7	Salient	2	16.4	0%

TABLE 3.4. Results of Comparative Metric Analyses between the Green and Dickenson Caches

CACHE	n	MAX. LENGTH		MAX. WIDTH		MAX. THICKNESS		PLT. REMNANT WIDTH		PLT. REMNANT DEPTH		CURVE INDEX	
		x	sd	x	sd	x	sd	x	sd	x	sd	x	sd
GREEN	17	141.65	7.50	30.49	3.21	13.03	3.05	6.61	2.19	2.41	0.83	13.91	2.33
DICKENSON	5	149.20	45.21	52.40	32.32	16.40	4.84	9.26	4.84	3.68	1.52	8.17	2.26
Mann-Whitney U Test	p value	.412		.004		.542		.724		.205		.003	

Note: n = 12 for platform remnant and n = 13 for curvature attributes. Measures are in millimeters.

60 percent (n = 3) of the blades had two flake scars; thus blades with two scars are most common in both assemblages. These two nonparametric data sets tentatively suggest that both the Green and Dickenson blades may have been selected relatively early in the core-reduction sequence, perhaps choosing for overall length and curvature rather than smaller, straighter, and cortex-free blades that occur during more advanced sequencing events (Bordes and Crabtree 1969).

Analysis of the bulb of force included seven samples from the Green cache and all five blades from the Dickenson cache. Eleven of the 12 blades (91.66 percent) exhibit salient or well-defined bulbs of force, with only Specimen 1.1990.1.6183/6188 (8.3 percent) containing a diffuse or weakly defined bulb of force. These subjective results suggest that the blades were detached with a relatively high level of applied force. Moreover, a secondary analysis of the ventral-surface and platform-remnant juncture identified Blade 62-120-02 of the Green cache and Blades 1.1990.1.6183/6188, 1.1990.1.6184, 1.1990.1.6185, and 1.1990.1.6187 from the Dickenson cache as exhibiting platform lipping. This attribute, although not definitive, presents the possibility of soft-hammer percussion in the detachment of blades rather than hard-hammer or indirect percussion (Andrefsky 1998; Collins 1999b; Crabtree 1982; Green 1963; Henry et al. 1976).

INTERPRETATIONS

The analysis of the Green and Dickenson blade caches revealed overall similarity and consistency in their technological attributes (Figure 3.8). Specifically, blade length and thickness values were statistically similar, keeping in mind the small sample size. The approximated mean length-to-width ratio, 5:1 for the Green cache and 3:1 for the Dickenson cache, illustrates the maximization of length as a standard characteristic. As such, these blades exhibit distinct morphological attributes that are characterized by length that is at least three times the width. Platform remnants recorded on the Dickenson blades tend to be slightly wider and thicker in comparison to the Green blades. The removal of outlier 1.1990.1.6183/6188 reduces the mean platform width to 7.12 mm, still comparable to the mean platform values for the Green cache.

Curvature presents another diagnostic attribute identified for Clovis blades, one that Bordes and Crabtree (1969) and Bradley et al. (2010:54) correlate with core morphology. As the reduction sequence advances, the curvature of each blade decreases, resulting in straighter blade cross sections. For the two samples analyzed in this study, the higher index values for the Green cache in comparison to the Dickenson cache suggest that the 1962 blades may have been detached slightly earlier in the core-reduction process. Intra-assemblage variability is expressed with indices ranging between 10.98 and 17.27 for the Green cache and between 6.40 and 12.10 for the Dickenson cache. One possible clue in support of this interpretation is revealed in Blade 62-120-03 from the Green cache.

This blade exhibits a crested ridge, or partial crested ridge, produced by bilateral flaking indicative of a lamé a crête technique. This use of this technique points toward the initial stages of blade core reduction (Bordes and Crabtree 1969; Crabtree 1982; Green 1963; Huckell 2007; Waters, Pevny, and Carlson 2011). Ridge maintenance carried out in preparation of blade removal is identified on Green cache Blades 62-120-3, 62-120-4, 62-120-6, and 62-120-7 (Huckell 2007:208). Moreover, the relative high frequency of cortical blades, 47.06 percent (n = 8) of the Green assemblage and 60 percent (n = 3) of the Dickenson assemblage, further supports the selection of blades from the early stages of blade core reduction.

These analyses suggest that the two blade caches recovered from the Clovis type site are similar in form and

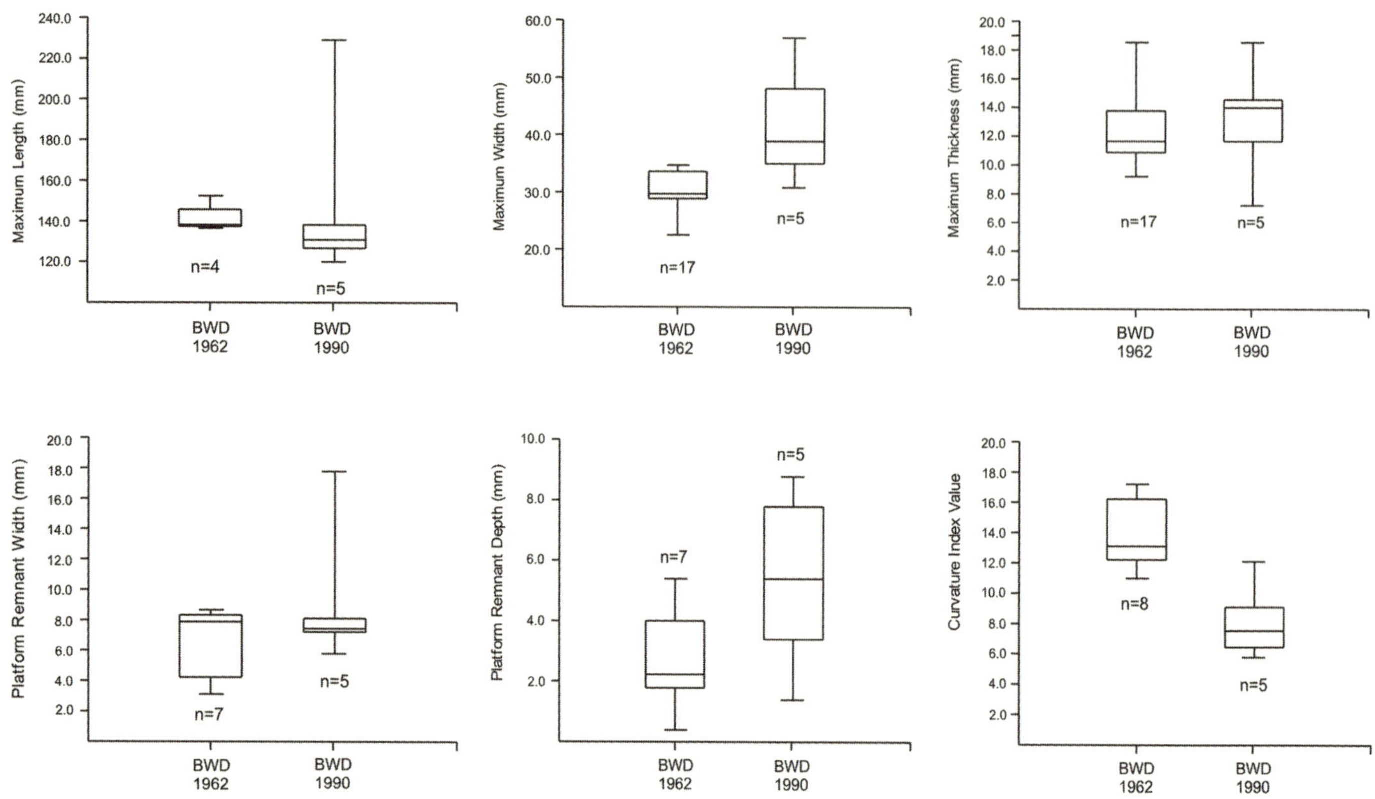

Figure 3.8. Box plot graphs displaying metric comparisons between the Green (1962) and Dickenson (1990) caches

are metrically comparable to one another, despite potentially representing different parts of the reduction continuum. The critical characteristics that distinguish Clovis technology, such as exaggerated curvature relative to width, length, small platform dimensions, and marked longitudinal curvature are all present in the Dickenson cache (Bradley et al. 2010:47; Collins 1999b:66). Paralleling Collins's (1999b) findings, the Dickenson cache probably is Clovis despite the uncertainty in its stratigraphic context. The implications for this study point toward a consistency in manufacture and selection.

CONCLUSIONS

Examination of the arroyo soil sequence reveals a depositional history that is temporally defined by the presence of diagnostic artifacts. Chronometric associations for Stratum IVb suggest that the sand and gravel deposit that underlies Stratum IVa dates between 12,100 and 13,400 RCYBP, demonstrating a late Pleistocene time frame for this basal unit. The depositional environment for Stratum IVa indicates an active arroyo characterized by water-lain sediments and freshwater shell. The presence of a blade tool is cautiously correlated to the blade cache, suggesting that these artifacts may be technologically and culturally contemporaneous with one another. Although unclear, the context of the single blade fragment in Stratum IVa, and by proxy the Dickenson cache, may reflect secondary deposition whereas the original placement of the cache would be outside of the channel proper. Movement into the channel would have occurred prior to the emplacement of Stratum IVa. This interpretation is further strengthened by the collection of a Midland-style point from Stratum IV and an Agate Basin point from Stratum III, each postdating the Clovis component at Blackwater Locality No. 1.

This chapter investigated whether a Clovis affiliation could be appropriately applied to the Dickenson blade cache. At present, there are no definitive answers; however, based on geologic positioning and technological parallels to the Green cache, it seems probable that it is Clovis. Observations regarding the possible provenience of the Dickenson cache raise questions as to the age of Unit IVa and the relationship between stratigraphic contacts, leaving some ambiguity as to spatial context of the cache. Operating under current paradigms that would have blade technology almost singularly linked to the Clovis culture, a Clovis affiliation for the Dickenson cache is posited (Collins 1999b; Collins and Lohse 2004; but see Roper 1999). The technological attributes of the blade cache fall well within the parameters set by Green (1963) and Collins (1999b). Finally, within a broader interpretive framework these analyses establish a foundation on which further investigations of early Paleoindian activities along the West Bank deposits and ancient landscapes of Blackwater Draw can be pursued.

Chapter 4

Clovis Caches and Clovis Knowledge of the North American Landscape

THE MAHAFFY CACHE, COLORADO

Douglas B. Bamforth

In 2008 landscapers in Boulder, Colorado, discovered a cache of flaked stone tools made from raw materials that occur naturally in areas scattered from northeastern Utah to Middle Park in the central Rocky Mountains, all on the opposite side of the Continental Divide from the cache. This paper discusses this discovery, arguing that the artifacts in the cache are terminal Pleistocene in age and probably Clovis in affiliation and that the cache has important implications for our understanding of Clovis ways of life. I begin, though, by considering the overall conceptual framework within which archaeologists interpret Clovis archaeology, to place my detailed discussion in a larger context.

CLOVIS FIRST? CLOVIS WHEN?

For decades, archaeologists agreed that the Clovis period represented the earliest human occupation of the Western Hemisphere south of the continental ice sheets. Viewing Clovis archaeology this way has fundamental implications for how we have made sense out of patterns in the known archaeological record for the Clovis period. In particular, given a range of Clovis radiocarbon dates that falls roughly between 11,500 and 11,000 B.C. (give or take a century or two), we have viewed Clovis people as new populations moving into a North American landscape that was changing rapidly and substantially at the very end of the Pleistocene.

Being the earliest migrants into new lands would have had profound implications for human beings (Kelly and Todd 1988; Meltzer 2009:209–238): the first occupants of North America would have had no knowledge of the kinds of resources that were available, of where they were available, of the dangers or opportunities lurking over the next hill, or of the terrain in general and so no information about how to get from place to place. They would also have had no one to ask about these and other matters and would have faced progressive change in the physical environment resulting from environmental shifts, which would have made preexisting information (and newly collected information) about many topics obsolete over time. If Clovis caches pertain to the first migrants into North America, we need to try to understand caching behavior in light of the limits on the knowledge those migrants could have had. However, as real as these limits must have been for the first people to arrive in the New World, there are two major reasons for arguing that they are not relevant to understanding Clovis caches or other Clovis archaeology.

The first of these is the increasing evidence that Clovis was not, in fact, first. Regardless of the contested status of many possibly pre-Clovis sites in North America (i.e., Holen 2006), multiple radiocarbon dates on the Monte Verde site in Chile predate Clovis (Dillehay 1989, 1997;

Meltzer et al. 1997). People coming from northeastern Asia can hardly have been in southern South America before they were in the north, whether they came down the coast or through the interior. Furthermore, there is increasing evidence for an archaeologically distinct—that is, non-Clovis—occupation in the Columbia Plateau and Great Basin of the northwestern part of North America ("Western Stemmed") that is as early as Clovis and that may well be slightly earlier (Beck and Jones 2010; Erlandson et al. 2011; Jenkins et al. 2012). If archaeological constructs like "Clovis" have the kinds of social meaning that, deep in our hearts, we know we all hope they have, this raises the possibility of multiple contemporary but socially distinct human groups in North America at the end of the Pleistocene.

Second, though, while we have often considered the unique adaptive problems that the earliest migrants to the New World would have faced, we less often considered the unique interpretive problems we face in trying to study those migrants. Chief among these is the problem of assessing the probability that we have seen, or ever will see, sites produced by the first arrivals. Common sense tells us that this probability is in the vicinity of zero. On one hand, it seems certain that in-migrating populations were very small and, regardless of how fast those populations might have grown, small and rare human groups produce small and rare archaeological sites, the least likely kinds of sites for archaeologists to find. Furthermore, the vagaries of site formation, preservation, and discovery always conspire to reduce the chances of finding any given site, and this is a worse and worse problem the farther back we go in time. Taken together, problems of detecting tiny mobile populations and of locating ancient hunter-gatherer sites suggest that we are not likely ever to see the remains of the first migrants to this continent.

And we do not have to rely only on common sense. Archaeologists have noted this problem for many years (Anderson and Gillam 2000; Bettinger and Young 2006; Hassan 1981; Prasciunas and Surovell in press; Toth 1991), although these arguments have received relatively little attention. The central issue that this problem raises is the magnitude of the lag between the date when people arrived in North America and the date at which they became archaeologically visible. Attempts to estimate this are varied but universally rest on estimates of how fast early populations grew and how many people North America could have supported. Varying these latter estimates obviously produces different estimates of this lag (and different authors use very different estimates), but all analysts agree that any reasonable set of estimates indicates that people must have lived in North America significantly longer than the available radiocarbon record suggests they did (see Prasciunas and Surovell in press for a particularly sophisticated example of this).

Together, these problems imply that the earliest migrants to North America are virtually certain to be archaeologically invisible, that they must have arrived substantially before Clovis times as we currently define them, and that we do not know when people first started making Clovis-style artifacts. This means, in turn, that the archaeology that we view as the residue of the first migrants to the continent actually represents people who lived many generations later in time than those first migrants. The Clovis people whom we can study on the basis of known archaeological material thus must have had substantial stores of sophisticated knowledge about the geography and resources of their regions of North America and, like all other human groups, social ties to groups in the regions around them. They lived on known landscapes that were certainly changing as the climate shifted, but the fact that they experienced long-term environmental change distinguishes them from few, and perhaps no, social groups in human history. This does not mean that Clovis people led lives that were exactly like those of any later human groups—they faced unique conditions and had to solve unique challenges. But it does mean that they faced these conditions and solved these challenges in places that they and thousands of their ancestors knew, and knew well.

Clovis tool caches, then, were left behind on landscapes that people recognized, remembered, and talked about. This paper considers one of these—the Mahaffy cache—with this in mind. I begin by describing how the cache was found and the evidence indicating that it is Clovis and then turn to describing the contents of the cache. I end by discussing some of what the Mahaffy cache tells us about the way that Clovis groups lived on the western North American landscape.

THE MAHAFFY CACHE: DISCOVERY AND CONTEXT

In the spring of 2008, landscapers working in the front yard of a house in the western portion of the city of Boulder, Colorado, uncovered a dense concentration of stone artifacts as they excavated a fish pond. The homeowner contacted the University of Colorado within 24 hours, making it possible to inspect the discovery location and, with the enthusiastic assistance of the landscaping crew, search for additional artifacts over the next two days.

The landscapers began their excavation with a backhoe and noticed the cache as they were subsequently trimming the edge of the pond area by hand. They report that the supervisor reached into the bank they were excavating with his hands approximately 40 cm apart and pulled out a solid mass of artifacts; workmen also recovered a few other pieces from their spoil piles. When archaeologists arrived, the landscapers identified backhoe spoils removed from sediment above the cache location as well as spoils removed from around the cache. Searching these different areas and screening all of the sediment we could recover from each of them through one-eighth-inch mesh produced no artifacts from above the cache and four small flakes from around it.

The landscapers completely removed the sediment around the cache while excavating the footing for a small stone bridge, making it impossible to see the pit into which the cache must have been placed. Careful inspection of subsurface deposits in the landscapers' excavation and in other places where they were visible revealed no traces at all of a larger archaeological site. Combined with the specific information on the concentration of artifacts that the landscapers found, this leaves little doubt that the cache is an isolated feature. Furthermore, while no archaeologist was able to observe evidence of a pit, no collection of artifacts left unprotected on the ground surface would remain within as small an area as the one that landscapers described: artifacts on the ground surface inevitably disperse horizontally over time (Bamforth and Dorn 1988; Bowers et al. 1983). Some of the smaller artifacts certainly dispersed slightly from the main concentration over time, but initial deposition in a pit seems indisputable.

Physical and Stratigraphic Setting

The cache was found at a depth of approximately 40 to 60 cm below the modern ground surface, but it is impossible to say how deeply it was buried below a recent natural ground surface: construction of roads and houses in its immediate vicinity since at least the 1940s has moved substantial amounts of earth and altered the topography (although searches of public records have not yet produced any information that makes it possible to reconstruct the degree of this alteration).

The landform in the area of Boulder where the cache was found is capped by Quaternary alluvium eroded from the mountains just to the west, but the cache itself was recovered from sediment within the drainage of Gregory Creek, which is incised into this alluvium. Gregory Creek runs out of the mountains at the north end of the Flatirons, a distinctive sandstone formation on the west edge of Boulder that is visible for great distances across the plains to the east; the creek joins Boulder Creek a short distance to the north of the cache location. The landscapers' excavations exposed three distinct layers of sediment in the cache location. The uppermost stratum appears to be the result of recent construction and is very distinct from the layers below it: it is light brown and clayey and contains recent debris (including mid-twentieth-century bottle glass and copper wire). This construction level caps the underlying sediment on three sides of the landscapers' excavation (the backhoe completely removed the fourth side), meaning that it must have extended over the intervening area and thus must have capped the sediment containing the cache.

There is a very sharp contact between this uppermost stratum and the sediment that contained the cache. This latter sediment is an intact and more ancient set of A/AC/C horizons that range from slightly plastic, dark sandy loam in the A horizon to lighter, nonplastic sandy loam in the AC horizon and lighter coarse sand in the C horizon (P. Birkeland, professor emeritus, Geology Department, University of Colorado, Boulder, personal communication 2010). The landscapers' description of the location where they found the artifacts corresponds roughly to the AC horizons, and traces of AC sediment adhering to some of the artifacts as well as staining of the entire collection by A horizon organics confirm this.

DATING THE MAHAFFY CACHE

Characteristics of the technology of a number of the artifacts in the Mahaffy cache are consistent with known Clovis artifacts (see below), but the cache contains no definitely Clovis diagnostics and we have no direct chronometric evidence of its age. Radiocarbon dates indicate that the A horizon above the cache formed during the fourteenth century (V. Holliday, personal communication 2011), but this tells us nothing about the age of sediment that contained the cache. However, Birkeland (personal communication 2008) states that at least some

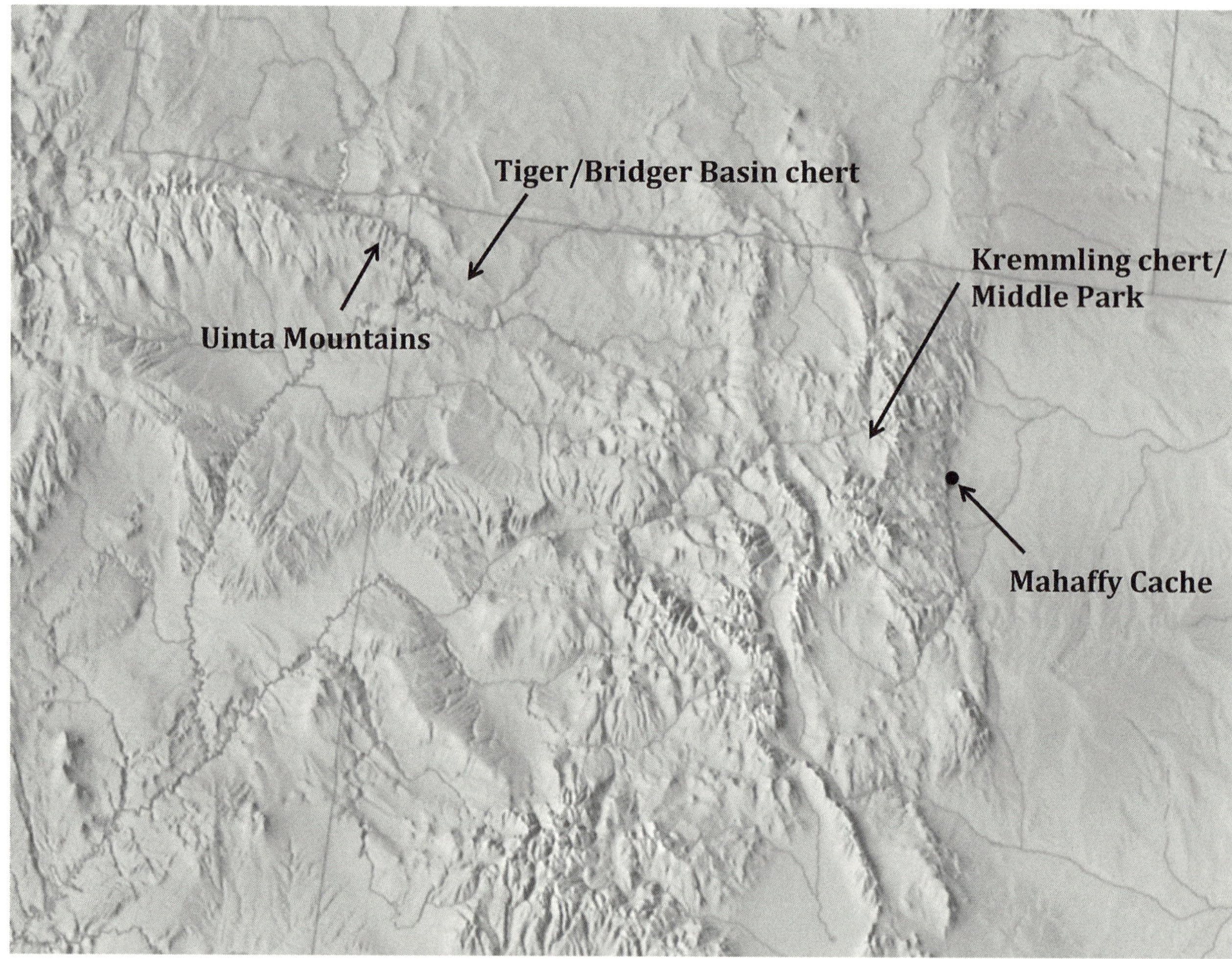

Figure 4.1. Locations of the Mahaffy cache and raw material sources

of the sediment within the channel of Gregory Creek was deposited during the late Pleistocene, although a refined chronology of this deposition does not exist.

Protein residue analysis using crossover immunoelectrophoresis (CIEP) of all of the artifacts in the cache found identifiable residues on four artifacts (Yohe and Bamforth 2013). These four appear to bear traces of protein from sheep, bear, horse, and camel. CIEP identifies protein residues at the taxonomic level of the family, and members of the sheep and bear families have been present in Colorado throughout the period when human beings have lived there. However, horses and camelids in the state date either to the Pleistocene or to the twentieth and twenty-first centuries. There is no evidence that horses or camels have lived at the location where the cache was found within the last century or so, and CIEP analysis of a sediment sample from the immediate vicinity of the cache produced no results of any kind. Furthermore, the landscapers damaged a few of the artifacts when they recovered them, and this damage shows relatively thick (as much as half a centimeter) weathering rinds on artifacts made from Tiger chert (see below). We cannot calibrate the thickness of these rinds to any absolute age, but they leave little doubt that the collection is older than the twentieth century. The CIEP results thus imply a Pleistocene age.

THE MAHAFFY CACHE: RAW MATERIAL SOURCES

Ancient knappers used four distinctly different raw materials to produce the Mahaffy cache artifacts, three of which we can identify with confidence and one of which we can identify less definitely (Figure 4.1). The bulk of the collection is made either from Kremmling chert or from a material that archaeologists variously refer to as Bridger Basin chert, Green River Formation chert, or Tiger chert.

Kremmling chert is a fine-grained, grayish-white silicate (properly, a chalcedony) found at the south end of Middle Park, west of the Continental Divide in the northern part of the Colorado Rocky Mountains. Tiger chert is a fossilized stromatolite that occurs in the Green River Basin of northwestern Colorado and southwestern Wyoming and is similarly fine-grained, grading from tan to black, often (but not always) with alternating bands of light and dark stripes. In some cases, including on a number of the Mahaffy cache artifacts, these stripes form quite spectacular patterns, but the clarity of these patterns results from long-term weathering; the stripes are only faintly visible on freshly flaked surfaces.

Finally, three bifaces were made from two different kinds of quartzite. Two of these are made from a fine-grained brownish-orange quartzite with red flecks that is identical to hand specimens from the Uinta Mountains in northeastern Utah. The third is made from a purplish-gray quartzite that is very similar (but not identical) to material from the Windy Ridge quarry at the north end of Middle Park (Bamforth 2006). It is different enough from the Windy Ridge material that it is unlikely to be from that precise source, but it falls generally within the range of similar material known from a number of locations in the mountains.

THE MAHAFFY CACHE: CONTENTS

The best-known Clovis caches tend to be dominated by points or point preforms, by relatively large bifaces, or by all of these kinds of artifacts. The largest portion of the Mahaffy cache, in contrast, consists of unmodified flakes, although worked pieces are present. Table 4.1 presents the frequencies of the artifact classes I describe below, Table 4.2 presents basic metric data on the individual bifaces in the cache, and Table 4.3 presents metric data on the nonbifacial artifacts. As Table 4.1 shows, the variety of artifacts in the cache fluctuates substantially across the range of material types just noted, and I therefore discuss the collection by stone source.

Kremmling Chert

The total of 23 objects made from this material includes 5 bifaces and 16 flakes, one of them retouched into an end scraper.

The five bifaces are quite diverse (Table 4.2). The largest of them (Figure 4.2) appears to have been the parent piece for most, and perhaps all, of the Kremmling chert biface thinning flakes of this material, although only one of these flakes can be refitted to it. This biface has fairly flat lateral and longitudinal cross sections, with each face shaped by a fairly small number (roughly half a dozen) of large flake removals, some of which extend beyond the biface's midline. There is evidence of two fractures on this piece that removed fragments along one of its edges rather than across its surface. One of these appears to have been intentional: a knapper struck a burin-like blow down one edge, removing a curved triangular flake some 13 cm long. This flake is not in the cache. A second, similar piece appears to have come off just inside this flake. However, this second piece has an irregular ventral surface with no force rings and no striking platform and is likely an accidental removal along a preexisting internal fracture (other such fractures are visible within the stone); it is even possible that it did not completely detach from the larger biface until after it was buried (Figure 4.2 shows the biface with this piece refitted to it). In contrast to very large bifaces elsewhere that appear to have served largely or completely as bifacial cores, substantial portions of the edges of this biface were regularized by finer flaking, and it may have been ready for use as a somewhat uncomfortably large knife or, more likely, a chopping tool.

The other four Kremmling chert bifaces fall into two categories (Figure 4.3). Three of them are basically smaller versions of the largest biface: their surfaces are shaped by a relatively small number of large flakes, with

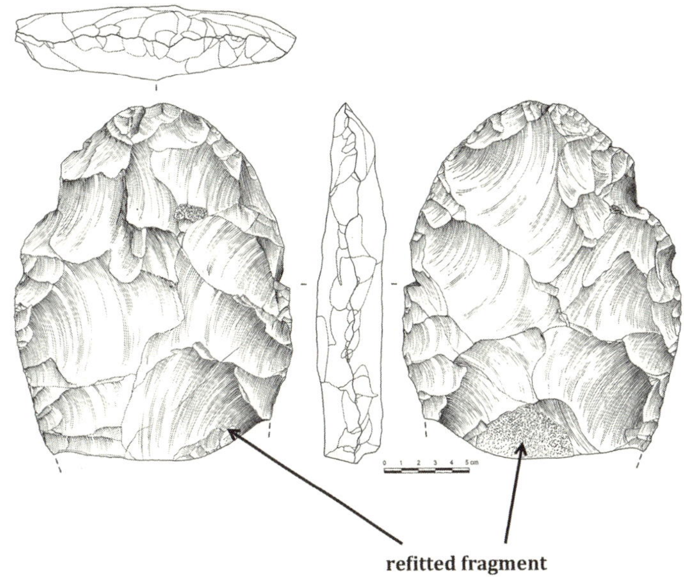

Figure 4.2. Largest Kremmling chert biface

TABLE 4.1. Frequencies of Artifact Categories by Raw Material in the Mahaffy Cache

		TIGER CHERT	KREMMLING CHERT	UINTA QUARTZITE	WINDY RIDGE-LIKE QUARTZITE	TOTAL
Biface	Count	2	6	2	1	11
	% within type	18.2%	54.5%	18.2%	9.1%	100.0%
	% within raw material	3.5%	27.3%	100.0%	100.0%	13.4%
Biface flake	Count	22	9	0	0	31
	% within type	71.0%	29.0%	.0%	.0%	100.0%
	% within raw material	38.6%	40.9%	.0%	.0%	37.8%
Small core-struck flake	Count	13	0	0	0	13
	% within type	100.0%	.0%	.0%	.0%	100.0%
	% within raw material	22.8%	.0%	.0%	.0%	15.9%
Backed piece	Count	0	6	0	0	6
	% within type	.0%	100.0%	.0%	.0%	100.0%
	% within raw material	.0%	27.3%	.0%	.0%	7.3%
Large core-struck flake	Count	7	0	0	0	7
	% within type	100.0%	.0%	.0%	.0%	100.0%
	% within raw material	12.3%	.0%	.0%	.0%	8.5%
Type 1 blade	Count	5	0	0	0	5
	% within type	100.0%	.0%	.0%	.0%	100.0%
	% within raw material	8.8%	.0%	.0%	.0%	6.1%
Type 2 blade	Count	2	0	0	0	2
	% within type	100.0%	.0%	.0%	.0%	100.0%
	% within raw material	3.5%	.0%	.0%	.0%	2.4%
Natural stone	Count	2	0	0	0	2
	% within type	100.0%	.0%	.0%	.0%	100.0%
	% within raw material	3.5%	.0%	.0%	.0%	2.4%
Indeter. flake	Count	4	1	0	0	5
	% within type	80.0%	20.0%	.0%	.0%	100.0%
	% within raw material	7.0%	4.5%	.0%	.0%	6.1%
Total	Count	57	22	2	1	82
	% within type	69.5%	26.8%	2.4%	1.2%	100.0%
	% within raw material	100.0%	100.0%	100.0%	100.0%	100.0%

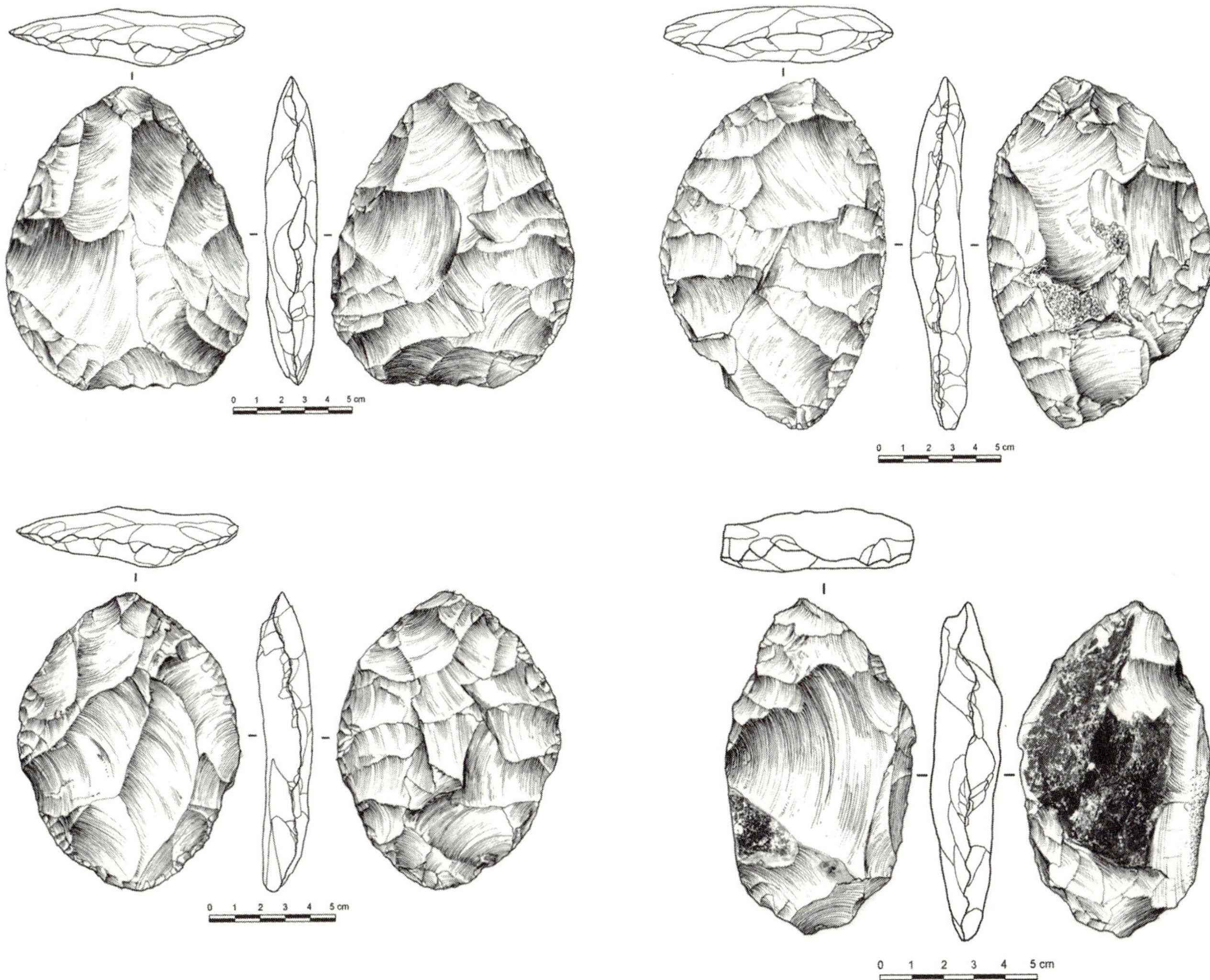

Figure 4.3. Kremmling chert bifaces

their edges then trimmed to finished form. One of them is triangular; two are ovate and bipointed. The last, and smallest, biface is made on a thin tabular fragment of stone and bears substantial traces of the original unworked (cortical) stone surface (Figure 4.3, lower right). Much of this piece is minimally worked, but there is a short section of prepared and useable edge adjacent to the pointed end. Residue from this tool reacted with camel protein.

With the exception of one technologically ambiguous piece (a narrow splinter of stone with its striking platform broken away), the flakes in this material are a mix of large biface thinning flakes (mean width = 60.7 mm) and core-struck flakes (Figure 4.4, biface thinning flakes; Figure 4.5, core-struck flakes). One of the biface flakes refits to the largest biface in the cache, but the color and consistency of the others suggest that all of the flakes in this category derive from this piece. The largest biface thinning flake is finely retouched along both of its lateral edges. The core-struck flakes are strikingly uniform. All six of them are roughly the same size and fit comfortably in the hand, and all have one steep and one acute lateral edge. In four cases the steeper edge is cortical and in two cases (including one cortical piece) it is at least partially retouched. These appear to have been selected to produce backed tools. Residue from one of them reacted with sheep protein.

Tiger Chert

The most common material in the cache by count is Tiger chert. It is also technologically the most diverse, including bifaces, blades, retouched and unretouched core-struck flakes, and biface thinning flakes.

TABLE 4.2. Dimensions of Individual Bifaces in the Mahaffy Cache

ARTIFACT NO.	LENGTH	WIDTH	MIN. THICKNESS[a]	MAX. THICKNESS[b]	W/MIN. *t*
MC-63	101.6	58.3	13.1	14.7	4.45
MC-65	122.4	52.3	13.7	15.6	3.82
MC-68	114.8	88.0	18.0	20.2	4.89
MC-70	123.2	102.3	19.2	21.0	5.32
MC-76	136.6	92.0	18.2	20.5	5.05
MC-78	161.1	80.0	18.6	22.4	4.30
MC-79	160.5	111.5	24.5	28.2	4.55
MC-80	199.5	114.9	14.2	20.5	8.09
MC-81	215.6	147.7	18.7	20.5	7.90
MC-82	212.3	101.4	41.0	55.4	2.47
MC-83	201.4	163.2	31.2	35.6	5.23

[a]Minimum thickness along midline in central third of biface.

[b]Maximum thickness along midline in central third of biface.

TABLE 4.3. Descriptive Statistics by Type for Nonbifacial Artifacts in the Mahaffy Cache

		LENGTH	WIDTH	THICKNESS	PLATFORM ANGLE	PLATFORM THICKNESS	PLATFORM WIDTH
Biface flake	Mean	55.5	42.0	6.6	84.2	3.9	12.1
	N	29	31	31	19	18	20
	Std. deviation	22.8	14.6	2.7	15.1	2.7	6.9
Small core-struck flake	Mean	39.7	31.1	6.5	79.0	5.0	16.2
	N	13	13	13	12	11	12
	Std. deviation	8.3	8.3	2.2	19.9	2.1	6.8
Backed piece	Mean	64.6	43.8	11.0	92.5	6.6	17.7
	N	6	6	6	6	6	6
	Std. deviation	11.0	6.2	3.8	21.6	2.9	6.6
Large core-struck flake	Mean	95.5	70.7	16.7	111.3	7.2	19.6
	N	7	7	7	4	4	4
	Std. deviation	29.5	20.3	5.7	14.4	2.5	6.4
Type 1 blade	Mean	139.1	47.4	18.2	94.0	7.1	15.3
	N	5	5	5	5	5	5
	Std. deviation	28.9	17.4	4.3	8.2	1.9	8.8
Type 2 blade	Mean	120.7	58.4	16.1	95.0	4.7	18.1
	N	2	2	2	2	2	2
	Std. deviation	2.1	17.3	.1	0.0	1.2	910.0
Stone	Mean	37.8	31.4	8.9			
	N	2	2	2	n/a	n/a	n/a
	Std. deviation	6.2	1.0	1.1			
Indeter. flake	Mean	42.0	30.9	6.0	80.0	4.5	16.4
	N	5	5	5	1	1	1
	Std. deviation	7.2	10.5	1.9			

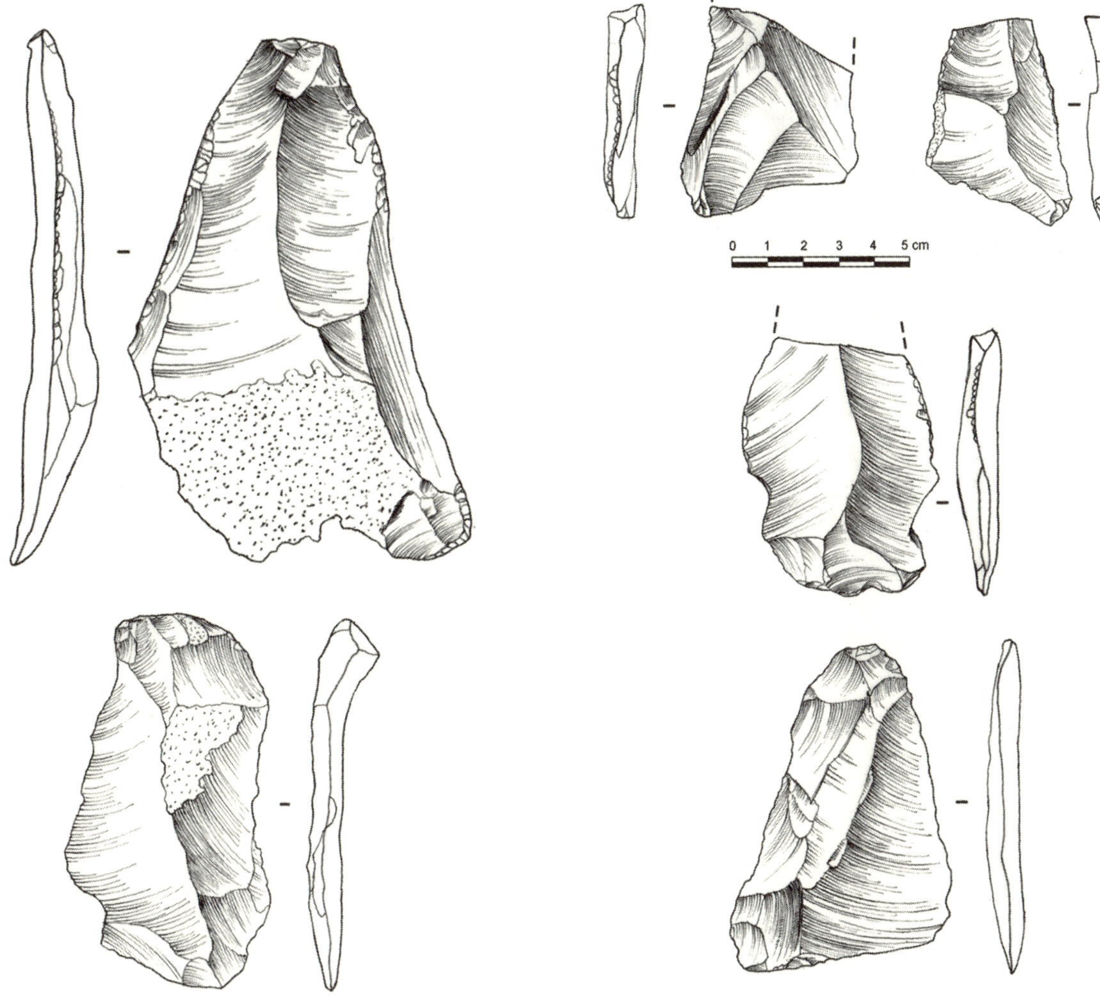

Figure 4.4. Biface thinning flakes in Kremmling chert

The two Tiger chert bifaces differ dramatically from one another. One of them (Figure 4.6) is morphologically more or less identical to a modern double-bitted axe, although it is not suitable for hafting. It was made on a brick-shaped block of stone and has flat cortical remnants on central portions of both lateral edges, the thickest part of the tool. Both ends of the tool are carefully flaked into sharp, rounded edges, with the remainder of the tool's surface shaped by removing large flakes. The other biface (Figure 4.7) is slightly larger than the Kremmling chert bifaces depicted in Figure 4.3 but is otherwise similar to them in shape and general reduction pattern. Both faces of this artifact appear to bear remnants of the surfaces of the large flake blank on which it was made, and there is an unworked section of edge (opposite the pointed end of the artifact) that may possibly be a remnant of the striking platform.

The collection includes seven "blades," meaning pieces that are at least twice as long as they are wide and that appear to have been the deliberate products of knapping (in contrast to production waste that is fortuitously useful); two of these show some marginal retouch. The Mahaffy cache blades fall into two types. Type 1 blades (n = 5) are true—that is, deliberately struck—blades (Figure 4.8). All five of these have cortical unfaceted striking platforms and dorsal scars from previous blades stuck parallel to them from adjacent platforms; four of the five bear at least some cortex on their dorsal faces. The two Type 2 blades (Figure 4.9) have noncortical platforms, one with an unprepared striking surface and the other with the striking surface carefully flaked but with virtually no preparation flakes on the adjacent dorsal surface of the piece. The orientations of previous flake removals indicated by remnant dorsal flake scars on

TABLE 4.4. T-tests Comparing Size for Tiger Chert and Kremmling Chert Biface Thinning Flakes

	RAW MATERIAL	N	MEAN	STD. DEVIATION	*t*	*df*	*p*
Width	Tiger chert	22	34.4	6.8	-8.10	29	.000
	Kremmling chert	9	60.7	11.1			
Thickness	Tiger chert	22	5.4	1.2	-5.54	29	.000
	Kremmling chert	9	9.5	3.1			
Length	Tiger chert	20	47.4	10.3	-3.31	27	.003
	Kremmling chert	9	73.4	32.2			

Type 2 blades are also more variable than on Type 1 blades, suggesting that they may be typological (that is, accidental) but not technological blades.

Strong similarities between the striking platforms on Type 2 blades and the striking platforms on a series of six large Tiger chert flakes (Figure 4.10) underscore this possibility. Three of these have their platforms trimmed away, but the others include one unfaceted noncortical form and three others with faceted platforms like those on the second Type 2 blade. The remainder of the Tiger chert flakes (Figure 4.11) appear to be a kind of grab bag of potentially useful pieces struck incidentally while making bifaces and trimming cores. As Table 4.4 shows, although the cache includes biface thinning flakes from both Kremmling and Tiger chert, such flakes in the former material are substantially larger than those in the latter material.

Finally, there are two small fragments of Tiger chert with no definite evidence of human alteration (one has flakes removed from its edge, but these could be accidental damage from exposure on the surface prior to collection or from transport). Neither of these is obviously useful in its present condition and neither is large enough to reduce into a useful item (Table 4.1 refers to these as "natural stone").

Quartzite

The three quartzite artifacts are all bifaces. One of these (in Uinta Formation quartzite) is technologically unsophisticated: it was made on a very large flake, with a substantial remnant of the unworked ventral flake surface still visible on one face (Figure 4.12). Residue from this biface reacted with horse antiserum. The other two (one each in Uinta Formation quartzite [Figure 4.13] and in Windy Ridge–like quartzite [Figure 4.14]) are perhaps the most spectacular items in the cache. These both have high width/thickness ratios (Figure 4.13: 8.09; Figure 4.14: 7.90) and were both shaped by small numbers of very large flakes and carefully flaked to finished form. Two flake scars on the Windy Ridge–like biface extend almost all the way across the artifact (Figure 4.14, right image). Residue from this biface reacted with bear antiserum.

SUMMARY

The Mahaffy cache includes a wide variety of artifacts, ranging from technically sophisticated bifacial knives to unmodified fragments of stone. We can organize this variety into four broad categories. The simplest of these includes the two small and unmodified fragments of Tiger chert, which seem more akin to souvenirs or children's possessions than to tools or potential tools. The second includes bifacial knives and choppers, made from all four of the materials in the collection. The two largest of these are unwieldy if held in one hand but would function well as choppers held in both hands (this is particularly true of the largest Tiger chert biface), but the others are well designed for use as knives and would work extremely well as skinning knives. The largest of the Kremmling chert bifaces (Figure 4.2) has clearly produced flakes that the people who left the cache thought were potentially useful; it is, in some sense, a bifacial core. However, relatively refined marginal flaking and fairly straight edges imply that it was on its way to becoming a bifacial tool. Archaeologists have often argued that Paleoindian technology relied heavily on the reduction of bifacial cores into bifacial tools but have rarely, if ever, provided

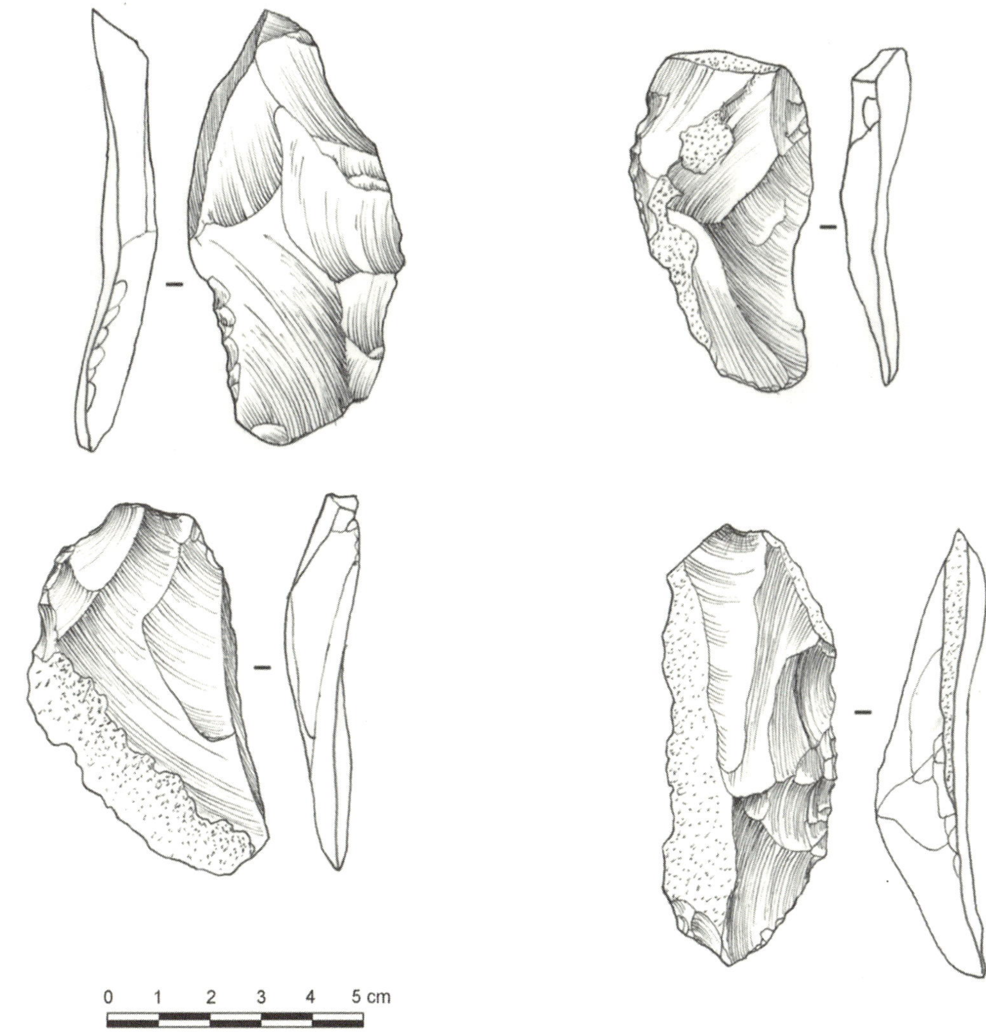

Figure 4.5. Core-struck, naturally backed and deliberately backed pieces, Kremmling chert

evidence that this was so (Bamforth 2002, 2003). This piece may be the only example of such reduction that we can actually document.

The third group includes pieces that are likely to be the deliberate products of knappers seeking large flakes and blades, and the fourth includes pieces that people appear to have selected from production waste generated by knappers making other kinds of tools or cores. These latter categories include artifacts made from both Tiger chert and Kremmling chert, although the specific forms of the artifacts of these different materials differ.

IF IT'S PLEISTOCENE, IS IT CLOVIS?

The term "Clovis" refers to an archaeological culture-historical unit defined first and foremost by the Clovis fluted point. So long as we were reasonably certain that the continent-wide distribution of these points told us that Clovis was the only such unit that could be defined at the end of the Pleistocene, and so long as we believed that the range of dates associated with Clovis points told us the duration of the Clovis period, it was reasonable to refer to all late Pleistocene discoveries as "Clovis," whether or not those discoveries included a fluted point. Green's (1963) attribution to the "Llano (Clovis) Complex" of a cache from late Pleistocene deposits at the Clovis type site that included blades but no points exemplifies this. I noted earlier, though, that we cannot be certain about either of these issues. The Mahaffy cache includes no Clovis points, and it includes a substantial number of artifacts made of stone from sources that are far enough west to raise the possibility that we might link it to the Western Stemmed

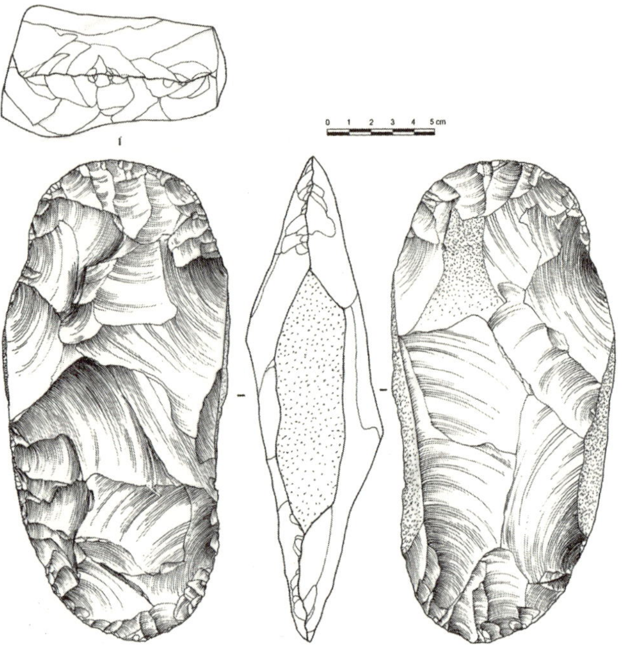

Figure 4.6. Largest Tiger chert biface

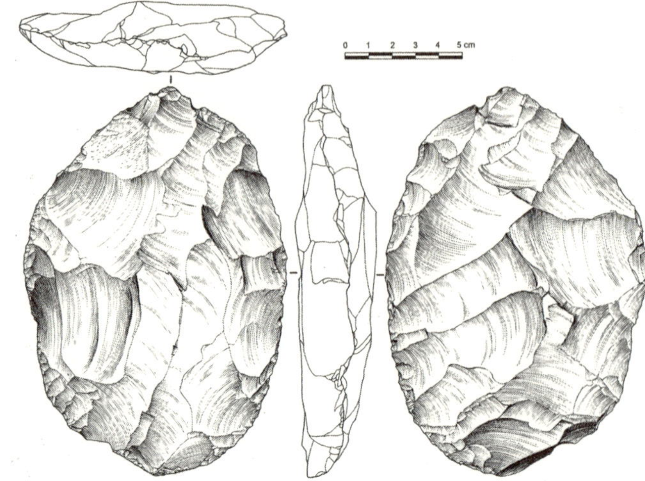

Figure 4.7. Second Tiger chert biface

occupation that is certainly as old as, and maybe older than, Clovis (Beck and Jones 2010; Jenkins et al. 2012). Is the Mahaffy cache Clovis?

Archaeologists have argued that we can recognize Clovis archaeology on the basis of specific kinds of tools in addition to Clovis-style points, as well as on the basis of particular patterns of tool production, but these arguments can be problematic. For example, we have often linked spurred end scrapers to the Paleoindian period, including the Clovis period (i.e., Hofman 1997; Rogers 1986). However, spurred end scrapers occur in stone tool assemblages dated to virtually every period in which archaeologists have specifically looked for them (M. Mitchell, personal communication 2008; Morris and Blakeslee 1987) and studies of modern stone tool users indicate that such scrapers are technological accidents, not culture-historical diagnostics (Weedman 2002).

More recent studies emphasize Clovis blade technology, with Clovis blades distinguished by curved longitudinal cross sections, carefully prepared and very small striking platforms, and other characteristics (Collins 1999b; Collins and Lohse 2004; Tunnell 1978). However, blades from undoubted Clovis levels at the Gault site, struck by undoubted Clovis blade makers, vary immensely in all of these traits (Collins and Lohse 2004): if there was a canon of Clovis blade production, individual Clovis stoneworkers interpreted it freely. Furthermore, Wilke et al. (2002) show that Central Plains Tradition farmers in eastern Nebraska systematically produced blades that are indistinguishable from those found in Clovis contexts. There are blades in the Mahaffy cache, but on the Great Plains, they are typologically as likely to date to the A.D. thirteenth century as the thirteenth millennium B.C.

Very generally, archaeologists have also often seen Paleoindian stoneworking and biface production in general, and Clovis stoneworking in particular, as gratuitously skilled, and they often infer, implicitly or explicitly, that such skill is diagnostic of early occupations in North America. This general inference, though, is incorrect: Indian stoneworkers in many times and places produced flaked stone artifacts as spectacular or (arguably) more spectacular than those made in Paleoindian times. Middle Woodland Hopewell mounds have produced thousands of "relatively large, broad [biface thinning] flakes with relatively little longitudinal curvature" that were often 15 cm or more long, implying production of very large bifaces with smooth, flat surface contours (Cowan and Greber 2002). Mississippian knappers produced large bifacially flaked maces and swords (Dye 2004), demonstrating knapping skills that rival or exceed those indicated by any Paleoindian artifact that has ever been found. Similar examples of superb stoneworking are widespread, although certainly not universal.

However, the substantial attention devoted to the Fenn Clovis cache (Frison and Bradley 1999), along with comparisons between artifacts in that cache and artifacts

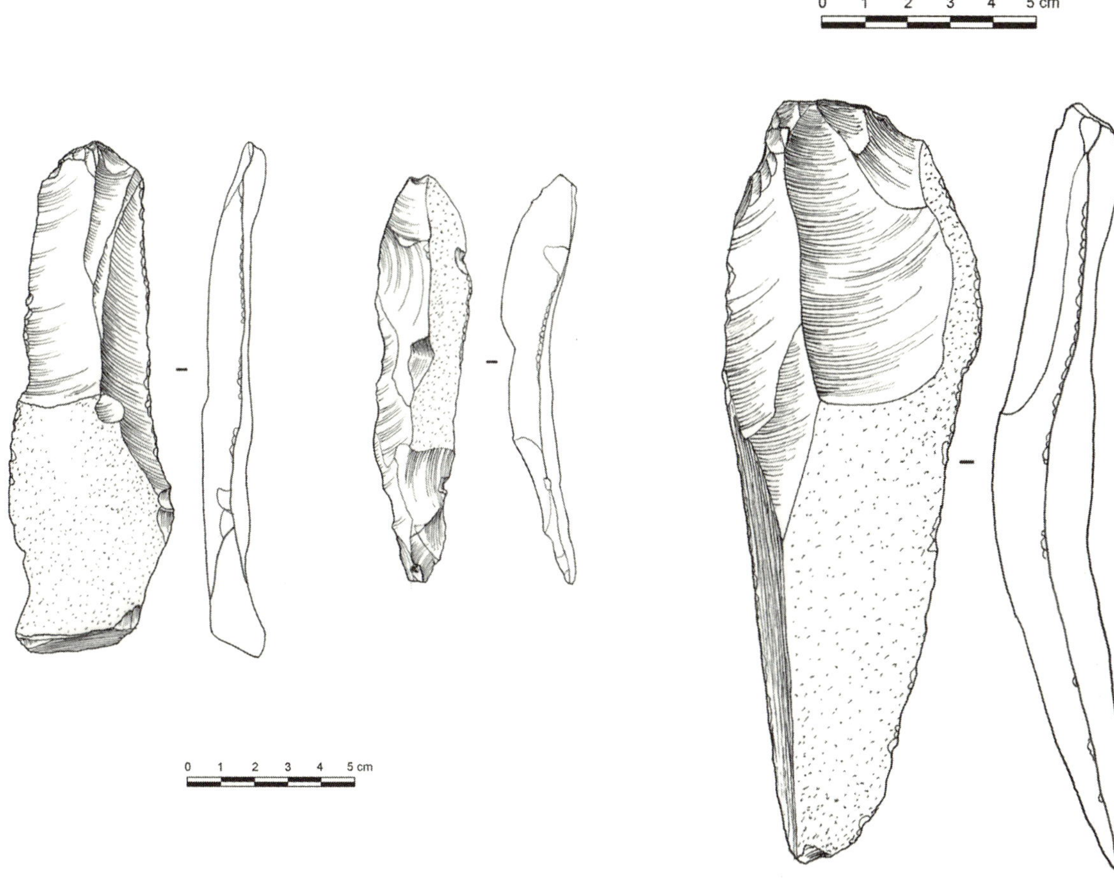

Figure 4.8. Examples of Type 1 blades

found elsewhere, has focused archaeological attention on patterns of biface reduction thought to be more specifically diagnostic of Clovis technology. Many—definitely not all—of the bifaces in the Fenn cache show overlapping sets of overshot thinning flakes struck in series at an angle across the face of the tool. Some—definitely not all—Clovis bifaces from other locations (for example, the Gault site [Collins et al. 2007] and the Sheaman site [Frison 1982c:154–155]) show this pattern as well, and Stanford and Bradley (2004) take such flaking as evidence of historical connections between Clovis and the western European Upper Paleolithic. Informal conversations with colleagues suggest that identifying overshot flaking is fast becoming the gold standard for identifying Clovis biface reduction.

There is no doubt that some Clovis knappers sometimes produced bifaces with some degree of the patterned flaking that is so evident on the Fenn cache material. However, there is equally no doubt that these bifaces are a minority of the ones made by Clovis people. Clovis points showing little or no evidence of overshot flaking are extremely common (see, for example, illustrations in Boldurian and Cotter [1999] and Frison and Todd [1986]), and Straus et al. (2005) argue that such points are overwhelmingly more common than points that do show overshot flaking. Callahan's (1979) intensive analysis and replication of eastern fluted points and production debris offers no evidence at all that Clovis knappers in that area relied systematically on serial removal of overshot flakes, or on overshot flaking in any form. The *presence* of a Fenn cache/Sheaman site–like pattern of flaking may be strong evidence of Clovis knapping, particularly in regions where post-Clovis groups did not emphasize gratuitously skilled stoneworking. However, its *absence* does not tell us that a particular artifact was not made by a Clovis knapper.

There are a few sequences of serial flake removals on some of the Mahaffy cache bifaces, but none of these extend along more than a portion of an edge and none of them removed flakes that we can accurately refer to as overshot (although some of the flakes removed from these bifaces, including some in these sequences, were certainly very large and often extend well past the midline). The clearest of these is on one of the Tiger chert bifaces (Figure 4.7, right), and includes three or four

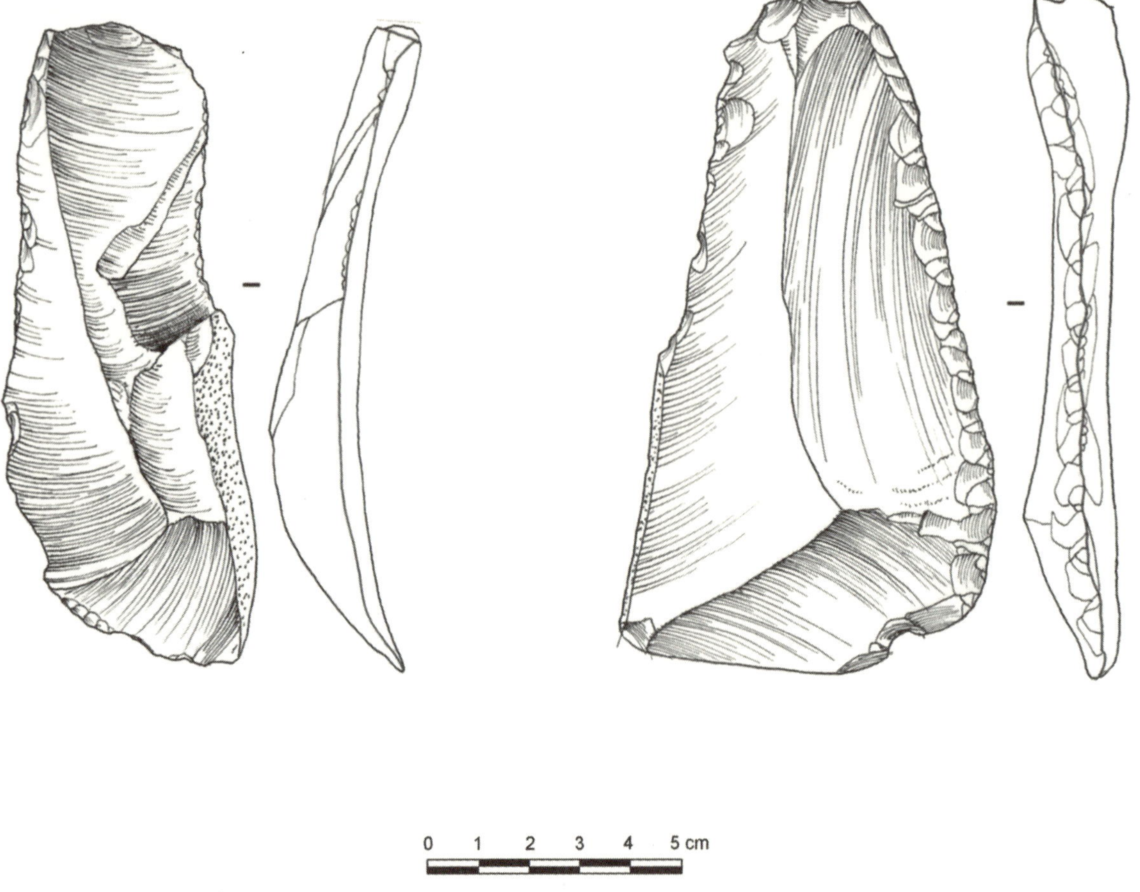

Figure 4.9. Type 2 blades

flakes, one of which (the uppermost in Figure 4.7, far right) may have been overshot. Two other bifaces, one in Uinta Mountains quartzite (Figure 4.12, uppermost scar in the right image) and one in Kremmling chert (Figure 4.3, lower right, center of the left image) have individual scars from flakes that we might classify as overshot, but these underscore the ambiguity of using this technique as a Clovis diagnostic. Overshot flaking is most often an error, and these last two pieces are among the least well-worked bifaces in the collection; in neither case is the single possibly overshot flake part of a regular series of patterned sequential removals. Patterns of bifacial flaking on the Mahaffy cache bifaces thus hint at the kinds of flaking seen on the Fenn artifacts and elsewhere, but they do not do much more than that.

However, several of the Mahaffy cache bifaces show fairly detailed morphological similarities to bifaces from definite Clovis contexts. The range of variation in the three intermediate-size Kremmling chert bifaces and the smaller of the two Tiger chert bifaces (including length:width ratios ranging from 1.4 to 2.0 and bipointed outline forms with asymmetric lateral edges combining one straighter and one more curved edge) is similar to the range of variation in the Clovis de Graffenried cache (Collins et al. 2007) and the Busse cache, which may also be Clovis (Hofman 1997), although the de Graffenried bifaces are notably thinner than those in the Mahaffy cache. We should be cautious, though, in drawing comparisons like this: the most triangular of the Kremmling chert Mahaffy bifaces is also extremely similar to Archaic-age bifaces that commonly occur in caches on the southern Plains.

The most spectacular similarity between a Mahaffy cache artifact and a Clovis artifact, though, is between the large Uinta quartzite biface (Figure 4.13) and biface 100 in the Fenn cache (Frison and Bradley 1999:102–104). The flaking patterns on these two artifacts differ in detail, but they are virtually exact copies of one another in size, width/thickness ratio, and outline form. These tools are so similar—for example, they share virtually identical idiosyncratic asymmetries at the tip and base—that they might almost have been made as copies of one another. We obviously cannot prove that this is so, but the stone they are made from derives from

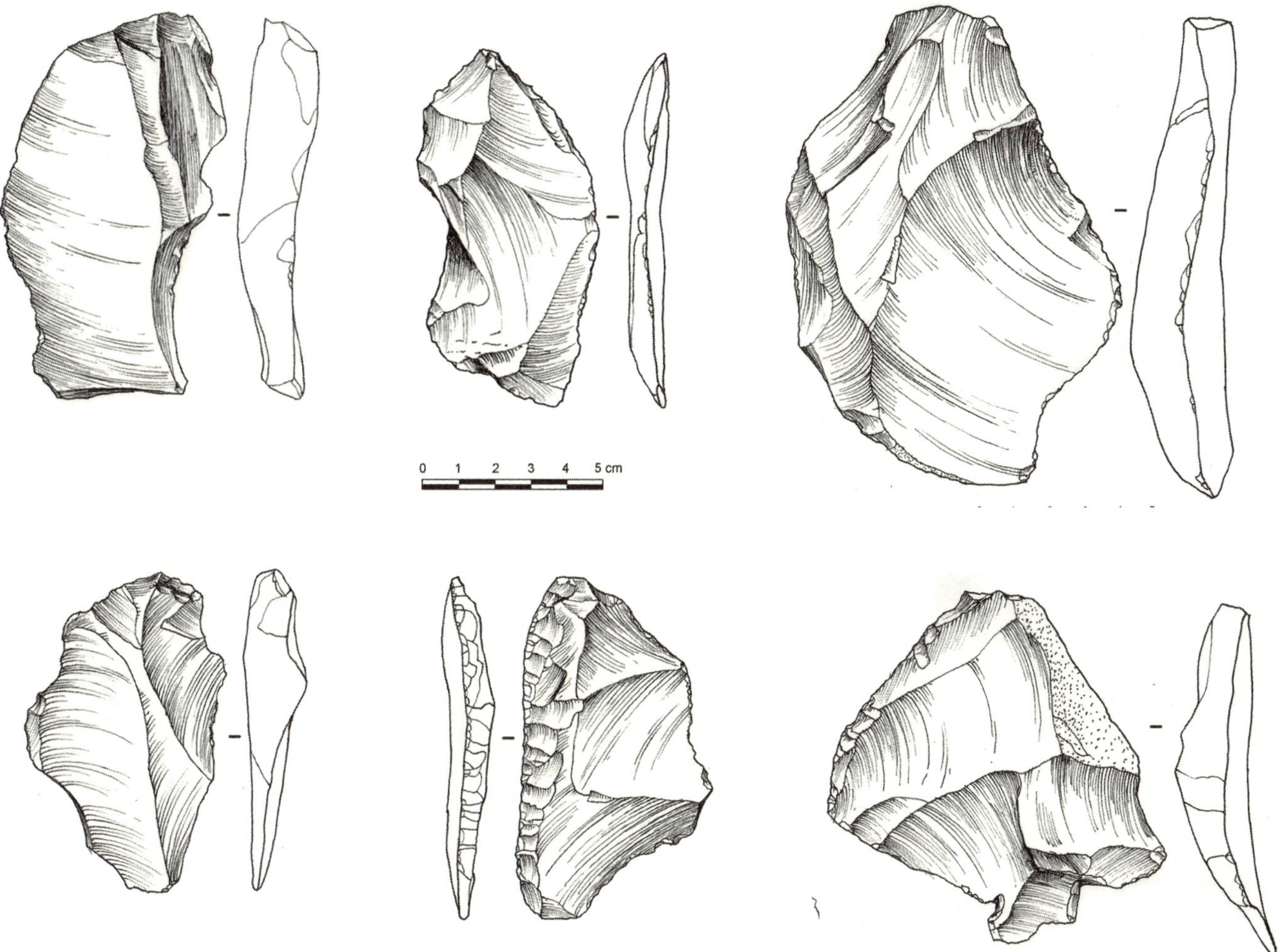

Figure 4.10. Examples of large core-struck Tiger chert flakes

sources that are close enough to one another that it is at least possible: the Mahaffy biface is made from quartzite from northeastern Utah and the Fenn biface is made from obsidian from sources just north of there, in southeastern Idaho.

Is the Mahaffy cache Clovis? The CIEP results and, in a very general way, the stratigraphic setting indicate that the Mahaffy cache dates to the late Pleistocene. Given this and the similarities between artifacts in the cache and artifacts elsewhere that are known to be Clovis makes it reasonable to argue that the cache is also Clovis, even though it contains no definite Clovis diagnostics.

GETTING HERE FROM OVER THERE: TRANSPORT TRACES

Artifacts found away from their raw material sources necessarily have a transport history, although we do not often consider how such a history might have affected them (but see Huckell et al. 2002). Transport across the Rocky Mountains has produced a variety of traces on the Mahaffy cache artifacts, including tiny (but macroscopic) mirror-like facets scattered on artifact surfaces ("bright spots"; Levi-Sala 1986; Vaughan 1985), rounding and polishing of dorsal flake ridges, impact traces on artifact surfaces, reduced reflectiveness of the high points of ventral force rings, and two forms of edge damage that are not typical of damage produced in use. These traces presumably result from contact with other stone artifacts and with other objects in containers with those artifacts. Bright spots, for example, form as a result of friction between pieces of microcrystalline silicates when there is moisture present, and movements of flakes against each other and against other objects can damage their edges. Dorsal ridge rounding and smoothing of the high points of ventral force rings are more likely the results of handling and of extended contact with other stone tools and probably with softer materials,

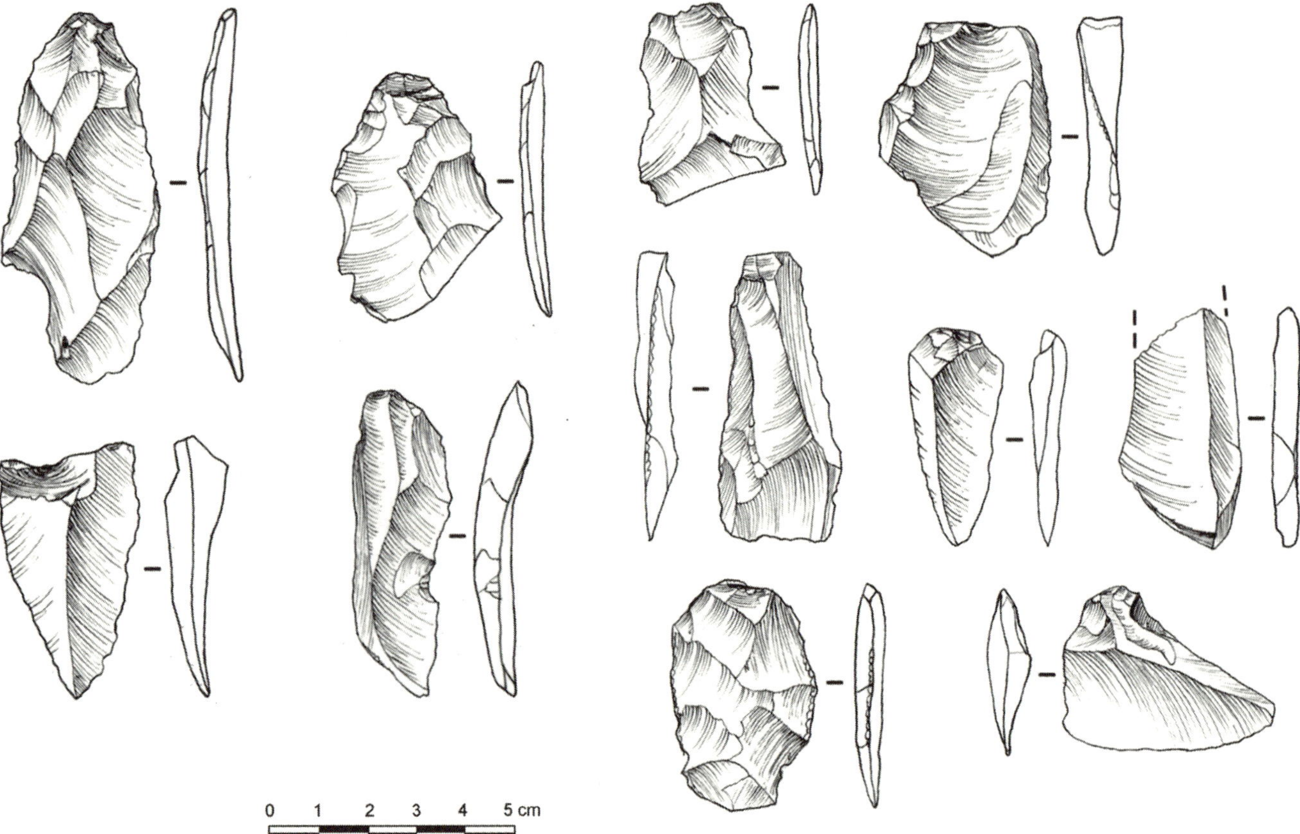

Figure 4.11. Examples of small Tiger chert biface and core-struck fakes

perhaps hide bags or wrappings in which tools were transported. Frison and Bradley (1999:81) and Huckell et al. (2002) report ridge rounding on experimental tools carried varying distances with and without padding in cardboard boxes and backpacks. In contrast, impact traces more likely result from momentary events, like bags being dropped on hard surfaces.

The edge damage on the Mahaffy cache artifacts requires more comment. Two general patterns of damage on the Mahaffy artifacts are particularly unlikely to have resulted from use. The first is a series of flakes on acute flake edges that produced irregular edges with many small projections, with these projections often defined by adjacent flakes that Keeley (1980:25) calls "half moon fractures" and that Hayden (1979:134–135) calls "snap fractures." Use of stone edges on material sufficiently hard to produce extensive damage rarely or never leaves these jagged projections (they break off), but nonuse forces often do. The second pattern is sets of overlapping series of small flakes removed unifacially with perfectly aligned distal margins. "Spontaneous retouch" (Newcomer 1976), formed when a flake rotates against a core as it is struck, generally shows this pattern of flake removal, but any process that exerts force simultaneously along a section of an edge can also produce it (contact with worked materials while a tool is in use almost always removes flakes one at a time, resulting in scars without perfectly aligned distal margins). Pressure along a section of an edge during transport offers an obvious mechanism that could produce this kind of damage.

Table 4.5 documents the frequencies of these traces on the different classes of artifacts and raw materials in the Mahaffy cache. The three quartzite pieces all show rounding of flake ridges on both faces, particularly on the ridges toward their center, implying that they were transported some distance in approximately their present form (cf. Huckell et al. 2002:Figures 4.2 and 4.5). Quartzite does not seem to form bright spots, though, and bifacial flaking makes it effectively impossible to distinguish transport damage from the very small components of production flaking. The traces on the other artifacts, though, show a more complex pattern.

Irregular edge damage is common in virtually all artifact categories, attesting to some form of fairly rough

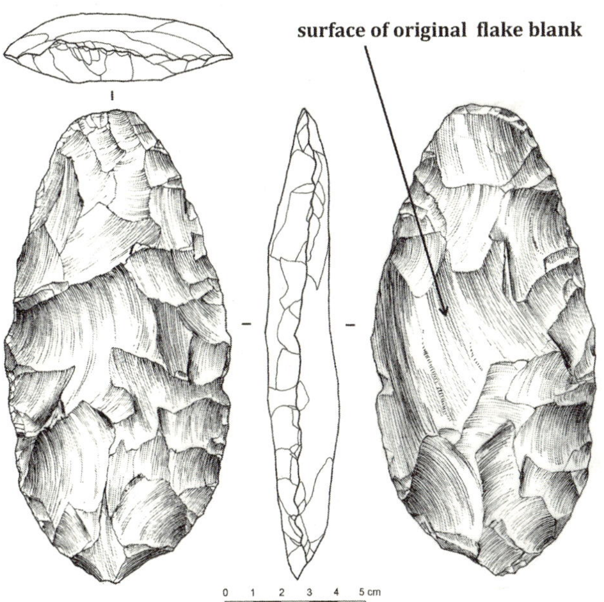

Figure 4.12. Smaller Uinta Formation quartzite biface

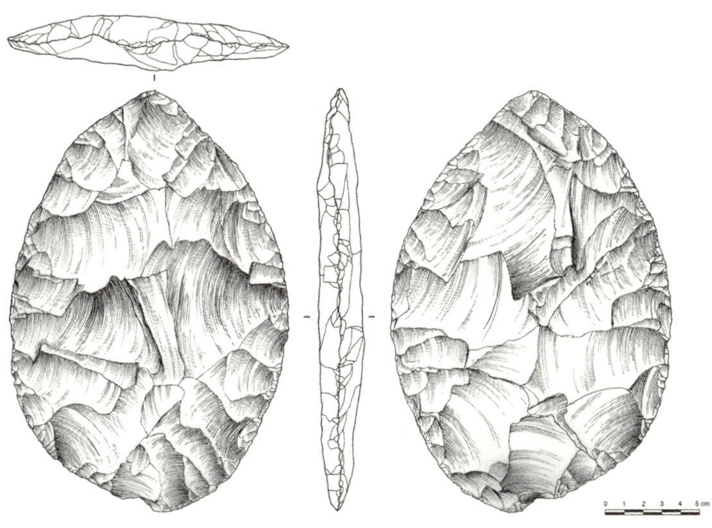

Figure 4.13. Larger Uinta Formation quartzite biface

handling during transport. Other traces, though, vary substantially among categories. Most generally, transport traces are less common on Kremmling chert artifacts than on Tiger chert artifacts, as we would expect given the different distances of these sources from Boulder. Although sample sizes are fairly small, the two most common categories of Kremmling chert artifacts (biface flakes and backed/potentially backed pieces) show very similar frequencies of these traces, suggesting similar treatment.

The Tiger chert artifacts, in contrast, show more complex patterns. Keeping variation in sample size among artifact categories in mind, there is a basic distinction between the larger, deliberately struck pieces (Type 1 and Type 2 blades and large flakes) and the pieces selected from production debris (small core-struck flakes and biface flakes). Most notably, the former show substantially higher frequencies of dorsal and ventral bright spots and of surface impacts than the latter. The near-universality of bright spots on the dorsal *and* ventral surfaces of these artifacts indicates that people transported them a considerable distance in the forms in which we see them today. Lower rates of these traces on selected production debris and consistently higher frequencies of dorsal than ventral bright spots suggest that this group of artifacts may have been produced and selected at a variety of times. Table 4.5 presents presence-absence data; close inspection of the collection indicates that bright spots are also more common per artifact among the larger pieces than the smaller

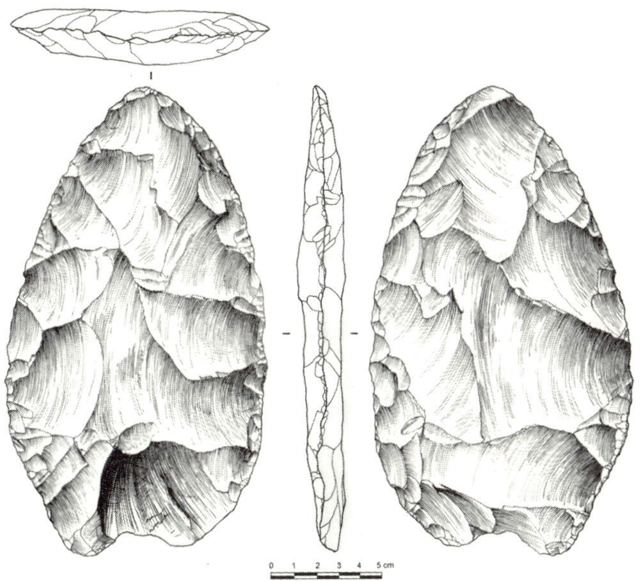

Figure 4.14. Windy Ridge–like quartzite biface

pieces. Bright spots imply artifact-to-artifact contact, and the generally higher rates of ridge rounding and ring smoothing among the smaller selected pieces than among the larger, deliberately produced pieces may reflect differences in the way they were packed or other variation in their production and transport histories. There is more than one potential explanation for this pattern—these groups of artifacts could have been moved independently of one another before coming together in the cache or they could simply have been produced, packed, and

TABLE 4.5. Frequencies of Transport Traces by Artifact Type

	MATERIAL	BRIGHT SPOTS (D)	BRIGHT SPOTS (V)	IMPACTS	RIDGES ROUNDED	FORCE RINGS ROUNDED	IRREG. DAMAGE	SPONT. RETOUCH	TOTAL ARTIFACTS IN TYPE
Biface	TC	1 50.0%	1 50%	1 50%	2 100%	0	0	0	2
	KC	1 16.7%	1 16.7%	0	4 66.7%	2 33.3%	0	0	6
Biface flake	TC	11 50.0%	5 22.4%	3 13.6%	20 90.9%	15 68.2%	18 81.8%	8 36.4%	22
	KC	3 33.3%	1 11.1%	1 11.1%	2 22.2%	1 11.2%	7 77.8%	0	9
Small core flake	TC	5 38.5%	0 23.1%	2 15.4%	8 61.5%	5 38.5%	10 76.9%	6 46.2%	13
	KC	n/a	n/a	n/a	n/a	n/a	n/a	n/a	0
Backed piece	TC	n/a	n/a	n/a	n/a	n/a	n/a	n/a	0
	KC	0	0	1 16.7%	0	1 16.7%	4 66.7%	2 33.3%	6
Large core flake	TC	5 71.4%	5 71.4%	4 57.1%	5 71.4%	4 57.1%	6 85.7%	2 28.6%	7
	KC	n/a	n/a	n/a	n/a	n/a	n/a	n/a	0
Type 1 blade	TC	5 100.0%	5 100.0%	5 100.0%	0	0 20.0%	1	0	5
	KC	n/a	n/a	n/a	n/a	n/a	n/a	n/a	0
Type 2 blade	TC	2 100.0%	2 100.0%	1 50.0%	1 50.0%	0	2 100.0%	0	2
	KC	n/a	n/a	n/a	n/a	n/a	n/a	n/a	0
Stone	TC	2 100.0%	2 100.0%	1 50.0%	1 50.0%	0	100.0%	0	2
	KC	n/a	n/a	n/a	n/a	n/a	n/a	n/a	0
Indeter. flake	TC	1 25.0%	0	0	4 100.0%	4 100.0%	4 100.0%	1 25.0%	4
	KC	0	1 100.0%	0	0	0	1 100.0%	0	1

Note: TC = Tiger chert. KC = Kremmling chert. Bright spots (D) = bright spots on dorsal surface. Bright Spots (V) = bright spots on ventral surface. Percentage figures are percentage of total artifacts in each type.

carried by different individuals—but it underscores the complexity of the life history of the collection.

SOME IMPLICATIONS OF THE MAHAFFY CACHE

We cannot think about caches in the same way that we think about most archaeological sites. Whether the city of Teotihuacan or a simple scatter of flakes and tools, the overwhelming majority of sites are accumulations of material representing multiple episodes of human action that took place over extended periods of time. In contrast, caches represent sets of objects that an individual or a small group of individuals selected and stored in what amounts to an instant. This makes it difficult to generalize from caches, particularly from single caches,

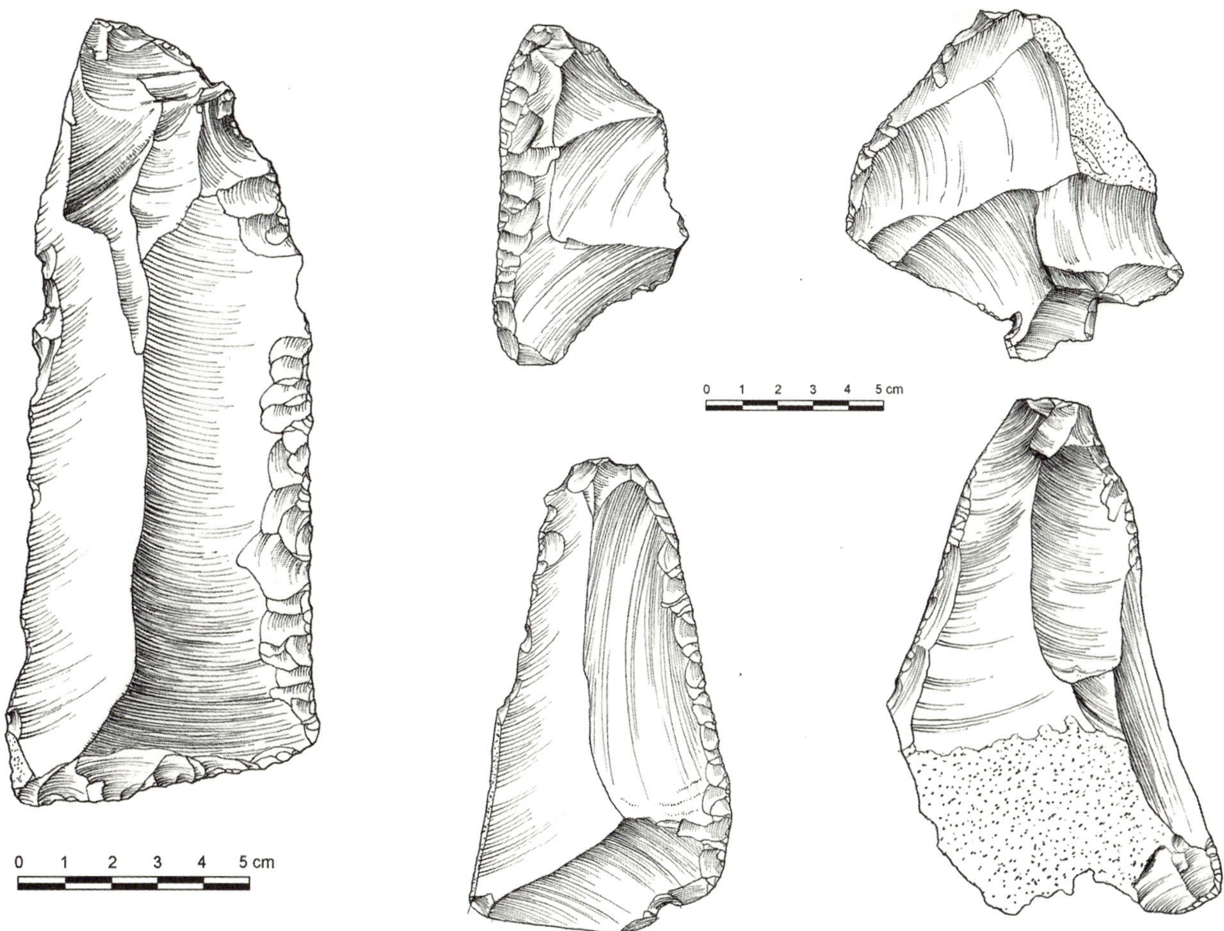

Figure 4.15. Retouched pieces. Note distinct scale for artifact on left. Artifact in lower right in Kremmling chert; all others in Tiger chert.

whose contents may have been manufactured by an individual in an hour or two based on judgments about future needs that depended on conditions experienced over very short periods of time.

This view of caches has powerful implications for understanding how the range of raw materials in the Mahaffy cache got to Boulder. Small numbers of exotic objects recovered from archaeological sites located great distances away from those objects' sources (as, for example, in the Paleoindian-age Allen [Bamforth 2007:176–178] or Bobtail Wolf [Root 2000:240–245] sites) may often have arrived individually through a variety of mechanisms (trade, individual travels, group travels) that can be extremely difficult to distinguish from one another. In cases like these, it can be difficult or impossible to determine whether or not the people occupying these sites at any single moment in the past had simultaneous access to the full range of materials we identify in our collections. For the Mahaffy cache, though, understanding how different materials came together in one place at one moment in time is central to making sense out of the behavior that the cache documents.

The distribution of transport traces across the different kinds of artifacts in the collection offers important information on this. Frison and Bradley (1999:81–82) note many of these same kinds of traces on artifacts in the Fenn cache but also observe that their frequency does not correlate with the distance from the area where the cache was found to the source of the material those artifacts were made from. As they discuss, this suggests that the objects in the Fenn cache "were transported in different ways and for different amounts of time." In the Mahaffy cache, though, the frequency of these traces *does* correlate with distance for the two materials represented in numbers of artifacts that we can analyze: transport traces of all kinds are overwhelmingly more common on Tiger chert than on Kremmling chert, although there appear to be two groups of Tiger chert artifacts with somewhat different specific transport histories. This is the pattern we would expect if the contents of the cache represent a single trek from northeastern Utah to Boulder, with the material carried the farthest subject to the greatest degree of wear and tear.

The raw materials represented in the Mahaffy cache also represent most of the sources of stone available along such a trek. The cache obviously does not include a map of the exact route the people who left it behind followed to get to the cache location, but the variety of stone sources suggests a trip up the Yampa River, over a pass through the northern part of the Gore Range into Middle Park, and then into the headwaters of the Colorado River and over one of the passes in or south of present-day Rocky Mountain National Park into the vicinity of Boulder. The people who left the cache could have taken this route, or a similar route, leisurely, over the course of a season or two, or rapidly, as a deliberate journey from one region to another.

Nothing in the cache tells us definitively about this, but evidence of the form in which people transported the cached artifacts may be consistent with something like the second of these options. The presence of transport traces on both the dorsal and the ventral faces of a large proportion of the Tiger chert flakes, blades, and retouched flakes leaves little doubt that we see these pieces in the forms in which people carried them. The blades and large flakes in this category were presumably made to be used, but many of the unmodified flakes appear more likely to have been selected as potentially useful from among those struck while making other tools. It seems unlikely, although not impossible, that pieces like these would linger for months in a toolkit, particularly because they are relatively small and have quite acute edges, making them useful for a limited range of tasks and difficult to resharpen. The retouched pieces in the collection speak more clearly to this. Regardless of raw material, it is clear that none of these have long or complex use-lives: edge modification of any kind is extremely limited, and no retouch modifies any edge more than minimally (Figure 4.15). Either knappers produced and carried these artifacts for an extended period of time almost without using them or they made them and carried them on a relatively rapid trip across the mountains.

The artifacts in any cache may have traveled independently of one another before people deposited them together, and I have noted that the artifacts in the Mahaffy cache may have changed hands as they moved across the mountains. They also may have been collected by different people who subsequently traveled together into the Boulder area; we cannot be certain. However, there is at least some reason to argue that Clovis people carried the cache in a single, relatively fast trip, and the sources represented in the cache represent most of the raw materials available in the area along any likely route from northeastern Utah to Boulder. This suggests a thorough knowledge of locations along this route where good-quality stone can be found.

Leaving the cache along Gregory Creek, in turn, suggests knowledge of where such stone cannot be found. Redeposited stone from mountain sources occurs in streambeds along the Colorado Front Range, but it is not common and tends to be highly fractured. There are more abundant and higher-quality sources of stone in some areas, but most of the open plains of eastern Colorado are stone poor, and there is virtually no flakeable material in Boulder County and adjacent areas.

People leave caches of artifacts on the landscape for more than one reason, including ideological and practical reasons. With the exception of the two tiny natural fragments of Tiger chert, the Mahaffy cache includes a range of useful pieces, including a number of unmodified flakes that seem to have been placed in the cache primarily because someone thought they might be good to have in the future. This strongly implies a utilitarian cache, left behind as a kind of insurance policy in a region where people knew that local sources of raw material were scarce or absent (cf. Bamforth and Woodman 2004; Binford 1979; Kornfeld et al. 1990; Thomas 1985). This implies, in turn, that the people who left the Mahaffy cache behind had a sufficiently repetitive pattern of land use that they expected to return to the Gregory Creek area. That is, the Mahaffy cache makes sense in the context of a mobile way of life led by hunter-gatherers with a fairly detailed knowledge of the landscape over a very large area. The distribution of the sources of the materials in the cache suggests that this area may have been much, much larger than the areas exploited by later groups along the Colorado Front Range, as widespread views of Clovis lifeways argue it should have been. But the level of knowledge of the landscape and the repetitive pattern of land use that the cache indicates also suggest that we cannot attribute the use of such a large area to the experience of being new migrants to unknown lands.

This last point underscores how much we still have to learn about North America's early occupants. The pattern of movement across the landscape that the Mahaffy cache implies fits well with long-standing expectations about Clovis ways of life, and as I noted earlier, the biface in Figure 4.2 fits very well with long-standing expectations of how Clovis technology should have reflected early use of the landscape. However, if we cannot realistically link Clovis archaeology to the earliest migrants to the New World—if that archaeology represents the ways of life of people many generations removed from those earliest migrants—long-standing explanations for patterns like those the cache indicates need to be revised.

CONCLUSIONS

The data from the Mahaffy cache expand our views of Clovis lives in important ways. As Yohe and Bamforth (2013) discuss, the CIEP data indicate that Clovis hunters used tools in the cache to process a number of animals that archaeologists have not found in studies of bone from Clovis sites. There is no compelling evidence that post-Clovis Paleoindian groups moved over unusually large areas (Bamforth 2009), but the Mahaffy data imply that at least some Clovis people probably did, as traditional views of their ways of life imply (i.e., Kelly and Todd 1988). And these data suggest that Clovis groups may have made long-distance moves rapidly, something that archaeologists have often implicitly assumed but are rarely able to address explicitly.

However, the knowledge of source locations and the expectation of return to the Boulder area that the cache suggests are not consistent with other important aspects of traditional views. Expected mobility and actual mobility are not necessarily the same thing (Kent 1991), but expectations grow from experience, and the Mahaffy cache implies that the experience of the people who left it behind was of repetitive patterns of land use. The Mahaffy cache itself offers one small view of Clovis ways of life, but the implications of what that view shows us point the way to new views of Clovis archaeology in general.

ACKNOWLEDGMENTS

Thanks first to Pat Mahaffy for his enthusiastic support for work on the cache. The landscaping crew who found the artifacts, and especially Juan Gonzalez and Jose Ramirez, provided important information on the discovery and helped to find stray items from the cache. Peter Birkeland, emeritus professor in geology at the University of Colorado, Boulder, provided critical stratigraphic information. The University of Colorado Archaeology Reading Group (Gerardo Gutierrez, Art Joyce, Payson Sheets, and Paolo Villa) improved this paper, as they have improved so many of my papers. The incomparable Eric Carlson drew the artifacts in Figures 4.2 through 4.15.

Chapter 5

The JS Cache

CLOVIS PROVISIONING THE SOUTHERN PLAINS LATE PLEISTOCENE LANDSCAPE

Leland C. Bement

INTRODUCTION

Artifacts clustered in tight association and found in isolation on the landscape are often identified as caches. Caches or caching behavior includes the intentional stashing of objects to be retrieved for use at some future time. As such, caching is an intentional act anticipated to be followed by the future need for the cached items. The context of the cached items leads to additional classification of the caches (Schiffer 1987). Funerary caches are those interred with the dead and are often viewed as representing the furnishings needed by the deceased in the afterlife or next life (Bement 1994; Kilby 2008), although they may also be votive, representing the social identity of the cemetery; or honorary, signaling the prestige level of the dead individual.

Caches not placed with the dead or in a cemetery context may have a more secular or mundane purpose often related to the subsistence organization of the group (Binford 1979, 1980; Hurst 2002; Schiffer 1987). Toolstone caches in areas devoid of suitable stone sources provide the makings for any item in a lithic tool kit. In these instances, the anticipated future need is not identified to specific function because any number of tool types can be fashioned from the lithic stores. Caches of tools, on the other hand, can signal the anticipated need for a particular task. In this case, a cache of hide scrapers portends the anticipated task of hide preparation, or a cache of grinding stones the need for plant processing. These items are placed in the area of anticipated use and as such provision that part of the landscape for a perceived future specific need. Kilby (2008) has divided these caches into three categories: insurance caches, seasonal/passive gear caches, and load exchange caches. Insurance caches contain general materials to meet the requirements of a wide variety of circumstances, whereas seasonal/passive gear caches are designed to meet the need of a select task or set of tasks within a set season of an annual round or a particular collecting task (Binford 1979). Load exchange caches reflect the decision making of the group to temporarily jettison objects in lieu of collected resources—a response to transport constraints (Kilby 2008).

Assigning a group of artifacts to one of the various categories (insurance, seasonal/passive, load exchange) is contingent upon the context of the find, the cache composition, and its placement within a particular cultural adaptation (economic system). The full array of caching behavior has been attributed to the Clovis techno-complex (Collins 2007; Kilby 2008). Similarly, the foraging subsistence systems of the Calf Creek/Andice (Middle Archaic) and Montell/Castroville (Late Archaic) cultures of the southern Plains and southern Plains periphery incorporate caching in their generalized subsistence mode that includes large-mammal (bison) hunting (Collins 2007:86). As stated by Collins (2007:86), "I would hypothesize that in Clovis, Calf

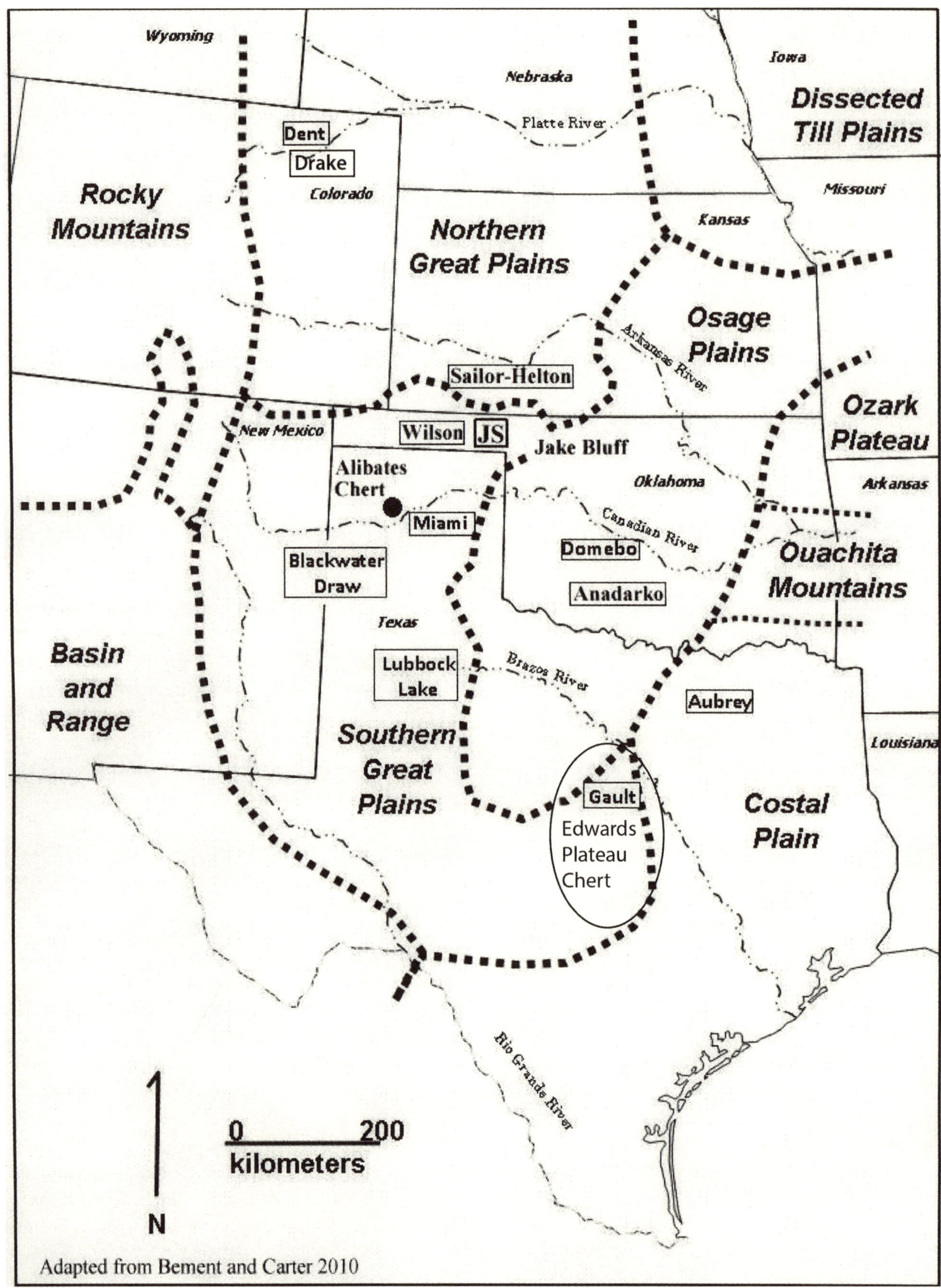

Figure 5.1. Map of the southern Plains with key sites and resources mentioned in the text

Creek/Andice, and Montell/Castroville times, foragers were based in central Texas *or similarly favorable environments* and that organized hunting parties at times traveled to outlying regions for big game. . . . Caching was an important means of ensuring that stone (and possibly other) materials were available to the hunting parties (and possibly to foraging parties as well)" (emphasis added).

One of the resources identified in the central Texas base camp area is the high-quality chert found on the Edwards Plateau (Figure 5.1). Projectile points and butchering tools of this material are associated with the Clovis-age Domebo mammoth kill in western Oklahoma (Leonhardy 1966), and caches of this material have been found in south central Oklahoma (Anadarko cache; Hammatt 1969). The movement of this chert over 400 km from the central Texas source and its association with hunting activities and caching activities supports Collins's hypothesis stated above. In this scenario, portions of present-day Oklahoma were once part of the hunting area frequented by central Texas Clovis hunters.

Another principal lithic toolstone utilized by Clovis groups is Alibates chert, which has a primary quarry outcrop area in the Texas panhandle. Clovis points and butchering tools of this material have been found at Clovis mammoth and bison kill sites at Blackwater Locality No. 1, New Mexico (Hester 1972); the Miami site, Texas panhandle (Holliday et al. 1994); and the Jake Bluff site in northwestern Oklahoma (Bement and Carter 2010). These sites identify the hunting areas repeatedly visited by Clovis hunters from a hypothesized but as-yet-unidentified base near the Alibates chert quarry area. Important caches of Alibates chert artifacts are the Drake cache (Stanford and Jodry 1988) and the Sailor-Helton cache (Mallouf 1994). The Drake cache from north-central Colorado consists of 13 complete or near-complete Clovis points, 11 of which are Alibates chert, and 1 hammerstone (Kilby 2008; Stanford and Jodry 1988). The cache is located over 580 km north of the Alibates quarry.

The Sailor-Helton cache of 40 blades, 115 flakes, and 10 large cores, all of Alibates chert, is an example of a Clovis utilitarian cache (Kilby 2008; Mallouf 1994). Its location in southwestern Kansas, almost 200 km north of the Alibates chert quarry area, suggests this cache served to provision seasonal activities, probably hunting, in an area almost devoid of similar-quality lithic sources.

A slightly smaller cache from the Oklahoma panhandle, consisting of tools made on 13 bifaces, 30 blades, and 69 flakes, is also dominated by Alibates chert (Graves et al. 2006). Known as the JS cache, this collection of tools provides the opportunity to analyze a utilitarian cache from the perspective of lithic reduction technology and tool use toward the goal of placing the find within the subsistence system and economic pursuits of a Clovis group. Building on the premise that the southern Plains Clovis adaptation consists of a combination of a generalist subsistence system and large-mammal hunting, expressed as annual movements between large base camps in rich ecotonal settings and seasonal large-mammal-hunting areas (Bement and Carter 2010; Collins 1999b), it is hypothesized that the JS cache was intended to provision a repeatedly visited productive seasonal hunting area for a Clovis group emanating from a base near the Alibates chert source.

An expectation arising from this hypothesis is that the cache was intended to supply stone material or tools for use in hunting/butchering activities. As such, the cache should contain material to make new tools or contain tools that are still useful for the intended tasks.

The purpose of this chapter is to provide a description of the JS cache and place it within a context of Clovis hunting organization. Following a brief narrative of the discovery of the cache, the 112 items are segregated by technological reduction criteria. Then a functional analysis is conducted based on tool edge morphology and edge angle.

THE JS CACHE

The JS cache (34BV180) consists of 112 artifacts found eroding from the right (east) bank of Bull Creek in western Beaver County, in the Oklahoma panhandle (Figure 5.1). The artifact concentration measured approximately 20 x 20 cm and was exposed in stratified sandy loam deposits approximately 2 m below surface (Figure 5.2). A profile cut near the find location exposed coarse, sandy alluvium over gravels deposited on sandstone bedrock. This sequence is common along Bull Creek. A distinct buried soil consisting of a thick A horizon generally forms within 1.5 m of the bedrock contact and has been dated to 11,000 radiocarbon years before present (Bement, Carter et al. 2007). This buried A horizon has been stripped from the deposits at the JS cache locality, probably during middle Holocene erosion of the Bull Creek valley.

The cache contains 13 bifaces, 30 blades, and 69 flakes. All items appear to be tools, used hard and put up dirty. The majority are made from Alibates chert (n = 94, 83.4

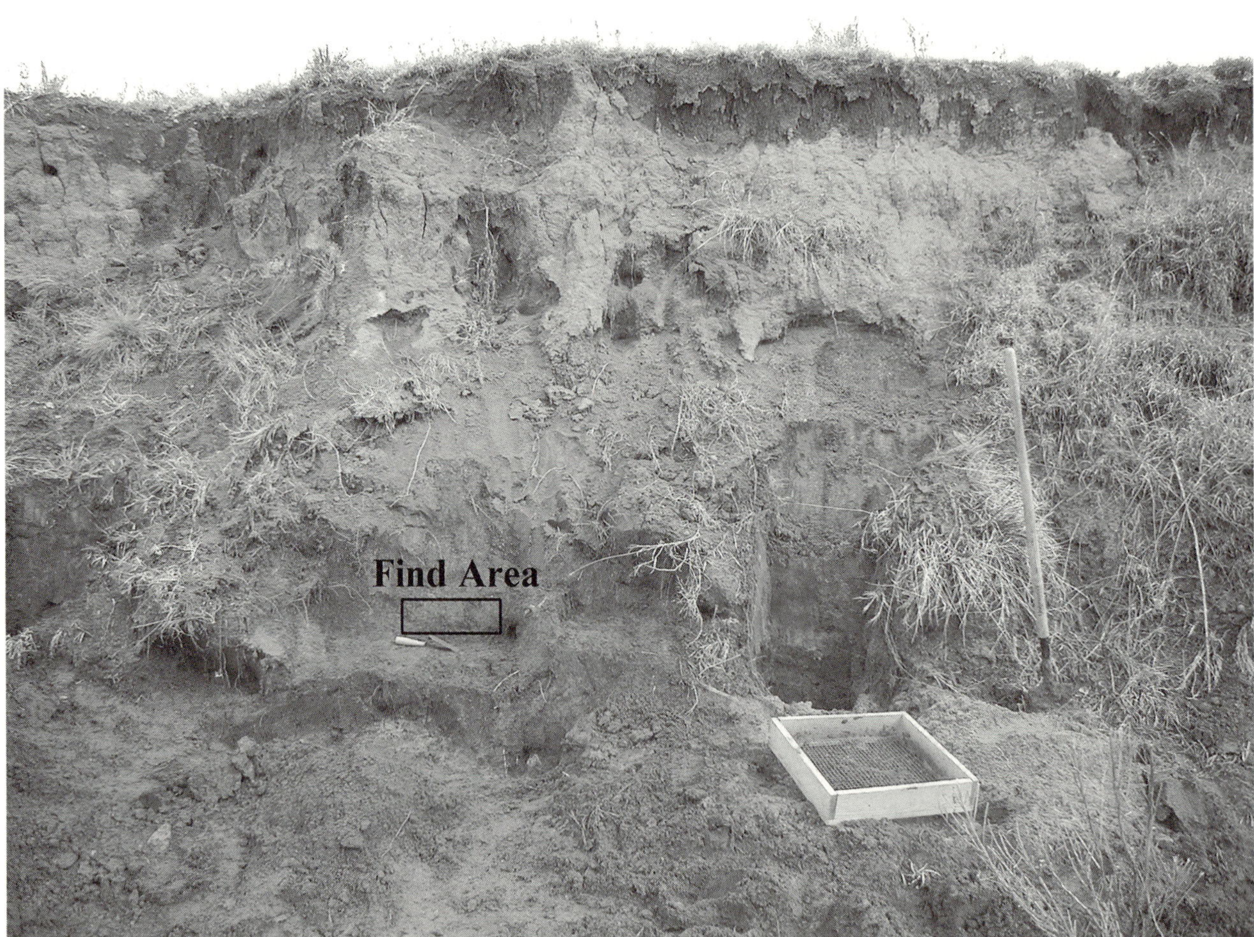

Figure 5.2. Find spot of the JS cache

percent) although Niobrara jasper ($n = 6$, 5.4 percent) and an unsourced quartzite ($n = 2$, 1.8 percent) are also represented (Table 5.1; Figure 5.3). The presence of one failed fluted preform (Figure 5.4), three overshot flakes, three bifaces with overshot flake scars, and film of red ochre on nine items (two blades, two bifaces, four flakes, one overshot flake; Table 5.1) lends credence to the Clovis attribution of this cache.

Although the placement of the various pieces was not documented by the cache discoverer, he thought the contents were stacked three or four deep. A three-tiered layering can be demonstrated. Roughly one-third of the cached items have a calcium carbonate coating on one surface; one-third display a milky-white patina on one surface (Table 5.1); and the remainder have neither a calcium carbonate coating nor a patina on a surface. No items have both calcium carbonate coating and patina. Since calcium carbonate coatings often indicate the lower surface of a buried artifact, those with this feature are interpreted to have been on the bottom of the cache. Patinas often form because of prolonged exposure to the sun and weather. Items with the patina are interpreted to be from the upper layer within the cache, with the patinated surface facing upward. Those items with neither coating nor patina would form the middle layer(s) of the cached items. There is no evidence of the kind of container holding the cache. However, it is assumed that some sort of bag was used. The presence of patina indicates that the objects on the top became exposed, possibly due to the deterioration of the bag. Patina also indicates the cache was not buried, or if buried, that it became uncovered. The sediments surrounding the cache suggest the package was set on the surface, which was eventually buried by a series of overbank deposits from the Bull Creek channel.

Understanding the life history of the cache begins with a technological accounting of the various pieces. The contents of the cache include large and small bifaces, flakes, and blades, each representing a different tool

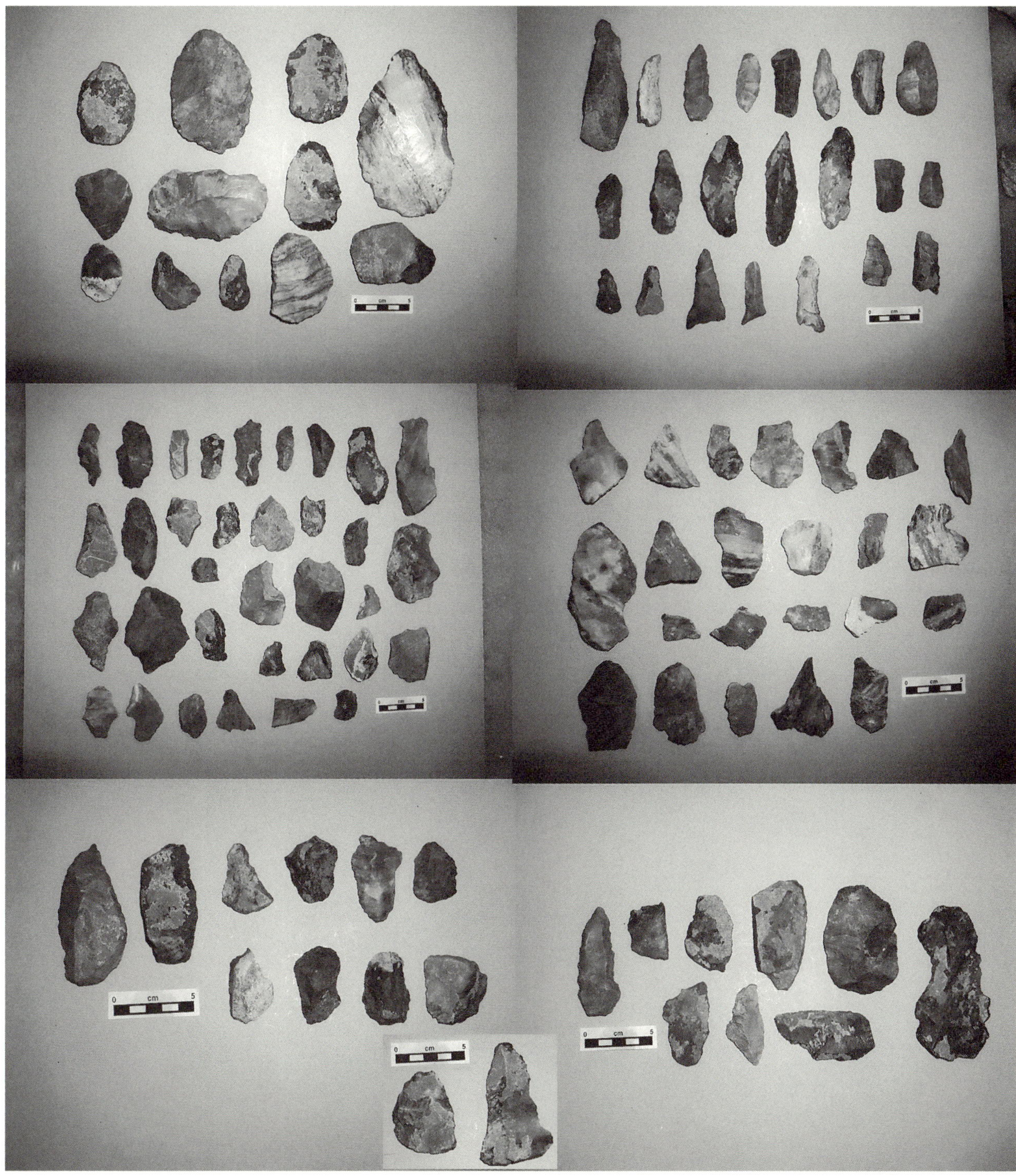

Figure 5.3. The artifacts of the JS cache

reduction strategy (Figure 5.5). Bifaces and flakes are closely intertwined since the flakes are struck from bifacial cores; the cores themselves form another trajectory to specific tool classes (Bradley et al. 2010; Collins 2007; Huckell 2007; Patten 2005). Blades, although similar to flakes in that they are struck from prepared cores, differ in form and the fact that the blade core is not integral to the production of a particular tool type in the fashion that biface cores become projectile points (Collins 1999b).

The bifacial core reduction sequence has received much attention, especially related to the production of Clovis projectile points (Bradley et al. 2010; Callahan 1979). In

Figure 5.4. Preform fluting failure, overshot flakes, and refit overshot flake

these studies, the reduction stages can be defined by width-to-thickness relationships that often follow shifts in flake-removal techniques (hard-hammer percussion, soft-hammer percussion, and pressure). Up to nine stages have been identified in Clovis projectile point production (Callahan 1979).

Another sequence related to biface reduction defines various technological stages on the basis of the width of the biface (Huckell 2007). In this sequence, initial biface reduction is characterized by the production of cores through deliberately spaced flake removals, followed by the sequential overlapping of flake removals. These two

TABLE 5.1. Attributes of the Specimens Contained in the JS Cache

Cat. No.	Material	Specimen	LENGTH	WIDTH	THICKNESS	WEIGHT	Patina	Ochre
1	Alibates	Blade	79.09	30.19	11.32	26.2	N	Y
2	Alibates	Biface[a]	29.28	42.45	7.52	11.1	N	Y
3	Alibates	Flake	57.8	36.1	10.23	19.4	N	Y
4	Alibates	Flake	81.15	42	14.3	60.5	N	Y
5	Alibates	Biface	79.67	56.48	18.87	84.8	N	Y
6	Alibates	Overshot	113.55	56	13.68	74.5	N	Y
7	Alibates	Flake	62.09	35.46	9.44	14.4	N	Y
8	Alibates	Blade	91.59	28.08	11.92	27.8	N	N
9	Alibates	Flake	42.56	26.65	6.5	5.7	N	N
10	Alibates	Flake	47.53	28.95	14.06	17.6	N	N
11	Alibates	Flake	44.46	29.95	15.06	20.4	N	N
12	Alibates	Flake	40.72	32.99	17.25	21	N	N
13	Alibates	Flake	58.45	28.36	11.59	13.8	N	Y
14	Alibates	Biface	143.19	81.51	30.96	324.7	Y	N
15	Niobrara	Flake	46.98	33.96	6.78	9.8	N	N
16	Niobrara	Flake	58.11	35.49	10.49	16.6	N	N
17	Alibates	Flake	50.09	30.6	12.55	16.1	N	N
18	Alibates	Flake	33.03	26.38	6.41	5.1	N	N
19	Alibates	Flake	49.86	26.62	5.08	6.1	N	N
20	Niobrara	Flake	45.89	27.55	8.37	10.2	N	N
21	Alibates	Flake	51.49	31.18	9.13	12.3	N	N
22	Alibates	Flake	51.88	33.07	8.46	10.5	N	N
23	Alibates	Flake	58.81	48.21	9.81	21.2	Y	N
24	Alibates	Flake	56.16	38.53	6.52	12.8	N	N
25	Alibates	Flake	47.22	26.81	6.74	8.6	N	N
26	Alibates	Flake	40.25	32.62	9.47	12.9	N	N
27	Niobrara	Biface	51.23	38.01	12.39	20.9	Y	N
28	Alibates	Flake	45.07	42.75	13.89	25.6	Y	N
29	Alibates	Flake	39.38	28.22	7.37	6.8	N	N
30	Alibates	Flake	60.75	43.7	23.64	45.6	Y	N
31	Alibates	Flake	90.89	69.26	13.66	71.5	N	N
32	Alibates	Flake	44.88	24.75	6.73	6.9	N	N
33	Alibates	Flake	61.89	37.08	8.2	18.1	N	N
34	Alibates	Flake	43.81	31.68	8.3	9.4	N	N
35	Alibates	Flake	84.6	58.8	18.08	88.4	N	N
36	Alibates	Flake	63.35	61.46	11.28	35	Y	N
37	Alibates	Blade	87.68	42.55	12.66	46.1	N	N
38	Alibates	Flake	64.03	31.72	8.77	19.2	Y	N
39	Alibates	Flake	79.7	48.77	11.43	30.4	Y	N
40	Alibates	Blade	137.46	46.5	14.42	85.6	Y	N
41	Alibates	Biface	77.58	49.95	16.91	66.4	N	N
42	Alibates	Flake	60.38	27.25	10.99	13.4	N	N

TABLE 5.1. *(continued)*

Cat. No.	Material	Specimen	LENGTH	WIDTH	THICKNESS	WEIGHT	Patina	Ochre
43	Alibates	Flake	52.79	27.63	12.33	15.9	N	N
44	Alibates	Biface	106.49	60.66	21.22	148	Y	N
45	Alibates	Blade	61.09	24.61	10.17	15.6	N	N
46	Alibates	Flake	63.9	28.06	11.19	17.4	N	N
47	Alibates	Flake	84.76	52.02	7.49	25.6	Y	N
48	Alibates	Overshot[b]	61.56	46.93	9.84	28.7	N	N
49	Alibates	Blade	111.54	31.63	22.07	73.4	N	N
50	Alibates	Blade	73.64	33.8	17.82	61.9	N	N
51	Alibates	Flake	77.29	53.95	14.2	57	N	N
52	Alibates	Flake	87.64	42.8	17.71	61.4	Y	N
53	Alibates	Overshot	88.51	54.33	13.44	42.9	N	N
54	Alibates	Blade	49.83	26.17	5.53	8	N	N
55	Alibates	Blade	100.55	33.58	9.88	37.1	N	N
56	Alibates	Blade	79.97	42.62	6.59	19.1	N	N
57	Alibates	Flake	76.24	44.58	13.74	49.4	Y	N
58	Alibates	Flake	36.67	23.23	5.89	5.3	N	N
59	Alibates	Flake	106.09	43.48	23.99	77.6	N	N
60	Niobrara	Flake	60.04	45.55	6.24	19	N	N
61	Alibates	Flake	62.02	29.93	12.36	22.1	N	N
62	Alibates	Blade	64.38	26.24	5.97	14	N	N
63	Alibates	Blade	55.38	19.74	6.42	10.6	Y	N
64	Alibates	Flake	46.81	30.4	8.44	12.3	N	N
65	Alibates	Flake	34.07	31.57	9.6	7.7	N	N
66	Alibates	Biface	76.96	52.76	20.84	94.7	Y	N
67	Alibates	Biface	108.57	70.8	13.97	141.8	N	N
68	Alibates	Biface	49.05	27.72	8.16	11.9	N	N
69	Alibates	Biface	75.54	55.99	14	65.4	Y	N
70	Alibates	Biface	79.95	52.28	11.82	63.7	Y	N
71	Alibates	Flake	69.18	47.25	10.52	27.1	N	N
72	Alibates	Flake	47.03	44.03	8.37	12.7	N	N
73	Alibates	Flake	54.78	30.92	12.48	16.9	N	N
74	Alibates	Biface[b]	62.95	54.93	11.27	43.6	N	N
75	Alibates	Flake	57.35	32.6	16.2	25.3	Y	N
76	Alibates	Flake	102.87	53.55	12.36	68.6	N	N
77	Alibates	Flake	38.56	20.73	4.89	3.9	N	N
78	Alibates	Flake	63.6	34.39	12.2	34.2	N	N
79	Alibates	Biface	53.01	37.64	18.87	27.7	N	N
80	Alibates	Flake	66.67	46.1	12.89	35.2	N	N
81	Alibates	Flake	60.75	37.91	11.31	18.8	Y	N
82	Alibates	Flake	67.63	49.71	19.64	49.8	Y	N
83	Alibates	Flake	54.49	38.77	10.02	20.7	N	N
84	Niobrara	Flake	79.59	55.53	7.69	30	N	N
85	Alibates	Flake	66.9	51.6	14.8	40.5	N	N
86	Alibates	Flake	45.27	28.37	8.73	12.7	N	N

Cat. No.	Material	Specimen	LENGTH	WIDTH	THICKNESS	WEIGHT	Patina	Ochre
87	Alibates	Flake	52.76	32	9.8	13.1	N	N
88	Alibates	Flake	51.7	25.19	11.27	14.5	N	N
89	Quartzite	Flake	45.03	43.86	10.18	14.5	Y	N
90	Alibates	Flake	47.49	34.87	8.45	9.8	N	N
91	Alibates	Flake	57.85	39.04	14.71	27	N	N
92	Alibates	Flake	36.95	28.04	7.56	9.5	N	N
93	Alibates	Blade	40.81	21.39	9.23	7.5	N	N
94	Alibates	Blade	63	26.67	11.29	12.8	Y	N
95	Alibates	Blade	68.87	19.16	10.74	14.3	N	N
96	Alibates	Blade	79.38	36.79	7.42	22.8	Y	Y
97	Alibates	Blade	86.59	41.77	15.12	47	Y	N
98	Alibates	Blade	98.66	40.96	15.19	65.5	Y	N
99	Alibates	Blade	72.79	28.29	11.8	26.5	N	N
100	Alibates	Blade	50.51	20.89	5.48	5.4	N	N
101	Alibates	Blade	83.11	32.78	16.62	47.4	N	N
102	Alibates	Blade	75.7	26.89	11.46	27.2	N	N
103	Alibates	Blade	73.37	42.09	16.34	45.5	N	N
104	Alibates	Blade	47.03	25.98	8.99	11.9	Y	N
105	Alibates	Blade	50.86	28.86	8.05	10.3	N	N
106	Alibates	Blade	73.73	30.36	8.95	21.4	N	N
107	Alibates	Blade	75.47	29.38	5.9	11.2	Y	N
108	Alibates	Blade	67.03	32	11.94	33.5	N	N
109	Quartzite	Blade	54.37	31.92	9.13	17.2	N	N
110	Alibates	Blade	68.93	29.8	17.89	32.5	N	N
111	Alibates	Flake	47.98	44.91	12.04	27	Y	N
112	Alibates	Flake	55.08	44.21	11.84	24.2	Y	N
					Total	3728.1 g		
						8.2 lbs.		

Note: All measurements in millimeters; weight in grams.

[a]Fluted preform failure.

[b]Specimen 48 refits to 74.

stages are delimited in the camp debris at the Murray Springs site in Arizona by a biface width of 65 mm (Huckell 2007). The primary biface (>65 mm width) may be employed as an expediency tool although its main purpose is the production of large flake tool blanks (Figure 5.5). Secondary bifaces (<65 mm width) are also employed in the production of flake tool blanks, although their main strategy is the production of bifacial tool forms such as knives; the ultimate goal is the production of projectile points.

In the JS cache, only 2 of the 13 bifaces are over 65 mm wide and can be classified as primary biface cores (Table 5.1). The remaining 11 bifaces have widths below 65 mm and are classified as secondary bifaces.

The flake reduction mode depends on the production of large flake blanks that can be further reduced into various tool forms, including large unifacially retouched flakes, gravers, side scrapers, small unifacially retouched flakes, end scrapers, and utilized flakes. By definition, larger flakes are produced from primary bifaces and smaller flakes from secondary bifaces (Figure 5.5).

Identifying the size of the biface is difficult from the flake blank, particularly if it has been further reduced into a tool. However, the length of the flake can be used to

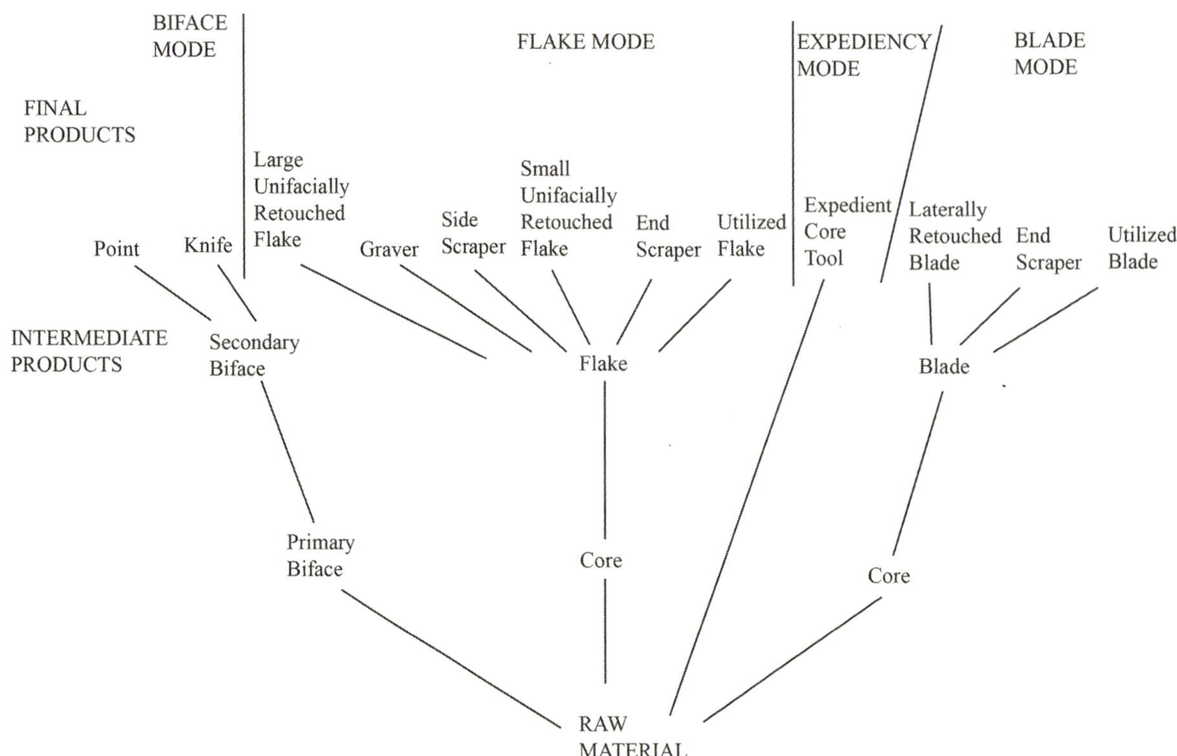

Figure 5.5 Clovis reduction sequences and tool production modes (after Huckell 2007)

identify the presence of a primary biface if the flake length exceeds the 65 mm delimiter for the biface width (flake length is determined by biface width except when the flake is removed along the longitudinal axis of the biface). In the JS cache there are only 17 flakes that are 65 mm or longer (Figure 5.6a). Overshot flakes can also be used to determine the width of biface cores, since the flake includes the opposing biface edge at its terminus. Of the three overshot flakes in the cache, two exceed the 65 mm delimiter. The third is from a narrower, thus secondary, biface.

Since many of the flakes are also tools, the flakes may be shortened due to resharpening of the distal end. To compensate for this, flake lengths were increased by 20 percent and 50 percent. A 20 percent increase in length expands the number of flakes from primary bifaces from 17 to 39 (Figure 5.6a). Increasing flake length by 50 percent expands this number further, to 60 of the 69 flakes. The 50 percent increase is probably excessive and the 20 percent totals are favored. By this analysis, the cache contains only two bifaces that can yield flakes of similar size to the rest of the cache (with a 20 percent increase in length). Thus the other 11 bifaces are no longer in the flake-production mode but are in the secondary biface tool category.

Another attribute that has been reported to be of use in understanding bifacial reduction strategies is flake thickness (Patten 2005). Through replicative studies, Patten (2005) has shown that flake thickness can predict the minimum thickness of the biface core. For example, a 10 mm-thick flake requires a core that is at least 25 mm thick. Flake thickness does not significantly vary with tool use or sharpening. For this reason, the flake thickness values from all the flakes can be employed in analysis without undergoing preanalysis alteration, as was employed in estimating flake length alteration with tool use.

To determine the required minimum thickness of the biface cores to produce all the flakes in the JS cache, all flake thicknesses were multiplied by 2.5 (Figure 5.6b), and their plot was compared with a plot of the thickness of the bifacial cores in the cache. The results show that 18 flakes require core thickness in excess of that contained in the cache; another 28 are in the size range of 1 core. The remaining 30 can be produced by the other 12 cores.

No blade cores were found in the cache. The blades and tools made on blades cannot be replaced without blade cores.

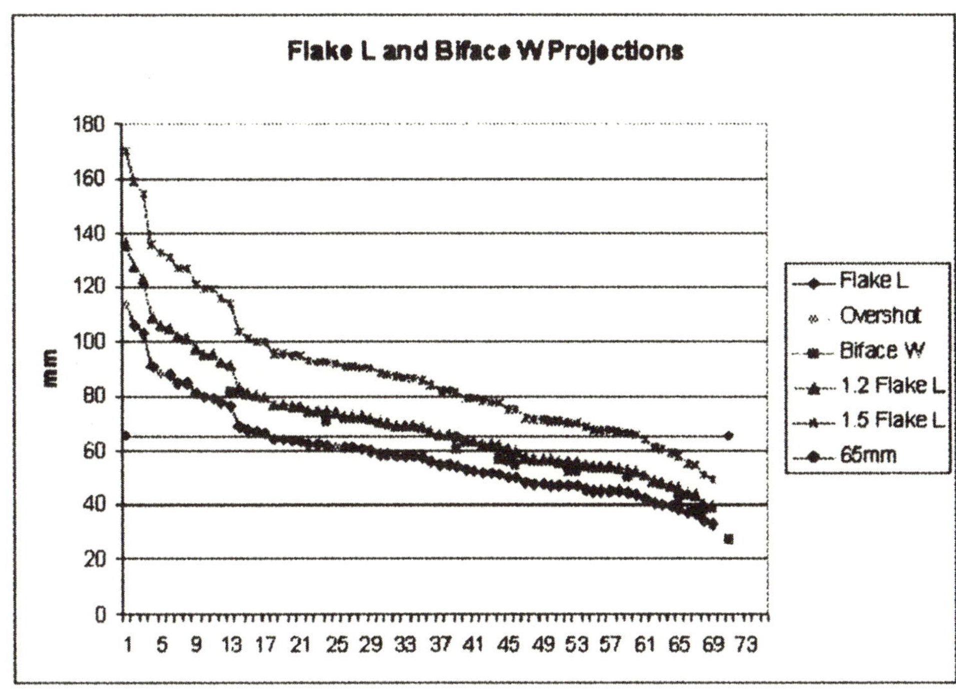

A.

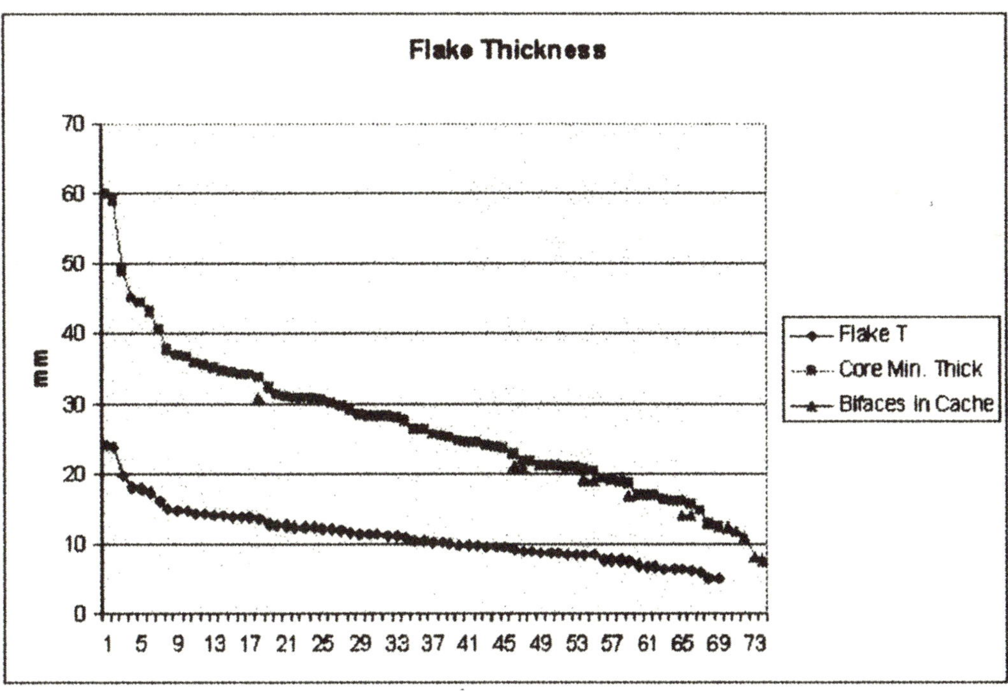

B.

Figure 5.6 Determining biface core fitness in producing the JS cache: (a) determining biface width from flake length (after Huckell 2007), and (b) determining biface thickness from flake thickness (after Patten 2005)

A single refit, an overshot flake on a small biface (Figure 5.4), has been identified in the assemblage. Several flakes appear to be from the same core, but no refits were possible.

From this analysis, it is shown that this cache no longer contains sufficient large cores to produce the array of tool forms contained in the cache, only the smallest. As such, the cache appears to have lost much of its ability to meet long-term needs, although it still contains useful tools, the limited ability to supply additional small tools, and a few bifaces that potentially could be made into projectile points.

FUNCTIONAL ANALYSIS

The interpretation that most, if not all, of the items in the JS cache are tools is based on the presence of retouch and/or patterned attritional removal along artifact edges. In an attempt to identify the tasks undertaken with these tools, a selection of 12 artifacts, including bifaces, flake tools, and blade tools, was subjected to protein residue, high-power microscopy, and edge angle analyses.

Protein residue analysis employing crossover immunoelectrophoresis (CIEP) was performed by the Paleo Research Institute (Puseman 2006). None of the artifacts provided positive results for animal or plant proteins, with the one exception of a positive match for human protein on one of the items. The human match could easily be attributed to modern handling of the artifact, although this has not been confirmed.

Microcopy was employed by Tom Loebel to analyze possible use-wear polish on the same 12 artifacts subjected to residue analysis. This analysis was hampered by the extensive battering found on all flake arises. This damage was interpreted as bag wear—the result of objects rubbing or clanging against one another during transport (Huckell et al. 2002). The presence and extent of bag wear precluded identification of use-wear polishes, even on specimens with formal flaking and retouch. The identification of bag wear on these 12 artifacts, however, suggests that the cached items had been moved from the

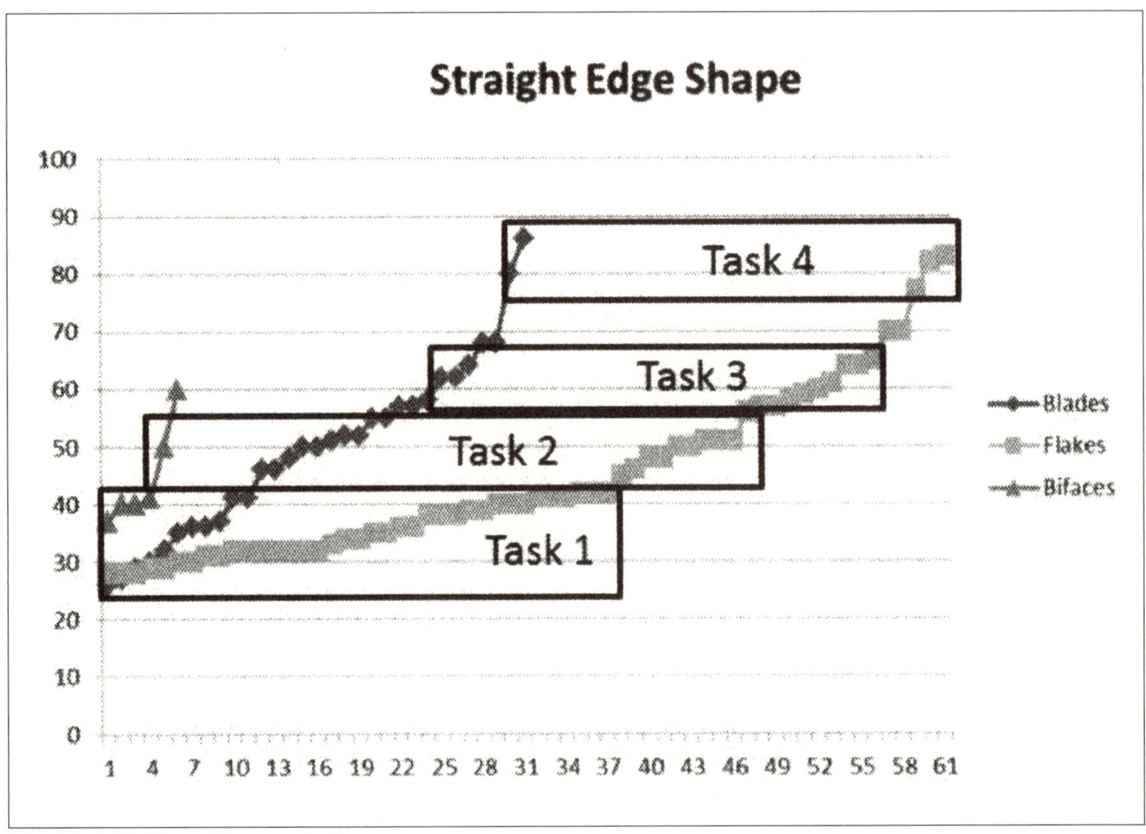

Figure 5.7 Distribution of edge angles on straight-edge units and breakdown of possible tasks

location of their last use (at least on these items). The analysis of additional specimens is needed to determine whether all artifacts in the cache are similarly worn.

Failing to gain insight into the function of the tools in the cache through residue and polish analysis, a less exacting functional analysis employing edge angle was undertaken (Wilmsen 1968). Low angle edges tend to be utilized in cutting modes, whereas steep angles are more indicative of scraping motions. Taken in conjunction with tool form (or edge shape), edge angle analysis can provide clues to the use and maintenance of stone tools. In the analysis of the JS cache, tool edges for all 112 specimens were first segregated by shape (straight, convex, concave, notch, projection) and then the angle of the use edge was taken by goniometer at the center of each edge segment and rounded to the nearest degree. A tool can have more than one use edge or edge segment. Use edges were identified on the basis of a continuous geometry without abrupt shape changes. A straight edge adjacent to a notch would be analyzed as two use edges, each with its own goniometric edge angle measurement.

Edge angles were plotted by lithic reduction class (biface, flake, blade) and edge shape (straight, concave, convex, notch, spur). Breaks between edge angle sequences within each edge shape are interpreted to represent either a shift in tool function (from a cutting to a scraping action or a change in the material being worked). Breaks in sequences could also indicate tool edge resharpening.

Straight use edges are identified on bifaces ($n = 6$ edge units), flakes ($n = 31$), and blades ($n = 31$) (Figure 5.7). Four tasks are delineated based on sequences of edge segment angles. Task 1 includes straight use edges with edge angles between 26 degrees and 41 degrees. Task 2 edges have angles between 42 degrees and 52 degrees. Task 3 edges have angles between 54 degrees and 67 degrees, and Task 4 edges have angles between 78 degrees and 86 degrees. Tasks 1 and 2 probably employ cutting motions and Tasks 3 and 4 are probably aligned with scraping motions.

Convex use edges occur on bifaces ($n = 19$ edge units), flakes ($n = 50$), and blades ($n = 27$) (Figure 5.8). Four tasks are identified for convex use edges. Task 1 specimens have edge angles between 21 degrees and 59

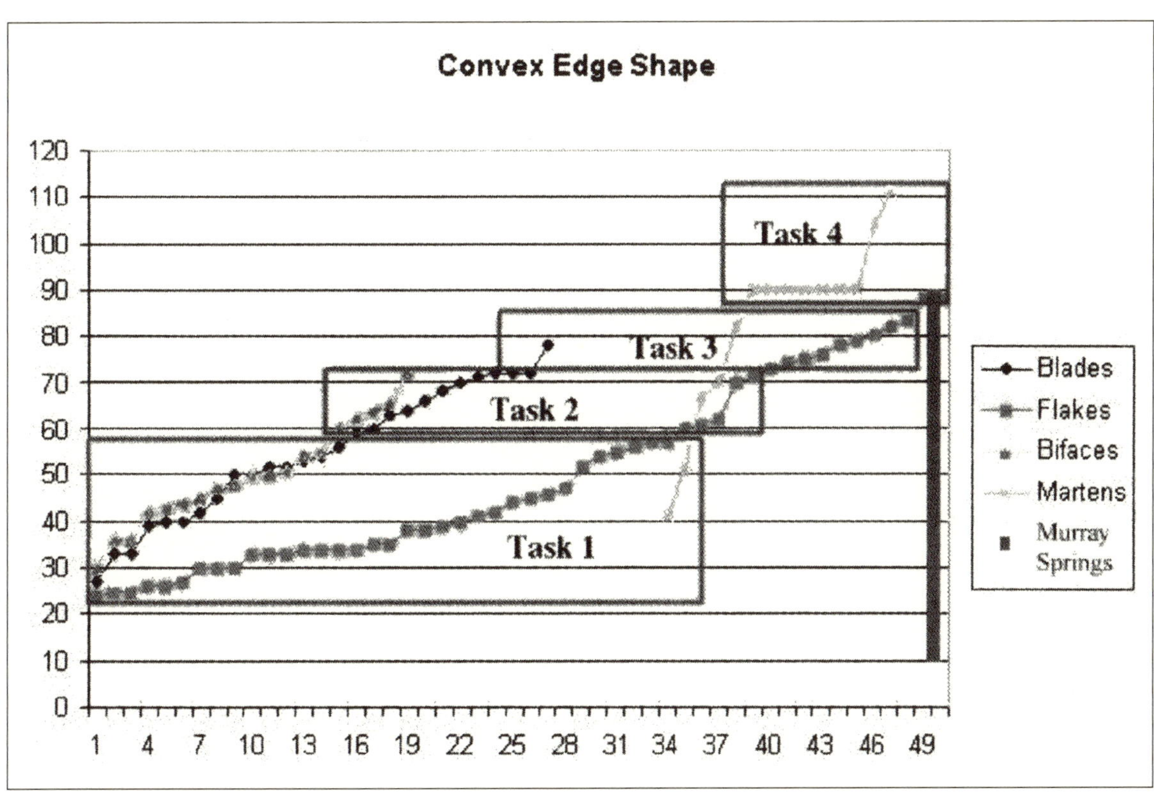

Figure 5.8 Distribution of edge angles on convex-edge units and breakdown of possible tasks. The edge angle distribution for the Murray Springs assemblage is also provided.

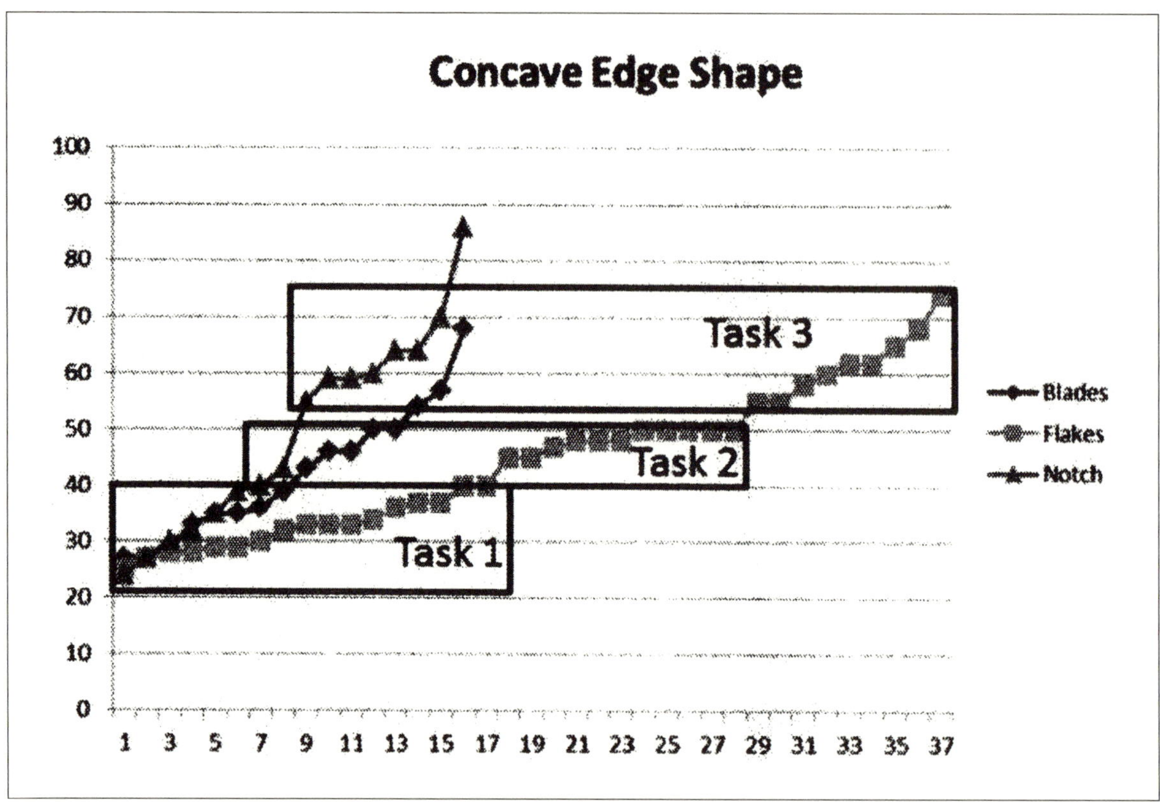

Figure 5.9 Distribution of edge angles on concave-edge units and notches and breakdown of possible tasks

degrees and probably represent cutting activities. Task 2 edges have angles between 60 degrees and 72 degrees and probably identify a scraping action. Task 3 edges have angles between 73 degrees and 87 degrees, indicating scraping activities. Task 4 edges—limited to two specimens—have angles of 88 degrees. These two artifacts are often referred to as end scrapers and their edge angle is consistent with end scrapers from the Clovis camp at the Martens site, Missouri (Kay and Martens 2004).

Concave use edges occur only on flakes (n = 37 edge units) and blades (n = 16) (Figure 5.9). Three tasks have been identified. Task 1 edges have angles between 25 degrees and 43 degrees and probably represent cutting activities. Task 2 edges have edge angles between 45 degrees and 51 degrees, representing scraping actions. Task 3 edges have angles between 54 degrees and 75 degrees and represent scraping actions.

A particular class of concave edge unit, the notch, is found on all three reduction classes. One notch is found on a biface, 12 on flakes, and 3 on blades. The edge angles for notches form two clusters: one between 23 degrees and 42 degrees, the other between 55 degrees and 70 degrees (Figure 5.9). The only notch on a biface has an edge angle of 86 degrees. Notches are assumed to function as spokeshaves; however, the two clusters suggest differences in their use. The lower edge angles possibly indicate a pushing spokeshave use and the steeper edge angle a scraping action.

The final edge unit shape is known as a projection or spur and probably functioned in a piercing or engraving action. Spurs were identified on flakes (n = 16 edge units) and blades (n = 4).

Edge angle analysis cannot identify the kinds of material being worked and thus is fairly limited in determining the range of activities or tasks to which the JS cache could have contributed. However, the edge angles on tools from the camp at the Murray Springs site provide a comparison from a hunting/processing context. The Murray Springs camp flake tool edge angle data range between 10 degrees and 90 degrees, providing a greater span of edge angles than that displayed by the JS cache artifacts, which range between 21 degrees and 90 degrees (Huckell 2007; Figure 5.8). The more acute angles on some of the Murray Springs flake tools may indicate that fresh (unretouched) utilized flakes are present in the collection. Such flakes are not in the JS cache. Overall, the JS cache implements are comparable to those in the Murray Springs assemblage and, as such, suggest a similar suite of activities. The JS cache probably functioned as a hunting camp assemblage.

DISCUSSION

The hypothesis that the JS cache is a provisioning cache that functioned to provide lithic tools for use during that part of the Clovis subsistence cycle that targeted large mammals gains support when the tool composition of the cache is compared with other site assemblages. The hunting camp at Murray Springs has been used to describe the lithic technologies employed by Clovis hunters. The JS cache tools can be placed into all categories of the Murray Springs classification except for the presence of minimally altered lithic cobbles and blade cores (Figure 5.10). In fact, the JS cache contains more implements (n = 112) that fit into this classification than the sites from which the classification was constructed (n = 54 tools, excluding debitage; Huckell 2007). The tool classification for Murray Springs also includes the tools associated with the various mammoth and bison kills in this reach of the San Pedro River. The comparable composition of the JS cache and San Pedro River assemblages indicate the cache is what should be expected to furnish the required tools for processing a series of successful Clovis kills such as those reported at and near the Murray Springs site (Haynes and Huckell, eds. 2007).

If the Murray Springs site and nearby portions of the San Pedro River are one of the mammoth patches or refugia envisioned by Gary Haynes (2002b), then the tool assemblages associated with those kills should reflect the range of tasks associated with Clovis large-mammal hunting and processing. To meet the anticipated needs of a similar group of Clovis hunters traveling to another mammoth patch would require transport of various tool types such as those itemized at the Murray Springs camp and vicinity. The array of tool forms and sizes contained in the JS cache fulfills this requirement. The presence of bag wear or transport damage on the JS assemblage is consistent with transport of the requisite assemblage to an area of anticipated need—in this case the Bull Creek area at a distance of 150 km from the Alibates chert quarry. Although no Clovis kills have been identified along Bull Creek, the presence of scattered mammoth, camel, and bison remains in stream deposits and the discovery of a large, unfluted, Alibates chert lanceolate point with elephant residue (Puseman 2004) suggests the possibility that these sites may be present or have once existed (Bement, Schuster, and Carter 2007).

To turn this discussion on its head, a cache of tools similar to the JS cache is sufficient to provision the processing needs of the hunters at the various kills at Murray Springs and those in the nearby San Pedro River area. The 112 items in the JS cache could provision two camps the size of that at Murray Springs, which contained 54 tools, if one excludes the raw material expended as debitage. This raises the question, was the Murray Springs camp assemblage furnished by a cache? And was this cache opened to furnish the other San Pedro kill activities (e.g., Lehner)? After all, a cache that is opened, used, and left scattered around is indistinguishable from a camp assemblage.

The JS cache is not alone in this portion of the southern Plains. As mentioned above, the Sailor-Helton cache of 40 blades, 115 flakes, and 10 large cores, all of Alibates chert (13.8 kg), was found north of the Cimarron River in southwestern Kansas (Kilby 2008; Mallouf 1994). Also in this area of the southern Plains is a group of eight Alibates chert blade tools and seven Alibates chert flake tools found eroding out of a plowed field along Fulton Creek in Oklahoma (Bement, Schuster, and Carter 2007). Known as the Wilson cache (34BV189), these implements are identical to ones in the JS cache, although confirmation of their cultural attribution awaits excavation of the site. Together with the JS and Sailor-Helton caches, these stockpiles of Alibates chert material and tools identify a regional node of anticipated, repeated Clovis use. The eventual identification of Clovis kills and processing camps is not unexpected.

A final attribute worth mentioning is the presence of red ochre on nine of the implements. Ochre on these nine artifacts is easily identified by the unaided eye. Additional examples of ochre staining are seen when other implements are viewed under low-power (20x) microscopy. It is likely that all implements bear some ochre, as it is easily transferred from one object to another. Red ochre is often found in suspected cemetery or burial contexts (Kilby 2008). The overwhelming evidence that the JS cache fulfilled utilitarian needs suggests ochre also had a utilitarian use. Perhaps the

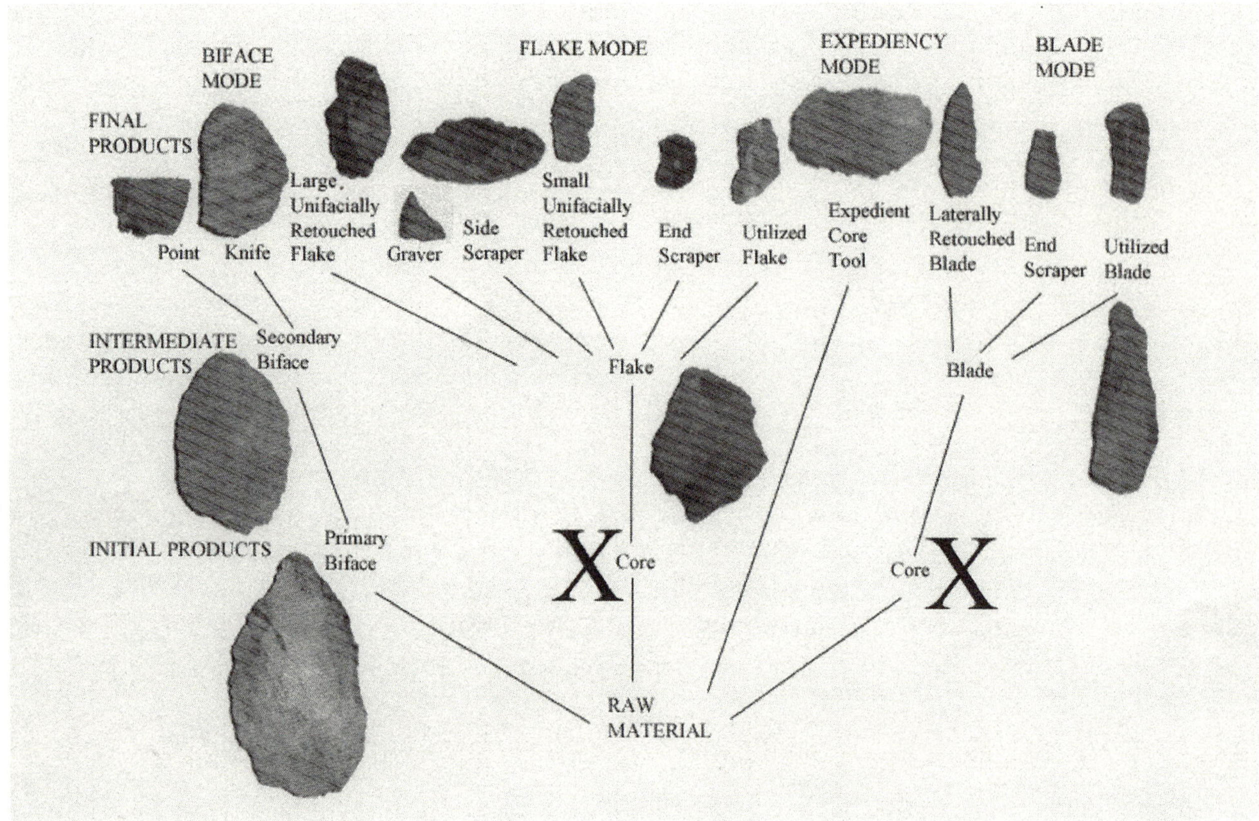

Figure 5.10. The JS cache specimens fill all classifications of the Huckell lithic reduction technology and tool classes except the raw material and blade core categories (adapted from Huckell 2007).

wicking property of hematite aided in tasks such as meat slicing and hide working where handheld tools became slick.

CONCLUSION

Caching behavior occurs in anticipation of future needs, whether the needs of the deceased in the afterlife or the needs of the living planning to return to productive procurement areas. As such, caching has a predictive quality: an implied repeated behavior at a particular place on the landscape. It also implies that a resource is predictable in space and time (seasonal or annual reliability). There is also an implied constraint of some sort, perhaps including a constraint on what can be carried, a constraint on availability of suitable raw material (for tool production), or a constraint on the time necessary to manufacture the tools even if raw material was available. Needs and constraints vary across time periods, geographic locations, and cultures. The earliest New World culture employing caching behavior is the Clovis culture.

The JS cache is interpreted to be a provision cache where stone tools and raw material were stashed in an accessible and easily identified place for the purpose of provisioning task groups (large-mammal hunters) visiting the area. As such, the tools contained in the cache are sufficient to cover the needs of the task group. As shown, the JS cache contains the array of tools seen in the hunting camp assemblage at Murray Springs, Arizona, and the kill-butchery assemblages from sites along the San Pedro River. The cache contains materials that can be employed as needed, thus foregoing the need for the group to transport these items.

When viewed from the perspective of the tool assemblages at the Murray Springs camp and other kill sites in the San Pedro River drainage, the JS cache contains the assorted tools expected in a seasonal gear cache. When viewed from the perspective of the JS and other provisioning caches, the Murray Springs camp assemblage and other San Pedro tool assemblages combined could have been supplied by a cache or series of caches, leading to the conclusion that the San Pedro valley was a productive hunting area or mammoth patch repeatedly visited by

Clovis hunters from a larger, extended-stay camp some distance away. The JS cache as a provisioning cache has broad implications for understanding Clovis hunting organization and land use practices.

To call for additional analyses of this and other caches is cliché. However, not to call for additional analyses neglects a treasure trove of information available from caches about the subsistence organization of southern Plains Clovis groups.

ACKNOWLEDGMENTS

Thanks to David Kilby and Bruce Huckell for including this material in the symposium on Clovis caches at the 2010 Society for American Archaeology meetings in St. Louis. The JS cache was found by avocationalists Terry Dorman and Bob Kerns. Their valued assistance in reporting the archaeological discoveries in the Oklahoma panhandle is greatly appreciated. Tom Loebel generously offered his time and expertise to look at a selection of tools. This is but one of many ongoing efforts to document Oklahoma prehistory supported mainly with private funds. This project was supported in part by a generous donation from Courson Oil and Gas. This chapter was improved by the suggestions of two anonymous reviewers and the editors. Their efforts are appreciated.

Chapter 6

The Carlisle Clovis Cache from Central Iowa

Matthew G. Hill, Thomas J. Loebel, and David W. May

INTRODUCTION

The peopling of the Americas marks the terminus of an epic dispersal of the genus *Homo*, commencing about 50,000 years ago as fully modern humans (*H. sapiens*) left Africa and culminating about 12,000 years ago with their appearance in South America. Documenting how these colonizers responded to various social and ecological circumstances is essential not only for understanding other prehistoric hominin radiations (Foley 2002) but also for contextualizing research on contemporary globalization processes such as immigration, resettlement, and smuggling as well as the introduction, spread, and impact of exotic plants and animals on endemic taxa. Exactly how these processes played out in North America is the source of recurrent contention. Questions persist about when people arrived here, where they came from, the routes they used to get here, the lifeways they practiced, and their role in the disappearance of multiple animal taxa (Meltzer 2009). Notwithstanding these unresolved matters, the first robust archaeological imprint on the landscape was generated by Clovis foragers (Kelly 2003a), and it is this "demographic and cultural baseline" (Fiedel 1999:110) that contributes most directly to the research presented here.

At first blush, the Clovis archaeological record appears profuse, diverse, and reasonably well understood. In reality, however, sites with contextually associated materials are scarce (as compared to finds of isolated points), excavated components are rarer still, chronological control is poor, and direct evidence of plant and animal exploitation is sparse. As outlined in Chapter 1 of this volume, among the most intriguing elements of this record are the caches, of which there are some 20 reported to date (Figure 6.1). Research on these caches and how they served Clovis foragers has matured from brief site reports (e.g., Anderson and Tiffany 1972; Butler 1963; Taylor 1969), to technological issues (e.g., Lahren and Bonnichsen 1974; Lyman et al. 1998; Wilke et al. 1991; Woods and Titmus 1985), to the current emphasis on their broader, systemic import as it relates to landscape learning, technological organization, and diet and subsistence behavior (e.g., Huckell et al. 2011; Kelly 2003b; Kilby 2008; Meltzer 2003a).

To this end, our goal in this chapter is to report on a cache of 43 Clovis artifacts that were recovered in 1968 near the small town of Carlisle in central Iowa (Figure 6.2). The Carlisle cache is significant for several reasons, most obviously as a collection of utilitarian gear—including 25 bifaces and 12 large flakes—that was stockpiled to back future hunting, butchering, and hide-processing activities in the area. Though lacking finished fluted points, the bifaces and large flakes display distinctive characteristics that are diagnostic of the reduction sequences employed by Clovis knappers. The collection thus provides an analytically tight snapshot of the organization of Clovis flaked stone technology. Furthermore, it was

Figure 6.1. Locations of confirmed Clovis caches (map created by Matthew G. Hill)

excavated by archaeologists from primary context, with the associated documentation offering clues on how the contents were packaged, emplaced, and buried. As such, it represents one of only a handful of contextually intact Clovis components in the Midcontinent as well as the easternmost example of a utilitarian Clovis cache published to date. Considered together with places like East Wenatchee and Simon in the Far West, Beach on the northern Plains, and de Graffenried on the southern Plains, the Carlisle cache stretches the geographic extent of Clovis caching practices to the eastern fringe of the Great Plains, upwards of 1,000 km east of CW and Drake in northeastern Colorado and Busse in northwestern Kansas. In addition, the geological context, including stratigraphic position and geochronology, has been established, providing information on the cache setting, its age, and the local Late Wisconsin environment.

THE CARLISLE CACHE

Location

The cache find spot is several hundred meters east of the Carlisle city limits, in northeastern Warren County, on a terrace overlooking the Des Moines and Middle Rivers, about 3 km west of the Des Moines River (Figure 6.2). The location is roughly equidistant between the dams of two large reservoirs on the Des Moines River, Saylorville Lake to the north and Lake Red Rock to the south. The terminal moraine of the Des Moines Lobe, which formed ca. 13,800 ^{14}C yr B.P., is located 10 km north-northwest of the location. The lobe retreated rapidly and by ca. 12,000 ^{14}C yr B.P. it was no longer active in Iowa, although it continued to issue melt water and outwash into its axial drainage, the Des Moines River, into Clovis times ca. 11,000 ^{14}C yr B.P. (Benn and Bettis 1985:12; Bettis et al. 1988:39–47; Bettis et al. 1996; Iverson 2005:51–53).

Discovery and Excavation

The cache was recovered during the salvage of a late prehistoric Oneota village, the Cribbs' Crib site (13WA105), by archaeologists from Iowa State University (Cole and Gradwohl 1969; DeVore 1990; Gradwohl 2003:24).[1] This effort was conducted in response to the partial destruction of the site by the U.S. Army Corps of Engineers as part of a levee construction project designed to protect southeastern Carlisle from the high-water levels of Lake Red Rock. Sediment for the levee was borrowed from the late prehistoric village area. Working in the shadow of heavy equipment from June 3 to July 19, 1968, workers excavated 130 features and 38 10 x 10 ft units (Figure 6.2). About half of the excavated features contain typical Oneota artifacts and ecofacts, including shell-tempered pottery, triangular arrow points, ground stone tools, and carbonized maize. Twenty-eight features in the northern part of the borrow area were destroyed before they could be salvaged. The balance of the excavated features were essentially sterile, with the exception of Feature 75 in the southeastern corner of the borrow area, which yielded a remarkable assemblage of bifaces, large flakes, and several small flakes. The feature was discovered and excavated by Jeff Hruska, an archaeology field school student, on the afternoon of July 12.

The corpus of information on the excavation of Feature 75 consists of entries in four field books, a plan map, a feature form, and a total of 19 35 mm Kodak Kodachrome slides. These materials document the general character and configuration of the cache, in addition to capturing clues related to its establishment and burial history. On July 12, Hruska writes, "Located cache pit containing 25 large biface knives, approx. 5 large scrapers, and an assortment of spalls and large flakes. These were photographed and removed."

Another field school student, David Seely, summarizes the discovery in the same vein: "During the afternoon a feature numbered 75 worked by Jeff Hruska was the hot pit for the day. Jeff's pit contained a concentration of knife blades and scrapers. The number was about 25 knife blades (all of them finely worked and made of a very good grade of flint) and a few scrapers and other flint artifacts."

The same with Nancy Osborn, a crew member: "Jeff Hruska found a cache of large flint knives to the far SW of the excavation—the area designated as feature 75, photographed, and the knives were removed."

The field supervisor, John Cole, sketched a plan map of the cache and described it in enthusiastic terms: "F 75 — scads of bifaces! (Hruska)"

The feature form completed by Cole on the day of discovery includes only one comment: "no discernible pit fill or limits—just a pile of artifacts."

The following day, July 13, Hruska more thoroughly assessed the context: "Skimmed area around the location of the flint cache, but no limits could be found. All material around & under the location of the flint appeared to be very sterile. Nothing besides the flint was found in or around F-75."

The photographic slides, all taken by John Cole on July 12, offer more information (Figure 6.3). The first (earliest) photograph in the series (Figure 6.3a) shows the cache shortly after it was exposed by the belly scraper and Hruska's initial probing of the find. It was originally manifest as a cluster of several bifaces, large flakes, and fragments thereof resulting from contact with the belly scraper. It appears that only a few artifacts were dislodged from primary context in this way. Working with a trowel, Hruska found the first artifacts, which included six near-surface bifaces and large flakes. These specimens, along with the dislodged biface, were set aside in a small pile. The second series of slides shows Hruska defining the margins and depth of the find using a trowel to chunk out the surrounding matrix, together with a small brush to clean the artifacts. Although most of the specimens remain obscured or partially obscured by sediment, the overall configuration begins to take shape. The final series was taken just prior to removal of the artifacts. In

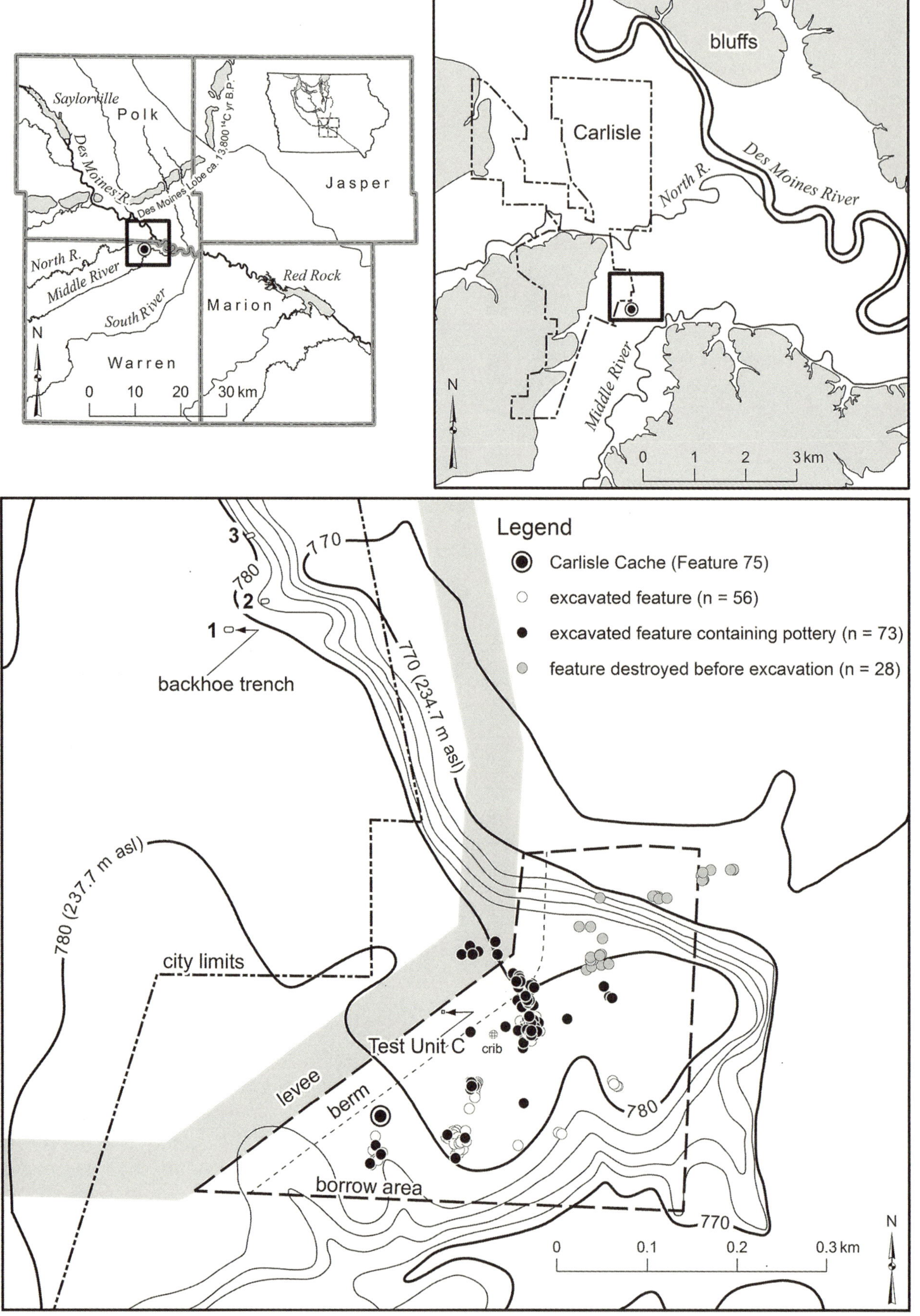

Figure 6.2. Location of the Carlisle cache (map created by Matthew G. Hill)

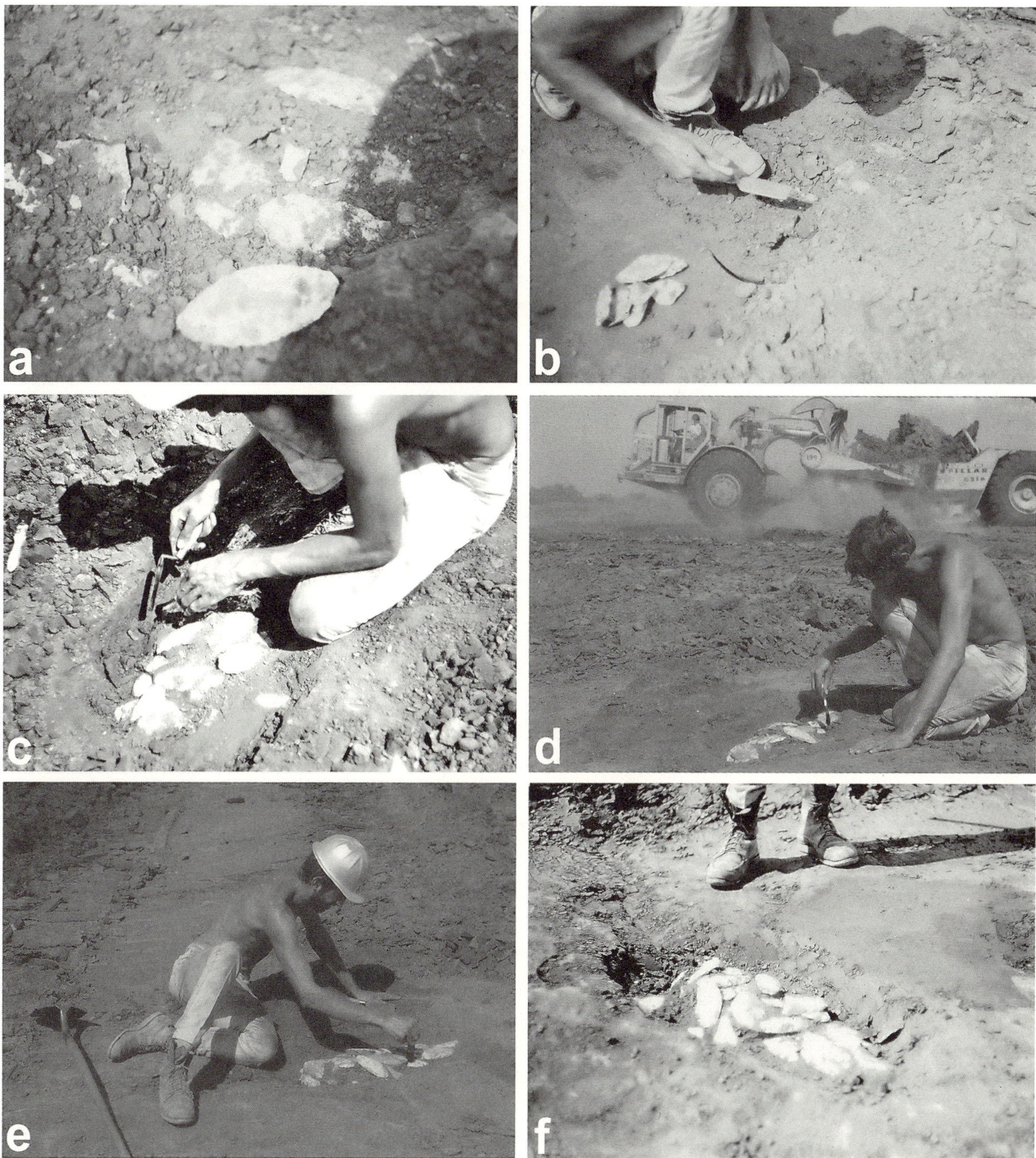

Figure 6.3. Excavation of the Carlisle cache: (a–b) discovery and probing; (c–f) exposure and demarcation. Large biface in the lower foreground of (a) is no. 4440. Distal piece of a small flake is visible in the center of (a) (see Figure 6.14, middle). Stacked bifaces in (b) are nos. 4440 (*top*) and 4427 (*bottom*). Flake blank no. 4452 is located second from left in (b) (photographs by John R. Cole).

Figure 6.4, the specimens are clean, a North arrow is present, and the excavation pit has been "squared up" by centering the cache within an ~2 x 3 ft unit.

The cache is elliptical in outline, measuring ~40 x 70 cm. It is oriented northwest–southeast and includes 25 bifaces, 12 large flakes, and 6 small flakes.[2] Ten bifaces and nine large flakes are identifiable in situ (Figure 6.4), while two other bifaces are visible in Figure 6.3a–b. The organized, compact arrangement of the artifacts, together with the absence of rust nicks and trails resulting from contact with modern tillage equipment, leaves no doubt that the cache lay undisturbed in primary context prior to discovery. The artifacts are generally arranged parallel to the long axis of the cache's outline (with the exception of two bifaces that are oriented transversely). They lay flat and are stacked several

Figure 6.4. Carlisle cache in situ (photograph by John R. Cole)

specimens deep in some places. The large flakes occur mostly on top of the bifaces and around the margins. Although recent compression and bend fractures raise the possibility that some artifacts were dislodged from primary context and inadvertently hauled away by the belly scraper, this does not appear to be likely. Damaged and reconstructed artifacts are essentially complete, and there are no fragmentary pieces representing "missing" bifaces or large flakes that were originally present in the cache.

Affiliation

Although the contents of Feature 75 are (and were at the time of discovery) anomalous by Oneota standards, the absence of a Clovis point or any other time-diagnostic artifacts makes it easy to understand its initial association with the late prehistoric component. The first cache of Clovis artifacts to come to light—the Simon cache from Idaho—was recovered in the fall of 1961 and reported on shortly thereafter in two short papers in an obscure venue (from the perspective of Iowa archaeology) (Butler 1963; Butler and Fitzwater 1965). Several months later, on February 27, 1962, at Blackwater Locality No. 1, New Mexico, a cache of 17 blades was found by F. Earl Green, who, in turn, promptly conducted a geological and technological assessment, publishing the results in *American Antiquity* (Green 1963). While this effort added blades to the identified Clovis toolkit, alerting archaeologists to the potential for similar finds (e.g., Hammatt 1969; Stoltman 1971), the Green cache offered little in the way of guidance for recognizing a Clovis connection for Feature 75 five years later. The Anzick cache from Montana was discovered in May 1968 and, like Simon, was also first reported on in an obscure venue (Taylor 1969). Anzick was introduced to the larger scientific community five years later in an article focusing on the bone rods, with only brief mention of the chipped stone artifacts, including Clovis points, bifaces, and several miscellaneous tools (Lahren and Bonnichsen 1974). The Rummells-Maske cache from Cedar County, Iowa, was headline news in regional archaeology for several years following its discovery in 1964, though since only finished fluted points were reported (Anderson and Tiffany 1972), it also did not call into question the affiliation of Feature 75. It is now clear, however, that the contents of this feature are assignable to the Clovis complex.

Geoarchaeological and technological evidence underpin this conclusion.

GEOARCHAEOLOGY

Basic geoarchaeological research on the landscape and stratigraphic position of the cache confirm the Clovis affiliation, an effort that was complicated by removal of find-spot sediments during levee construction. Fortunately, the associated field documentation contains two important clues bearing on this problem. First, and most significant, are the photographic slides, particularly Figure 6.4, which appears to capture the truest colors of the alluvium encasing the cache. Using this image, the matrix is brown to dark brown with yellowish-brown mottles. The second clue comes from Test Unit C (Figure 6.2), where a complete stratigraphic profile was described. The plow zone (Ap horizon) (~0–30 cm) is described as dark brown silt loam, the "intact cultural zone" (i.e., Oneota) (~30–73 cm) as dark grayish-brown to dark brown silt loam, and the sterile subsoil below as dark yellowish-brown silty clay loam (DeVore 1990:52).

Field investigations conducted in the vicinity of the find spot in September 2009 uphold these observations as well as offer new details (Figure 6.2). For this research, the study area is a pasture about 500 m north-northwest of the find spot, within the Carlisle city limits. The landform here consists of an extensive, undisturbed terrace remnant standing about 7.5 m (25 ft) above the modern low-water Des Moines River at 238.98 m (784 ft). It is situated on the west side of the Des Moines River Valley south of the North River and north of the Middle River near their confluences with the Des Moines River where the Des Moines River Valley is especially wide and occupies a large, buried valley system (Salisbury et al. 1968:86). The terrace is a Late Wisconsin–Early Holocene landform that we correlate with the High Terrace of Bettis and Benn (1984:217), located up-valley of the City of Des Moines. A point-type terrace (Bettis et al. 1988:46), it has been protected and preserved from later Holocene erosion by the uplands in Carlisle that form the divide between the North and Middle River Valleys. It is also noteworthy that in the vicinity of the find spot, the Des Moines River Valley is wide (5.1 km [3.15 mi]). This width probably accounts for local preservation of the High Terrace, in a similar manner to the pattern of High Terrace preservation found up-valley near Saylorville Lake (Bettis and Benn 1984:Figure 2). Late Holocene channel belts of the Des Moines River did not reach the find spot, perhaps as a result of sediment inputs from the North and Middle Rivers that diverted them from the western margins of the Des Moines River Valley.

Three backhoe trenches provided access to the alluvial stratigraphy beneath the High Terrace (Figure 6.2). Trench 1 was located on the highest and most level area of the High Terrace, while Trenches 2 and 3 were located at the margin of the terrace on the upper portion of the scarp descending to the Late Holocene channel belt. Trench 1 exposed ~1.6 m of early Holocene alluvium associated with the Gunder Member of the DeForest Formation (Bettis 1992; Bettis and Littke 1987). Trench 2 exposed Late Holocene alluvium associated with the Roberts Creek Member of the DeForest Formation. Trench 3, like Trench 1, exposed alluvium associated with the Gunder Member of the DeForest Formation. Properties of the alluvium here suggest a point-bar facies (Allen 1970:141–142; Wolman and Leopold 1957) of the Gunder Member is exposed; the deposits are laminated, dip to the west, and are generally coarser in texture near the base of the trench. Of these, Trench 1 is most directly relevant for reconstructing the stratigraphic position of the cache.

Alluvium Exposed In Trench 1

Trench 1 exposed ~1.6 m of alluvium belonging to the Early Gunder Member. This sediment package is informally recognized in northeast Iowa (Baker et al. 1996) and southern Minnesota (Baker et al. 2002). The degree of clay translocation as well as colors, which are indicative of the degree of oxidation and reduction, provide the basis for this conclusion. Below the plow zone (Ap horizon) colors range from very dark grayish brown to dark brown. At the very base of the trench the alluvium is more oxidized (dark yellowish brown) with many prominent strong brown mottles (Table 6.1). Trench 1 also exposed a Late Holocene gully near its east end containing black (10YR 2/1) to very dark brown(10YR 3/2) silty-loam alluvium. Wood charcoal from the gully—the only piece found in any of the three trenches—was dated to 962 ± 35 B.P. (AA87100).

Pertinent to our reconstruction, the alluvium between depths of 237.78 m and 237.92 m is brown to dark brown in color (Table 6.1). This matches the color of the alluvium around the cache and on which the cache was resting (Figure 6.4). Our reconstructed position thus places the cache just over 1 m below the uneroded High Terrace surface (Figure 6.5), with the caveat that since there is likely slight lateral variability in the alluvium, the cache

TABLE 6.1. Soil Description of Trench 1, Profile A

SOIL HORIZON	ELEVATION (m asl)	DESCRIPTION
Ap	238.99-238.79	Very dark brown (10YR 2/2, moist) silt loam; moderate, fine, platy structure; very friable consistence; abrupt, smooth boundary; many fine roots; plow zone.
A	238.79-238.44	Very dark grayish brown (10YR 3/2, moist) silt loam; moderate, very fine, subangular blocky structure; very friable consistence; gradual, smooth boundary; many fine roots.
ABt	238.44-238.28	Dark brown (10YR 3/3, moist) silt loam; moderate, fine, subangular blocky structure; very friable consistence; common, thin, continuous, dark yellowish brown (10YR 3/4, moist) clay skins and organic coatings on ped faces; gradual, smooth boundary; few fine roots.
Bt1	238.28-237.92	Dark brown (7.5YR 4/4, moist) light silt loam; few, fine prominent, dark yellowish brown (10YR 4/6) mottles in lower several centimeters of unit; moderate, medium, subangular blocky structure; very friable consistence; many, thin, continuous, brown (10YR 5/3, moist) clay skins on ped faces; clear, smooth boundary.
Bt2	237.92-237.78	Brown-dark brown (10YR 4/3, moist) silty clay loam; many fine, prominent dark yellowish brown (10YR 4/6, moist) mottles; moderate, medium, subangular blocky structure; friable consistence; many thin, continuous, brown (10YR 5/3, moist) clay skins on ped faces; clear, smooth boundary.
Bt3	237.78-237.60	Dark yellowish brown (10YR 3/4, moist) silty clay loam-silty clay; many, fine and medium, prominent, strong brown (7.5YR 4/6, moist) mottles; moderate-strong, medium, angular blocky structure; firm consistence; many thick, continuous, dark yellowish brown (10YR 3/4, moist) clay skins on ped faces; abrupt, wavy boundary; cracks and shrinks when dried.
C1	237.60-237.51	Dark brown (7.5YR 4/4, moist) loam-sandy loam; many medium, distinct, strong brown (7.5YR 4/6, moist) mottles; moderate, coarse, horizontally laminated structure; friable consistence; abrupt, smooth boundary.
C2	237.51-237.45	Pale brown (10YR 6/3, moist) silt loam; many medium, prominent strong brown (7.5YR 4/6, moist) mottles; single lamination within horizontally laminated silt loam-sandy loam; very friable consistence; abrupt, smooth boundary.
C3	237.45-237.42	Strong brown (7.5YR 4/6, moist) sandy loam; single lamination within horizontally laminated silt loam-sandy loam; very friable consistence; abrupt, smooth boundary.
C4	237.42-237.40	Pale brown (10YR 6/3, moist) silty clay loam; common, fine-medium, prominent, strong brown (7.5YR 4/6, moist) mottles; single lamination within laminated silt loam-sandy loam; friable consistence; abrupt, smooth boundary.

may in fact have rested slightly higher or deeper below the High Terrace.

Six optically stimulated luminescence (OSL) assays verify these stratigraphic correlations as well as establish an absolute age for deposition of the cache. Although this technique is often used to date eolian sediments, it has proven successful in dating alluvium (e.g., Waters, Forman et al. 2011; Waters, Forman, Stafford, and Foss 2009). Four OSL ages are available for Trench 1 (Table 6.2). The ages are both stratigraphically consistent (Figure 6.5) and within the range of previously reported calibrated radiocarbon ages for alluvium from the Early Gunder Member (Baker et al. 2002), with a single exception. For reasons that are not clear, the result for sample 2 (7910 ± 550) is anomalous.

Using the basal OSL age in Trench 1 and adding one standard deviation (i.e., 13,870 + 1290 years) and using the upper OSL age and subtracting one standard deviation (i.e., 10,980 – 850 years), the Early Gunder sediment package in Trench 1 was deposited between 15,160 and 10,130 years ago, using A.D. 2010 as the OSL reference year. In order to render these OSL ages meaningful for comparison to published, uncalibrated radiocarbon ages, 60 years were then subtracted from the OSL ages so that they could be compared to the radiocarbon reference year of A.D. 1950. OxCal 4.1 (Bronk Ramsey 2009), in conjunction with the

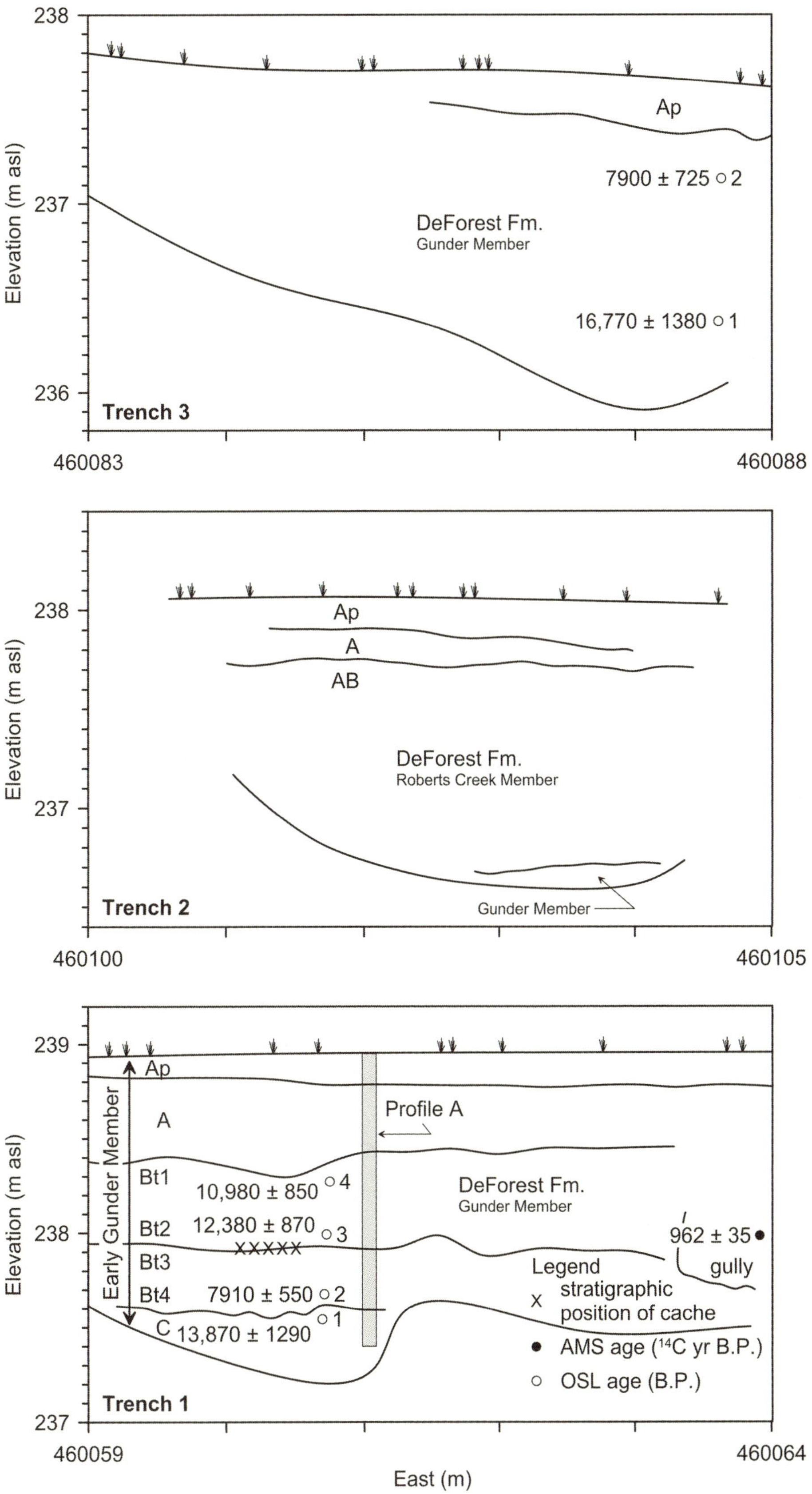

Figure 6.5. Stratigraphic profiles for Trenches 1–3 (NAD 1983, UTM Zone 15 N) (illustration created by Matthew G. Hill)

TABLE 6.2. Optically Stimulated Luminescence Ages for Trench 1 and 3 Sediments

FIELD NO.	UIC LAB NO.	DEPTH (m)	ELEVATION (m asl)	ALIQUOTS	EQUIVALENT DOSE (Gray)[a]	U (ppm)[b]	TH (ppm)[b]	K^2O (%)[b]	H_2O (%)	A VALUE[c]	COSMIC DOSE (mGray/YR)[d]	DOSE RATE (mGray/yr)	OSL AGE (yr)[e]
Tr. 1 OSL 4	2641	0.65	238.272	30	39.51 ± 2.32	3.0 ± 0.1	8.7 ± 0.1	1.76 ± 0.02	10 ± 3	0.046 ± 0.04	0.19 ± 0.02	3.60 ± 0.18	10,980 ± 850
Tr. 1 OSL 3	2651	0.93	237.992	30	47.17 ± 2.07	3.2 ± 0.1	9.2 ± 0.1	1.90 ± 0.02	10 ± 2	0.044 ± 0.04	0.18 ± 0.02	3.81 ± 0.19	12,380 ± 870
Tr. 1 OSL 2	2652	1.25	237.677	30	43.48 ± 1.25	2.6 ± 0.1	10.0 ± 0.1	2.24 ± 0.02	10 ± 3	0.054 ± 0.05	0.17 ± 0.02	4.11 ± 0.20	7910 ± 550
Tr. 1 OSL 1	2678	1.38	237.543	30	29.29 ± 1.99	1.3 ± 0.1	4.7 ± 0.1	1.62 ± 0.01	10 ± 3	–	0.17 ± 0.02	2.11± 0.11	13,870 ± 1290
Tr. 3 OSL 2	2722	0.71	237.133	29	27.86 ± 1.92	2.9 ± 0.1	11.3 ± 0.1	2.27 ± 0.02	10 ± 3	–	0.19 ± 0.02	3.52 ± 0.18	7900 ± 725
Tr. 3 OSL 1	2653	1.47	236.376	30	27.42 ± 1.44	1.2 ± 0.1	3.8 ± 0.1	1.15 ± 0.01	10 ± 3	–	0.17 ± 0.02	2.55 ± 0.13	16,770 ± 1380

Note: Samples assayed at the Luminescence Dating Research Laboratory, University of Illinois, Chicago (UIC).

[a]4 to 11 μm quartz fraction analyzed under blue-light excitation (470 ± 20 nm) by single aliquot regeneration protocols (Murray and Wintle 2003), except for UIC lab nos. 2653, 2678, and 2722, for which the 150–250 quartz fraction was analyzed.

[b]U, Th, and K_2O content analyzed by inductively coupled plasma-mass spectrometry, Activation Laboratory Ltd., Ontario, Canada.

[c]Alpha efficiency factor from Aitken and Bowman (1975).

[d]From Prescott and Hutton (1994).

[e]Ages calculated using the central age model of Galbraith et al. (1999). All errors are at 1 sigma and ages calculated from the reference year A.D. 2010.

IntCal04 calibration curve (Reimer et al. 2004), was used to convert OSL ages into uncalibrated radiocarbon ages. This conversion reveals that the Early Gunder dates to 12,705–8955 uncalibrated radiocarbon years B.P. Applying the same technique to OSL sample 3 (12,380 ± 870) narrows the age of the cache position to 11,280–9985 B.P. The upper end of this age range dovetails with current age estimates for the Clovis complex (Haynes et al. 2007; Waters and Stafford 2007; Waters, Stafford, Redmond, and Tankersley 2009), while the lower end is far too young.

Two OSL ages are available for Trench 3 (Table 6.2 and Figure 6.5). Using the age-conversion method outlined above, the uncalibrated radiocarbon ages equivalent to OSL sample 1 are between 12,835 B.P. and 14,790 B.P. This range of ages is too old for the Gunder Member (Baker et al. 2002; Baker et al. 1996), suggesting that the sample was not exposed sufficiently to sunlight prior to deposition (Murray et al. 1995). OSL sample 2 is equivalent to 6200–7790 B.P., which is consistent with uncalibrated radiocarbon ages reported for the Gunder Member elsewhere in the Des Moines River Valley (Baker et al. 2002; Baker et al. 1996).

Sediment samples from horizons described in the field also were collected and analyzed in order to better characterize both the fluvial depositional environment (Folk and Ward 1957) and the degree of soil formation in the alluvium (Birkeland 1999). Results are presented in Table 6.3 and Figure 6.6 and are discussed from bottom to top. A lithologic discontinuity at 237.597 m, especially apparent in the sand fraction, most probably reflects a channel avulsion on the aggrading floodplain responsible for moving the Des Moines River channel away from the study area (i.e., eastward). The dominance of silt and clay deposition (elevations 237.597 m to 237.917 m) is typical of a backswamp area away from the active channel (Aslan and Autin 1998; Grenfell et al. 2009). The reconstructed stratigraphic position of the cache is on the surface of these fine-grained deposits. The return to increased sand content at 237.917 m signals a return of the channel to a location nearer the study area, probably as a result of another avulsion. The steady fining-upward trend from 237.917 m to the surface of the A horizon (238.786 m) is consistent with overbank sedimentation on an aggrading floodplain by analogy to studies of historical floodplain sedimentation (Magilligan 1992). It appears, then, that the cache was probably buried more rapidly at first and then more slowly during the period of floodplain aggradation.

Stable carbon isotope and soil organic carbon (SOC) records preserved in Trench 1 sediment provide more

TABLE 6.3. Particle-Size Distribution in Sediment Samples from Trench 1, Profile A

ELEVATION (m asl)	% SAND	% SILT	% CLAY
238.786-238.978	25.8	61.3	12.9
238.669-238.786	17.0	67.2	15.8
238.549-238.669	17.2	63.8	19.0
238.429-238.549	19.2	63.1	17.7
238.257-238.429	19.6	61.4	19.0
238.087-238.257	24.5	58.6	16.9
237.917-238.087	23.6	58.4	18.1
237.817-237.917	5.0	69.1	25.9
237.707-237.817	0.0	65.6	34.4
237.597-237.707	1.7	60.9	37.4
237.514-237.597	32.8	46.1	21.1
237.446-237.514	35.0	43.8	21.2

Note: Samples assayed by laser diffraction, Geography Laboratory, University of Kansas; adjusted clay and silt percentages are reported (see Buurman et al. 2001; Eshel et al. 2004; Konert and Vandenberghe 1997).

information on environmental conditions during deposition of the alluvium as well as during coeval and subsequent pedogenesis. Although SOC in alluvium is a mixture of carbon of unknown proportions derived from basin-wide SOC (depositional), combined with carbon as a result of in situ pedogenesis, it provides an environmental record comparable to other proxies of climate and vegetation (Baker et al. 1998; Cordova et al. 2011). As illustrated in Figure 6.6 (Table 6.4), an up-profile increase reaches the lower boundary of the Ap horizon. Any fluctuations in SOC imparted by differing depositional rates, particularly individual floods, have been erased by more than 10,000 years of pedogenesis. The very faint bulge in SOC above 237.8 m may represent the remnant of a buried A horizon.

The $\delta^{13}C$ data reveal an up-profile trend in values becoming less negative through time, with values near -20‰ at the base and -15‰ at the top (excepting the top two samples, which derive from the Ap horizon [i.e., plow zone]) (Figure 6.7, Table 6.4). The vegetation thus changed from a mixed C_3-C_4 environment to a C_4 environment during deposition of Trench 1 alluvium. To put it another way, C_4 plants contributed to about half of the overall soil organic matter at the bottom of the profile and to over three-quarters at the top. Moreover, this change was underway as early as ca. 14,000 B.P. ($\delta^{13}C$ values -20.4‰) and complete by ca. 11,000 B.P. ($\delta^{13}C$ values ~-16.0‰). It appears then that during Clovis times the central Des Moines River Valley floodplain was vegetated mostly

TABLE 6.4. $\delta^{13}C$, Derived Percentage of C_4 Plant Biomass, and Organic Carbon Content in Sediment Samples from Trench 1, Profile A

ELEVATION (m asl)	$\delta^{13}C$ (‰)	C_4 PLANT BIOMASS (%)	ORGANIC CARBON (%)
238.880-238.978	-16.7	73.5	0.8840
238.780-238.880	-16.4	75.4	0.7693
238.680-238.780	-14.8	87.0	0.9929
238.580-238.680	-14.7	88.2	0.9031
238.480-238.580	-14.6	88.4	0.7933
238.380-238.480	-14.9	86.5	0.6386
238.280-238.380	-14.7	87.5	0.4295
238.180-238.280	-15.3	83.4	0.2710
238.080-238.180	-16.0	78.3	0.2028
237.980-238.080	-16.6	74.1	0.2081
237.880-237.980	-17.3	69.5	0.2232
237.780-237.880	-18.5	60.9	0.2025
237.680-237.780	-19.3	54.9	0.2631
237.580-237.680	-20.4	46.9	0.2412
237.480-237.580	-20.4	47.1	0.1225

Note: Samples assayed at Keck Paleoenvironmental and Environmental Stable Isotope Laboratory, University of Kansas.

with warm-season grasses, for example, big bluestem (*Andropogon gerardii*), little bluestem (*Schizachyrium scoparium*), Indian grass (*Sorghastrum nutans*), and switch grass (*Panicum virgatum*) (Brown 1985:35–36). This conclusion is in line with the paucity of wood charcoal contained in Early Gunder alluvium.

The presence of an obvious C_4 environment by ca. 11,000 B.P. does not square with several other reconstructions in the region that also span the Late Wisconsin–Holocene transition. The comparative sequences considered here, reported by Leavitt et al. (2007), are from, most notably, Indianola, Iowa, 20 km south-southwest of Carlisle; Lincoln, Nebraska, 300 km west; and Glencoe, Minnesota, 350 km north. Prior to ca. 11,000 B.P., Glencoe has a strong C_3 signal ($\delta^{13}C$ values -25.0‰ to -24.6‰), followed by a transitional period characterized by a weak mixed C_3-C_4 signal between ca. 10,000–9000 B.P. ($\delta^{13}C$ values -23.7‰ to -21.16‰). For the balance of the Holocene, from ca. 8000 B.P. to present, the location records mixed signals ($\delta^{13}C$ values -19.4‰ to -16.7‰). The Lincoln sequence is similar save for the fact that the $\delta^{13}C$ values are ~1–3‰ less negative for the respective 1,000-year interval, which is not unexpected given its more westerly location. Indianola, on the other hand, embraces a strong C_3 signal for 8,000 years, from ca. 12,000 B.P. ($\delta^{13}C$ value -25.6‰) to ca. 4000 B.P. ($\delta^{13}C$ value -23.5‰). In summary, these study sites do not witness $\delta^{13}C$ values around -16.0‰ until middle to late Holocene times, upwards of 6,000–9,000 years later than in Trench 1.

The proximate cause of the Trench 1 $\delta^{13}C$ sequence is attributed to local geomorphological processes. Between ca. 12,600 and 11,000 B.P., the Des Moines River transported melt water and outwash from the Des Moines Lobe in a braided stream system (Bettis et al. 1988:10–14; Iverson 2005:55). Due to extensive lateral migration and accretion, plant succession on relatively stable alluvial landforms was frequently "reset" by erosion and floods, which buried, drowned, or otherwise removed existing valley-bottom vegetation. Since retreat of glacial ice out of the drainage basin ca. 11,000 B.P., the "channel pattern has been meandering. . . . In the early Holocene (approximately 10,500–8,000 years B.P.) overbank deposition of silt loam and loamy alluvium occurred across the broad floodplain" (Benn and Bettis 1985:13). The situation, coupled with a developing warmer, drier climatic pattern, was thus ripe for C_4 plants to establish (and sustain) an early foothold in the valley bottom, at least in the vicinity of Trench 1. Support for this idea comes from observations that C_4 plants hold a competitive edge over C_3 plants in disturbance situations due to greater invasibility (Smith and Knapp 1999) and, additionally, that these plants prosper as climatic variability increases and climatic extremes become more frequent (White et al. 2001). It follows that the floodplain was excellent bison habitat, thus making it an attractive potential resource patch for Clovis foragers.

CACHE CONTENTS

As a direct result of the careful excavation and documentation methods employed by Jeff Hruska and John Cole, the analytical potential and integrity of the Carlisle cache as a source of information on Clovis technology and caching practices is exceptional. A total of 43 artifacts make up this assemblage—25 bifaces, 12 large flakes, and 6 small flakes—with a combined weight of 4.13 kg (9.11 lbs). The specimens are in pristine condition, save for some recent damage resulting from compression by and/or contact with heavy equipment. None of the edges show signs of use wear under high magnification. With one

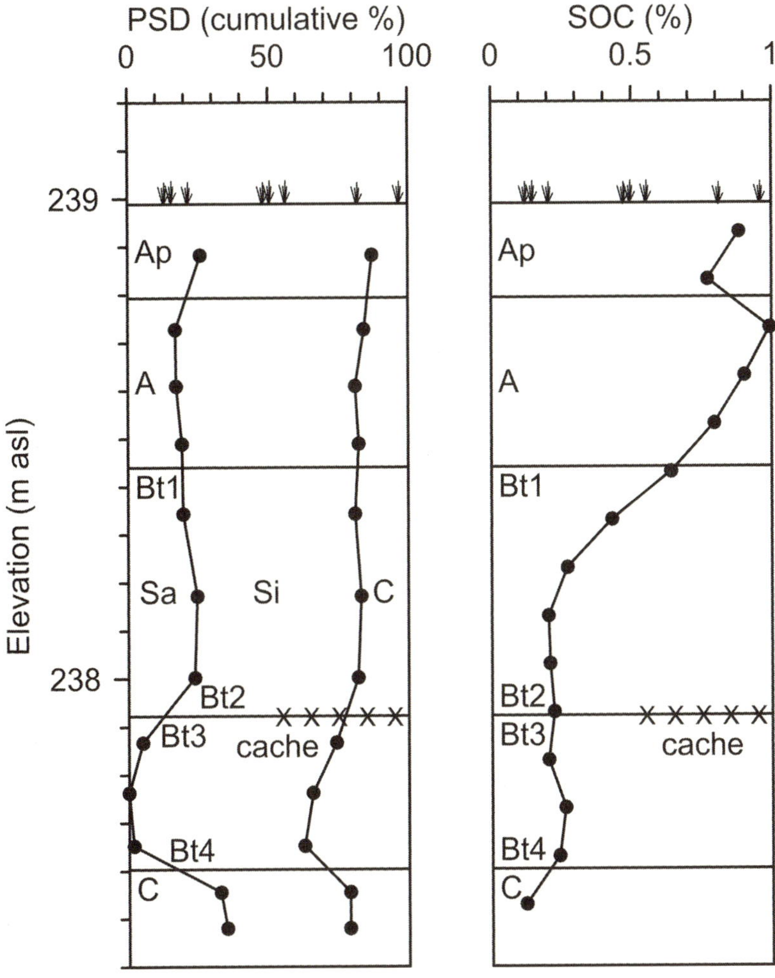

Figure 6.6. Particle-size distribution and soil organic carbon profiles for Trench 1, Profile A. Sampling interval for particle-size distribution is one sample for horizons less than 15 cm thick and three samples (i.e., bottom, middle, and top) for thicker horizons. Sampling interval is 10 cm for soil organic carbon (illustration created by Matthew G. Hill).

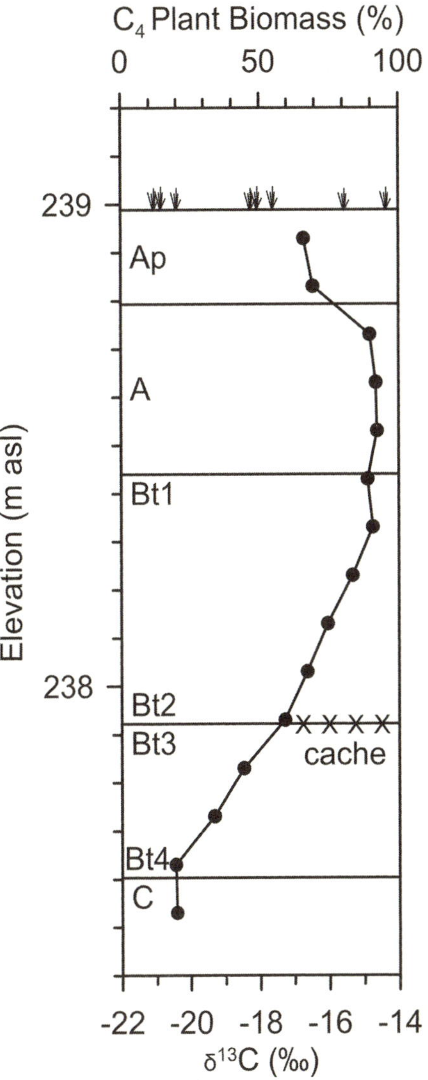

Figure 6.7. $\delta^{13}C$ and C4 plant biomass profiles for Trench 1, Profile A. Sampling interval is 10 cm (illustration created by Matthew G. Hill).

exception, they are made on high-quality varieties of Burlington chert. The closest host rock for this toolstone is about 200 km southeast of Carlisle, in southeastern Iowa and northeastern Missouri, in the vicinity of the confluences of the Iowa, Skunk, and Des Moines Rivers with the Mississippi River (Morrow 1994:123–124) (Figure 6.8). The exception is a small flake made on Warsaw chalcedonic chert (Toby A. Morrow, personal communication 2012). This toolstone occurs in small nodules (10–40 cm in diameter) in the Skunk River Valley (Morrow 1994:124), which stretches from southeast to north central Iowa and roughly parallels the Des Moines River Valley to the west (Figure 6.8).

Bifaces

The discovery of artifacts associated with mammoth remains at Blackwater Draw, New Mexico; Dent, Colorado; and Miami, Texas, during the 1930s established the Clovis fluted point as the diagnostic artifact of the Clovis complex (Howard 1943). Since then, our understanding of Clovis lithic technology has increased substantially and it is now clear that Clovis bifaces and associated manufacture debris can also be telling, especially when multiple specimens are available for analysis (Bradley et al. 2010:56–106). Evidence from quarry-related sites such as Gault (Collins and Hemmings 2005; Waters, Pevny, and

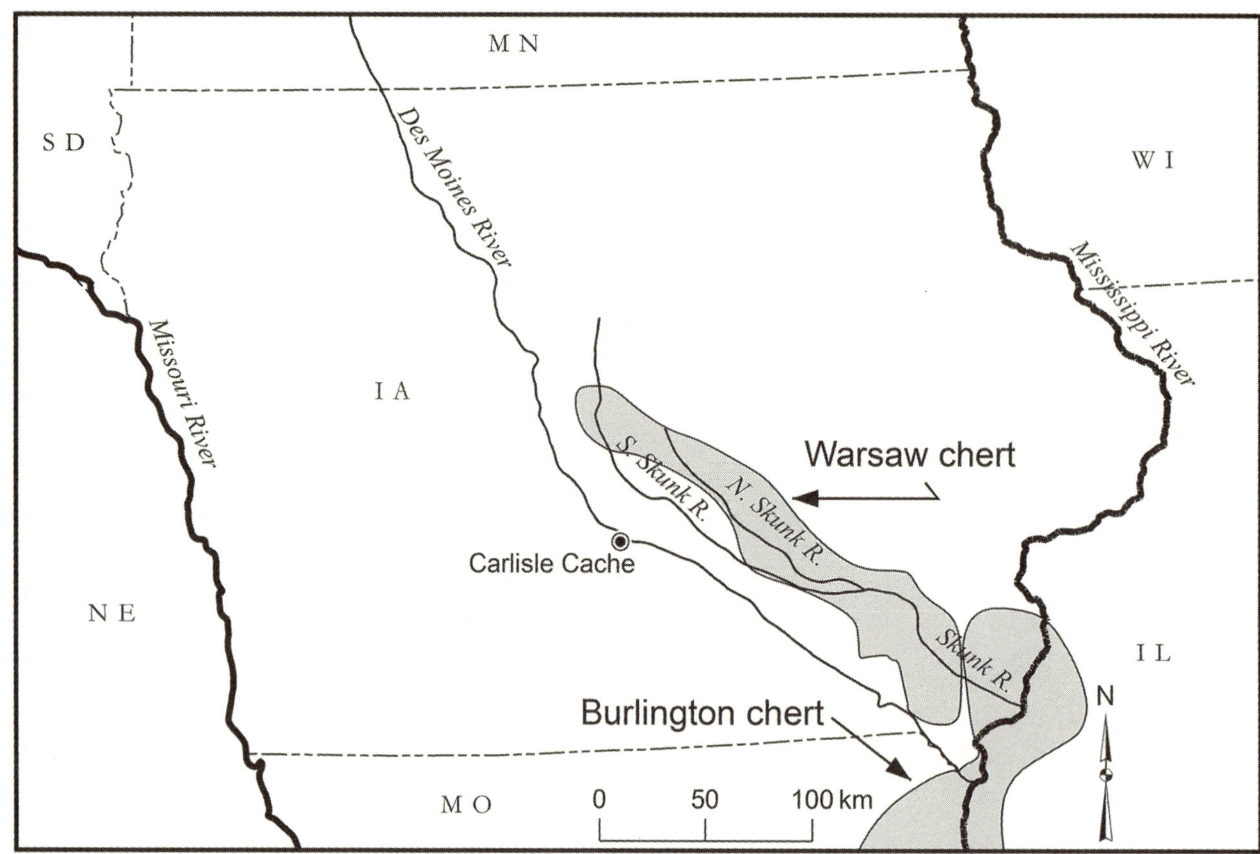

Figure 6.8. Outcrop sources of tool stone in the Carlisle cache (after Morrow 1994:Figure 6) (map created by Matthew G. Hill)

Carlson 2011), Pavo Real (Collins et al. 2003), and Adams (Sanders 1990); from kill camps, namely Murray Springs (Huckell 2007) and Aubrey (Ferring 2001); and from small, single-component sites like Sheaman (Bradley 1982) have proven crucial in this regard. The single most distinctive characteristic of this technology is controlled overshot and full-facial flaking, that is, the intentional removal of thinning flakes that tend to expand rapidly and terminate well past the midline of the biface. Opposed overshot and full-facial flaking is a diagnostic variant of this technique that occurs less frequently. Other typically Clovis technological traits include the use of direct soft-hammer percussion, the detachment of a few large, widely spaced flake scars from each face of bifaces, and remnant square-edge facets on one or both ends and/or the lateral margins, as well as end thinning, all of which served to facilitate the production of large, thin bifaces. The Carlisle bifaces (and large flakes) display these hallmarks (Figure 6.9, Table 6.5).

The Carlisle bifaces are large, display-flattened biconvex cross sections of uniform thicknesses. They fall into three groups based on their outline: large ovoid, medium ovoid, and willow leaf. The presence of either cortex or unflaked and stained tabular remnants on the lateral margins and/or faces of 23 specimens indicates natural morphological variation in tabular Burlington chert selected as toolstone. Using the scheme outlined by Bradley and associates (2010:83–91), the reduction of three bifaces was terminated relatively early in the sequence, as signaled by the presence of remnants of original, exterior toolstone surfaces on either one or both faces or lateral margins. The rest of the specimens are middle interval bifaces, and they generally overlap in overall size and morphology with those from several other Clovis caches, including Fenn, Simon, and Anzick (Figure 6.10). The Carlisle middle interval bifaces are, however, generally thinner, with a mean width-to-thickness ratio of 4.4 (range 3.8–5.3), compared to 4.7 (2.9–8.3) at Fenn, 5.1 (2.9–9.3) at Anzick, and 5.6 (4.3–7.6) at Simon (Bradley et al. 2010:Table 3.5).

Initial biface manufacture involved the removal of several large, widely spaced overshot and full-facial thinning flakes from each face. These early thinning flakes tend to expand rapidly and terminate well past

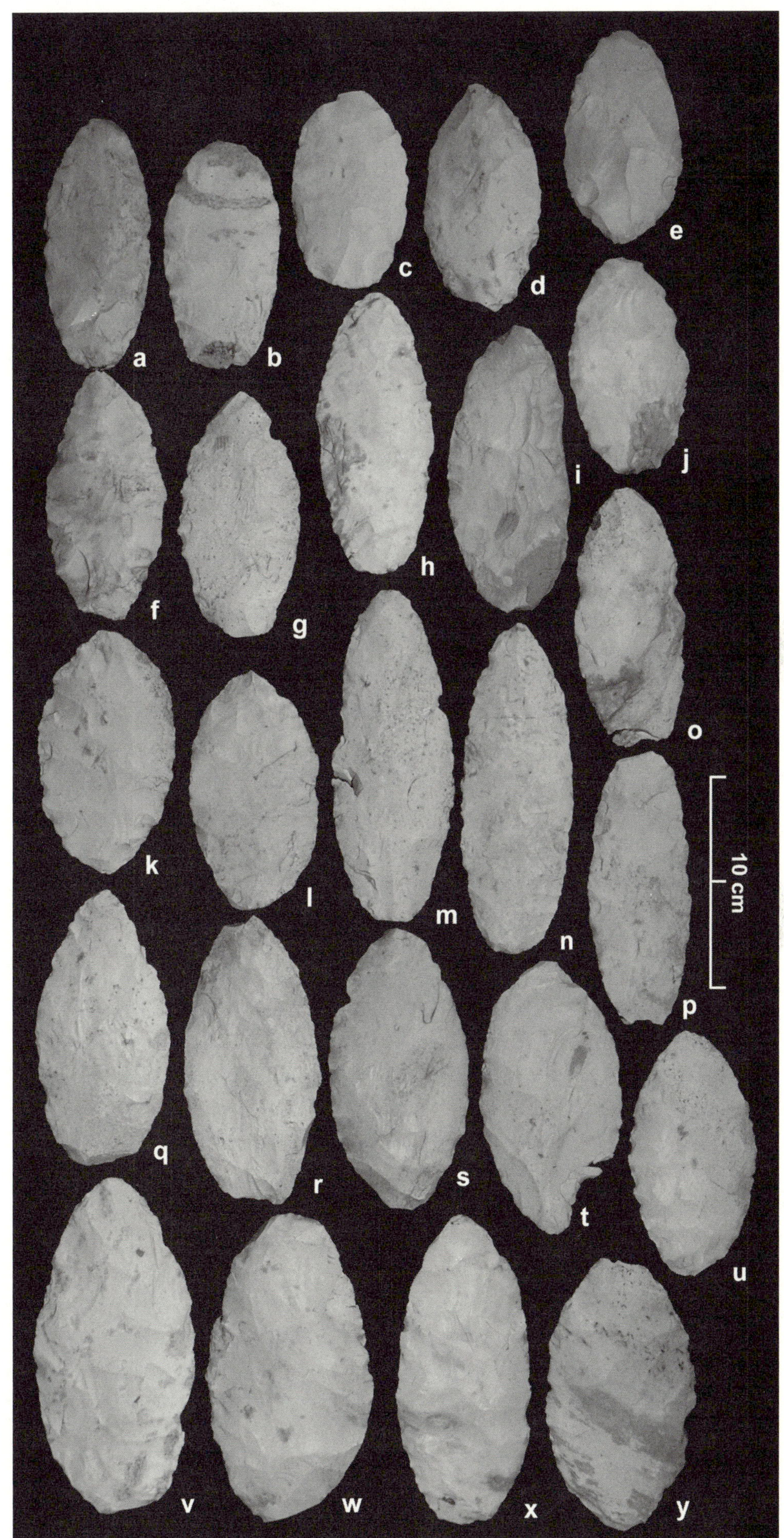

Figure 6.9. Carlisle cache bifaces (photograph by Matthew G. Hill)

TABLE 6.5. Metric and Nonmetric Information on Carlisle Cache Bifaces

	Metric[a]						Nonmetric[b]						
NO.	FIG. 6.9	L (mm)	W (mm)	T (mm)	WT (g)	W/T RATIO	INTERVAL	OSA	OSAt	OSB	OSBt	FACET LOC.	END THIN.
4424	m	156.2	60.5	14.4	139.7	4.2	Middle	0	0	0	0	D	+
4425	o	(122.0)	55.0	14.5	102.8	3.8	Middle	0	2	0	0	D	-
4426	y	134.8	74.9	15.4	181.8	4.9	Middle	0	2	0	0	P	+
4427	g	117.4	60.5	14.0	107.1	4.3	Middle	0	0	0	0	L	-
4428	a	127.8	54.8	14.0	104.6	3.9	Middle	0	0	0	0	D	-
4429	q	132.9	68.2	14.2	137.8	4.8	Middle	0	0	1	0	P, D	-
4430	u	115.9	63.1	14.2	103.6	4.4	Early	0	0	0	0	P	-
4431	x	150.4	67.5	15.4	174.2	4.4	Middle	0	0	0	0	I	+
4432	n	155.2	55.3	13.9	127.5	4.0	Middle	2	0	1	1	D	-
4433	s	133.4	68.3	16.3	170.4	4.2	Middle	0	0	0	1	P, D	-
4434	k	(114.7)	60.6	12.8	93.2	4.7	Middle	1	0	0	0	P, D	-
4435	e	110.0	60.5	13.7	96.3	4.4	Early	1	0	0	0	P, D	+
4436	t	128.9	70.9	13.4	124.0	5.3	Middle	0	0	0	0	D	-
4437	l	116.3	68.8	13.3	118.7	5.2	Middle	0	0	0	0	P, D, L	+
4438	c	101.1	58.8	13.1	88.3	4.5	Middle	0	1	0	0	P, D	+
4439	f	121.1	61.2	16.1	119.5	3.8	Middle	0	0	0	0	P, L	-
4440	w	152.5	83.8	16.0	221.1	5.2	Middle	0	1	0	0	P, D	-
4441	h	137.5	57.2	14.4	123.0	4.0	Middle	0	0	2	0	P, D	-
4442	v	167.2	80.0	18.1	266.6	4.4	Middle	0	0	1	1	P	-
4443	j	108.2	60.7	11.5	82.5	5.3	Middle	0	0	0	1	D	-
4444	i	138.0	59.9	16.0	135.4	3.7	Early	0	0	2	0	L	-
4445	b	117.8	59.5	15.3	109.9	3.9	Middle	0	0	3	0	D	-
4446	r	137.9	67.7	16.7	164.0	4.1	Middle	1	0	0	0	P	-
4447	p	(136.8)	50.1	12.0	83.1	4.2	Middle	1	0	1	0	I	-
4448	d	113.1	62.8	15.1	119.4	4.2	Middle	0	0	0	0	P, D	-

[a]Length (L), width (W), thickness (T), weight (Wt). Values in parentheses indicate the measurement is incomplete due to recent damage.
[b]Number of complete overshot scars, side A/B (OSA/OSB); number of "trimmed" overshot scars, side A/B (OSAt/OSBt). Facet location: proximal (P), distal (D), lateral (L), indeterminate due to damage (I). End thinning: present (+), absent (-).

the midline or along the opposite margin of the tabular blank (Figure 6.11b). No fewer than nine middle interval bifaces display one or more complete controlled overshot flake scars on one or both faces, while another six display overshot scars that are lightly "trimmed" along the opposing margin (Figure 6.11a, d). At least three of these specimens are thinned with the opposed overshot technique (Figure 6.11b). Remnant edge facets are preserved on the lateral margins and/or ends on 23 bifaces, and at least one facet on 16 specimens is manifest as an unflaked, weathered surface. End thinning is present on six bifaces (Figure 6.11c).

The incidence of these technological details is similar to those documented in other assemblages. No less than 41 percent (9/22) and not more than 68 percent (15/22) of the middle interval bifaces display overshot thinning. These figures compare favorably to the middle interval bifaces in the Fenn (11/24, 46 percent) and Simon caches (7/12, 58 percent).[3] And in a sample of 157 Clovis bifaces and finished points, Stanford and Bradley (2012:Table 6.1) report that half (50–55 percent) of the 86 middle interval bifaces were thinned using the overshot technique.[4]

Twenty-three (92 percent) of the bifaces retain remnant edge facets. Comparative data on this attribute are

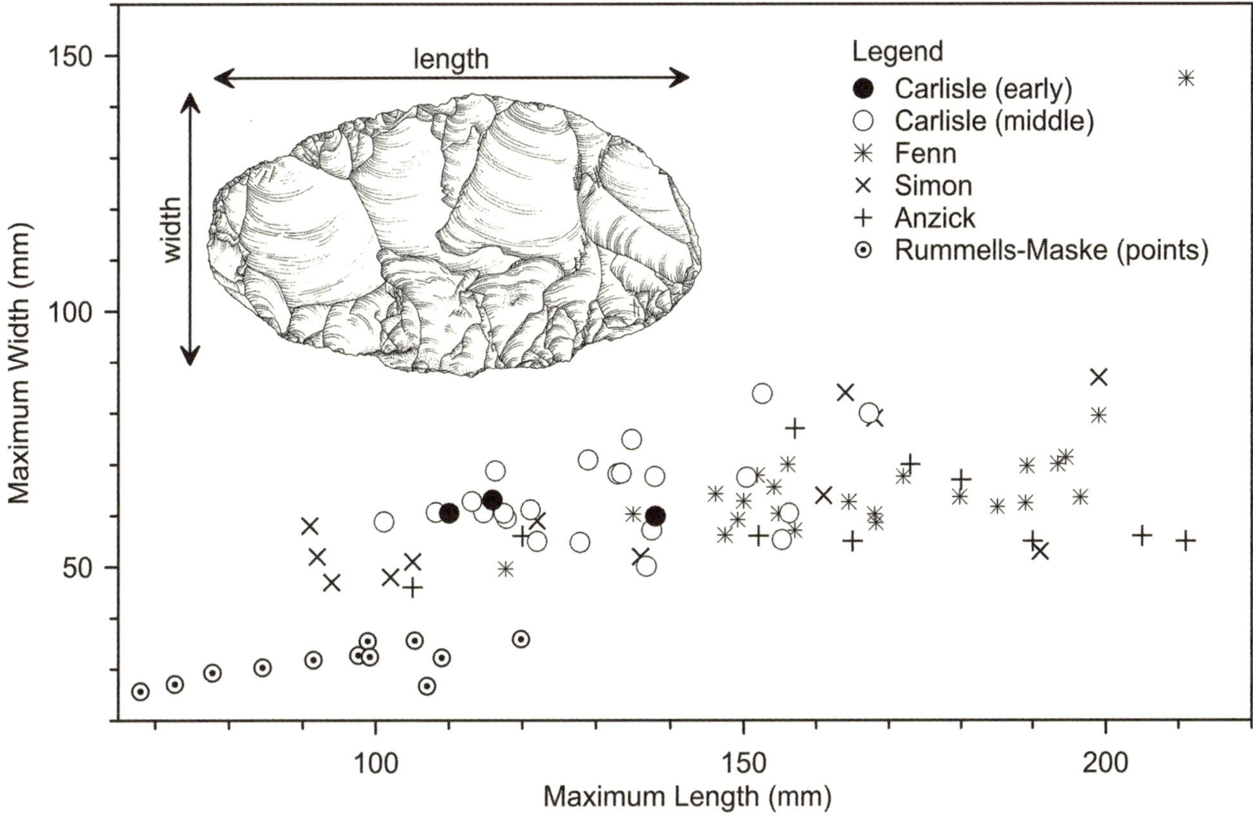

Figure 6.10. Size comparison of middle interval bifaces in several caches and the Rummells-Maske points. The three early interval bifaces in the Carlisle cache are also included (illustration created by Matthew G. Hill).

not available from the Clovis cache literature, nor is it obtainable from published illustrations. However, we glean from Bradley et al. (2010:56–106) that the presence of remnant edge facets is a fairly common feature of cached bifaces. Although the reasons behind this practice are not entirely clear, it appears to relate simply to the size and shape of the original toolstone tablets since many of the facets in the assemblage present unflaked, weathered surfaces. In other words, a primary goal during early-interval production involved maintaining maximum length, as controlled by the size of the natural tabular blanks employed in the production of each biface. Retaining small sections of unflaked tabular edges provides effective natural striking platforms that facilitate the removal of additional thinning flakes. This strategy thus extends the utility of early- and middle-interval bifaces by serving as a potential source of small, thin flake blanks for expedient tools. As well, these unflaked tabular edges are frequently left at the proximal ends of the Carlisle bifaces. Such naturally beveled edges could have served as striking platforms in the subsequent removal of end thinning flakes.

Although the bifaces could have served as a source of flakes in the production of small, expedient tools, we infer that the foremost plan was to stockpile them for future conversion into Clovis points. If necessary, an experienced Clovis knapper could have completed this task with less than a day's work (Callahan 1979:23; Huckell et al. 2011:973). The near-pristine finished fluted points from Rummells-Maske (Morrow and Morrow 2002) (Figure 6.10), which are also made on Burlington chert, offer support for this scenario. Converting the Carlisle bifaces into finished points of the same general size as those from Rummells-Maske would have required minimal time and effort, all else being equal.

Large Flakes

Twelve hand-sized flakes, interpreted as unifacial tool preforms, complement the bifaces (Figure 6.12). These artifacts display telltale markers of Clovis technology, including a high degree of ridge-centered platform preparation involving isolation, faceting, and grinding; use of direct soft-hammer percussion; overshot flakes

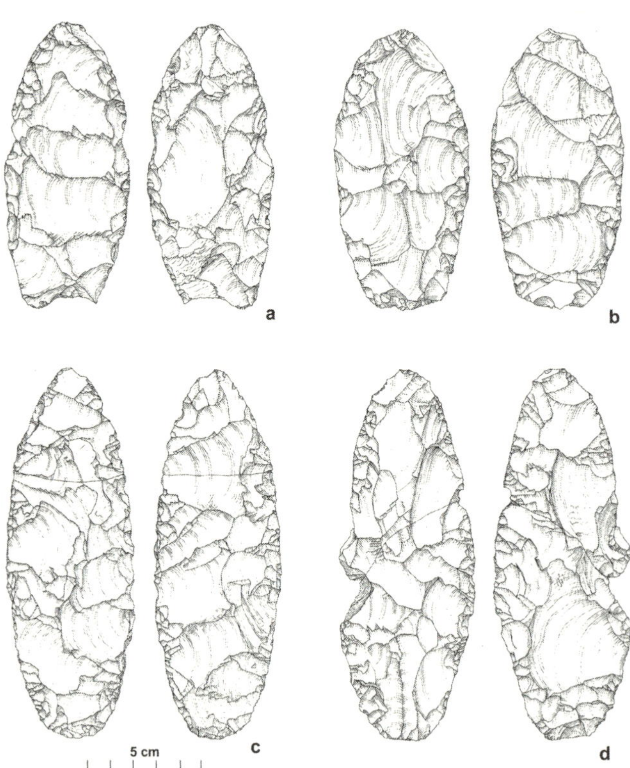

Figure 6.11. Illustrations of selected Carlisle cache bifaces that exemplify certain Clovis technological characteristics: (a) no. 4425, (b) 4445, (c) 4424, (d) 4432. Recent compression damage is readily apparent on the proximal end of (a) and on the lateral edge of (d). Recent bend fractures are visible on (c) and (d) (illustrations by Sarah Moore).

with a distinctive distal curve as well as remnants of square margins along distal edges; and flat flakes displaying wide spacing between removals and/or signs of previous overshot or full-face flake removals on their dorsal surfaces. Employing these characteristics, two general categories are present: the first consists of seven flat flakes, the second of five overshot flakes (Table 6.6).

The flat flakes are generally long and thin, exhibiting minimal curvature or ventral rippling. Five were struck from isolated and heavily-abraded, unfaceted, tabular core platforms centered on or near dorsal ridges on tabular margins, while the other two were struck from heavily-abraded, bifacially-prepared platforms. Each of these specimens shows remnants of previous full-face flake removals on the dorsal surface. The overall morphology of the flat flakes suggests they were most probably destined for conversion into handheld butchery and scraping tools.

In contrast, the overshot flakes are generally short and thick, exhibiting pronounced curvature just prior to distal termination. Three are distinctively triangular in outline, while the other two are blade-like. Four flakes were detached from simple, well-prepared platforms set on tabular margins. The fifth flake was struck from a biface core platform. All but one preserve traces of previous overshot or full-face flake removals on the dorsal surface. The presence of square edges (i.e., tabular remnants) on the distal terminations or unflaked facets indicates that these are early interval overshot flakes. In addition, the presence on these flakes of platforms set on tabular margins, together with overshot flake scars on the middle interval bifaces, indicates overshot thinning was applied throughout the reduction sequence; thus, overshot thinning was intended, controlled, and employed repeatedly during manufacture. The three triangular flakes appear to represent end scraper blanks intended for hide processing. The two blade-like flakes may also represent end scraper blanks or preforms for some other tool type.

Two conjoin groups provide further insight on the organization of technology. Conjoin no. 1 is a mechanically reconstructed flake sequence involving six flat flakes and one overshot flake (Figure 6.13). It reveals the systematic reduction of a large tabular chert block with the intent to produce large flakes. The core was reduced from a single face by a series of large flakes being struck from opposed margins by soft hammer. Flake platforms were placed directly on abraded and minimally prepared unflaked and weathered tabular core surfaces. These removals produced a series of six large, flat flakes of relatively uniform thickness that, in most cases, traveled across nearly the entire core surface. The last specimen in the conjoin, an overshot flake, was placed to remove an angular corner

Figure 6.12. Carlisle cache large flakes (dorsal view) (photograph by Matthew G. Hill)

and resulted in a large triangular flake. We interpret this flake as an end scraper blank.

Conjoin no. 2 is a "second-order" refit (Petraglia 1992:165) comprising two overshot flakes, one flat flake, and a biface (no. 4431) that share a unique pattern of blue mottling and a singular, distinctive vug. The conjoin provides clear evidence for the systematic application of overshot/full-facial thinning during biface manufacture as well as for culling of large, early interval flake removals from debitage. The latter is especially noteworthy since it shows that subsequent removals were (already) too small to be preferentially selected for future use.

The conjoins provide the basis for two key observations. First, overshot and full-facial thinning began early in the reduction sequence of tabular cores to bifaces and to large flakes. Second, conjoin no. 1 demonstrates intentional reduction of large tabular cores solely for the production of large flake blanks. Although closely associated with biface manufacture and employing the same basic knapping techniques, this formal trajectory of reduction marks a poorly known aspect of Clovis technological organization that merits future contemplation and research. Cores were systematically reduced for bifaces as well as for large flakes, sometimes with the intention of conveying and caching them together, as in the Carlisle cache.

Figure 6.13. Conjoin no. 1 (photograph by Thomas J. Loebel)

Figure 6.14. Carlisle cache small flakes (dorsal view, except for lateral fragment, lower right, which is not possible to orient) (photograph by Matthew G. Hill)

TABLE 6.6. Metric and Nonmetric Information on Carlisle Cache Large Flakes

			Metric[a]							Nonmetric		
No.	Fig. 6.12	Category	L (mm)	W (mm)	T (mm)	Wt (g)	PW (mm)	PT (mm)	PEA (deg.)	Conjoin Group	Platform	Dorsal Flake Scars (n)
4449	e	Overshot	74.0	51.2	15.9	47.1	10.7	4.8	78	1	Simple	4
4450	d	Overshot	73.4	57.5	15.0	60.2	17.2	2.6	73	2	Simple	7
4451	l	Flat	85.4	74.5	12.9	71.5	13.7	5.6	56	2	Simple	7
4452	h	Flat	98.4	49.0	18.5	144.8	20.3	9.2	87	1	Simple	6
4453	i	Flat	104.7	56.3	12.9	57.7	29.9	10.2	55	1	Prepared	4
4454	k	Flat	76.5	75.4	12.3	52.9	20.1	5.3	80	1	Prepared	9
4455	f	Flat	102.2	84.2	9.8	91.7	28.3	11.2	73	1	Simple	9
4456	g	Flat	124.2	61.8	10.3	73.3	12.6	3.8	60	1	Simple	5
4457	b	Overshot	106.2	50.9	12.9	53.1	6.2	2.3	82	–	Prepared	8
4458	j	Flat	90.2	102.7	14.9	104.5	31.4	10.1	78	1	Simple	13
4459	c	Overshot	76.0	56.1	12.5	32.6	5.7	2.9	84	2	Simple	6
4460	a	Overshot	86.4	51.2	14.4	50.7	16.2	9.2	90	–	Simple	8

[a]Length (L), width (W), thickness (T), weight (Wt), platform width (PW), platform thickness (PT), platform edge angle (PEA).

Small Flakes

Six small flakes and fragments, including five made from Burlington chert and one made from Warsaw chalcedonic chert, round out the cache contents (Figure 6.14). These specimens stand in stark contrast to the balance of the collection, which forms a technologically cohesive package of bifaces and large flakes. The circumstances surrounding the cache's discovery raise the possibility that these artifacts may in fact be associated with the Oneota component and were inadvertently recovered as part of the cache. However, convergent evidence warrants their inclusion and, as a group, they contribute details on its genesis.

Four Burlington flakes refit to produce two separate biface thinning flakes. One conjoin forms a complete flake, while the other comprises medial and proximal pieces. In the second instance, the proximal end and a distal corner of the proximal piece display recent damage. In both conjoins, though, analogous weathering and staining of exterior surfaces and fracture edges indicate the refits mend old breaks. The distal break on the medial piece in the second refit is also an old fracture. The fifth Burlington specimen, which represents a third flake, is a lateral fragment resulting from two intersecting bend fractures that, again, occurred in antiquity. The Warsaw flake is a distal fragment with an old proximal break.

We interpret the small flakes as fortuitous accompaniments, or "riders" (in the sense used by Binford 1978a:74). The three Burlington flakes—two refits plus the isolated fragment—are made from varieties of this toolstone that were also used to produce several bifaces and large flakes. These specimens are debitage that was likely unintentionally packaged with the bifaces and large flakes at the location of manufacture as part of transport preparations. Relative to the cache, the closest source of Warsaw chert is the Skunk River Valley, some 40–50 km east of the find spot in the central Des Moines River Valley. Downstream in southeastern Iowa, it is available close to the Des Moines River as well as close to sources of Burlington (Figure 6.8). Thus, while it is not possible to pinpoint the source of this toolstone, it was not available at the location where the bifaces and large flakes were knapped, which almost certainly happened in the Burlington source area. For this reason, we suspect the small Warsaw flake preexisted as residue in a bag used to transport the bifaces and large flakes to the find spot, perhaps much like small debris that accumulates in the bottom of a student backpack.

Examination of the small flakes under high magnification reinforces this conclusion. Each specimen displays generalized wear, polish, and abrasion on the ventral and dorsal faces along with light edge rounding and random edge damage. These modifications are interpreted as "transport wear" resulting from friction and jostling during transport.

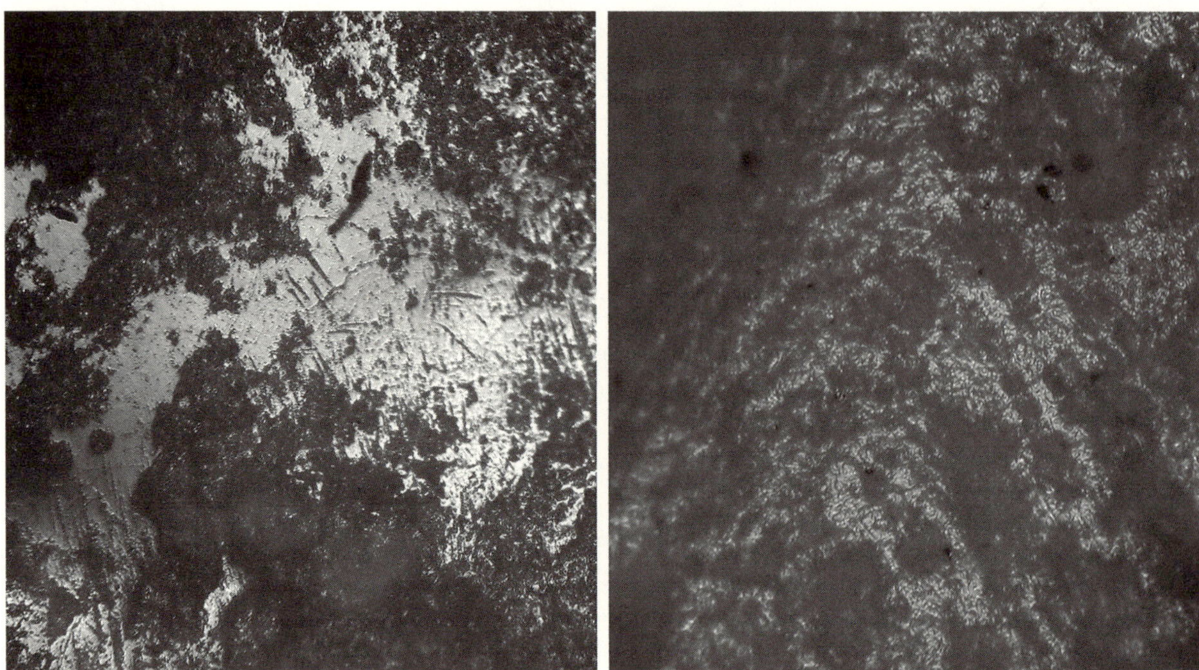

Figure 6.15. Photomicrographs (100x) of stone-on-stone (*left*) and hide polish (*right*) on the "down-side," and "up-side," respectively, of biface no. 4442. Stone-on-stone polish is characterized by truncation of microtopography and a bright, flat polish with crisp, well-defined edges, while dry hide wear typically shows as a dull, pitted, interlinked polish accompanied by rounded flake-scar ridges (photographs by Thomas J. Loebel).

PACKING, EMPLACEMENT, AND BURIAL

Several lines of evidence indicate that the contents of the cache were not only bundled inside a bag during transport to the ground-surface find spot but also remained enclosed until their eventual burial. Transport wear in the form of small patches of light to medium stone-on-stone (SOS) polish are visible under high magnification (100x) on the higher flake-scar ridges and/or the broader flake-scar troughs of many of the bifaces and large flakes (Figure 6.15). Generalized microwear interpreted as hide polish also exists on the face of some specimens (Figure 6.15). Considered together, these subtle modifications reflect wear that developed at locations where artifacts were in direct and constant contact with other chipped stone artifacts and/or hide during transport. It follows that the items were not individually wrapped but rather were tightly bundled together or, perhaps, bound into several smaller bundles, inside a transport bag. Microwear resulting from contact with bone, antler, or wood is not present and suggests the cache did not include artifacts made from these materials.

Two other observations indicate that the contents originally rested on the surface in a bundle, perhaps remaining inside a transport bag. First, the specimens uniformly lack a well-developed patina. While patina formation is a complex phenomenon (Van Nest 1985), the effective absence of patina on artifacts of this age is rather unusual, suggesting they were shielded from the elements after their arrival at the find spot. Incremental burial in alluvium, combined with deterioration of organic packaging material, appears to have occurred roughly concurrently. Although three large flakes and a biface situated along the southwest margin appear to have slipped away from the main axis of the cache (Figure 6.4), this scenario brings the orderly arrangement of the contents into focus, suggesting that organic covers had not fully deteriorated before the majority of the cache was buried.

Second, SOS polish occurs on both faces of most bifaces and large flakes; however, in seven specimens, SOS and hide polish occur on opposite faces (Table 6.7). We attribute this pattern to the artifact's location within the bundle. Those showing SOS on both faces held interior positions, while those showing SOS and hide polish on opposing faces held exterior positions, with the "hide side" facing outward and thus making contact with hide packaging material. Furthermore, it appears the artifacts were emplaced as such. Working back and forth between the artifacts and the photographic slides, the "up-side" can be determined for 19 specimens (Figure 6.4). As predicted, the hide side is the up-side and SOS is the down-side on three in situ specimens. Biface no. 4442 exhibits

TABLE 6.7. Summary of Microwear Polish (Transport Wear) on Carlisle Cache Bifaces and Large Flakes

	Biface		Large Flake	
POLISH	FACE A	FACE B	FACE A	FACE B
Stone-on-stone	24	21	9	11
Hide	1	4	2	0
Stone-on-stone and hide	0	0	0	0
indeterminate	0	0	1	1

this pattern (Figures 6.4 and 6.15). Instances of the reverse pattern do not occur.

An alternative version of this formational scenario invokes intentional burial. The field notes and photographic slides indicate that the color (and presumably texture) of the matrix encasing the artifacts was indistinguishable from the surrounding sediment. Although this observation is significant, its interpretation is ambiguous. All else being equal, if the package were placed into a pit intended to hold it and then covered with the excavated sediment, detecting the pit margins would be extremely difficult given some 11,000 years of subsequent pedogenesis. The presence of such a pit might be more apparent if the fill was distinctly different—as seen in many prehistoric pit features—but this is not the case here. In addition, the items were lying flat, not on their edges or at various angles, as might be expected if the packaged contents (or individual specimens) had been positioned against pit walls. This scenario is, of course, moot if the cache originally rested on the surface. There is one clue, however, contradicting the idea that the cache was intentionally buried: the three flakes and the biface that are figured to have slipped away from their original positions near the top of the cache. Though possible, it is difficult to imagine how these specimens could have migrated laterally in a buried context while none of the others did so.

Why the cache was left at this location as opposed to some other place is conjectural. Around the time of emplacement, the area was a grassy, aggrading the valley bottom. In general, travel was easy. Local topography was dominated by an open, monotonous landscape, with the exception of major river confluences. Currently, the Des Moines River is situated some 3 km east of the find spot, while the Middle River is located about 0.5 km south. Their confluence is roughly 6 km to the southeast. The situation was undoubtedly different at the close of the Late Wisconsin, although precisely how is impossible to say. We can say with confidence that the rivers had wide channels sweeping from valley margin to valley margin. It is therefore possible that the confluences of the Middle and/or North Rivers and the Des Moines River were in closer proximity to the find spot during Clovis times and that, when considered together with the bluffs to the northwest and southeast (Figure 6.2), this may have been a locally prominent, strategic place to stow the cache.

FUNCTION

The Carlisle cache consists of unfinished tools made on nonlocal toolstone, with a series of bifaces and large flakes intended as preforms for projectile points and unifacial tools, respectively. It exemplifies a function-specific, personal gear cache (though we argue below that it was available for anyone to use, not just a single person). Such caches occur at places where "non-local staged raw materials were stored with the tools necessary to fabricate finished items" (Thomas 1985:33). The fact that the cache lacks fabricators (e.g., flint-knapping gear) does not preclude this assessment—perhaps fabricators were not included or, alternatively, they consisted of organic items that did not preserve.

Summarizing (and greatly simplifying) Morrow's (1994) discussion of selected regional toolstone resources, south central Iowa is not endowed with primary sources of abundant, high-quality toolstone of the sort often sought for tool manufacture by Clovis knappers. The northwest quarter of the state is also "chert-deficient" (Morrow 1994:108). The situation is somewhat better in eastern Iowa, where bedrock exposures may host chert suitable for use as toolstone. Still, most Clovis points and preforms reported to date are made on Mississippian-age chert from southeastern Iowa and adjacent areas, with Burlington by far the preferred toolstone (Morrow and Morrow 1994). This pattern is not unexpected considering Burlington chert's convenient package sizes, its local abundance, and its superior flaking properties. However, it is difficult to say if the Carlisle cache was established in response to a known absence of suitable toolstone in an area used recurrently by

Clovis foragers or if it marks an initial trip into an unmapped, large river valley. Whatever the case may be, oral tradition and everyday conversation would have kept this critical bit of information circulating for some time (Binford 1978b, 1979:257, 1983:114; Minc 1986; Nelson 1969:374). For example, Binford (1983:206) reports that "almost every man could provide me with an accurate list of cached tools dispersed over an area of nearly a quarter of a million kilometers," a knowledge repository that would sweat a modern supply chain analyst. To put this figure into perspective, the State of Iowa covers 145,000 km^2.

The cache has a robust hunting/butchering signature, and although the targeted prey is not clear, it can be narrowed to two taxa. During the Late Wisconsin the region hosted a diverse large herbivore bestiary, including caribou (*Rangifer* sp.), mammoth (*Mammuthus* sp.), mastodon (*Mammut* sp.), elk-moose (*Cervalces* sp.), bison (*Bison* sp.), muskoxen (*Ovibos* sp.), and horse (*Equus* sp.) (Hay 1912; Long and Yahnke 2011; Schultz and Martin 1970; Semken and Falk 1987). However, these taxa were at least regionally extinct by the time the cache was established, with the exception of bison and mammoth (Faith and Surovell 2009; Saunders et al. 2010). As discussed above, the area was grassland, dominated apparently for the first time by tall, warm-season prairie grasses (Wells 1970). While these grasses offer poor forage for mammoth (and other monogastrics), bison thrive on these varieties (Guthrie 1984a; Knapp et al. 1999), and); paleozoological evidence indicates that bison numbers exploded at this time (Hill et al. 2008). In fact, extinct bison remains occur in the area, including a *B. antiquus* cranium from "near Carlisle" and five *B. occidentalis* crania from "Polk County, Iowa" (McDonald 1981:Tables 23 and 27) (Figure 6.2). It is therefore reasonable to suggest that bison drew Clovis hunters to central Iowa. Extending this idea further, herd movement may have been structured by a steep seasonal foraging gradient (Guthrie 1984a:269) (aided by periglacial conditions in central and northern Minnesota [Dyke 2004]) that pulled animals northward during the primary growing season along Iowa's distinctive, elongated (north–south trending) drainage structure. Such movements would have been relatively foreseeable by Clovis hunters, who in turn planned their activities accordingly, establishing facilities such as the Carlisle cache.

Support for this scenario is provided by the distribution of 107 Clovis points and preforms recorded by Morrow and Morrow (1994). Most of these finds occur in counties along the Des Moines and Iowa Rivers (Figure 6.16). About one-third of the specimens, including 18 points from Louisa County, are from counties in southeastern Iowa, where outcrops of Burlington chert also occur. Twenty of the 21 points in Cedar County derive from the Rummells-Maske cache. Interestingly, these finds do not cluster around the modern large cities, as they do in other areas (Shott 2002), or along interstate highway corridors, where construction and development activities may bias the sample. Moreover, the Office of the State Archaeologist, in Iowa City, has been especially active in the search for archaeological sites since 1959, as have numerous private consulting firms, an effort that has benefited from the annual cultivation of over three-quarters of the state's total area.[5] Against this backdrop, the distribution of points and preforms appears to capture the general pattern of Clovis land use in Iowa, which may reflect patterns of behavior related to bison procurement.

Despite these inferences, the organized nature of the cache contents leads us to suspect that the raison d'être for the cache's contents was not executed. This situation is not unusual. The archaeological and ethnographical literature contains numerous cases where passive gear (Binford 1979:256) was not put (back) into play for reasons unknown. Archaeological examples include the 2,000-year-old duck decoys from Lovelock Cave, Nevada (Tuohy and Napton 1986) and the 9,000-year-old net from Sheep Mountain, Wyoming (Frison et al. 1986), as well as Mississippian-age hoes and related agricultural material from rock shelters in southwestern Illinois (Winters 1981:27). These items were most probably intended for seasonal use, to be employed over a period of time (years?) before falling into disuse and/or eventually disappearing from collective memory.

Many reasons may be given for why passive gear is sometimes not reactivated. To list a few obvious possibilities, resource distributions and availabilities change and people move or die and their memories fade, though, in light of Binford's remark (above) it is unlikely that a healthy forager would forget such information. Use of the Carlisle cache may have failed simply because it rested on a rapidly aggrading floodplain surface and was quickly covered in Early Gunder alluvium. Plus, the location may not have been physically marked, since at the time this was a rock-scarce environment. The limestone bluffs to the west, which could potentially have served as a source of rock, were mantled with Late Wisconsin Peoria loess during this period (Bettis et al. 2003), which may have made finding suitable marker rock not worth the effort. Wood, on the other hand, was

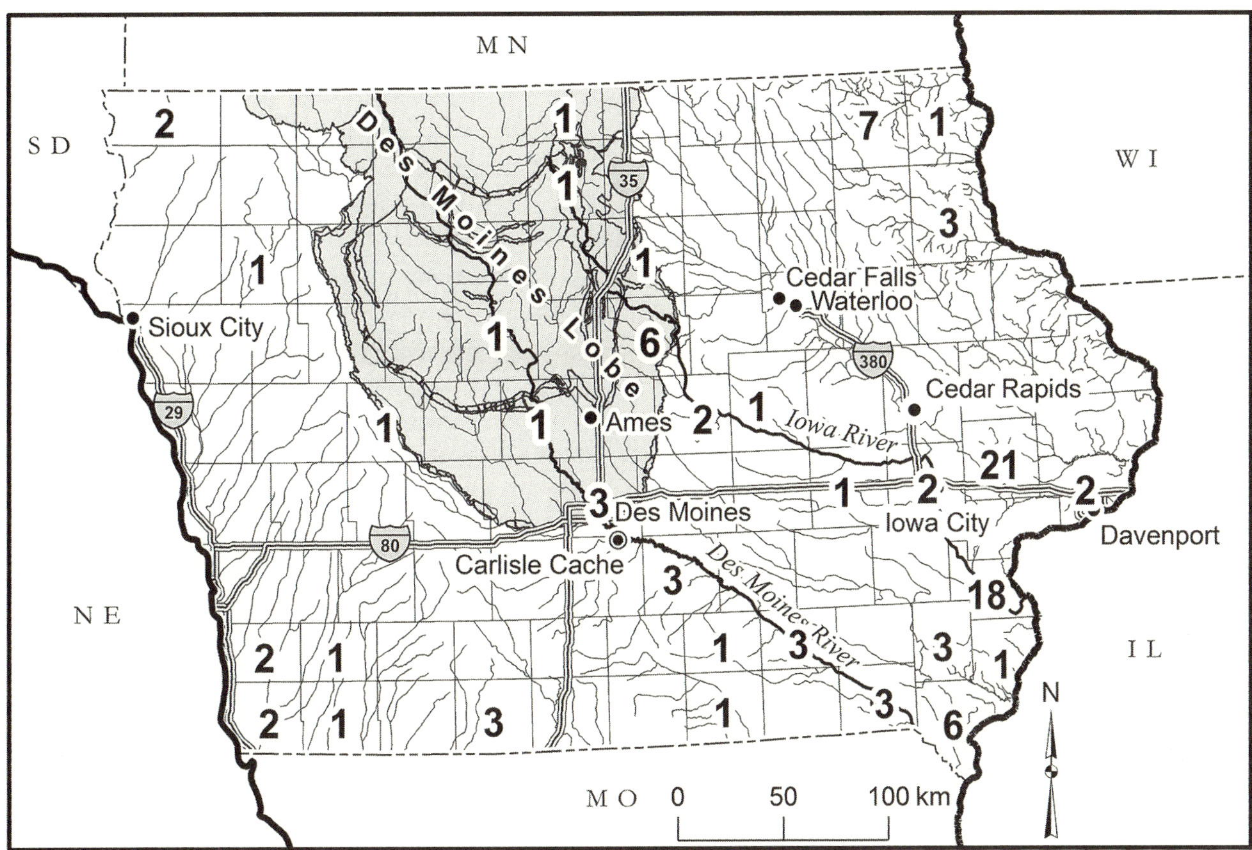

Figure 6.16. Distribution of Clovis points and preforms in Iowa, summarized by county (map created by Matthew G. Hill)

probably within relatively easy reach in most places in the Des Moines River Valley, based on the vegetational history of central Iowa following deglaciation (Kim 1986). However, if the location was signaled by a wood marker of some sort, it was probably not substantial, perhaps resembling the ritual tripod documented by Fitzhugh and Golovnev (1998:Figure 5) and susceptible to destruction by occasional floods that reshaped the immediate physiography, making relocation efforts doubly challenging.

CONCLUSIONS

The Carlisle cache is a substantial addition to the Clovis archaeological record. It offers empirical information on the life history of an intact cache and on flaked stone technology, as well as general insights on the local Late Wisconsin environment. These observations implicate the development of Clovis settlement system models, including aspects of technological organization, mobility and land use, and subsistence. As an initial contribution along these lines, a simple model of Clovis bison hunting, land use, and technological organization in central Iowa is presented below, incorporating inferences drawn from other localities and assemblages.

1. The Carlisle artifacts were cached on the surface of an aggrading floodplain. The position of the Des Moines and Middle Rivers during Clovis times, relative to the cache, is unknown. However, the channels were wide and sweeping from valley margin to valley margin, thereby sustaining savanna/open grassland dominated by warm-season grasses on the floodplain and making this landform prime habitat for ruminant grazers, specifically bison, and especially for nursery herds in the summer months. Easy travel, rapidly increasing bison populations, plenty of water, and a reliable supply of wood would have made these tracts of land especially attractive to Clovis foragers, at least seasonally, and they appear to have visited them relatively frequently.

Additional support for this simple model has recently been documented at several sites in the Beaver River drainage system in northwestern Oklahoma. Briefly, the JS cache totals 112 artifacts (3.73 kg), including 66 flakes, 30 blades, 12 bifaces, and 3 large overshot flakes (Bement, Chapter 5; Graves et al. 2006). Alibates silicified dolomite, which outcrops some 200 km southwest of the find spot, is by far the most common toolstone present. The site of Jake Bluff provides complementary evidence of Clovis bison hunting (Bement and Carter 2010). Here a small bison herd was stampeded into an arroyo cut into a low hill bordering the Beaver River floodplain and killed. Three of the four Clovis points recovered at the site are made on Alibates. Significantly, initial use of the locality occurs at ca. 10,800 B.P., which coincides with a change in floodplain vegetation, from communities dominated by warm-season plants by 11,000 B.P. to ones characterized by roughly equal percentages of warm- and cool-season plants at 10,000 B.P. (Bement, Carter et al. 2007). Taken together, the combined Beaver River record, coupled with inferences drawn from research on the Carlisle cache, reveals a pattern of Clovis land use on the central Great Plains in which specific, often distant, floodplain environments were visited recurrently for bison hunting. The Aubrey site in north central Texas (Ferring, ed. 2001) appears to represent another instance of this general land use strategy.

The Carlisle cache confirms the long-standing suspicion that Clovis sites in Iowa have been preserved by deep burial in early postglacial valley fill in the large river valleys (Benn and Bettis 1985:17; Bettis and Benn 1984:216, Table 5). Similar alluvial architecture may characterize other tributary confluences, thereby providing a starting point for the discovery of new sites. If our land use model is accurate, multiple site types should be found in these locales, with bison kill-butchery sites showing the greatest relative archaeological visibility. Evaluating this idea will not be easy, requiring appropriate discovery methods, a visionary research team with expertise in fluvial geomorphology, yeoman's work, and of course, generous funding (e.g., Mandel 2008). The cache further suggests that the current distribution of Clovis points and preforms is biased toward upland settings where appropriately aged sediments are better exposed.

2. The location and character of the cache contents combined with the distribution of Clovis points and preforms throughout Iowa suggest a mobility strategy based on patterned, perhaps seasonal, residential movement oriented up and down the larger rivers draining the Des Moines Lobe (upstream) and incorporating the Burlington chert source area (downstream). The presence of a Skunk River Valley toolstone—Warsaw chalcedonic chert—bolsters this inference while also providing evidence for movement across drainage divides. In the case of the Carlisle cache, planned upstream movement along the Des Moines River was initiated shortly after the bifaces and large flakes were manufactured in the Burlington source area. To put it another way, toolstone procurement was embedded (Binford 1979:259) within the settlement system, while at the same time it employed tactics such as caching tool preforms at strategic locations to facilitate movement into and between highly productive food resource patches, especially those that did not contain desirable toolstone.

3. Bison drew Clovis foragers into central Iowa and perhaps as far north as southern Minnesota. Following a steep seasonal foraging gradient northward, herd movement was probably highly predictable and relatively fast-paced due to the time- and space-transgressive nature of the growing season. In response, Clovis groups employed elements of a foraging strategy (Binford 1980) during these periods, characterized by high rates of residential mobility, in order to maintain close contact with the itinerant food supply (as used broadly by Kelly and Todd 1988:234). Residential mobility was comparatively reduced during the balance of the year (and logistical ranges were increased) as groups made their way back downstream, perhaps within a different drainage network in order to gather fresh information for planning future trips upstream. This may explain how Warsaw chert entered the cache. It suggests that a source for this toolstone was visited after an intense period of upstream activity in order to replenish tool kits for use on the downstream, return trip to the Burlington source area. Few tools made on Burlington survived the round trip; those that did arrived largely exhausted and were jettisoned when the tool kit was overhauled (cf. Gramly 1980; Hill 1994; Hofman 1992; Ingbar 1994).

4. Gearing up included manufacturing new points for immediate use and tool preforms destined to be cached on the landscape for future use. The fact that the cache includes only preforms is taken as evidence that it functioned as an open-use stockpile, that is, available for anyone to use when necessary. As Simon Paneack, a Nunamiut informant, put it, "Good men always say 'what can I carry that may help someone in the future'" (Binford 1979:257; see also Marlowe 2010:253). The logic behind this strategy is simple: it ensures that the toolstone has been subjected to quality-control assessment, thereby reducing the risk of failure during subsequent manufacturing activities. Equally important is the observation that converting a middle interval biface into a finished point of appropriate size and shape to fit a foreshaft is much easier to accomplish than tailoring a

foreshaft to fit a finished point. In this light, it is perhaps not surprising that most Clovis caches do not include finished points (Kilby 2008:Table 14). This implies that the function of caches that do contain multiple finished points—Drake, Anzick, East Wenatchee, Fenn, Simon, and Rummells-Maske—are fundamentally different in a functional sense. Parenthetically, these observations provide an analytical framework for addressing variation in the basal morphology of Clovis points (and the relative lack thereof in Folsom points, for example [Ahler and Geib 2000:800]).

5. Ethnographic observations on task differentiation in foraging societies (Kelly 1995; Kuhn and Stiner 2006:954–956; Waguespack 2005), particularly those in which meat is a staple food item, lead us to conclude that the Carlisle cache was established to satisfy the anticipated, task-specific needs of both men and women. In this scenario, the middle interval bifaces were intended to be converted into weapon tips for use by men in hunting. The large, flat flakes are interpreted as blanks for handheld tools used by men and women in various butchering, processing, and scraping activities, while the large, overshot flakes are reasonably considered as preforms for hafted end scrapers intended for use primarily by women in hide processing. In other words, the cache was constructed with everyone in mind, as opposed to being developed for a narrower segment of society. To push this idea a bit further, the items were attended to the cache find spot by a small, mixed group of foragers during the course of residential movement and activity. This notion may help explain the contents of other caches. For instance, the large number of essentially identical finished points in the Rummells-Maske cache may be the work of one or two hunters who, during a routine logistical foray, emplaced them for future use. The fact that the points are finished indicates that this is not an open-use cache; instead, the points were tailored to fit particular foreshafts.

6. Finally, the Carlisle cache anchors the distinctive aspects of Clovis flaked stone technology in the region and, more importantly, provides insight on the organization of the technology. From the vantage point of this cache, the assemblage was designed to accommodate three main activities: hunting, butchering, and hide processing. In preparing for extended forays away from prime toolstone sources, greater emphasis was placed on gearing up weaponry components than on butchery and hide-processing tools, in anticipation of a relatively higher rate of point turnover due to damage or loss in hunting (cf. Sellet 2004). While the bifaces could have served as a source of small flakes for expedient tools, they are far too small to have served efficiently as bifacial cores (cf. Bamforth 2003), as inferred for several other caches, including Anzick (Wilke et al. 1991), Watts (Kilby 2008:112–114), and Crook County (Bradley et al. 2010:Figure 3.4). Instead, bifaces and large flake blanks were made from tabular cores at the toolstone source, with intentions of future conversion into weapon tips and a multitude of unifacial tools, respectively. This finding confirms Eren's (2013; Eren and Andrews 2013) experimentally derived prediction that large, flat flakes like those in the Carlisle cache were made with functional flexibility and longevity in mind. If pressed, one of these flakes (or a relatively large unifacial tool) could readily be transformed into a diminutive weapon tip, as seen at Morrow-Hensel in western Wisconsin (Hensel et al. 1999:26).

This twofold system of biface and flake production enabled Clovis foragers to prosper off-quarry no matter whether spoor steered them into mapped or unmapped areas (cf. Kelly and Todd 1988). Technological and subsistence confidence was managed by performing early interval biface work at quarry sources, thereby decreasing the chances of off-quarry, late interval (point) manufacturing failures, and by regularly carrying substantial numbers of point and unifacial tool preforms. Such items were occasionally cached in areas where tool kits were prone to rapid depletion based on a history there of kill-butchery events, as well as at previously unvisited locations judged to have good potential for similar activities during anticipated future movements.

ACKNOWLEDGMENTS

We express our sincere thanks to Bruce Bradley, Mike Collins, Andy Hemmings, Dave Meltzer, Bob Patten, and Dennis Stanford for sharing their thoughts on the Carlisle cache and other things Clovis with us. Other individuals who helped out in one way or another include Art Bettis, Nancy Coinman, Steve Forman, Marlin Hawley, Bill Johnson, Larry Keeley, Brad Koldehoff, John Lambert, Vandana Loomba, Toby Morrow, Carrie O'Rourke, Dave Rapson, and Chris Widga. Kudos to Adam Holven for bringing the cache to our attention during collections maintenance. Jeff Hruska recalled the discovery and excavation of the cache, though, in the end, he was unable to proffer information not recorded in his field notes. The artifact illustrations in Figure 6.11 were prepared by Sarah

Moore (deceased), an outstanding illustrator and an even better person. And finally, we are indebted to the Iowa Science Foundation, which sponsored the geoarchaeology, and to Don Bartholomew, who granted access to his pasture for this work.

NOTES

1. "Cribbs' Crib" is derived from the landowner's surname and a woven metal mesh corncrib that formerly stood in the site area (Figure 6.2). We use "Carlisle cache" for Feature 75 to avoid confusion with the Oneota component.
2. DeVore (1990:Table 13) reports 48 flakes from the cache. This number includes the 12 large flakes and the 6 small flakes. The remaining specimens are pseudo-microflakes resulting from compression by heavy equipment, as evidenced by fresh fracture edges, the absence of striking platforms, and the fact that they refit to damaged bifaces and large flakes.
3. To arrive at these figures, we examined illustrations of the bifaces (Frison and Bradley 1999 [for Fenn]; Woods and Titmus 1985 [for Simon]) that Bradley et al. (2010:Table 3.5) classify as middle interval specimens. Santarone (2007:Table 1) supplies information to cross-match the Simon illustrations and specimens. Also, the values for Simon could potentially be slightly higher since only one face of biface no. 5381 is illustrated in Woods and Titmus (1985:Figure 4a). However, the illustrated face of this specimen shows no overshot flaking, nor does it appear likely on the opposite face (Butler 1963:Figure 5b).
4. We are not quite sure what to make of these results. The data set is a convenience sample, including specimens from different site types and recovery contexts, thereby obfuscating interassemblage comparisons.
5. Iowa covers 145,003 km^2, or 55,986 mi^2 (Prior 1991:30). Data compiled by the USDA National Agricultural Statistics Service indicates the percentage of land cultivated annually decreased steadily between 1964 and 2007, from an astonishing 94 percent (136,615 km^2, 52,747 mi^2) to merely 85 percent (124,430 km^2, 48,043 mi^2).

Chapter 7

Determining a Cultural Affiliation for the CW Cache from Northeastern Colorado

Mark P. Muñiz

Lacking a projectile point or solid radiocarbon date, archaeologists often face a significant problem in establishing a cultural affiliation for surface-collected stone artifact assemblages. When these kinds of assemblages are recovered in regions where surface and near-surface deposits may contain significant antiquity, the assemblage may conceivably date to any one of a number of prehistoric cultures that span millennia. This situation describes the context from which the CW cache was originally recovered. The CW cache was found as a tight surface concentration eroding from the margin of a playa located on private land in north central Lincoln County, Colorado, approximately 28 km northeast of Limon (Figure 7.1). The cache was collected by two individuals who visited the site about six years apart in the 1990s and eventually reported the find to Steve Holen (then curator of archaeology, Denver Museum of Nature & Science) in 2004. Although the collectors indicated generally where the cache came from, they did not pinpoint the exact physical location. The locale was not radiocarbon dated because the years that passed between the discovery and reporting allowed the original matrix to erode away. The general morphology of the artifacts suggested a possible Clovis affiliation, but the lack of a diagnostic projectile point hampered initial attempts to make a more certain determination.

In cases where a surface assemblage lacking projectile points is made up of bifaces, a careful analysis of the morphology, production strategy, and metric attributes compared to other bifaces from known cultural contexts may reveal a probable cultural affiliation. This is because strategies for manufacturing bifaces and projectile point preforms can involve culturally unique methods for thinning the biface, shaping the outline form, and finishing the base (e.g., Whittaker 1994). The probability of determining a cultural affiliation may be further increased when additional lines of evidence are considered, such as the geomorphic context of the find site, the raw materials used, how the artifacts have weathered over time, and long-term cultural patterns of landscape utilization.

An inherent problem with using the approach outlined above to determine a prehistoric cultural affiliation for the CW cache, or any similar assemblage, is the possibility of independent invention or stochastic variation that coincidentally results in similar morphologies for bifaces made by different cultures at different times. For example, large, well-made bifaces have been documented at Paleoindian, Woodland, and Late Prehistoric sites.

Large Paleoindian bifaces have been found in Clovis caches (e.g., Anzick, Crook County, Fenn, Simon) and at other sites such as Agate Basin, Big Black, Bobtail Wolf, Blackwater Draw, Gordon Creek, Kriesel, Lime Creek, and Tim Adrian (Anderson 1966; Boldurian 1991; Bradley 1982; Breternitz et al. 1971; Carr and Boszhardt 2003; Frison and Bradley 1999; Hicks 2002; Jones and Bonnichsen 1994; Mehringer 1988; O'Brien 1984; Root et

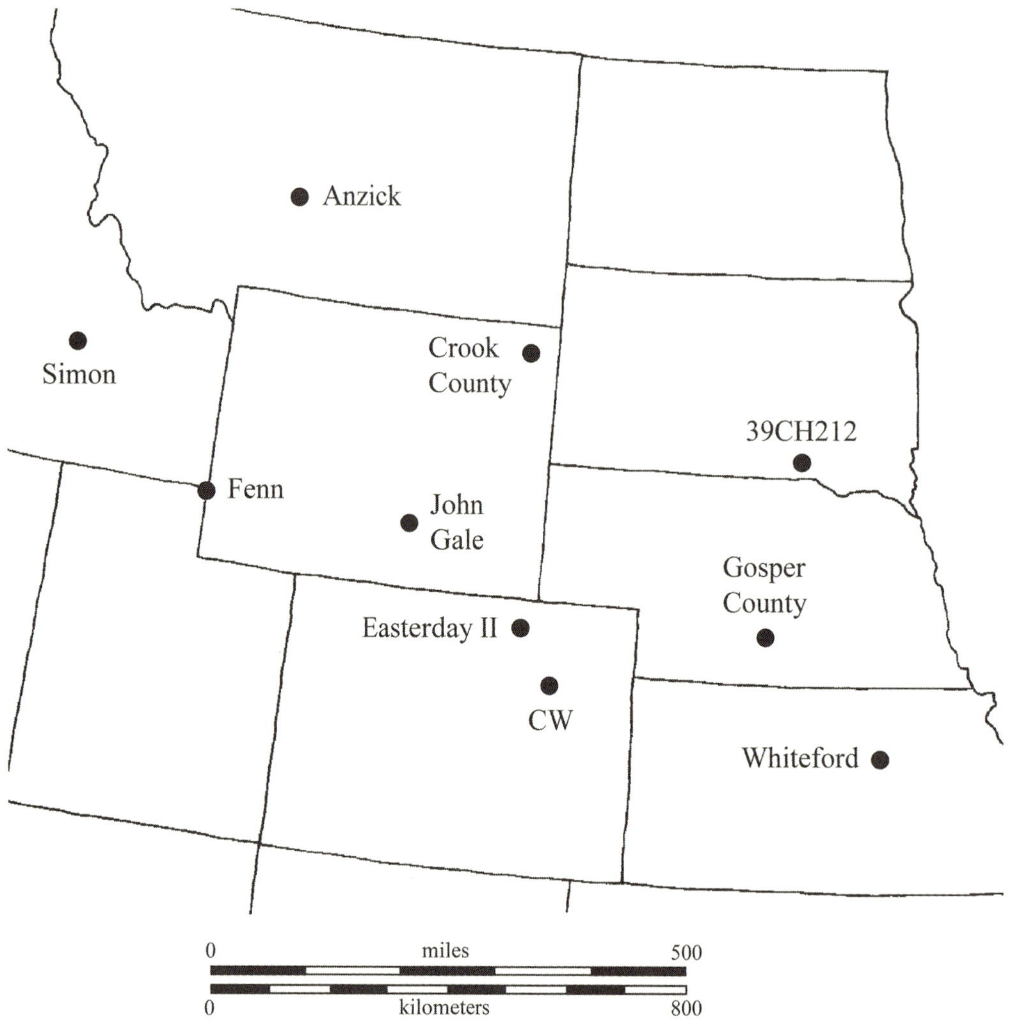

Figure 7.1. Map of biface cache sites with artifacts analyzed in this study

al. 1999; Tankersley 1998, 2002; Wilke et al. 1991; Woods and Titmus 1985; Wormington 1957). Typically these Paleoindian sites date between about 9,500 and 11,000 radiocarbon years before present.

Following the Paleoindian period, examples of large Archaic bifaces come from the Eva site in western Tennessee (Lewis and Lewis 1961:51–53). Woodland specimens have been documented in northeastern Iowa (Logan 1976:116–117) and the Illinois River Valley (Montet-White 1968). The long Mississippian "swords" (Kneberg 1952; Lewis and Kneberg 1958) are examples of some of the most skilled stoneworking in the North American precontact archaeological record.

Closer to Colorado, Late Plains Archaic and Shoshone groups of Wyoming made large, skillfully crafted bifacial knives (Frison 1991b:129, 133, 134). Late Prehistoric groups in Kansas and Nebraska also produced large, thin, finely made bifaces (Steinacher and Carlson 1998:243; Wedel 1986:107). Reynolds (1990) illustrated large, thin ceremonial bifaces included with Smoky Hill phase Central Plains Tradition (CPT) burials at the Whiteford site in central Kansas, and Fosha (1993) published another example of this biface type recovered from site 39CH212 in South Dakota. Basham and Holen (2006) reported on the Late Prehistoric Easterday II cache recovered from the Riverside Reservoir in northeastern Colorado. These Late Prehistoric sites in Colorado, Kansas, and South Dakota date between about A.D. 900 and 1500. Given that finely made bifaces were produced by both Paleoindians and Late Prehistoric peoples living in the same region over 8,000 years apart, we must ask, are there recognizable attributes of the CW cache that can be used to associate it with a specific prehistoric culture?

CW CACHE

The CW cache consists of 9 complete and nearly complete bifaces, 2 partial bifaces, and 3 large flakes, for a total of 14 pieces (Figure 7.2). Fresh breaks and nicked edges indicate that some of the bifaces were damaged relatively recently by agricultural machinery. All pieces in the cache are made from White River Group silicate, the nearest occurrence of which is at Flattop Butte, Colorado, 160 km to the north. For all of the artifacts one surface is significantly patinated, and for several pieces the opposite face is encrusted with calcium carbonate ($CaCO_3$) that is occasionally greater than 1 mm thick. These surface weathering characteristics on alternate faces indicate that the cache lay in a relatively undisturbed horizontal position for a very long time.

The two owners of the CW cache allowed their artifacts to be initially examined for one day during the summer of 2004, at which time metric attributes, photographs, and general notes were collected. Two years later, one of the collectors briefly loaned five of the bifaces (A1–A5) for an intensive analysis of the production strategy used to make them. Some of the production characteristics for the remaining sample could be integrated into this study based on field notes and photographs. Any future analysis of the second owner's portion of the cache is not expected to change the outcome of this research. To my knowledge, the two collectors still possess their respective portions of the cache. A high-magnification microwear analysis was not performed, although there is no macroscopic evidence of use wear along the edges. Based on visual inspection, the CW cache artifacts are not coated with ochre. Lengths for complete bifaces range from 11.1 to 14.0 cm with a mean of 12.6 cm; widths range from 5.8 to 8.0 cm and average 6.7 cm; and thickness ranges from 1.1 to 1.6 cm with a mean of 1.3 cm (Table 7.1). Two of the three flakes (A7 and B5) included in the cache were produced from biface reduction and thinning but unfortunately a refitting analysis was not possible. The third flake (A6) may have been removed from a prepared unidirectional core but is not technically a blade. More detailed analysis is required before the flakes can be better described, and they will not contribute to the remainder of this study.

The nine complete and nearly complete CW cache bifaces are classified as primarily late-stage bifacial cores, with one or two examples approaching an early-stage projectile point preform. The criteria used to classify them are described below. The pieces mostly exhibit an ovate outline form with rounded to flat bases. A common technique for reducing the pieces was the removal of large flakes oriented about 45 degrees to the long axis that traveled across the midline. Of the five bifaces reexamined in 2006 (A1–A5), three have evidence of longitudinal thinning flakes that originate from the base (i.e., wider, more squared end), though none are technically fluted, and one has two longitudinal thinning flakes that originate at the distal (i.e., pointed) end. A single biface (A2) has a flake scar that came within 5 mm of removing the opposite margin, which is the closest example of overshot flaking observed on any of the bifaces. Flake scars on the bifaces frequently end in wide, expanding terminations and were most probably made with soft-hammer percussion. One broken biface (A5) with serial collateral flaking may have been on the verge of becoming a point preform. The overall use of pressure flaking was very restricted and was employed mainly to standardize the edge morphology rather than as a finishing technique that might be used on a projectile point or more formal knife.

Figure 7.3 illustrates the general pattern of reduction used to shape bifaces A1–A5. The numbers within flake scars or regions of flake scars indicate a relative order of removal, so that areas labeled "1" have flakes removed prior to areas labeled "2" and so on. Bifaces A1–A3 demonstrate a sequential flaking pattern that allowed entire regions of flake scars to be mapped in order of removal, while bifaces A4 and A5 show a more complex pattern that required numbering of individual flake scars. Overall, there are two different flaking patterns.

Biface A1 shows a clockwise flaking pattern on the left face that begins at the distal end and exhibits more of an opposed pattern on the right face. Both lateral margins were worked in the same order relative to each other. Figure 7.4 illustrates the A1 flake scars in detail. The left face of A3 follows the same basic clockwise strategy evident on the left face of A1. The right face of A3 was treated similarly, with the left-margin flaking continuing all the way to the distal end.

The left face of A2 shows a counterclockwise flaking pattern beginning at the distal end. The flake scar intersection at the midline of the right face indicates that the left margin was shaped before the right margin. The right face of A2 preserves evidence of large flakes extending some 4.5–5.0 cm across the face with one terminating within 5 mm of the opposite edge. While portions of the distal and basal areas show flake scars that may precede the large flakes just described, smaller, younger flake scars obscure the sequence by intersecting the older flake

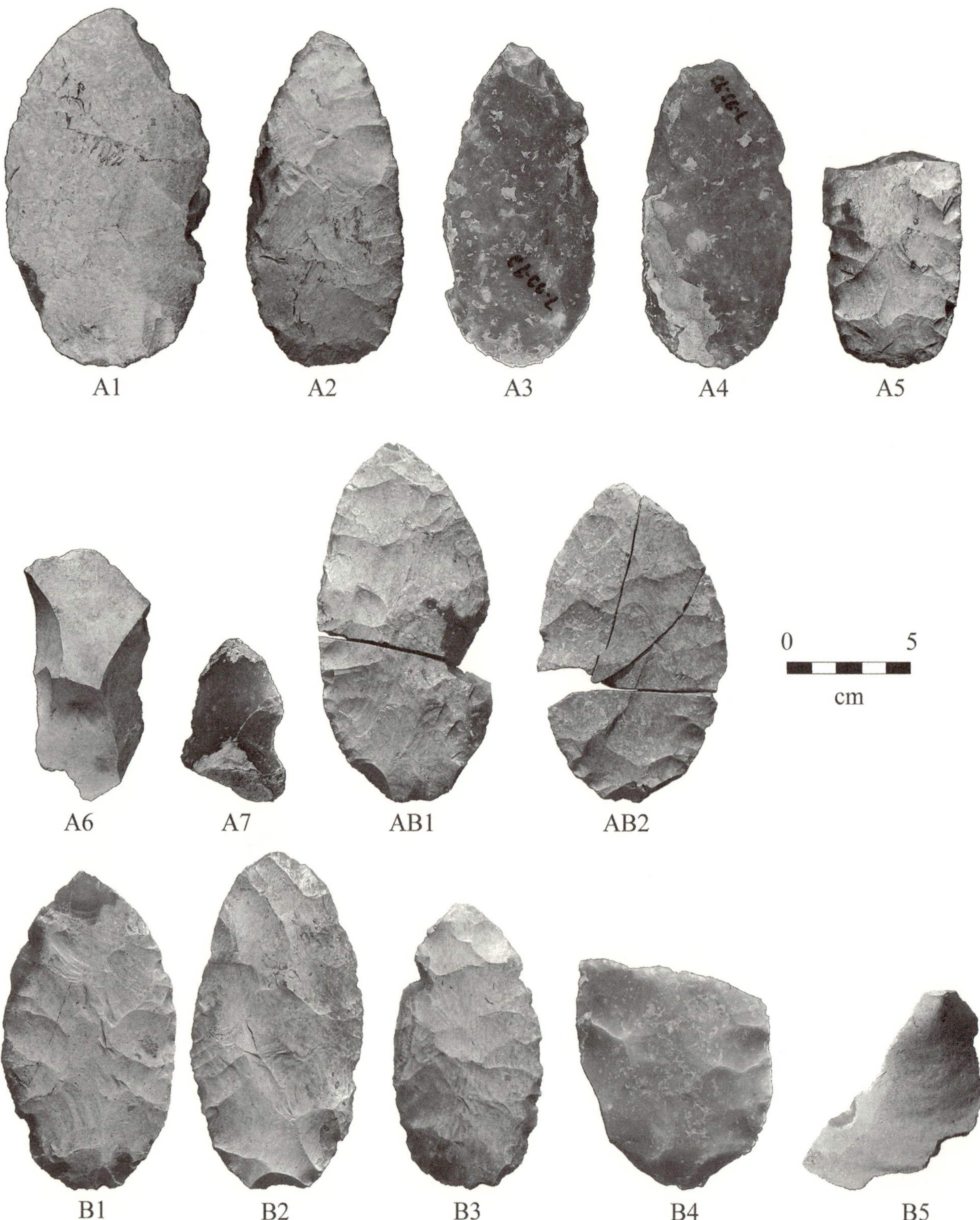

Figure 7.2 CW cache bifaces (A1–A5, AB1, AB2, B1–B4) and flakes (A6, A7, B5) exhibiting white patination and yellow calcium carbonate encrustation; labels correspond to Table 7.1 metric attributes and descriptions

TABLE 7.1. CW Cache Metric Data and Attributes

SPECIMEN NO.	CLASS	LENGTH[a]	WIDTH	THICKNESS	WIDTH/ THICKNESS	FLAKING PATTERN	COMMENTS
A1	Biface	13.66	7.96	1.48	5.38	Broad percussion	Edge damage along both lateral margins
A2	Biface	12.75	6.33	1.25	5.06	Broad percussion	Slight edge damage along 3 cm of one lateral margin
A3	Biface	12.32[b]	5.97	1.23	4.85	Broad percussion	Post-depositional edge damage along both lateral margins and distal end
A4	Biface	11.81	5.88	1.1	5.35	Broad percussion, longitudinal thinning flake removed from one end	Slight edge damage along 1.25 cm of one lateral margin
A5	Biface	8.3[b]	5.78	1.15	5.03	Broad percussion, fairly regular on one face	Basal half of square-based preform, modern break, ~1 cm of edge damage along one lateral margin
A6	Flake	9.63	4.5	1.69	2.66	–	Somewhat blade-like, "H" flake-scar pattern on dorsal surface
A7	Flake	6.3	4.9	–	–	–	Probable biface thinning flake
AB1	Biface	14.04	7.13[b]	1.56	4.57	Broad percussion, random	Two refitted halves (A&B), missing 3 cm from lateral margin—otherwise complete
AB2	Biface	12.5[b]	7.73[b]	–	–	Broad percussion	Four refitted pieces (A&B), still missing a piece, significant modern edge damage
B1	Biface	13.11	7.04	1.3	5.42	Random collateral	Complete
B2	Biface	12.43	7.02	1.17	6.0	Random collateral	Probably complete
B3	Biface	11.11	5.96	1.24	4.81	Broad collateral	Some edge damage along lateral margin
B4	Biface	8.76[b]	7.43	1.4	5.31	–	Proximal basal half with modern break
B5	Flake	9.3	4.6	–	–	Blade-like flake	Early-stage biface reduction flake

Note: Raw material for all specimens is White River Group silicate from Flattop Butte, Colorado.

[a]Length, width, and thickness recorded in centimeters.

[b]Slight breakage has minimally affected measurement.

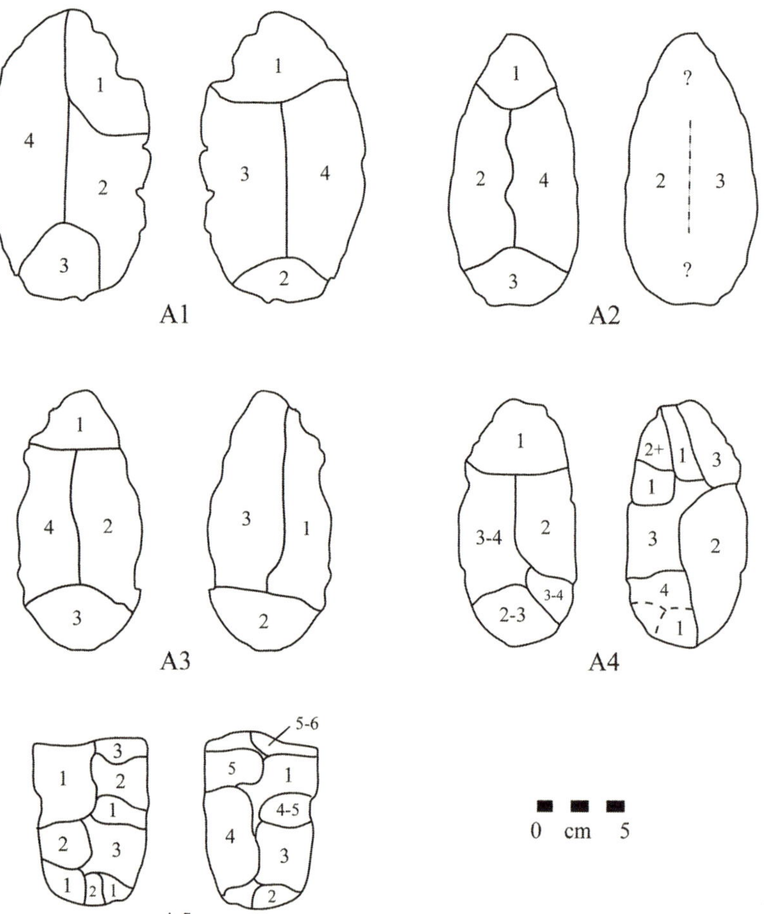

Figure 7.3 CW cache biface flaking patterns; ordered by sequential removals

scar edges, and the complete sequence for A2 cannot be determined.

In general, bifaces A1–A3 show a flaking pattern that followed a zoned approach such that the flint-knapper progressed by removing flakes along a lateral sequence in a more-or-less uninterrupted order. The flake scar pattern also indicates that the bifaces were consistently flaked in a manner that generated wide and flat flakes that could have been used as excellent cutting and graving tools and possibly also for end scraper blanks.

Bifaces A4 and A5 depart from the previous pattern (Figure 7.3). With A4 we see that while the left face has a somewhat clockwise flaking pattern, the right face differs considerably. The right face shows that the flint-knapper changed the strategy described previously for bifaces A1–A3 by removing specific flakes out of sequence from the clockwise/counterclockwise lateral progression. The flake scars of A4 are illustrated in more detail in Figure 7.4.

Biface A5 (recently broken) demonstrates the departure from the A1–A3 pattern even more dramatically. The flake scars on both faces of A5 show that the knapper flaked the piece in a less patterned way that probably arose as situational needs developed while creating the squared-off base and straighter margins. Figure 7.4 illustrates the individual flake scars in detail. The base of A5 is noticeably squared and the sides are much more parallel when compared to the other 10 bifaces in the cache. The overall morphology of A5 and the change in flaking pattern are consistent with this biface and with A4 being transitional between a late-stage bifacial core and an early-stage projectile point preform.

With the overall metric attributes and production strategy for the CW cache described, this study will now analyze multiple lines of evidence in order to determine whether the artifacts can be associated with any of the precontact cultural traditions in the region that are known to have cached bifaces. Lines of evidence include raw material and landscape utilization; culturally specific biface reduction and production strategies; and attribute and morphometric analyses.

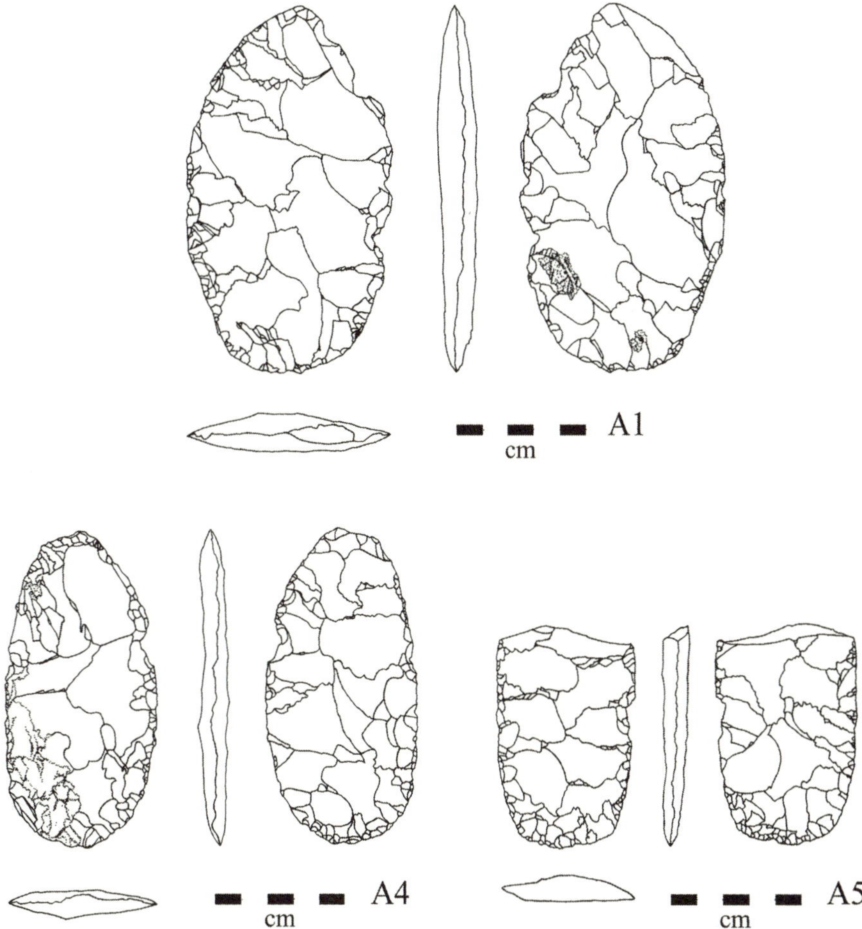

Figure 7.4 CW cache flake scar patterns for bifaces A1, A4, and A5

RAW MATERIAL USE AND LANDSCAPE UTILIZATION

The entire CW cache is made from White River Group silicate (chalcedony), most probably from the Flattop Butte quarry. The Flattop Butte quarry is a member of the White River Group Formation that outcrops in restricted areas of northeastern Colorado, eastern Wyoming, northwestern Nebraska, southwestern South Dakota, and southwestern North Dakota. Holen (2001a, 2010, Chapter 10) has demonstrated that Clovis peoples frequently utilized Flattop chalcedony and moved it as much as 600 km to the east and southeast onto the central Plains, up to 475 km to the south, and as much as 175 km to the southwest into the Front Range of the Rocky Mountains. High-quality Black Forest silicified wood outcrops not far to the west of the CW cache, and there are abundant secondary cobbles of Black Forest silicified wood, basalt, and various cherts and good-quality quartzites in the vicinity of the cache location. Based on available data and observations of private collections, later Paleoindian groups utilized these sources but Clovis groups in northeastern Colorado largely ignored them.

In contrast, Late Prehistoric peoples in eastern Colorado relied primarily on locally available stone, with the Easterday II cache serving as a unique exception. Gilmore (1999:247–255) provided information on lithic raw material use for three Middle Ceramic period sites that temporally overlap with the CPT and are located in the Platte River drainage of eastern Colorado. The occupants at Happy Hollow Rock Shelter, 5AH417, and 5AH15 (about 195 km northwest, 105 km west, and 50 km west-northwest of the CW cache, respectively) used a variety of lithic raw materials that were generally locally available. Quartzites, petrified wood, and various secondary chert and jasper cobbles supplied the bulk of the materials (Gilmore 1999). This is somewhat surprising given that the Happy Hollow Rock Shelter is only about 80 km west of the high-quality Flattop Butte outcrop. Muñiz and Holen (2005) found similar results in a survey of the Arikaree River drainage that contains the CW cache site. Two CPT sites were recorded in Yuma County, some 105 km northeast of the CW cache location. At 5YM218, only 1 of 239 artifacts was made of Flattop chalcedony, while at 5YM220 none of the 123 artifacts were made of this material. The Easterday II cache, recovered from the Riverside Reservoir located 97 km west-southwest of Flattop Butte, stands as an exceptional example of a Late Prehistoric site where Flattop chalcedony was used to make 99 bifaces (Basham and Holen 2006). Admittedly, data on lithic raw materials used at 31 other Middle Ceramic period sites recorded on the plains of eastern Colorado (Gilmore 1999) are not published and could add further support to the Easterday II pattern. Overall, the use of White River Group silicates to make the CW cache is consistent with the larger pattern of Clovis raw material preferences for the region.

The second line of evidence that suggests a Clovis association for the CW cache is the geomorphic setting of the find spot—along the margin of an upland playa associated with a well-developed paleosol. Of the five Clovis sites recorded in eastern Colorado that have been tested or excavated (see Chenault 1999; Holen 2001a; and Stanford 1999 for summary descriptions), the Dutton and Claypool sites are directly associated with playa settings (Dick and Mountain 1960; Stanford 1979, 1999; Stanford and Albanese 1975). In contrast, the Klein site is situated on a low ridge along the Kersey Terrace, the Drake cache occurred in an upland setting, and the Dent site is located at the border between uplands and an alluvial valley. Muñiz and Holen (2005) recorded a fluted point site in eastern Colorado that is either Clovis or Folsom and is situated adjacent to several small upland playas. Although the total number of sites is small, it appears that Clovis peoples actively utilized upland playas in eastern Colorado, possibly because these settings would have held water, provided habitat for edible plants, and attracted large game.

Late Prehistoric sites in eastern Colorado, including the CPT and Middle Ceramic period sites, have a much more diverse landscape distribution than exhibited by Clovis. Of 26 CPT and Middle Ceramic sites described by Gilmore (1999) and recorded by Muñiz and Holen (2005), only 1 is located near an upland playa. The remainder are situated in rock shelters or bedrock scarps (38.5 percent), along drainage divides (26.9 percent), along creeks or in open settings (23.1 percent), or on buttes or bluff tops (7.7 percent). While this Late Prehistoric sample is much larger than the Clovis sample, it is important to note that no Clovis sites have been found in rock shelter or bedrock scarp settings or on top of hills or ridges dividing creeks and drainages, which are the preferred CPT/Middle Ceramic period settings. Even though the Clovis sample is small, the significant differences between the early Paleoindian and Late Prehistoric environments, subsistence strategies, and probably social organization suggest that the geomorphic difference in Clovis and Late Prehistoric site locations in eastern Colorado is real and not a function of differential site preservation or discovery. Thus the position of the CW cache adjacent to a playa is much more consistent with land use patterns exhibited by Clovis than Late Prehistoric cultures.

A well-developed buried soil was identified in the same area where the CW cache was recovered and underwent preliminary field analysis by David May. May (2005:102–103) described the paleosol as consisting of a black A horizon (20–35 cm thick) overlying a grayish-brown or brownish-gray Bt horizon rich in secondary calcium carbonate deposits. Late Wisconsinan Peoria loess was identified directly below the Bt horizon. This paleosol appears to contain the Pleistocene-Holocene transition in the base of the A horizon and overall is consistent with observations of characteristics for the Brady soil. Mason and others (2008) documented region-wide soil development for the central and northern Great Pains that correlates the Brady and Leonard paleosols to the late Pleistocene–early Holocene transition. Through a combination of radiocarbon and optically stimulated luminescence dating, Mason and colleagues timed the soil-forming period as initiating between 15 and 13.5 cal ka and terminating between 10.5 and 9 cal ka (approximately 12,750–8000 ^{14}C yr B.P.). The presence of a likely Brady/Leonard paleosol outcropping and eroding on the modern ground surface adjacent to the playa where the CW cache was recovered opens the possibility that the cache dates to the early Paleoindian period. Furthermore, the presence of a buried Bt horizon with abundant calcium carbonate is consistent with expectations for a depositional setting that resulted in calcium carbonate encrustation on the CW bifaces.

BIFACE REDUCTION AND PRODUCTION STRATEGIES

The CW cache bifaces are not automatically assumed to have been solely intended for projectile points, and they are treated here first as bifacial cores for flake production and second as preforms that could be transformed into projectile points. This analysis considers the boundary between a bifacial core and a preform to occur at the conceptual transition point where the core ceases to *primarily* produce flake blanks for other tools and instead becomes the object of tool production itself. Without going into the minds of the ancient flint-knappers, this boundary can be approximated based on functional requirements of flake tools and projectile points, as described below.

The biface knapping strategies employed for the CW cache are compared here to those used at five Clovis sites and four Late Prehistoric sites in the western Plains and adjacent Rocky Mountain regions. Bifaces from these nine sites were selected for comparison because they represent skillful flint-knapping by cultures that practiced biface caching. Furthermore, the bifaces from these sites are made on good-quality raw materials, share aspects of reduction strategy, and occur in the same general region, and their metric and production data are accessible from direct measurements and publications with high-quality, scaled line drawings. Caches are uniquely suited to examination of both bifacial core reduction and preform/point production because they represent "frozen" moments in time that preserve examples of each of these stages and often include transitional forms as well. Furthermore, caches are not subject to mixing from later occupations, as might occur at a camp site or quarry.

The Clovis sites include well-known caches from the Anzick (Jones and Bonnichsen 1994; Lahren and Bonnichsen 1974; Wilke et al. 1991), Crook County (Tankersley 2002), Fenn (Frison and Bradley 1999), and Simon sites (Butler 1963; Woods and Titmus 1985) (Figure 7.1) as well as two Edwards chert bifaces from Gosper County, Nebraska (Holen 2002).

The Late Prehistoric sites used in this study include the Easterday II cache from northeastern Colorado (Basham and Holen 2006); the Whiteford site in central Kansas (Reynolds 1990); site 39CH212 from southern South Dakota (Fosha 1993); and the John Gale cache (Miller et al. 1991) from south central Wyoming. The Easterday II cache consists of 99 bifaces, two bifacially worked flakes, and a single unifacial scraper, all made from Flattop Butte chalcedony (Basham and Holen 2006). The John Gale cache includes 18 bifaces made from Green River chert and transported east from the source area into south central Wyoming (Miller et al. 1991). The Whiteford site contained four very well crafted bifaces that were found among burial offerings (Reynolds 1990). The biface recovered from 39CH212 is associated with the same cultural practices that account for the Whiteford pieces (Fosha 1993). Although the Whiteford and 39CH212 bifaces were not deposited as a single cache like the other assemblages, they are included because Reynolds's (1990) detailed analysis documented the production process and the high flint-knapping skill that was required to make them. Additionally, their sizes overlap with some of the Clovis bifaces and they are roughly central Plains contemporaries with the Late Prehistoric manufacturers of the Easterday II cache.

STAGES OF BIFACE REDUCTION AND PRODUCTION

To analyze morphological and metric attributes of Paleoindian and Late Prehistoric samples and compare them to the CW cache, a classification scheme was developed that analyzed these objects primarily as cores. This approach differs from those developed by Callahan (1979, 1991), Bradley and colleagues (2010), and others that seek to understand Paleoindian biface production largely with the goal of producing projectile points. The approach presented here is more in line with theoretical perspectives discussed by Kelly (1988) and colleagues (Kelly and Todd 1988), Kuhn (1994, 1996), and Morrow (1996), and with analyses by Huckell (2007) and Smallwood (2012). Although bifacial core reduction is conceived here as occurring along a continuum as flakes are removed to produce tools as needed, the classification system is divided into "stages" based on shared attributes and morphology in order to be more comparable with other published analyses.

The main variables of the classification scheme developed here include: (1) presence of cortex and degree of surficial (nonmarginal) flaking as indications of post-blank modification; (2) outline symmetry as an indication of the transition from mid- to late-stage core and eventually to preform; and (3) maximum thickness as an indicator of potential flake production. Because these three attributes are free of expectations regarding projectile point manufacture and specifically fluting, they work to classify bifacial cores based on overall morphology along a continuum of reduction, regardless of maximum length and width, and are thus applicable to technological strategies used from the Paleoindian through the Late Prehistoric periods. This scheme emphasizes thickness over width because biface width can be quite variable and still produce usable flake blanks for different applications.

Since the classification scheme is designed to be sensitive to bifaces functioning as cores, the transition points between each stage are primarily determined by the potential to produce a flake of sufficient thickness to function as a tool. This assumes that most durable flake tools will need a thickness of at least 2.5–5.0 mm, although thinner flake tools have been recorded. Further, if the bifacial core *could* (but not *will*) eventually be turned into a point preform, the point on average will range between 5 and 10 mm in thickness. These estimates are consistent with flake tools and points recorded throughout the Paleoindian period (e.g., Bradley 1982, 2009a; Bradley and Frison 1987; Carr and Boszhardt 2003; Frison 1975, 1982a, 1982b; Frison and Stanford 1982a, 1982b; Huckell 2007; Ingbar and Frison 1987; Justice 1987; Morrow and Morrow 2002; Muñiz 2005, 2009, 2013; Smallwood 2012).

The six bifacial stages used for this analysis begin with a blank and progress through early-stage bifacial core (ESBC), mid-stage bifacial core (MSBC), and late-stage bifacial core (LSBC) before reaching the preform and finished tool (e.g., projectile point, knife) stages (Table 7.2, Figure 7.5). When the CW cache is classified with these bifacial core continuum stages, all 11 bifaces fall into the LSBC stage, with 2 close to becoming preforms.

Table 7.2 provides the attributes for the classification system and indicates that there is a wide range of acceptable thicknesses for bifacial cores in the blank and ESBC stages. After bifaces reach a maximum thickness of 30 mm, the potential to produce flake tool blanks begins to decline and the biface may move through the subsequent stages more quickly with fewer total flake removals than what was required to achieve the 30 mm thickness. The absolute number of flakes produced by any core is relative to the initial size and shape of the blank.

Figure 7.5 illustrates a model for the relative utility and duration of bifacial core stages. The y-axis indicates the potential for the core to produce usable flake blanks. The x-axis tracks the progression of the core from blank to finished tool and indicates a relative amount of time the core may stay in each stage. The estimate for temporal duration of each stage is based on the relationship between steadily reducing core mass and functional requirements of the products (including both flake blanks and bifacial tools). The y-axis intercept with the curve indicates flake blank production potential, and the area under the curve for each stage is a relative measure of bifacial core utility. The range of dotted curves for the blank stage indicates variability based on the initial blank size and shape. However, the model expects that the blank will transition rather quickly into an early-stage bifacial core after sufficient cortex has been removed and initial edging has prepared platforms for controlled flake removal. Thus, the duration of the blank stage is short. The model also allows for thin flake blanks (<2.5 mm) to be produced during point production (e.g., channel flakes) but notes the relative potential for flake tool production is very low. As indicated in Table 7.2, maximum thickness is a primary variable restricting the potential to produce usable flake blanks, and the key thresholds of 30, 20, and 10 mm are illustrated along the top of the Figure 7.5 curve. This modeled relationship is nonlinear in terms of both the number of flakes removed per stage and the amount of time the biface may remain at each stage. Given that individual flake thickness varies, an actual curve documenting this process for a complete assemblage is expected to be sinusoidal but trending in the same basic direction. The model is generally consistent with studies of Clovis biface manufacturing throughout the United States (e.g., Bradley et al. 2010; Huckell 2007; Smallwood 2012; Wilke et al. 1991; Woods and Titmus 1985).

If the model is accurate, the implications are important because it indicates that after the maximum thickness passes below 30 mm the core use-life becomes relatively short. In Smallwood's (2012) terms, the "tempo" of reduction should increase, as fewer flake removals result in a greater rate of morphological change to the core compared with earlier stages. Once the biface enters the last stage of its life as a core, with maximum thickness between 20 and 10 mm, its function may irrevocably shift into that of a preform or bifacial tool, as it has largely lost the capacity to produce useful flake blanks. It is argued here that during this short period as a late-stage bifacial core, culturally distinctive styles of biface knapping become more apparent and take on new significance as the "flake producer" becomes a tool that is shaped to meet certain cultural expectations of function, performance, and style. Smallwood (2012)

TABLE 7.2. Bifacial Core Continuum Stages

STAGE	CORTEX	OUTLINE FORM[a]	EDGING	FACIAL FLAKING	THICKNESS	FLAKE TOOL POTENTIAL[b]
Blank	Raw cobble, primary flake, blocky chunk with moderate to complete cortical coverage	Random, depends on type of source material	≤ half the margin flaked	Little to none	Variable, depending on type of source material, but > 31 mm at minimum	Variable
Early-stage bifacial core	Moderate amount may still be present	May be quite asymmetrical	> half the margin flaked	Few comedial or transmedial flakes indicating early flake production	≥ 31 mm	High
Mid-stage bifacial core	Minor amount may still be present	May be asymmetrical	> half to all the margin flaked	Comedial and/or transmedial flakes cover face(s)	30–21 mm	High-moderate
Late-stage bifacial core	Nearly or completely absent	Moderate to high symmetry	Margin flaked to standardize edges/platforms	Comedial and/or transmedial flakes cover both faces	20–11 mm	Moderate-low
Preform	Nearly or completely absent	High symmetry	Margin flaked to standardize edges/platforms	Comedial and/or transmedial flakes cover both faces	≤ 10 mm	Very low
Finished bifacial tool	Absent	High symmetry	All of the margin flaked to standardize edges and remove platform remnants	Comedial and/or transmedial flakes cover both faces with edge retouch	≤ 10 mm	Exhausted

[a]Symmetry may be a subjective determination; low: lateral halves are very different from each other; moderate: lateral halves resemble each other with differential proportions; high: lateral halves are almost exactly the same.

[b]Flake tool potential refers to the capacity of the bifacial core to produce a flake of sufficient thickness to make a tool such as a utilized flake, flake knife, scraper, graver, etc.

noted a similar pattern in the point at which regionally distinctive flint-knapping strategies became apparent in Clovis bifaces from the Southeast. It is not until the final stage of the bifacial core's use-life, when it shifts into a preform, that morphological constraints are imposed to prepare it to become a hafted tool. Unique cultural requirements of hafting play a key role in constricting basal morphology (Keeley 1982) in ways that bifacial cores are immune to and that change over time, as demonstrated by projectile point morphology. If this model is accurate, it also predicts that when a biface is cached as a prepared blank or an early- to mid-stage core, we are much less likely recognize unique cultural production strategies because the primary function of the object is to produce flakes—a more generalized technological strategy shared by *many* precontact cultures through time. This is another reason why biface caches are so critically important for research on lithic technology; they often include multiple examples of complete forms for early- to midproduction stages that can be correlated with later stages and finished tools that demonstrate culturally unique flint-knapping strategies.

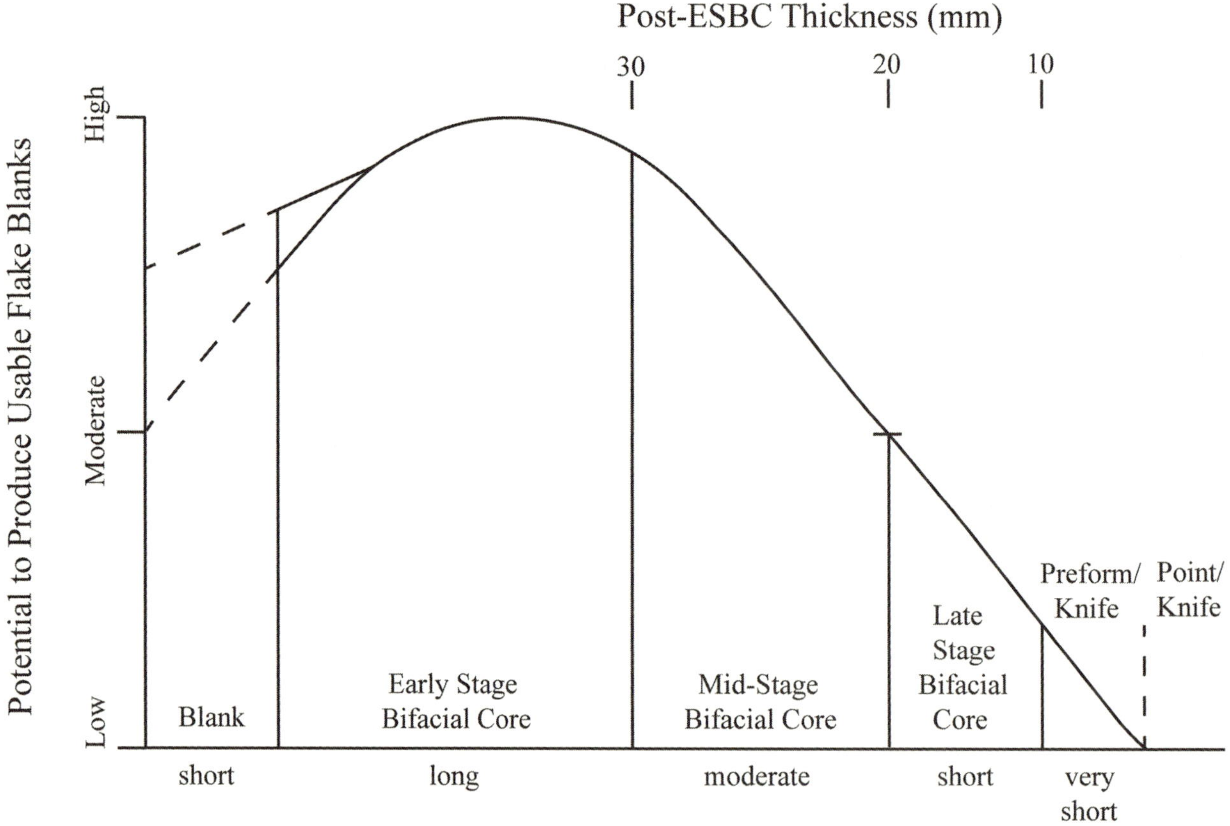

Figure 7.5 Bifacial core use-life curve. X-axis represents use-life phases (longer segments = more time) and y-axis represents potential flake blank production (higher intersect = more flakes).

LATE PREHISTORIC BIFACE KNAPPING STRATEGIES

The Easterday II cache represents a good example of the total bifacial core reduction trajectory employed by Late Prehistoric peoples in northeastern Colorado. Twenty-one of the cores still retain cortex, 76 cores represent varying stages of reduction and flake production, and 2 of the bifaces have been formally shaped (Basham and Holen 2006). The outline shapes of the bifacial cores range from rectangular, to ovoid-rectangular, to oval, to round, and overshot flaking was employed on about 30 percent of the sample. The use of overshot flaking on these Late Prehistoric bifacial cores is important, as Bradley and colleagues (2010) have proposed that this flaking technique—when combined with other production attributes—may be diagnostic of Clovis. Basham and Holen (2006:6) noted a characteristic pattern of core reduction for the Easterday II cache in which flakes on one face were removed perpendicular to the direction of those on the opposite face. This strategy resulted in each side of the biface having a very different flake scar pattern and may have resulted from a method for maintaining a flat overall surface contour. This pattern differs significantly from that observed on the CW cache pieces.

The John Gale biface cache originally included 18 bifaces recovered in 1936, and 17 of those were analyzed in detail and the results later published (Miller et al. 1991). Miller and colleagues (1991) describe the production process as stemming from plano-convex flakes that approximately fit into Stages 2 and 3 of the widely known Callahan (1979) model. The authors describe the bifaces: "Dorsal surfaces generally exhibit more flake removals and flaking sequences than ventral surfaces. . . . Most dorsal scars, however, run perpendicular or diagonal to the long axis, and parallel to each other. Flake scars seldom cross the midline of the biface and hence do not thin the piece, but remove inter-flake ridges and other prominent features that once projected from the blank. . . . Ventral flake removals were used to thin bulbs of percussion and large conchoidal ripple marks" (Miller et al. 1991:48). The manufacturing approach produced generally ovoid, ovate, and oval bifaces with frequent remnants of the original ventral flake surfaces. The presence of remnant ventral flake surfaces has also been occasionally noted on Clovis biface production (Bradley et al. 2010).

The Whiteford and 39CH212 bifaces represent CPT artifacts that were shaped to a completed stage of production and as such are not strictly comparable to the same stages of production exhibited by the CW cache. However, the pieces are large and were made by highly skilled flint-knappers, and Reynolds (1990) provides a detailed description of the method used to make them that also applies to the 39CH212 biface reported by Fosha (1993). The basic production sequence, as described by Reynolds (1990:9–16), started with a thin, tabular piece of Niobrarite (i.e., Smoky Hill jasper) that was reduced via direct percussion, creating a series of flakes that crossed the midline. Overshot flaking was not employed. A series of pressure flakes was then removed along flake arrises to further thin the margins of the biface before one or more rounds of small pressure flakes were again removed from the edges, until an alternately beveled, diamond-shaped knife was produced (Reynolds 1990). The pattern created by this strategy left flake scars that are oriented approximately parallel to each other and consistently perpendicular to the long axis of the piece. Overlapping lateral margins indicate a strongly sequenced flake removal for both the direct percussion and pressure flaking stages.

The three Late Prehistoric biface assemblages share similarities with the CW cache pieces in the form of overshot (Easterday II) and diagonal flaking (John Gale). However, there are also striking differences, such as: different outline forms; the perpendicular orientation of flakes from opposite faces at Easterday II; the use of plano-convex flake blanks at John Gale; and the use of tabular core blanks and highly patterned perpendicular percussion and pressure flake-removal sequences at Whiteford and 39CH212.

PALEOINDIAN BIFACE KNAPPING STRATEGIES

Bradley (1982, 1991, 1993) and Bradley and colleagues (2010) described the general sequence of Clovis flint-knapping techniques used to produce bifacial cores, preforms, and points that applies to many Great Plains and Rocky Mountain sites. Huckell (2007) conducted an in-depth analysis of Murray Springs and Upper San Pedro Valley Clovis bifaces and Smallwood (2012) published a comprehensive morphological analysis of Clovis bifaces from the southeastern United States.

Bradley and colleagues (2010:64) were careful to note that while most Clovis biface manufacture produces debitage and bifaces that "could be found in any number of assemblages world wide," there are certain aspects that even if "not numerically dominant" are "distinctive and even diagnostic." Some of the more culturally diagnostic traits for early-stage Clovis bifaces discussed by Bradley and colleagues include square edge remnants along bifacial margins, end thinning (i.e., flaking the longitudinal axis rather than the latitudinal axis), and distinctive platform preparation combined with overshot (i.e., outré passé) flaking. Huckell's and Smallwood's analyses generally support these observations, with a lesser emphasis placed on the role of overshot flaking as a diagnostic trait.

Bradley and colleagues (2010) stated that 63 percent of their "middle interval" biface sample (e.g., Callahan Stages 3 and 4) have overshot flake scars and end thinning continues to be practiced; however, there does not seem to be a well-patterned sequence for removing large thinning flakes. Huckell (2007) also observed that large flakes removed from the "primary bifaces" at Murray Springs were strategically placed but lacked the sequential pattern evident in the subsequent "secondary bifaces." Smallwood (2012) noted the frequent use of end thinning as a means to remove mass in the early to middle stages of Clovis biface reduction in the Southeast. Despite differences in raw material package size and initial blank shapes, Smallwood recorded increased standardization of morphological ratios for middle-to-late-stage Clovis bifaces from multiple sites and isolated find locales. This standardization indicated a shared basic template for biface reduction strategy throughout the Southeast.

In an earlier publication, Bradley (1993) observed a distinct shift that occurred when Clovis flint-knappers transitioned from using the biface as a core to thinning and shaping the biface into a preform. He stated that compared to the earlier bifacial core stage, once a biface entered the point or knife preform stage, "the flake removal sequence tended to be serial along a single margin, and flake size and spacing was substantially reduced" (Bradley 1993:253). Lacking evidence for a culturally diagnostic Clovis pattern at this stage, Bradley and colleagues (2010:83) recently noted that "there does seem to be a greater than random occurrence of flake removals on single faces that alternate between margins." Huckell's

(2007) Murray Springs analysis also recorded sequential flake removal and reduced size and spacing of flake placement for the secondary bifaces. However, Huckell considered the secondary bifaces as fully functional implements, rather than primarily preforms as Bradley emphasized.

Moving to the Clovis preform stage, Bradley and colleagues describe the following characteristics: "continued use of intentional overshot flaking . . . albeit less frequent, flake scars become smaller but maintain relatively wide spacing and sequencing is still selective and still occasionally alternates. . . . End thinning, by definition, becomes fluting" (Bradley et al. 2010:93). The CW cache late-stage bifacial cores exhibit broad, flat flake scars that thinned and shaped the pieces with notable convergent and diagonal patterns that compare well to Clovis bifaces from the Anzick, Crook County, Fenn, and Simon caches. A pattern that is closer to a serial collateral reduction strategy is present on A5 (the early-stage point preform) and is consistent with similar-stage bifaces from Anzick, Fenn, and Simon. As Figure 7.3 illustrates, a pattern of serial flake removal from the margin is present in a clockwise pattern on one or both faces for A1, A3, and possibly A4 and in a counterclockwise pattern for A2. Biface A5 and one face of A4 are also consistent with Bradley's (1993) observations for the basic Clovis point and/or knife production strategy. The more random flake-removal sequence of A5 and one face of A4 is consistent with a transition from a bifacial core to an early-stage point preform that employs the basic Clovis strategy, as noted above by Bradley and colleagues (2010).

COMPARATIVE ANALYSIS

While the narrative descriptions of bifacial production strategies are informative, a quantitative analysis of knapping patterns was performed to objectively compare the CW bifaces with the Late Prehistoric and Clovis samples. The goal of this analysis was to establish a range of variation for the occurrence of cortex, specific flake-scar patterns, and edge treatments for Clovis and Late Prehistoric bifaces and then compare the CW cache to these results. This study analyzed original artifacts from CW and Easterday II and high-quality casts and published data for Simon and gathered additional data from publications with scaled, black-and-white line drawings of flake-scar patterns for the remainder of the samples (Butler 1963; Fosha 1993; Frison and Bradley 1999; Holen 2002; Miller et al. 1991; Reynolds 1990; Tankersley 2002; Wilke et al. 1991; Woods and Titmus 1985). In the case of assemblages for which published illustrations showed only one face, or for broken bifaces, it is recognized that the nonillustrated face and missing portion may contain additional knapping patterns. Even with this limitation, this study provides a first approximation of the quantitative frequency and associated variation for biface production characteristics that have before now largely been proposed as diagnostic of specific cultures based on qualitative interpretations.

The knapping characteristics analyzed for this study are: presence of cortex; flake patterns, including convergent, comedial, transmedial, diagonal, longitudinal (end thinning), and overshot (outré passé); the presence of square edge remnants; and patterned edge retouch used to both prepare and remove platform remnants (Figure 7.6). Each biface in the analysis was coded for the presence or absence of these characteristics and thus each characteristic was evaluated independently. The single occurrence of a characteristic resulted in the biface being coded with its presence even if it occurred on only one of the two faces. Except for the presence of patterned edge retouch, small marginal flakes that did not penetrate into the interior of the bifaces were not coded; their presence is often ubiquitous and unrelated to larger flake-scar patterning resultant from producing flakes, thinning, and shaping a biface. Coding for the presence of convergent flaking did not automatically result in a positive code for the presence of diagonal and comedial flaking, even if some of the convergent flakes were oriented diagonally to the long axis and many flakes met near the middle of the biface. Convergent flaking was evaluated as an overall pattern rather than by the presence of a single flake occurrence, as is possible with overshot and longitudinal end flaking. Including the 11 CW LSBC specimens, a total of 190 bifaces were used for this study. The Clovis sample includes: 11 MSBC (Anzick = 4, Crook County = 2, Fenn = 2, Fuller = 1, Simon = 2); 57 LSBC (Anzick = 8, Crook County = 5, Fenn = 28, Gosper County = 2, Simon = 14); and 12 preforms (Anzick = 3, Fenn = 2, Simon = 7). To be consistent with the CW cache, all Clovis preforms were nonfluted but may have retained evidence of earlier stage end thinning. The Late Prehistoric sample includes 4 MSBC (all Easterday II); 82 LSBC (Easterday II = 80, John Gale = 2); and 13 preforms (all Easterday II).

The frequencies of occurrence for each biface knapping characteristic were determined for each production stage at a 95 percent confidence interval following methods explained by Drennan (1996, 2004) and converted to proportions before being plotted at a 95 percent confidence interval. Statistically significant differences between the samples can be determined from these plots by comparing the mean of one sample with the error range from the other samples. If the mean of a sample does not intersect the error range of another, then there is a statistically significant difference between the two samples (Drennan 1996, 2004). Figures 7.7 and 7.8 illustrate the results in groups of four. Overall, for the seven biface sample populations, the frequency proportion plots show that at 95 percent confidence there is often a large amount of variability, expressed as error ranges that overlap between the Clovis and Late Prehistoric samples. Fortunately, 8 of the 12 instances of samples with <10 percent error range occurred with the Clovis and Late Prehistoric LSBC samples, which correspond most closely to the CW LSBC sample and serve to strengthen the overall interpretations of the analysis.

The two biface knapping characteristics with the most statistically significant differences between the comparative samples are longitudinal flaking (i.e., end thinning) and the presence of cortex (Figure 7.7). Although Bradley and colleagues (2010) included longitudinal flaking as a diagnostic Clovis trait (when combined with other traits), the results show a lower proportion of longitudinal flaking on the Clovis sample than the Late Prehistoric. The Late Prehistoric bifaces also have a higher proportion of pieces with cortex than Clovis; however, there is a clear trend indicating reduction in cortex frequency as both sample sets move from MSBC through LSBC to the preform stage. In both cases, the CW LSBC sample more closely resembles Clovis and shares a very close similarity in proportion of longitudinal flaking with the Clovis MSBC and preform groups.

The third most marked difference between the samples occurs with the use of convergent flaking (Figure 7.7). The LSBC and preform categories show a statistically significant difference between Clovis and the Late Prehistoric samples. In this instance the CW LSBC error overlaps the Late Prehistoric frequency proportion even though the means are quite different.

Comedial flaking shows a difference in means between the six baseline samples, with significant differences between the MSBC and preform categories for Clovis and Late Prehistoric (Figure 7.7). The CW cache has an error range that overlaps with both, although the mean is closer to the Late Prehistoric mean.

The use of transmedial and diagonal flaking show similar mixed results (Figure 7.8). For both

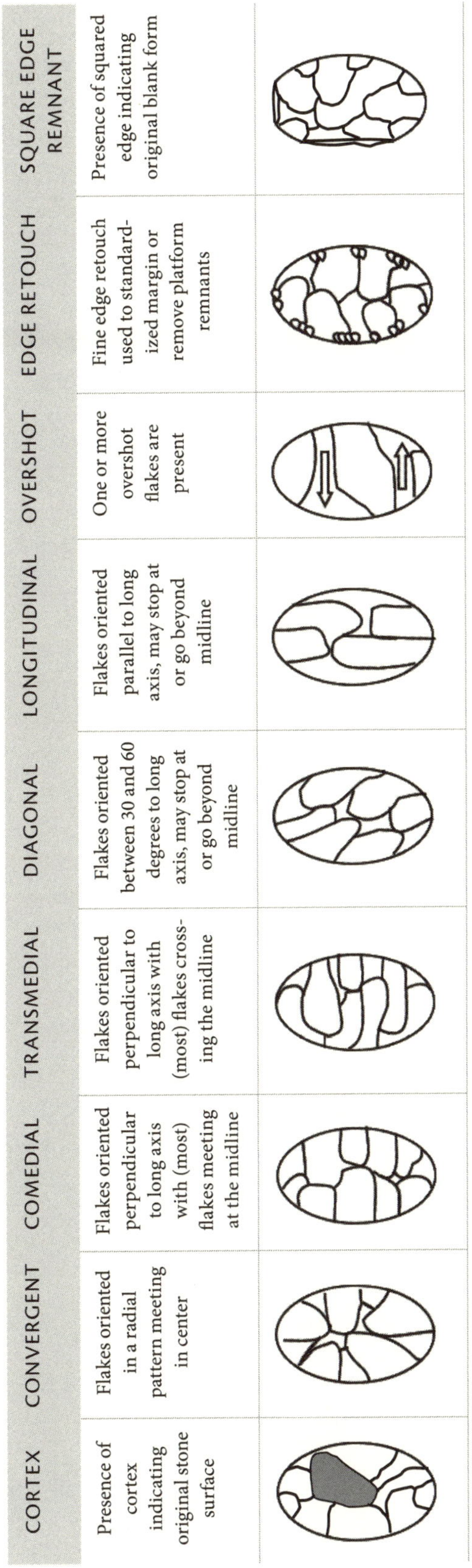

CORTEX	CONVERGENT	COMEDIAL	TRANSMEDIAL	DIAGONAL	LONGITUDINAL	OVERSHOT	EDGE RETOUCH	SQUARE EDGE REMNANT
Presence of cortex indicating original stone surface	Flakes oriented in a radial pattern meeting in center	Flakes oriented perpendicular to long axis with (most) flakes meeting at the midline	Flakes oriented perpendicular to long axis with (most) flakes crossing the midline	Flakes oriented between 30 and 60 degrees to long axis, may stop at or go beyond midline	Flakes oriented parallel to long axis, may stop at or go beyond midline	One or more overshot flakes are present	Fine edge retouch used to standardized margin or remove platform remnants	Presence of squared edge indicating original blank form

Figure 7.6. Definitions for coding presence of flake scar patterns used in this analysis

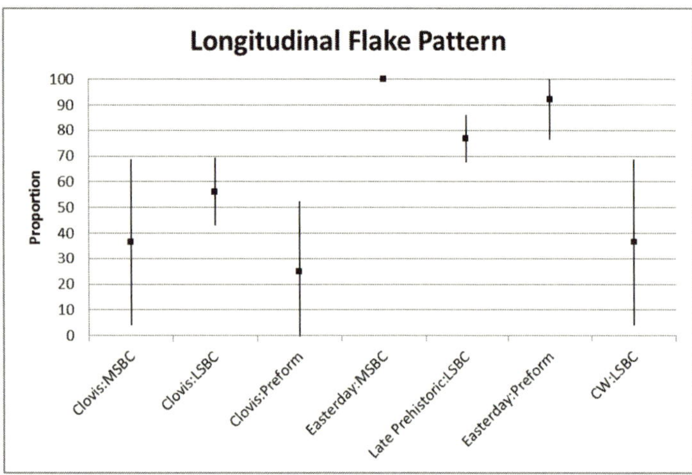

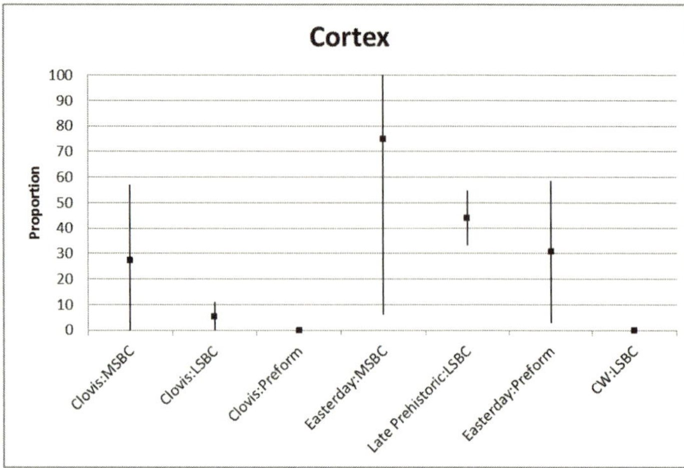

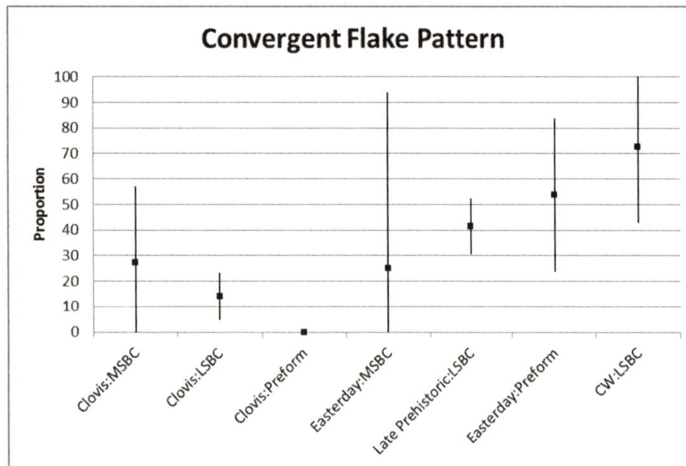

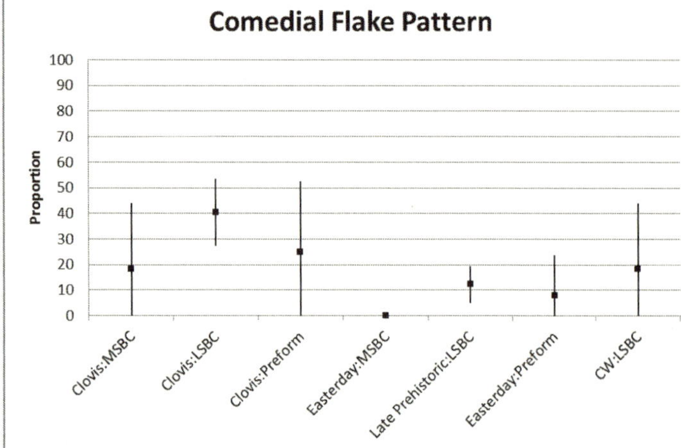

Figure 7.7. Frequency proportions at 95 percent confidence interval for the presence of cortex and longitudinal, convergent, and comedial flake scar patterns

characteristics there are nearly significant differences among the various stage categories; however, the means are often similar enough that even relatively small error ranges result in statistical overlap. The frequency proportion for the CW cache more closely matches the Clovis samples for transmedial flaking and overlaps with both Clovis and Late Prehistoric for the use of diagonal flaking.

The final two characteristics, square edge remnants and overshot flaking, show the most overlap in error ranges and thus indicate the greatest variability in how often these approaches are evident in the Clovis and Late Prehistoric samples (Figure 7.8). Of the two, the mean for the proportional frequency of square edge remnants is slightly higher in the Late Prehistoric sample, whereas the Clovis sample has on average a greater frequency of overshot flaking except in the MSBC category. These results are unexpected in light of Clovis biface analyses that have identified square edge remnants and a greater proportion of overshot flaking as diagnostic traits (e.g., Bradley et al. 2010; Wilke et al. 1991). The CW cache lacks any true overshot flakes and so does not overlap with either of the two comparison groups, but the frequency proportion of square edge remnants is closer to the Late Prehistoric sample than to Clovis.

Overall, these results show two important things. First, biface knapping characteristics such as overshot flaking and the presence of square edge remnants that have been cited as possibly diagnostic of Clovis manufacture strategies fail to show statistically significant differences with the Late Prehistoric sample when frequency proportions are compared at the 95 percent confidence interval. Additionally, evidence for comedial, transmedial, and convergent flaking resulted in mixed outcomes, with some production stages showing clear distinctions and others having similar means and overlapping error ranges. Somewhat unexpectedly, the presence of cortex and the

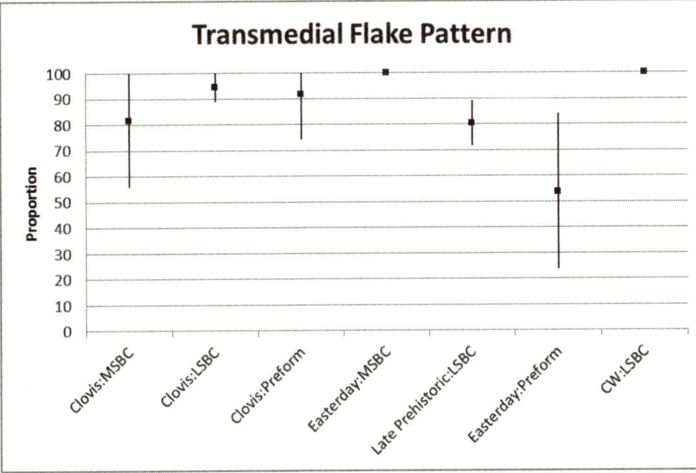

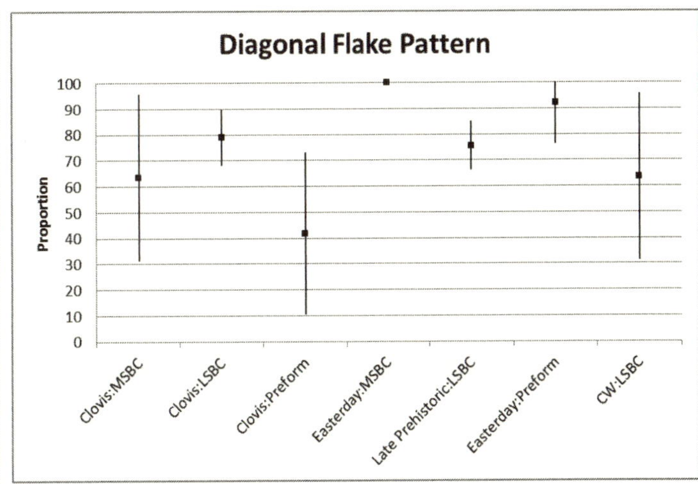

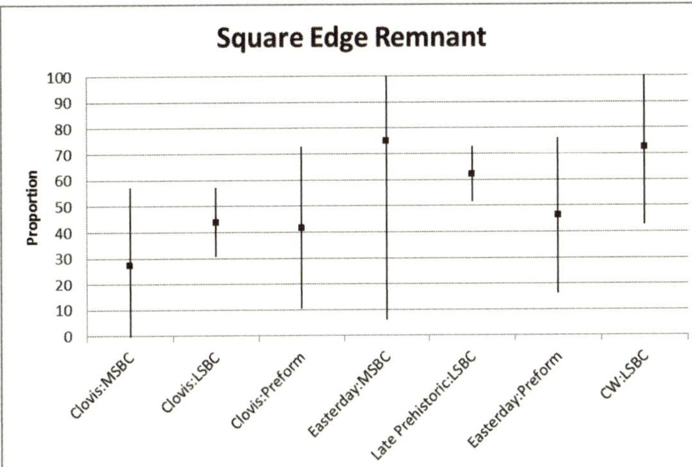

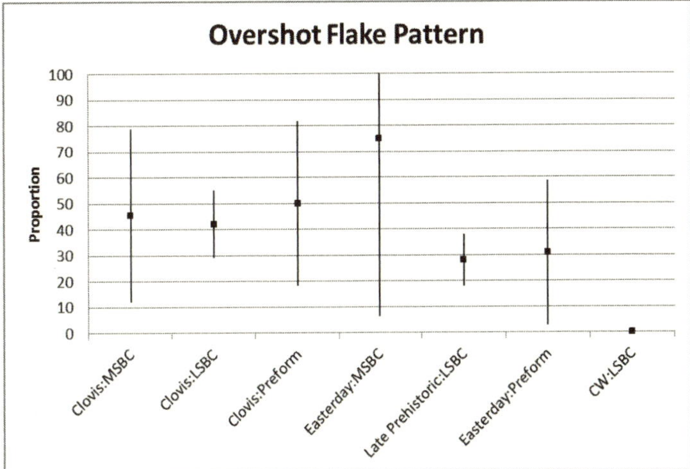

Figure 7.8. Frequency proportions at 95 percent confidence interval for transmedial and diagonal flake scar patterns as well as square edge remnants and overshot flaking

use of longitudinal flaking turned out to be better indicators of Clovis and Late Prehistoric knapping strategies for each biface stage. The second important outcome is that the frequency proportions for the CW cache were more similar to Clovis four times, Late Prehistoric twice, both of them once, and neither of them once as well. Although there is statistical overlap for many of the stages, these results indicate that the CW cache is more similar to Clovis and also show that no single flaking characteristic should be used alone as a culturally diagnostic trait.

MORPHOMETRIC ANALYSES

Flake scar patterning is indicative of different knapping strategies but it does not reflect scalar differences that indicate other important aspects of how bifaces function within a technology. Even if bifacial cores served a similarly flexible role for Clovis and Late Prehistoric knappers, one very important difference is that when the core transitioned into a point preform, the size of the final product varied significantly between the two. The fact that both groups of knappers were creating similar flake-scar patterns should not obscure the potential for significant differences in shape and size that inherently result from cultural decisions about how a point preform is produced. In order to evaluate these potential differences, the following variables were statistically analyzed for the three sample populations: outline form; maximum length, width, and thickness; and ratios comparing length, width, and thickness.

In order to compare the 11 CW cache bifaces to similar-stage bifaces from the Paleoindian and Late Prehistoric comparative samples, bifaces categorized as MSBC, LSBC, and preform were selected, resulting in a total sample of 204 specimens: 16 from Anzick (MSBC = 4, LSBC = 9,

TABLE 7.3. Frequencies of Outline Forms by Culture and Biface Stage

SAMPLE	STAGE	OVAL	OBLONG	OBLONGATE	ELLIPTIC	OVOID	OVATE	LANCEOLATE	DELTOID	TRIANGULOID	TRAPEZOIDAL	SPATULATE	TOTAL
Shapes													
Clovis	MSBC	2	0	0	0	0	3	1	0	1	2	1	10
Clovis	LSBC	7	4	1	3	0	20	21	0	0	1	0	57
Clovis	Preform	0	0	0	0	1	3	8	0	0	0	0	12
CW	LSBC	2	1	0	0	1	7	0	0	0	0	0	11
Late Prehistoric	MSBC	0	1	0	0	0	1	0	1	0	0	1	4
Late Prehistoric	LSBC	22	14	8	5	10	32	0	3	0	0	3	97
Late Prehistoric	Preform	3	2	2	0	0	3	0	2	0	0	1	13
Total		36	22	11	8	12	69	30	6	1	3	6	204

Note: MSBC = mid-stage bifacial core; LSBC = late-stage bifacial core.

Preform = 3); 7 from Crook County (MSBC = 2, LSBC = 5); 32 from Fenn (MSBC = 2, LSBC = 28, preform = 2); 2 from the Gosper County site (LSBC = 2); 22 from Simon (MSBC = 1, LSBC = 14, preform = 7); 97 from Easterday II (MSBC = 4, LSBC = 80, Preform = 13); and 17 from John Gale (LSBC = 17). Pieces lacking complete metric measurements due to breakage or lack of published data were removed from statistical analysis as appropriate for each category.

As with flake scar patterns, outline shapes were standardized for the current analysis to provide a consistent terminology. The basic shapes were taken from botanical terms for leaves as well as standard geometric forms. Each of the bifaces in the analysis was matched to 1 of 11 possible shapes or identified as too irregular for classification. Table 7.3 illustrates the shapes that were represented by the total biface sample and provides the frequency distributions of each; Figure 7.9 illustrates the proportions.

The frequency distribution indicates that the ovate outline form is the most popular for all three subsamples (Clovis, Late Prehistoric, and CW). The next three most frequent outline forms—oval, lanceolate, and oblong, in that order—show a different pattern. The Late Prehistoric sample accounts for 72.4 percent of the oval and oblong sample while Clovis bifaces account for 100 percent of the lanceolate outline form. While the CW cache has three bifaces that are either oval or oblong, it lacks any lanceolate forms. Of the remaining outline forms, the Late Prehistoric sample dominates deltoid (100 percent), oblongate (90.9 percent), ovoid (83.3 percent), spatulate (83.3 percent), and elliptic (62.5 percent), while the Clovis sample dominates trapezoidal and trianguloid (100 percent each), although these final two forms are made up of a very small sample. Generally, the results show a rather clear distribution between a more restricted range of forms favored by Clovis and a wider range of outline shapes utilized more frequently (but not exclusively) by Late Prehistoric knappers. The majority ($n = 7$) of the CW cache falls within the ovate category. Although the remaining four CW bifaces have outlines favored by Late Prehistoric knappers, the overall shape of the proportion curve more closely follows the Clovis pattern. The primary difference between the CW and Clovis curves is that CW lacks lanceolate outline forms.

A comparison of the maximum length, width, and thickness and of ratios of these for the CW cache and the Clovis and Late Prehistoric samples is more revealing than the results of the outline-shape analysis. Figures 7.10–7.12 illustrate scatter plots of length to width, length

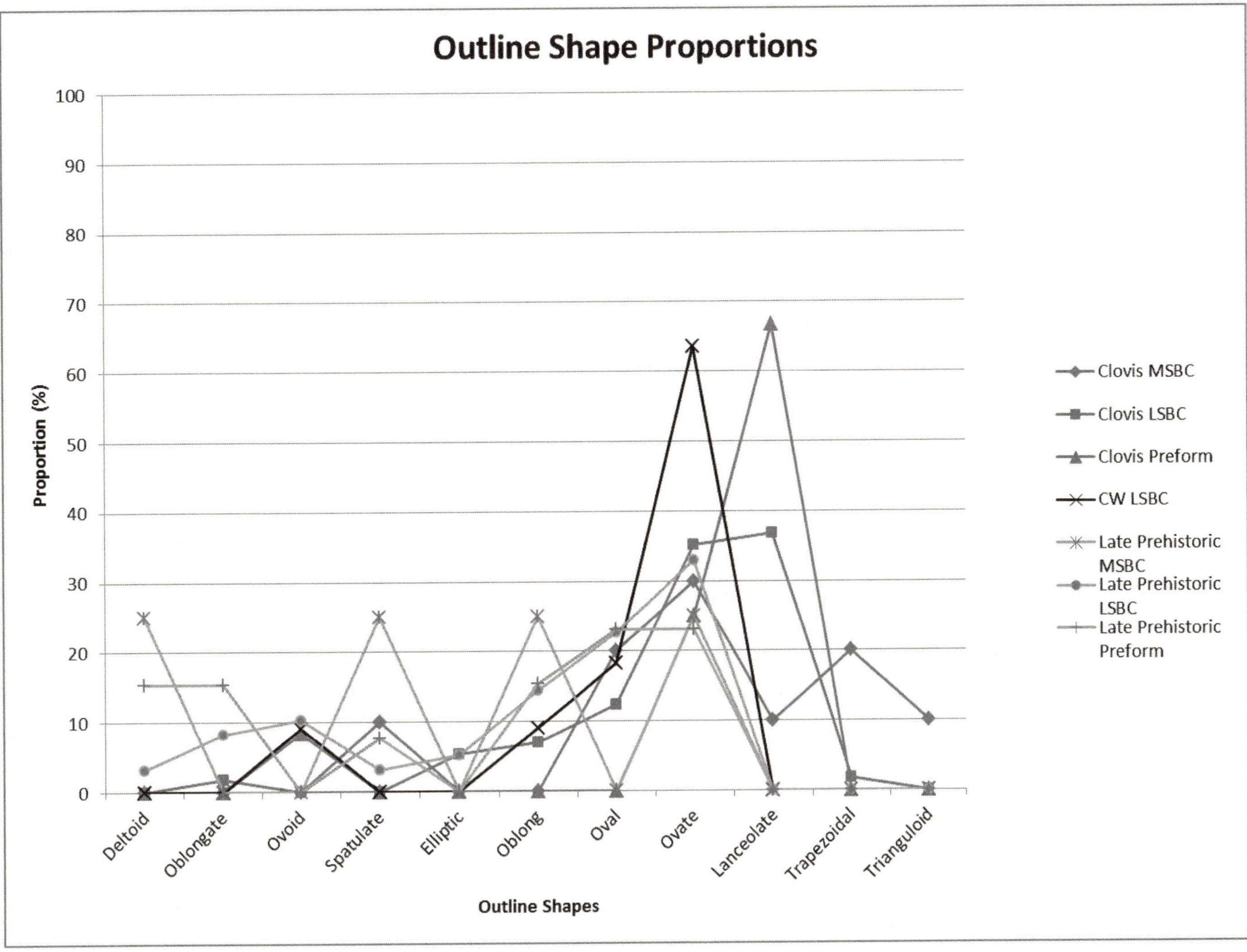

Figure 7.9. Plotted frequency proportions for outline shapes (n = 204)

to thickness, and length to width divided by thickness, respectively. In all plots there is a clear break between the Late Prehistoric sample (on left) and the Clovis sample (on right), and the CW cache consistently clusters with the Clovis sample. The primary factor affecting the distribution is maximum length; the Late Prehistoric bifaces are shorter than the Clovis ones. This pattern probably reflects the restrictions on size imposed by different needs of flake tools and bifaces and may directly result from the difference between minimum acceptable lengths of Clovis spear points and Late Prehistoric arrowheads. There are only one or two specimens from each group that cluster on the other side of the boundary as defined by the straight line in each scatter plot. The Late Prehistoric outliers are two MSBC pieces that represent the longest and thickest specimens; the Clovis outliers are two LSBC pieces from Simon that are the two shortest pieces in that sample. In both of these plots, the CW cache consistently clusters with LSBCs from Crook County, Fenn, Gosper County, and Simon and also with preforms from Anzick and Simon. When comparing all three metric dimensions in the form of a scatter plot for length and width/thickness ratio (Figure 7.12), we see the same outliers for both the Clovis and Late Prehistoric samples. In this plot the CW cache clusters on the Clovis side of the dividing line near LSBCs from Crook County and Fenn and preforms from Simon.

Based on the results of the scatter plots, the CW cache was compared with a series of t-tests against samples from Anzick (LSBC and preform), Crook County (LSBC), Fenn (LSBC), Gosper County (LSBC), Simon (LSBC and preform), Easterday II (LSBC), and John Gale (LSBC). Although the scatter plots indicate a strong similarity between CW bifaces and specific Clovis bifaces, the t-tests were run to evaluate the probability that the similarity in means between the samples could occur through chance

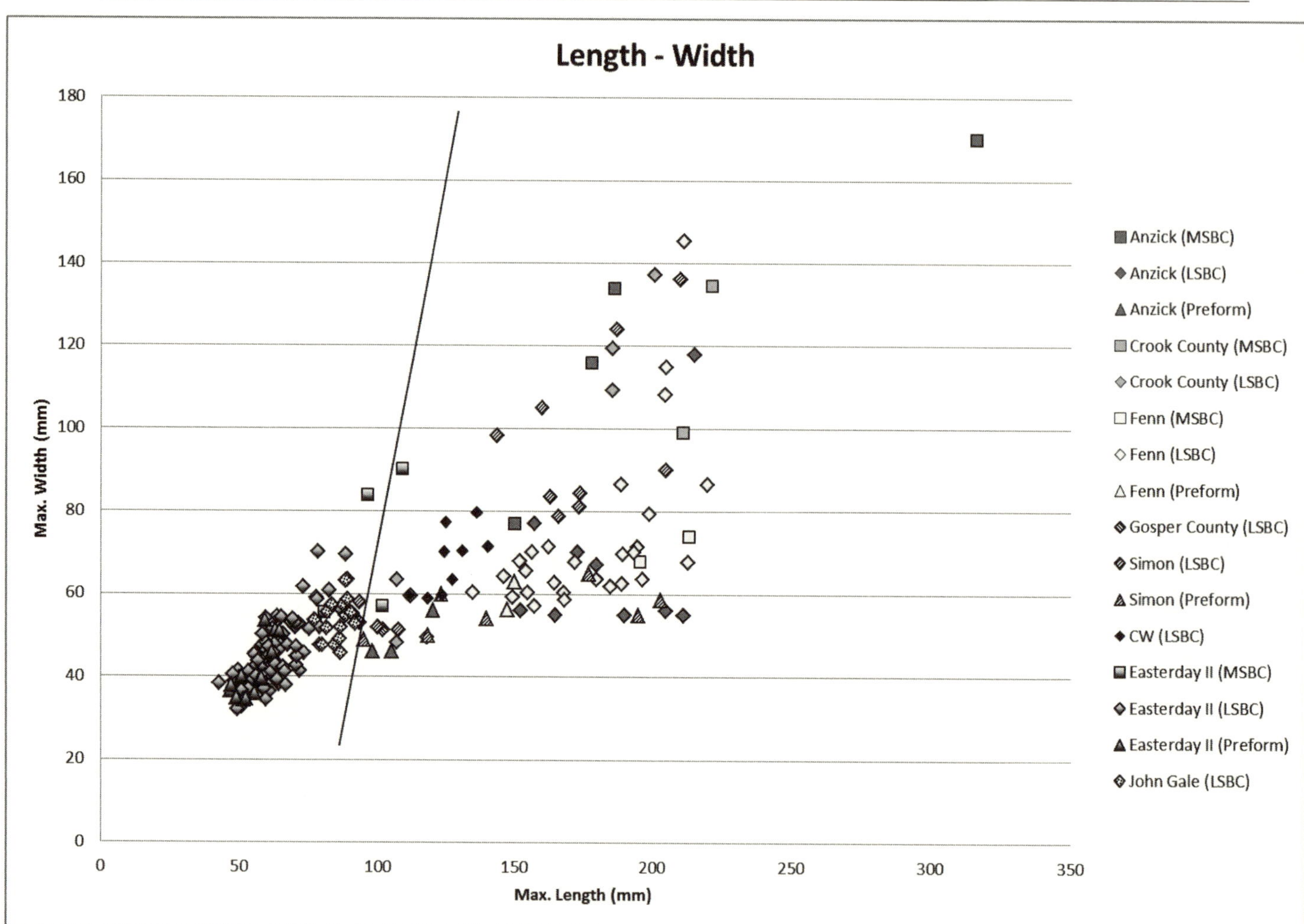

Figure 7.10. Scatter plot for length and width; line separates Late Prehistoric sample (*left*) and Clovis sample (*right*)

alone (Table 7.4). Specimens that lacked accurate dimensional data due to breakage were excluded and all tests were run in Microsoft Excel. The results indicate statistically significant differences in means of at least two of the three metric indices (ratios excluded) between CW and the Anzick preforms as well as between LSBCs from CW and from Fenn, Simon, Easterday II, and John Gale. Given the variability in raw material package size and idiosyncratic flint-knapping behavior, perhaps these results are not that surprising. However, in spite of these two potential sources of variability, the t-tests failed to show any statistically significant difference for length, width, and thickness between CW and Crook County LSBC samples and for width and thickness between CW and Anzick and CW and Gosper County LSBC samples. The lack of significant differences in at least two of the three metric attributes for CW and the three Clovis samples is more suggestive of a Clovis affiliation than the scatter plots alone, given that the scatter plots compare specific individuals while the t-tests compare entire sample populations with cumulative variability.

To evaluate the relationship between metric variables that record specific dimensions (maximum length, width, and thickness) concurrently with ratios that record aspects of overall shape (ratios for width/thickness and length/width), a cluster analysis was conducted on the total sample of bifaces described above. The cluster analysis used an unweighted pair-group average (UPGMA) and a Euclidean distance measure and was run in PAST 2.17. The UPGMA joins clusters based on the average distance between all members in each group and the Euclidean distance is converted to a relative measure of similarity. The results of the analysis are presented in a cladistic diagram with a measure of distance along the x-axis and the individually numbered bifaces oriented along the y-axis (Figure 7.13). A distance measure for any two bifaces is determined by adding the cumulative distance of each vertical branch required to connect the

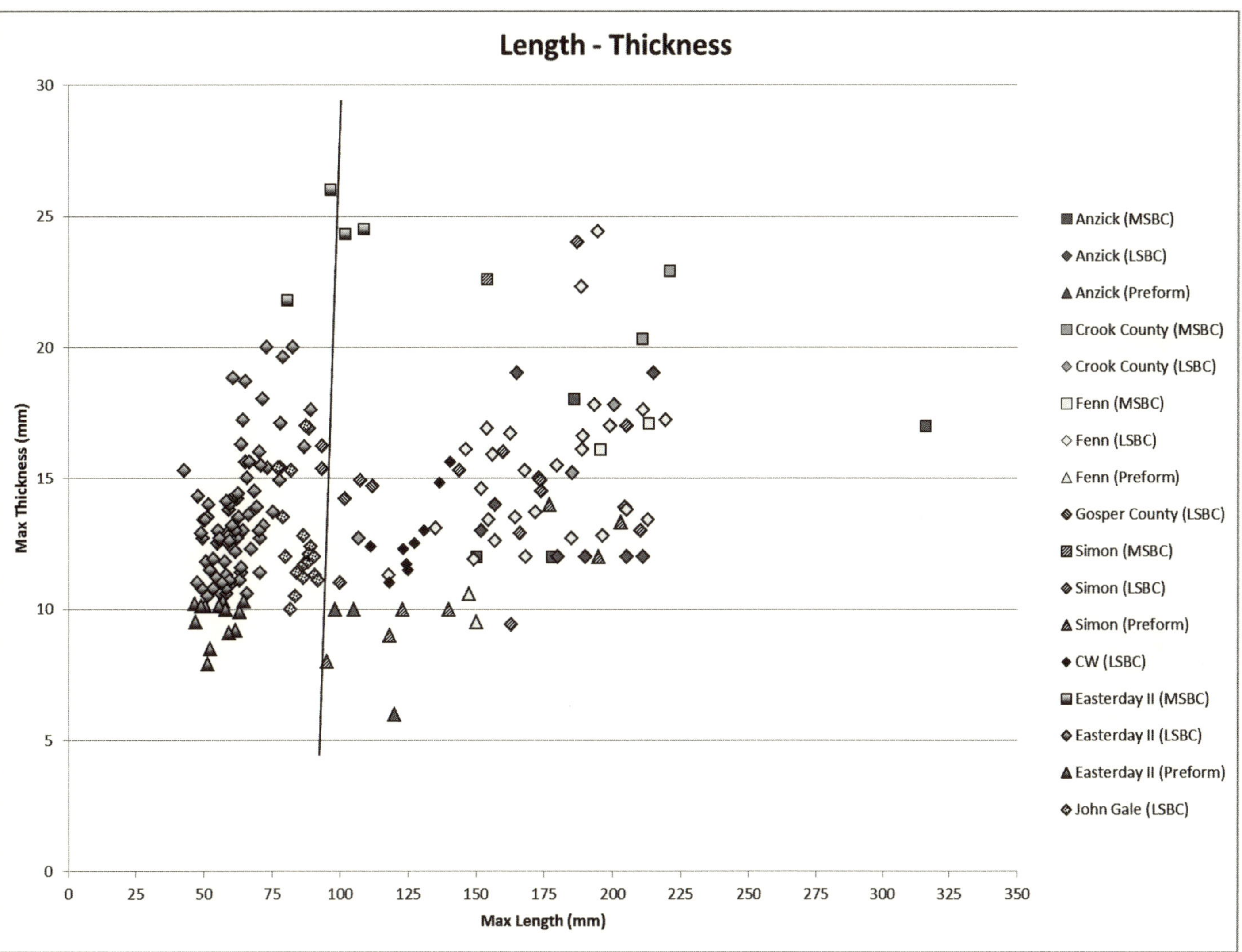

Figure 7.11. Scatter plot for length and thickness; line separates Late Prehistoric sample (*left*) and Clovis sample (*right*)

pieces. Following this method, a distance measure of 440 is the maximum possible distance (MPD) of the two most dissimilar pieces in the total sample.

The cluster analysis resulted in seven main branches. Branch 1 (on left) is populated by all of the John Gale sample, 25 Easterday II LSBCs, and 2 LSBCs from Simon that represent the two shortest pieces from that assemblage. The 44 bifaces of Branch 1 are relatively homogenous with a cumulative distance measure of 36 (8.2 percent MPD).

Branch 2 contains 69 bifaces composed entirely of the Easterday II cache with 56 LSBCs and 13 preforms. The cumulative distance measure is the lowest for any branch on the diagram at 28 (6.4 percent MPD) and is consistent with the interpretation that this biface assemblage may have been made by a single knapper (Basham and Holen 2006).

Branch 3 contains 25 bifaces composed of the most diverse set of sites for any of the branches and includes 9 of the CW cache bifaces. Five CW bifaces are clustered on the leftmost subdivision with a distance measure of only 31 (7.0 percent MPD), indicating tight morphological similarity for the group. All five Clovis sites are included on this branch, with three preforms each from Anzick and Simon and the remainder composed of LSBCs from the other Clovis sites. This is the most frequent occurrence of preforms ($n = 6$) for any of the branches and supports the earlier interpretation of some of the CW bifaces being close to a preform stage. There are also two Easterday II bifaces attached to the right side as an outlying subdivision. The Easterday II bifaces represent the three longest pieces in that sample. The cumulative distance measure for Branch 3 is 76 (17.3 percent MPD) and this drops to 63 (14.3 percent MPD) if the Easterday II outliers are excluded.

Branches 4 and 5 are similar regarding the number of specimens included (12 and 19, respectively), the

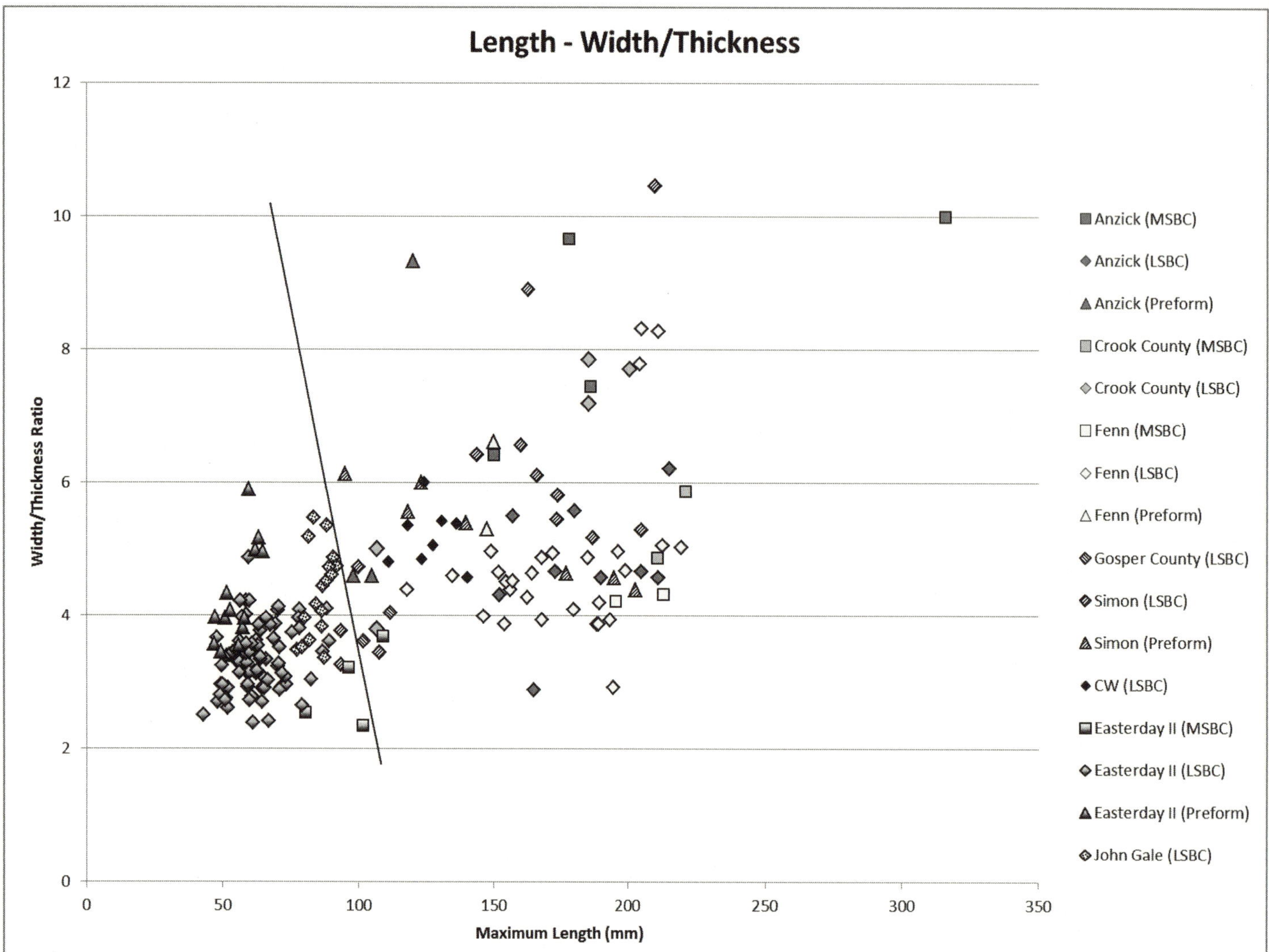

Figure 7.12. Scatter plot for length and width/thickness ratio; line separates Late Prehistoric sample (*left*) and Clovis sample (*right*)

respective distance measures of 60 (13.6 percent MPD) and 64 (14.5 percent MPD), and the sites represented (Anzick, Crook County, Fenn, and Simon). The general distributions of MSBC and LSBC bifaces are also similar, with Branch 5 also having two preforms from Simon. The single biggest difference between them would appear to be that Branch 5 is dominated by Fenn (63.2 percent of the sample) while Branch 4 has a much more even site distribution.

The sixth branch has 33 bifaces and includes the final 2 from CW as well as 16 from Fenn, 9 from Simon, and 6 from Anzick. It is important to note that the second branch where the CW bifaces occur also contains the second-highest frequency of preforms ($n = 4$), with two each from Fenn and Simon. The outlying subdivision on the left side of this branch is made up of three Simon bifaces that represent some, but not all, of the longest pieces from that site sample. Branch 6 has a cumulative distance measure of 70 (15.9 percent) and this drops to 46 (10.5 percent) if the Simon outlier subdivision is removed.

The seventh branch is composed of only two bifaces (MSBC and LSBC) from Anzick and Fenn. These pieces are unusually large and clearly do not fit well with any of the other groups. The cumulative distance measure for this branch is 358 (81.4 percent MPD).

Overall, the cluster analysis demonstrates a clear distinction between Clovis and Late Prehistoric MSBC, LSBC, and preform bifaces for variables related to size (maximum length, width, thickness) and distribution of mass (ratios of width/thickness and length/width). At a gross scale, the diagram shows tightly clustered Late Prehistoric bifaces on the left and more variable, but still rather similar, Clovis bifaces on the right. The cumulative distance measure when the Late Prehistoric Branches 1

TABLE 7.4. Results of t-test at 95 Percent Confidence Interval as *p* Values

CW COMPARED WITH . . .	ANZICK LSBC	ANZICK PREFORM	CROOK COUNTY LSBC	FENN LSBC	GOSPER LSBC	SIMON LSBC	SIMON PREFORM	EASTERDAY LSBC	JOHN GALE LSBC
Length	*0.000*	*0.014*	0.215	*0.000*	*0.019*	*0.048*	0.186	*0.000*	*0.000*
Width	0.980	*0.003*	0.174	0.284	0.068	*0.026*	*0.004*	*0.000*	*0.000*
Thickness	0.237	*0.003*	0.071	*0.002*	0.183	*0.041*	*0.044*	0.311	0.533

Note: LSBC = late-stage bifacial core; italicized p values reject null hypothesis of equality of means.

and 2 are combined is 54 (12.3 percent MPD), whereas the combined measure for Clovis Branches 3–6 is 218 (49.5 percent MPD). In general, one would expect that the Late Prehistoric sample should exhibit less variability since it comprises two sites, whereas the Clovis sample comprises five. With this in mind, it is remarkable how tightly clustered the Clovis sample actually is, and this speaks to the cultural continuity of this technological tradition through time in the study region. Smallwood (2012) found an analogous degree of overall morphological homogeneity within three different regions of the Southeast using a very large sample of Clovis bifaces. The CW cache bifaces cluster with bifaces from all of the Clovis sites in this study and this indicates that they would not appear out of place (morphologically) in any of these assemblages.

CONCLUSION

In the mid-1990s a cache of 11 well-made bifaces and 3 large flakes was recovered by two collectors from private land in northeastern Colorado and was reported to Steve Holen, then curator of archaeology at the Denver Museum of Nature & Science, in 2004. Five of the bifaces were loaned for additional brief study in 2006. Based on the overall morphology of the CW cache bifaces, they were initially categorized as late-stage bifacial cores with at least two nearing early-stage point preforms. The cache artifacts are made from White River Group chalcedony that most probably originated from Flattop Butte, approximately 160 km north of the site. The restricted range of variation in metric attributes, consistency in manufacturing strategy, and use of a single raw material indicate that the CW cache may have been made by a single flint-knapper.

The use of White River Group silicate, evidence of weathering and $CaCO_3$ encrustation, and the geomorphic setting of the find site are all consistent with the CW cache being of Clovis origin. In order to better quantify such an association, this study further examined flake-scar patterns and metric attributes and compared those data against samples of Clovis and Late Prehistoric bifaces in order to determine whether an archaeological cultural affiliation could be substantiated.

An analysis of the flake scar patterns determined that the CW cache was generally more similar to Clovis. However, a surprising outcome was that hallmark traits of Clovis technology—overshot flaking and square edge remnants—were actually used more frequently in the Late Prehistoric sample. More sensitive indicators of culturally specific biface knapping strategies were longitudinal flaking and the presence of cortex, and the CW cache resembled the Clovis sample in these respects. Analysis of outline forms also showed that there was substantial overlap between the samples. While the ovate shape was most preferred by all groups, Clovis bifaces were mainly ovate and lanceolate and were more restricted than the highly variable Late Prehistoric shapes. The CW cache shared some outline forms with both groups but generally had more in common with the Clovis sample.

The metric attributes for length, width, and thickness and the resulting ratios were analyzed with t-tests and a UPGMA cluster analysis. The t-tests indicated that the CW cache is most similar to Clovis LSBCs and preforms. The cluster analysis demonstrated that the CW cache consistently clusters with all of the Clovis sites in the sample and often with Clovis point preforms.

Geomorphic setting, raw material use, flake scar patterning, morphology, and metric attributes all indicate that the CW cache is associated with the Clovis culture. In conjunction with the Drake Clovis cache (Stanford and Jodry 1988), the CW cache provides another important example of Clovis caching behavior on the northeastern Colorado plains. Caching this type of biface assemblage provided flexibility for Clovis peoples in that: (1) the three flakes could have been used for cutting or scraping tools; (2) thinning flakes could have been removed from some of the bifaces to provide additional

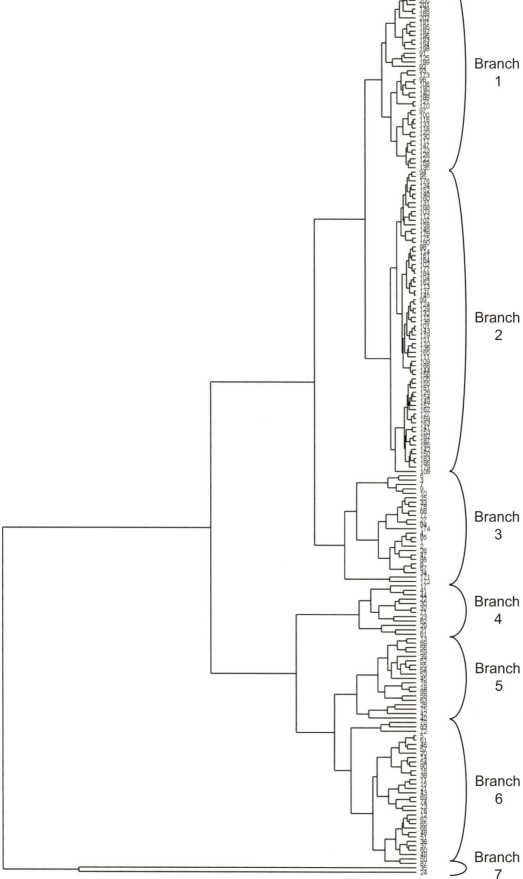

Figure 7.13 UPGMA Euclidean distance cluster diagram for metric attributes and derived ratios. Number labels correspond to: CW = 1–11; Anzick = 12–27; Crook County = 28–34; Fenn = 35–66; Gosper County = 67–68; Simon = 69–91; Easterday II = 92–188; John Gale = 189–204.

cutting, graving, and scraping tools; (3) the bifaces themselves could have been turned into other tools not necessarily on a projectile point trajectory; and, (4) at least 11 large projectile points could have been made from the bifaces in their cached form.

This study serves as an important example of how a surface-collected artifact assemblage lacking a diagnostic projectile point can be carefully analyzed with different techniques to provide multiple lines of evidence for determining an archaeological cultural affiliation. Fortunately, the results of this study all pointed to the same conclusion, and a site that could have been considered a culturally unidentified surface scatter can now be included among the earliest sites in Colorado. Hopefully the analysis presented here will serve as a reminder not to rely strictly on the presence or absence of a single diagnostic artifact class (i.e., projectile point) when evaluating the importance of a site, nor should Paleoindian archaeologists rely too heavily on a single flaking characteristic to identify Clovis. We should instead look at the full suite of production characteristics and any other lines of evidence available to us that may be indicative of cultural affiliations and patterns of ancient lifeways.

ACKNOWLEDGMENTS

This research was made possible by the interest and support of the two private collectors who initially found the site and the landowner who allowed survey and subsurface sampling of the site stratigraphy. The names of these individuals are not listed at their request to protect their anonymity. This study originally began as a joint effort with Steve Holen, then curator of archaeology for the Denver Museum of Nature & Science. He deserves recognition for the very significant contribution he made to further it along and the comments he made on earlier drafts of this paper that served to improve the work. Thanks also to Bruce Huckell and David Kilby for inviting this research into their symposium on Clovis caches and for extending the offer to include it in the final publication. Matt Tornow at St. Cloud State University deserves thanks for his insight on methods of cluster analysis. Any inadvertent omissions or misinterpretations of fact or sources are solely the responsibility of the author.

Chapter 8

But How Do We Know If It's Clovis?

AN EXAMINATION OF CLOVIS OVERSHOT FLAKING OF BIFACES AND A NORTH DAKOTA CACHE

Bruce B. Huckell

Caches offer rare, valuable insights into the ways in which people solved issues of supplying themselves with lithic toolstone and other materials in areas that might lack natural sources or where future foraging activities drawing upon such caches were anticipated. In some cases, culturally diagnostic artifacts were included in the caches, making it possible to link a given cache to a particular culture-historic group and thus allowing insights into how that group organized lithic material procurement, reduction, transportation, and consumption. However, as many of the chapters in this volume show, in the absence of such diagnostics other lines of evidence need to be considered in order to link a cache to a given cultural tradition and its system of technological organization. This chapter considers a large biface cache from North Dakota that, although discovered in 1970, lacked obviously diagnostic artifacts that would permit simple determination of its age and affinity.

The goals of this chapter are four. First, the discovery and later history of what is known as the Beach cache are described, and its assemblage is presented in general terms. Second, approaches to the classification and analysis of Clovis bifaces are reviewed. Third, given the potential value of a technological signature—overshot flaking of bifaces—for identifying Clovis, it is important to explore it more fully and consider analytical approaches to its study. The chapter shows how overshot flaking varies in its expression and develops ways to measure its use. Fourth, using the approaches developed for evaluating overshot flaking, the Beach cache bifaces are analyzed and compared with those from East Wenatchee and Fenn, two undoubted Clovis caches.

RECOGNIZING CLOVIS CACHES

As discussed in the first chapter, it's been 50 years since the first Clovis cache—the Simon cache in south central Idaho—came to archaeological attention (Butler 1963; Butler and Fitzwater 1965). Its recognition as Clovis was straightforward, because it included 5 Clovis fluted points among the 33 artifacts that made up its contents (although see Santarone, Chapter 2 for a current estimate of its assemblage size and composition). By 1985 it was clear that the remainder of the artifacts were bifaces of varying sizes and degrees of reduction (Woods and Titmus 1985). The Simon cache became a sort of standard for northern Plains/Columbia Plateau/Pacific Northwest Clovis caches, and while subsequent discoveries in that region—Anzick (Lahren 2001; Owsley and Hunt 2001; Wilke et al. 1991), Drake (Stanford and Jodry 1988), East Wenatchee (Gramly 1993; Mehringer 1988; Mehringer and Foit 1990), Fenn (Frison and Bradley 1999), Crook County (Tankersley 1998, 2002:104–134)—expanded slightly on the range of artifact forms, all produced Clovis points.

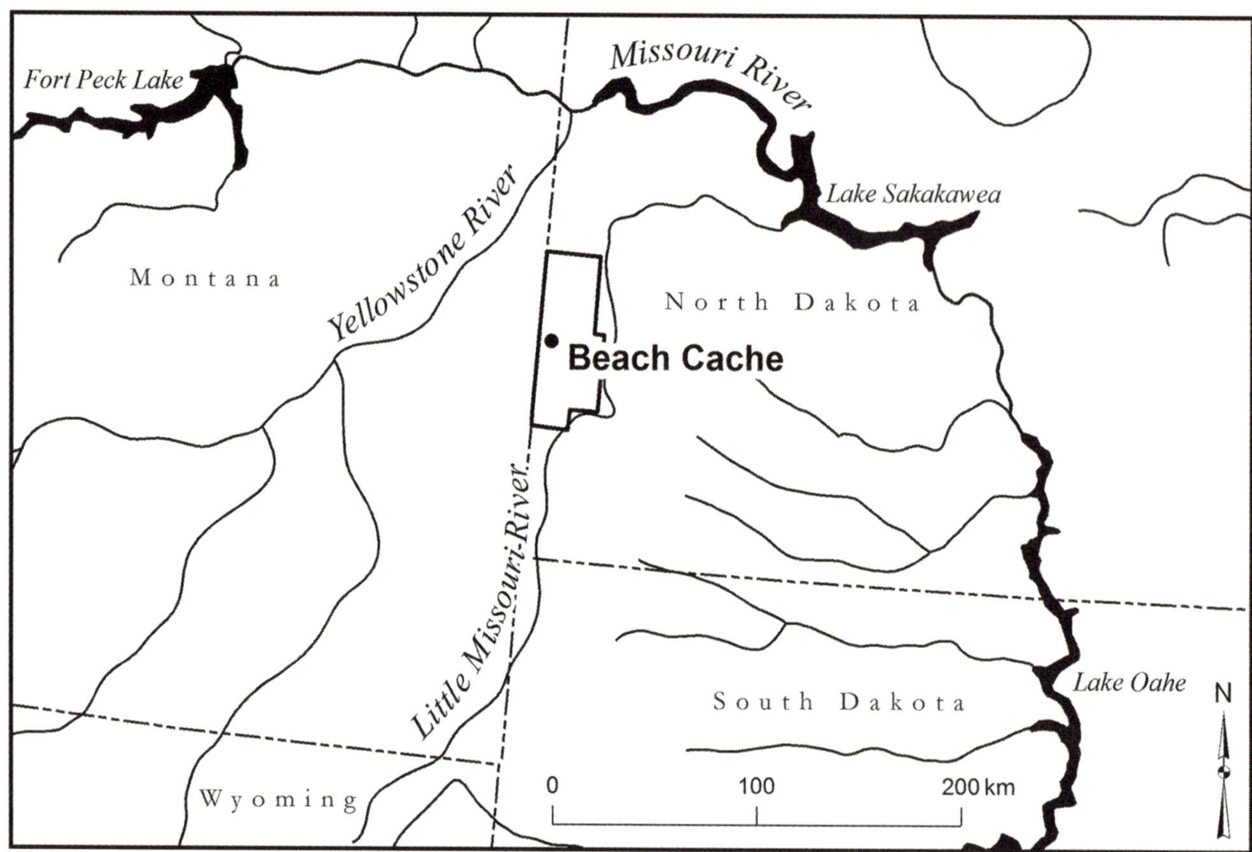

Figure 8.1 Map showing the location of the Beach cache in western North Dakota. Small rectangle around site is Golden Valley County (map created by Matthew G. Hill).

Like other caches discussed in this volume, such as Mahaffy (Bamforth, Chapter 4), Carlisle (Hill et al. Chapter 6), and CW (Muñiz, Chapter 7), the Beach cache is dominated by generalized bifaces and lacks points. The challenge presented by the Beach cache was that although sizeable, it lacked Clovis points; how then could it—and others of similar composition—be attributed to Clovis or any other northern Plains prehistoric cultural complex? In fact, Stan Ahler analyzed a portion of the Beach cache in 1986 (Ahler 1987), and after comparing the bifaces metrically and morphologically to the Simon cache bifaces, he concluded that it wasn't Clovis. However, his analysis occurred shortly before the time when the significance of overshot flaking as a potentially distinctively Clovis technological signature began to be widely appreciated.

HISTORY OF THE BEACH CACHE

During the summer of 2005, Gary Vaughn, who had taken a class on Paleoindian archaeology from me at UNM, sent me an e-mail message about a collection of flaked stone tools owned by his wife's cousin, Alan Miller, a resident of the small town of Beach in southwestern North Dakota, just 3.2 km from the Montana border. Intrigued by a few large bifaces and one apparent blade in images of the cache artifacts, David Kilby and I visited Beach in October 2006.

Like many caches, this one was exposed to the modern world by plowing; it was discovered by Miller in 1970 during a pheasant hunt in a recently harvested cornfield (Huckell and Kilby 2009; Huckell et al. 2011). The site is positioned approximately 16 km northeast of Beach at an elevation of 835 m (2,740 ft) within the rolling prairie that typifies this part of the Missouri Plateau (Figure 8.1). The first artifacts he found were a few meters below the crown of an east-west trending ridge, on its south-facing slope, within the headwaters region of a tributary to Elk Creek. Over the next five years he collected 55 artifacts, 53 of them generalized bifaces and the other 2 blades (Figure 8.2a). Most of these he found as scattered specimens in the plow zone, but 8 or 10 (including one blade tool) came from a single, small pit near the crown of the ridge. In

Figure 8.2a. Miller sample of the Beach cache artifacts (2006 photograph). Bifaces on the dark cloth to the left are all WRGS; bifaces on the light cloth to the right are of multiple raw materials, including quartzite (lower two rows).

Figure 8.2b. Abernethy sample of the Beach cache artifacts (1975 photograph, taken by Ted Trinka the day that they were excavated)

1975 Don Abernethy, the landowner, and some friends discovered and dug up another 80 bifaces in the same area explored by Miller (Figure 8.2b); it is likely that these artifacts were an undisturbed portion of the same cache. Thus, approximately 135 artifacts made up the cache. One of Abernethy's friends and a participant in the discovery, the late Bob Jagd, recalled in 2007 that the artifacts came from 8–10 pits, each the "size of a volleyball," which were concentrated within an area some "4–5 yards" in diameter. Each pit contained 8 or 10 artifacts, he told us. Over the years since the mid-1970s several attempts by Miller and Abernethy to learn about the age and affinity of the artifacts they had found essentially came to naught, because the archaeologists to whom they showed the bifaces did not know what to make of their age or function.

We examined both Miller's and Abernethy's collections, photographing, measuring, and recording the attributes of flake scars on each artifact. Many of Miller's artifacts came from the plow zone and were broken or damaged by plowing; very few of those in Abernethy's collection exhibited damage from cultivation. We observed overshot-terminated flake scars on many of the bifaces, a feature suggesting that they were potentially Clovis; a single retouched blade tool and an unretouched blade also supported this assignment. After handling and analyzing the 100 or so extant artifacts, we were struck by the range of variation in size and shape. There were certainly large bifaces similar in size and flaking to those we'd handled in other Clovis cache assemblages, but over half were small, variable in shape and flaking, and if found alone, most likely wouldn't be called Clovis.

Beach Cache Artifacts

The artifacts recovered from the cache at the time we first recorded them in 2006 are listed by type and raw material in Table 8.1. Originally a total of approximately 135 were recovered, but by 2006 that number had been reduced as some of Abernethy's artifacts were sent off to museums or universities and never returned, or were given as gifts. We documented 98 bifaces, only 4 of which exhibited lateral margins regularized by finer flaking; most displayed large percussion flake scars, often with intact negative bulbs of percussion, and uneven margins. Seven different lithic material types were identified, including White River Group silicates (WRGS; Hoard et al. 1993); Rainy Buttes silicified wood (RBSW; Loendorf et al. 1984); quartzite, some most likely from Spanish Diggings (Dorsey 1900; Reher 1991) or some of the Black Hills outcrops (Church 1999; Miller 2010), or a mix of the two; dark chalcedony (probably silicified lignite but not Knife River flint, based on lack of fluorescence); and agate and chert from unknown sources. Hartville chert (Miller 2010) was represented by a single retouched blade tool (Figure 8.2a, specimen to left of large broken biface in upper right). Nearly all of the artifacts displayed well-developed patina on one surface and, unless removed by cleaning, a 0.5–1.0 mm thick coating of calcium carbonate and carbonate-cemented sediment on the

TABLE 8.1. Artifacts from the Miller and Abernethy Samples Making Up the Beach Cache

LITHIC MATERIAL TYPE	BIFACES (COMPLETE)	BIFACES (FRAGMENTARY)	BLADES/FLAKES	TOTAL
Agate	1			1
WRGS	53	5		58
Chert (unsourced)	3			3
Dark chalcedony	9	2	1	12
Hartville Uplift chert			1	1
Petrified wood	3			3
Porcellanite	3			3
Quartzite	5	7		12
RBSW	7	1		8
Total	84	15	2	101

Note: WRGS = White River Group silicate; RBSW = Rainy Buttes silicified wood.

opposite surface. This differential weathering and secondary carbonate accumulation demonstrated that the artifacts had lain buried in the same position for an extended period of time, presumably from their deposition in the pits until they were disturbed by cultivation in the 1970s. Further, some artifacts with patinated surfaces had large patches where the patina was absent; we suspect that such gaps in the patina reflect instances where one artifact partially overlay another, protecting it from the percolating, probably slightly acidic, water that promoted patination.

The four bifaces that display finer retouch include one large porcellanite knife (Figure 8.3a; also see Figure 8.2b, second row of artifacts nearest the camera position), two large quartzite midsections (Figure 8.3b, c), and one smaller quartzite specimen (Figure 8.3d). The porcellanite biface is 263.1 mm long, 80.2 mm wide, and 13.2 mm thick, and it displays a slight asymmetry, with one convex margin and one nearly straight one; it is percussion flaked and exhibits extensive fine marginal retouch. The two large midsection fragments—one 142 mm long and the other 154 mm long—and the smaller (86 mm long) specimen missing one end are symmetrical. All three are percussion flaked and their margins evened by selective pressure flaking. It is tempting to view the midsection fragments as parts of projectile points, but they lack any indications of fluting or margin grinding and the transverse snap breaks are not necessarily the result of impact damage. They are therefore classified as possible bifacial knives. The small biface also lacks any indications, such as margin grinding, that it served as a projectile point; it is also classified as a small bifacial knife. Based on current knowledge, none of the four are obviously diagnostic of Clovis or any other cultural complex, although Frison (1982c:Figures 2.91A and B, specimens a and b) illustrates a biface similar in size and morphology to the small Beach biface as well as a fragment of a large biface, both from the Sheaman Clovis site. The larger one displays what appears to be fine pressure retouch along one margin, perhaps suggesting that it was a knife similar to the large Beach specimen shown in Figure 8.3a.

The retouched blade tool (Figure 8.2a, right-hand group, third artifact right of scale) is made of Hartville Uplift chert. It is 146.3 mm long, 26.3 mm wide, and 20.1 mm thick. It has a small, bifacially prepared (faceted) ground striking platform and displays extensive, invasive unifacial retouch along one lateral margin and finer retouch or damage along the other. It is triangular in cross section, and the distal portion of the exterior ridge shows a series of flakes designed to straighten it.

The remainder of the bifaces and biface fragments display considerable variation in size and flaking (Figure 8.2). In general the WRGS bifaces are smaller and the quartzite and porcellanite ones are larger. Figure 8.4 shows a scatter plot of the length and width dimensions for each complete biface (n = 83) that demonstrates this distribution of size by raw material. Neutron activation analysis has shown that the WRGS bifaces are derived from an exposure of small nodules atop Sentinel Butte, a prominent landmark approximately 19 km south of the cache site (Huckell et al. 2011). The nodules there are generally small (5–10 cm in maximum dimension), although occasional larger, more tabular pieces may be up to 30 cm in maximum dimension. Both RBSW and Spanish Diggings or Black Hills

Figure 8.3. Finished bifacial artifacts in the Beach cache: (a) knife; (b) and (c) point or knife fragments; (d) small knife.

quartzite, by contrast, are available in larger initial piece sizes from their primary source areas, approximately 85 km and 250–500 km to the south, respectively (Church 1999; Loendorf 1984; Reher 1991). Thus, some of the variation in the Beach cache bifaces is likely the product of raw material piece size. Some of the quartzite bifaces (Figure 8.2a, right side, lower row), one of the porcellanite bifaces (Figure 8.2a, specimen at upper right), and one of the WRGS bifaces (Figure 8.2a, left side, second row from top, second specimen from right) are of asymmetrical form, with one convex margin and one straighter margin. They resemble the finished knife (Figure 8.3a) and may be preforms for similar knives. In addition, they are similar to large, asymmetrical bifaces from the Fenn (Frison and Bradley 1999:Plates 54, 55), Anzick (Wilke et al. 1991:Figure 2), Simon (Butler 1963:Figures 4a–c), Busse (Kilby 2008:Figure 13, specimen right of artifact 10), and de Graffenried (Collins et al. 2007:Figures 3, 4) caches.

CLOVIS BIFACE MANUFACTURE

It is common for archaeologists to apply more specific descriptive terms to bifacially flaked artifacts, usually predicated on an assessment of what purpose the biface was intended to serve or what its position may have been in a sequence of reduction "stages" leading to a finished artifact (Shott 1996). These terms include commonly used standards such as "blank," "preform," and "biface core." More specifically for what he termed the Eastern U.S. fluted point tradition, Callahan (1979) proposed a system of five specific biface "stage" designations (1 = obtaining the blank, 2 = initial edging, 3 = primary thinning, 4 = secondary thinning, and 5 = shaping), based on archaeological evidence and his experimental replication studies. These stages were differentiated based on increasing regularity in morphology and facial flatness coupled with decreasing width/thickness ratios. Four additional stages (6–9) were added for Clovis point manufacture from a Stage 5 biface. Sanders (1990: 23), in his analysis of the Adams site in western Kentucky, reduced the number of stages to seven from Callahan's nine; however, the first five stages of his scheme are identical to Callahan's.

In their study of the Simon cache, Woods and Titmus (1985) identified three reduction sequences leading to larger (Sequence A, >12 cm) and smaller (Sequence B, <12 cm) Clovis points and another (Sequence C) that entailed manufacture of very large bifaces. Sequences A and B each contained discrete manufacturing stages based on

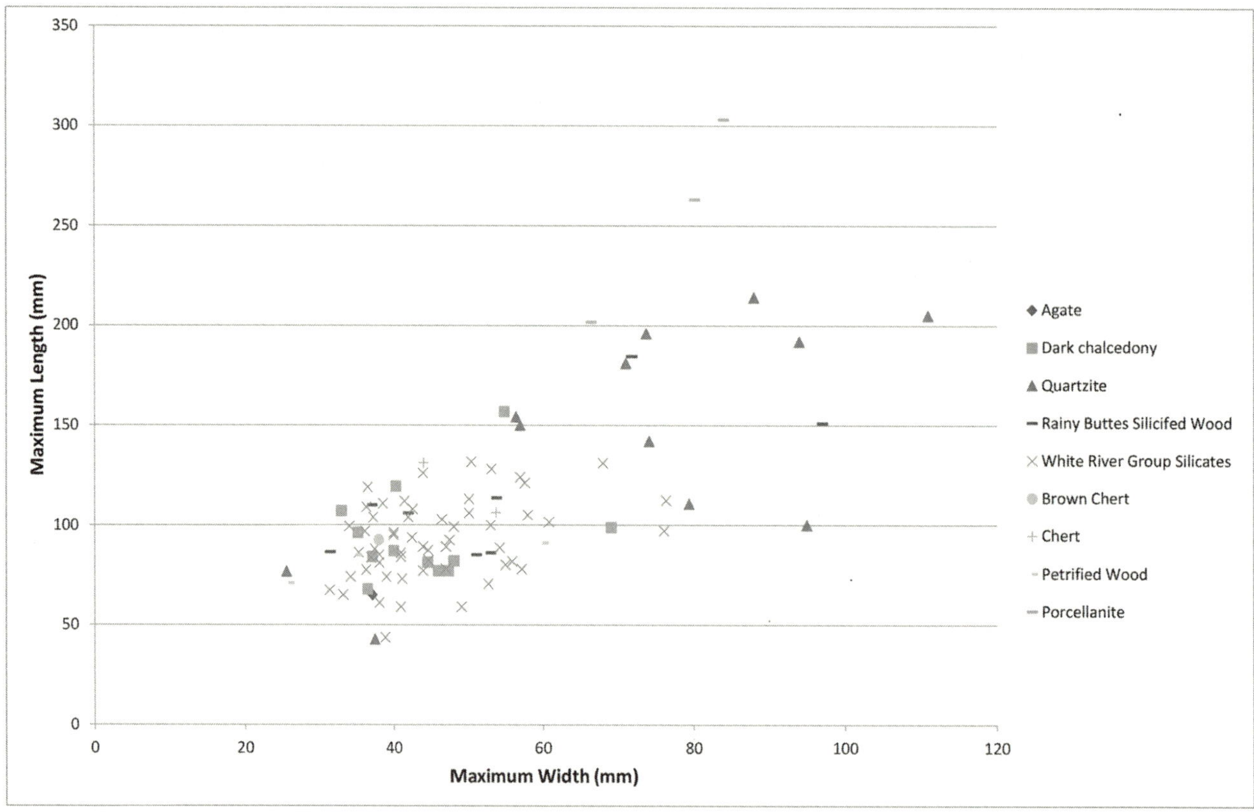

Figure 8.4. Scatterplot of length and width of complete Beach cache bifaces by lithic material type

"overall symmetry, margin morphology, width/thickness ratios, number of flakes per tool face, and characteristics of the negative bulb of force" (Woods and Titmus 1985:3–4).

Wilke et al. (1991) used a less detailed classification system to categorize the Anzick cache bifaces, including "bifacial flake core," "percussion-flaked bifacial blank," and "percussion- and pressure-flaked bifacial preform"; these forms were linked together by a reduction sequence beginning with the bifacial flake core (an "immediate" reduction strategy geared toward the manufacture of large biface reduction flakes for tool production) and ending (an "ultimate" strategy) with the production of a Clovis point.

A two-category system of "primary biface" and "secondary biface" has been proposed for archaeological specimens from the Murray Springs site (Huckell 2007), with larger, primary bifaces being episodically reduced to smaller (secondary) bifaces and ultimately Clovis points. Primarily for the Gault site but including other western Clovis sites, Bradley and his collaborators (2010) developed and employed a three-part division of "early interval biface," "middle interval biface," and "late interval biface," the latter being equivalent to a Clovis point preform. They employ "interval" to describe the biface product of a reduction "phase," which they define as the biface and its by-products (debitage). "Phase" is, in their view, different from and preferable to "stage" for discussing a reduction continuum, although the distinction seems minor.

A separate study of lithic artifacts from another portion of the Gault site was reported by Waters, Pevny, and Carlson (2011). They described an assemblage of bifaces from the site that they divide into primary bifaces, secondary bifaces, preforms, and completed points. The distinctions among these categories are predicated on "metric data, plan view and cross-section morphology, edge sinuousity, presence of cortex, degree of platform preparation and edge beveling, flake-removal techniques, flaking pattern, flake-scar morphology, and the presence or absence of final endthinning, commonly referred to as fluting" (Waters, Pevny, and Carlson 2011:84). Primary bifaces are larger, more cortical, thicker, and less refined than secondary bifaces; preforms are more regular in size and cross section and the base has been fluted, but the final shaping and edge grinding that appear on completed points are absent from preforms.

Finally, Smallwood (2012), in an analysis of bifaces from three Eastern U.S. fluted point sites (Topper,

Carson-Conn-Short, and Williamson), divided bifaces into early, middle, and late reduction stages, utilizing such attributes as presence/absence of cortex, extent of flaking, edge sinuosity, flake removal technique, and flaking index.

All of these classificatory typological approaches share the underlying assumption that the bifaces are parts of a predictable, staged reduction sequence leading from an initial larger bifacial form to the manufacture of a Clovis point. Given the differences in size among the Beach cache bifaces, as well as among the four finished bifaces in the sample, it is not clear whether such an assumption is valid for the Beach cache, so these artifacts are treated here as an assemblage of undifferentiated "bifaces," without attempting any technological or typological subdivision. The same approach will be used in comparing bifaces from the Fenn and East Wenatchee caches to the Beach specimens.

To further characterize and describe the technological features of the Beach bifaces, it is necessary to delve into the particulars of overshot flaking, to explore the variation in the employment of this remarkable knapping strategy, and to examine its linkage to Clovis. The following section discusses overshot flaking and offers some analytical terms and conventions for investigating this phenomenon. Next overshot flaking as seen on the Beach bifaces is described and then compared to that on bifaces from Fenn and East Wenatchee, undoubted Clovis caches that I have been able to study in detail. A final section offers an independent line of evidence of cultural-temporal context from 2007 through 2012 excavations at the Beach cache site.

OVERSHOT FLAKING CONSIDERED

The detachment of a flake that terminates by overshooting and removing a portion of the edge or end of the objective piece opposite the platform is well known among knappers and is often accompanied by profanity rather than feelings of satisfaction. Such flakes were recognized as "outrepasse" by Jacques Tixier in 1963 (Tixier 1974) in the Old World and by Don Crabtree (1972:80) a few years later in the New World, who applied the term to flakes removed from both cores and bifaces. "Overshot termination" was introduced by Callahan (1979) in his study of biface knapping in eastern U.S. fluted point industries, and I follow his usage here. As it pertains to the bifaces considered in this study, "overshot" refers to a flake struck from one margin that travels, or was intended to travel, completely across the piece and removes some portion of the opposite margin. It should be noted that "partial overshot flakes" has been proposed by Dickens (2007) to describe flakes that remove part but not all of thick, typically cortical, square edges on some bifaces (see Waters, Pevny, and Carlson 2011:Figure 54). This category is not used herein.

Experiments by Callahan (1979) and Dibble and Whittaker (1981) were the first to isolate the conditions necessary for the production of overshot-terminated flakes. Dibble and Whittaker, who studied flake production in a controlled laboratory setting, discovered that overshot terminations were probable with large exterior striking platform angles (those with a mean of 76.7 degrees, ranging from 67.3 to 86.1 degrees). Subsequent experimentation also suggested that overshot terminations were linked to greater platform depths or thicknesses (Dibble and Pelcin 1995; Dibble and Rezek 2009:1950). These experiments were done on glass, flaked with ball bearings by Hertzian fracture, which differs significantly from the bending fracture that occurs with biface manufacture (Cotterell and Kamminga 1987). Callahan, discussing results from his hands-on knapping experimentation with biface manufacture, found overshot flakes to result from (1) bevel (exterior platform) angles greater than 75 degrees; (2) striking "too straight in," and/or (3) striking "with too much force over a gently convex surface" (Callahan 1979:86). Positioning the striking platform slightly below the center plane (a plane created by the intersection of the two surfaces of the biface, marked by the margins) of the biface, toward the side from which the flake will be detached, also enhances the probability of removing flakes with overshot terminations (see Callahan 1979:Table 11c). Note that these studies all suggest that exterior platform angle plays a critical role in overshot flake removals, regardless of the type of fracture. It is important to recognize that the variables discussed here—exterior platform angle, angle of blow, force of blow, and position of platform relative to the biface center plane—are, to a large extent, controlled by the knapper, which in turn means that they can be manipulated intentionally to facilitate the production of overshot flakes.

Until the early 1980s, overshot-terminated flakes were viewed as knapping errors; Callahan (1979:86, 111–112, 149–150) offered several tips on how to avoid producing them during biface manufacture. Bradley's (1982) study of refitted debitage from the manufacture of a biface at the Sheaman (Wyoming) site suggested that repeated, controlled overshot flaking had been done intentionally by Clovis knappers. Since then, overshot flaking has been recognized on bifaces from multiple Clovis sites across North America (for examples, see Bradley 1982; Bradley et al. 2010; Frison and Bradley 1999; Huckell 2007; Sanders 1990; Waters, Pevny, and Carlson 2011; Yahnig 2004) and potentially as far south as northern Venezuela (Pearson and Ream 2005). The manifestation of overshot flaking on Clovis bifaces and points has been treated in some detail from the Gault quarry/workshop site (Bradley et al. 2010:68–77; Waters, Pevny, and Carlson 2011:103–112), and the abundance of overshot flaking suggests that it was a commonly employed technique. For example, Waters, Pevny, and Carlson (2011) reported that 21 percent of both primary and secondary bifaces from Gault Excavation Area 8 exhibited overshot flaking, and 79 complete and distal fragments of overshot flakes (plus 58 partial overshot flakes) were also recognized among the biface reduction debitage. Bradley et al. (2010:Table 3.1) reported that 61 percent of all bifaces they examined from a sample of bifaces from Gault and caches exhibited at least one overshot flake. If overshot-terminated flakes were the result of random knapping errors, they should be expected in frequencies no greater than 5 or at most 10 percent across an assemblage.

Overshot flaking has also been recognized in later Paleoindian site assemblages, including Midland and Agate Basin contexts at the Hell Gap site (Bradley 2009b, 2010). Further, although bifaces manufactured by later groups may show occasional overshot flakes, there is at present no evidence that post-Clovis knappers regularly used controlled overshot flaking as a manufacturing strategy to the same degree that Clovis knappers did. Thus, particularly when considered in light of the fact that its successful application involves manipulation of striking platform variables, surface topography, and applied force, the potential value of overshot flaking as a biface knapping strategy diagnostic of Clovis may be appreciated. This is not to say that it was the sole technique by which Clovis biface reduction proceeded, as noted by several investigators (Bradley 1982; Bradley et al. 2010; Callahan 1979; Huckell 2007; Waters, Pevny, and Carlson 2011; Wilke et al. 1991; Woods and Titmus 1985). Other approaches to biface reduction have been identified, and in addition to overshot flakes Bradley and colleagues (2010:Figure 3.11) identify such flake types as overlapping (transmedial), full-face, diving, end thinning, comedial, invasive, and marginal. These flake types may correspond in general to other approaches to flake removal that have slightly differing goals or that represent different solutions to the problems associated with the manufacture of a biface with regularity in form, cross section, desired width/thickness ratio, facial regularity, and basal (or tip) thinning. Fuller discussion of these flake types and approaches is outside the scope of this study, however, and it is overshot flakes that are the focus.

Variation in Overshot Flaking

It is unfortunately the case that most often overshot flaking is simply reported to be present on artifacts at a site, and little or no detailed description of its frequency or variation in its application is presented. Recognition of overshot flaking is more complicated than it might first appear, both because of variation in the successful execution of overshot flaking and due to the effects of continued reduction after removal of an overshot-terminated flake. In the first instance, although the intent may have been to detach an overshot flake, flakes struck from one margin may not always reach and remove the opposite margin. This may be due to some slight flaw in execution on the part of the knapper, including platform construction or the angle at which or force with which the blow was struck, or the response of the lithic material to the blow. Second, subsequent knapping may remove the distal overshot termination and/or the proximal portion of the scar (see Bradley et al. 2010:72–73). Operations such as regularizing the biface margin where the overshot termination occurred, constructing striking platforms for flake removals on the opposite face of the biface (or even the same face), as well as continued knapping to refine the size and shape of the biface will all contribute to the loss of evidence of overshot flaking. However, the relative amount of post–overshot flaking is key—less will result in a higher likelihood that some portion of the overshot flake will remain. In both cases, one can only say that the flake may have terminated in an overshot if subsequent flake scars were detached from where the termination (or platform) occurred or infer that a flake was an "unsuccessful" attempt to overshoot the opposite margin. Of course, a flake terminating close to the opposite margin is hard to describe as "unsuccessful" biface thinning; Bradley et al. (2010:Figure 3.11) identify similar flakes as "full-face" and Smallwood (2012) terms them "overface" flakes. Flakes that nearly reach but do not overshoot the opposite margin are viewed in this study as instances of intentional overshot flaking in which a flake simply failed to reach the opposite margin.

In order to try to better characterize the extent of its use, I believe it is important to try to capture all the evidence of overshot flaking available on archaeological specimens. *Overshot-terminated flake* (OTF) is best reserved for those flakes that clearly ended in an overshot termination; *possible overshot-terminated flake* (POTF) is suggested for those instances in which flake terminations closely approach but do not overshoot the opposite margin or for flakes whose terminations have been removed or obscured by subsequent flaking. Examples of Beach cache bifaces with these flake scars appear in Figures 8.5–8.7. Note that with continued reduction of the biface by a knapper using a flake-removal strategy that does not employ overshot flakes, any previous OTF scars will be gradually removed or at least reduced in area, to the point where it is increasingly difficult to determine whether a particular scar remnant was or was not an overshot flake (Bradley et al. 2010:71–72; Dickens 2007). Bradley and his colleagues (2010) have described these scars as "full-face" and avoided including them in their analyses of overshot flaking, which, as they note, has the probable effect of underestimating the frequency with which this technique was employed. For this study I have attempted to include them by tabulating their frequency separately from clear OTF scars. The recognition of POTF scars is something of an analytical challenge, and hard-and-fast criteria for identifying them are elusive. As a rule of thumb, I suggest that large scar remnants ending within 1–10 mm of the margin be evaluated as potential POTF scars. Determining whether subsequent flaking has obscured the termination is also important in identifying POTF scars; small, post-overshot flake scars are frequently evident along the margin where the overshot termination occurred. Caution should be used in identifying POTF scars near the tip of a biface, where the lessened distance between lateral margins may increase the probability of an overshot termination.

Another source of variation is the extent of overshot flaking apparent on a single artifact. In some cases, only one or two isolated OTF/POTF scars may be evident, while in other instances much or most of the surface of the biface exhibits overshot flaking. The former condition is termed *selective overshot flaking* and the latter *systematic overshot flaking*. Again, differentiation of these may depend somewhat on an analyst's judgment, but for the analysis here I will specify that bifaces with systematic overshot flaking must exhibit at least three contiguous (laterally overlapping) overshot or possible overshot flake scars on one or both faces. The flakes may all originate from the same margin, or from opposing margins. There is not a distinct boundary separating selective and systematic overshot flaking, and they are perhaps best conceived of as parts of a continuum in the application of overshot flaking to biface manufacture. That is, use of overshot flaking can range from single removals as part of the reduction process up to patterned, contiguous removals that also serve as a projectile point finishing technique in certain instances (Frison and Bradley 1999: Plates 1–6; Gramly 1993:32, 33b, 34b). With these distinctions and conventions in mind, let us turn to the Beach cache and explore overshot flaking on its bifacial artifacts.

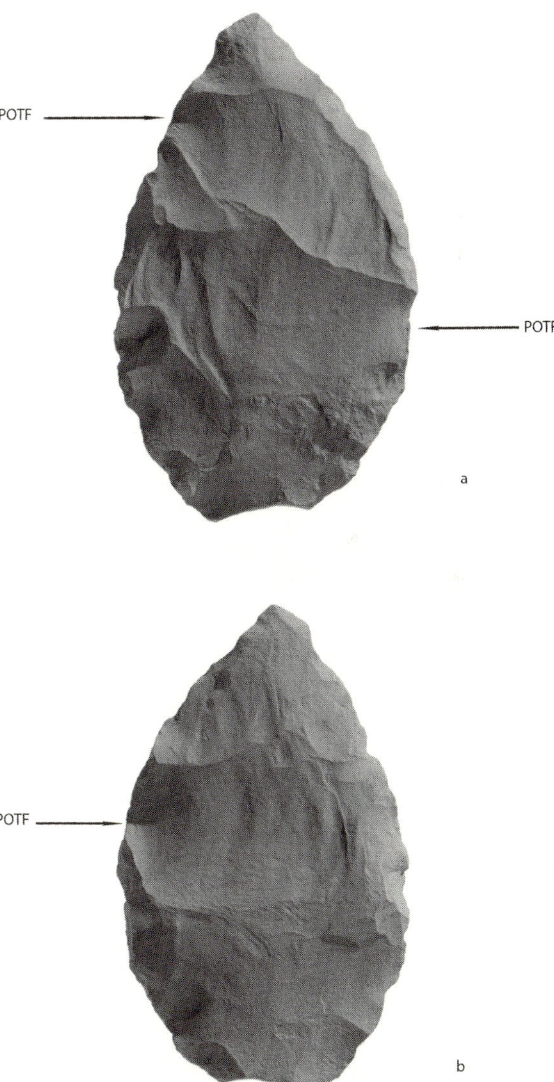

Figure 8.5. Three-dimensional scans of a Beach cache biface showing possible overshot-terminated (POTF) scars on both faces; length of (a) is 151 mm. Note that the lower scar on face a comes within 1 mm of overshot terminating, while the upper scar on face a has had its termination completely removed by subsequent retouch.

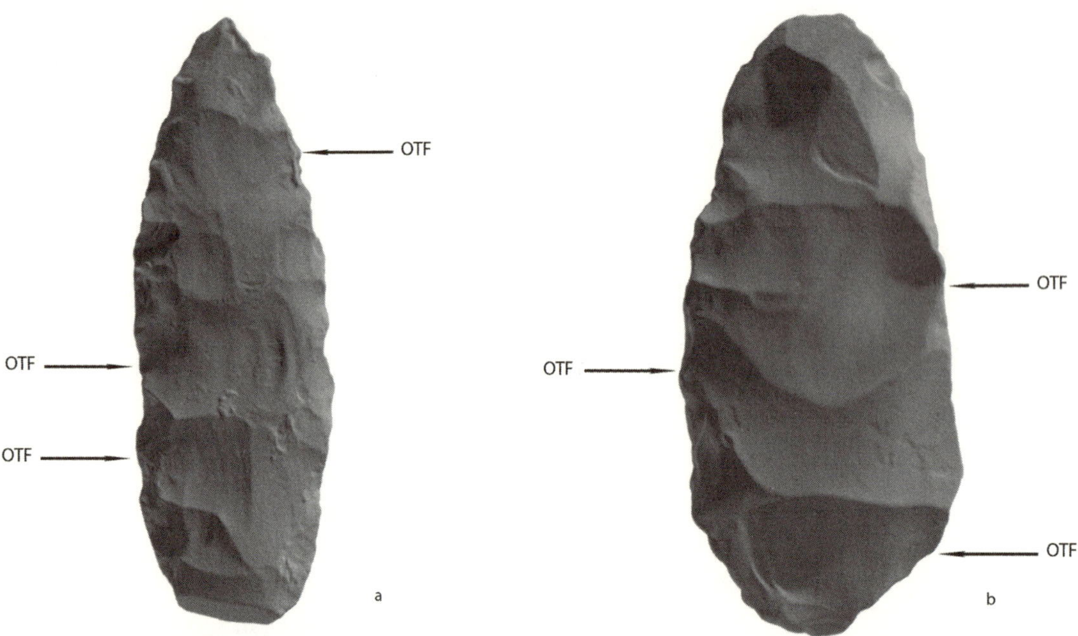

Figure 8.6. Three-dimensional scans of two Beach cache bifaces with overshot-terminated (OTF) scars. Length of (a) is 67 mm, length of (b) is 99 mm. The overshot terminations of the lower two scars on (a) are both partly but not completely removed by subsequent retouch.

Figure 8.7. Three-dimensional scans of three Beach cache bifaces with both overshot-terminated and possible overshot-terminated (OTF/POTF) flake scars. Length of (a) is 78 mm, length of (b) is 109 mm, length of (c) is 132 mm.

Overshot Flaking on the Beach Cache Bifaces

Of the 98 Beach cache bifaces, 84 are complete and 55 (65.5 percent) of them exhibit one or more OTF/POTF scars while the remaining 29 (34.5 percent) lack them (Table 8.2). Of the 15 fragmentary (broken by plowing) bifaces, 9 (60 percent) show one or more OTF/POTF flake scars; they are not treated further in the following analyses. Table 8.2 presents data on the 55 complete bifaces with and without OTF/POTF flaking by raw material type; in Table 8.3 those bifaces with overshot flaking are treated in greater detail. Three possible conditions—OTF only, POTF only, and both OTF/POTF—are recognized for overshot flaking. The number of overshot flake scars is totaled for both faces of each specimen, which for OTF and POTF ranges from one through eight; by definition, bifaces with both OTF and POTF scars must have at least two, and the number per specimen ranges up to fourteen. Table 8.3 reveals that bifaces with only OTF total 8 (14.5 percent), while those with POTF account for 21 of the 55, or 38.2 percent; 26 bifaces (47.3 percent) have both OTF

TABLE 8.2. Counts and Percentages of Overshot Flaked and Not Overshot Flaked Complete Bifaces in the Beach Cache by Raw Material Types

MATERIAL TYPE	BIFACE *n*	OVERSHOT FLAKED	NOT OVERSHOT FLAKED
WRGS	53	33 (62.26)	20 (37.74)
RBSW	7	5 (71.43)	2 (28.57)
Quartzite	5	5 (100.00)	
Dark chalcedony	9	6 (66.67)	3 (33.33)
Petrified wood	3	2 (66.67)	1 (33.33)
Porcellanite	3	2 (66.67)	1 (33.33)
Agate	1	1 (100.00)	
Chert	3	1 (33.33)	2 (66.67)
Total	84	55	29

Note: Frequency (percentage); WRGS = White River Group silicate; RBSW = Rainy Buttes silicified wood.

TABLE 8.3. Frequencies of Beach Cache Bifaces Showing OTF, POTF, and OTF/POTF Flake Scars by Raw Material Type

		OTF SCARS ONLY			POTF SCARS ONLY						BOTH OTF AND POTF SCARS					
No. of overshot flakes per biface		1	2	3	1	2	3	4	6	8	2	3	4	5	8	14
Biface *n*	Material															
33	WRGS	3	1	1	5	5	2	1		1	6	5	2	1		
5	RBSW	1						1			1	1			1	
5	Qzite	1							1		2	1				
6	Dk. chal.				3			1			1		1			
2	P. wood		1			1										
2	Porcel														1	1
1	Agate												1			
1	Chert											1				
55	total	5	2	1	8	6	2	3	1	1	10	8	4	1	2	1

Note: WRGS = White River group silicate; RBSW = Rainey Buttes silicified wood; Qzite = quartzite; Dk. chal. = dark chalcedony; P. wood = petrified wood; Porcel = porcellanite

and POTF scars. Combining the OTF and OTF/POTF categories, 34 of the 55 bifaces (61.8 percent) display at least one flake with a clearly overshot termination. Looking at the numbers of bifaces under each category of overshot flaking, it is evident that in all three categories there is a clear tendency for the modal classes to be specimens with one or two overshot flakes. Thus, although overshot flaking appears to have been used frequently by the artisans who produced the Beach cache bifaces, it is typically limited to a small number of overshot-terminated or possibly overshot-terminated flakes on most specimens. Still, 5 bifaces with only POTF exhibit 4 or more possible overshot flake scars, and 2 bifaces with both OTF and POTF display 8 overshot flake scars and one has 14 indicating that these knappers could and did employ the technique more extensively on some bifaces.

How does the use of overshot flaking vary among raw material types in the Beach cache? Although there are considerable differences in sample size by material type, variation is apparent in the percentages of the type of overshot flaking by material type; generally smaller percentages of bifaces of all material types show only OTF scars, while those with both OTF and POTF scars are most abundant (Table 8.3). Note that despite known variation in original piece size (small nodule size for the Sentinel Butte WRGS, large for quartzite and porcellanite, intermediate for RBSW), overshot flaking is consistently applied across the material types. For WRGS,

Figure 8.8. Both faces of two Beach cache bifaces showing systematic overshot flaking. Length of smaller biface is 201 mm. Larger biface broken and damaged by plowing.

TABLE 8.4. Systematic Overshot Flaking on Beach Cache Bifaces by Raw Material Type

MATERIAL TYPE	NO. OF OVERSHOT BIFACES	NO. WITH SYSTEMATIC OVERSHOT FLAKING	PERCENTAGE WITH SYSTEMATIC OVERSHOT FLAKING
WRGS	33	5	15.15
RBSW	5	2	40.00
Porcellanite	2	2	100.00
Total	40	9	22.50

Note: WRGS = White River Group silicate; RBSW = Rainy Buttes silicified wood.

62.26 percent are overshot flaked; for RBSW the percentage is 71.43; and for quartzite and porcellanite 100 percent are overshot flaked (Table 8.2). Use of this approach to reduction can thus be described as consistent, regardless of material type, among the Beach cache bifaces.

Table 8.4 presents data on the frequency of systematic overshot flaking on the Beach cache bifaces by raw material type. As defined above, systematic overshot flaking requires three contiguous OTF/POTF flake scars on the same face; these scars may originate from the same margin or from the opposing margin, so long as their lateral margins adjoin. Systematic overshot flaking was present on nine bifaces of three of the eight distinct lithic materials in the cache: WRGS ($n = 5$, or 15.15 percent of the 33 overshot-flaked WRGS bifaces), RBSW ($n = 2$, or 40 percent of the 5 overshot-flaked RBSW bifaces), and porcellanite ($n = 2$, which is 100 percent of the overshot-flaked bifaces of this material). The two porcellanite bifaces exhibit systematic overshot flaking on both faces of the specimen; the others have it on only one face (Figure 8.8). As would be anticipated by the predominance of bifaces with small numbers of overshot flakes in the OTF, POTF, and OTF/POTF categories (Table 8.3), selective use of overshot flaking is predominant in the Beach cache.

The picture that emerges is that, while common, overshot flaking tends to be somewhat sparingly used on individual artifacts among the Beach cache bifaces. How does the frequency of its use compare with biface assemblages from caches that included Clovis points? To examine this question, the same analytical approaches were used to evaluate the bifaces from the Fenn and East Wenatchee caches.

OVERSHOT FLAKING ON THE FENN AND EAST WENATCHEE CACHE BIFACES

I participated in the analysis of the artifacts from both the Fenn and East Wenatchee caches in 1989 and retained metric data and the excellent line drawings of Sarah Moore for both faces of each artifact; this allowed me to examine them for OTF/POTF scars and selective/systematic use of overshot flaking. Thirty-four complete, non–projectile point bifaces were reported from the Fenn cache by Frison and Bradley (1999), while the East Wenatchee cache yielded 20 complete bifaces (Huckell et al. in review). Fourteen of the East Wenatchee bifaces exhibit overshot flaking, and all 34 of the Fenn bifaces have it (Table 8.5). Parenthetically, the six East Wenatchee bifaces that lack overshot flaking, are all large flakes that display extensive remnants of original interior and exterior flake surfaces. They are thus edge-trimmed flakes that reflect an earlier portion of the process of reduction of a flake to create a biface (see Gramly 1993:39 for two examples).

Tables 8.6 and 8.7 present the results of the OTF and

TABLE 8.5. Quantities of Bifaces with and without Overshot Flaking in the Beach, Fenn, and East Wenatchee Caches

	OVERSHOT FLAKED	NOT OVERSHOT FLAKED	TOTAL
Beach	55 (66.3)	28 (33.7)	83
Fenn	34 (100.0)	0	34
East Wenatchee	14 (70.0)	6 (30.0)	20

Note: Frequency (percentage).

TABLE 8.6. Frequencies of Fenn Cache Bifaces Showing OTF, POTF, and OTF/POTF Flake Scars by Raw Material Type

		OTF SCARS ONLY	POTF SCARS ONLY					BOTH OTF AND POTF SCARS				
No. of overshot flake scars per biface		3	2	3	4	5	6	3	4	5	6	7
Biface *n*	Material											
16	Agate			2	4	3			2	3	1	1
12	GRFC		1	4	1		1	1		4		
6	Obsidian	1		2				1	2			
34	Total	1	1	8	5	3	1	2	4	7	1	1

Note: GRFC = Green River Formation chert

TABLE 8.7. Frequencies of East Wenatchee Cache Bifaces Showing POTF and OTF/POTF Flake Scars by Raw Material Type

		OTF SCARS ONLY				BOTH OTF AND POTF SCARS		
No. of overshot flake scars per biface		2	3	4	6	3	4	6
Biface *n*	Material							
13	Agate[1]	1	3	3	1	3	1	1
1	Agate[2]	1						
14	Total	2	3	3	1	3	1	1

Note: No bifaces had OTF scars only; Agate[1] and Agate[2] refer to separate varieties of agate

POTF analyses of the bifaces from the two caches by raw material type. All but one of the East Wenatchee bifaces are of the same agate, while the Fenn cache has three raw material types—Green River Formation chert (GRFC), agate, and obsidian. Across the entire sample of Fenn bifaces, those with only POTF scars (18, or 52.9%) are nearly equal in number to those with both POTF and OTF scars (15, or 44.1 percent); one biface has only OTF scars (Table 8.6). A difference between the Beach cache and the Fenn cache may be seen by comparing the total number of bifaces with 1, 2, 3, 4, or 5 overshot flake scars per biface. Under the POTF category, the Fenn cache mode is 3 scars per biface, followed closely by those with 4 scars. For Fenn bifaces with both OTF and POTF scars, the modes are 4 and 5 flake scars. The modal value for Beach bifaces with only POTF scars is 1, followed by 2; for Beach bifaces with both OTF and POTF scars the mode is 2 (compare Tables 8.3 and 8.6). Thus the Fenn bifaces exhibit greater numbers of overshot flakes per biface than do the Beach bifaces.

Turning to the 14 East Wenatchee bifaces with overshot flaking (Table 8.7), bifaces with only POTF scars make up 64.3 percent of the sample (9 bifaces), while those with both OTF and POTF scars make up the remaining 35.7 percent, or 5 bifaces. None featured only OTF scars. The relatively small sample of overshot-flaked bifaces from this cache makes it more difficult to identify any clear trends in the relative abundance of bifaces by number of overshot flake scars per biface. Among those with only POTF scars, a broad distribution with modes at 3 and 4 flake scars per biface is present; for bifaces with both OTF and POTF scars, the mode is 3. In general, it appears that there are more bifaces in the higher scar count categories for the East Wenatchee cache than for Beach (compare Table 8.3 to Table 8.7).

Comparing the East Wenatchee cache bifaces to those in the Fenn cache, there is a tendency for there to be fewer East Wenatchee bifaces in the higher overshot flake scar per biface categories (see Tables 8.6 and 8.7). Table 8.8 provides a summary of the relative frequencies of bifaces with OTF scars only, POTF scars only, and both OTF and POTF scars, combining all lithic material types for each of the three caches. It is clear that despite variation in the relative percentages of these categories

TABLE 8.8. Comparison of Overshot Flake-Scar Types among the Beach, Fenn, and East Wenatchee Cache Bifaces of all Materials

	OTF ONLY	POTF ONLY	BOTH POTF AND OTF	TOTAL
Beach	8 (14.56)	21 (38.18)	26 (47.27)	55 (53.40)
Fenn	1 (2.94)	18 (52.94)	15 (44.12)	34 (33.01)
East Wenatchee		9 (64.29)	5 (35.71)	14 (13.59)
Total	9 (8.74)	48 (46.60)	46 (44.66)	103 (100.00)

Note: Frequency (percentage)

among the three caches, the caches are roughly similar. It is also evident that bifaces with only POTF scars are abundant in relation to those with only OTF scars and that bifaces with both OTF and POTF scars are also common. This highlights the potential importance of identifying and recording POTF scars on Clovis bifaces rather than relying solely on the presence of extant OTF scars to assess the frequency of use of overshot flaking. Continuing reduction will modify and potentially eliminate many, perhaps most, overshot flake scars, unless manufacture is halted while such scars are still evident or unless there is a desire on the part of the knapper to retain the biface in relatively unaltered fashion. The latter situation may be seen on some fluted points in the Fenn (Frison and Bradley 1999:Plates 1–4) and East Wenatchee (Gramly 1993:29, 32, 34b, 35b) caches. The figure presented by Bradley and colleagues (2010:Figure 3.26) underscores the importance of POTF (for them, overface) scars in the treatment of overshot flaking—note the few scars with intact overshot terminations in comparison to several other scars that reach almost to the opposite margin.

The relative frequency of systematic overshot flaking was also examined for the Fenn and East Wenatchee bifaces. The results of this analysis—along with the Beach cache data—are shown in Table 8.9. Seven Fenn cache bifaces—four of Green River Formation chert and three of agate—exhibit systematic overshot flaking, while three of the East Wenatchee cache bifaces have systematic overshot flaking. With respect to the Fenn cache, these numbers correspond to systematic overshot flaking on 33.3 percent of the Green River Formation chert bifaces and 18.8 percent of the agate bifaces. For East Wenatchee, 21.4 percent of the agate bifaces were systematically overshot flaked. As can be seen in Table 8.9, these percentages are slightly higher than the 15.2 percent of WRGS bifaces with systematic overshot flaking in the Beach cache. Although not the focus of this analysis, it is worth observing that both the East Wenatchee and Fenn caches contain Clovis points with beautiful systematic overshot flaking (Frison and Bradley 1999:Plates 1–4, 6, 12, 24; Gramly 1993:29, 32, 34b, 35b). It appears to have been used as a strategy for finishing these points, not simply for the thinning of a biface earlier in the reduction process, as seems to be reflected in the bifaces examined in this study. This is another aspect of overshot flaking that merits closer analysis in the future.

COMPARISONS AMONG THE THREE CACHES

Turning to more in-depth comparisons among the three caches, as discussed above there is variation in the relative numbers of overshot flake scars on the bifaces from each. Beach seemed to have relatively lower numbers of OTF/POTF scars on most bifaces than Fenn or East Wenatchee. To determine whether the differences between the caches are statistically significant, Kolmogorov-Smirnov two-sample tests were conducted. The combined totals of bifaces in each of the three categories (OTF only, POTF only, combination of OTF/POTF) from each cache were used without regard to lithic material type. The first comparison showed that at a $p = .01$ level, the categorical distributions of bifaces with only POTF scars were significantly different between the Beach and Fenn caches ($D_{obs} = .6111$, $>D_{crit} = .5236$). A second comparison demonstrated that the categorical distributions of bifaces with both OTF and POTF flake scars were also different ($p = .01$) between Beach and Fenn ($D_{obs} = .5590$, $>D_{crit} = .5284$). Because only one Fenn cache biface displayed OTF scars only, no analytical comparison of bifaces in this category was possible. Thus, in two categories the bifaces in the Fenn cache display significantly more overshot flake scars than those in the Beach cache.

TABLE 8.9. Systematically Overshot-Flaked Bifaces in the Beach, Fenn, and East Wenatchee Caches

CACHE	MATERIAL TYPE	NO. OF OVERSHOT BIFACES	NO. WITH SYSTEMATIC OVERSHOT FLAKING	PERCENTAGE WITH SYSTEMATIC OVERSHOT FLAKING
Beach				
	WRGS	33	5	15.2
	RBSW	5	2	40.0
	Porcellanite	2	2	100.0
Fenn				
	GRFC	12	4	33.3
	Agate	16	3	18.8
East Wenatchee				
	Agate	14	3	21.4

Note: WRGS = White River Group silicate; RBSW = Rainy Buttes silicified wood; GRFC = Green River Formation chert.

Kolmogorov-Smirnov two-sample tests were also used to compare the numbers of overshot flake scars per biface between the Beach and East Wenatchee caches. No significant differences existed at the $p = .01$ level between the bifaces in the two caches with only POTF scars ($D_{obs} = 11$, $<D_{crit} = 13$), but between those with both OTF and POTF scars there are ($D_{obs} = 18$, $<D_{crit} = 13$); the East Wenatchee cache lacks bifaces with only OTF scars, so no comparison is possible. The same test procedure was used to compare the distribution of POTF scar category for the East Wenatchee and Fenn bifaces, with the same results—no significant differences were present in the numbers of overshot flake scars per biface ($D_{obs} = 8$, $<D_{crit} = 12$). For bifaces with OTF and POTF scars, significant differences are evident ($D_{obs} = 13$, $>D_{crit} = 11$). Again, the small sample size for East Wenatchee plays a role in these results.

Is it possible that other variables play a role in measuring the relative abundance of overshot flaking on bifaces from the three caches? One that comes to mind is biface length—perhaps it is the case that longer bifaces offer more opportunity for knappers to employ overshot flaking. As shown in Figure 8.4, most of the WRGS bifaces from Beach are short in comparison to those of other materials in the cache, particularly quartzite and porcellanite. Further, the Fenn and East Wenatchee bifaces are longer on average than the Beach bifaces and exhibit more overshot flake scars. If it is true that shorter lengths lead to fewer opportunities for overshot flaking, is there a way to develop a comparison among the caches that is sensitive to size differences? A simple expression was settled on to serve this purpose:

$$\frac{\Sigma os}{\Sigma L}$$

where Σos is the total number of all OTF, POTF, and OTF/POTF scars on all bifaces and ΣL is the summed length of all the bifaces with overshot flaking. Lower values of the expression reflect less frequent use of overshot flaking, and increasingly higher values suggest relatively more use of overshot flaking. This expression was applied to the Beach, Fenn, and East Wenatchee bifaces by raw material type; the results are shown in Table 8.10 along with means and standard deviations of length. Figure 8.9 provides a visual representation of the distribution of these ratio values.

What is most striking is that the ratio values for Beach WRGS (0.0259), Fenn agate (0.0250), and East Wenatchee agate (0.0251) are practically identical. Fenn GRFC (0.236), Beach dark chalcedony (0.0221), and Beach petrified wood (0.0228) have slightly lower values, while Beach RBSW (0.0281) is somewhat higher. The Beach porcellanite bifaces have the highest value (0.0436), while Beach quartzite (0.0142) and Fenn obsidian (0.0185) have the lowest. These results support the proposition that if biface length is taken into account, the relative numbers of overshot flake scars among the most abundant raw materials in the three caches is actually quite similar. That is, the knappers who made these bifaces applied the technique of overshot flaking to the reduction process in a similar manner and frequency when relative length is factored into comparisons. Thus raw material piece size is a factor that should be considered in analyses of this type. Use of overshot flaking as a reduction technique

TABLE 8.10. Lithic Material, Length, and Size-Corrected Values for Biface Length and Quantities of Overshot Flake Scars in the Beach, Fenn, and East Wenatchee Caches

CACHE	MATERIAL	BIFACE *n*	ΣL	MEAN L	SD L	Σos	Σos / ΣL
Beach							
	WRGS	33	3130.5	94.86	17.75	81	.0259
	RBSW	5	640.3	128.06	35.41	18	.0281
	Quartzite	5	988.9	197.78	11.17	14	.0142
	Dark chalcedony	6	588.7	98.11	29.13	13	.0221
	Porcellanite	2	504.7	252.34	50.66	22	.0436
	Petrified wood	2	175.8	87.90	3.10	4	.0228
Fenn							
	GRFC	12	2035.9	169.66	30.42	48	.0236
	Agate	16	2922.0	182.63	22.38	72	.0246
	Obsidian	6	1081.9	180.32	24.28	20	.0185
East Wenatchee							
	Agate	14	1990.7	142.19	29.87	50	.0251

Note: L = length (measured in millimeters); SD = standard deviation; os = overshot flake scar; WRGS = White River Group silicates; RBSW = Rainy Buttes silicified wood; ; GRFC = Green River Formation chert. Single bifaces of chert and agate from beach are omitted.

seems to crosscut raw materials, despite the fact that the mean lengths of the Fenn and East Wenatchee agate bifaces are 48–88 mm greater than the Beach WRGS biface mean length (Table 8.10).

Turning to the outliers in Figure 8.9, the two Beach porcellanite bifaces are both systematically overshot flaked, so the fact that they produced the highest ratio value is not surprising. The lowest ratio values—Beach quartzite and Fenn obsidian—are a bit more difficult to explain. They are texturally quite different from one another, and it might be anticipated that, due to its glassy texture, obsidian should be easier to reduce by overshot flaking. Quartzite, although of high quality, is a bit coarser than the cherts, petrified woods, and agates, so perhaps its small ratio value reflects its greater difficulty of fracture. That both obsidian and quartzite produced low ratio values is at first glance somewhat unexpected; however, one similarity between the bifaces of these two materials is that they are relatively wide in comparison to bifaces of the other materials. The mean width for Beach quartzite bifaces is 87.52 mm, which is from 12 to 47 mm greater than the mean widths of the other materials. Fenn obsidian bifaces have a mean width of 84.82 mm, which is from 11 to 26 mm greater than other material mean widths. Student's t-tests comparing the mean widths reveal no significant differences between the Beach quartzite and Fenn obsidian bifaces at a $p = .05$ level. The t-tests also showed some unanticipated results, however. For example, as might be expected from their significantly shorter lengths, Beach WRGS bifaces had significantly different ($p = .05$) mean widths when compared to East Wenatchee agate bifaces, Fenn agate bifaces, and Fenn GRFC bifaces. The mean widths of East Wenatchee and Fenn agate bifaces were not significantly different at $p = .05$; East Wenatchee agate bifaces were barely significantly different from Fenn GRFC bifaces at the $p = .05$ level but not different at the $p = .01$ level.

On the basis of these results, it is hypothesized that the wider the biface, the more difficult it may be to employ the overshot reduction technique. Thus, when comparing the frequencies of overshot flaking, it is potentially important to take both the length and width dimensions of the bifaces into consideration.

DISCUSSION AND CONCLUSIONS

This study began with the goal of determining whether a technological signature—overshot flaking—could serve to evaluate the question of whether the bifaces recovered from the Beach cache could be assigned to Clovis. A second goal was to take a closer look at the

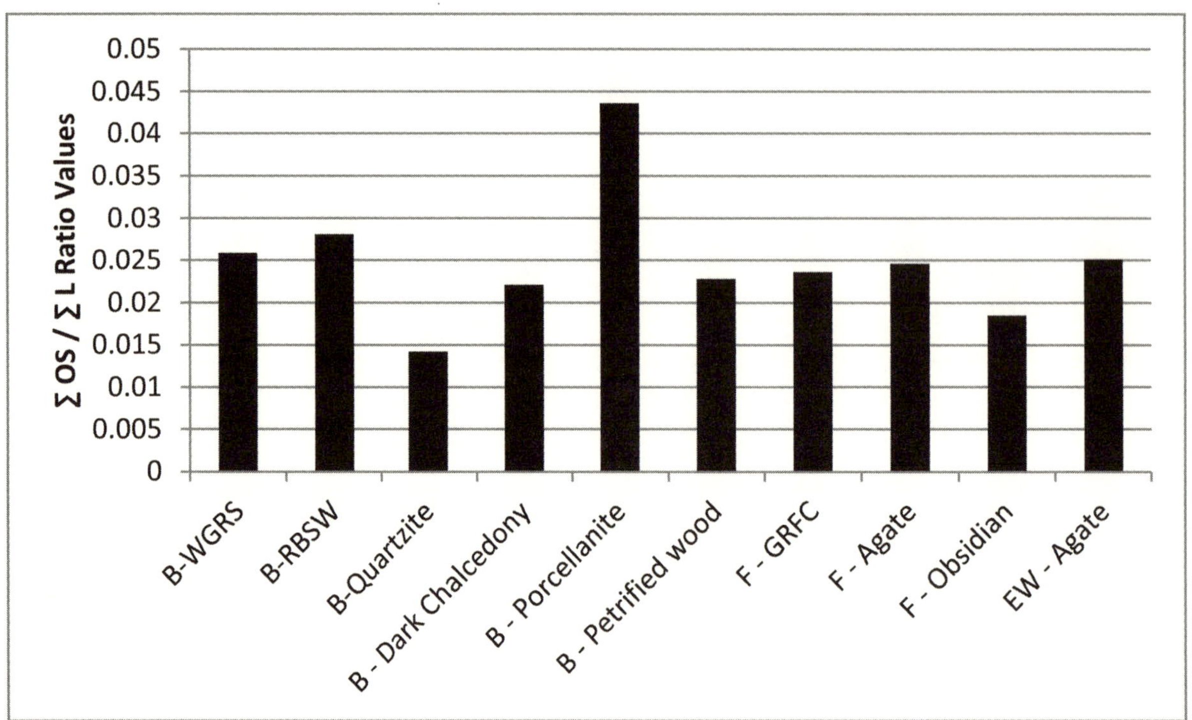

Figure 8.9. Histogram of the relative frequency of overshot flaking as adjusted for biface length among the Beach (B), Fenn (F), and East Wenatchee (EW) caches, by material type

phenomenon of overshot flaking and to develop analytical approaches to delve more deeply into the variation present in this remarkable knapping technique. Comparison of non–projectile point bifaces from the East Wenatchee and Fenn Clovis caches was accomplished using a more fine-grained approach to categorizing and analyzing the bifaces from the three cache assemblages.

The mechanical basis underlying overshot flaking consists of at least three components—a steep (67–86 degree) exterior platform angle, a forceful ("too much force") blow struck at a low angle to the face (too "straight in"), and a striking platform set below the center plane of the piece. Critically, these variables are under the direct control of the knapper, and therefore if overshot flaking is routinely employed as a reduction technique the signature flake scars should be relatively abundant. However, recognition of overshot flaking is complicated by the fact that subsequent flake detachments may frequently remove the actual overshot termination of the flake or, in some cases, an attempted overshot flake may not actually have reached the opposite edge of the biface. The concepts of *overshot-terminated flake* (OTF) and *possible overshot-terminated flake* (POTF) were introduced to describe variation in the outcome of overshot flaking, including the success of execution of overshot flaking as well as the loss of the overshot flake terminations by subsequent reduction. Application of these concepts to the three cache biface samples revealed that POTF scars are more abundant than OTF scars in all. Further, recognition of the difference between selective and systematic use of overshot flaking may also permit another aspect of variation in overshot flaking to be recognized. Systematic overshot flaking was defined as the presence of three or more contiguous OTF/POTF flake scars on the same face; selective overshot flaking consists of one or two noncontiguous or contiguous OTF/POTF scars on the same face. Their employment of systematic overshot flaking underscores the extent to which Clovis knappers were able to control the technical elements of this strategy.

The comparison of the three caches in terms of the use of overshot-terminated flaking accomplishes one of the goals of this research: to determine whether or not the employment of overshot flaking in the bifaces recovered from the Beach cache is or is not similar to its use in the reduction of bifaces that are part of the Fenn and East Wenatchee caches, both of which contain Clovis projectile points. The analyses presented here suggest that while differences exist among the caches, they are of degree rather than kind. Overshot flaking is common in all three caches, ranging from a high of 100 percent of the 34 Fenn bifaces, to 14 of 20 East Wenatchee bifaces (70 percent), to 55 of 83 complete bifaces in the Beach cache (66.3 percent). In all three caches

(Table 8.6), overshot-flaked bifaces with POTF scars make up the largest part of the sample, followed closely by those with a mixture of bifaces with OTF scars and POTF scars. Bifaces displaying only OTF scars are uncommon but actually relatively more abundant in the Beach sample than in the other two. So, while Beach cache bifaces may display fewer POTF scars, OTF scars, or OTF/POTF scars per biface than those in the other two caches, after adjusting for the relatively smaller size of the most abundant lithic material (WRGS) in the Beach sample, the differences are lessened and the relative use of overshot flaking is very similar.

The Beach cache does appear, on technological grounds, to be Clovis. However, can we be certain that intentional, controlled use of overshot flaking is truly restricted to Clovis? This is a question for which there is no certain answer at this time. I have yet to see biface assemblages from post-Clovis Paleoindian or Archaic sites in the Southwest or Plains that exhibit any use of overshot flaking at frequencies akin to those reported in this study. Bradley et al. (2010:76, Table 3.2) examined over 400 bifaces from the Archaic deposits at the Gault site and reported that less than 1 percent exhibited overshot flake scars. However, evidence of this strategy has been illustrated by Odess and Rasic (2007:Figure 6) from the Nogahabara I site in Alaska, dated to ca. 10,740–11,850 cal B.C. They suggest it was used to produce large flake blanks from bifacial cores made on small obsidian nodules. Similarly, the Easterday II cache from northeastern Colorado consists of 99 biface cores, a pair of bifaces, and a scraper, all of WRGS. The cache, thought to be of late prehistoric age, is suggested to represent transported cores (bifaces) used for flake production (Basham and Holen 2006). Some are said to exhibit overshot-terminated flakes, but the actual frequency of overshot flaking is not reported. Note that the investigators of both the Easterday II and Nogahabara sites share the inference that overshot flaking served for the production of flake blanks, rather than for the manufacture of bifaces, as seems to be the primary purpose of Clovis overshot flaking. This is not to say that overshot flakes were not used as tools by Clovis groups, but rather that these flakes were a secondary byproduct. Finally, Bradley (2009b, 2010) noted the presence of overshot flaking on bifaces from the Agate Basin and Hell Gap levels at the Agate Basin and Hell Gap sites but did not find it in Folsom assemblages; however, Root and his colleagues (1999) observed it on some Folsom bifaces from Lake Ilo. In the absence of more deimtailed description and quantitative analysis of non-Clovis bifaces, it is challenging to be certain that intentional overshot flaking is *uniquely* diagnostic of Clovis. It remains to be seen to what extent the technique may have seen use over time and space.

The paths forward in the investigation of overshot flaking are, in my estimation, three. First, I would suggest that analyses of overshot flaking on biface assemblages from securely post-Clovis contexts be accorded a high priority; a cache such as the one from the San Jon site (Roberts 1942; see Huckell and Kilby Chapter 1) is an example of an important assemblage to be analyzed. The results of such analyses should help to determine the degree to which overshot flaking—and in particular systematic, controlled overshot flaking—can be established as a reductive strategy distinctive of Clovis. Only when a much greater number of such assemblages have been studied can the variation in use of overshot flaking over time and across space be determined.

Second, this examination hopefully points out productive methods for the comparison of bifaces from other caches, both those known to be Clovis (such as Simon, Anzick, and Crook County, for example) as well as those of uncertain age and cultural affiliation. Application of these approaches to other caches would augment what was learned from the Beach, Fenn, and East Wenatchee cache bifaces and help us to better understand how overshot flaking varies among Clovis caches. Use of the same analytical approach for the study of post- or non-Clovis bifaces will provide a firm basis for their comparison to Clovis as well.

Third, an important task that remains is the development of ways in which to securely identify and incorporate POTF scars in the analysis of overshot flaking. As discussed above, due to the impact of continuing reduction, an approach that limits the study of overshot flaking solely to those scars that retain overshot terminations will underestimate the use of this technique. Particularly in the absence of debitage, as is the case with most cache sites, we have only bifaces to study. However, flake scars on bifaces that others have termed "full-face" (Bradley et al. 2010) or "overface" (Smallwood 2012) have been identified here as POTF. After concluding the analysis of the Beach, East Wenatchee, and Fenn bifaces, I would suggest that if the terminations of flake scars that approach but do not overshoot the opposing edge are intact and unaffected by subsequent flaking, full-face or overface may be appropriately used to classify those scars. If the terminations of the scars have been modified by subsequent flaking, POTF is more appropriate. The biface shown in Figure 8.5a is a good example of the differences in these two scar types: the face shown has a clear POTF scar near its tip and a clear full-face/overface scar just below and contiguous to it. Ultimately, this approach may permit a more precise and replicable characterization of variation in knapping technique and the outcomes (flake scars) of techniques; such an approach recognizes to the extent possible the certain and likely employment of controlled overshot flaking.

Our ability to precisely characterize overshot flaking of bifaces, and to understand how it varies within particular cultural/technological traditions as well as across them, is still in its developmental stages. Its importance for the identification of caches and other sites that lack finished project points as Clovis is great, and it is imperative that we continue to refine our understanding of this knapping strategy and its role in Clovis and other technological traditions.

POSTSCRIPT: ANOTHER LINE OF EVIDENCE

Beginning in 2007 we excavated 1m x 1m test pits into the general area where Alan Miller and Don Abernethy remembered finding the cache. Most units revealed a plow zone resting directly atop Paleocene-age Ft. Union Formation claystone. However, one unit produced the proximal end of a blade of RBSW, which rested at the base of the plow zone atop a fine sand deposit. Subsequent deepening of this unit showed the sandy deposit to be eolian and to have filled an erosional cut in the Paleocene claystone. In 2009 additional units were excavated to investigate the extent of the eolian deposit (Huckell et al. 2011). Within one unit a large (75 mm long, 50 mm wide, 9.5 mm thick) RBSW flake was discovered in the eolian deposit below the plow zone; upon collection it proved to be a nearly complete overshot-terminated biface reduction flake. The presence of edge damage along one lateral margin suggested that it had been utilized. Approximately 35 cm from it and at the identical elevation was a small piece of charcoal. It was submitted to the Arizona AMS Radiocarbon Laboratory, and in 2010 it returned an age of 11,626 +/- 68 B.P. (13,550 cal B.P.) (AA-88825). This age is slightly beyond or just within the early end of the known or possible range of Clovis dates (Haynes 2002b), being within one standard deviation of two assays from the Aubrey Clovis site in Texas (Ferring, ed. 2001). It is some four centuries older than the oldest Clovis dates accepted by Waters and Stafford (2007; but also see Haynes et al. 2007). While it is only a single assay, it does provide potential support for the technological assessment of the Beach cache as Clovis. Subsequent excavations have revealed numerous additional pieces and flecks of charcoal in the vicinity, which may reflect the scattered remains of a hearth. In addition, more than a dozen flake tools and several pieces of debitage have been recovered from the eolian deposit within a 6 m by 6 m area, suggesting the presence of a short-term camp or work area associated with the cache. Investigations continue.

ACKNOWLEDGMENTS

Thanks first and foremost to Alan Miller and Donald Abernethy for finding the Beach cache and to Gary Vaughn for reporting it to me. Ever since the first visit that David Kilby and I made to Beach, Al and Don proved eager partners in our efforts to document and investigate the cache. Don and his wife, Rella, have allowed us to excavate in the area of the cache in the now-retired field and treated us to memorable feasts of all kinds during the fieldwork and other visits. Don and Rella, Ted Trinka, and the late Bob Jagd not only shared their memories of excavating the cache pits but donated the artifacts they had recovered from the cache to the North Dakota Heritage Center in 2009, a generous and thoughtful gift to future generations of North Dakotans. Ted also generously permitted the reproduction of his photograph of the cache artifacts, which appears as Figure 8.2b. Gary Vaughn has donated countless hours of volunteer work in the field, and UNM graduate students Christina Sinkovec, Caroline Gabe, Chris Merriman, and Matt O'Brien, and my wife, Lisa Huckell, have done excellent work during the continuing excavations. I am indebted to Jim Holmlund of Western Mapping, Inc., for the fine 3-D scans of the Beach artifacts, some of which appear in Figures 8.5–8.7, and to Matt O'Brien for the plots and graphs in Figures 8.4 and 8.9. Matthew G. Hill created the map that appears as Figure 8.1, for which I am grateful. The National Geographic Society provided critical support for the artifact recording, lithic material sourcing, and fieldwork in 2007 and 2008 (NGS grants 8232-07 and 8531-08). The Maxwell Museum of Anthropology also provided funds to make possible the 2009–2011 field seasons. I am also grateful to my friends and colleagues for their participation in the 2010 Society for American Archaeology symposium on Clovis caches. They have taught me a lot, and their contributions to this volume ensure that we will continue to learn about Clovis lithic technology and organization.

Sadly, in July 2012 Don Abernethy passed away; it is to his memory that this chapter is dedicated.

Chapter 9

Putting the Specialization Back in Clovis

WHAT SOME CACHES REVEAL ABOUT SKILL AND THE ORGANIZATION OF PRODUCTION IN THE TERMINAL PLEISTOCENE

Jon C. Lohse, C. Andrew Hemmings, Michael B. Collins, and David M. Yelacic

In this chapter we advance the proposal that part-time specialization in tool production was an important aspect of some Clovis economic organization. In support of this proposition, we present data from a portion of the Hogeye cache from Bastrop, Texas (Hemmings et al. 2006; Jennings 2013) and evaluate these data against detailed descriptions and measurements from two previously reported and well-illustrated caches, de Graffenried (Collins et al. 2007) and Fenn (Frison and Bradley 1999). Artifacts in many documented Clovis caches can be objectively characterized as displaying high-quality craftsmanship when compared with debris recovered from camp site, workshop, or domestic contexts (Kilby 2008). Indeed, based partly on cached assemblages, complex, well-executed workmanship has been used as a defining technical trait for Clovis technology in general (Collins 1999a). This phenomenon results to some degree from sampling bias in which parts of Clovis tool kits are commonly represented among biface caches, as well as from the types of differences observed in use-life and reduction stage in Clovis caches compared with other, noncache contexts. Nevertheless, the relations and conditions of production that can be reconstructed for some cached Clovis implements is suggestive of uneven economic organization, in which some toolmakers were considerably more skilled or spent more of their time in tool making (or both) than others.

Our assessment of some of the Hogeye specimens combines measurements of important dimensions with descriptive analyses characterizing stage of reduction and other objective traits such as consistency in point outline and knapper approaches to thinning and shaping bifaces. We also employ statistical analyses of width and thickness variation to compare specimens within each cache and between caches. Based on patterned variations seen within and between Hogeye, de Graffenried, and Fenn, we conclude that many Clovis caches probably represent the work of a disproportionately small number of knappers working within the context of age- and sex-based divisions of labor. Two related concluding hypotheses that we present based on this analysis are: (1) that producing stone tools in anticipation of future need seems to reflect individual-level variation in terms of aptitude and performance and (2) that this "embedded specialization" was a critical element of larger cultural practices that reflect some focus on megafaunal predation. Both conclusions require much additional study, but our analysis has important implications for understanding how specialization may have been expressed among prehistoric societies and also for how archaeologists model "generalized" versus "specialized" Clovis economic and adaptive practices.

THE PROBLEM OF SPECIALIZATION AND WHAT IT MEANS TO CLOVIS

Almost all discussions of specialization in Clovis focus on whether or not Clovis peoples were specialized big-game hunters. This model was crystallized in Paul Martin's (1984) overkill hypothesis, the idea that hyper-efficient Clovis hunters pursued big animals, including mammoth, across the Bering Land Bridge, down an ice-free corridor, and into the central continent, where these large herbivores were hunted into extinction. Gary Haynes (2002a) has supported versions of this view, but with the caveat that dispersing Clovis hunters were targeting animal populations already stressed as a result of environmental and climate change. Although the overkill model no longer receives wide support among archaeologists (Grayson and Meltzer 2003; but see Haynes, ed. 2009 for more complete treatment), the question of whether Clovis societies included specialized big-game hunters is unresolved. More precisely, scholars are still seeking consensus regarding the importance of megafauna to Clovis diets.

In response to the overkill hypothesis, many researchers have presented evidence for broad-spectrum Clovis diets (e.g., Ferring, ed. 2001; Johnson 1991; Meltzer 1993), seemingly calling into question whether Clovis hunters were primarily focused on highly ranked taxa, including mammoth. Yet the association between Clovis artifacts and large herbivore elements seems undeniable, and the question has recently shifted to demonstrating the centrality of megafaunal resources in Clovis diets. In 2003 Waguespack and Surovell (2003) looked at 33 assemblages in order to measure diet breadth and reconstruct Clovis prey choices. They found that proboscideans are by far the most common taxon by minimum number of individuals (or MNI) found in Clovis contexts and are also the taxon that is found at the most Clovis sites. Based on these results, they conclude that "Clovis hunting behaviors appear more closely aligned with specialized, rather than generalized, strategy" (Waguespack and Surovell 2003:348).

Grayson and Meltzer (2002, 2003) have recently critiqued this model in their review of 76 sites where extinct fauna and artifacts were reported. Of these, in only 14 cases were humans confidently fingered as agents of death or dismemberment. Based on this low figure, Meltzer (2009) concludes that Clovis hunters not only were not responsible for overkill, but they also probably focused on large game only rarely. Using optimal foraging theory, Byers and Ugan (2005) also hypothesize that early Paleoindians *ought* to have pursued a wide range of prey and that specializing in large taxa was profitable only under narrow circumstances that, in their opinion, were uncommon at best.

More recently, Waguespack (2007) argues that, as the highest-ranked resources on the Clovis landscape, mammoths were likely to have been targeted when available. Lower-ranked prey, too, were commonly taken under certain circumstances. However, the key to understanding subsistence activities relating to diet breadth depends on situation and context. Both high- and low-ranked prey clearly were important in certain circumstances, but this point does not obviate the demonstrated exploitation of megafauna by Clovis hunters. In order to contextualize the degree to which Clovis hunters may have depended on proboscideans, Surovell and Waguespack (2008) quantify the documented occurrences of proboscidean-bearing sites in the Old and New Worlds. They conclude that, with the possible exception of Lower Paleolithic Iberia, the 14 occurrences of Clovis mammoth and mastodon associations demonstrate the highest frequency of subsistence exploitation of Proboscidea anywhere in the prehistoric world. This figure becomes even higher when factoring in at least some of the many reported occurrences of human-mammoth associations that have been reported in Mexico (Arroyo-Cabrales et al. 2006). Even allowing for problems of preservation and site identification, they conclude that Clovis reliance on mammoth and mastodon was higher than that of virtually any other global Ice Age hunting society.

Cannon and Meltzer (2004) seem to come close to acknowledging this problem when they question whether it is appropriate to generalize early Paleoindian foraging strategies at a continental scale and note that assemblage differences should occur at sites with different functions. This observation opens the possibility that different *kinds* of people responsible for different parts of Clovis diets created or contributed to different kinds of sites (e.g., Chilton 2004; Waguespack 2005). Put differently, current thought on Clovis subsistence economies seems to accommodate a scenario wherein some people focused on gathering or trapping small game while others may have focused on large, highly ranked taxa when they were available. This variable contribution to Clovis diets accounts for variations in site types as well as the presence and frequency of anatomical remains of prey characterized by differences in body mass.

To the degree that this brief summary characterizes current statements on Clovis diet specialization, in our view the debate seems to overlook how Clovis economic activities were organized for the purpose of hunting big animals. With respect to the question of whether Clovis peoples included specialized big-game hunters, most focus has been placed on diet breadth, which might stand as a proxy for how band-level task groups organized their labor. Based on abundant evidence of diverse diets, it is clear that Clovis society *in general* did not focus exclusively on large herbivores. Mammoth and other large game were taken under certain circumstances, while in other contexts subsistence activities focused on small game. Yet, based on technological debris from residential camps like Gault, *some* people obviously spent a great deal of time preparing tool kits involved in hunting large animals. Conflating diet-breadth decisions with other economic activities, including the manufacture and use of different parts of Clovis tool kits, leaves archaeologists poorly able to understand how labor arrangements were scheduled, negotiated, or expressed as an important component of larger, society-wide adaptive strategies. In response, our focus here is on technological behavior associated with gearing up for logistically organized big-game hunting. We distinguish hunting as a separate activity from gearing up, where we currently find better evidence for specialization.

TOWARD UNDERSTANDING EMBEDDED SPECIALIZATION IN HUNTER-GATHERER SOCIETIES

We argue that the way the concept of specialization has been dealt with in Clovis scholarship has impeded our understanding of the ways in which terminal Pleistocene economies were organized to facilitate cultural adaptations across an enormous and highly diverse landscape. Anthropologists commonly associate economic specialization with complex societies (see reviews by Clark 1995; Costin 1991). Indeed, for some, economic specialization is one of the defining traits of complex (chiefdom- or state-level) societies and is decidedly *not* to be found among "simple" band-level groups. Concerning economic activities at the band level of integration, for example, Elman Service (1962:108) argues that "there are no special economic groups or special productive units such as guilds or factories, no specialized occupational groups, no economic institutions such as markets, no special consuming groups or classes. The economy, in short, is not separately institutionalized, but remains merely an aspect of kinship organization; in the usual modern sense of the word, there is no formal economy at all."

To the extent that Paleoindian societies were not integrated by markets or production guilds, this statement is accurate. Yet it overlooks the potential for behavioral complexity in terms of how productive activities were organized in ways having to do with individual-level aptitude and skill. It also overlooks the important role of task groups in successful adaptive strategies, whether or not those groups exist in the context of kin-based networks.

The views of Service and others are starkly at odds with abundant ethnographic data regarding uneven performance at the level of the individual among forager bands (e.g., Hill and Kintigh 2009; Wiessner 1996). Based on evidence of individual-level behavioral specialization that is *not* focused on diet breadth among some sociable animal groups (e.g., Araújo and Gonzaga 2007; Sargeant et al. 2005; van Schaik and Pradhan 2003), it could easily be argued that specialization in certain undertakings defines not only complex human societies but nearly *all* animal societies (Bolnick et al. 2003). In addition to individual specialists, specialized task groups are well established in hunter-gatherer studies. For example, Binford's (1980) forager-collector continuum, a model that is most often used to describe archaeological site patterning on the landscape, is fundamentally a working hypothesis for how economic production can be organized and carried out by persons who possess skills, aptitudes, and abilities that set them apart from others. Binford (1980:10) notes that "logistically organized task groups are generally small and composed of skilled and knowledgeable individuals. They are not groups out 'searching' for any resource encountered; they are task groups seeking to procure *specific resources* in specific contexts" (emphasis in original). In our view, it is significant that some archaeologists (e.g., Cross 1991; Seeman 1985) have looked at specialization among hunter-gatherers in ways that are not predicated on stages of evolutionary complexity.

Taking a cross-cultural view of specialization allows researchers to examine how technological production may have been organized in Clovis societies by identifying important linkages between resource availability, different approaches to sequencing or scheduling production, the development of skill arising from divisions of labor, relations between individuals and task groups, and considerations of efficiency and standardization. An important study by John Clark and William Parry (1990) used historical and ethnographic data to define the full range of how specialization can be organized, including in ways that allow scholars to decouple the concept from questions of social complexity. According to the minimal definition shared among the many case studies reviewed by Clark and Parry, specialists are simply those who produce goods used by others. John Cross (1991:65) defines specialization somewhat more specifically by considering the

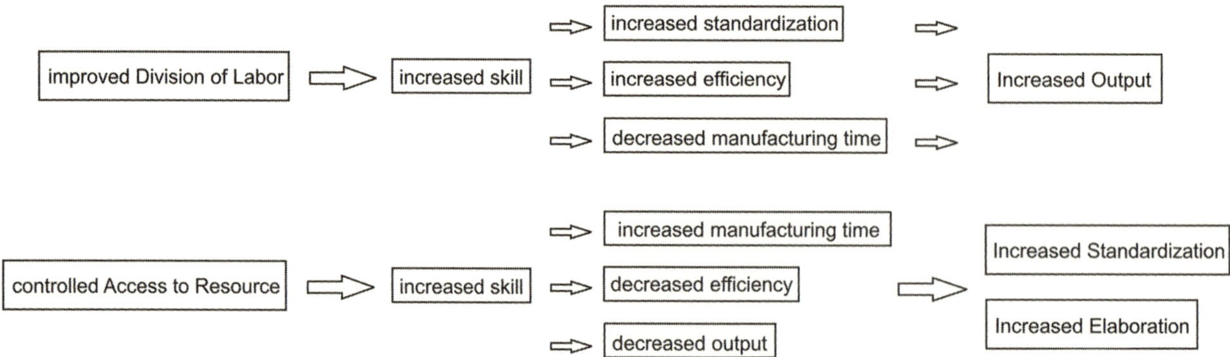

Figure 9.1. Models of economic production defined by Adam Smith (top) and Bronislaw Malinowski (bottom). Smith's model describes specialization as a means to increase production efficiency and standardized output, while Malinowski's model shows the decreased availability of increasingly elaborate prestige goods. In each version, specialized production shares common attributes but is organized differently depending on intended objectives and also control relationships between producers and consumers.

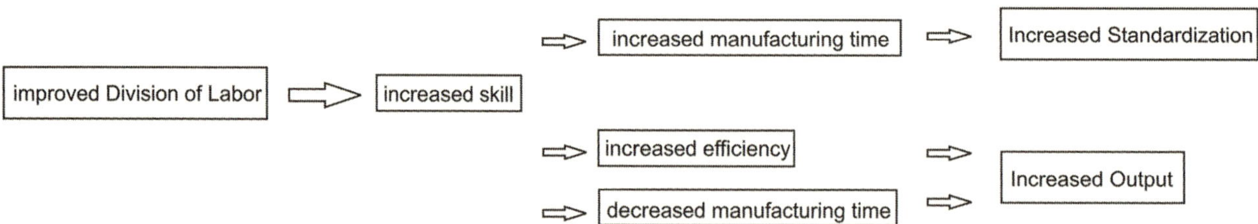

Figure 9.2. Alternative configuration of specialization and its possible implications with respect to Clovis

relative volume of production. For Cross, specialization is "a situation in which a large portion of the total production of a class of items is generated by a small segment of the population." By this definition, a specialist either spends more time on his or her task or is highly skilled so that she or he produces a higher quantity of a given good in the same amount of time as another person. One important emphasis found in Cross's approach to specialization is on relations that exist between producers and consumers. Kenneth Ames (1995) retained Cross's emphasis on time but contextualized specialization in relation to kinship-based modes of production that presumably would have characterized band-level societies like Clovis. For Ames, "embedded specialists" are those who produce in the context of their kin or communal roles; their work is part of local or domestic economies, yet they spend a larger share of their time at it than do others. This progression in how specialization is defined greatly advances the theoretical understanding of this concept by archaeologists and can help researchers model the organization of some Clovis labor-based task groups. We see Cross's emphasis on producer-consumer relations and Ames's concept of embeddedness as particularly suitable for application to prehistoric hunter-gatherers.

Using important historical studies of specialized economic production, Clark and Parry (1990) defined two poles along which specialization can be organized. In one example, eighteenth-century factory workers increased their production of pins from 20 to over 4,000 per day (Smith 1970 [1776]). Through increased division of labor, each worker improved his or her skill and thereby reduced manufacturing time, increased standardization, and increased production efficiency. All of these improvements in the production process led to increased output. In the other example, some Polynesian chiefs controlled raw material used for making special axes; the limited availability of key resources resulted in increases in worker skill and also tethered those workers and their output to controlling individuals (Malinowski 1922). As a result, specialists spent more time at their work but actually decreased their productivity. However, the axes that were produced were more elaborate and standardized than before (Figure 9.1).

These two case studies define a "field" of specialization and help demonstrate how it might appear in different cases, including among terminal Pleistocene foragers like Clovis peoples. Clear labor divisions lead to increased skill; archaeologists can see this as *differences* in skill level (see Bamforth and Finlay 2008; Lohse 2010, 2011). Skilled producers can either increase or decrease the amount of time they spend manufacturing tools; neither can be easily measured without associated production debris. However, higher skill and more time spent manufacturing can translate into increases in both standardization and success rates at the individual level. Stylistic elaboration may also indicate skill and, together with consistent approaches to the overall design process, can also help suggest the presence of minimal numbers of producers. Increased time spent on production can be offset by strategies that raise efficiency and help to bring up output (Figure 9.2).

In evaluating alternative configurations of specialization and what they mean for Clovis economic behavior, it is important to consider the relationship between skill and either standardized or increased output. In some cases analysts can hypothesize about the work of skilled individuals through observation of idiosyncratic stylistic traits or through statistical comparisons. Alternatively, archaeologists might examine how efficiency was increased by organizing production into sequential steps or stages of reduction. As we show, this strategy is readily seen in many Clovis caches. Importantly, making a case for Clovis embedded specialization by linking technological attributes with behavioral approaches to standardizing production or increasing output does not require analysts to associate a given cache with the work of a single knapper. Rather, we see the production of cached bifaces and other implements as part of a larger economic system that included highly skilled toolmakers whose contributions to some assemblages are disproportionately represented compared with other band members (in the sense used by Bamforth 1991). From this perspective, our objective is not to identify *an* individual knapper but rather to characterize discrepancies in Clovis technological production that reflect uneven degrees of productive skill and time or labor investment.

THE HOGEYE CLOVIS CACHE

Here we present the results of our analysis of a portion of the Hogeye cache, which was recovered by owners of a sand quarry near Bastrop, Texas. Our analysis was conducted in a single visit to the home of the cache owners in early December 2004. At that time we viewed a total of 24 artifacts (Jennings [2013] has since reported data for all 52 pieces). We took a number of precise measurements (Table 9.1), classified the specimens by reduction stage, described the condition of the pieces and their flaking patterns, and photographed each face of all specimens (through oversight, only one face of Specimen 21 was photographed). Our initial assignment of reduction stages was based on the approximate morphology of each specimen and also on certain important flaking details. While complete Clovis biface reduction sequences have been described elsewhere (e.g., Bradley et al. 2010), the Hogeye cache seems to represent only late-middle to late-stage reduction. Ovate forms, our earliest reduction stage, represent the beginning of a formal or regular outline and show a relatively consistent thickness partly achieved through overshot flaking. Lanceolate preforms follow this stage and are defined by straight bases and near-parallel sides. Overshot flaking occurs at this stage as well, as does end thinning (early fluting) on some specimens. Once achieved, lanceolate forms are carefully reduced in terms of length, width, and thickness to what we identify as a nearly complete but still unfinished stage, unfinished points. All of these are fluted on at least one face, and thinning by overshot has been replaced by more judicious use of biface thinning flakes and edge margin trimming.

In order to assess how accurately these categories reflect intentional stages in the shaping of each piece along a trajectory toward late-stage preforms, we converted width and thickness measurements to ratios (Table 9.2). It was felt that no useful information could be derived from length measurements since so many of the specimens were missing either their tips or bases.

The portion of the cache we saw included 3 ovate bifaces, 8 lanceolate bifaces, and 13 late-stage preforms (Figures 9.3, 9.4). All are of Edwards chert, many have calcium carbonate encrusted on one or both faces, and many show mechanical and/or heat damage from the quarry operation. All clearly evince Clovis technological traits, including controlled overshot flaking and, for later-stage pieces, fluting. In our assessment, none of the late-stage preforms qualifies as an actual Clovis point since all lack final edge trimming, shaping, and basal grinding. Presumably these final steps would have been undertaken prior to hafting and use but were not considered necessary steps for completing whatever scheduled interval of gearing up that this cache represents.

TABLE 9.1. Measurements (in mm) and Descriptions of Hogeye Bifaces

SPEC. NO.	FORM	LENGTH	WIDTH	THICKNESS	COMPLETE?	FLUTED?
2	Ovate	122.5	60	7.7	y	n
3	Ovate	103.6*	55.5	11.6	n—medial frag	n
6	Ovate	141.7	67	9.3	n—distal tip missing	y
1	Lanceolate preform	122.5	48.4	10.4	y	n
4	Lanceolate preform	82.8*	57.4	10.6	n—basal frag	y
5	Lanceolate preform	143.7	49.6	9.6	n—distal tip missing	y
7	Lanceolate preform	142.5	55.8	15.8	n—distal tip missing	y
8	Lanceolate preform	123.4	57.1	10.7	n—distal tip missing	y
9	Lanceolate preform	122	50.4	8.7	n—basal ear missing	y
10	Lanceolate preform	120.3	48.1	10	y	y
11	Lanceolate preform	114.7	53.1	9.4	y	y
12	Unfinished point	114.1	41.4	9.4	y	y
13	Unfinished point	109	34.5	8.3	y	y
14	Unfinished point	108	39.2	8.1	n—distal tip and basal ear missing	y
15	Unfinished point	105.5	34.4	9.2	y	y
16	Unfinished point	98.9	30.2	6.7	n-basal ear missing	y
17	Unfinished point	97.5	33.7	8.2	y	y
18	Unfinished point	97.4	33.8	7.8	y	y
19	Unfinished point	93.2	32.6	7.3	n—distal tip and basal ear missing	y
20	Unfinished point	90.3	30.3	8.1	y	y
21	Unfinished point	89.3	29.7	8.2	y	y
22	Unfinished point	88.4	31.8	8.2	n—both basal ears broken	y
23	Unfinished point	85.7	31.8	7.3	n—distal tip and basal ears missing	y
24	Unfinished point	65.1*	35.4	7.9	n—basal section only	y

Note: Length measurements with an asterisk are incomplete and are not considered useful.

TABLE 9.2. Proportional Ratios of Width / (Width + Thickness) and Thickness / (Width + Thickness)

SPEC. NO.	FORM	W / (W + TH)	TH / (W + TH)
2	Ovate	0.886	0.113
3	Ovate	0.827	0.172
6	Ovate	0.878	0.121
1	Lanceolate preform	0.823	0.176
4	Lanceolate preform	0.844	0.155
5	Lanceolate preform	0.837	0.162
7	Lanceolate preform	0.779	0.220
8	Lanceolate preform	0.842	0.157
9	Lanceolate preform	0.852	0.147
10	Lanceolate preform	0.827	0.172
11	Lanceolate preform	0.849	0.150
12	Unfinished point	0.814	0.185
13	Unfinished point	0.806	0.193
14	Unfinished point	0.828	0.171
15	Unfinished point	0.788	0.211
16	Unfinished point	0.818	0.181
17	Unfinished point	0.804	0.195
18	Unfinished point	0.812	0.187
19	Unfinished point	0.817	0.182
20	Unfinished point	0.789	0.210
21	Unfinished point	0.783	0.216
22	Unfinished point	0.795	0.205
23	Unfinished point	0.813	0.186
24	Unfinished point	0.817	0.182

Subsequent to our analysis, Mike Waters of Texas A&M University was also given the opportunity to examine the cache. At this time it became clear that the 24 specimens we saw were actually a portion of a larger assemblage that also included a collection of 13 bifaces known at the time as the Wall cache. Kilby (2008) refers to this smaller assemblage as the Bastrop County cache; it had been loaned to Waters for study by the owner, who had apparently purchased or acquired it apart from the original assemblage. Waters has since visited the cache site, where he and his colleagues recorded the archaeological and geological context of the find spot and conducted controlled excavations that recovered additional specimens. The Hogeye cache now numbers 52 artifacts and has been extensively documented (Jennings 2013).

In our classification, ovate bifaces have biconvex outlines with weakly defined tips and bases and retain a number of overshot flake scars with retouched terminations. No serious hinge or step terminations are visible on any of the three bifaces. Even though the distal and proximal ends of Specimen 3 (see Figure 9.3) are missing, this piece is included in this category based on its strongly convex shape. Importantly, none of these artifacts (including Specimen 3) shows any evidence of end thinning. Neither of the two that have intact bases (Specimens 2 and 6; see Figure 9.3) has a squared base, which marks another important distinction between this form and lanceolate bifaces.

Lanceolate bifaces (see Figure 9.3) have parallel to biconvex margins, squared bases, and better-defined converging tips. Additional marginal retouch was performed to further shape the outlines of these pieces compared with the ovate forms. Overshot flaking is present on most but not all specimens. The few bifaces that do not display this trait clearly show possible overshot flakes whose terminations were removed by subsequent marginal retouch. Importantly, all but one of these bifaces show evidence of having been basally thinned by longitudinal

Figure 9.3. Ovate (specimens 2, 3, and 6) and lanceolate (1, 4, 5, 7–11) bifaces in the portion of the Hogeye cache discussed here (photo by M. Collins)

flakes. Analysis of bifaces in various stages of reduction from Gault and other Clovis contexts (Bradley et al. 2010:83, 93) shows how many of the end thinning (fluting) scars were removed through subsequent thinning and shaping, before late-stage preforms were fluted as one of the final steps in the production of finished points.

The late-stage preforms we analyzed are all considered to be unfinished points; as noted, none have any basal edge grinding, which is common among completed Clovis points, and all lack last-stage edge trimming. All of these specimens have well-defined outlines shaped by intensive marginal retouch and consistently concave bases. Eight bases are intact enough that distinct "ears" can be seen. Specimens with complete or mostly complete bases also show a distinct asymmetry, with one ear dropping lower than the other (see Specimens 13, 15, 16, 17, 19, 20, 21, and 24 in Figure 9.4). In our view, it is compelling that so many of the Hogeye unfinished points share this stylistic trait, which appears to have been entirely nonfunctional in nature. All of these artifacts are excurvate in outline, all are fluted, and all fluting preceded final basal retouch. In general, these 13 artifacts have a great deal in common in terms of morphology, the sequence with which certain operations were performed, and idiosyncratic style.

These 24 Hogeye specimens reflect a staged approach to reducing bifaces in a number of ways. Variation in form, traits, and measurements occurs within each stage, but this variation lessens with further reduction. Although our reduction categories are subjectively based on outline and form, they are confirmed by certain technological traits. For example, some distinction appears

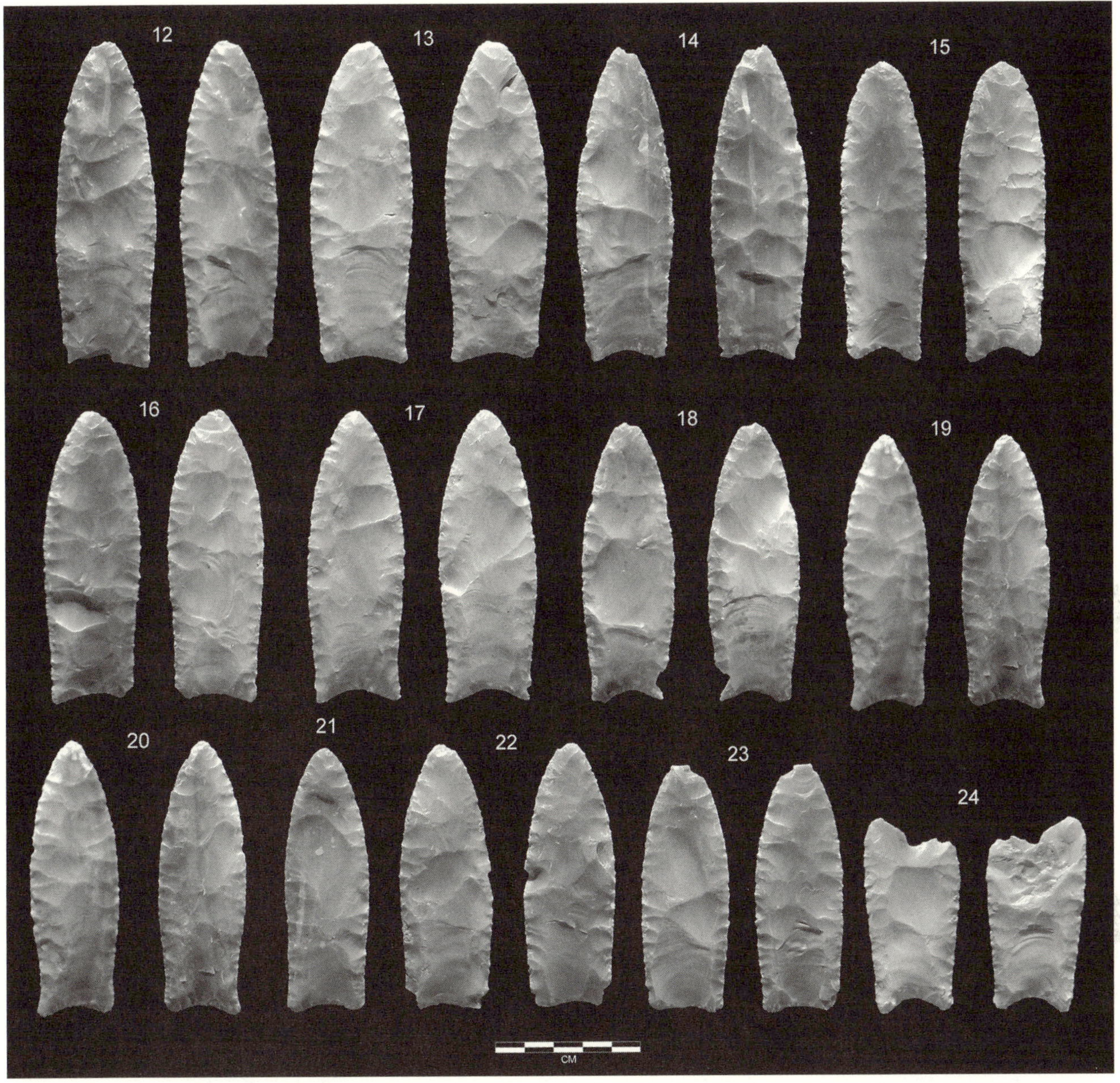

Figure 9.4. Late-stage preforms from the part of the Hogeye cache presented here. Only one face of specimen 21 was photographed (photo by M. Collins).

between ovate and lanceolate bifaces in terms of basal shaping and thinning; ovate bifaces were not end thinned while all but one lanceolate artifact were. Staging is also indicated by comparing both the dimensions and proportions of the artifacts. Since many of the tips and bases were broken, we only use width and thickness measurements. When plotted by these dimensions, these three stages can be distinguished, with ovate bifaces the most dispersed and unfinished points forming the smallest cluster (except for a single outlier; Figure 9.5). Importantly, there is no overlap between unfinished points and lanceolate preforms.

The artifacts also retain their groupings when compared in terms of width and thickness proportions (Figure 9.6), although unfinished points and lanceolate bifaces overlap slightly and there are a couple of outliers. Evaluating proportions in addition to absolute measurements helps to show standardization in terms of how intended outcomes or objectives were achieved. These values reveal that while the unfinished points are both thinner and less wide than lanceolate bifaces, they are consistently thicker *by proportion* than lanceolate bifaces. This makes sense if analysts think of shaping lanceolate preforms by marginal retouch, which occurs more

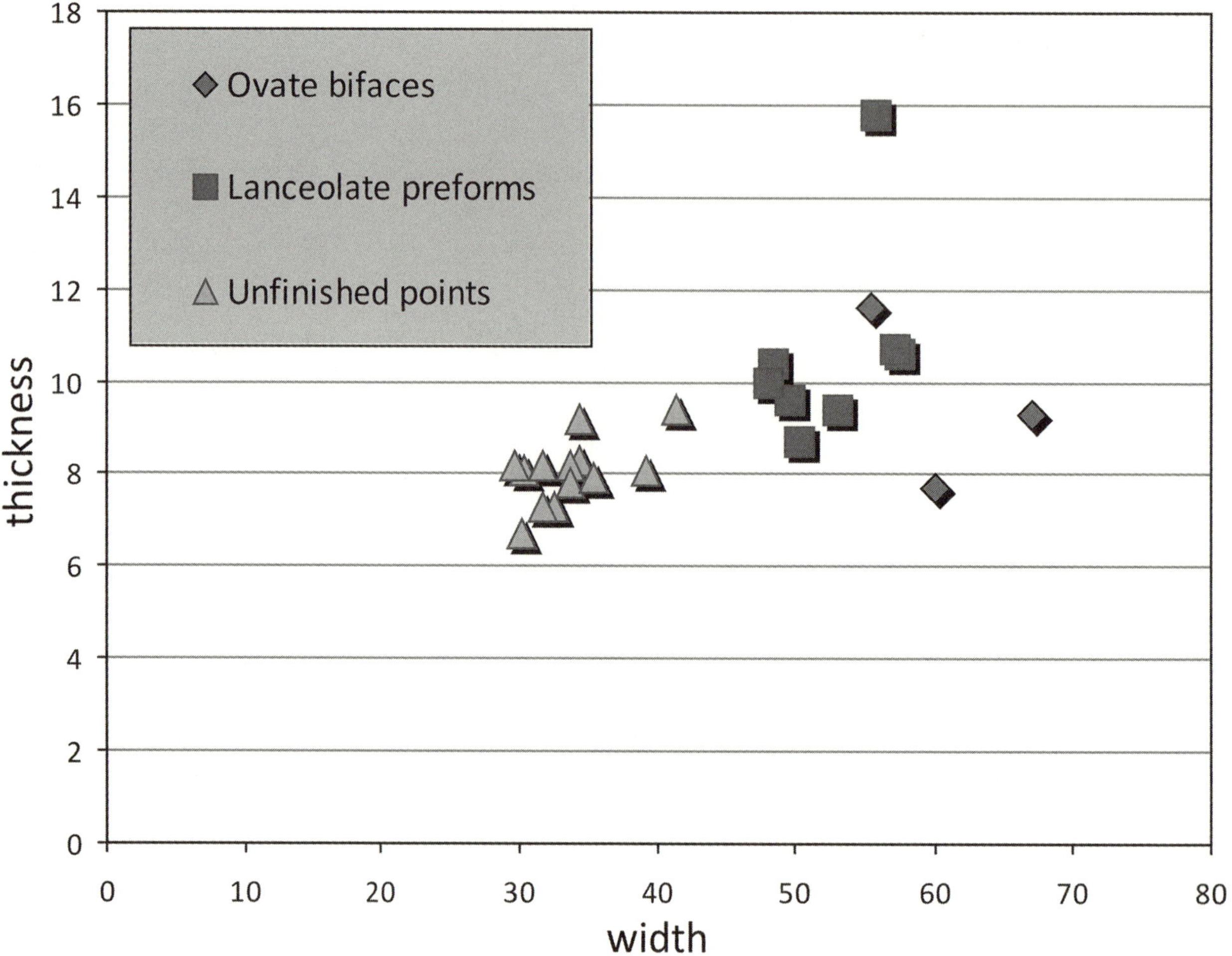

Figure 9.5. Hogeye specimens (n = 24) plotted by width and thickness

intensively at this stage than in the previous one; comparatively short flakes that do not carry to or across a biface's midline make that specimen narrower without significantly altering its thickness. It appears as if the knapper(s) of this assemblage consistently achieved the desired thickness for these specimens at the lanceolate biface stage; virtually all subsequent adjustments involved finalizing the margins.

When stylistic observations of these specimens are considered together with metric and proportional data, a circumstantial case can be made that this cache represents the work of a very small number of knappers. Supporting evidence is seen in the clarity of the technological staging and also in the absolute measurements and proportions. Additional support comes from the shared stylistic traits on the unfinished points. Presumably, if more knappers were involved in making this cache, more technical approaches and more variation in knapper performance would be seen. These conclusions can also be drawn from examinations of the de Graffenried and Fenn caches.

De Graffenried

The de Graffenried cache consists of five specimens, including four oval bifaces and one late-stage preform (Figure 9.7). The lanceolate preform is highly comparable to the unfinished points from Hogeye in that no edge grinding is present and final margin trimming and shaping were not carried out. Based on oral and historical accounts, this cache may have been recovered from within or near the Gault site (Collins et al. 2007). All five pieces are made of a variety of Georgetown chert found at Gault. Like Hogeye, de Graffenried shows a distinctly staged approach to biface reduction, although the small size of this cache precludes more detailed assessments of what it represents in terms of strategies for increasing biface production efficiency. Given the similarity in size, dimensions, and

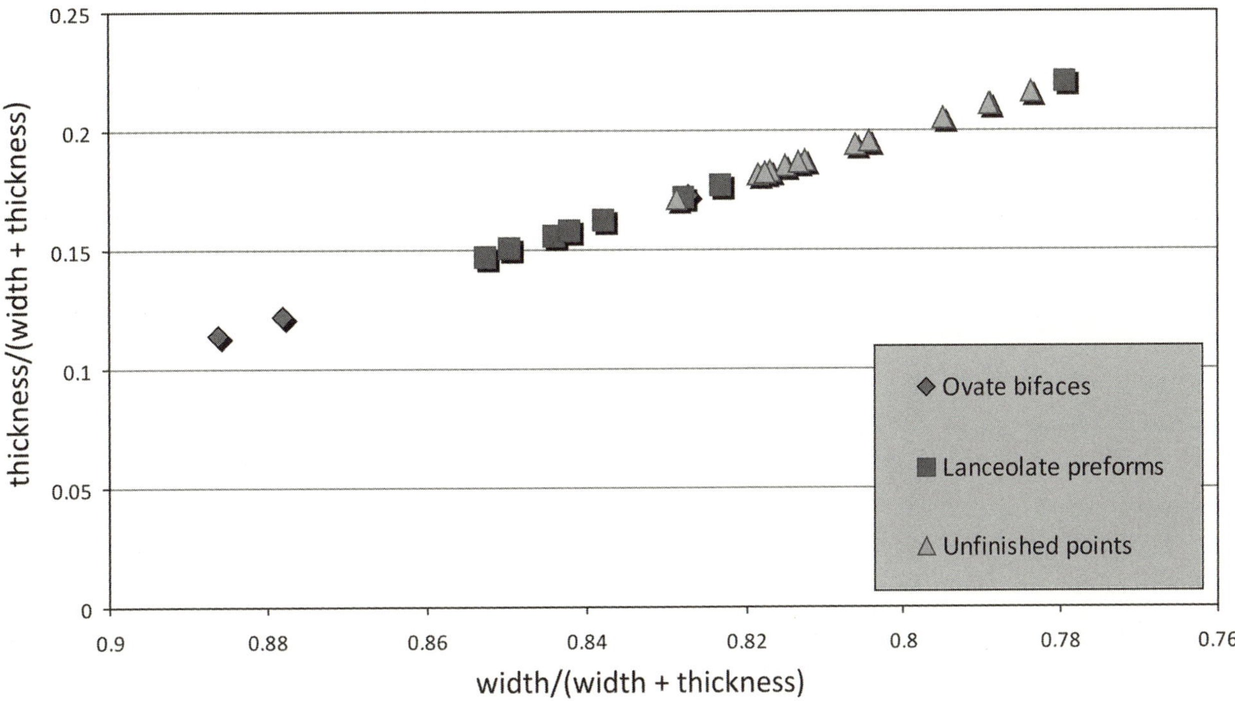

Figure 9.6. Proportional ratios based on width and thickness for 24 Hogeye specimens

proportions of the four oval bifaces (Figure 9.8), a circumstantial case can be made that this cache also represents the work of a very small number of knappers. Clearly, however, a larger sample of specimens would be necessary to substantiate this point.

Fenn

One of the best-studied Clovis caches is Fenn, recovered near the converging corners of Utah, Wyoming, and Idaho (Frison and Bradley 1999). This collection consists of 54 whole and broken points, preforms, lanceolate bifaces, and oval and round bifaces (two additional specimens, a crescent and a blade, are not discussed here). Six different materials types are represented, including Utah agate, Green River chert, obsidian, red jasper from northern Wyoming, quartz, and an unknown material.

The Fenn cache includes forms that, as in Hogeye and de Graffenried, appear to represent different stages of reduction down to almost finished but not yet used points. Unlike Hogeye and de Graffenried, however, Fenn also contains Clovis points that have been used and resharpened and even a few that have been broken, presumably from use. In their study, Frison and Bradley (1999) label pieces as "points" and "bifaces," terms that carry no information concerning stage of reduction. However, some pieces are similar to stages defined for the Hogeye and de Graffenried collections, such as lanceolate preforms and round or oval bifaces. By examining published illustrations and descriptions, we created categories approximating those used for Hogeye and de Graffenried for the Fenn specimens. These categories include round bifaces, oval or ovate bifaces, lanceolate bifaces (also preforms), and points (Table 9.3). Using these categories to compare Fenn with Hogeye and de Graffenried creates some problems in terms of how reduction is represented among the three assemblages, since staging is not as clearly expressed in Fenn as in the other two caches. However, these problems are relatively minor and are overcome by our statistical evaluation of the three caches (see below).

Round bifaces ($n = 3$) are large and nearly perfectly round in outline. Large thinning flakes extending beyond the midline are easily visible on these pieces; many carry all the way across a face to the opposing margin. Little or no marginal retouch is evident on these specimens. Ovate bifaces ($n = 4$) have converging distal and proximal ends and are significantly less wide than round bifaces. Margin trimming is only slightly more well defined than that seen on the round bifaces. Based on form and flaking attributes alone, we suggest that these two categories may reflect approximately the same stage of reduction. Lanceolate bifaces/preforms ($n = 25$)

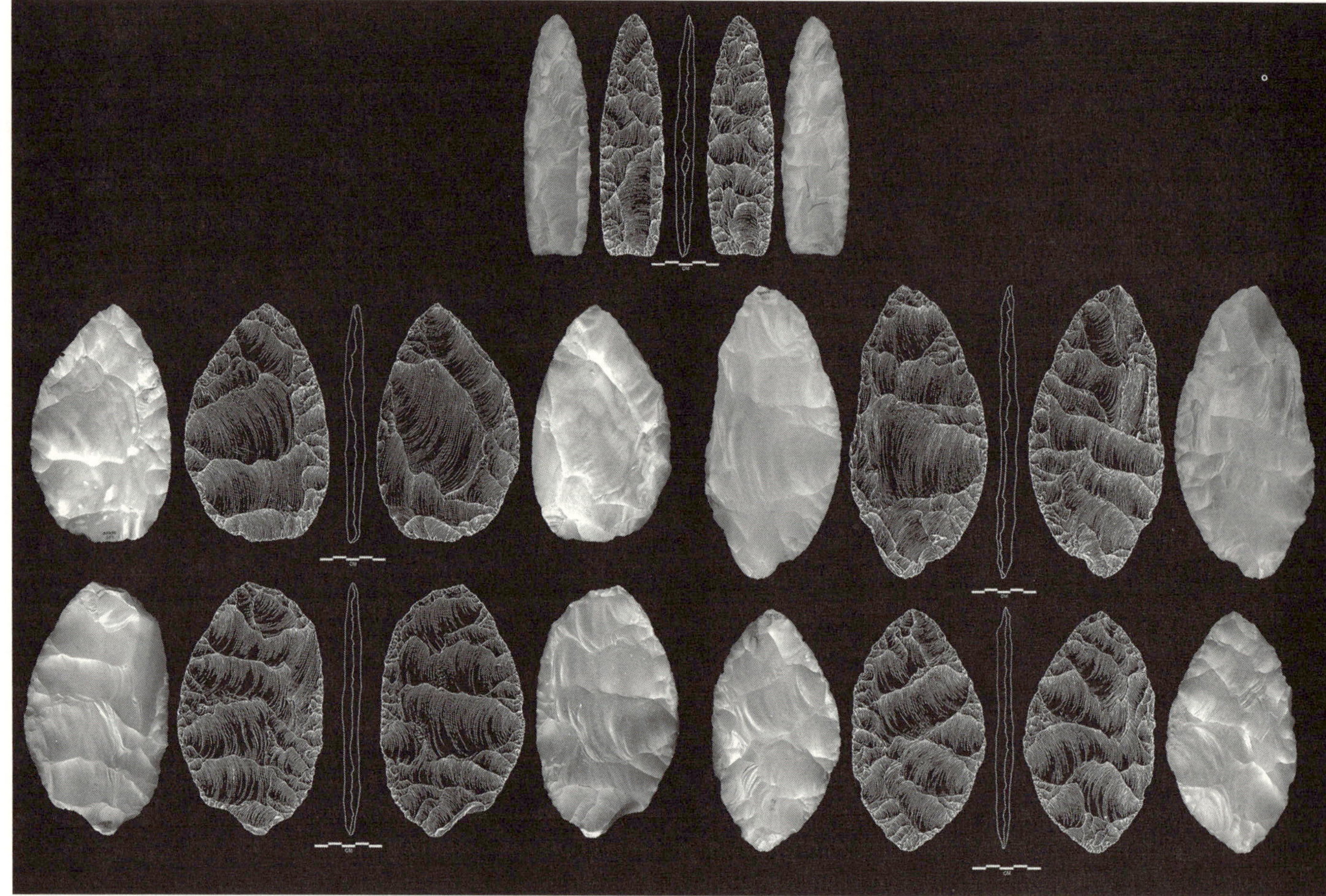

Figure 9.7. The five bifaces making up the de Graffenried cache (photos by M. Gardner and line drawings by F. Weir, used with permission)

have converging tips, convex outlines, and squared bases. Many show end thinning yet lack the kinds of final-stage margin shaping found on unfinished points in Hogeye. This category is problematic since many of the lanceolate bifaces/preforms made on Utah agate are finely worked and appear to be very near completion; these probably correspond most closely with unfinished points in the Hogeye and de Graffenried samples. However, other lanceolate bifaces, especially those of Green River chert, are considerably earlier in reduction. The variation of raw material in this category seems to reflect diversity in terms of knapper approaches to staging reduction. Points (n = 22) were identified as such by Frison and Bradley and have all of the attributes of the Hogeye unfinished points. However, several show evidence of having been resharpened after use while three or four are broken at or near their midsection. In general, more variation in staged reduction is represented in Fenn than in the other two caches.

When plotting the Fenn bifaces by width and thickness alone, points separate from the other bifaces with the exception of two specimens, which overlap with the loose cluster of lanceolate preforms (Figure 9.9). Interestingly, the three round bifaces fall well to the right on this graph, with wide but relatively thin measurements. In this respect they strongly resemble the oval bifaces from de Graffenried, although the thickness measurements of the Fenn specimens are slightly greater than those from de Graffenried (see Figure 9.8). However, unlike Hogeye and de Graffenried, distinctions between forms become lost when width and thickness proportions are considered (Table 9.4). Except for round bifaces, the artifacts are virtually indistinguishable in terms of proportion. To some degree, this overlap may reflect the imprecision of evaluating these specimens by reduction stage using only published descriptions and illustrations. Nevertheless, it is compelling that points and lanceolate preforms overlap completely when plotted by proportion. This pattern

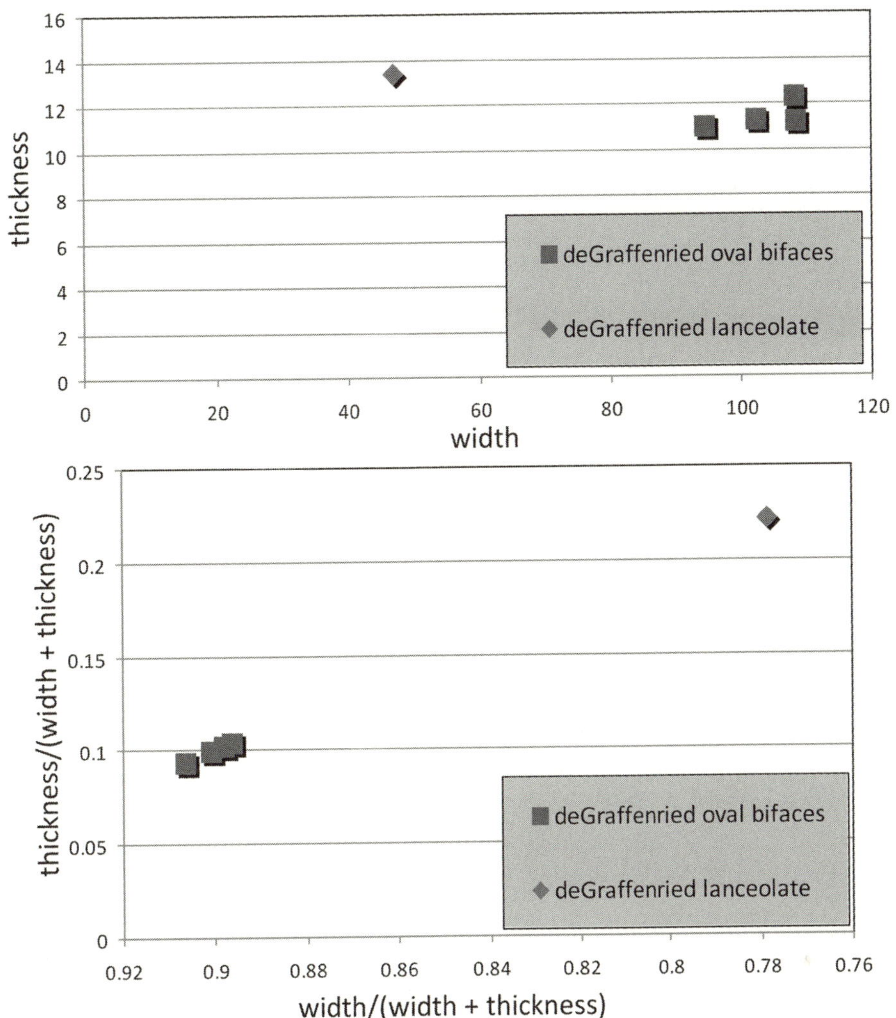

Figure 9.8. The de Graffenried cache artifacts by width and thickness values (top) and by proportion of width and thickness values (bottom). Each graph clearly shows the staged and also standardized approach to the production of these two biface forms. See Collins et al. (2007) for measurements of these artifacts.

supports our contention that, unlike Hogeye and de Graffenried, the Fenn materials represent greater variation in how thinning and reducing Clovis bifaces to late-stage preforms and finished points was accomplished.

In their analysis of the Fenn material, Frison and Bradley address the possibility of individual-level specialization by considering flaking style. They describe several finished points characterized by distinctive diagonal flaking that is so consistently well done that they conclude it may be the work of a single individual (Figure 9.10). This style appears on points of different materials, including both points made on jasper and many of the 11 points made of agate. However, the pattern is absent from others, specifically on two of the three quartz points. In addition, we note that raw material diversity increases by reduction stage, using the categories we identify. Only two material types are found among round bifaces, three for ovate and lanceolate preforms, and yet points are made using all six materials. This suggests that some very late-stage artifacts, specifically points, *may have been* contributed by people with different access to materials or who had different priorities for staging biface reduction.

DISCUSSION

Making a case that some Clovis caches are the result of knappers working under conditions of specialization requires using multiple lines of evidence simultaneously, and what works well for one cache does not necessarily translate to others. Models that can be tested with cache data need to be informed by some of the cross-cultural principles that attend different forms of specialization. Globally, many instances of specialization share an emphasis on modifying production by increasing standardization, output, or both. In some cases, this is accomplished

TABLE 9.3. Data for Fenn Bifaces Taken from Frison and Bradley (1999:Table 1), Except "Form" (Assigned during This Study)

CATALOG NO.	MATERIAL	FORM	WEIGHT	LENGTH	WIDTH	THICKNESS
135	A	Lanceolate	119.5	149.2	59.2	11.9
132	A	Lanceolate	183.1	185	61.8	12.7
130	A	Lanceolate	186.7	168	60.3	15.3
134	A	Lanceolate	156	168.2	58.6	12
126	A	Lanceolate	217	179.8	63.7	15.5
124	A	Lanceolate	260.5	195.5	68	16.1
125	A	Lanceolate	224.1	196.5	63.6	12.8
133	A	Lanceolate	179	151.8	67.9	14.6
127	A	Lanceolate	118.8	150	62.9	9.5
131	A	Lanceolate	217.4	212.7	67.7	13.4
123	A	Lanceolate	252.5	189.2	69.7	16.6
129	A	Lanceolate	229.2	189	62.5	16.1
122	A	Lanceolate	328.9	213	74.1	17.1
128	A	Lanceolate	282.2	193.4	70.1	17.8
119	G	Lanceolate	135.3	157	57.1	12.6
114	G	Lanceolate	78.1	117.7	49.6	11.3
115	G	Lanceolate	111.1	147.5	56.2	10.6
113	G	Lanceolate	162.3	164.5	62.7	13.5
109	G	Lanceolate	398.4	219.5	86.5	17.2
118	G	Lanceolate	136.6	135	60.3	13.1
112	G	Lanceolate	306.5	199	79.5	17
117	G	Lanceolate	158.2	146.2	64.3	16.1
116	G	Lanceolate	150	154.7	60.4	13.4
103	O	Lanceolate	181.8	172	67.7	13.7
102	O	Lanceolate	175.2	154.1	65.6	16.9
110	G	Ovate	206.5	162.5	71.5	16.7
105	O	Ovate	365.2	188.5	86.6	22.3
101	O	Ovate	196.3	156	70	15.9
104	O	Ovate	316.3	194.5	71.4	24.4
108	G	Round	384.5	204.5	108.2	13.9
111	G	Round	440.7	205	114.8	13.8
100	O	Round	640.7	211	145.5	17.6
140	A	Point	20.5	77.8	32	6.8
142	A	Point	36.3	107.5	36.5	7.9
146	A	Point	24.9	79.4	39.4	8.3
141	A	Point	32.5	103.7	34.4	7.3
143	A	Point	31.3	114.6	33.7	6.9
144	A	Point	38.6	123.1	34.6	7.6
145	A	Point	41.6	133.7	38.2	7.3
138	A	Point	18.6	93.1	26.6	6.6
139	A	Point	23.7	91.9	31.6	6.6
136	A	Point	92.2	171	47.8	8.9

CATALOG NO.	MATERIAL	FORM	WEIGHT	LENGTH	WIDTH	THICKNESS
137	A	Point	156.9	212.5	53.8	11.7
153	Q	Point	29.3	101.4	32.7	8.1
154	Q	Point	28.3	99.9	33.2	7
155	Q	Point	26.1	86	34.5	7.9
121	G	Point	32.6	105.5	37.6	7.2
120	G	Point	23	79.4	37	7.2
147	G	Point	31.2	85.1	35.1	8.5
148	J	Point	28	82.9	37.6	8.1
149	J	Point	79.6	152	46.3	9
106	O	Point	33.2	76.8	43.2	8.2
107	O	Point	32.3	110.2	38	8.2
150	–	Point	62.9	150.7	40.6	8.6

Note: A = Utah agate; G = Green River Formation chert; O = obsidian; J = red jasper; Q = quartz; – = unknown.

by developing and maintaining skill differentials between producers or by increasing the efficiency with which production is carried out. Differences in skill often imply that a great deal more time was spent honing and maintaining physical abilities and cognitive awareness of production requirements (Pelegrin 1990; see Lohse 2011) and, consequently, on production itself. Strategies for increasing production efficiency can be noted in terms of staging reduction, while methods for distinguishing skilled from unskilled production are increasingly identified by archaeologists (e.g., Bamforth and Finlay 2008; Geribàs et al. 2010).

Identifying standardization is also difficult and can be approached in different ways. In our evaluation of three caches, we see common (standard) approaches to staging reduction; identifying such standardized approaches is important to our study not only because it allowed knappers to produce bifaces more efficiently through task scheduling, and as such was an important component of specialization, but also because it is shared among the three assemblages we evaluate. Elsewhere it is apparent that, although staged reduction characterizes some other Clovis biface assemblages, reduction staging *per se* does not characterize *all* biface production (Bradley et al. 2010:77–79). In other words, even though reduction stages are clear in some cases, not all Clovis biface production appears to have been as clearly staged as we see in Hogeye, de Graffenried, and Fenn. In our view, this has important implications for identifying cases of specialist production apart from "ordinary" production at domestic camp sites. For example, at Gault (Bradley et al. 2010) and Murray Springs (Huckell 2007), biface production appears as a continuous sequence occurring over several episodes of thinning and shaping, at times interrupted by the actual use of these implements.

In addition to standardized approaches to biface design and manufacture, we recognize certain idiosyncratic attributes that may indicate individual-level elaboration. Specifically, these include asymmetrical bases on Hogeye unfinished points and diagonal flaking on many of the Fenn points. By itself, neither attribute is an overly compelling argument for individual-level specialized production, yet these traits cannot be accounted for with any functional explanation. The fact that not all Fenn points were finished using diagonal flaking suggests that more than one individual contributed to this assemblage, a conclusion that is supported in part by our reduction stage and proportional data. This particular trait of the Fenn material complicates comparison of these caches using the same procedures. Although width and thickness values and proportions confirm a single approach to biface reduction at Hogeye, proportions do not work as well for analyzing the Fenn material. However, because the diagonal flaking used on Fenn points removes both width and thickness while the late flaking on Hogeye materials mostly affects width, analysts should not be discouraged to find that proportional measurements are not as useful for Fenn as for other caches. It turns out that technological standardization is both complemented and complicated by idiosyncratic variation like basal ears in Hogeye and diagonal flaking in Fenn. Both caches show standardization, but in different ways.

A final approach to understanding standardization involves the use of nonparametric statistics to quantify

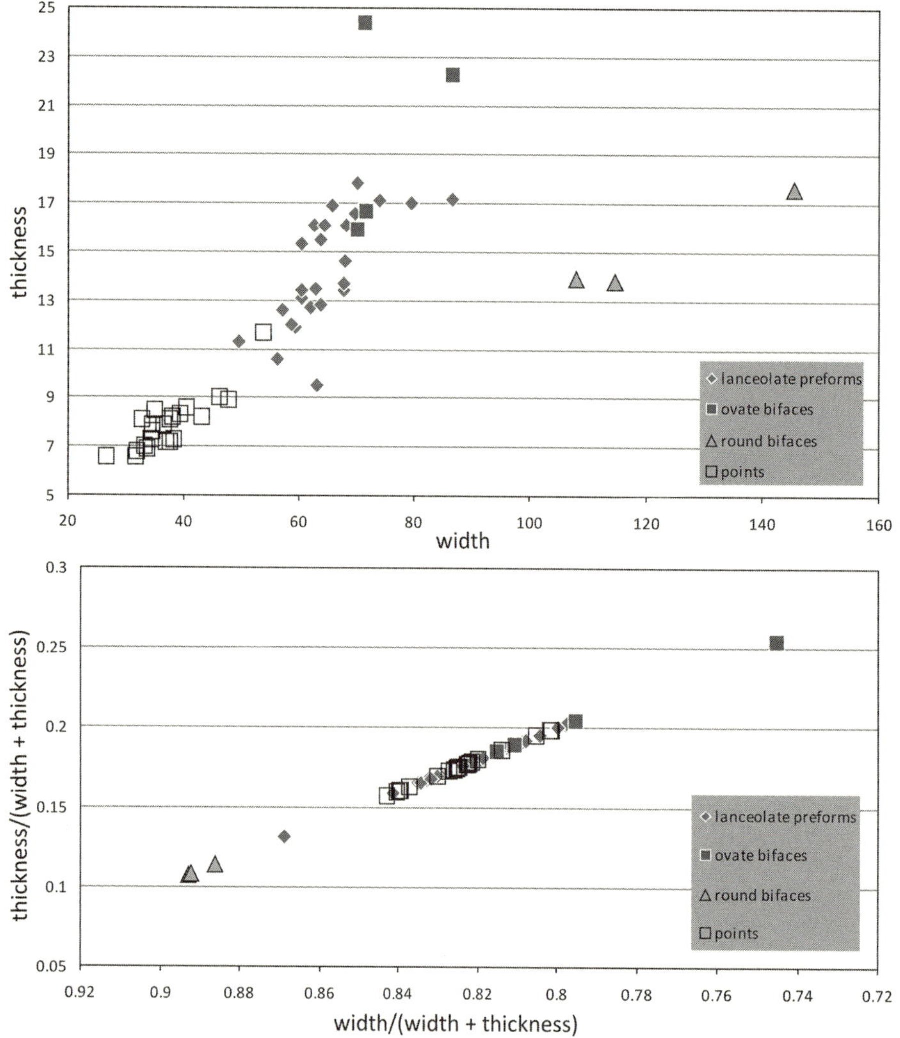

Figure 9.9. Fenn cache materials plotted by width and thickness measurements (*top*) and by proportional ratios of width and thickness (*bottom*). See Frison and Bradley (1999:Table 1) for measurements used for these graphs.

variation within and between different reduction groups for each of the three caches. We assume that metric variation reflects different approaches taken by the knapper(s) who contributed to each cache. Although even skilled knappers can exhibit variation in their work (Finlay 2008), we see greater amounts of variation as possible evidence that multiple knappers contributed to the assemblage(s) in question. Analyses showing that certain intracache reduction categories are defined by remarkably low degrees of variation can provide indirect support for our proposition that relatively few knappers produced those bifaces. Here we compare round and ovate bifaces from Fenn, Hogeye, and de Graffenried; lanceolate preforms from Fenn and Hogeye; and points from Fenn and Hogeye.

Descriptive statistics, including mean, median, standard deviation, and coefficient of variation, as well as a variety of nonparametric inferential statistical tests were used to examine variation by cache and reduction group. For inferential statistics, we employed Mann-Whitney, Kruskal-Wallis, Kolmogorov-Smirnov, and Median tests. Mann-Whitney and Kruskal-Wallis tests examine the variation within and among two and more than two samples, respectively (Daniel 1990; Zar 1999). A goodness-of-fit test, Kolmogorov-Smirnov compares frequency distributions between two groups. The median test uses samples' medians to determine whether or not two or more groups represent the same, or similar, populations. These tests measure variation, dispersion, and central tendencies of at least two samples.

For these comparisons, we used the same proportional ratios between width and thickness measurements that have been previously presented. These ratios allow us to assess relative degrees of standardization in biface

TABLE 9.4. Proportional Ratios of Width / (Width + Thickness) and Thickness / (Width + Thickness) of Fenn Bifaces

CATALOG NO.	FORM	W / (W + TH)	TH / (W + TH)
135	Lanceolate	0.832	0.167
132	Lanceolate	0.829	0.170
130	Lanceolate	0.797	0.202
134	Lanceolate	0.830	0.169
126	Lanceolate	0.804	0.195
124	Lanceolate	0.808	0.191
125	Lanceolate	0.832	0.167
133	Lanceolate	0.823	0.176
127	Lanceolate	0.868	0.131
131	Lanceolate	0.834	0.165
123	Lanceolate	0.807	0.192
129	Lanceolate	0.795	0.204
122	Lanceolate	0.812	0.187
128	Lanceolate	0.797	0.202
119	Lanceolate	0.819	0.180
114	Lanceolate	0.814	0.185
115	Lanceolate	0.841	0.158
113	Lanceolate	0.822	0.177
109	Lanceolate	0.834	0.165
118	Lanceolate	0.821	0.178
112	Lanceolate	0.823	0.176
117	Lanceolate	0.799	0.200
116	Lanceolate	0.818	0.181
103	Lanceolate	0.831	0.168
102	Lanceolate	0.795	0.204
110	Ovate	0.810	0.189
105	Ovate	0.795	0.204
101	Ovate	0.814	0.185
104	Ovate	0.745	0.254
108	Round	0.886	0.113
111	Round	0.892	0.107
100	Round	0.892	0.107
140	Point	0.824	0.175
142	Point	0.822	0.177
146	Point	0.825	0.174
141	Point	0.824	0.175
143	Point	0.830	0.169
144	Point	0.819	0.180
145	Point	0.839	0.160
138	Point	0.801	0.198
139	Point	0.827	0.172
136	Point	0.843	0.156
137	Point	0.821	0.178
153	Point	0.801	0.198

TABLE 9.4 *(continued)*

CATALOG NO.	FORM	W / (W + TH)	TH / (W + TH)
154	Point	0.825	0.174
155	Point	0.813	0.186
121	Point	0.839	0.160
120	Point	0.837	0.162
147	Point	0.805	0.194
148	Point	0.822	0.177
149	Point	0.837	0.162
106	Point	0.840	0.159
107	Point	0.822	0.177
150	Point	0.825	0.174

manufacture in two different yet related ways. The relationship between width and thickness was calculated in two ways:

1. Width / (width + thickness) (henceforth referred to as W / (W + Th))

2. Thickness / (width + thickness) (henceforth referred to as Th / (W + Th))

Results of Statistical Comparisons

For descriptive statistics (Table 9.5), we focus on trends in variation as expressed by coefficient of variation (CV), which are unitless and therefore comparable (Zar 1999:40). Considerable differences in CV between W / (W + Th) and Th / (W + Th) of any particular artifact class (i.e., category and site) indicate that changes in thickness have a greater effect on the ratio than equal changes in width. These differences imply that Th / (W + Th) is more sensitive to variation, although both proportions can be used to identify standardization and within-category variation.

Ratios of W / (W + Th) and Th / (W + Th) for ovate and round bifaces show the greatest amounts of variation among all biface forms. Ovate artifacts from de Graffenried, however, had the lowest CVs across any artifact form or cache. The stark contrast in CVs for de Graffenried ovate bifaces and for similar artifacts at Fenn and Hogeye is not attributable to the smaller size of the sample from de Graffenried but rather indicates precision in terms of repeatedly achieving similar width and thickness dimensions for the four bifaces in this cache. Regarding the other two caches, Fenn has more variation than Hogeye, in both W / (W + Th) and Th / (W + Th), which may support our assertion that the Fenn cache represents the work of multiple knappers.

Lanceolate preforms are present only in Fenn and Hogeye, and in general these artifacts from these two caches show marked decreases in variation in relation to ovate and round bifaces. Whereas W / (W + Th) CVs for preforms from these two assemblages are relatively similar, Th / (W + Th) CVs differ considerably. Hogeye's greater lanceolate preform Th / (W + Th) CV indicates that although both sites' assemblages are similar in width, the thickness of lanceolate preforms from Hogeye is more variable. Comparing means and medians of the Th / (W + Th) for the two collections, Hogeye lanceolate preforms are thinner than similar artifacts from the Fenn cache.

Not surprisingly, points have the lowest CVs of all reduction categories (with the exception of de Graffenried ovate bifaces). Fenn points are less variable than those from Hogeye. Based on this fact alone, one might conclude that there were regional differences in skill level between the northern and southern Plains.

Some general trends can be seen in the descriptive statistics for cached bifaces across reduction categories and by cache. First, variation generally decreases as artifacts undergo further reduction. From this analysts can conclude that, under most scenarios, it may be difficult to find supporting evidence of minimal numbers of knappers from earlier-stage artifacts using measures of variation. Ovate bifaces from de Graffenried, which show far lower CVs than any other artifact or cache category, are an important exception. Also, differences in variation appear among comparable artifacts from different caches or sites. Lanceolate bifaces from Fenn and Hogeye are

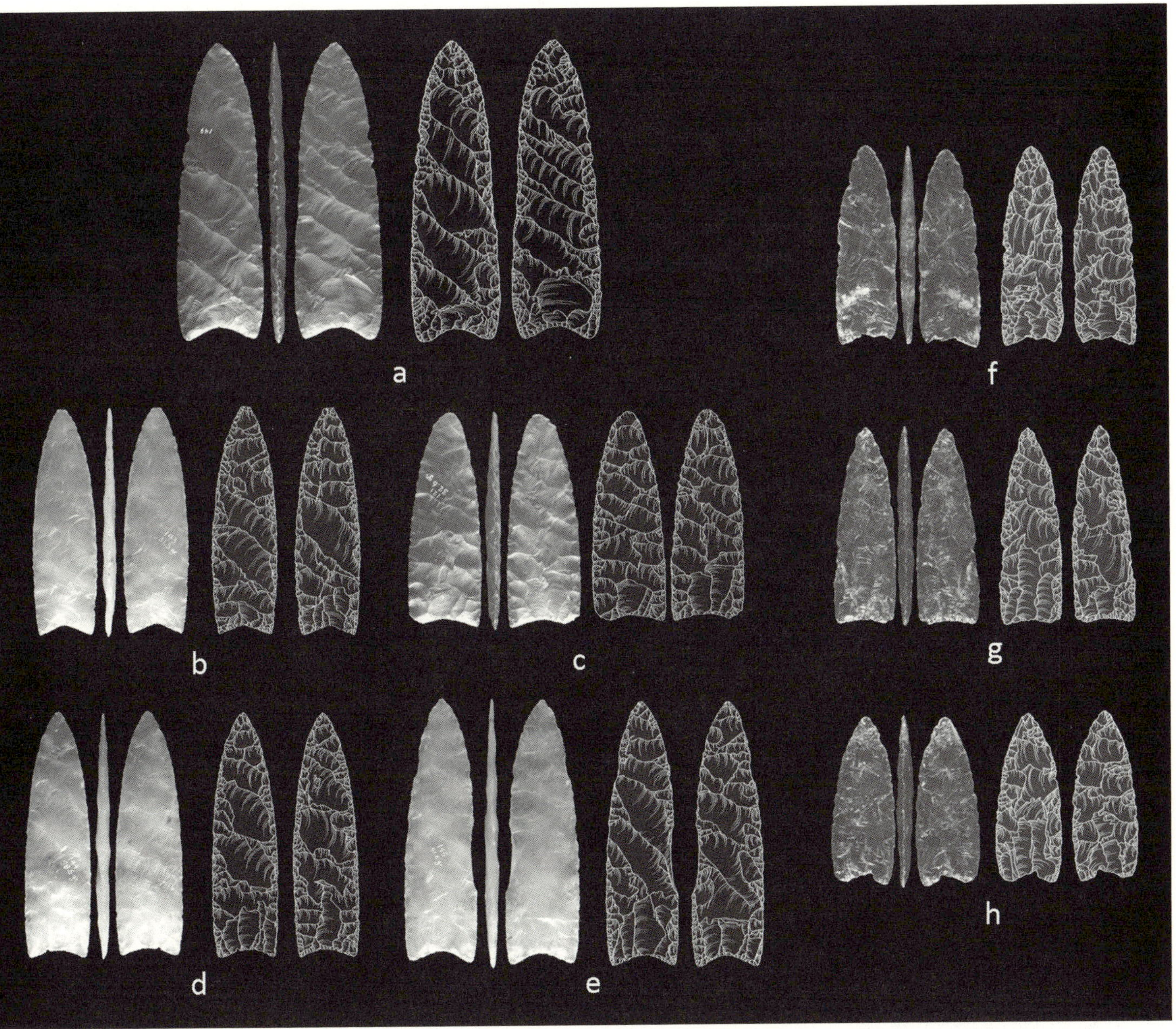

Figure 9.10. Examples of Fenn points of different materials that show and do not show diagonal flaking style: (a) red jasper; (b), (d), (e) Utah agate; (c) Green River chert; (f), (g), (h) quartz. Quartz points are reworked yet clearly lack the flaking pattern (reproduced with permission from Bruce Bradley; original photographs by Pete Bostrom and line drawings by Sarah Moore). All are shown in proportionally correct size in relation to each other.

roughly comparable in terms of CV, while points from Fenn and Hogeye also favorably compare. Not only does variation in general decrease with reduction, but rates of increasing standardization appear to be relatively constant within assemblages from the same cache.

In order to verify these observations, we performed a number of inferential statistical tests (Table 9.6) using as our null hypothesis the proposition that variation is equivalent between sites with respect to reduction category. We evaluated cache assemblages by reduction category using two different degrees of confidence, an alpha level of 0.01, and an alpha level of 0.05. Kruskal-Wallis and Median tests applied to round and ovate bifaces from Fenn, Hogeye, and de Graffenried indicate that at the 0.01 alpha level, the null hypothesis of equal variation and medians among the caches is not rejected. That is to say that width-to-thickness ratios for round and ovate bifaces from Fenn, Hogeye, and de Graffenried are not significantly different in terms of variation and medians. With the 0.05 alpha level, however, the same

TABLE 9.5. Descriptive Statistics for Hogeye, Fenn, and de Graffenried Reduction Groups

	POINTS		LANCEOLATE PREFORMS		OVATE AND ROUND BIFACES		
	Fenn	Hogeye	Fenn	Hogeye	Fenn	Hogeye	de Graffenried
W / (W + Th)							
n	22	13	25	8	7	3	4
Mean	0.825	0.807	0.820	0.832	0.834	0.864	0.900
Median	0.825	0.813	0.822	0.840	0.815	0.878	0.898
SD	0.012	0.014	0.017	0.024	0.057	0.032	0.004
CV	1.452	1.713	2.113	2.835	6.893	3.710	0.497
Th / (W + Th)							
n	22	13	25	8	7	3	4
Mean	0.175	0.193	0.180	0.168	0.166	0.136	0.100
Median	0.175	0.188	0.178	0.160	0.185	0.122	0.102
SD	0.012	0.014	0.017	0.024	0.057	0.032	0.004
CV	6.848	7.158	9.616	14.053	34.594	23.538	4.489

Note: Width and thickness ratios for Hogeye and Fenn are included in Tables 9.2 and 9.4, respectively. Values for de Graffenried are from Collins et al. (2007:Table 1). SD = standard deviation; CV = coefficient of variation.

null hypothesis of equal variation and medians is rejected for W / (W + Th) yet retained for Th / (W + Th). In other words, width is significantly different among round and ovate bifaces from these caches while thickness remains fairly consistent.

Results of Mann-Whitney, Median, and Kolmogorov-Smirnov tests on two samples of lanceolate preforms, Fenn and Hogeye (de Graffenried has only one lanceolate preform and so was not included), indicate that at an alpha level of 0.01, the null hypothesis of equal variation, medians, and distribution frequencies failed to be rejected in terms of W / (W + Th) and Th / (W + Th). Again, an alpha level of 0.05 yielded slightly different results, but this time for variation in both width and thickness. At this reduced confidence level, the same null hypothesis was rejected for variation but failed to be rejected for medians and distribution frequencies. This indicates that with a less rigorous alpha level, variation in lanceolate preforms in terms of W / (W + Th) and Th / (W + Th) is significantly different between the Fenn and Hogeye caches, although medians and distribution frequencies are statistically similar.

Points from Fenn and Hogeye were subjected to Mann-Whitney, Median, and Kolmogorov-Smirnov tests. At both alpha levels of 0.01 and 0.05, the null hypotheses of equal variation and medians were rejected, meaning that variation and medians of points from the two caches are significantly different. In other words, variation, medians, and distribution frequencies of points are significantly different among these two assemblages.

Discussion of Statistics

Together, descriptive and inferential statistics applied to artifacts from Fenn, Hogeye, and de Graffenried identify important trends with respect to standardization in the production of Clovis bifaces and points. Based on our analyses, variation in width and thickness decreases from earlier to later reduction stages. Moreover, relative to width, thickness is a more variable attribute throughout the manufacturing process, though it, too, decreases along the tool-making continuum. These trends were indicated by descriptive statistics and substantiated by nonparametric tests.

The low CV values for Fenn and Hogeye indicate remarkable standardization with respect to W / (W + Th) ratios, and we argue that these low values are most easily explained in terms of each cache representing the work of a minimal number of knappers. This conclusion receives some support from the still-low CVs for W / (W + Th) for

TABLE 9.6. Nonparametric Inferential Statistics Results for Hogeye, Fenn, and de Graffenried Reduction Groups

	POINTS			LANCEOLATE PREFORMS			ROUND AND OVATE BIFACES[a]		
	p value	a level 0.05	0.01	*p* value	a level 0.05	0.01	*p* value	a level 0.05	0.01
W / (W + Th)									
Mann-Whitney Test	0.000	Reject	Reject	0.036	Reject	Retain	-	-	-
Kruskal-Wallis Test	-	-	-	-	-	-	0.017	Reject	Retain
Median Test	0.000	Reject	Reject	0.085	Retain	Retain	0.017	Reject	Retain
Kolmogorov-Smirnov Test	0.000	Reject	Reject	0.055	Retain	Retain	-	-	-
Th / (W + Th)									
Mann-Whitney Test	0.000	Reject	Reject	0.036	Reject	Retain	-	-	-
Kruskal-Wallis Test	-	-	-	-	-	-	0.060	Retain	Retain
Median Test	0.00	Reject	Reject	0.085	Retain	Retain	0.060	Retain	Retain
Kolmogorov-Smirnov Test	0.000	Reject	Reject	0.055	Retain	Retain	-	-	-

Note: Width and thickness ratios for Hogeye and Fenn are included in Tables 9.2 and 9.4, respectively. Values for de Graffenried are from Collins et al. (2007:Table 1).

[a]Includes de Graffenried.

Fenn and Hogeye lanceolate bifaces. The higher CVs for Th / (W + Th) indicate, as noted above, that thickness measurements are much more sensitive to variation than width, and we observe that, in general, the same trends hold true for this measurement as for W / (W + Th). With respect to earlier-stage categories, the extremely low CV for de Graffenried ovate bifaces is remarkable, and this small assemblage probably offers the best indirect evidence of a single knapper of any of the artifacts considered in our study.

Our use of nonparametric statistics allowed us to discern important differences between the apparently low CVs between Fenn and Hogeye in terms of medians and variation. Statistically, the amount of internal variation seen within the Fenn and Hogeye points shows that the Fenn assemblage displays much greater standardization in terms of width and thickness than Hogeye. From this, one can suggest that the relative degree of knapper skill seen in Fenn is higher than that of Hogeye, so long as "skill" is expressed through standardized output. An alternative explanation is that Hogeye's greater degree of variation reflects a higher number of contributing knappers than seen in Fenn points, although our earlier observations do not support this conclusion. In either case, the production of these artifacts was not carried out under identical circumstances with respect to skill and standardization, and perhaps in the size of the task group responsible for producing points.

CONCLUSIONS

In this study we argue that at least some parts of certain Clovis biface caches are the result of occupational specialization on the part of toolmakers. Here specialization does not refer to full-time or industrial-scale production, which are characteristics of complex prehistoric economies. Further, specialization is not to be confused with narrow diet breadth. Rather, we see the labor role of certain individuals, people who were disproportionately responsible for manufacturing the weapons systems that were important in hunting proboscidean prey, as firmly embedded in the kin-based economic structures that characterize many band-level societies, the views of Elman Service and others notwithstanding. An important element of specialization that sets most hunter-gatherers apart from "complex" societies is that specialized production does not necessarily involve control over labor. Rather, relations of production often remain largely (i.e., long-term in duration) egalitarian until scales of organization exceeded what could be effectively negotiated through face-to-face interactions (Lee 1990).

Similar instances of specialized production have been recognized for Paleolithic societies elsewhere. For example, Soffer (1985) argues that the production of prismatic blades in the Central Russian Plain around 20,000 years ago represents some form of part-time craft production. Conkey (1985) identifies carved Middle Magdalenian objects such as spear throwers from the French Pyrenees that indicate a close adherence to formalized rules of production, perhaps associated with specialized ritual production. Closer to our study region, Bamforth (1991) notes that post-Clovis fluted points occur in much higher frequencies at communal kill sites than at camp sites on the North American Plains and that unfluted points commonly occur in nonkill site contexts dating to the same periods. His implication is that many of the fluted points (which are harder to make) actually used for hunting were made by a smaller segment of the population than was engaged in making points. With these cases in mind, we conclude that the kind of embedded specialization that we argue was associated with Hogeye, de Graffenried, Fenn, and perhaps other Clovis caches was an important adaptive feature of North American forager economies during the terminal Pleistocene.

Based on our study, at least two additional concluding hypotheses can be offered regarding specialization in Clovis societies. First, statistical analyses indicate that, except under unusual circumstances, only very late-stage bifaces (unfinished points) reveal the kinds of standardization that we see as indicative of specialized production. Earlier stages of reduction, including round or ovate and lanceolate biface preforms are often indistinguishable according to width and thickness variation. Specimens from different caches can of course be identified based on material and perhaps stylistic traits. But, aside from de Graffenried, we are able to distinguish the work of a very small number of toolmakers only in the very last stages of reduction. Importantly, this is also the stage where idiosyncratic elaboration seems to appear. Artifacts that represent this final stage of production are notably scarce in camp site and production contexts where bifaces representing all degrees of reduction down to but excluding unfinished points are present along with broken, resharpened, and discarded points. To the degree that studies like Bamforth's (1991) evaluation of fluted and unfluted points in camp and communal hunting contexts accurately reflect the proportions in which these points were made and used, the clear implication is that the output of only a relatively few knappers was actually used in logistically organized hunting excursions. It is possible that the absence of suitable samples of very late-stage forms from most noncache contexts may contribute to the low amount of attention North American scholars have historically given to specialized Clovis production.

A second concluding hypothesis, following from the first, is that the evidence presented here most likely indicates *individual*-level specialized production. At least in some cases, as illustrated by cache contents, the labor output of only a very small number of workers is represented among parts of tool kits that were used to hunt and kill large herbivores. This conclusion warrants discussion in light of what archaeologists know or surmise about other economic activities, such as hunting, that involve larger task groups. Recent analysis at the Bull Brook site in Massachusetts (Robinson et al. 2009) confirms the original assessment that this site results from a single occupation event that may have been scheduled for a communal caribou hunt. The Casper site (Frison, ed. 1974) is interpreted as a communal, mass bison kill site belonging to the Hell Gap complex in central Wyoming. Many other mass Paleoindian bison kill sites (e.g., Cooper [Bement 2007] and others [Carlson and Bement 2013]) can and should be interpreted as communal efforts as well (Frison 1988). Saunders (1992) suggests Clovis mammoth hunting may have targeted family units (although Frison [1988] argues that opportunistic culling of individuals had a higher probability of success), a broadly shared Paleolithic strategy that may be at least 27,000 years old (e.g., Fladerer 2001) and that would necessarily involve multiple hunters working in concert. The kinds of special-purpose task groups that would have been involved in forays organized around logistical hunting of highly ranked large prey characterize Binford's (1980) collector form of organization. They also seem theoretically at odds with the generalized foraging strategy that many archaeologists have argued for Clovis (see above). Nevertheless, the likely presence of such specialized task groups adds another layer of complexity to the individual-level specialization that we interpret for some Clovis-period labor scheduling and economic organization. This is not to say that additional economic strategies were not also present, potentially including other instances of specialized as well as nonspecialized production. Each of these strategies represents an important aspect of Clovis adaptive behavior in need of further research before archaeologists can fully understand the spread of Clovis cultural patterns in the terminal Pleistocene.

The debate about whether Clovis peoples were specialized large-game hunters has not significantly advanced our understanding of Clovis specialization, hunting or otherwise. Consequently, aside from furthering our general knowledge about diet breadth, this issue has failed to contribute substantially to what we know about Clovis economic adaptations and strategies. Knowing whether Clovis people were specialized big-game hunters will require developing and testing models that quantify how people spend their time hunting or that measure different rates of success relating specifically to taking large herbivores. In this study, which focuses on gearing up, we look at the staged manufacture of bifaces and points from cache contexts that were intended for use in logistical big-game hunting and make the case that this task was carried out under conditions of specialization. Considering where caches are found (Kilby 2008), it seems clear that this kind of specialized production was an important aspect of Clovis economic adaptation in certain regions of Pleistocene North America.

In many Clovis caches we see the effect of increased skill in terms of high success rates (none of the bifaces we looked at are failures) and intracache standardization in width and thickness values and proportions. Additionally, we observe idiosyncratic variation like asymmetry in basal ears or diagonal flaking and, for Hogeye and de Graffenried, technological approaches to staged reduction that suggest restricted ideas about knapping and tool design. Staging at Fenn is present but is harder to see, perhaps indicating that more than one person made that cache. Each of these traits is a key aspect of specialized systems of economic production, and understanding how production was organized in terms of specialization as well as generalized production helps archaeologists understand the Clovis cultural phenomenon. We hope that our observations on Clovis economic production will help spur future attention to these important topics.

For Nancy,
Best regards,
Steve Holen

Chapter 10

Clovis Lithic Procurement, Caching, and Mobility in the Central Great Plains of North America

Steven R. Holen

INTRODUCTION

The central Great Plains region is well suited to address the research question of Clovis lithic procurement, caching, and mobility (Figure 10.1). This type of research is possible because the region contains relatively well-known lithic material sources that are macroscopically distinct and are separated by large areas with few or no lithic resources (Holen 1991, 2001a), which makes tracking Clovis peoples' movements via lithic raw material use reasonably accurate. Vast areas with little or no good lithic material required mobile hunter-gatherer groups to carry large quantities of lithic material with them. Caching of these lithic materials provisioned the landscape for times when the group was passing through the area and lithic supplies became low. Lithic caching on the central Great Plains offers a glimpse into Clovis planning strategies to provision this landscape with high-quality, reliable toolstone in a vast area that is impoverished of high-quality lithic resources.

Regional models of Clovis adaptation are available for the southern Plains (Johnson 1991), the northwestern Plains (Frison 1978, 1991b), and the northeastern United States (Ellis and Lothrop 1989) and more general models of Clovis settlement and subsistence at a continental scale have been developed (Bonnichsen and Turnmire 1991; Haynes 2002b; Kelly and Todd 1988; Meltzer 1993, 2009). However, prior to the work of Holen (2001a), the only model treating Clovis adaptations to the vast central Plains was that of Greiser (1985), which was very brief and unfortunately lacked empirical verification. This lack of research and model development for Clovis on the central Plains stems from the fact that very few Clovis sites have been excavated and only a few preliminary reports of surface-collected material have been published (Blackmar 2001; Hofman and Hesse 2001; Hofman and Gottsfield 2010; Holen 2003; Myers 1987; Prasciunas 2011). Surface-collected artifacts housed in museums and private collections must be included in any research effort because the amount of data available from the few excavated Clovis sites on the central Plains is limited. Only when excavated site data are supplemented with surface data can Clovis mobility be viewed at a high enough resolution that meaningful interpretations can be drawn. This chapter presents the results of a study designed to develop a model of Clovis lithic procurement, caching, and mobility during the Pleistocene-Holocene transition on the central Plains.

BACKGROUND

In order to interpret Clovis mobility on the central Plains, we must have a general idea of (1) what the environment was like and how it changed during the Clovis era; (2) the present knowledge of Clovis lithic procurement and

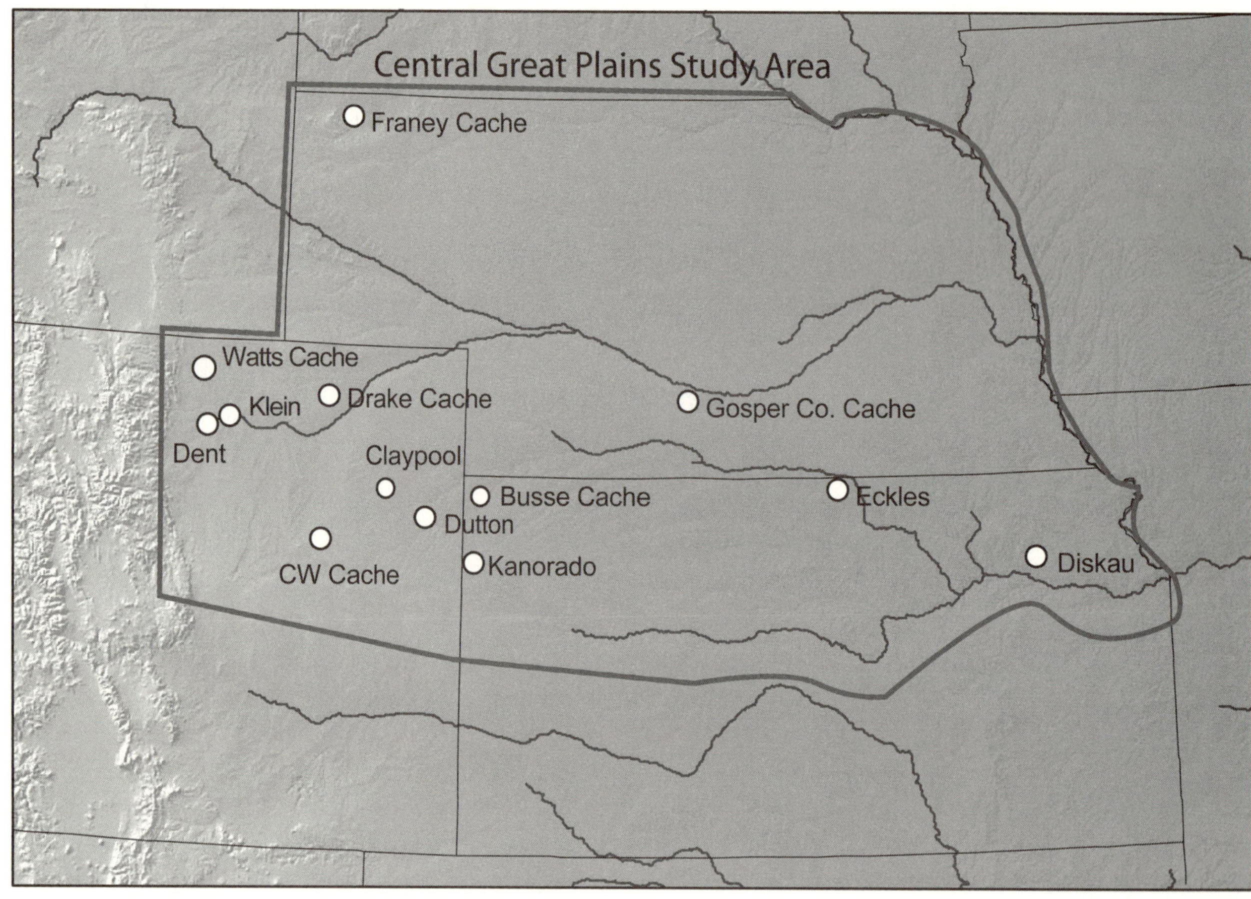

Figure 10.1. Central Plains study area with known Clovis sites.

mobility from previously recorded sites and surface collections; and (3) the lithic landscape that provided the raw material from which we can interpret Clovis mobility.

Paleoenvironmental Setting

Extending southward from the Laurentide ice sheet, the Des Moines and James lobes, in Iowa and North and South Dakota, respectively, reached maximum southward expansion at 14,000 RCYBP (Clayton and Moran 1982). By 11,000 RCYBP the southern glacial margin had retreated back into Canada. South and west of these glacial lobes, the remainder of the central Plains had a significantly different climate than that of today. Many researchers have documented that late Pleistocene vertebrate, invertebrate, and floral communities were "disharmonious" or "intermingled" when compared with modern biotic distributions (Elias 1991; Graham 1976, 1979, 1985; Graham and Semken 1976; Guthrie 1968, 1990b; Hibbard 1960; Lundelius 1989; Wright 1970, 1981). But as Guthrie (1990b:51) has stated, "The seemingly exotic faunal mixtures of the Pleistocene are not disharmonious, it is the present that is so atypical." In other words the Holocene is quite different from the Pleistocene biotic regime.

To summarize a diverse array of paleoenvironmental data, during the Last Glacial Maximum, at 20,000 RCYBP the eastern edge of the central Plains was forested with spruce and mixtures of spruce and deciduous species. Farther west, forests were limited to the river valleys and escarpments. In the area that is now western Kansas and Nebraska and eastern Colorado, the uplands were a vast grassland steppe. Stag moose, mastodon, and sloth inhabited the eastern woodlands while mammoth, horse, camel, and bison dominated the western grasslands. After 12,000 RCYBP palynological evidence suggests the spruce forests began disappearing from the eastern and northern central Plains. At first spruce was replaced by deciduous species and later by prairie as the climate became more arid. This shift probably reflects the beginning of a more seasonal climate with less effective precipitation during the summer.

Climate change during the late Pleistocene appears to have been very rapid. Centuries before the Younger Dryas onset at 10,900 RCYBP, significant climate change began causing biotic community alterations. Both humans and megafauna were living through stressful climatic conditions during this period, experiencing increased seasonality and a warming climate.

The Clovis era is considered to span 10,900–11,400 RCYBP (Haynes 1992, 1993; Haynes 2002b). However, new radiocarbon ages from several important Clovis sites suggest a range of 10,850–11,050 RCYBP (Waters and Stafford 2007). Radiocarbon ages from sites in Texas indicate that the Clovis occupation at Aubrey may extend back to 11,550–11,590 RCYBP (Ferring 1995) and between 11,400–11,500 RCYBP at Wilson-Leonard, a probable Clovis site that does not contain Clovis points (Collins 1999b). It is apparent that Clovis peoples experienced significant climate change and biotic reorganization in as little as 200 or as much as 600 years.

Rapid climatic change between 11,000 and 12,500 RCYBP caused severe stress to biotic communities on the central Plains (Graham 1991; Guthrie 1990b; Martin and Nuener 1978; Meltzer and Mead 1983). Researchers have estimated the number of extinctions at the end of the Pleistocene at between 32 and 38 genera (Graham 1991; Grayson 1989; Meltzer and Mead 1983) that included as many as 39 species (Martin and Nuener 1978). Research by Graham, Guthrie, Lundelius, and others (Graham 1979, 1985, 1991; Graham and Lundelius 1984; Graham et al. 1996; Lundelius 1989; Guthrie 1982, 1984a, 1984b, 1990a, 1990b) points out that loss of habitat is the ultimate cause of extinction and most, if not all, of these species probably would have become extinct even if humans were not present. Humans certainly hastened the extinction of some species and may have been the major cause of mammoth and mastodon extinction.

Most megafauna that would have been prey species for Clovis hunters appear to have become extinct by about 10,800–11,000 RCYBP, leaving bison to play a very important role in Clovis adaptation as bison populations expanded at the end of the Pleistocene. This expansion occurred in part because bison were well adapted to the shift from mid- and tallgrass to shortgrass prairies that began during the Clovis era (Epp 1995; Guthrie 1980, 1984b; Martin et al. 1985). Another significant factor is that *Bison antiquus* populations were at least somewhat migratory on a seasonal basis (Guthrie 1982; Jefferson and Goldin 1989), and this would have allowed them to "catch the same species of plants in early stages of growth" (Guthrie 1984b:268) as the new plant growth progressed northwestward across the Great Plains. Research on migrant versus sedentary ungulate behavior (Fryxell et al. 1988; Epp 1995) concludes that migratory ungulates always outcompete sedentary ungulates when their ranges overlap significantly and that in grassland-woodland ecosystems the migratory ungulates may outnumber their sedentary counterparts by as much as ten to one.

Bamforth (1988) concludes that morphological changes in bison physiology were probably correlated with behavioral changes regarding herd size and the timing and range of seasonal migrations. Based on the relationship between bison ecology and climatic patterns at the end of the Pleistocene, Bamforth (1988:149) predicts that while bison body sizes became smaller, herd sizes increased.

Although Clovis is often associated with mammoth hunting, the Jake Bluff site in Oklahoma (Bement and Carter 2005), the Aubrey site in Texas (Ferring 1995), the Blackwater Draw site in New Mexico (Hester 1972), and the Murray Springs site in Arizona (Haynes 1982; Haynes and Huckell 2007) all contain bison killed by Clovis hunters. In fact, bison is the primary prey species at Jake Bluff and Murray Springs and may be the major prey species at Aubrey. These data suggest that Clovis populations responded to the Pleistocene extinctions by focusing their hunting strategies on bison. This is not to suggest that Clovis peoples focused solely on megafauna to the exclusion of smaller faunal and floral resources; however, it seems clear that bison were important prey species after the beginning of the Pleistocene extinction event. The focus on bison hunting by post-Clovis cultures such as Folsom and Goshen adds further evidence to support this interpretation (Hofman 1999; Frison 1996).

Central Plains Clovis Sites

Thirteen Clovis sites—seven in Colorado, four in Kansas, and two in Nebraska—with some published information are located within the area of the central Plains identified for this study (Figure 10.1). Previous research completed at these sites includes reports of major excavations and documentation of surface-collected materials. Each site is described briefly below, beginning with kill and occupation sites, followed by caches.

The Dent site along the South Platte River near Greeley, Colorado, was excavated in 1933 by a crew from the Colorado Museum of Natural History; it was the first scientifically excavated Clovis site in North America at which spear points directly associated with mammoths were found (Brunswig 2007; Figgins 1933; Saunders 2007). The remains of 15 mammoths and two complete Clovis points and one broken biface were recovered in what may have been a gully trap.

Situated in an upland playa lake in eastern Colorado, the Dutton site consists of a Clovis component overlying a pre-Clovis level excavated in the mid-1970s by the Smithsonian Institution (Stanford 1979; Stanford and Graham 1985). Diagnostic artifacts include one Clovis projectile point and other associated Clovis lithic tools.

The Klein site is a surface collection from a late Pleistocene terrace along the South Platte River in northeastern Colorado (Zier et al. 1993) consisting of two projectile points and a biface tip, probably part of a projectile point, all made of unidentified lithic materials. Test excavations at the site did not locate any undisturbed cultural deposits.

Located in northeastern Colorado, the Claypool site was reported by Bert Mountain, an avocational collector (Dick and Mountain 1960; Stanford and Albanese 1975). The site produced two Clovis projectile points found in a blowout near a mammoth skeleton. Test excavations by Dick in 1953 and later by Stanford in 1975 did not locate any intact Clovis cultural deposits.

The Kanorado site was first excavated as a paleontological site in 1976 and 1981 by the Denver Museum of Natural History. It was later reinvestigated by a joint team from the Denver Museum of Nature & Science and the University of Kansas (Mandel et al. 2004), when it was discovered that three late Pleistocene/early Holocene sites existed along a one-mile stretch of Middle Beaver Creek in far western Kansas. All three sites contain Folsom-age and Clovis-age cultural components in a buried A horizon soil. No diagnostic Clovis artifacts have been found; however, the lithic and faunal components have been dated to 10,950 ± 60 and 11,085 ± 20 RCYBP, suggesting a Clovis cultural affiliation.

Discovered on White Rock Creek in north central Kansas (Holen 2010) where artifacts had eroded out of a late Wisconsin terrace fill, the Eckles site artifacts were not found in situ. Clovis artifacts (Figure 10.2) from the site include 3 projectile points, 1 preform, 2 broken bifaces, 6 gravers, 9 end scrapers, 12 utilized or retouched flakes, 20 pieces of debitage, and 27 biface reduction flakes. Although the Eckles site Clovis assemblage was not recovered in situ, the 80 artifacts are clearly part of the Clovis component because (1) the assemblage includes diagnostic Clovis points and preforms; (2) all of the artifacts are made of the same material, Flattop chalcedony (White River Group silicates [WRGS]) that was moved eastward from the source (Hoard et al. 1991, 1993; Holen 2010); (3) the bifacial reduction flakes, end scrapers, and gravers made from Flattop chalcedony are consistent with Clovis technology at other sites; (4) no later archaeological components in the vicinity of the site used WRGS; and (5) very few artifacts made from this purple WRGS are found this far east in Kansas and southern Nebraska, which indicates it is not a lithic source commonly used by later occupants in the area (Holen 2001a).

Tools and bifacial manufacturing debris suggest that the Clovis occupants discarded a worn-out Flattop chalcedony tool kit at the Eckles site and made a new set of tools, including projectile points of the same lithic material. Evidence of the reduction of large bifaces, in the range of 9.4 cm to 12–15 cm in width, is present in the form of large, thin bifacial reduction flakes produced by soft-hammer percussion. Later-stage bifacial reduction is evident from the presence of smaller bifacial thinning flakes and from the projectile point preform broken during manufacture. Other probable activities at the Eckles site include hide working, as indicated by the end scrapers, and butchering, as evidenced by the bifaces and flake tools. Gravers may have been used for bone carving and/or woodworking and at least one tool was recycled from an end scraper to a beaked graver. Burned lithic material suggests that hearths were present at the site. The range of activities represented by the Clovis assemblage suggests that the Eckles site was a residential camp that was probably located near a recent kill.

The Diskau site is situated in an upland area west of the Blue River in northeastern Kansas. It consists of a large surface collection of lithic tools and debitage, and test excavations yielded remains of mammoth and camel. Schmits and Kost (1985) and Schmits (1987) list a total of 123 formal chipped stone tools from a surface collection at the site, in addition to numerous pieces of debitage that apparently refer to the Clovis component, although an Archaic component is also present. Shaped tools include " 8 projectile points, 26 knives, 62 scrapers, 15 gravers, 2 spokeshaves, 2 perforators, 1 drill, 1 *piece d'esquille*, 3 discoids, and 4 biface fragments" (Schmits 1987:69). Schmits (1987) and Schmits and Kost (1985) note a high percentage of nonlocal lithic materials, with Smoky Hill jasper being the most common. Other materials include Flattop chalcedony (WRGS), Knife River flint, silicified wood, quartzite, white chert, and unidentified gray chalcedony. The Diskau assemblage is highly

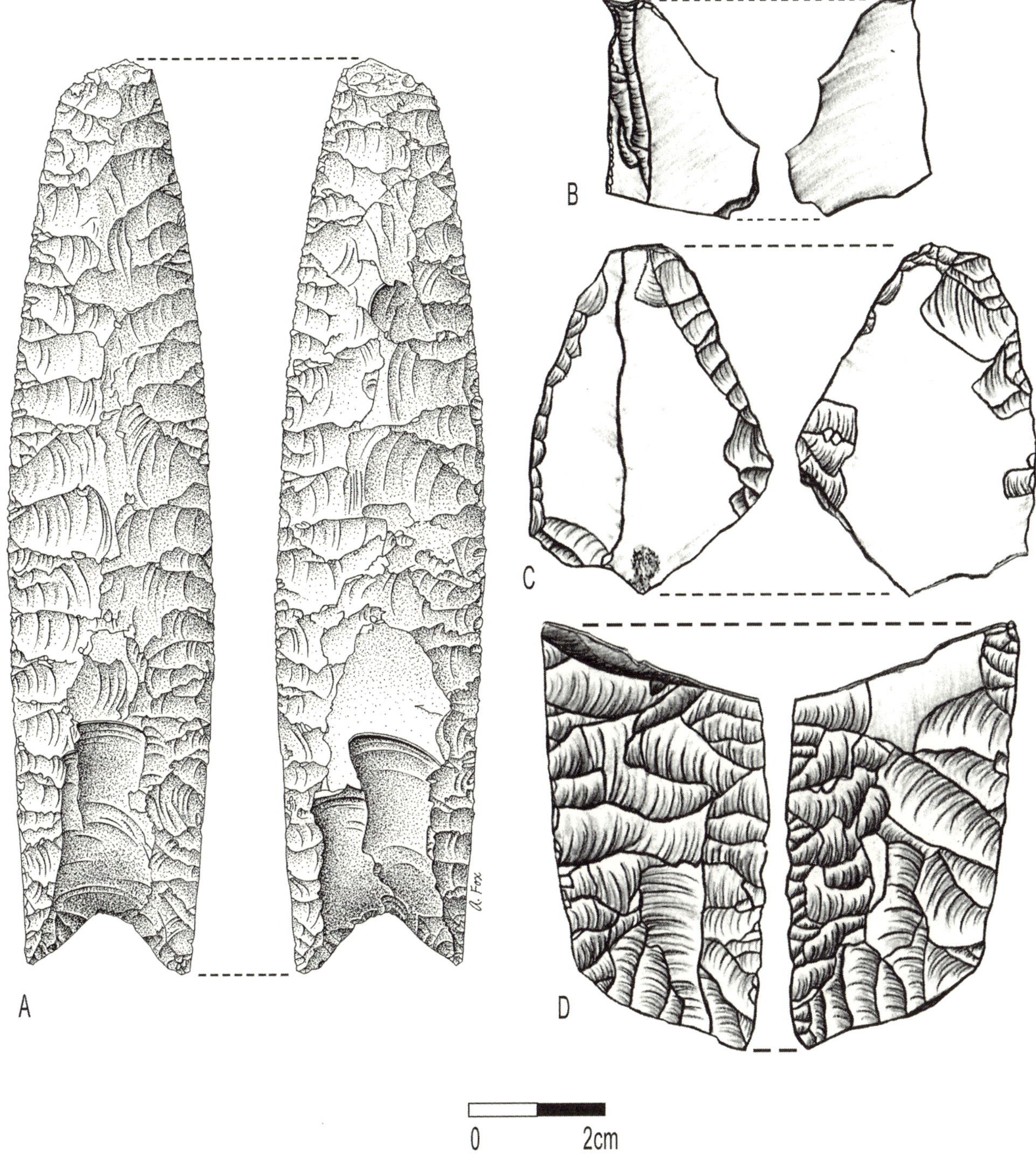

Figure 10.2. Eckles site artifacts: bifaces and flake tools

curated and heavily utilized; it appears to represent the discard of tools made from raw materials arriving primarily from the west, but from other directions also. This lithic material may have been replaced with a new tool kit produced with chert from nearby Permian outcrops. Camel and mammoth faunal remains at the site may indicate this was also a kill/processing situation near a camp site.

Found near the foothills of the Colorado Rockies in northeastern Colorado near Fort Collins (Kilby 2008, Chapter 11), the Watts cache consists of three large bifaces and three projectile point preforms. Kilby identifies five of the six artifacts as being made of a material similar to Cloverly quartzite from the Hartville Uplift area of eastern Wyoming, based on a website article by Bob Patten. Some of the quartzite may come from the Windy Ridge quartzite outcrop (Bamforth 2006) near the Continental Divide in the Rocky Mountains west of the cache location (Jason LaBelle, personal communication 2011). The sixth artifact is made of a reddish-purple chert and the source is unidentified. This cache will not be considered in the overall discussion of Clovis lithic procurement and mobility because the sources of the lithic material are uncertain.

The Drake cache in northeastern Colorado was found by avocational collectors and later tested by Stanford of the Smithsonian (Stanford and Jodry 1988; Stanford 1997). It consists of 13 Clovis projectile points, some of which have been resharpened, one hammerstone, and some small fragments of what appears to be ivory. Eleven of the projectile points are made of Alibates chert from the Texas Panhandle, one point is made of Edwards chert from central Texas, and one is made of an unknown chalcedony.

The CW cache in northeastern Colorado was found by avocational collectors on the edge of an upland playa lake in Lincoln County (Holen and Muñiz 2005; Muñiz, Chapter 7). It consists of 11 late-stage bifaces made of WRGS whose reduction trajectory appears to be toward the production of Clovis projectile point preforms. Three large flakes were also found with the cache.

Two Clovis early-stage projectile point preforms were part of the Gosper County cache, an apparent cache found in a south central Nebraska construction area in 1939 (Holen 2002). These two artifacts are made of Edwards chert from central Texas.

The Busse cache is located in Sherman County in northwestern Kansas (Hofman 1995, 1997). It appears to be a utilitarian Clovis cache consisting of 90 lithic artifacts, including large bifaces, blades, gravers, flakes, and flake tools, with a total weight of 7.3 kg. Both biface and blade technology are present in the assemblage. Streaks of red ochre were present on some of the artifacts. All but three of the artifacts are made of Smoky Hill jasper, the nearest source of which is 100 km to the east. Two flake gravers are produced of Hartville chert from east central Wyoming.

The Franey cache was found in Dawes County, northwest Nebraska, at Crow Butte (Grange 1964). Kilby (2008, Chapter 11) analyzed the cache and determined that it is most probably a Clovis cache. The cache consists of 75 artifacts, including 35 blades, 10 flake tools, 26 unmodified flakes, 1 biface, 1 core, 1 mollusk shell from the Atlantic coast, and 1 chip. The long-distance movement of Hartville chert may support the Clovis cultural affiliation, as does the thickness of the calcium carbonate encrustation. However, late prehistoric peoples on the western central Plains moved lithic materials at least 258 km (Basham and Holen 2006), and there was an extensive late prehistoric/protohistoric blade technology used to produce end scrapers on the central Great Plains (Wilke et al. 2002). These two facts suggest that caution should be exercised in accepting a Clovis cultural affiliation for this cache and at present it appears best not to consider this cache in the overall discussion of Clovis mobility and caching.

Four cache sites—CW, Drake, Busse, and Gosper County—and two sites—Diskau and Eckles—are the most important for understanding Clovis long-distance lithic movements in the central Plains. Other finds of large bifaces that may have been parts of caches also provide useful information (Holen 2001a, 2001b). Two other Clovis caches from the southern Plains, Sailor-Helton (Mallouf 1994) and the JS cache (Bement, Chapter 5), are included in the discussion of Clovis mobility in the central Plains because they represent movement of southern Plains lithic material into the central Plains. The Mahaffy cache (Bamforth, Chapter 4), found at the boundary between the central Plains and the Rocky Mountain foothills in Boulder, Colorado, is another interesting example of lithic material moving into the western edge of the central Plains from sources far to the west.

The Central Plains Lithic Landscape

In the central Plains, localized deposits of high-quality bedrock lithic material are separated by vast areas where little to no lithic material is available (Figure 10.3; Holen 1991). For example, the area between west central Kansas/southwest Nebraska and the foothills of the Rocky Mountains to the west has only one major bedrock source of high-quality lithic material, at Flattop Butte in northeastern Colorado. Other lithic material in cobble form from northeastern Colorado includes basalt, Black Forest silicified wood, and some cherts and silicified sediments that were not heavily utilized by Clovis peoples, who apparently preferred bedrock sources to cobbles. Another northeastern Colorado cobble source is clear chalcedony from the little-known Holiday Springs, a high-quality lithic material that was used only occasionally by Clovis peoples.

In order to study Clovis lithic procurement it is necessary to understand a lithic landscape that is much larger than the central Plains because Clovis peoples brought lithic material into the study area from distant sources.

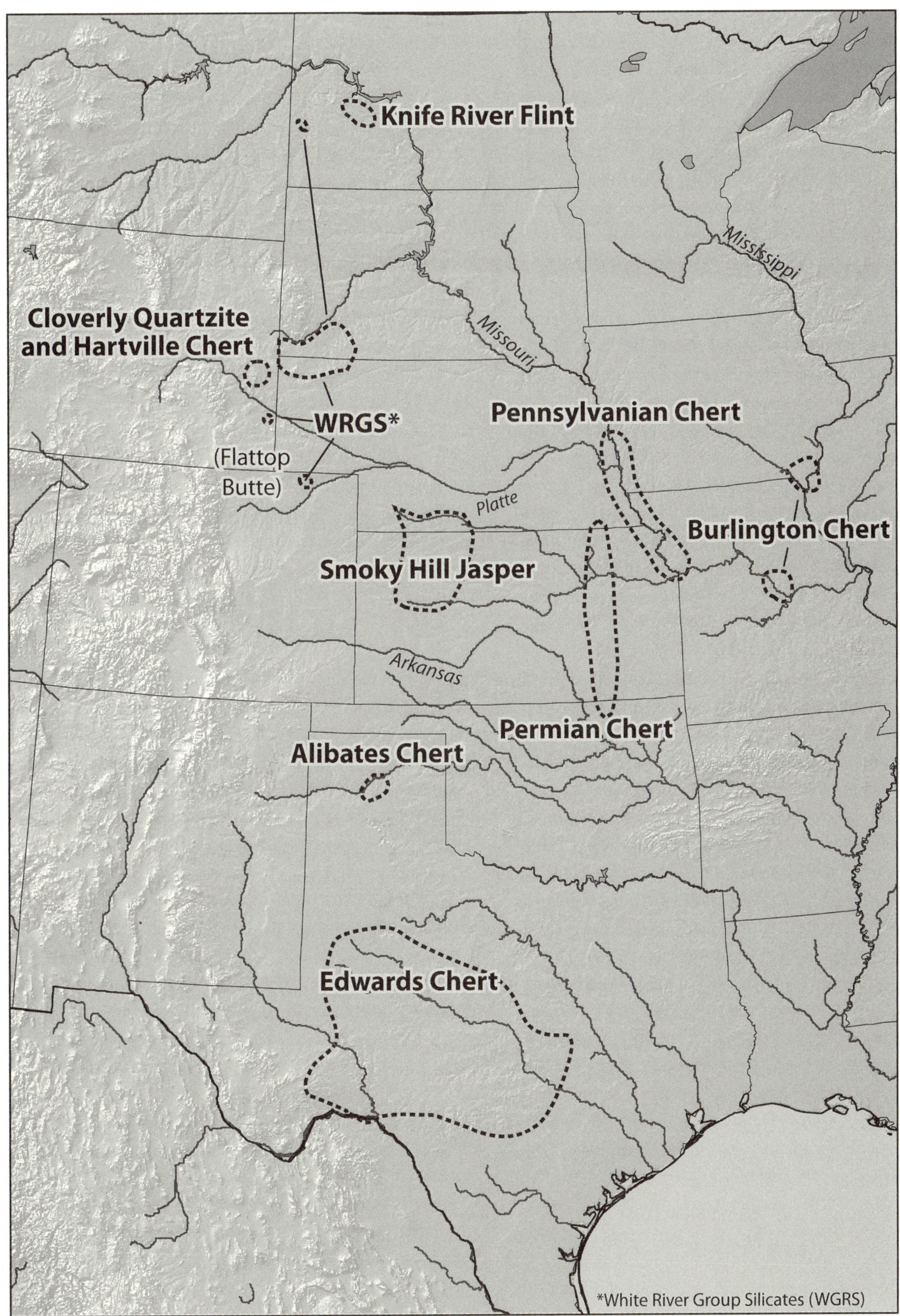

Figure 10.3. Map of major lithic material sources referred to in this study

The lithic landscape discussed in this study encompasses an area that extends 1,660 km south to north, running from central Texas to western North Dakota (Figure 10.3), and stretches 1,100 km east to west, from southeastern Iowa and central Missouri into eastern Wyoming. Eleven major lithic sources are described in this study (Table 10.1): Knife River flint (KRF), which is the most northerly source; Cloverly quartzite (a.k.a. Spanish Diggings quartzite) and Hartville chert, which are the most westerly sources; White River Group silicates (WRGS), which include Flattop chalcedony from northeastern Colorado and sources in eastern Wyoming, northwestern Nebraska, southwestern South Dakota, and southwestern North Dakota; Smoky Hill jasper (a.k.a. Niobrara jasper, Republican River jasper) from the center of the study area; Pennsylvanian chert (a.k.a. Nehawka chert) from the eastern central Plains; Permian chert, including Florence A and B varieties from east central Kansas; Burlington chert, the most easterly source, from southeastern Iowa and central Missouri; Alibates chert from the panhandle of Texas; Edwards chert, the most southerly source, from central Texas; and clear chalcedony, which may have multiple sources, including the Holiday Springs source in northeastern Colorado.

In addition to the 11 major sources, there are 6 other sources that make minor contributions (Table 10.1). These include: Reed Springs chert (a.k.a. Boone chert) from bedrock sources in northwestern Arkansas and northeastern Oklahoma; basalt (a.k.a. trachite), which occurs in secondary cobble deposits on the plains of eastern Colorado and western Kansas; Tongue River silicified sediment/Morrison Formation quartzite, which outcrops along the Front Range of the Rocky Mountains in Colorado and occurs in cobble form in northeastern Colorado as well as in the Powder River Basin in southeastern Montana and northeastern Wyoming; nonobsidian volcanic glass, which may outcrop in the Rocky Mountains of Wyoming or Colorado; Phosphoria chert, which outcrops in north central Wyoming but has recently been identified near Laramie, Wyoming; and Black Forest silicified wood. Black Forest wood outcrops as logs in primary context southeast of Denver, Colorado. This silicified wood is also widely dispersed as cobbles along the South Platte River and Arikaree River drainages in eastern Colorado, southwestern Nebraska, and western Kansas. Silicified wood outcrops within the Colorado Rocky Mountains.

Seventeen lithic types are generally identifiable at the macroscopic level, but the use of ultraviolet light and microscopic examination aid in classifying those materials that are not. Table 10.1 provides detailed descriptions and references for the 17 lithic sources.

As Figure 10.3 illustrates, three major lithic sources (WRGS/Flattop chalcedony, Pennsylvanian chert, and Smoky Hill jasper) occur completely within the study area and two additional major sources (Permian chert and some WRGS outcrops) straddle its boundaries; other lithic source areas occur completely outside the study area. The effect of this is an unavoidable sampling bias in the representation of lithic movements. For example, KRF, Alibates chert, and Edwards chert outcrop well outside the central Plains, and as a result this study documents only long-distance movements of these materials and will always show them moving toward the central Plains (i.e., into the study area). On the other hand, lithic source areas that outcrop within the central Plains will have a bias toward showing shorter-distance movements relative to the previous example. Smoky Hill jasper occurs at the center of the study area and is perhaps the most sensitive to trends in directionality because the users of this material can be tracked in any direction away from the source.

Sampling and Methods

Thirteen Clovis sites in the study area do not provide enough lithic data to study Clovis lithic procurement patterns and mobility. In order to overcome this lack of spatial data regarding Clovis lithic procurement and mobility, additional data were gathered from surface-collected projectile points and preforms in museums and private collections, based upon three criteria. First, the artifact had to be diagnostic of Clovis technology. This limited the range of tools to projectile points and preforms. Technology utilized to produce Clovis points and preforms is adequately described in the literature and widely recognized (Bradley 1982, 1991; Bradley et al. 2010; Wilke et al. 1991). The second criterion was that all specimens had to come either from museum collections with good documentation or from private collections where the owner either found the specimen or was familiar with the details of the find. Artifacts that had been sold, traded, or otherwise removed from the original collector were generally not used. Third, a minimum of county-specific locational data for the artifacts had to be available. Six projectile points used in the database could not be provenienced to less than two or three contiguous counties; however, they could be placed within a known geographic area (i.e., along a specific river or near a named landform) and so they were included.

TABLE 10.1. Major and Minor Lithic Sources Identified in the Central Plains Clovis Sample

PRIMARY SOURCE TYPES	LOCATION	FORMATION	DESCRIPTION	REFERENCES
Alibates chert (a.k.a. Alibates Agatized Dolomite)	Canadian River in the central Texas Panhandle and in cobble form along the Canadian River to the east	Alibates member of the Quartermaster Formation of the Permian Series	High-quality banded agate with red, purple, white, and yellow colors	Banks 1990; Hofman 1991; Wyckoff 1993
Burlington chert	Southeastern Iowa and central Missouri	Mississippian-age limestone	High-quality chert is a distinctive creamy-white color	Morrow 1994; Ray 2007
Clear chalcedony	Along Front Range of Colorado and Wyoming, into the plains of northeastern Colorado at Holiday Springs, into western Nebraska	Tertiary deposits; also may include some chalcedonies from the Ogallala Formation	Generally good-quality chalcedony ranging from milky white to translucent; material in Ogallala small and not as good	Carlson and Peacock 1975; Muñiz and Holen 2005
Cloverly quartzite (a.k.a. Spanish Diggings quartzite)	Hartville Uplift, east central Wyoming and southern Black Hills in South Dakota	Cloverly Formation; Hartville Uplift of east central Wyoming and equivalent Fall River Formation in the southern Black Hills/Bearlodge Mountains, Wyoming	High-quality, fine-grained quartzite of several colors, including purple, light gray, and gold	Church 1996; Francis 1991; Miller 1991; Reher 1991
Edwards chert	West central Texas	Cretaceous-age Edwards Formation	High-quality chert occurs in several color varieties but shades of gray, blue, and brown are the most common; bedrock and stream gravel	Banks 1990; Hofman 1991
Hartville chert	Beds: Hartville Uplift, east central Wyoming; cobbles: in the North Platte and Platte River drainage in Nebraska and the Chadron and Broadwater Formation cobble beds in western Nebraska	Mississippian-age Madison limestone in the Guernsey Formation	High-quality brown, tan, pink, or yellow chert with black dendritic inclusions	Francis 1991; Miller 1991; Reher 1991
Knife River flint	South central North Dakota in Dunn and Mercer Counties	Cobble deposits at main source and secondary alluvial and glacial deposits to the east of the primary source	Chocolate-colored high-quality silicified lignite coal, often with small, light-colored fossil plant inclusions	Ahler 1977; Ahler and VanNest 1985; Root 1993
Pennsylvanian chert (a.k.a. Nehawka chert)	Extreme eastern and southeastern Nebraska, western Iowa, and northeastern Kansas	Limestone of the Pennsylvanian System	High-quality, generally gray in color but includes off-white and black	Carlson and Peacock 1975; Gradwohl 1969; Holen 1983, 1991; Morrow 1994; Reid 1980
Permian chert (Florence A and B varieties)	Flint Hills from north central Oklahoma, in a band across east central Kansas, into southeastern Nebraska	Limestone of the Chase Group of the Permian series	Several varieties of gray cherts, the best quality is Florence D with predominantly dark- and light-gray banded colors	Banks 1990; Blasing 1984; Carlson and Peacock 1975; Holen 1983; Vehik 1984
Smoky Hill jasper (a.k.a. Niobrara jasper, Republican River jasper)	North central Kansas and south central Nebraska in tributaries of the Kansas River, and in east central Nebraska in the Loup River Valley	Top of the Smoky Hill member of the Niobrara Formation in soft limestone	Variable quality, including brown, yellow, red, white, and green colors	Banks 1990; Carlson and Peacock 1975; Holen 1983, 1989
White River Group silicates (WRGS), includes Flattop chalcedony	Northeastern Colorado, eastern Wyoming, northwestern Nebraska, southwestern South Dakota, southwestern North Dakota	Chadron and Brule Formations of the White River Group	Good- to high-quality, including primarily purple, pink, white, and gray colors	Carlson and Peacock 1975; Greiser 1983; Hoard et al. 1991, 1993; Huckell et al. 2011; Koch and Miller 1996; Miller 1991; Nowak et al. 1984

TABLE 10.1 *(continued)*

PRIMARY SOURCE TYPES	LOCATION	FORMATION	DESCRIPTION	REFERENCES
Minor lithic sources				
Reed Springs chert (a.k.a. Boone chert)	Northwestern Arkansas, northeastern Oklahoma, and southern Missouri	Boone formation, Mississippian Age	Light to dark gray and off-white mottled chert	Ray 2007
Basalt (a.k.a. trachite)	Eastern Colorado, western Kansas	Secondary cobble deposits, original source unknown	Varying quality, generally fine grained, dark gray to black	None
Phosphoria chert	North central and south central Wyoming	Minnekahta Formation	High-quality, colors include red, purple, gray, and other colors	Francis 1991; Miller 1991
Silicified wood (includes Black Forest Formation sources as well as other unidentified sources)	Widespread from primary deposits south of Denver, Colorado, along rivers eastward into western Kansas and Nebraska	Some use of Black Forest Formation sources from south of Denver as well as secondary stream cobbles to the east	Varying from high-quality to coarser materials, wide variety of colors, including yellow, tan, dark and light brown, gray, white, and clear	Black 2000; Holen 1983, 2001a
Tongue River silicified sediment; Morrison Formation quartzite	Bedrock: in Powder River Basin in southeastern Montana and northeastern Wyoming; along the Front Range in Colorado with cobble sources to the east	Bedrock and secondary cobble sources are widely dispersed	Fine-grained quartzite consistency, mottled with reds, yellow, gray, and brown	Black 2000
Volcanic glass (not obsidian)	Rocky Mountains	Unknown	Opaque black, soft, light volcanic glass	None

These data have certain limitations. Clovis groups may have used, lost, and discarded projectile points differently than the rest of their tool kit. Projectile points may have been transported longer distances than other tools within an assemblage, possibly through exchange or movement of people between bands. These data also do not inform us about complete assemblage composition or reduction sequences employed as tool kits were transported and used across the landscape.

Despite these limitations, and because of the paucity of excavated or surface site assemblages, investigation of central Plains Clovis land use patterns becomes feasible only by utilizing site-based evidence combined with region-wide Clovis projectile point and preform surface samples. Previous studies by Tankersley (1989) and Loebel (2005) in the Midwest and several chapters in Ellis and Lothrop (1989) concerning the northeastern United States have successfully used this strategy to study Clovis lithic procurement and mobility.

Whether or not Paleoindians acquired exotic raw materials through direct or indirect procurement is not easily determined. Many researchers have addressed this issue for areas outside the central Plains (Ellis and Lothrop 1989; Gardner 1977; Goodyear 1979; Hofman 1990, 1991, 1992, 1999; Meltzer 1989; Snow 1980; Wilmsen 1973; Wittoft 1952). Archaeologists working in the Great Plains and in the eastern United States generally agree that Paleoindian settlement mobility is the primary reason for the direct procurement and movement of high-quality lithic materials over long distances. This study follows these earlier studies in positing that Clovis bands directly procured the large majority of their lithic supply during the yearly round. Researchers also generally agree that a small amount of lithic material was exchanged. Evidence cited for exchange is based on the relative proportion of a specific raw material in relation to the distance from its source. For example, lithic materials that are moved very long distances and make up a small percentage of an assemblage are typically considered to result from exchange, whereas if the same raw material made up a high percentage of an assemblage that was not too far away from the source, it would often be interpreted as direct procurement. There is no standard distance or proportion of an assemblage that is used as a cutoff in determining whether a raw material was directly or indirectly procured, and such assessments are often made based on the researcher's understanding of what is typical for a region or culture.

RESULTS

Data were obtained for a total of 244 Clovis projectile points and preforms from the central Plains study area, including diagnostic projectile points from the sites discussed above. This data set consists of 231 fluted projectile points, 9 fluted preforms, 2 unfluted preforms, and 2 unfluted projectile points. Artifacts in this group originated from a variety of surface contexts, most commonly blowouts in sand dune areas (e.g., Wray dune field, Nebraska Sand Hills) and gravel bars in streams and rivers (e.g., Blue River, Little Blue River, Kansas River, South Platte River). Upland settings (e.g., bordering the Platte River and Missouri River, Colorado Piedmont, Nebraska Loess Hills, northwestern Nebraska, western Kansas) and tributary valley settings (e.g., Republican River drainage, Salt Creek drainage, White Rock Creek) also contribute significantly to the sample. Lithic sources were identified for 204 of the 244 projectile points and preforms (Figure 10.4). The remaining 40 artifacts either could not be identified to lithic type ($n = 24$), or the source of the material was not known ($n = 16$). Most of the unidentified chert and chalcedony has probable sources in the Rocky Mountains or secondary cobble deposits near the mountains. Lithic source data are presented in Figure 10.4. Frequencies for each raw material are represented by the first (solid black) bar, the percentage of the total of artifacts identified to lithic source is represented by the second bar, and the percentage of the total sample made up of the raw material is represented by the third (gray) bar. Table 10.2 provides summary statistics for each of the 10 major lithic types identified to source.

White River Group Silicates (WRGS)

Projectile points and preforms made of WRGS ($n = 55$) represent the most frequently used raw material in the sample. Projectile points and preforms thought to be derived from the Flattop Butte source in northeastern Colorado number 53, with the remaining 2 artifacts coming from either the Wyoming or South Dakota outcrops. Major source areas of WRGS can be distinguished using neutron activation (Huckell et al. 2011), and previous studies linked WRGS artifacts from the Eckles Clovis site to Flattop Butte (Hoard et al. 1991, 1993). Average distance from the Flattop Butte source calculated for 51 of the WRGS points and preforms was 181.3 km.

There is good evidence of the long-distance movement of WRGS, in the form of two large bifaces found 125 km and 200 km east of the Flattop Butte source (Holen 2001b) and large bifacial reduction flakes found at the Eckles site at a distance of 450 km from the source (Holen 2010). Eight projectile points made of WRGS, or 14.8 percent of the sample ($n = 53$), were moved more than 400 km. The longest distance recorded in the study area for movement of a projectile point, 565 km, was in the Salt Creek drainage in east central Nebraska. WRGS tools (not points or preforms) discarded at the Diskau site are 590 km from the nearest source and represent the longest known movement of this lithic material by Clovis people.

TABLE 10.2. Summary Statistics for the 10 Major Lithic Sources Identified in the Study Area

LITHIC TYPE	SAMPLE SIZE	MINIMUM DISTANCE (km)	MAXIMUM DISTANCE (km)	MEAN DISTANCE (km)	STANDARD DEVIATION (km)	PREDOMINANT DIRECTION OF MOVEMENT
WRGS	55	0	565	168.6	146.0	SE (45.5%)
Smoky Hill jasper	34	0	220	115.1	70.0	W (41.2%)
Alibates chert	24	325	640	551.0	70.9	NW (52.4%)
Pennsylvanian chert	24	0	510	76.3	175.2	Local (79.2%), W (12.5%)
Hartville chert	23	190	615	311.1	123.8	SE (52.2%)
Knife River flint	10	510	875	737.0	133.1	S (60%)
Permian chert	10	50	440	238.5	148.6	NW (60%)
Burlington chert	5	330	490	383.0	62.0	W (60%)
Cloverly quartzite	5	100	375	225.0	106.1	S (40%), E (40%)
Edwards chert	5	850	975	932.0	51.1	N (80%)

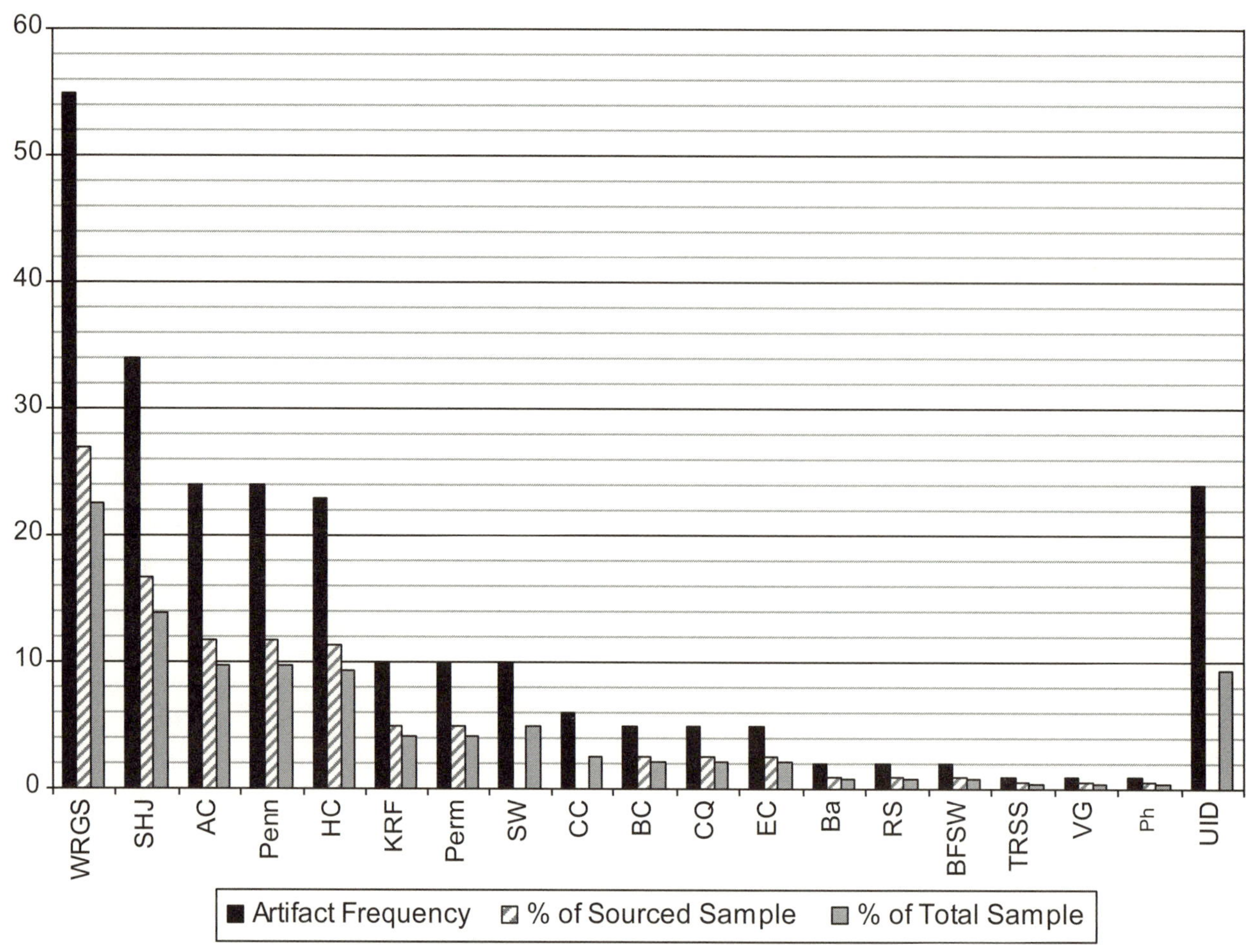

Figure 10.4. Artifact frequency, percentage of sourced sample, and percentage of the total sample for each major and minor raw material source identified in the study, as well as unidentified sources (n = 244)

Of the 53 WRGS specimens with data on direction of movement, 45.5 percent traveled southeast from the source and an additional 23.6 percent traveled east. Movement to the south (14.5 percent) and southwest (9.1 percent) is also evident. Southeastern movement of WRGS accounts for 33.9 percent of the sample of 65 Clovis projectile points recovered in the Wray dune field in northeastern Colorado, and these points represent movements between 95 and 185 km. Eleven late-stage bifaces from the CW cache are not included in list of 244 projectile points and preforms because they have not quite reached the preform stage of reduction (Holen and Muñiz 2005; Muñiz, Chapter 7). They deserve mention, however, because they were found cached 165 km south-southwest of the source.

Previously reported movements of WRGS to the South Platte River drainage occur between 60 km and 200 km from the quarry source. Recent documentation of WRGS Clovis points in southeastern Colorado indicates that the material was moving a minimum of 300 km to the south, and one report of a WRGS point in the Oklahoma Panhandle (Hofman and Wyckoff 1991) is a minimum of 450 km from Flattop Butte. These data are excellent examples of how Clovis peoples repeatedly quarried chalcedony from Flattop Butte, a restricted point source, and then traveled east to what is now eastern Nebraska and Kansas and to the southeast, into southern Colorado and the Oklahoma Panhandle. However, not all movement and caching of WRGS are long-distance movements, as demonstrated by the discovery of WRGS bifaces in the Beach cache in southwestern North Dakota, just 13 km from the outcrop at Sentinel Butte (Huckell et al. 2011).

Smoky Hill Jasper

The second most abundant lithic material utilized in the study area is Smoky Hill jasper, represented by 34 specimens (13.9 percent of the total artifact class). For those specimens for which direction of movement could be determined, artifacts carried to the west of the source account for 41.2 percent, while eastward movement accounts for 26.5 percent. Movement from the source toward the northwest and north each account for 8.8 percent of the sample. Of the 34 artifacts, 27 (79.4 percent) were moved more than 40 km. The average distance that these 27 artifacts were moved is 145 km. This includes both movements to the east into the Blue River drainage in Kansas and to the west into the Wray dune field in Colorado. The longest recorded movement of Smoky Hill jasper is for a projectile point found 220 km to the west-northwest along the South Platte River in Colorado. One Clovis point made of Smoky Hill jasper is recorded in western Oklahoma, south of the source area (Hofman 1990; Hofman and Wyckoff 1991).

Movement and caching of Smoky Hill jasper west or northwest of the source are represented at the Busse cache in northwestern Kansas (Hofman 1995, 1997). Large bifaces, large blades, and smaller blades are present in the Busse cache. The pattern of westward movement and caching of Smoky Hill jasper indicates that this lithic material was moved in the form of large bifacial cores at least 100 km to the west.

Alibates Chert

Alibates chert and Pennsylvanian chert tie for the third most represented lithic type, each with 24 specimens, or 9.8 percent of the total sample. Alibates chert outcrops outside of the study area far to the south in the Texas Panhandle. All recorded Alibates projectile points in the central Plains region represent long-distance movement to the north (37.5 percent), northeast (5.9 percent), or northwest (52.4 percent). The average distance these specimens were moved is 551 km, with the longest distance being 640 km to the Little Blue River located in southeastern Nebraska. One projectile point was found in western Kansas 325 km from the source. Another Alibates projectile point from White Rock Creek in north central Kansas was found 560 km from the source.

Movement distances of Alibates into the Blue River and eastern Republican River drainages in Kansas and Nebraska are generally less than those into northeastern Colorado. The Drake cache in northeastern Colorado, for example, has always seemed an anomaly because it contains 11 Alibates projectile points that were moved 600 km from the source area. Two additional Alibates points were recorded from Logan County, one in the South Platte River (560 km) and one in an upland setting (600 km) relatively near the Drake cache. The Wray dune field of northeastern Colorado and southwestern Nebraska produced eight additional Alibates Clovis points, some 490–500 km from the source. With the addition of these 10 newly reported Alibates points moved to the northwest, the Drake cache now fits within a broader pattern of Clovis peoples bringing Alibates into northeastern Colorado.

Northward movement of Clovis Alibates tools other than projectile points is also evident at the Sailor-Helton cache, found in southwestern Kansas (Mallouf 1994), and at the JS site in northwestern Oklahoma (Bement, Chapter 5). Alibates Paleoindian flake tools found in surface sites in northeastern Colorado and southwestern Nebraska that also contain Alibates Clovis projectile points indicate that tool kits were moving north along with projectile points.

Pennsylvanian Chert

Twenty of the 24 Pennsylvanian chert specimens were produced locally (less than 40 km from the source), and all of them were found in the vicinity of the Missouri River and Lower Kansas River. The remaining three points and one preform were moved an average distance of 457.5 km, with the longest recorded distance at 510.0 km. Movements to the west and northwest into the Nebraska Sand Hills, the South Platte River, and the Wray dune field were recorded. Based on this sample, Pennsylvanian chert points and preforms appear to have been discarded more locally in the central Plains. However, when the lithic material was transported to the west and northwest, it has been found at long distances from the source.

Hartville Chert

Hartville chert points and preforms ($n = 23$) represent 9.4 percent of the total sample. Although the average movement of Hartville chert is 309.1 km, this may reflect the lack of recorded Clovis projectile points in the Nebraska Panhandle, which is closer to the source. Given the location of the Hartville Uplift in eastern Wyoming, just outside of the study area, it is not unexpected that 52.2 percent of the sample was moved to the southeast, with southern (26.1 percent) and eastern movements (21.7 percent) making up the remainder.

Hartville chert points and preforms have been found as far away as eastern and southeastern Nebraska as well as northeastern Colorado. Two points were found along the Little Blue River, 615 km from the source. Movement of projectile points in the range of 200–400 km is common and movements of 400–700 km represent 17.4 percent of the Hartville point and preform sample. A small Hartville chert core and two pieces of Cloverly quartzite debitage were found on a site containing a Clovis component along Salt Creek in east central Nebraska. This core is 600 km east-southeast of the source area. Hartville chert artifacts (not points or preforms) at the Diskau site along the Blue River in northeastern Kansas are 740 km from the source. One large Hartville chert bifacial core that is probably Clovis was found in east central Nebraska some 435 km east of the quarry area.

Knife River Flint (KRF)

Even though KRF outcrops far to the north of the study area in west central North Dakota, it is tied with Permian chert and non–Black Forest silicified wood as the sixth most frequently used raw material in this sample from Clovis peoples on the central Plains. Ten KRF specimens make up 4.1 percent of the total sample and represent material moved the second-longest average distance (757 km) from its source area. The location of the primary quarries accounts for the predominant southward (60 percent) and southeastern (40 percent) movement of this material. Although KRF is found in secondary contexts far to the east and southeast of the outcrop area, these cobbles are probably not large enough to produce average size Clovis preforms and points.

Knife River flint was widely distributed throughout the study area and has been found in northwestern Nebraska, the Nebraska Sand Hills, and the Wray dune field as well as along the Little Blue and Missouri Rivers. The most noticeable movement pattern is down the Missouri River, where KRF accounts for 20 percent of the total sample of points or preforms found in this region. In comparison, it accounts for only 3.1 percent of points and preforms from the Wray dune field, at a comparable distance from the source but on the opposite side of the central Plains.

Permian Chert

Permian chert outcrops extensively in the Flint Hills of Kansas and in southeastern Nebraska but accounts for only 10 specimens, or 4.1 percent of the total sample. This material was generally moved from 100 to 330 km to the northwest (60 percent), with movement to the west (10 percent), north (10 percent), northeast (10 percent), and south (10 percent) making up the remainder. One point made of the Florence A variety from the southern Flint Hills was moved 380 km northwest to northern Kansas. The greatest distance that Permian chert was moved is 440 km to the northwest into the Nebraska Sand Hills.

Clear Chalcedony

Clear chalcedony may be from multiple sources that are not well documented, although some probably came from the Holiday Spring source area in northeastern Colorado. Clear chalcedony is represented in the sample by six projectile points, three of which were found in the Blue River drainage in northeastern Kansas and southeastern Nebraska and the other three found in the South Platte River and the Wray dune field in northeastern Colorado. More research is needed to identify the exact source or sources of the clear chalcedony used to make these points.

Burlington Chert

Five points made of Burlington chert represent western and northwestern movements of the material away from its sources. Three of the points were found along the Missouri River bluffs, and the source for this material is probably in southeastern Iowa (Billeck 1998). However, it seems just as likely that the chert came from sources in central Missouri, because the Missouri River may have served as a natural route for movements of this lithic material to the northwest. Distances from the southeastern Iowa source to the find spots were calculated at 360–375 km. One Burlington chert point found in the Little Blue River area is 330 km from that source. A large point midsection found in the east central Nebraska Loess Hills was moved 490 km, the longest movement of Burlington chert. This midsection represents one of the two largest projectile points recorded during this study. The fact that the point was so large and distant from the source, and apparently was broken during its first usage, suggests that the movement of newly manufactured and very large points occurred across the central Plains. Burlington chert is also reported from the Diskau site on the Blue River in northeastern Kansas.

Cloverly Quartzite

Five Cloverly quartzite specimens were recorded in the study area. The distances for the movement of Cloverly quartzite were calculated from the Wyoming source rather than the outcrops in the southern Black Hills, although two of the points were recovered in northwestern Nebraska near the Black Hills. Two other points were found in eastern Colorado, with the longest distance recorded at 375 km from the Wray dune field. The locations of the Cloverly sources within the study area demonstrated directions of movement to the south, east, and southeast. Kilby (2008) identifies five of the six artifacts from the Watts cache in northeastern Colorado as similar to the Hartville source of quartzite, although they may also be derived from the Windy Ridge source area in the Rocky Mountains to the west.

Cloverly quartzite outcrops near Hartville chert, but the chert was used more than 4.5 times as frequently as Cloverly quartzite for the production of Clovis projectile points in this sample. While this finding may represent a bias on the part of Clovis toolmakers against Cloverly quartzite and in favor of Hartville chert, the quartzite has been recovered at Clovis sites that are great distances from the source. One surface site containing a Clovis component in the Salt River drainage in east central Nebraska has two pieces of Cloverly debitage, and the Diskau site in northeastern Kansas has one Cloverly quartzite tool.

Edwards Chert

Edwards chert, originating far south of the study area, in central Texas, represents the most distant source of lithic material that contributes more than a single specimen to the projectile point ($n = 3$) and preform ($n = 2$) categories. Distances from the chert source for the five artifacts range from 850 km for the point found in the Wray dune field to 975 km for the point from the Drake cache in Logan County, Colorado. The average distance from the source for the five specimens is 932 km, the longest average distance that any lithic material was moved in this study.

Five Edwards chert specimens demonstrate significant contrasts in stages of manufacture. Two of the artifacts are point preforms, although they may have been too thick to produce high-quality points. These two artifacts were found together at a construction site in Gosper County in south central Nebraska and were probably part of a cache (Holen 2002). Two specimens from northeastern Colorado, including the point from the Drake cache, are large projectile points that may have never been resharpened. The fifth specimen is a point base manufactured on a large flake. Preforms; large, newly manufactured points; and points made on large flakes are probably only part of the lithic inventory that moved north from the raw material source.

I also observed several other Edwards chert artifacts that have characteristics of Clovis technology but are not diagnostic points or preforms. These include two prismatic blades (in the sense used by Collins 1999b) from the South Platte River in Keith County, Nebraska; a small biface/wedge found near a Clovis point made of WRGS on a site in the Salt Creek drainage in northern Lancaster County, Nebraska, that was moved 1,020 km from the source; and the tip of a thick biface from the Little Blue River in southeastern Nebraska. Thick biface tips like this example and the two from the Eckles site (Holen 2010) may represent a diagnostic Clovis tool type. These bifaces may have been failed projectile preforms that became too thick and were instead used as flake cores until they broke.

Miscellaneous Minor Sources

Seven points in the sample represent five minor lithic sources. Two points made of basalt were found in western Kansas and eastern Colorado. Two points made of Reed Springs chert, which outcrops in northwestern Arkansas and northeastern Oklahoma, were found on the Kansas River near its confluence with the Blue River and on the Little Blue River in southern Nebraska and were carried between 350 and 450 km. A single specimen recovered from the Wray dune field was made of Tongue River silicified sediment or Morrison chert that probably derived from secondary cobble deposits in northeastern Colorado or outcrops of Morrison Formation quartzite along the Front Range of the Rocky Mountains. Another single point is made of nonobsidian volcanic glass with a probable source in the Rocky Mountains of Wyoming or Colorado. One point found in the Wray dune field in northeastern Colorado is made of Phosphoria chert from Wyoming.

Silicified Woods

Although non–Black Forest Formation silicified wood was used as frequently as KRF and Permian chert, the distance that it traveled cannot be calculated because we do not know the exact source areas for this lithic material. Ten Clovis points made of non–Black Forest silicified wood were found in northeastern Colorado, and this diverse material may be from multiple sources in the Rocky Mountains. Two other points in the sample are identified as Black Forest wood and were found in northeastern Colorado, but it is not known if the toolstone was derived from primary or secondary sources and a distance of movement cannot be determined.

DISCUSSION

Results of this study indicate that there are four broad patterns of lithic raw material movement by Clovis peoples on the central Plains. The first is from the High Plains on the western edge of the study area to the east, southeast, and south and is best represented by movement of WRGS, Hartville chert, and Cloverly quartzite. The second is the movement of Alibates chert and Edwards chert northwest and north from the southern Plains in Texas to the central Plains. The third is from the eastern edge of the study area to the west, as documented by the movement of Burlington, Pennsylvanian, and Permian chert. Movement of KRF to the south and southeast is the fourth.

The most robust pattern of Clovis mobility on the central Plains is evident in the movement of High Plains lithic sources far to the east and south. Repeated movement of Flattop chalcedony from a single point source outcrop to multiple locations on the central Plains indicates that Clovis peoples knew the Flattop source well and often included a stop at that location in their mobility schedule. Large bifaces, preforms, projectile points, and other tool forms made of WRGS, Hartville chert, and Cloverly quartzite found in tool kits to the east indicate that Clovis bands moved off the High Plains and carried these lithic materials to locations that contained good toolstone, timber, and other resources on the central or eastern central Plains. Small quantities of Smoky Hill jasper artifacts moving east may be the result of stops in western Kansas and southwestern Nebraska before continuing eastward.

Eastward movement of High Plains lithic materials suggests Clovis band movements of 500 to 600 km (Figure 10.5). Kill and butchery events would necessitate the transport of lithic resources into areas with few or no lithic materials available to enable the Clovis bands to produce new tool kits. The Eckles site, 450 km east of the Flattop chalcedony source, probably represents one such retooling event when transported lithic materials were utilized after a kill. Alternatively, the Diskau site, situated near a Permian chert source, indicates that a largely depleted tool kit of western source material was abandoned when the Clovis band arrived at the new source area. Clovis artifacts made of western source materials have not been found east of the Permian and Pennsylvanian chert outcrops on the eastern central Plains. Documentation of WRGS Clovis points in southeastern Colorado and one point in the panhandle of Oklahoma support an important movement of western central Plains lithics to the south.

Clovis movement of high-quality Alibates chert and Edwards chert from the southern Plains to the western central Plains (Figure 10.6) also left a significant record in the sample used for this study. Northern and northwestern movement of lithic material from the southern Plains has also been noted by Kilby (2008:168, Chapter 11). The Drake cache is predominantly Alibates chert but also contains one Edwards chert point; some points in this cache were used and resharpened, suggesting it may be a utilitarian cache. Alibates chert Clovis points from northeastern Colorado and southwestern Nebraska, in addition to many Alibates Paleoindian flake tools (some of which are probably Clovis artifacts), suggest the movement of entire tool kits, not just projectile points. Evidence of extensive movement of Alibates to the north is present at the Sailor-Helton cache in southwestern Kansas (Kilby 2008, Chapter 11; Mallouf 1994). The presence of Edwards chert prismatic blade tools, thick point preforms, flake tools, a thick biface, and a small biface/wedge of probable Clovis origin all suggest that this material was also moved northward in the form of tool kits. It is hypothesized that Clovis bands on the southern Plains were moving between Edwards chert and Alibates chert quarry areas and exchanging lithic materials. These data suggest that Clovis bands were moving northward into the central Plains a minimum of 500–600 km from the Alibates quarries, carrying both Alibates chert and Edwards chert acquired through band interactions on the southern Plains.

Movement of Pennsylvanian and Permian cherts from the eastern central Plains to the west and northwest (Figure 10.6) is less pronounced than the movement of High Plains materials to the east and south and southern Plains materials to the north. Only eight projectile points and one preform were documented more than 200 km to the west from these eastern sources. No other Clovis tools made of these lithic materials have been identified in western locations. Lack of evidence of Permian and Pennsylvanian tool kits may in part be a reflection of the lack of significant site-specific assemblages in the western central Plains. Another possible factor, however, is that

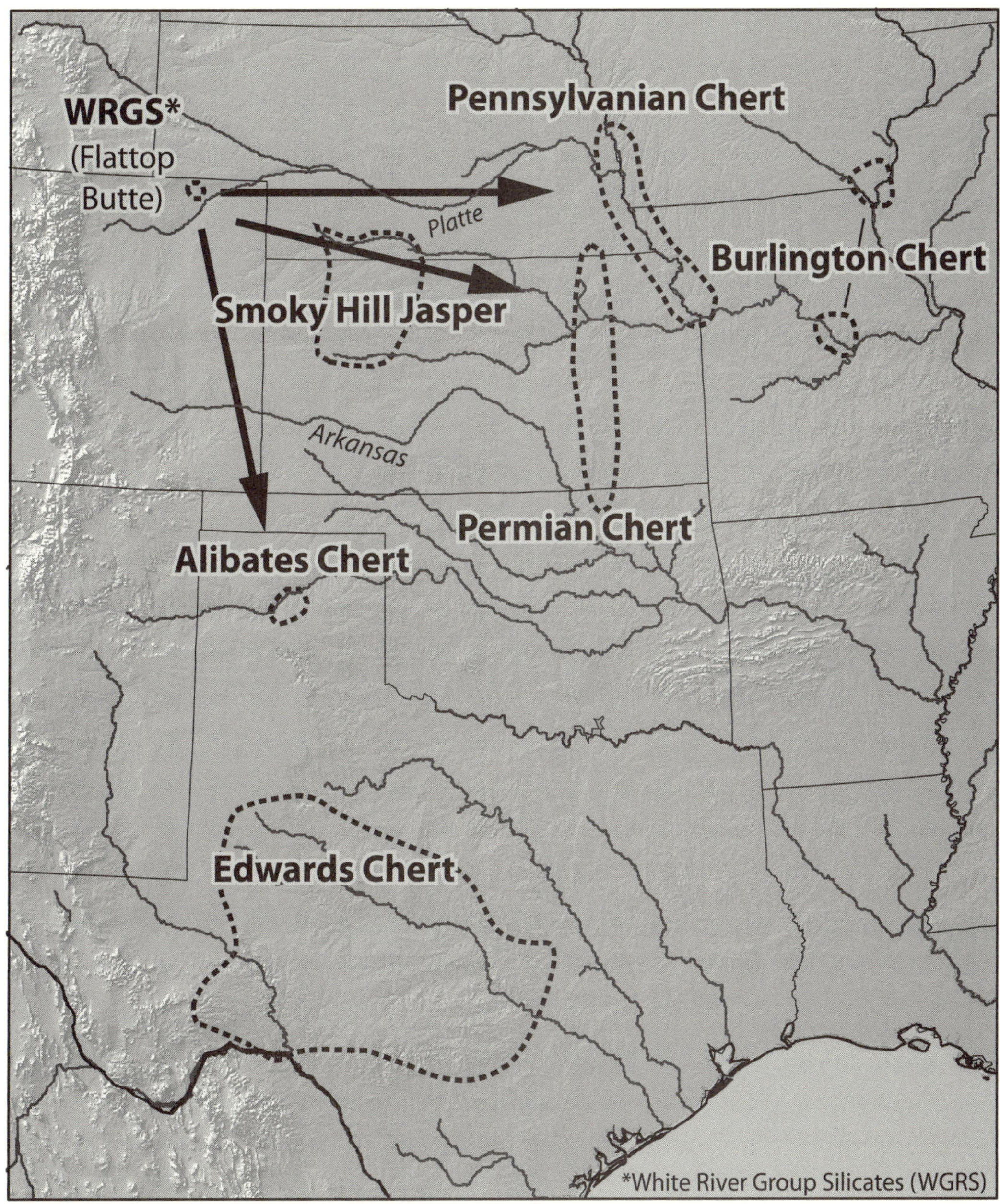

Figure 10.5. Hypothesized direction of Clovis band and lithic movements in the fall

the quality of most Permian and Pennsylvanian cherts may not be as good as much of the western High Plains lithic material.

It is clear from studies over broad areas of North America that Clovis peoples preferred high-quality lithic materials, primarily from bedrock sources (Goodyear 1979). Clovis peoples may not have been able to consistently produce large bifacial cores from Permian and Pennsylvanian cherts because these raw materials often occur as smaller nodules. The longest Clovis point recorded in the present study produced from either of these two cherts is only 8.4 cm long. On the other hand, very high-quality Hartville chert, WRGS, Edwards chert, Alibates chert, and Burlington chert all have examples of projectile points more than 10 cm long, with some in the range of 12–17 cm. Therefore, Permian chert may commonly have been transported in the form of small preforms, completed projectile points, and completed patterned artifacts; the same may be true for Pennsylvanian chert. However, some larger nodules of high-quality Pennsylvanian chert are known to occur. This may explain the relative lack of eastern chert

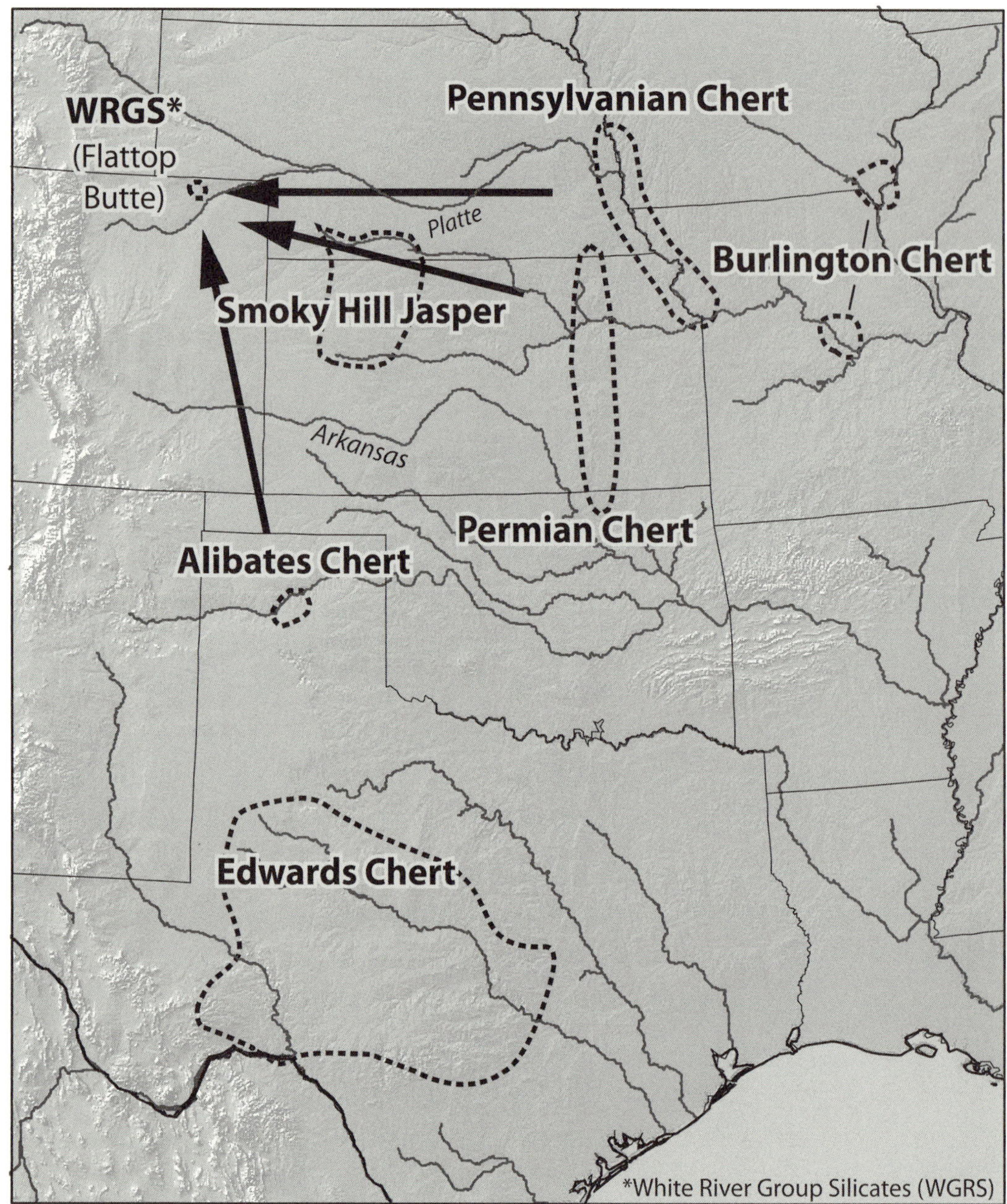

Figure 10.6. Hypothesized direction of Clovis band and lithic movements in the spring

projectile points and tools on the western High Plains. This mobility strategy may also account for the predominance of westward (41.2 percent) movement of Smoky Hill jasper toward the High Plains, compared to eastward movement (26.5 percent) of this material. Clovis bands moving west would have passed through areas with Smoky Hill jasper outcrops and could have geared up before reaching the High Plains and so would not have had to carry as much Permian and Pennsylvanian cherts.

Based on these observations, we may hypothesize that if Clovis peoples did prefer High Plains lithic sources to eastern Plains sources, they may have preferentially cached western source materials in the form of large bifaces or early-stage preforms east and south of the Flattop Butte source area, as indicated by the find of large bifaces east of the source area, bifacial reduction flakes from a large core at the Eckles site, and the CW cache south of the source area. Caching western raw materials east of the primary source area in a landscape poor in lithic materials would reduce the need to move large quantities of less preferable eastern toolstone back to the west during a return trip because the better-quality High Plains toolstone would be

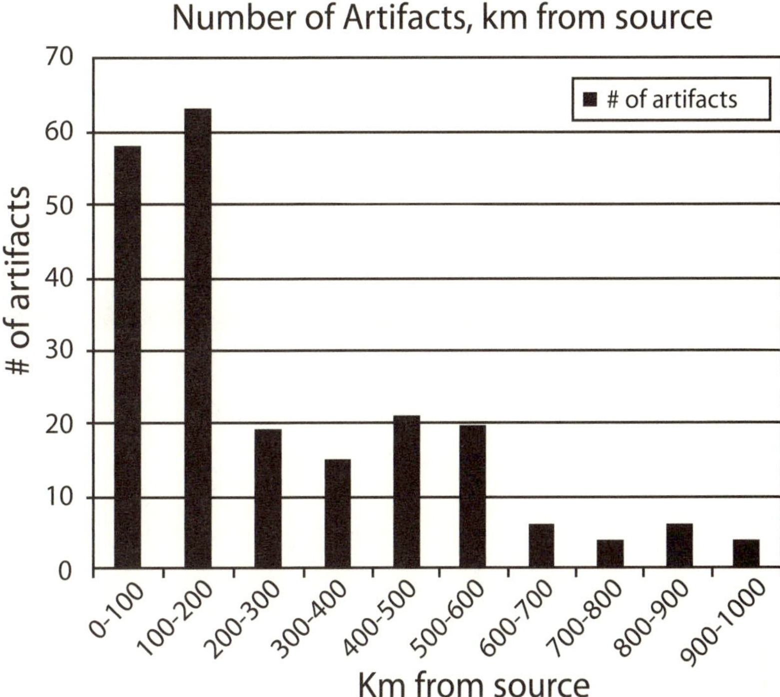

Figure 10.7. Distances that Clovis peoples moved projectile points

accessible before the primary quarries were reached. However, the Busse cache suggests that Clovis bands cached Smoky Hill jasper west of the source, indicating they had recently passed through this source area on the way west. Additional discoveries of Clovis caches on the central Plains are required to evaluate this hypothesis.

Long-distance movement of Knife River flint to the south and southeast is the final pattern of Clovis raw material movement on the central Plains. Movement of Clovis KRF artifacts between 675 and 875 km along the Missouri River and as much as 1,500 km into Illinois (as seen at the Bostrom site [Tankersley 1995; Tankersley and Morrow 1993]) suggests the Missouri River may have played an important role in Clovis mobility. A few KRF artifacts documented in the central Plains study area indicate that north–south movement occurred between the central and northern Plains, but more data are necessary to derive a meaningful interpretation of the pattern.

These data indicate that Clovis bands were frequently moving both east and west across the breadth of the central Plains and north and south between the central and southern Plains. Research by Blackmar (2001) demonstrated a widespread Clovis presence in Texas and the southern Plains, and combining lithic material source data from her study with the results presented here may further refine the north–south mobility pattern. More than 28 percent of the projectile points in this study identified to lithic source were moved more than 400 km. Band mobility from 400 to 600 km was apparently common. This study indicates that band mobility greater than 600 km occurred less often, as indicated by the decrease noted in the number of projectile points being moved more than that distance (Figure 10.7).

Tantalizing evidence of possible band aggregation is present at one site in the study area. The Diskau assemblage contains a high percentage of lithic material from far-western sources. However, there may also be Burlington chert and KRF artifacts at the site. If these diverse lithic materials exist together in the same component, then one explanation is that there was more than one band present at the site. These possible band aggregation events, similar to those proposed by Hofman (1994) for Folsom sites, would probably have included exchange of lithic materials.

It appears that some lithic movements cannot be explained within the context of bands moving long distances and carrying lithic material they acquired during the yearly round. Evidence of indirect procurement is circumstantial and consists of single projectile points made of lithic material from a source over 600 km away (Figure 10.7), with little other evidence of tool kits made of the same material moving comparably long distances. Based on the results of this study, 600 km is the maximum distance entire tool kits were moved from most lithic resources before being discarded. When points occur alone, and at distances greater than 600 km from the source, they are likely the result of indirect procurement. That is, they represent the exchange of lithics or people between bands after they moved the lithic material long distances. This study identifies five examples of probable lithic exchange.

A good candidate for exchange is the very large midsection of the Burlington chert Clovis point found in east central Nebraska. This point would have been 15–17 cm long before it was broken. Distance from the southeastern Iowa source area is 490 km, the longest movement of this lithic material recorded. This distance is about 125 km farther than any other recorded movement for Burlington chert Clovis points.

Two projectile points made of Reeds Spring chert from northwestern Arkansas were found in northern Kansas and southern Nebraska, between 350 and 450 km from the source. No other evidence of this chert being used for Clovis tools has been observed anywhere in the study area. These two points are probably examples of exchange.

Very long distance movement of Knife River flint (737 km average distance) may be the result of exchange, especially the finds of KRF Clovis points on the western central Plains. The large majority of KRF lithic movement appears to be down the Missouri River valley, which also raises the possibility of the use of boats to transport this lithic material long distances downstream.

Evidence of exchange also comes from the presence of Edwards chert in the central Great Plains. We know from the Drake cache in northeastern Colorado that Edwards chert was moved with Alibates chert because both lithic types were found in the same cache. Other Edwards chert Clovis projectile points occur an average of 932 km from the source, including three projectile points and two preforms. Also, two Clovis blades have been identified that were moved more than 900 km from the source. The fact that this lithic material is more than 300 km south of the Alibates quarry area suggests that movements by Clovis bands on the southern Plains between the Edwards chert and Alibates chert quarries and subsequent exchange of lithic materials between these bands best explain the presence of these two lithic types far to the north in the central Great Plains.

The Model

Having demonstrated that Clovis groups traveled over long distances, we can now place this mobility within the context of Clovis subsistence patterns. Clovis populations in the central Plains and nearby areas of the High Plains probably reacted to increased climatic warming and seasonality and the attendant biotic reorganization with two adaptive strategies. It is hypothesized here that the first strategy was to increase mobility and the second was to focus primarily on bison as a prey species. The reason for selecting these options has to do primarily with how bison adapted to environmental changes at the end of the Pleistocene.

Neither humans nor bison were adapted to the climatic change of the late Pleistocene and the resulting effects on biotic communities. Migration would have been the most economical adaptation to help mitigate the effects of a shorter peak in new grass growth (Guthrie 1984b:268, Figure 13.2) and reduced precipitation that resulted from the environmental shift. By increasing the distance of seasonal migration in order to forage on higher-protein grasses throughout the year, bison could increase the duration of access to peak forage. Bison that traveled from the High Plains to the southern or eastern central Plains could increase their access to green forage by about four weeks and also find sheltered areas in wooded river valleys that were less prone to heavy winter snow cover. When spring returned, bison could travel back to the north and west following the growth of grass to peak nutrition, again extending the period of peak forage nutrition by several weeks. This strategy would be especially important during calving season. During the summer months the Clovis bands would have moved into northeastern Colorado when short grasses like buffalo grass would reach their peak period of nutrition. Northeastern Colorado also had hundreds of playa lakes that, while diminished in size due to increased aridity and seasonality, still held substantial water in the middle of high-quality grass forage areas. Evidence of this use of playa lakes by Clovis peoples is evident from the Dutton site, the CW cache site, and a playa in western Kansas as well as surface finds of Clovis artifacts near several other playas in northeastern Colorado. It should be noted that seasonal data on Clovis sites and the fauna that Clovis peoples at these sites utilized is not presently available from the few excavated Clovis sites on the central Great Plains, nor is good temporal control of Clovis sites.

While other, less migratory megafauna became increasingly scarce, bison provided a reliable resource that Clovis groups could hunt during the Pleistocene-Holocene transition. Clovis mobility patterns on the central Plains became more influenced by the movement of bison as humans became more economically dependent upon them. Specialization in bison procurement began in the Clovis period, as evidenced at Jake Bluff, Aubrey, Blackwater Draw, and Murray Springs, and was heightened during the Folsom and Goshen era beginning about 10,800 RCYBP.

This model of Clovis mobility assumes that groups on the Great Plains were dependent on hunting terrestrial game as their primary subsistence strategy (in the sense used by Kelly and Todd 1988). Plant foods also formed an important part of the Clovis diet, and the suggested seasonal mobility pattern would have allowed people to take advantage of an extended growing season for floral resources. As Clovis groups moved north and west during spring, edible plants would become available over a longer period of time as the Plains "greened up."

Consistency of Clovis technological traits over vast areas of North America suggests that repeated band interactions played an important role in maintaining the Clovis techno-culture and probably also in scheduling Clovis mobility. If Clovis bands were dependent on highly mobile faunal resources such as bison, and were thus highly mobile themselves, a need would exist for reference points on the landscape in order to interact with other Clovis bands at certain times of the year (Bamforth 1988; Hofman 1994; MacDonald 1999; Surovell 2000). High-quality lithic quarries would have made excellent fixed locations to serve as meeting points for band interactions and to allow groups to retool.

Flattop Butte in northeastern Colorado provides one of the best examples of possible band aggregation locations in the central Plains. More than 25 percent of this study's projectile points and preforms, one large biface, and many other tool types attest to the importance of this lithic source to Clovis populations on the central Plains. Based on the data from the study area and the model developed here, Clovis bands may have congregated near Flattop Butte in the late summer or early fall to gear up by producing large bifaces for trips to wintering localities. Some of the destinations of the various bands might have been sheltered wooded valleys of eastern Nebraska, the Flint Hills of east central Kansas, and northern to central Texas, all areas that also contain lithic resources. Other Clovis bands may have departed for the foothills of the Rocky Mountains, to residential camp sites like those used by the later Folsom peoples at the Lindenmeier site (Wilmsen and Roberts 1978) near the Colorado-Wyoming border. These late summer to early fall band aggregations would have allowed exchange of resource information and rare commodities from distant sources and, possibly most important, the transfer of mates between the small bands (Hofman 1994; MacDonald 1999; Surovell 2000).

Cementing social ties between bands may have allowed individuals access to new procurement areas during times of resource shortages. This would provide a significant adaptive advantage in the rapidly changing environment of the Pleistocene-Holocene transition. Even though this study suggests there probably was some general patterning in the territories utilized by Clovis bands, for such a system to be effective at the end of the Pleistocene, territorial boundaries must have remained fluid.

A settlement-subsistence model of Clovis adaptations on the central Plains presented here supplants the earlier model of Clovis subsistence and settlement proposed by Greiser (1985) and is more similar to Kelly and Todd's (1988) and Waguespack and Surovell's (2003) models than to those suggested by either Meltzer (1993) or Johnson (1991). Evidence presented here supports portions of the Kelly and Todd and Waguespack and Surovell models, suggesting a heavy reliance on terrestrial fauna. Also supported are the parts of Kelly and Todd's model indicating high residential and logistical mobility, the lack of long-term food storage, and the use of high-quality lithic resources and a tool kit manufactured from large bifaces. The primary difference between the Kelly and Todd model and the one presented here is in the area of resource knowledge and population interactions between bands. Kelly and Todd deemphasize reliance on floral resources and unique areas on the landscape, such as restricted, point-source lithic quarries. Their model also deemphasizes the role of band interactions based on the unlikely assumption that population density was so low that bands would not have met on a regular basis.

The model presented here assumes that human populations on the Great Plains were very familiar with each other and with the faunal and floral resource base and the locations of lithic resources and unique geographic features of the landscape. This long-extant population must have established itself on the Great Plains long before the Clovis techno-complex developed (Holen 2006, 2007). Multidirectional long-distance movement of high-quality lithic material indicates intimate knowledge of the landscape and its resources and supports this interpretation. In other words, Clovis populations were not moving into new territories while settling a new continent. Instead, a dramatic climatic change forced adaptive responses to biotic reorganization, causing pre-Clovis populations to become highly mobile and heavily reliant on migrating terrestrial game. This initiated the efficient use of bifaces made from high-quality lithic resources as pre-Clovis populations adapted to the end of the Pleistocene by developing "Clovis" lithic technology from the late Upper Paleolithic technology that they had brought with them to the Americas. Similarities between the two that may be indications of transition have previously been noted by C. V. Haynes (1982, 1987). Furthermore, these Clovis bands would have maintained necessary interactions by meeting at unique places on the landscape at regular and agreed upon times of the year. These unique places would likely include resource procurement areas like lithic quarries. Bands could socialize, exchange information, intermarry, exchange goods that might not be available in other areas, and generally maintain intergroup bonds while strengthening survival skills.

CLOVIS CACHING IN THE CENTRAL GREAT PLAINS

Clovis caching fits within the mobility and lithic procurement system model presented above. High-quality lithic material was moved into areas with few or no good lithic resources to provision the landscape for times when these resources would be needed. There are two major trends in Clovis caching on the central Great Plains (Figure 10.8). First is the movement of Flattop chalcedony to the south, east, and southeast. The CW cache is located 165 km to the south of Flattop Butte on the edge of an upland playa lake and consists of 11 bifaces and 3 flakes. It appears to be a utilitarian cache meant for retrieval. There are no high-quality lithic resources in the area where the cache was deposited, only a few cobbles of Black Forest silicified wood and quartzites.

No actual caches of Flattop chalcedony have been found east or southeast of Flattop Butte; however, two large Clovis bifaces that were probably parts of caches have been found to the east in the Platte River drainage. The area where these two bifaces were found contains only relatively small cobbles from the Platte River, none of which would be good for producing Clovis projectile points. One biface (Holen 2001b) was found on a northward tributary of the Platte River just into the Nebraska Sand Hills, some 200 km east of the source area. The second biface (Holen 2001a) was found 125 km east of the source in a gravel pit in the South Platte River. Other evidence of the long-distance movement of Flattop chalcedony bifaces comes from the Eckles site in northern Kansas, where large bifacial flakes were being removed from a flake core. Whether this material was transported directly from the source or derived from cached material is unknown. The Platte River would have offered a natural travel corridor to Clovis groups moving east and southeast to eastern Nebraska and northeastern Kansas. Clovis groups then could have crossed the relatively short distance between the Platte River and Republican River drainages in south central Nebraska to reach White Rock Creek, a tributary of the Republican. One other example of possible caching of high-quality western source lithic material to the east is the large Hartville chert bifacial core that was found in east central Nebraska some 435 km east of the quarry area (Figure 10.8).

There is one example of caching of medium-quality lithic material to the west of its source and that is the Busse cache (Hofman 1995, 1997). This cache was found 100 km west of the source of Smoky Hill jasper. In the area where this material was cached there is no good lithic material, just a few small cobbles from stream sources.

Clovis peoples moved high-quality lithic material from the southern Plains to the north and northwest very long distances and cached it. The primary lithic material that was moved to the north and cached is Alibates chert from a source along the Canadian River in the Texas Panhandle. Two caches, the JS cache in northwestern Oklahoma about 150 km from the source and the Sailor-Helton cache in southwestern Kansas 200 km from the source, are in areas where there are few or no good sources of high-quality lithic material. Clovis peoples moved Alibates chert very great distances to the northwest. The Drake site contains 11 Clovis points made of Alibates chert that were cached about 600 km from the source.

Edwards chert from central Texas was also being moved north by Clovis populations, based on evidence from western Oklahoma, where the Domebo mammoth kill site contains Edwards chert projectile points and tools (Leonhardy 1966). One point made of Edwards chert was found in the Drake cache, indicating that Alibates and Edwards lithic materials were being moved long distances in the same assemblage.

In south central Nebraska the Gosper County cache indicates that Edwards chert was being cached 930 km from the source. The cache consists of two projectile point preforms, and more material may have been present in the construction area. Once again, the cache was found in an area where there are only small cobbles available in the Platte River as a lithic source. Edwards chert

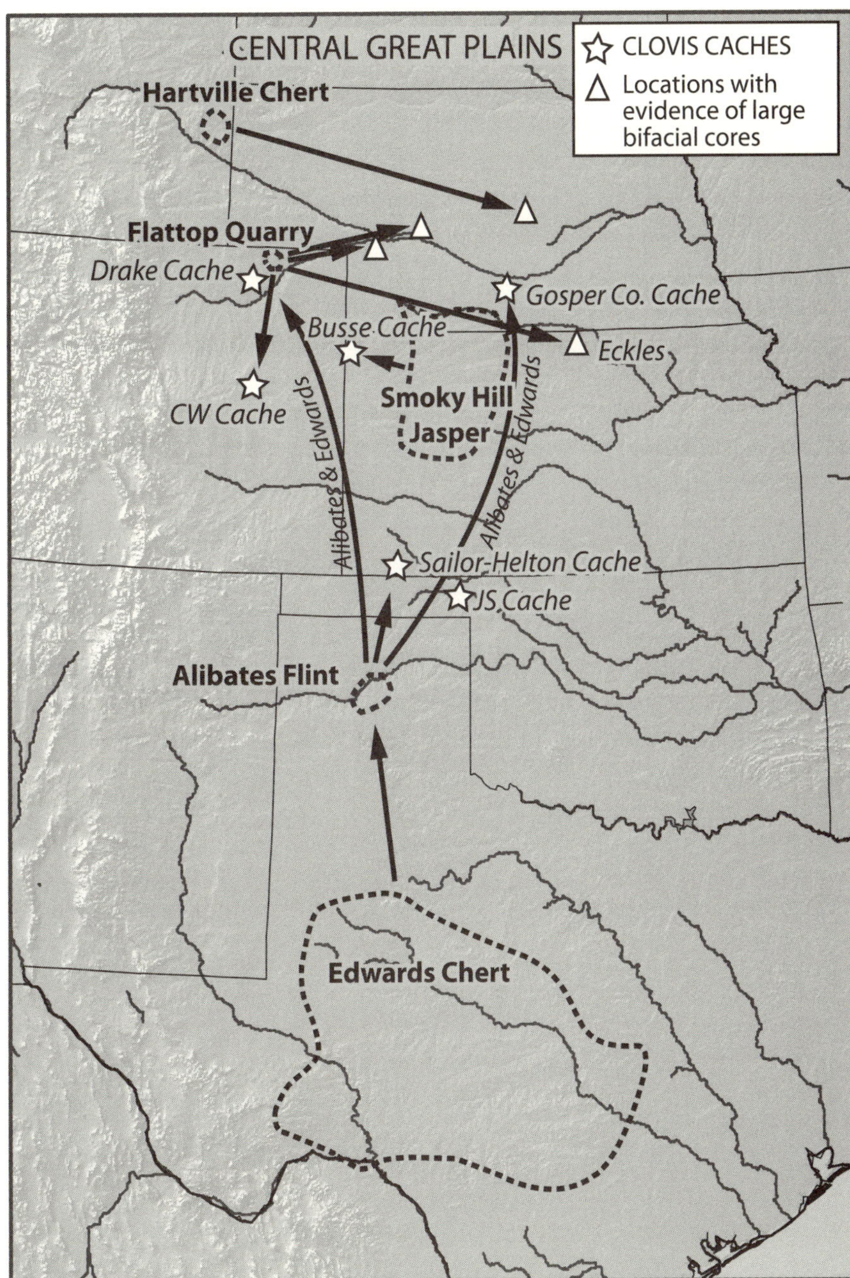

Figure 10.8. Clovis caching and movement of large bifaces in the central Great Plains

must have been moved north through extensive deposits of Smoky Hill jasper to reach the point where it was found. This cache represents the longest distance between a cache of Clovis lithic material and the source yet known in North America.

CONCLUSION

This study presents a preliminary attempt to understand lithic procurement, caching, and mobility of Clovis populations in the central Great Plains of North America. Evidence of Clovis adaptation at the Pleistocene-Holocene boundary suggests that human populations were highly adaptable and able to withstand a rapid change in climate and biotic organization. On the central Plains, lithic procurement data suggest that some groups adapted by migrating long distances, up to 600 km, probably on a seasonal basis (Figures 10.5, 10.6). Robust patterns of movement of Flattop chalcedony from northeastern Colorado across the breadth of the Plains to the east and southeast, as well as movement of Alibates chert and Edwards chert from Texas northward into the central Plains was documented. Weaker patterns of chert being moved from the eastern central Plains to the west and of Knife River flint being carried southward toward the central Plains were also documented. Lithic material was cached in areas of the central Plains where there were no good lithic resources in order to provision the landscape with good toolstone.

One reason why Clovis groups carried toolstone over very long distances may be related to patterns of seasonal bison migration as bison adapted to the shorter duration of the peak of new plant growth (Guthrie 1984b:268, Figure 13.2) that resulted from increased seasonality at the end of the Pleistocene. As many megafaunal prey species went extinct, Clovis hunters would have been left with bison as a primary prey species. Bison kills in Oklahoma, Texas, New Mexico, and Arizona attest to this early Clovis specialization in bison hunting. This model is similar to Clovis lithic procurement and mobility models that are linked to seasonal movement of caribou in the Illinois-Wisconsin area (Loebel 2005), the Great Lakes, and the Northeast (Ellis and Deller 2000; MacDonald 1968; Simons 1997; Spiess et al. 1998).

Finally, this research has demonstrated the benefits of using surface-collected data from museum and private collections as a methodology in the study of early Paleoindian lithic procurement, mobility, and land use patterns. With appropriate documentation, private collections have tremendous research potential for studies of early human groups that left a minimal archaeological signature because of low population density, high mobility, and geomorphic processes that have destroyed or deeply buried many sites. Hopefully, additional data from Clovis sites and collections of Clovis materials will allow the model developed here to be tested and refined.

ACKNOWLEDGMENTS

I would like to thank the following people for assistance with the research that led to this chapter. Kathleen Holen read and commented on several drafts of this document. Jack Hofman and Rolfe Mandel were very helpful in the early stages of this research. Dick and Carol Eckles allowed me to record the very important Eckles site Clovis collection. Angie Fox, of the University of Nebraska State Museum, completed the illustrations of the Eckles site artifacts. Eric Parrish completed the graphics for this chapter. I would also like to thank the many collectors who allowed access to their Clovis artifacts; without this data the research could not have been completed.

Chapter 11

Direction and Distance in Clovis Caching

THE MOVEMENT OF PEOPLE AND LITHIC RAW MATERIALS ON THE CLOVIS-AGE LANDSCAPE

J. David Kilby

≈

INTRODUCTION

The relatively frequent caching of tools by Clovis people is becoming increasingly evident (as these chapters attest) and appears to set Clovis apart from subsequent Paleoindian groups in the North American Plains and western mountains. The initial discoveries of caches (Butler 1963; Butler and Fitzwater 1965; Grange 1964; Green 1963; Hammatt 1970) were treated as anomalies to be inspected individually. However, a watershed of sorts occurred in the early 1990s when caching began to be recognized as a regular part of Clovis organization (e.g., Frison 1991a, 1991b; Stanford 1991). Functional interpretations of caches identified them as generalized or specialized tool kits (e.g., Grange 1964; Hammatt 1970; Mallouf 1994) and burial assemblages, perhaps more ritual than functional (e.g., Frison 1991b; Stanford and Jodry 1988; Wilke et al. 1991; Woods and Titmus 1985), often depending upon which specific cache or caches constituted the subject of study. More recently, researchers including David Meltzer (2002), Gary Haynes (2002b), Michael Collins (1999b), Bruce Huckell (1999), several authors in this volume, and me (Kilby 2008; 2011) have increasingly viewed caches in relation to other kinds of sites and in the context of organizational strategies.

A recurring perspective is that Clovis caches represent the precautions of initial colonizers who were new to a region and thus unfamiliar with local resource distributions; they were insurance against resource shortages as colonizing populations first made their way across an unknown continent. Wilke et al. (1991:243–244) referred to caches as "a coherent technological adaptation among the initial colonizers of the New World." More specifically, Meltzer (2002:38; 2004) proposed that "Clovis groups were so *new* to the landscape they didn't know and could not predict where or when they were next going to find vital resources. By leaving caches scattered about the landscape, as they moved away from known sources, they created artificial supply depots, and thus compensated for their lack of knowledge." Haynes (2002b:247) argued that if caches represent a strategy associated with colonization, they are single-event phenomena with limited potential for aiding in the understanding of colonization as a process. The purpose of this chapter is to evaluate Clovis caches as signatures of colonization—in other words, to test the idea that Clovis caches represent a strategy on the part of the initial colonizers of North America to supply unexplored or poorly explored regions with essential stone resources.

THE PROVISIONING AND EXPLORATION HYPOTHESES

The proposition that caches served as fixed points for resupply as the New World was explored can be broken down into two hypotheses: (1) that Clovis caches served to provision areas where suitable raw material was unavailable or was not known to exist, and (2) that they are associated with the initial exploration and colonization of the North American landscape. A number of testable predictions logically follow from these hypotheses. In a scenario where caches served to artificially supply the landscape, we should expect caches to occur in areas that are impoverished with regard to quality lithic raw materials. It is possible that if caches were indeed established as part of explorations of areas that were entirely unknown, they might occasionally have been unknowingly placed near existing raw material sources; however, the chances of such coincidence seem unlikely and we should expect the strongest pattern to reflect the purposeful placement of caches where raw materials were scarce. A second implication is that, for reasons of efficiency, the distances that raw materials were transported for caching should not significantly exceed the distance between the nearest available source and the cache location, assuming that the nearest source was known.

For the second hypothesis, that caches functioned to facilitate initial exploration, at least three testable implications can be derived. First, we should expect caches to be diverse and/or generalized with regard to tool forms. If one is uncertain as to what specific resources and opportunities lie ahead, it follows that a tool kit that could meet a variety of unexpected conditions would be preferred. This could be achieved by caching a diverse range of finished tools or by caching a set of generalized forms (e.g., large bifaces, generalized cores, flake blanks, etc.) that could be reduced into more task-specific tools as unforeseen needs arose. Second, we should expect Clovis caches to be distributed throughout the continent, at least within the nonglaciated regions. The simple reason for this is that regardless of the order in which different regions were colonized, every area would have to have been initially explored at some point. Last, if Clovis caches are associated with the initial exploration and colonization of the continent, we can expect the direction that raw materials were moved before being cached to correspond to the directions in which people were moving. With the well-supported assumption that the first explorers of the New World entered the continent from northeastern Asia, it should be expected that caches reflect generally southward and eastward population movement. This large-scale pattern should hold true regardless of what initial entry route was taken (i.e., coastal or ice-free corridor).

Both of these hypotheses can be addressed using data from the caches themselves, including the lithology of the cached items. Linking individual artifacts to geologic sources of lithic raw materials provides a key avenue to understanding the organization of lithic technology as well as the movement of groups of prehistoric people across the landscape (e.g., Amick 1996; Holen 1991; Huckell and Kilby 2002; Huckell et al. 2011; Ingbar 1994; Meltzer 2006). In cases where an artifact of a particular raw material can be identified to its geologic source, its presence in an assemblage provides a limited area on the landscape, in addition to that provided by the location of the cached assemblage itself, to which movements of people can be traced. In order to do so, it is important to consider secondary geologic sources, where stone has been redeposited by alluvial or glacial processes, as potential source areas for lithic raw materials. Furthermore, because the raw material sources must have been visited before sites containing those raw materials were occupied, the locations of the source and the site provide a glimpse of the overall directionality of human movements. In other words, the identification of a specific raw material of known origin in an archaeological assemblage provides two points on the landscape between which a prehistoric person traveled, and the order in which they visited these points provides a general indication of the direction traveled. These indications are strengthened when multiple raw materials in an assemblage are identified to source.

The validity of this approach is, of course, limited by the degree to which exchange can be ruled out as a process by which raw materials were moved around the landscape. This is a difficult and sometimes insurmountable problem when researching more sedentary prehistoric cultures but is unlikely to present a significant obstacle with regard to Clovis. While it might be expected that stone was occasionally exchanged by Clovis people, evidence for substantial exchange of lithic raw materials among early Paleoindians is lacking (Meltzer 1984). Evidence for extensive exchange networks in North America in general postdate the Paleoindian period by several millennia, perhaps due to the combination of low population densities and highly mobile lifestyles that characterized late Pleistocene foraging societies. For the purposes of this chapter it is assumed that exchange played an insignificant role in the acquisition and movement of lithic raw materials among western Clovis groups and that the presence of a particular raw material indicates a visit to a primary or secondary geologic source for that material.

The remainder of this chapter presents raw material data for a group of 17 Clovis caches (Table 11.1) and utilizes these data to evaluate the likelihood that caching was related to provisioning the landscape to facilitate the initial exploration and colonization of the continent. In doing so, particular attention is given to reconstructing the distances stone was transported and the directions in which Clovis groups transported them.

LITHIC RAW MATERIALS IN CLOVIS CACHES

The raw materials identified in the 17 caches are presented in Table 11.2. In some cases, these identifications can be made with a fair amount of confidence because the raw material is distinctive in regard to some particular attribute (e.g., color variations, fossil inclusions, UV fluorescence, etc.) or because thorough descriptions of the named raw material source have been published. In other cases specific raw material identifications are made with less confidence and represent best estimations based upon current information. I assume that these identifications are correct, although admittedly they are tentative. More accurate or precise identifications may be made in the future that might require the modification of some of these conclusions.

The most important reason for identifying specific raw material sources is to have the ability to measure the distance and direction that the materials have been transported. This too is a complex issue, because specific raw materials may outcrop continuously or sporadically over a large area, or they may be displaced as secondary occurrences scattered over significant distances by geological processes, or they may be easily confused with materials with similar characteristics. Also, the actual distance a particular material has been transported by humans is impossible to determine due to the inability to reconstruct the exact path taken. Straight-line distance from source to recovery site is used instead and is measured from the cache find location to the nearest documented source that corresponds to the characteristics of the raw material in question. In some cases (e.g., Edwards chert), distance is measured to the location of a specific variant of the material that is represented in the cache. In cases where considerable natural transport and dispersal of a raw material from its primary source has been documented (e.g., Alibates chert [Wyckoff 1993]), distance is measured from each cache to the closest location where raw materials of appropriate quality (especially with regard to nodule size) are found today. Measurements are estimated to the nearest kilometer using the straight-line measuring tool available in Google Earth software. It should be noted that the Fenn cache presents a special case because its exact find location is not known. Measurements for the Fenn cache are made from the point where the boundaries of Utah, Idaho, and Wyoming meet. While raw material identification, source area recognition, and measurement are clearly complex, and the methods used here to address them are admittedly simple, I believe that this approach makes the best use of the information at hand and enables the detection of some general patterns by means of comparison.

Table 11.2 presents the raw materials that make up each cache in order of abundance by weight. Center points for source locations are presented in Figure 11.1.

TRANSPORT DISTANCE

The hypothesis that caches served to supply areas of the landscape that lacked adequate or known raw material sources with readily available stores of raw material has two testable implications. First, caches should be located in areas that either lack adequate or known raw materials, and thus transport distances should be long. Second, the distance that raw materials in caches were transported should not significantly exceed the distance to the nearest known source.

The range in distances from cached artifacts to raw material sources is great (Table 11.2). The de Graffenried cache is unique in that it was located practically at the source of its raw material (it is estimated to be at a distance of 1 km, both to account for the uncertainty of its find location and to give it a positive value for mathematical purposes). Evidence of the greatest distance for raw material transport comes from the Drake cache, where a single artifact manufactured from raw material from the Edwards chert source was transported over 950 km. The distribution of distances from caches to raw material sources appears to be relatively normally distributed between these two extremes (with the distance from the source of Edwards chert to the Drake cache as somewhat of an outlier), with an expected right skew reflecting decreasing frequency as distance increases (Figure 11.2).

TABLE 11.1. Clovis Caches Included in This Investigation

ASSEMBLAGE	ARTIFACT CLASSES							PRIMARY REFERENCES
	Bifaces	Points	Cores	Blades	Flakes	Other[a]	Total Items	
Anadarko, OK	2		4	26			32	Hammatt 1970; McKee 1964
Anzick, MT	62	8		1	9	6	86	Jones and Bonnichsen 1994; Taylor 1969; Wilke at al. 1991
Beach, ND[b]	99			4			103	Huckell and Kilby 2009; Huckell et al. 2011
Busse, NM	13		1	33	30	1	78	Hofman 1995
Crook County, WY	7	1		1			9	Tankersley 1998
de Graffenried, TX	4	1					5	Collins et al. 2007
Dickenson, NM				4	1		5	Montgomery and Dickenson 1992a
Drake, CO		13				1	14	Stanford and Jodry 1988
East Wenatchee, WA	20	14		4	8	12	58	Gramly 1993; Huckell et al. in review; Lyman et al. 1998; Mehringer 1988
Fenn, UT/WY	35	20		1			56	Frison 1991a; Frison and Bradley 1999
Franey, NE	1		1	35	36	1	74	Grange 1964
Green, NM				17			17	Green 1963
Keven Davis, TX				14			14	Young and Collins 1989; Collins 1996
Pelland, MN				9			9	Stoltman 1971
Sailor-Helton, KS			10	40	115		165	Mallouf 1994; Helton 1957
Simon, ID	28	7					35	Butler 1963; Butler and Fitzwater 1965; Muto 1971; Woods and Titmus 1985
Watts, CO	6						6	Bob Patten n.d.; Kilby 2008

[a]Includes bone and ivory rods (Anzick and East Wenatchee), a hammerstone (Drake), a marine shell (Franey), and an abrader (Busse)

[b]Includes 2 additional blades recovered during 2007 fieldwork

TABLE 11.2. Lithic Raw Material Data for Cache Analysis

CACHE	PRIMARY				SECONDARY				TERTIARY				QUATERNARY				QUINARY				NEAREST OTHER	
	Source	Distance (km)	Weight (g)	%	Source	Distance (km)	Weight (g)	%	Source	Distance (km)	Weight (g)	%	Source	Distance (km)	Weight (g)	%	Source	Distance (km)	Weight (g)	%	Source	Distance (km)
Anadarko	Edwards chert (Sweetwater)	352	4123.9	72.00	Alibates chert	135	1603.9	28.00													Alibates chert	135
Anzick[a]	Hartville Uplift chert	590	11082.5	66.60	Moss agate	618	5225.1	31.40	Phosphoria chert	197	166.4	1.00	Porcellanite	377	166.4	1.00					Big Horn Mtns	197
Beach	Sentinel Butte chert (WRGS)	19	3200.8	34.86	Spanish Diggings quartzite	490	2708.8	29.50	Rainy Buttes Silicified Wood	86	1177.5	12.82	Hartville chert	500.00	60.20	0.66	Other	Unk.	2034.1	22.15	Sentinel Butte chert (WRGS)	19
Busse	Niobrara Jasper	100	7798.9	99.79	Fossiliferous chert	Unk.	13.2	0.17	Moss agate	408	1.9	0.02	Hartville chert	387	1.6	0.02					Niobrara Jasper	100
Green	Edwards chert (Abilene)	392	678.9	100.00																	Alibates chert	209
Dickenson	Edwards chert (unspecified)	310	448.1	100.00																	Alibates chert	209
Crook County	Green River Formation chert	588	2697.5	99.78	Hartville chert	261	6.0	0.22													Porcellanite	65
de Graffenried	Edwards chert (Georgetown)	1	1284.2	100.00																	Edwards chert (Georgetown)	1
Drake	Alibates dolomite	584	417.0	81.48	Edwards chert (unspecified)	955	49.8	9.73	Chalcedony (Laramie Fm)	140	45.0	8.79									Chalcedony (Laramie Fm)	140
East Wenatchee	Agate	50	4342.9	80.56	White chalcedony	Unk.	603.1	11.19	Gray chalcedony	Unk.	245.1	4.55	Brown chert	Unk.	199.8	3.71					Ephrata agate	50
Fenn	Utah Agate	358	3481.6	41.2	Green River Formation chert	130	2772.8	32.8	Obsidian (SW Idaho)	150	1942.6	23.0	Big Horn Mtns. / red jasper	360	107.8	1.3	Crystal	Unk.	83.6	1.0	Green River Formation chert	130
Franey	Hartville chert	120	1022.5	52.01	Yellow jasper	22	903.7	45.97	Green chert	Unk.	39.8	2.02									Yellow jasper	22
Keven Davis	Edwards chert (Georgetown)	205	313.8	86.00	Tan chert	Unk.	51.1	14.00													Edwards chert (Georgetown)	205
Pelland	Knife River chalcedony	670	156.5	100.00																	Knife River chalcedony	670
Sailor-Helton	Alibates dolomite	155	13763.1	100.00																	Alibates chert	155
Simon	Unidentified gray chert (Amsden?)	585	4026.0	50.49	Quartz crystal	Unk.	1124.9	14.11	Big Horn Mtns. / Phosphoria chert	593.0	778.4	9.76	Green River Formation chert	461	310.4	3.89	Other	Unk.	1733.7	21.74	Idaho obsidian	216
Watts	Spanish Diggings quartzite	230	4385.9	98.28	Phosphoria chert	390	76.7	1.72													Chalcedony (Laramie Formation)	75

Note: WRGS = White River Group silicates

[a]Because casts from Anzick were analyzed, weights are estimated from size and raw material percentages are based upon number of specimens rather than weight.

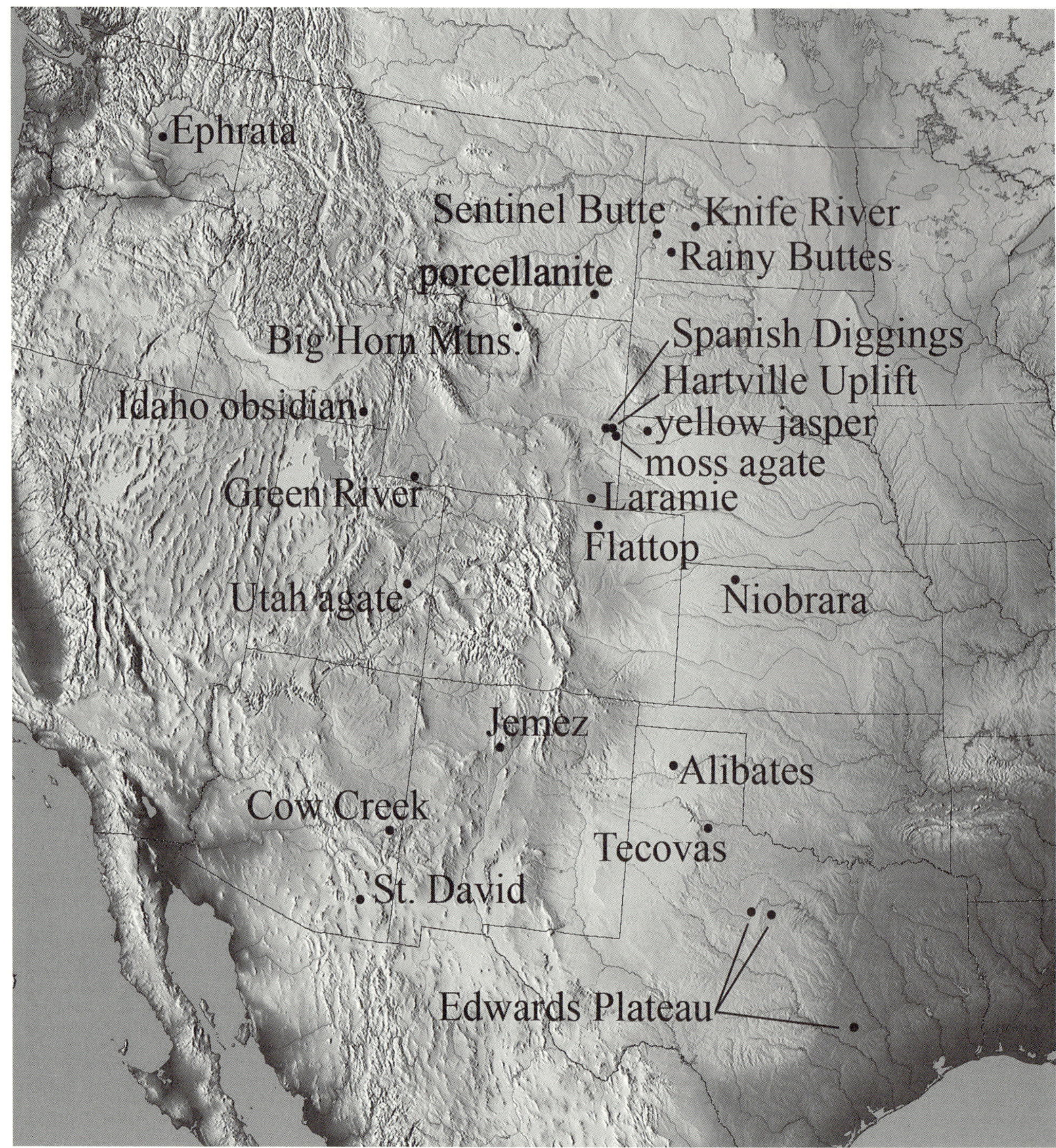

Figure 11.1. Locations of primary sources for lithic raw materials discussed in text

A simple measure of distance to raw material sources for any specific cache is complicated by the number of raw materials present, the proportion of each type of raw material in the assemblage, and the proximity of each cache location to known sources that do not appear in the cache. For example, while 81 percent of the Drake cache is made of stone from the Alibates source located 585 km away and 10 percent (one artifact) is made of Edwards chert 955 km distant, 9 percent (one artifact) is made from chalcedony available only 140 km away. Accordingly, it is difficult to estimate, based on any single source, whether the distance between cache location and raw materials should be considered relatively low or relatively high.

In order for a single value to represent the variation in distances to multiple raw material sources within an individual cache, the measure must be based not only upon the distances to the sources but also the proportion of the

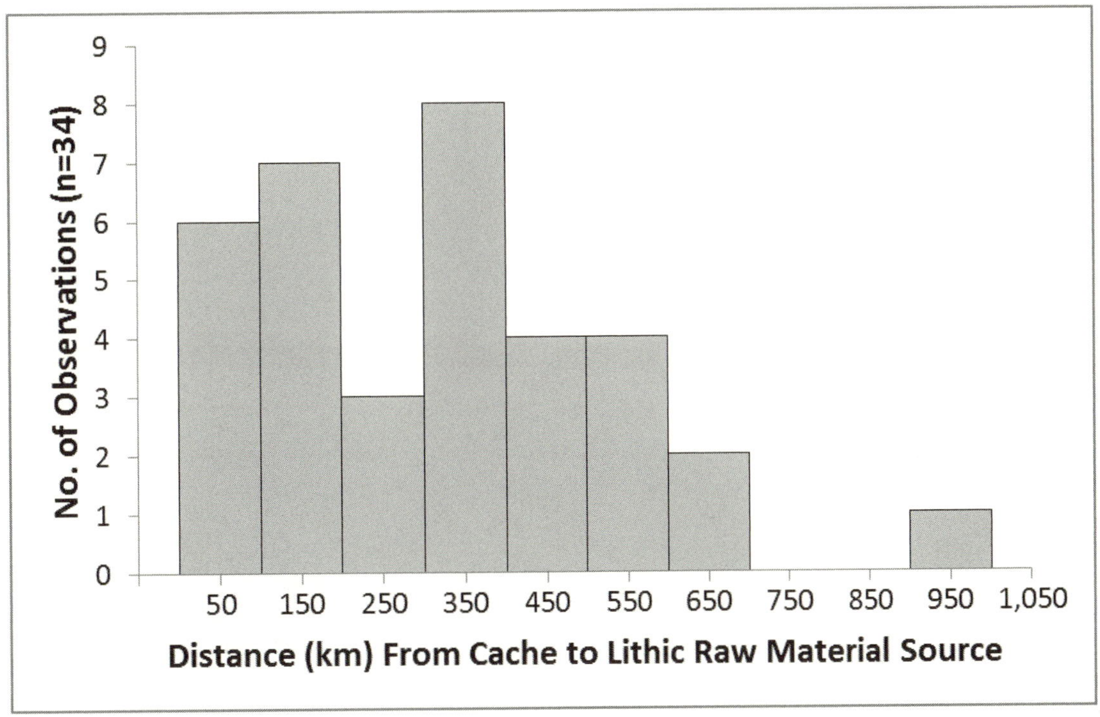

Figure 11.2. The distribution of distances from geologic sources of lithic raw materials to caches in which they occur

assemblage that source represents. Thus, the value needs to be not an average of the distances but an average weighted by proportion. The following formula is used to weight the averages:

$$ATD = (D_{rm1} * P_{rm1}) + (D_{rm2} * P_{rm2}) \ldots / \Sigma P$$

where *ATD* is average transport distance, *D* is distance (km), *P* is the proportion (percentage by weight), and *rm* is the material source. It should be noted that the formula only takes into account raw materials identified to source (i.e., raw materials for which there are distance measures). Accordingly, the sum of *P* is always 100. Relative transport distance is thus calculated by ignoring artifacts of raw materials unidentified to source. The validity of this measure is supported by the fact that in all but one case (Simon) raw materials identified to source represent more than 80 percent of the assemblage. The calculation of average transport distance for each cache assemblage is presented in Table 11.3.

Average transport distances range from 1 km in the case of de Graffenried, where all the artifacts are made of Edwards chert that outcrops nearby, to 683 km in the case of Simon, where artifacts are made from several distant raw materials. It should be pointed out, however, that only 54 percent of the Simon materials are identified to source, and the high average transport distance may reflect a bias toward identifying more distant sources. A more reliable maximum of 670 km is found in the case of Pelland, where all artifacts are made from Knife River flint found at that distance.

Measuring the distance from a cache to the nearest available source requires estimating which sources Clovis groups knew. For the sake of simplicity, the population of known raw material sources is taken to be those that are present in any of the cache assemblages as well as kill and camp sites from the same regions (Kilby 2008). It is clear that Clovis people were using stone from these sources and, assuming again that acquisition was not by long-distance trade, that they knew their locations. Certainly these groups can be expected to have been aware of and utilized other sources as well, but the recurring use of many of the sources present in the Clovis assemblages analyzed here suggests that they were commonly used and preferred resources.

Nearest source distance (NSD) is thus a measure of distance from a cache to the nearest raw material source known to have been utilized, regardless of whether or not it occurs within the particular cache in question.

If caches are for moving stone to stoneless areas, the distance to the nearest source (NSD) should be relatively high. More importantly, the ratio of nearest source

TABLE 11.3. Calculation of Average Transport Distance (ATD) for Caches

CACHE	$(D_{rm1}*P_{rm1})$	$(D_{rm2}*P_{rm2})$	$(D_{rm3}*P_{rm3})$	$(D_{rm4}*P_{rm4})$	P	ATD
Anadarko	25,343.3	3,780.0	0.0	0.0	100.00	291.2
Anzick	39,294.0	19,405.2	197.0	377.0	100.00	592.7
Beach	662.3	14,455.0	1049.2	330.0	77.84	211.9
Busse	9,978.6	0.0	9.9	7.9	99.83	100.1
Green	39,200.0	0.0	0.0	0.0	100.00	392.0
Dickenson	31,000.0	0.0	0.0	0.0	100.00	310.0
Crook County	58,669.5	57.9	0.0	0.0	100.00	587.3
de Graffenried	100.0	0.0	0.0	0.0	100.00	1.0
Drake	47,582.6	9,292.5	1,230.9	0.0	100.00	581.1
East Wenatchee	4,028.0	0.0	0.0	0.0	80.56	50.0
Fenn	14,748.2	4,265.2	3,447.9	459.2	99.00	231.5
Franey	6241.1	1,011.3	0.0	0.0	97.98	74.0
Keven Davis	17,629.2	0.0	0.0	0.0	86.00	205.0
Pelland	67,000.0	0.0	0.0	0.0	100.00	670.0
Sailor-Helton	15,500.0	0.0	0.0	0.0	100.00	155.0
Simon	29,538.3	0.0	5,787.7	1794.6	54.39	682.5
Watts	22,604.7	670.3	0.0	0.0	100.00	232.8

distance to average transport distance (NSD:ATD) associated with a cache also should be high. This ratio provides a measure of the distance to the nearest source relative to the distances to other sources within a given cache (Table 11.4). For caches that served to move stone to stoneless areas, we can expect that distance to nearest source accounts for a higher proportion of the ATD, thus resulting in a ratio with a higher value. Under the simplest conditions, if the sole function of caches was to move stone to stoneless areas, the NSD and the ATD should be the same, resulting in a value of one.

The relationship between distance to nearest source and ATD is presented in Figure 11.3, along with the hypothetical 1:1 (y = x) expectation. The patterns evident in the figure and in Table 11.4 indicate that a group of five caches (Busse, East Wenatchee, Keven Davis, Pelland, and Sailor-Helton) conform precisely to the expectation for moving stone to stoneless areas. Six caches (Anadarko, Beach, Dickenson, Fenn, Franey, Green, and Watts) conform more closely to the expected relationship but do not match it precisely. For these six, an increase in ATD still correlates with increasing NSD, but ATD is consistently greater, suggesting that while they do not represent the simple movement of raw materials to areas that lack them entirely, they may represent the movement of *greatly preferred* raw materials to areas where they are otherwise lacking. Preferences may not have been uniform; that is, individual groups may have been partial to certain raw materials for a number of reasons, perhaps including color and pattern as well as technical attributes of workability. In contrast, four caches (Anzick, Crook County, Drake, and Simon) deviate substantially from this expectation, suggesting that their existence is not easily explained in simple terms of supplying areas of low abundance. In these four cases, it appears that stone has been moved long distances and placed in areas where adequate stone is available relatively close by. A more focused analysis of cache function resulted in the identification of two of these (Anzick and Simon) as likely ritual caches, perhaps associated with burials (Kilby 2008:216–219); one other (Crook County) perhaps represents a circumstantial load exchange (Kilby 2008:214–216). The Drake cache, which does not conform well to expectations for supplying stone to stoneless areas but otherwise compares well to expectations for insurance caching (Kilby 2008:209–212), may represent an extreme case of the transport of preferred raw materials.

Thus, with the caveat that no single function is sufficient to explain the existence of Clovis caches (Kilby 2008:244), the majority of cache assemblages do meet expectations for supplying the landscape with raw materials, and thus caches probably did serve to guard against coming up short with regard to lithic raw materials. I hesitate to use the term *insurance* loosely in this context, because that term is used elsewhere (Binford 1979; Kilby

TABLE 11.4. Ratio of Nearest Source Distance (NSD) to Average Transport Distance (ATD) for Lithic Raw Materials

ASSEMBLAGE	NSD (km)	ATD (km)	NSD/ATD
Anadarko	135	291.2	0.464
Anzick	197	592.7	0.332
Beach	19	211.9	0.090
Busse	100	100.1	0.999
Green	209	392.0	0.533
Dickenson	209	310.0	0.674
Crook County	65	587.3	0.111
de Graffenried	1	1.0	1.000
Drake	140	581.1	0.241
East Wenatchee	50	50.0	1.000
Fenn	130	231.5	0.562
Franey	22	74.0	0.297
Keven Davis	205	205.0	1.000
Pelland	670	670.0	1.000
Sailor-Helton	155	155.0	1.000
Simon	216	682.5	0.316
Watts	75	232.8	0.322

2008; Schlanger 1981) to denote a more specific caching behavior. However, several of these caches do meet that specific definition rather neatly.

DIRECTION OF TRANSPORT

Identification of raw material sources provides the rare opportunity to track the direction of movement of stone, and of the people carrying it, across the landscape. The geographic relationships between raw material sources and archaeological sites have been used to estimate the general directions in which the groups were traveling prior to inhabiting individual Folsom sites (e.g., Huckell and Kilby 2002:21–27; Meltzer 2006:273–274) and Clovis sites (e.g., Huckell 2007; Huckell et al. 2011). Similarly, viewing the geographic patterns from the perspective of cache assemblages can shed light upon directionality of raw material transport prior to the deposition of Clovis caches and allows us to literally retrace some of the steps taken by the Clovis groups who set aside those bundles of stone tools.

Figure 11.4 illustrates the direction of movement of raw materials from sources to caches for all raw materials identified to source. In the area from Texas to northeastern Colorado there is a consistent pattern that represents the transport of Edwards chert and Alibates chert in northerly and northwesterly directions from their sources (Figure 11.4a). Only in the case of the Anadarko and Drake caches is there evidence of raw materials (Alibates chert and Laramie Formation chert, respectively) being moved southward. In both of these cases, the raw materials carried south make up a smaller portion of the assemblage than those moved northward. The caches in this region thus represent the transport of southern raw materials northward onto the Plains and, in the case of the Drake cache, along the Rocky Mountain front. In the majority of cases it appears that materials were being moved from their sources to areas of relatively low raw material abundance (an exception is the Drake cache, which was placed within about 120 km of the Flattop chalcedony source of White River Group silicates, common in other Clovis assemblages, including the CW cache). This suggestion is strengthened by the fact that there are caches in roughly all directions north from the Edwards Plateau source area, except in the direction of the Alibates source, where additional raw material could be anticipated as one moved north. It also bears noting that while both Edwards and Alibates chert were cached as far north as northeastern Colorado, none of the materials from that region (e.g., Hartville chert, Laramie Formation chert, Niobrara chert, White River Group

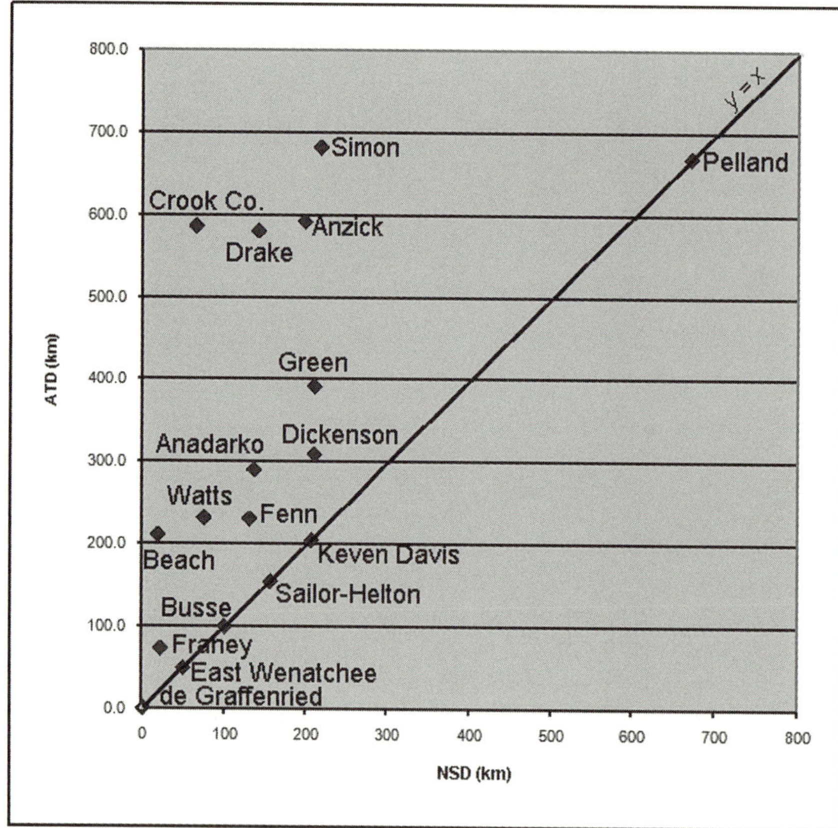

Figure 11.3. Relationship of average transport distance (ADT) to nearest source distance (NSD) for caches

silicates) appear to have been transported and cached far to the south.

To the north, in the central and northern Plains and Rocky Mountain area, the pattern is more complex (Figure 11.4b). The multiple directions from which materials in each assemblage originate clearly suggest more cyclical patterns of movement across the landscape. For example, based upon the relative abundances of raw materials in the Anzick cache, it is not too difficult to envision a route leading northeastward from the Bighorn Mountains (Phosphoria chert) to the Powder River Basin (porcellanite), then southward to the Hartville Uplift (Hartville chert and moss agate) before turning back to the northwest toward the Anzick cache location where these materials were ultimately deposited. To the northeast, the Beach cache represents the transport of materials almost directly northward, with a proportionate decrease in specific raw materials with increasing distance from their source (Figure 11.4c). The Pelland cache records the transport of Knife River flint primarily eastward, albeit slightly northward. The locations of both the Beach and Pelland caches stand out as almost certainly having been close to the margins of the Laurentide ice sheet and Lake Agassiz during the Clovis time period. Though not included in this analysis, the CW cache (Holen, Chapter 10; Muniz, Chapter 7), which contains White River Group silicates transported 165 km south from the Flattop Butte source to the cache location, stands out as one of the few instances (along with the Watts cache) in which substantial amounts of raw materials were moved relatively short distances directly southward.

Despite the greater variability in direction of transport in the north relative to areas to the south, two patterns remain consistent. First, while a small minority of materials were transported southward before being cached, there remains a clear trend of raw material movement to the north and west. The Watts cache represents an exception, as it records the transport of a substantial amount of quartzite from the Spanish Diggings source, along with a small amount of Phosphoria chert, for a relatively short distance almost directly southward before being cached. Additionally, the Pelland cache records a primarily east-northeast route. The preponderance of

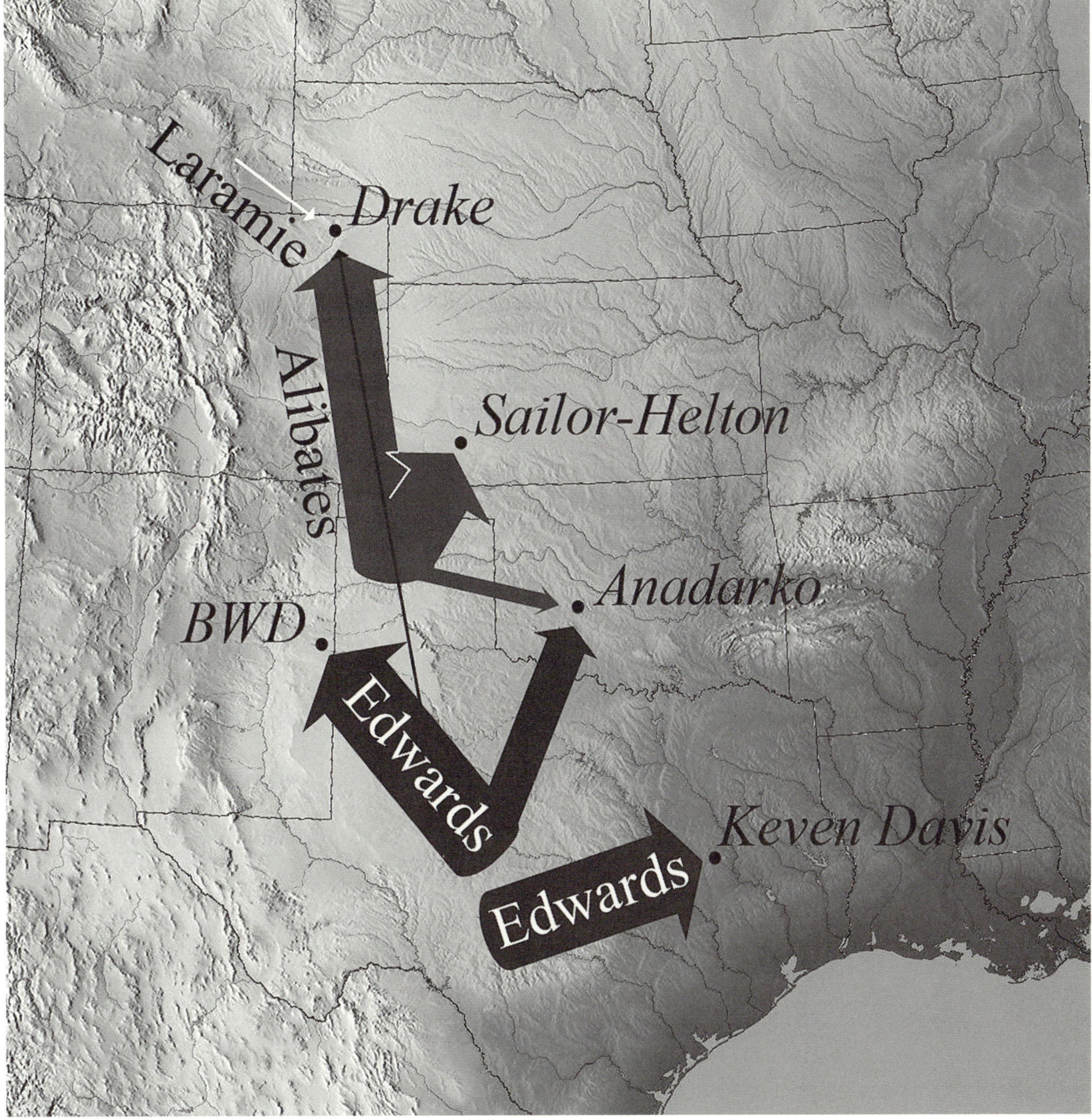

Figure 11.4a. Directions of raw material transport prior to caching for the southern Plains. Line thickness reflects the percentage of the total raw material in a cache contributed by that source.

data, however, reflect northward and westward transport of raw material prior to caching. Second, while materials were clearly transported through other source areas, the cache locations indicate that materials were deposited when moving away from areas of abundance. As in the southern region, no northern caches were located in the areas between the major raw material sources.

The northerly and westerly trend in the transport of raw materials in caches is clearly demonstrated by measurements of the bearing from raw material sources to cache locations (Table 11.5; Figure 11.5). The pattern is highly significant (χ^2 = 12.941; *df* = 5, 34; $p < .025$). Calculation of adjusted χ^2 residuals indicates that the source of variation driving that significance is the number of observations for the 300–360° range (d = 3.08; Z_{crit} = ±1.96,α = .05). Indeed, Figure 11.5 illustrates that only 13 percent by weight of raw material identified to source is associated with bearings between 60 and 240°;

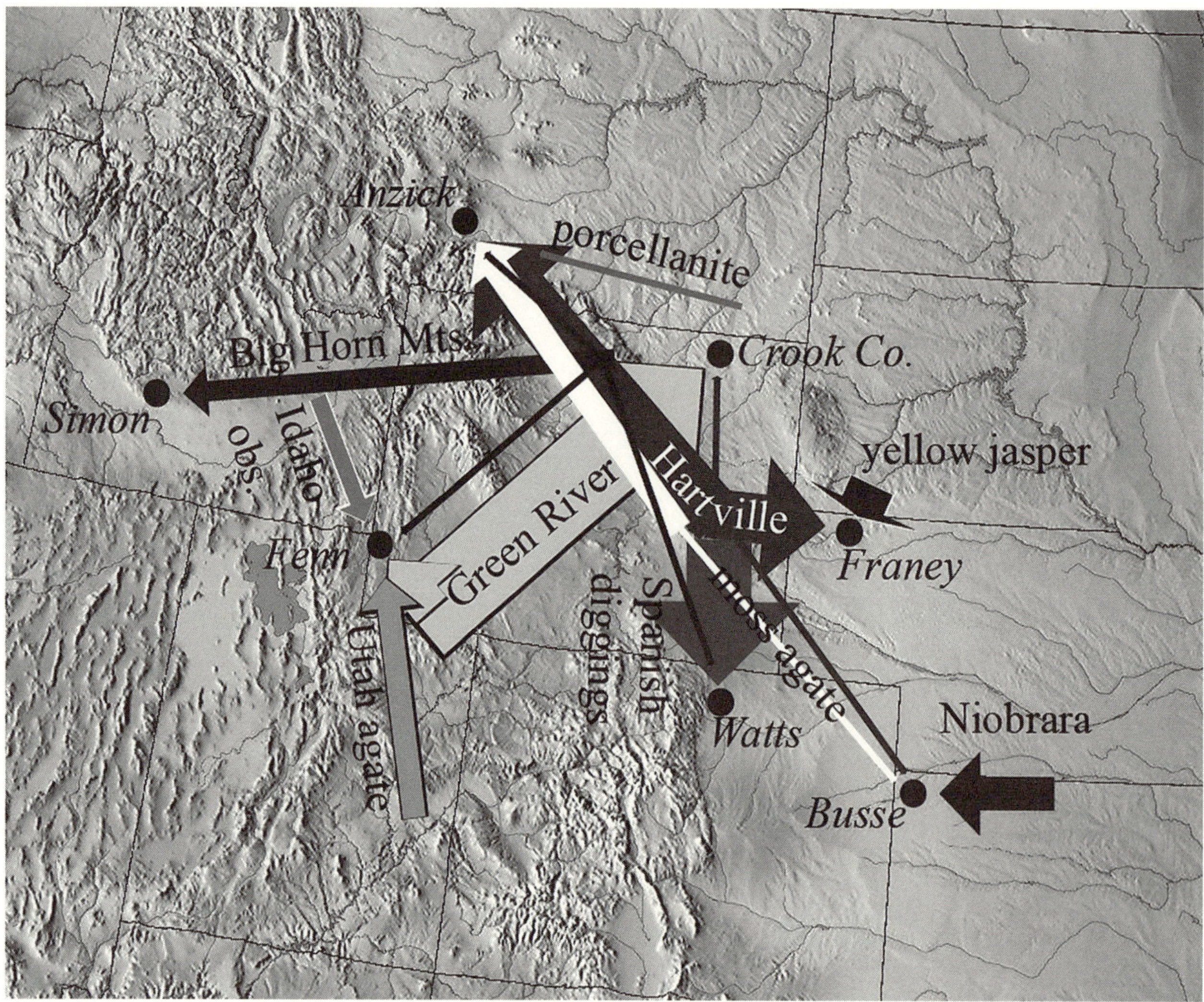

Figure 11.4b. Directions of raw material transport prior to caching for the central Plains and Rockies. Line thickness reflects the percentage of the total raw material in a cache contributed by that source.

the remaining 87 percent was transported to the north or west.

DISCUSSION

The locations of Clovis caches relative to raw material sources and the distances raw materials were transported relative to the nearest alternative sources both generally meet the expectations for the hypothesis that caches served to supply the landscape with lithic raw materials. The variation among Clovis assemblages that have traditionally been identified as "caches" is great and in all likelihood cannot be uniformly explained in reference to a single function, and at least four caches included here (Anzick, East Wenatchee, Fenn, and Simon) are identified elsewhere (Kilby 2008) as most likely being ritual deposits possibly once associated with human burials ("afterlife caches"). Utilitarian caches too probably represent a number of different specific functions; however, the raw material data suggest that a concern for raw material supply is in all likelihood a unifying factor among all of the caches and goes quite a long way toward explaining their existence.

The second set of predictions was derived from the hypothesis that Clovis caches are associated with the initial exploration and colonization of the North American landscape. The first expectation is that caches should have been ideal for meeting a variety of unforeseen needs and thus should consistently be either generalized or diverse with regard to artifact classes. What we should *not* expect is caches consisting of a single class of specialized

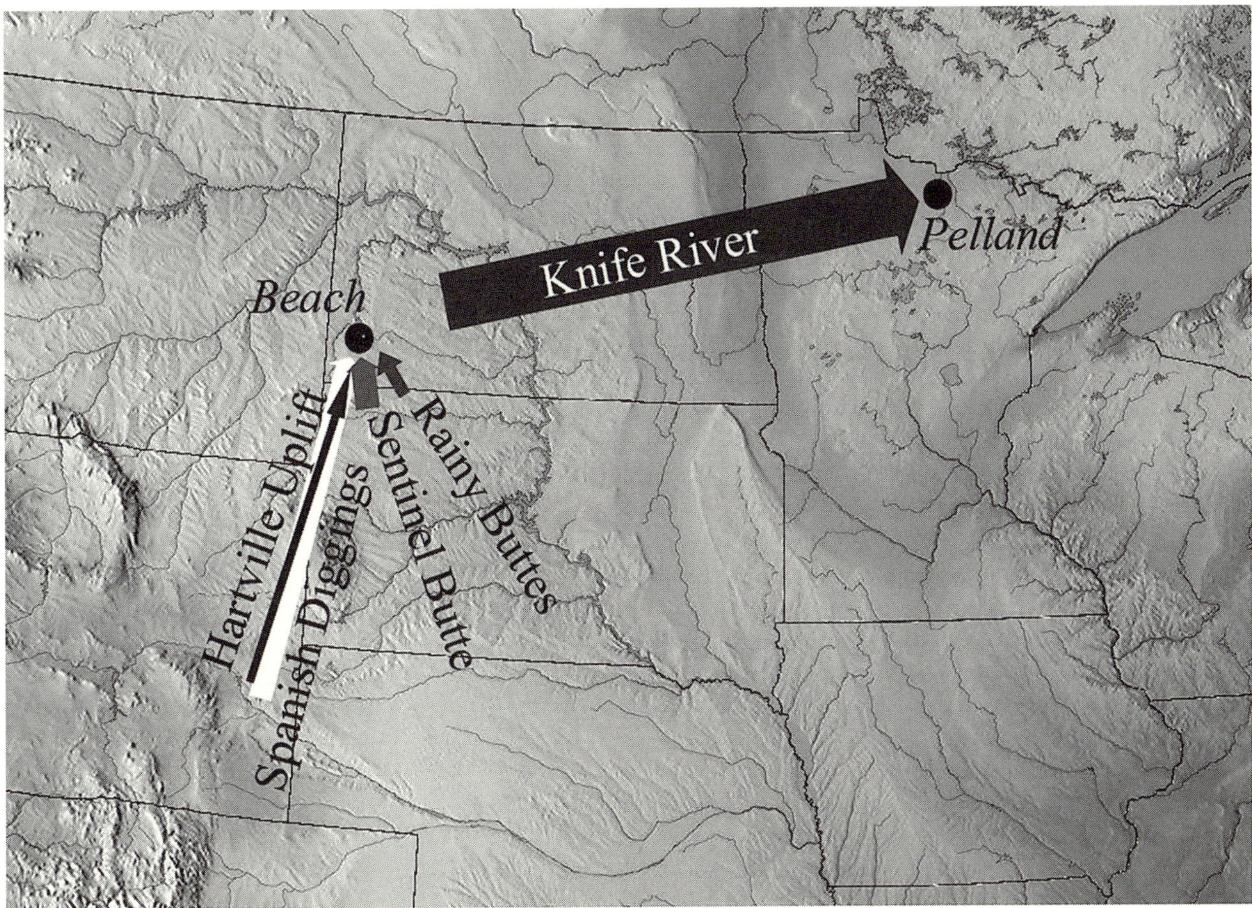

Figure 11.4c. Directions of raw material transport prior to caching for the northern Plains. Line thickness reflects the percentage of the total raw material in a cache contributed by that source.

tools, yet caches consisting entirely of finished projectile points or blades are just that. Although not explored in depth in this chapter, numerous caches are conspicuously homogenous (Table 11.1), with some consisting of a single specialized artifact form (e.g., Drake, Green, Pelland, Keven Davis, etc.). Further, more intensive investigation of diversity in artifact classes among Clovis caches (Kilby 2008:130–134) demonstrates considerable variability, as opposed to consistency, among artifact diversity values for caches. The expectations for this hypothesis are thus not well supported by patterns in artifact diversity and generality.

Another expectation that logically proceeds from the exploration hypothesis is that due to the fact that every region was necessarily explored for the first time at some point, caches should be distributed throughout the continent. Based upon the current data, including the 17 caches focused upon here, the additional caches covered in the chapters of this volume, and a handful of others, Clovis caches occur in the northern Rockies and across the Great Plains, eastward into the upper Midwest, and perhaps throughout the Great Lakes area (Kilby and Huckell 2013). They are thus far conspicuously absent from the North American East Coast, Southeast, Southwest, West Coast, and Mexico. I suspect that this distribution may be real and may be directly related to the distribution of economic reliance on highly migratory animals (such as mammoth and bison in the West and perhaps caribou in the upper Midwest and Great Lakes), but it stands in clear contrast to the expectations of the exploration hypothesis.

Last, I predicted that if caches were primarily associated with exploration and colonization, the result should be the movement of people, and thus raw materials, in a generally southward and eastward direction as populations swept across the continent. As described above, the data reveal a strong pattern of generally northward and westward movement from raw material sources to the locations where they were eventually cached. The hypothesis is no better supported by raw material evidence for

TABLE 11.5. Direction of Transport for Raw Materials in Caches

RAW MATERIAL SOURCE	CACHE	WEIGHT (g)	% OF TOTAL WEIGHT	BEARING FROM SOURCE TO CACHE
Alibates	Drake	417.0	0.5	330
Alibates	Anadarko	1603.9	2.0	100
Alibates	Sailor-Helton	13,763.1	17.2	20
Big Horn Mtns.	Watts	76.7	0.1	155
Big Horn Mtns.	Fenn	107.8	0.1	230
Big Horn Mtns.	Anzick	166.4	0.2	305
Big Horn Mtns.	Simon	4,804.4	6.0	260
Edwards	Drake	49.8	0.1	340
Edwards	Keven Davis	313.8	0.4	50
Edwards	Dickenson	448.1	0.6	305
Edwards	Green	678.9	0.8	305
Edwards	Anadarko	4,123.9	5.2	30
Ephrata	East Wenatchee	4,342.9	5.4	270
Green River Fm.	Simon	310.4	0.4	300
Green River Fm.	Crook County	2,697.5	3.4	45
Green River Fm.	Fenn	2,772.8	3.5	325
Hartville	Busse	1.6	0.0	135
Hartville	Crook County	6.0	0.0	360
Hartville	Franey	1,022.5	1.3	85
Hartville	Beach	60.2	0.1	5
Hartville	Anzick	11,082.5	13.8	310
Idaho obsidian	Fenn	1,942.6	2.4	145
Knife River	Pelland	156.5	0.2	75
Laramie Fm.	Drake	45.0	0.1	115
Moss agate	Busse	1.9	0.0	135
Moss agate	Anzick	5,225.1	6.5	310
Niobrara chert	Busse	7,798.9	9.7	265
Porcellanite	Anzick	166.4	0.2	280
Rainy Buttes	Beach	1,177.5	1.5	315
Sentinel Butte	Beach	3,200.8	4.0	360
Spanish Diggings	Watts	4,385.9	5.5	185
Spanish Diggings	Beach	2,708.8	3.4	0
Utah agate	Fenn	3,481.6	4.3	345
Yellow jasper	Franey	903.7	1.1	360

the direction of movement across the landscape. David Meltzer (personal communication, 2008) has pointed out (and, I believe, is right) that, even if the populations were colonizing in a generally southeastward direction, exploration of any given area might have been from some other direction. Still, even if it is accepted that exploration and colonization occurred in a less linear fashion, it is difficult to imagine that the northern Rockies and northern Plains remained unexplored until after the southern Plains had been colonized. Specifically for Clovis, spatial gradients in radiocarbon dates do not support a scenario in which Clovis groups were present on the southern Plains before they were present on the northern Plains (Hamilton and Buchanan 2007).

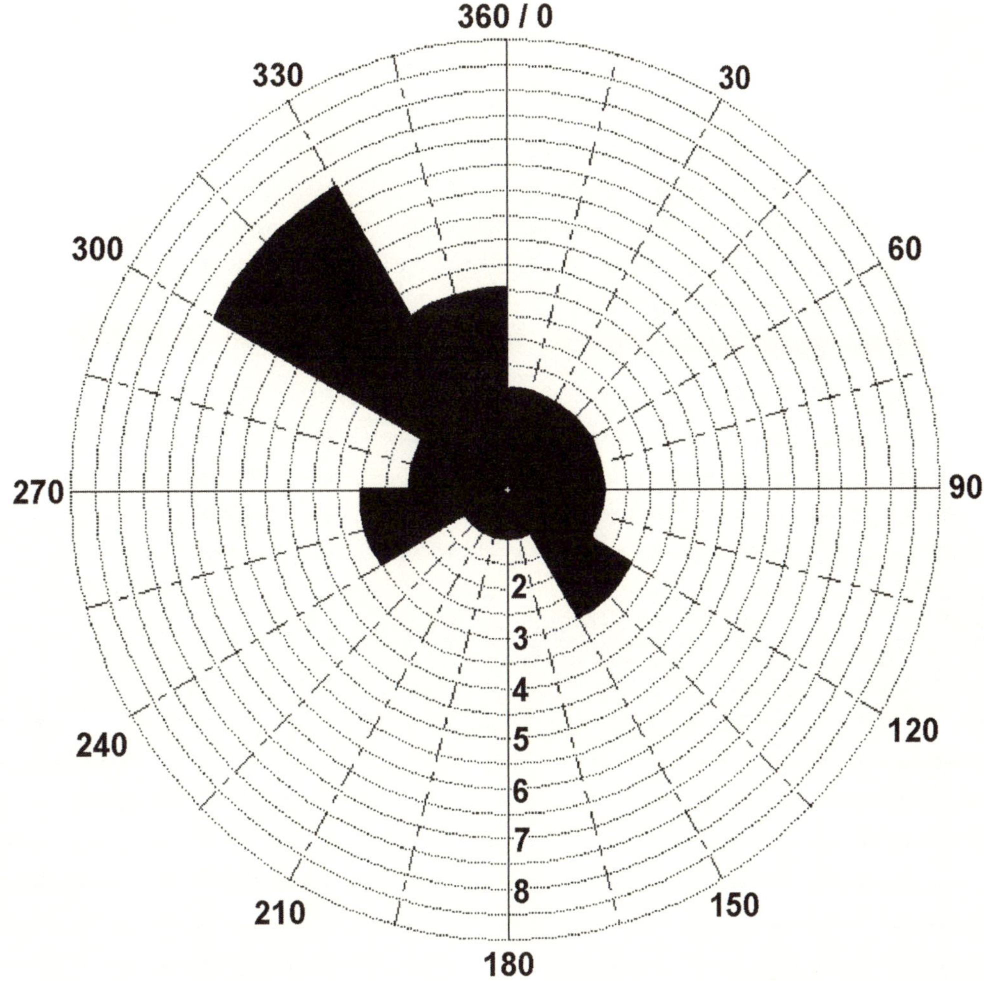

Figure 11.5. Rose diagram depicting the frequency of bearings in degrees (n = 34) from raw material sources to cache locations

The direction of movement evidenced by the cached raw materials might be seen as supporting an argument that Clovis technology actually developed in the Southeast and then spread westward from there (e.g., Mason 1962; Stanford and Bradley 2002). This argument is primarily based upon the greater number and greater variety of fluted points in the Southeast, but demonstrating it is hampered by the paucity of chronometric dates from that area. One of two conditions is necessary for this argument to be supported: either the origin of colonizing populations lies somewhere in the East (Stanford and Bradley 2002; Bradley and Stanford 2004), or Clovis technology was developed in the East among some preexisting population (Waters and Stafford 2007; but see Haynes et al. 2007; Hamilton and Buchanan 2007) and then spread westward and northward into unoccupied territory. Though both of these possibilities have been debated, neither is well supported by current data, and I do not consider either scenario to be a satisfactory explanation of the direction of movement evident in Clovis caches.

Because the opposite of the predicted southward and eastward movement is clearly evident in raw material distributions, we must reconsider explanations for Clovis caches as a colonization phenomenon. An alternative perspective is that materials were cached by people who already knew the landscape and corresponding resource distributions quite well and moved raw materials in accordance with this knowledge. In this scenario, the movement of raw materials northward was by design. The presence of small amounts of raw materials from the north in caches dominated by more southerly raw materials not only fits poorly with an initial exploration model (for how could those materials be present in the cache if the area of their origin had not yet been explored?) but also strongly suggests a cyclical pattern of movement. The pattern is perhaps clearest in the northern Plains and Rockies, where directional lines of transport crisscross each other and suggest a complex network of human movements.

I suggest that raw material needs for a given Clovis group that moved cyclically within a region may have been different when moving north than when moving south. Furthermore, one might expect this difference, like the movements themselves, to have been seasonally patterned. I envision a situation in which it was important to transport surplus raw materials when moving northward in the spring, perhaps following forage and game animals northward as the weather warmed. Patterns in the seasonality of early Paleoindian kills indicate a preponderance of kills in the warm season and early cool season (Hill 2007:256–262; Todd et al. 1996), and the hunting component of the subsistence economy may have been particularly emphasized in the summer and fall. Surplus materials could be cached in order to sustain raw material needs throughout the season spent on that portion of a group's range. If supplies ran low toward the end of a long season in that portion of the range, caches would provide necessary surplus material to draw upon as the optimal hunting season continued or as the group backtracked at the end of the season with raw material in short supply.

CONCLUSIONS

By identifying tangible locations that must have been visited in order to acquire them, lithic raw materials that can be identified to source from any archaeological site can be richly informative of the mobility and range of the groups who used them. As a particular class of site, caches (particularly utilitarian caches) add another dimension to this relationship because they arguably represent strategies for artificially extending the availability of those raw materials into new geographic areas. The main focus of this chapter has been to evaluate the likelihood that the primary reason for artificially supplying the landscape was to facilitate its exploration by groups that were entirely new to it. Specifically, observations on the distances and directions that lithic raw materials were transported prior to being cached have been used to determine whether the caches indeed served to provision the landscape, which it appears they did, and whether they indeed served to facilitate exploration and colonization, which it appears they did not.

Instead, the patterns support a model of cyclical range use by groups who not only knew the landscape well but also knew with some certainty where they were likely to be in the future and what they were likely to need while there. Further, it was proposed that this cycle of land use might relate to seasonal differentiation in subsistence economy, specifically summer and fall hunting, by groups with a well-developed knowledge of resource structure.

It has proved tempting to tie estimates of range familiarity among Clovis groups to colonization debates; that is, to argue that if there is evidence that the occupants of a particular Clovis site or of a particular area were knowledgeable with regard to local environmental conditions, then Clovis groups must not have been the original colonists of that landscape. Alternately, it could be argued that Clovis groups must have been first people on the landscape because there is evidence from particular Clovis sites that the occupants were wide ranging and did not exploit the full range of locally available resources. Neither of these arguments allows for changes in landscape familiarity within the temporal range of Clovis. It is important to bear in mind that while, even by a most conservative estimate, the Clovis period lasted at least 200 years (Waters and Stafford 2007) and perhaps as much as 800 years (given dates of 11,550 RCYBP at Aubrey, Texas [Ferring 1995; Ferring, ed. 2001], and 10,760 RCYBP at Jake Bluff, Oklahoma [Bement and Carter 2010]), only the *initial* generation of colonizers was new to the landscape. Assuming that the fundamental characteristics of an area can be learned over a few decades of hunting and gathering, it follows that only a fraction of the Clovis period might relate to initial landscape learning. Thus, while a given Clovis site may represent a group of Clovis colonizers unfamiliar with an area, it should not be expected that *each* Clovis site will reflect this situation regardless of whether or not Clovis was first. On the contrary, any Clovis record that reflects colonizing behavior would likely be swamped by the more abundant Clovis record of inhabitants who were familiar with their range.

Likewise, patterns in caching behavior that suggest intimate familiarity with the landscape have no bearing upon whether or not the initial colonizers of the New World possessed Clovis technology. Due to the lack of precise dates for Clovis caches and the dim prospects for procuring them in abundance anytime in the near future, we cannot easily position the caches within a certain portion of the Clovis time period (Kilby and Huckell 2013). If the proposition that caches were utilized as part of a cyclical pattern of range use is correct, it might indicate that in those places where the strategy of caching was in use, it was indeed in use throughout the entirety of the Clovis period.

Chapter 12

Opportunities and Challenges in Working with Clovis Caches

SOME CONCLUDING THOUGHTS

J. David Kilby and Bruce B. Huckell

In the 50 years that have elapsed since they were first identified, Clovis caches have been reported in the professional archaeological literature with increasing frequency. The first two were reported in 1963 (Butler 1963; Green 1963), though neither was identified as a cache until somewhat later. Frison reported 5 Clovis caches in 1991 (Frison 1991a); by 1999, 9 assemblages had been confidently identified as Clovis caches (Collins 1999a:41–43); the number had increased to at least 16 by 2008 (Kilby 2008), and at the time of the publication of this volume the number of probable Clovis caches appears to exceed 25. We believe that this pattern reflects a combination of an increasing awareness of caches as a recurring assemblage type within Clovis, an evolving perspective on the technological and morphological characteristics of artifacts that identify them as Clovis, and the simple fact that there appear to be large numbers of Clovis caches scattered across central North America. For these same reasons, we expect that new Clovis caches will continue to be recognized with increasing frequency in the near future.

Many artifacts in Clovis caches embody an impressive degree of skill and artistry that often seems to set them apart from those in other Clovis assemblages, despite the fact that they reflect the same general technology. Research increasingly indicates that the differences between cached artifacts and those from other Clovis contexts are more apparent than real, and with a few exceptions artifacts from caches are comparable to those wielded by Clovis tool users on a daily basis (e.g., Collins 1999a; Huckell 1999; Wilke et al 1991). Comparative analyses indicate that Clovis points from caches reflect the same allometric trajectory as do those from kill and camp sites (Buchanan et al. 2012) and that even the largest Clovis bifaces from caches are reflected in the overshot and refitted flakes from noncache sites (Kilby 2008:225–229). As research on Clovis caches proceeds, and perhaps intensifies, it is worth asking why Clovis caches should be considered unusual in comparison to other assemblage types at all. Why approach them any differently than collections of lithic and osseous artifacts from other Clovis contexts such as kill, camp, and quarry sites? The fundamental characteristic that differentiates cache assemblages from other Clovis assemblages is that the artifacts from caches do not appear to have been abandoned because they were worn out or broken but instead appear to have been removed from the system at earlier stages in their potential use-lives. They stand out because they are not the depleted artifacts that were routinely abandoned at kill or camp sites. A second characteristic that sets caches apart from other assemblages is that they arguably represent anticipatory behavior. In other words, most caches reflect expectations for what might be needed in the future on particular parts of the landscape. For these reasons, Clovis caches have more than aesthetic value; they provide a unique window into Clovis lithic technological organization.

SOME UNUSUAL RESEARCH OPPORTUNITIES PROVIDED BY CLOVIS CACHES

As a site class, caches provide unique opportunities to address at least five major avenues of investigation that are of critical importance for Clovis research: lithic tool manufacture and maintenance, the composition of Clovis tool kits, mobility and land use strategies, Clovis social organization, and regional diversity in Clovis adaptations. While the chapters in this volume go beyond these fundamental research issues, each addresses at least one, and many address a combination of these issues from the perspective of a single cache or through comparison of multiple assemblages.

Lithic Tool Manufacture and Maintenance

Lithic tool manufacture and maintenance was guided by a series of social and economic strategies collectively referred to as technological organization (Binford 1979; Nelson 1991). For lithic tools and materials, technological organization represents a continuum of reduction strategies wherein raw material is acquired, shaped, and reshaped, potentially passing through a variety of stages or forms, until it is discarded or lost. Archaeologists can observe points along this continuum through tools and manufacturing debris. Because the vast majority of known Clovis sites appear to have been kill or camp sites, most Clovis tools from them represent the final point in this reduction continuum—discard or loss—and flake debris from shaping and reshaping them. A fundamental problem, then, is that archaeological reconstruction of the artifact forms present in a working tool kit and any corresponding interpretation of technological organization are rendered somewhat narrow or speculative if only discarded forms are considered. Artifacts from caches provide a way around this dilemma in that they represent forms at earlier points along the reduction continuum to complement existing data from camp or kill sites. In conjunction with the study of the initial stages of tool manufacture at lithic material sources and related workshops (Bradley et al. 2010; Waters, Forman et al. 2011), cache assemblages provide an exceptional source of information about manufacturing technology, the consumption of tools, and the forms in which lithic material was transported.

Windows into the Composition of Clovis Tool Kits

In addition to investigations at the scale of individual artifacts, caches potentially provide a window into the transported Clovis tool kit that we are otherwise lacking, and they may allow the most accurate representations of what a Clovis person would have carried in travels across the late Pleistocene landscape. All of the chapters herein touch on this theme. As noted above, as tools at some point in their use-lives between quarrying and discard, cached artifacts also provide tangible evidence of the forms in which raw material was transported and maintained. For example, by comparing caches to quarry/workshop sites, Collins (1999a, 1999b) and Huckell (2007) have argued that, unlike bifacial cores, which clearly were regularly transported, blade cores were more typically reduced at or near sources of raw material, and only the resulting blades were entrained for transport. Bifaces of a variety of shapes and sizes were clearly a key focus of Clovis technological organization, as shown by the caches discussed in this volume. These bifaces range from completed points, point preforms, knives, and cores to a suite of unfinished specimens at more advanced stages of manufacture; there are suggestions that bifaces filled a number of roles for Clovis foragers (cf. Huckell 2007; Kelly 1988; Wilke et al. 1991). Blades, blade-like flakes, and simple flakes were also part of the suite of lithic forms that were transported and cached.

Mobility and Land Use Practices

Caches also provide data points on the landscape from which aspects of Clovis land use can be inferred. We argue that the geographic locations of caches that served a utilitarian purpose (i.e., the storage of material for later retrieval) indicate points on the landscape to which Clovis groups planned to return; further, this willingness to invest material in the landscape suggests a degree of confidence on the part of those who placed the cache that future movements were predictable. Moreover, in some cases the specific forms of items (e.g., shaped formal tools as opposed to early-stage biface cores) provide evidence as to the anticipated activities on those parts of the landscape. In other cases, the cached forms suggest less-specific needs beyond sharp edges provided by flakes, blades, or blade-like flakes (Bement, Chapter 5; Condon et al., Chapter 3). The lithic raw material sources represented within the assemblages provide evidence of at least some portion of the overall territories covered by these groups over the course of an annual cycle, as well as the general directions of their movements (Frison 1991a; also see Bamforth, Chapter 4; Bement, Chapter 5; Holen, Chapter 10; Kilby, Chapter 11). Caches that may be more ritual than utilitarian in function (perhaps not intended for retrieval), such as Anzick (Wilke et al. 1991) and perhaps Simon (Santarone, Chapter 2), can also provide insight into Clovis lithic reduction and raw material use and are valuable in reconstructing directionality of movement.

Social Organization and Ritual Behavior

Caches that are not primarily utilitarian offer rare opportunities for insight into Clovis ritual behavior and social organization. Based largely upon the association of the Anzick cache with human remains (and the relatively high visibility of Anzick compared with the F. E. Green cache), Clovis caches were initially inferred by some (e.g., Stanford 1991) to primarily reflect burial traditions. Anzick (Wilke et al. 1991) remains the only cache associated with human remains, although artifacts from the Simon, Fenn, and some components of the East Wenatchee caches are coated with red ochre. The use of ochre in and of itself is an indication that a cache may have been deposited with no intention of future retrieval. Though a minority of caches are identified as having served a primarily ritual function (Kilby 2008), these caches possess a relatively untapped potential to inform on Clovis ideology. As Wilke et al. (1991:268) observe, the assemblage from Anzick might be perceived as a mortuary "teaching kit" with all of the "elements of *information* for an effective lithic technological system in the afterlife" (emphasis in original).

Other social organizational aspects of Clovis are potentially reflected in the manufacturing methods and techniques exhibited in the cached items themselves. Lohse and others (Chapter 9) investigate the possibility of craft specialization among Clovis as evidenced by projectile points from caches.

Regional Variation in the Clovis Period

The geographic distribution of Clovis caches in general and, more specifically, the distribution of particular kinds of caches suggest regional variation in Clovis behavior and potentially aid in identifying geographic variants of the Clovis archaeological culture. Regional heterogeneity in the functions and distribution of caches suggests that, despite a degree of technological uniformity across the North American continent, Clovis strategies were not uniform. Instead, caching behavior appears to be an adaptation to regional conditions. Not only do cache contents and functions vary geographically, but caches have been recovered from only a limited portion of the Clovis range. Known Clovis caches occur along a trajectory extending northward from the southern Plains through the northern Plains and Rocky Mountains, spilling eastward into the northern Midwest and Great Lakes area (Figure 1.1). It is worth noting that both the North American West and the Great Lakes were home to prey animals that may have undertaken large-scale seasonal migrations (i.e., mammoth and bison, and caribou, respectively). The challenges posed by mobile prey with a patchy and poorly predictable distribution may go a long way toward explaining why caches occur within the ranges of such prey. In contrast, the environments of other areas of the North American continent where cache assemblages are thus far conspicuously absent may not have been characterized by resource incongruities throughout the Clovis time period. If Clovis caches were part of the Clovis land use strategy in the southeastern United States, where large numbers of Clovis points have been reported, they are thus far undetected. The distributions of lithic raw materials and subsistence resources in these areas may have been consistent enough that material caching was not warranted. It is also possible that the diet breadth of Clovis groups in the Southeast differed significantly from that of groups farther west and north.

As our inventory of Clovis caches increases, it is also becoming apparent that specific kinds of caches—both utilitarian and ritual—are geographically patterned as well. For example, utilitarian caches of blades and flakes are primarily a central and southern Plains phenomenon (Kilby in press). Apparently utilitarian caches of finished points and bifaces tend to be more common in the central and northern Plains. Four caches identified by Kilby (2008) as ritual caches—Anzick, East Wenatchee, Fenn, and Simon—suggest that the practice of ritual caching appears to have been a component of a burial tradition limited to the northern Rocky Mountains of what is now the United States. Their distribution does not overlap with that of any other kinds of Clovis caches. Whether this is a sampling phenomenon remains to be determined, but it is perhaps not surprising that ritual caches would occur within the same region as those that seem to be utilitarian. The transportation and placement of stone and bone objects in anticipation of future use might well have a logical extension in providing for the needs of the departed in the next world.

CHALLENGES INHERENT TO CLOVIS CACHE RESEARCH

In order to fully realize the research potential of caches, we are faced with addressing a number of challenges inherent in the nature of caches as sites and as assemblages. Because caches are a unique class of archaeological site and assemblage, they present some additional problems for those who endeavor to formulate inferences regarding past human behavior from collections of artifacts. The primary problematic issues for the archaeological investigation of caches include defining "cache" as an assemblage class and assigning cultural-temporal affiliation to a collection of items identified as a cache. In addition to these primary issues, matters regarding context and recovery, assemblage size and completeness, and authenticity provide additional challenges for cache research. Many of the chapters in this volume wrestle with some these challenges as they relate to the particular caches under investigation.

Defining "Cache"

An initial and fundamental problem lies in defining precisely what does and what does not constitute a cache and how that is recognized in the material record. As traditionally defined, a cache is expected to represent storage of goods for use at some later time. As used in the Clovis archaeological literature, however, the term "cache" has been used to represent a variety of concepts regarding collections of artifacts. At present there is no single satisfactory definition of what constitutes a Clovis cache, and there is even less agreement as to what role these assemblages played in the lives of Clovis hunter-gatherers. An intensive examination of cache function made it clear that no single functional interpretation can be applied to Clovis caches (Kilby 2008).

Collins (1999a:173) summarizes well the traditional, often implicit, criterion for caches as "tightly clustered groups of artifacts identified as Clovis." That all such groupings do not necessarily represent the result of caching behavior in a technical sense is a nagging issue recognized by Collins and others (e.g. Frison 1991a; Huckell 1999; Kilby 2008; Meltzer 2002; Wilke et al. 1991). It is particularly those groups of artifacts that may represent burial or other ritual assemblages that complicate a simple scenario of artifact storage for "cached" assemblages. If, however, burial assemblages represent collections of essential resources to accompany the dead into an afterlife, they may not be so different in composition or size from caches intended for later retrieval by the living. This is more or less what was proposed for afterlife caches by Thomas (1985) and specifically for Clovis burial caches by Wilke et al. (1991) and Huckell (1999:5).

The term "cache" has enjoyed vague and perhaps semantically liberal usage among Clovis researchers. Despite its imprecision, we stop short of recommending discontinuation of use of the term. It is well entrenched in the archaeological literature and vernacular language, and archaeologists appear to be in agreement that "cache" is a useful term to identify a collection of artifacts that was intentionally set aside (as opposed to being discarded, abandoned, or lost), regardless of doubts that some of them (afterlife caches, as they are defined here) may ever have been intended for retrieval.

We endorse a relatively broad definition of the Clovis cache, because a fuller understanding of the character and function of tightly clustered assemblages of Clovis artifacts remains a goal, as opposed to a presumption, of current research. Caches (at least those in the western United States) can be to some extent defined by default; that is, they do not appear to correspond to other proposed site types. Other components of a proposed working definition of Clovis caches emphasize positive evidence. We propose (following Kilby 2008:37) that Clovis caches should meet four criteria: (1) they do not appear to correspond to other proposed site types for Clovis groups, such as kill, camp, or quarry sites (although they may occur as discrete features within these); (2) they are composed of implements and materials that are tightly clustered in space, usually within a few centimeters of one another (though they may be dispersed by natural or cultural postdepositional processes); (3) the residue of their manufacture or maintenance is not present; and (4) the only activities they directly reflect are those associated with the act of their deposition.

Assigning Cultural-Temporal Affiliation

Caches of lithic artifacts are not entirely uncommon in the North American archaeological record, particularly among populations that ranged over large territories and were dependent on access to high-quality lithic raw material. Caches of Archaic period lithic tools and materials are well known from the Plains (e.g. Tunnell 1978; Hurst 2002; Wiseman et al. 1994). Paleoindian groups that postdate the Clovis period, particularly Agate Basin (Carr and Boszhardt 2003), Plainview (Hartwell 1994), and Cody (Ingbar and Frison 1987), are known to have deposited lithic artifact caches as well, but apparently at much lower frequency. Because contextual information is often poorly known or entirely unavailable for cache assemblages (as discussed below), cultural-temporal affiliation is best ascertained through technological and stylistic hallmarks when diagnostic artifacts are not present.

The attribution of caches to the Clovis culture is ideally based upon diagnostic Clovis artifacts, such as fluted projectile points and beveled bone or ivory rods, and supported by chronometric dating; however, it is becoming apparent that the majority of caches do not include projectile points, and very few have been radiometrically dated. Projectile points and late-stage preforms occur in a minority of known caches, currently including Anzick, Crook County, de Graffenried, Drake, East Wenatchee, Fenn, Hogeye, and Simon. Only Anzick and Beach have closely associated dates; East Wenatchee and Green occur in demonstrably Clovis-age stratigraphic contexts. Lacking these, Clovis affiliation is supported by technological hallmarks, such as systematic overshot flaking on bifaces (Bradley 1982, 1993; Huckell 2007) and prismatic blades produced from prepared cores (Collins 1999a, 1999b). Huckell (Chapter 8) evaluates the utility of a systematic analysis of overshot flaking as a diagnostic technological attribute of Clovis bifaces; in Chapter 6 Hill and his colleagues, as well as Muñiz in Chapter 7, explore other analytical approaches and distinctive technological signatures for Clovis biface manufacture.

For many potential Clovis caches that lack bifacial tools, blades and blade-like flakes are the artifacts that are most suggestive of Clovis affiliation, as reflected in several of the chapters in this volume (Bamforth, Chapter 4; Bement, Chapter 5; Condon et al., Chapter 3). Blades are a regular component of assemblages from secure Clovis contexts; however, these artifacts are known from later prehistoric contexts in some areas as well. Most notably, blade reduction technology is recognized in Upper Republican sites (Roper 1999), and these overlap geographically with the range of Clovis caches. Collins's (1999b) important comparative analysis of blade technologies, itself inspired by the goal of evaluating the cultural-temporal affiliation of the Keven Davis cache, succeeded in isolating a number of distinctively Clovis technological features of blades (also see Condon et al., Chapter 3). As for caches that contain only early-stage bifaces, the assignment of Clovis affiliation for blade and flake caches is based upon an assessment of whether the majority of technological features is consistent with artifacts from secure Clovis contexts or with those from secure non-Clovis contexts. The problem of attribution in cache research particularly highlights the critical importance of studies that aim to identify characteristic technological and stylistic attributes of artifacts from secure Clovis contexts that can be used to reliably assign cultural-temporal affiliation in the absence of more traditionally diagnostic artifacts.

Context and Recovery

The circumstances of cache discoveries vary but generally involve industrial earth removal, cultivation, or erosional events and recovery by avocationalists; recovery by professional archaeological excavation is a rare exception. Of the 22 cache assemblages considered in this volume, 7 were discovered at the surface and have limited stratigraphic information. Eleven were discovered during agricultural or industrial activity (plowing, grading, construction, etc.), and the conditions under which two (Fenn and de Graffenried) were found are completely unknown. With regard to recovery, only in the Carlisle cache (Hill et al., Chapter 6) and portions of the East Wenatchee cache (Gramly 1993; Mehringer 1988) was the majority of the assemblage collected through professional excavation.

The conditions under which these assemblages are discovered and recovered typically result in very limited information concerning the stratigraphic context of the assemblage, the presence or absence of a pit, the spatial relationships of items within the cache, and whether related features occurred nearby. While some of this information can be gleaned from interviews with the finders of the assemblages or their current owners, it is often incomplete or in some cases contradictory. Lacking notes from professional investigations, the best way to proceed is to rely upon that information that is consistently supported by numerous informants or by additional observations. When caches are brought to professional attention, even if years have passed since their original discovery, it is important to conduct field investigations at the find spot whenever possible. The recovery of additional artifacts or fragments of artifacts can provide greater certainty about the accuracy of the memories of the original discoverer (Huckell, Chapter 8; Kilby 2008:96; Stanford and Jodry 1988) and can help to identify deposits of late Pleistocene age from which the cache may have come (Bamforth, Chapter 4; Hill et al., Chapter 6).

Assemblage Size and Completeness

It is difficult, and perhaps impossible, to ascertain to what extent a cache assemblage as it currently exists accurately represents what was originally deposited (Huckell, Chapter 8; Lohse et al., Chapter 9; Santaroneet et al., Chapter 2). Several factors affect cache completeness. Perhaps the most obvious limitation is the decomposition of organic artifacts. Bone or ivory is occasionally preserved; however, it may never be known what amount of bone, wood, leather, or plant material may have once accompanied a cache. Some lithic items originally relating to the cache may never be recovered. They may be overlooked (particularly if they are not formal tools) or transported away from the majority of the assemblage by natural (e.g., fluvial or eolian action, erosion) or cultural (e.g., industrial equipment, construction) processes. Further, the possibility always exists that some portion of the original assemblage was removed by those who created it or by other discoverers at any point in prehistory. Finally, postrecovery processes that potentially affect assemblage completeness include sharing of artifacts among multiple individuals (for examples, see Huckell, Chapter 8; Lohse et al., Chapter 9; Stanford and Jodry 1988), as well as the loss or trade of particular items by the assemblage owners.

In addition to the loss of items, caches may actually gain items through time. The simplest way this might happen is that items that are coincidentally deposited near the cache might be added in during recovery. Another (and perhaps more common) scenario is that items may get mixed into the cached assemblages as larger collections are donated or traded or when the original owners pass away and their heirs do not know exactly which specimens in the collection belong to the cache. This appears to be the case with the Watts cache, in which four artifacts donated along with the cache do not appear to belong with it (Kilby 2008:112).

Even if complete, cache assemblages tend to be small. The number of artifacts in the potential Clovis caches treated in this volume range from 3 to 165 items. Theoretically a cache assemblage (or at least its lithic contents) could be considered for comparative purposes a population as opposed to a sample. Because a cache may never be confidently regarded as complete, however, each is most conservatively viewed as a sample of some once-larger assemblage. These small frequencies frustrate robust statistical comparisons and require the use of techniques that account for small sample sizes.

Authenticity

Antiquities draw remarkable prices among private collectors; Paleoindian projectile points are often valued in the thousands of dollars even as individual artifacts, and complete Clovis caches have been valued in the hundreds of thousands or millions of dollars. The monetary value placed on these items has unfortunately resulted in the occasional forgery—the manufacture of artifacts by modern knappers with the intention of passing them off as authentic. Clovis flint-knapping skill is by no means easy to duplicate, but a handful of modern flint-knappers with exceptional skill and knowledge of Clovis lithic technology can produce specimens that are extremely difficult to differentiate from prehistoric artifacts. An example of a nearly perfect attempt to pass off a collection of modern replicas as an authentic Clovis cache is the so-called Woody's Dream cache reported by Preston (1999). In this case, the replicator carefully left projectile points slightly imperfectly finished, ground the bases, simulated edge damage and surface weathering, and even broke and resharpened tips. The points were successfully sold to a collector after passing scrutiny by some of the most experienced Clovis archaeologists but finally were recognized as fraudulent when in-depth examination revealed traces of plastic residue and red clay (rather than red ochre) on their surfaces.

Perhaps the only way to address the issue of authenticity is to be aware of the possibility that Clovis caches can be faked and to remain vigilant about both the small details of manufacture and weathering as well as the reliability of information on the origin of the collection. That stated, we have not found convincing reasons to believe that any of the assemblages investigated in this research are not authentic, and we are proceeding under the assumption that they are indeed of Clovis age. It is apparent that many of these issues cannot be resolved with absolute certainty. Decisions in some cases come down to subjective judgment on the part of the investigator. Perhaps the best procedure is to be explicit about the available evidence in support of that judgment, to acknowledge uncertainties where they exist, and to seek the opinions of other researchers well versed in Clovis lithic technology.

CONCLUDING THOUGHTS

Clovis caches will continue to be identified with increasing frequency as we become more aware of them and their identifying characteristics. While many "discoveries" consist of identifying existing privately or publicly held collections as Clovis caches, we are optimistic that new assemblages will be discovered in place. Given the paucity of information reflecting the archaeological contexts of Clovis caches, it is critical that caches discovered in place are subjected to carefully controlled excavation, with attention focused upon recovering information on both the landscape and stratigraphic contexts of the assemblage, as well as on spatial associations among the lithic artifacts themselves and other items that may be associated. Some fundamental information on which to focus includes relative (stratigraphic) temporal data and chronometric dating; depositional context (evidence for burial, surface deposition, or covering); evidence of bundling or wrapping of artifacts in containers; evidence of specific markers or nearby landscape features that could have aided in cache recovery; and association with particular landforms or natural corridors of travel (e.g., watercourses, springs, ridges, or upland passes). For assemblages identified in existing collections, efforts should be focused upon reconstructing and recording such information as precisely as is possible, ideally through interviews with those who discovered the cache or their descendants. With an increasing sample of Clovis caches available for analysis, progress can be made toward better understanding their distribution in both time and space and toward interpreting their roles in the organization of mobility, subsistence, and technology.

The majority of Clovis caches investigated thus far appear to represent temporary material storage, with apparent anticipation on the part of those making the cache that the contents would prove useful at some point in the future. That these assemblages remained in place to be found by people in the past century or in this one indicates that they were not recovered. They likely represent cases in which the cache was lost, forgotten, or abandoned. It is probably impossible to know how many caches were made and then successfully recovered by their makers, but we can speculate with some certainty that recovery must have been the case for the great majority of utilitarian caches. Vastly greater numbers of Clovis caches must once have existed, and it is virtually certain that the assemblages that remained buried until the present are but a small sample of the original population. It follows that Clovis caches should not be viewed solely as anomalous or special archaeological assemblages but are better understood as part of a regular strategy for meeting the challenges of high mobility and of the spatially and temporally variable resource structure that Clovis people faced throughout much of North America.

References Cited

Agogino, George A., and Irwin Rovner

1969 Preliminary Report of a Stratified Post-Folsom Sequence at Blackwater Draw, Locality No. 1. *American Antiquity* 34:175–176.

Ahler, Stanley A.

1977 Lithic Resource Utilization Patterns in the Middle Missouri Subarea. In Trends in Middle Missouri Prehistory: A Festschrift Honoring the Contributions of Donald J. Lehmer. Memoir 13. *Plains Anthropologist* 22:132–150.

1987 Notes to Al Miller Concerning Analysis and Interpretation of a Lithic Biface Cache Found near Sentinel Butte, North Dakota, Referred to as the Beech [*sic*] Cache. Unpublished report manuscript in possession of Bruce B. Huckell.

Ahler, Stanley A., and Phil R. Geib

2000 Why Flute? Folsom Point Design and Adaptation. *Journal of Archaeological Science* 27:799–820.

Ahler, Stanley A., and J. VanNest

1985 Temporal Change in Knife River Flint Reduction Strategies. In *Lithic Resource Procurement: Proceedings from the Second Conference on Prehistoric Chert Exploitation*, edited by S. C. Vehik, pp. 183–198. Occasional Paper No. 4, Center for Archaeological Investigations, Southern Illinois University, Carbondale.

Aitken, M. J., and S. G. E. Bowman

1975 Thermoluminescent Dating: Assessment of Alpha Particle Contribution. *Archaeometry* 17:132–138.

Allen, John R. L.

1970 *Physical Processes of Sedimentation*. Elsevier, New York.

Ames, Kenneth M.

1995 Chiefly Power and Household Production on the Northwest Coast. In *Foundations of Social Inequality*, edited by T. Douglas Price and Gary M. Feinman, pp. 155–187. Plenum Press, New York.

Amick, Daniel S.

1996 Regional Patterns of Folsom Mobility and Land Use in the American Southwest. *World Archaeology* 27:411–426.

Anderson, Adrian D., and Joseph A. Tiffany

1972 Rummells-Maske: A Clovis Find-Spot in Iowa. *Plains Anthropologist* 17:55–59.

Anderson, David G.

1990 The Paleoindian Colonization of Eastern North America: A View from the Southeastern United States. In *Early Paleoindian Economies of Eastern North America*, edited by Kenneth B. Tankersley and Barry L. Isaac, pp. 163–216. Research in Economic Anthropology Supplement 5. JAI Press, Greenwich, CT.

Anderson, David G., and Michael K. Faught

2000 Paleoindian Artifact Distributions: Evidence and Implications. *Antiquity* 74:507–513.

Anderson, David G., and J. Christopher Gillam

2000 Paleoindian Colonization of the Americas: Implications from an Examination of Physiography, Demography, and Artifact Distribution. *American Antiquity* 65:43–66.

Anderson, Duane C.

1966 The Gordon Creek Burial. *Southwestern Lore* 32:1–9.

Andrefsky, William

1998 *Lithics: Macroscopic Approaches to Analysis*. Cambridge

Manuals in Archaeology. Cambridge University Press, Cambridge.

2005 *Lithics: Macroscopic Approaches to Analysis.* 2nd ed. Cambridge University Press, Cambridge.

Araújo, Márcio S., and Marcelo O. Gonzaga

2007 Individual Specialization in the Hunting Wasp *Trypoxylon* (*Trypargilum*) *Albonigrum* (Hymenoptra, Crabronidae). *Behavioral and Ecological Scoiobiology* 61:1855–1863.

Arroyo-Cabrales, Joaquin, Oscar J. Polaco, and Eileen Johnson

2006 A Preliminary View of the Coexistence of Mammoth and Early Peoples in Mexico. *Quaternary International* 142–143:79–86.

Aslan, Andres, and Whitney J. Autin

1998 Holocene Flood-Plain Soil Formation in the Southern Lower Mississippi Valley: Implications for Interpreting Alluvial Paleosols. *Geological Society of America Bulletin* 110:433–439.

Baker, Richard G., E. Arthur Bettis, Rhawn F. Denniston, Luis A. Gonzalez, L. E. Strickland, and Joseph R. Krieg

2002 Holocene Paleoenvironments in Southeastern Minnesota—Chasing the Prairie-Forest Ecotone. *Palaeogeography, Palaeoclimatology, Palaeoecology* 177:103–122.

Baker, Richard G., E. Arthur Bettis, D. P. Schwert, D. G. Horton, Craig A. Chumbley, Luis A. Gonzalez, and Mark K. Reagan

1996 Holocene Paleoenvironments of Northeast Iowa. *Ecological Monographs* 66:203–234.

Baker, Richard G., Luis A. Gonzalez, M. Raymo, E. Arthur Bettis, Mark K. Reagan, and J. A. Dorale

1998 Comparison of Multiple Proxy Records of Holocene Environments in Midwestern USA. *Geology* 26:1131–1134.

Bamforth, Douglas B.

1988 *Ecology and Human Organization on the Great Plains.* Plenum, New York.

1991 Flintknapping Skill, Communal Hunting, and Paleoindian Projectile Point Variation Typology. *Plains Anthropologist* 36:309–322.

2002 High-Tech Foragers? Folsom and Later Paleoindian Technology on the Great Plains. *Journal of World Prehistory* 16:55–98.

2003 Rethinking the Role of Bifacial Technology in Paleoindian Adaptations on the Great Plains. In *Multiple Approaches to the Study of Bifacial Technologies*, edited by Marie Soressi and Harold L. Dibble, pp. 209–228. University of Pennsylvania Museum of Archaeology and Anthropology, Philadelphia.

2006 Hunter-Gatherer Mining and Hunter-Gatherer Land Use on the Continental Divide: The Windy Ridge Site. *World Archaeology* 38:511–527.

2009 Projectile Points, People, and Plains Paleoindian Perambulations. *Journal of Anthropological Archaeology* 28:142–157.

Bamforth, Douglas B. (editor)

2007 *The Allen Site: A Paleoindian Camp in Southwestern Nebraska.* University of New Mexico Press, Albuquerque.

Bamforth, Douglas B., and Ronald I. Dorn

1988 On the Nature and Antiquity of the Manix Lake Industry. *Journal of California and Great Basin Anthropology* 10:209–226.

Bamforth, Douglas B., and Nyree Finlay

2008 Introduction: Archaeological Approaches to Lithic Production Skill and Craft Learning. *Journal of Archaeological Method and Theory* 15:1–27.

Bamforth, Douglas B., and Peter C. Woodman

2004 Tool Hoards and Neolithic Use of the Landscape in Northeastern Ireland. *Oxford Journal of Archaeology* 23:21–44.

Banks, Larry D.

1990 *From Mountain Peaks to Alligator Stomachs: A Review of Lithic Sources in the Trans-Mississippi South, the Southern Plains, and Adjacent Southwest.* Memoir 4, Oklahoma Anthropological Society, Norman.

Basham, Matthew P., and Steven R. Holen

2006 Easterday II Cache: A Flake Core Cache from Weld County, Colorado. *Southwestern Lore* 72:1–14.

Beck, Charlotte, and George T. Jones

2010 Clovis and Western Stemmed: Population Migration and the Meeting of Two Technologies. *American Antiquity* 75:81–116.

Bement, Leland C.

1994 *Hunter-Gatherer Mortuary Practices during the Central Texas Archaic.* University of Texas Press, Austin.

2003 Clovis Bison Hunting at the Jake Bluff Site, NW Oklahoma. *Current Research in the Pleistocene* 20:5–7.

2007 Bonfire Shelter: A Jumping Off Point for Comments for Byerly et al. *American Antiquity* 72:366–372.

Bement, Leland C., and Brian J. Carter

2005 *Buffalo Chips in the Mammoth Patch: Investigating Clovis Bison Hunting at the Jake Bluff Site, NW Oklahoma.* Prehistoric People of Oklahoma No. 5. Oklahoma Archaeological Survey, Norman.

2010 Jake Bluff: Clovis Bison Hunting on the Southern Plains of North America. *American Antiquity* 75:907–933.

Bement, Leland C., Brian J. Carter, R. A. Varney, Linda Scott Cummings, and J. Byron Sudbury

2007 Paleo-environmental Reconstruction and Bio-stratigraphy, Oklahoma Panhandle, USA. *Quaternary International* 169–170:29–50.

Bement, Leland C., Kurt Schuster, and Brian J. Carter

2007 *Archeological Survey for Paleo-Indian Sites along the Beaver River, Beaver County, Oklahoma.* Archeological Resource Survey Report No. 54. Oklahoma Archeological Survey, University of Oklahoma, Norman.

Benn, David W., and E. Arthur Bettis

1985 *Archaeology and Landscapes in Saylorville Lake, Iowa.*

Field Trip Guide, Association of Iowa Archaeologists' Summer Meeting, Center for Archeological Research, Southwest Missouri State University, Springfield.

Bettinger, Robert L., and David A. Young

2006 Hunter-Gatherer Population Expansion in North Asia and the New World. In *Entering America*, edited by D. B. Madsen, pp. 239–253. University of Utah Press, Salt Lake City.

Bettis, E. Arthur

1992 Soil Morphologic Properties and Weathering Zone Characteristics as Age Indicators in Holocene Alluvium in the Upper Midwest. In *Soils in Archaeology: Landscape Evolution and Human Occupation*, edited by Vance T. Holliday, pp. 119–144. Smithsonian Institution Press, Washington, D.C.

Bettis, E. Arthur, and David W. Benn

1984 An Archaeological and Geomorphological Survey in the Central Des Moines River Valley, Iowa. *Plains Anthropologist* 29:211–227.

Bettis, E. Arthur, and John P. Littke

1987 *Holocene Alluvial Stratigraphy and Landscape Development in Soap Creek Watershed, Appanoose, Davis, Monroe, and Wapello Counties, Iowa*. Open File Report 87-2. Geological Survey Bureau, Iowa Department of Natural Resources, Des Moines.

Bettis, E. Arthur, Daniel R. Muhs, Helen M. Roberts, and Ann G. Wintle

2003 Last Glacial Loess in the Conterminous USA. *Quaternary Science Reviews* 22:1907–1946.

Bettis, E. Arthur, John Pearson, Mark Edwards, David M. Gradwohl, Nancy Osborn, Timothy J. Kemmis, and Deborah J. Quade

1988 *Natural History of Ledges State Park and the Des Moines Valley in Boone County*. Iowa Natural History Association Guidebook No. 6/Geological Society of Iowa Guidebook No. 48. Iowa City.

Bettis, E. Arthur, Deborah J. Quade, and Timothy J. Kemmis

1996 *Hogs, Bogs, and Logs: Quaternary Deposits and Environmental Geology of the Des Moines Lobe*. Guidebook Series No. 18. North-Central Section Annual Meeting, Geological Society of America, Iowa Department of Natural Resources, Geological Survey Bureau, Des Moines.

Billeck, William T.

1998 Fluted Point Distribution in the Loess Hills of Southwestern Iowa. *Plains Anthropologist* 43:401–409.

Binford, Lewis R.

1978a *Nunamiut Ethnoarchaeology*. Academic Press, New York.

1978b Dimensional Analysis of Behavior and Site Structure: Learning from an Eskimo Hunting Stand. *American Antiquity* 43:330–361.

1979 Organization and Formation Processes: Looking at Curated Technologies. *Journal of Anthropological Research* 35:255–273.

1980 Willow Smoke and Dog's Tails: Hunter-Gatherer Settlement Systems and Archaeological Site Formation. *American Antiquity* 45:4–20.

1983 *In Pursuit of the Past*. Thames and Hudson, New York.

Birkeland, Peter W.

1999 *Soils and Geomorphology*. 3rd ed. Oxford University Press, New York.

Black, Kevin D.

2000 Lithic Sources in the Rocky Mountains of Colorado. In *Intermountain Archaeology*, edited by D. B. Madsen and M. D. Metcalf, pp. 132–147. University of Utah Press, Salt Lake City.

Blackmar, Jeannette M.

2001 Regional Variability in Clovis, Folsom, and Cody Land Use. *Plains Anthropologist* 46:65–94.

Blasing, Robert K.

1984 Prehistoric Sources of Chert in the Flint Hills. Manuscript on file at the Nebraska State Historical Society, Lincoln.

Boldurian, Anthony T.

1990 Lithic Technology at the Mitchell Locality of Blackwater Draw: A Stratified Folsom Site in Eastern New Mexico. Memoir 24. *Plains Anthropologist* 35(130).

1991 Folsom Mobility and Organization of Lithic Technology: A View from Blackwater Draw, New Mexico. *Plains Anthropologist* 36:281–295.

Boldurian, Anthony T., and J. L. Cotter

1999 *Clovis Revisited*. University Museum, University of Pennsylvania, Philadelphia.

Bolnick, Daniel I., Richard Svanbäck, James A. Fordyce, Louie H. Yang, Jeremy M. Davis, C. Darrin Hulsey, and Matthew L. Forister

2003 The Ecology of Individuals: Incidence and Implications of Individual Specialization. *American Naturalist* 161:1–28.

Bonnichsen, Robson

1977 *Models for Deriving Cultural Information from Stone Tools*. Mercury Series No. 60. National Museum of Man, Ottawa, Canada.

Bonnichsen, Robson, and Karen L. Turnmire, eds.

1991 *Clovis: Origins and Adaptations*. Center for the Study of the First Americans, Oregon State University, Corvallis.

Bordes, François, and Don E. Crabtree

1969 The Corbiac Blade Technique and Other Experiments. *Tebiwa* 12:1–21.

Bowers, Peter M., Robson Bonnichsen, and David M. Hoch

1983 Flake Dispersal Experiments: Noncultural Transformation of the Archaeological Record. *American Antiquity* 48:553–572.

Bradley, Bruce A.

1982 Flaked Stone Technology and Typology. In *The Agate Basin Site: A Record of the Paleoindian Occupation of the Northwestern High Plains*, edited by George C. Frison and Dennis J. Stanford, pp. 181–208. Academic Press, New York.

1991 Lithic Technology. In *Prehistoric Hunters of the High Plains*, 2nd ed., edited by George C. Frison, pp. 369–395. Academic Press, San Diego, CA.

1993 Paleoindian Flaked Stone Technology in the North American High Plains. In *From Kostenki to Clovis: Upper Paleolithic–Paleo-Indian Adaptations*, edited by O. Soffer and N. D. Praslov, pp. 251–262. Plenum Press, New York.

1996 Clovis Ivory and Bone Rods. In *Le travail et l'usage de l'ivoire au Paléolithique Supérieur*, edited by J. Hahn, M. Menu, Y. Taborin, Ph. Walter, and F. Widemann, pp. 259–273. Instituto Poligrafico e Zecca dello Libreria dello Stato, Centro Universitario Europeo per I Beni Culturali, Ravello, Italy.

2009a Appendix K: Data, Codes, and Descriptions of Attributes Used in Projectile Point and Biface Analysis. In *Hell Gap: A Stratified Paleoindian Campsite at the Edge of the Rockies*, edited by Mary Lou Larson, Marcel Kornfeld, and George C. Frison, pp. 414–422. University of Utah Press, Salt Lake City.

2009b Bifacial Technology and Paleoindian Projectile Points. In *Hell Gap: A Stratified Paleoindian Campsite at the Edge of the Rockies*, edited by Mary Lou Larson, Marcel Kornfeld, and George C. Frison, pp. 259–273. University of Utah Press, Salt Lake City.

2010 Paleoindian Flaked Stone Technology on the Plains and in the Rockies. In *Prehistoric Hunter-Gatherers of the High Plains and Rockies*, 3rd ed., edited by Marcel Kornfeld, George C. Frison, and Mary Lou Larson, pp. 463–497. Left Coast Press, Walnut Creek, California.

Bradley, Bruce A., Michael B. Collins, and C. Andrew Hemmings

2010 *Clovis Technology*. Archaeological Series 17. International Monographs in Prehistory, Ann Arbor, MI.

Bradley, Bruce A., and George C. Frison

1987 Projectile Points and Specialized Bifaces from the Horner Site. In *The Horner Site: The Type Site of the Cody Cultural Complex*, edited by George C. Frison and Lawrence C. Todd, pp. 199–232. Academic Press, Orlando, FL.

Bradley, Bruce A., and Dennis J. Stanford

2004 The North Atlantic Ice-Edge Corridor: A Possible Paleolithic Route to the New World. *World Archaeology* 36:459–478.

Bradley, James W., Arthur E. Spiess, Richard A. Boisvert, and Jeff Boudreau

2008 What's the Point?: Modal Forms and Attributes of Paleoindian Bifaces in the New England Maritimes Region. *Archaeology of Eastern North America* 36:119–172.

Breternitz, David A., Alan C. Swedlund, and Duane C. Anderson

1971 An Early Burial from Gordon Creek, Colorado. *American Antiquity* 36:170–182.

Bronk Ramsey, Christopher

2009 Bayesian Analysis of Radiocarbon Dates. *Radiocarbon* 51:337–360.

Brown, Lauren

1985 *Grasslands*. Knopf, New York.

Brunswig, Robert H.

2007 New Interpretations of the Dent Mammoth Site: A Synthesis of Recent Multidisciplinary Evidence. In *Frontiers in Colorado Paleoindian Archaeology*, edited by R. H. Brunswig and B. L. Pitblado. University Press of Colorado, Boulder.

Buchanan, Briggs, J. David Kilby, Bruce B. Huckell, Matthew J. O'Brien, and Mark Collard

2012 A Morphometric Assessment of the Intended Function of Cached Clovis Points. *PLoS ONE* 7(2): e30530. doi:10.1371/journal.pone.0030530.

Butler, B. Robert

1963 An Early Man Site at Big Camas Prairie, South-Central Idaho. *Tebiwa* 6:22–33.

Butler, B. Robert, and R. J. Fitzwater

1965 A Further Note on the Clovis Site at Big Camas Prairie, South-Central Idaho. *Tebiwa* 8:38–40.

Buurman, Peter, Th. Pape, J. Arjan Reijneveld, Fokke de Jong, and E. van Gelder

2001 Laser-Diffraction and Pipette-Method Grain Sizing of Dutch Sediments: Correlations for Fine Fractions of Marine, Fluvial, and Loess Samples. *Netherlands Journal of Geosciences* 80:49–57.

Byers, David A., and Andrew Ugan

2005 Should We Expect Large Game Specialization in the Late Pleistocene? An Optimal Foraging Perspective on Early Paleoindian Prey Choice. *Journal of Archaeological Science* 32:1624–1640.

Callahan, Errett

1979 The Basics of Biface Knapping in the Eastern Fluted Point Tradition: A Manual for Flintknappers and Analysts. *Archaeology of Eastern North America* 7:1–180.

1991 Out of Theory and Into Reality: A Comment on Nami's Comment. *Plains Anthropologist* 36:367–368.

Cannon, Michael D., and David J. Meltzer

2004 Early Paleoindian Foraging: Examining the Faunal Evidence for Large Mammal Specialization and Regional Variability in Prey Choice. *Quaternary Science Reviews* 23:1955–1987.

Carlson, Gayle F., and Curtis A. Peacock

1975 Lithic Distribution in Nebraska. In *Lithic Source Notebook*, edited by R. A. Thomas. Section of Archaeology, Division of Historical and Cultural Affairs, Milford, DE.

Carlson, Kristen, and Leland Bement

2013 Organization of Bison Hunting at the Pleistocene/Holocene Transition on the Plains of North America. *Quaternary International* 297:93–99.

Carr, Dillon H., and Robert F. Boszhardt

2003 The Kriesel Cache: A Late Paleoindian Biface Cache from Western Wisconsin. *Plains Anthropologist* 48:225–236.

Chenault, Mark L.

1999 Paleoindian Stage. In *Colorado Prehistory: A Context for the Platte River Basin*, edited by K. P. Gilmore, M. Tate, M. L. Chenault, B. Clark, T. McBride, and M. Wood, pp. 51–90. Colorado Council of Professional Archaeologists, Denver.

Chilton, Elizabeth

2004 Beyond "Big": Gender, Age, and Subsistence Diversity in Paleoindian Societies. In *The Settlement of the American Continents: A Multidisciplinary Approach to Human Biogeography*, edited by C. Michael Barton, Geoffery A. Clark, David R. Yesner, and Georges A. Pearson, pp. 162–172. University of Arizona Press, Tucson.

Church, Tim

1996 Lithic Resources of the Bearlodge Mountains, Wyoming: Description, Distribution and Implications. *Plains Anthropologist* 41:135–164.

1999 Investigations into Prehistoric Lithic Procurement in the Black Hills Uplift, South Dakota and Wyoming. *Island in the Plains* 1:61–104.

Clark, John E.

1995 Craft Specialization as an Archaeological Category. *Research in Economic Anthropology* 16:267–294. JAI Press, Greenwich, CT.

Clark, John E., and William J. Parry

1990 Craft Specialization and Cultural Complexity. *Research in Economic Anthropology* 12:289–346. JAI Press, Greenwich, CT.

Clark, William Z., Jr., and Arnold C. Zisa

1976 Physiographic Districts of Georgia. Georgia Department of Natural Resources. Reprinted in electronic format, http://georgiainfo.galileo.usg.edu/physiographic/physiodist.htm, accessed December 30, 2010.

Clayton, Lee, and Stephen R. Moran

1982 Chronology of Late Wisconsinan Glaciation in Middle North America. *Quaternary Science Reviews* 1:55–82.

Cole, John, and David M. Gradwohl

1969 Emergency Archaeology at Site 13WA105, Red Rock Reservoir, Iowa, 1968 (abstract). *Plains Anthropologist* 14:309–310.

Collins, Michael B.

1996 *The Keven Davis Cache (41NV659) and Clovis Blade Technology in the South Central United States*. Report submitted to the Office of the State Archaeologist, Texas Historical Commission, Austin.

1999a Clovis and Folsom Lithic Technology on and near the Southern Plains: Similar Ends, Different Means. In *Folsom Lithic Technology: Explorations in Structure and Variation*, edited by Daniel S. Amick, pp. 12–38. Archaeological Series 12. International Monographs in Prehistory, Ann Arbor, MI.

1999b *Clovis Blade Technology: A Comparative Study of the Keven Davis Cache*. University of Texas Press, Austin.

2007 Discerning Clovis Subsistence from Stone Artifacts and Site Distributions on the Southern Plains Periphery. In *Foragers of the Terminal Pleistocene in North America*, edited by Renee B. Walker and Boyce N. Driskell, pp. 59–87. University of Nebraska Press, Lincoln.

Collins, Michael B., and C. Andrew Hemmings

2005 Lesser-Known Clovis Diagnostic Artifacts I: The Bifaces. *La Tierra* 32:9–20.

Collins, Michael B., Dale B. Hudler, and Stephen L. Black

2003 *Pavo Real (41BX52): A Paleoindian and Archaic Camp and Workshop on the Balcones Escarpment, South-Central Texas*. Studies in Archeology 41, Texas Archeological Research Laboratory, University of Texas at Austin, and Report 50, Archeological Studies Program, Environmental Affairs Division, Texas Department of Transportation, Austin.

Collins, Michael B., and Jon C. Lohse

2004 The Nature of Clovis Blades and Blade Cores. In *Entering America: Northeast Asia and Beringia Before the Last Glacial Maximum*, edited by David B. Madsen, pp. 159–183. University of Utah Press, Salt Lake City.

Collins, Michael B., Jon C. Lohse, and Marilyn Shoberg

2007 The de Graffenried Collection: A Clovis Biface Cache from the Gault Site, Central Texas. *Bulletin of the Texas Archeological Society* 78:101–124.

Condon, Keith W., and Jerome C. Rose

1997 Bioarchaeology of the Sloan Site. In *Sloan: A Paleoindian Dalton Cemetery in Arkansas*, edited by Dan F. Morse, pp. 8–13. Smithsonian Institution Press, Washington, D.C.

Condon, Peter C.

2000 Analysis of Two Blade Caches of Potential Clovis-Age, Recovered from Blackwater Locality No. 1, Roosevelt County, New Mexico. Poster presented at the 65th Annual Meeting of the Society for American Archaeology, Philadelphia, PA.

Conkey, Margaret W.

1985 Ritual Communication, Social Elaboration, and the Variable Trajectories of Paleolithic Material Culture. In *Prehistoric Hunter-Gatherers: The Emergence of Cultural Complexity*, edited by T. Douglas Price and James A. Brown, pp. 299–323. Academic Press, New York.

Cordova, Carlos E., William C. Johnson, Rolfe D. Mandel, and Michael W. Palmer

2011 Late Quaternary Environmental Change Inferred from Phytoliths and Other Soil Related Proxies: Case Studies from the Central and Southern Great Plains, USA. *Catena* 85:87–108.

Costin, Cathy Lynne

1991 Craft Specialization: Issues in Defining, Documenting, and Explaining the Organization of Production. *Archaeological Method and Theory* 3:1–56.

Cotterell, Brian, and Johan Kamminga

1987 The Formation of Flakes. *American Antiquity* 52:675–708.

Cowan, Frank L., and N'omi Greber

2002 Hopewell Mound 11: Yet Another Look at an Old Collection. *Hopewell Archaeology* 5:1–7.

Crabtree, Don E.

1972 *An Introduction to Flintworking.* Occasional Papers of the Idaho State University Museum, Number 28. Pocatello.

1982 *An Introduction to Flintworking.* Idaho Museum of Natural History, Pocatello.

Cross, John R.

1991 Craft Specialization in Nonstratified Societies. *Research in Economic Anthropology* 14:61–84. JAI Press, Greenwich, CT.

Curran, Mary Lou, and John R. Grimes

1989 Ecological Implications for Paleoindian Lithic Procurement Economy in New England. In *Eastern Paleoindian Lithic Resource Use*, edited by C. J. Ellis and J. C. Lothrop, pp. 41–74. Westview Press, Boulder, CO.

Daniel, I. Randolph Jr., and Michael Wisenbaker

1989 Paleoindian in the Southeast: The View from Harney Flats. In *Eastern Paleoindian Lithic Resource Use*, edited by C. J. Ellis and J. C. Lothrop, pp. 323–351. Westview Press, Boulder, CO.

Daniel, Wayne W.

1990 *Applied Nonparametric Statistics*, 2nd ed. PWS-KENT Publishing, Boston.

Deller, D. Brian

1989 Interpretation of Chert Type Variation in Paleoindian Industries, Southwestern Ontario. In *Eastern Paleoindian Lithic Resource Use*, edited by C. J. Ellis and J. C. Lothrop. Westview Press, Boulder, CO.

Deller, D. Brian, and C. J. Ellis

1984 Crowfield: A Preliminary Report on a Probable Paleo-Indian Cremation in Southwestern Ontario. *Archaeology of Eastern North America* 12:41–70.

1992 *Thedford II: A Paleoindian Site in the Ausable River Watershed of Southwestern Ontario.* Memoirs No. 24. Museum of Anthropology, University of Michigan, Ann Arbor.

Deller, D. Brian, C. J. Ellis, and James R. Keron

2009 Understanding Cache Variability: A Deliberately Burned Early Paleoindian Tool Assemblage from the Crowfield Site, Southwestern Ontario, Canada. *American Antiquity* 74:371–397.

DeVore, Steven L.

1990 The Cribbs' Crib Site (13WA105): The Archaeology and Ecology of an Oneota Village in the Central Des Moines River Valley. *Journal of the Iowa Archaeological Society* 37:46–87.

Dibble, Harold L., and Andrew Pelcin

1995 The Effect of Hammer Mass and Velocity on Flake Mass. *Journal of Archaeological Science* 22:429–439.

Dibble, Harold L., and Zeljo Rezek

2009 Introducing a New Experimental Design for Controlled Studies of Flake Formation: Results for Exterior Platform Angle, Platform Depth, Angle of Blow, Velocity, and Force. *Journal of Archaeological Science* 36:1945–1954.

Dibble, Harold L., and John C. Whittaker

1981 New Experimental Evidence on the Relation Between Percussion Flaking and Flake Variation. *Journal of Archaeological Science* 8:283–296.

Dick, Herbert W., and Bert Mountain

1960 The Claypool Site: A Cody Complex Site in Northeastern Colorado. *American Antiquity* 26:223–235.

Dickens, William A.

2007 Clovis Biface Lithic Technology at the Gault Site (41BL323), Bell County, Texas. *Current Research in the Pleistocene* 24:78–79.

Dillehay, Tom D. (editor)

1989 *Monte Verde: A Late Pleistocene Settlement in Chile.* Vol. 1, *Paleoenvironment and Site Context.* Smithsonian Institution Press, Washington, D.C.

1997 *Monte Verde: A Late Pleistocene Settlement in Chile.* Vol. 2, *The Archaeological Context and Interpretation.* Smithsonian Institution Press, Washington, D.C.

Dorsey, George A.

1900 *An Aboriginal Quartzite Quarry in Eastern Wyoming.* Field Columbian Museum Publication 51, Anthropological Series 2:231–243, plates 28–39. Chicago, IL.

Drennan, Robert D.

1996 *Statistics for Archaeologists: A Common Sense Approach.* Plenum Press, New York.

2004 *Statistics for Archaeologists: A Common Sense Approach.* 2nd ed. Springer, New York.

Duncan, Mack S.

2002 Fall Line. In *New Georgia Encyclopedia.* Electronic document, http://georgiaencyclopedia.org/nge/Article.jsp?id=h-721, accessed December 30, 2010.

Dye, David H.

2004 Art, Ritual, and Chiefly Warfare in the Mississippian World. In *Hawk, Hero, and Open Hand*, edited by R. F. Townsend, pp. 191–206. Yale University Press, New Haven, CT.

Dyke, Arthur S.

2004 An Outline of North American Deglaciation with Emphasis on Central and Northern Canada. In *Quaternary Glaciations Extent and Chronology*, part 2, *North America*, edited by Jürgen Ehlers and Philip L. Gibbard, pp. 371–406. Elsevier, Amsterdam.

Elias, Scott A.

1991 The Timing and Intensity of Environmental Changes during the Paleoindian Period in Western North America: Evidence from the Fossil Record. In *Megafauna and Man: Discovery of America's Heartland*, edited by L. D. Agenbroad, J. I. Mead, and L. W. Nelson, pp. 11–14. Scientific Papers 1. Mammoth Site of Hot Springs, South Dakota.

Ellis, Christopher J.

1989 The Explanation of Northeastern Paleo-Indian Lithic Procurement Patterns. In *Eastern PaleoIndian Lithic*

Resource Use, edited by C. J. Ellis and J. C. Lothrop, pp. 139–164. Westview Press, Boulder, CO.

Ellis, Christopher J., and D. Brian Deller

2000 *An Early Paleo-Indian Site Near Parkhill, Ontario.* Mercury Series, Archaeological Survey of Canada Paper No. 159. Canadian Museum of Civilization, Gatineau, Quebec.

Ellis, Christopher J., and Jonathan C. Lothrop (editors)

1989 *Eastern Paleoindian Lithic Resource Use.* Westview Press, Boulder, CO.

Emerson, William K., and Morris K. Jacobson

1976 *The American Museum of Natural History Guide to Shells: Land, Freshwater, and Marine from Nova Scotia to Florida.* Alfred A. Knopf, New York.

Epp, Henry. T.

1995 Migration Six Implies Extinction. Paper Presented at the Plains Anthropological Society Meetings, Saskatoon, Saskatchewan.

Eren, Metin I.

2013 The Technology of Stone Age Colonization: An Empirical, Regional-Scale Examination of Clovis Unifacial Stone Tool Reduction, Allometry, and Edge Angle from the North American Lower Great Lakes Region. *Journal of Archaeological Science* 40:2101–2112.

Eren, Metin I., and Brian N. Andrews

2013 Were Bifaces Used as Mobile Cores by Clovis Foragers in the North American Lower Great Lakes Region? An Archaeological Test of Experimentally Derived Quantitative Predictions. *American Antiquity* 78:166–180.

Erlandson, Jon M., Madonna L. Moss, and Matthew Des Lauriers

2008 Living on the Edge: Early Maritime Cultures of the Pacific Coast of North America. *Quaternary Science Reviews* 27:2232–2245.

Erlandson, Jon M., Torben C. Rick, Todd J. Braje, Molly Casperson, Brendan Culleton, Brian Fulfrost, Tracy Garcia, Daniel A. Guthrie, Nicholas Jew, Douglas J. Kennett, Madonna L. Moss, Leslie Reeder, Craig Skinner, Jack Watts, and Lauren Willis

2011 Paleoindian Seafaring, Maritime Technologies, and Coastal Foraging on California's Channel Islands. *Science* 331:1181–1184.

Eshel, Gil, Guy J. Levy, Uri Mingelgrin, and Michael J. Singer

2004 Critical Evaluation of the Use of Laser Diffraction for Particle-Size Distribution Analysis. *Soil Science Society of America Journal* 68:736–743.

Faith, J. Tyler, and Todd A. Surovell

2009 Synchronous Extinction of North America's Pleistocene Mammals. *Proceedings of the National Academy of Sciences of the United States of America* 106:20641–20645.

Ferring, C. Reid

1995 The Late Quaternary Geology andArchaeology of the Aubrey Site, Texas. In *Ancient Peoples and Landscapes*, edited by Eileen Johnson, pp. 273–281. Museum of Texas Tech University, Lubbock.

2001 Archaeology of the Aubrey Clovis Site. In *The Archaeology and Paleoecology of the Aubrey Clovis Site (41DN479), Denton County, Texas*, edited by C. Reid Ferring, pp. 121–202. Center for Environmental Archaeology, Department of Geography, University of North Texas, Denton.

Ferring, C. Reid (editor)

2001 *The Archaeology and Paleoecology of the Aubrey Clovis Site (41DN479), Denton County, Texas.* Center for Environmental Archaeology, Department of Geography, University of North Texas, Denton.

Fiedel, Stuart J.

1999 Older Than We Thought: Implications of Corrected Dates for Paleoindians. *American Antiquity* 64:95–115.

Figgins, Jesse D.

1933 A Further Contribution to the Antiquity of Man in America. *Proceedings of the Colorado Museum of Natural History* 12(2).

Finlay, Nyree

2008 Blank Concerns: Issues of Skill and Consistency in the Replication of Scottish Later Mesolithic Blades. *Journal of Archaeological Method and Theory* 15:68–90.

Fitzhugh, William W., and Andrei V. Golovnev

1998 The Drovyanoy 3 Shaman's Cache: Archaeology, Ethnography, and "Living Yamal." *Arctic Anthropology* 35:177–198.

Fladerer, F. A.

2001 The Krems-Wachtberg Camp-Site: Mammoth Carcass Utilization Along the Danube 27,000 Years Ago. In *The World of Elephants: Proceedings of the 1st International Congress, Rome, 16–20 October 2001*, edited by G. Cavarretta, P. Gioia, and M. R. Palombo, pp. 432–438. Consiglio Nazionale delle Ricerche, Rome.

Foley, Robert A.

2002 Adaptive Radiations and Dispersals in Hominin Evolutionary Ecology. *Evolutionary Anthropology* 11:32–37.

Folk, Robert L., and William C. Ward

1957 Brazos River Bar: A Study in the Significance of Grain Size Parameters. *Journal of Sedimentary Petrology* 27:3–26.

Fosha, Michael R.

1993 A Niobrarite Biface from South Dakota. *Newsletter of the South Dakota Archaeological Society* 23:1–4.

Francis, Julie E.

1991 Lithic Resources of the Northwestern High Plains: Problems and Perspectives in Analysis and Interpretation. In *Raw Material Economies Among Prehistoric Hunter-Gatherers*, edited by A. Montet-White and S. R. Holen. Publications in Anthropology 19. University of Kansas, Lawrence.

Frison, George C.

1975 Archaeology of the Casper Site. In *The Casper Site: A Hell Gap Bison Kill on the High Plains*, edited by George C. Frison, pp. 1–112. Academic Press, New York.

1978 *Prehistoric Hunters of the High Plains.* Academic Press, New York.

1982a Folsom Components. In *The Agate Basin Site: A Record of the Paleoindian Occupation of the Northwestern High Plains*, edited by George C. Frison and Dennis J. Stanford, pp. 37–75. Academic Press, New York.

1982b Hell Gap Components. In *The Agate Basin Site: A Record of the Paleoindian Occupation of the Northwestern High Plains*, edited by George C. Frison and Dennis J. Stanford, pp. 135–142. Academic Press, New York.

1982c The Sheaman Site: A Clovis Component. In *The Agate Basin Site: A Record of the Paleoindian Occupation of the Northwestern High Plains*, edited by George C. Frison and Dennis J. Stanford, pp. 143–157. Academic Press, New York.

1988 Prehistoric, Plains-Mountain, Large-Mammal, Communal Hunting Strategies. In *The Evolution of Human Hunting*, edited by M. H. Nitecki and D. V. Nitecki, pp. 177–223. Plenum Press, New York.

1991a The Clovis Cultural Complex: New Data from Caches of Flaked Stone and Worked Bone Artifacts. In *Raw Material Economies Among Prehistoric Hunter-Gatherers*, edited by A. Montet-White and S. R. Holen, pp. 321–333. Publications in Anthropology 19. University of Kansas, Lawrence.

1991b *Prehistoric Hunters of the High Plains*. 2nd ed. Academic Press, New York.

Frison, George C. (editor)

1974 *The Casper Site: A Hell Gap Bison Kill on the High Plains*. Academic Press, New York.

1996 *The Mill Iron Site*. University of New Mexico Press, Albuquerque.

Frison, George C., Robert L. Andrews, James M. Adovasio, Ronald C. Carlisle, and Robert Edgar

1986 A Late Paleo-Indian Animal Trapping Net from Northern Wyoming. *American Antiquity* 51:352–361.

Frison, George C., and Bruce A. Bradley

1999 *The Fenn Cache: Clovis Weapons and Tools*. One Horse Land & Cattle Company, Santa Fe, New Mexico.

Frison, George C., and Dennis J. Stanford

1982a Appendix. In *The Agate Basin Site: A Record of the Paleoindian Occupation of the Northwestern High Plains*, edited by George C. Frison and Dennis J. Stanford, pp. 371–382. Academic Press, New York.

1982b Agate Basin Components. In *The Agate Basin Site: A Record of the Paleoindian Occupation of the Northwestern High Plains*, edited by George C. Frison and Dennis J. Stanford, pp. 76–135. Academic Press, New York.

Frison, George C. and Dennis S. Stanford (editors)

1982c *The Agate Basin Site: A Record of the Paleoindian Occupation of the Northwestern High Plains*. Academic Press, New York.

Frison, George C., and Lawrence C. Todd

1986 *The Colby Mammoth Site: Taphonomy and Archaeology of a Clovis Kill in Northern Wyoming*. University of New Mexico Press, Albuquerque, New Mexico.

Fryxell, John M., John Greever, and A. R. E. Sinclair

1988 Why Are Migratory Ungulates So Abundant? *American Naturalist* 131:781–798.

Galbraith, Rex F., Richard G. Roberts, Geoff M. Laslett, Hiroyuki Yoshida, and Jonathan M. Olley

1999 Optical Dating of Single and Multiple Grains of Quartz from Jinmium Rock Shelter, Northern Australia, Part 1, Experimental Design and Statistical Models. *Archaeometry* 41:339–364.

Gardner, Samuel

2006 Clovis Lithic Technology at Gault: Our Evolving View of Technological Organization at the End of the Pleistocene. Poster presented at the 64th Plains Anthropological Conference, Topeka, KS.

Gardner, William M.

1977 The Flint Run Paleo-Indian Complex and Its Implications for Eastern North American Prehistory. In *Amerinds and Their Paleo-environments in Northeastern North America*, edited by W. Newman and B. Salwen, pp. 257–263. Annals of the New York Academy of Sciences 288.

Geribàs, Núria, Marina Mosquera, and Josep Maria Vergès

2010 What Novice Knappers Have to Learn to Become Expert Stone Toolmakers. *Journal of Archaeological Science* 37:2857–2870.

Gilmore, Kevin P.

1999 Late Prehistoric Stage. In *Colorado Prehistory: A Context for the Platte River Basin*, edited by K. P. Gilmore, M. Tate, M. L. Chenault, B. Clark, T. McBride, and M. Wood, pp. 175–307. Colorado Council of Professional Archaeologists, Denver.

Goodyear, Albert C.

1979 *A Hypothesis for the Use of Cryptocrystalline Raw Materials Among Paleoindian Groups of North America*. Research Manuscript Series 156. University of South Carolina, Institute of Archaeology and Anthropology, Columbia.

2005 Evidence for Pre-Clovis Sites in the Eastern United States. In *Paleoamerican Origins: Beyond Clovis*, edited by Robson Bonnichsen, Bradley T. Lepper, Dennis Stanford, and Michael R. Waters, pp. 103–112. Center for the Study of the First Americans, Texas A&M University Press, College Station.

Gradwohl, David M.

2003 From Turin to 2002: Reflections on My Career in Iowa Archaeology. *Journal of the Iowa Archaeological Society* 50:11–50.

Graham, Russell W.

1976 Late Wisconsin Mammalian Faunas and Environmental Gradients of the Eastern United States. *Paleobiology* 2:343–350.

1979 Paleoclimates and Late Pleistocene Faunal Provinces in North America. In *Pre-Llano Cultures of the Americas: Paradoxes and Possibilities*, edited by R. L. Humphrey and

D. Stanford, pp. 49–69. Anthropological Society of Washington, Washington, D.C.

1985 Diversity and Community of the Late Pleistocene Mammal Fauna of North America. *Acta Zoologica Fennica* 170:181–192.

1991 Evolution of New Ecosystems at the End of the Pleistocene. In *Megafauna and Man: Discovery of America's Heartland*, edited by L. D. Agenbroad, J. I. Mead, and L. W. Nelson, pp. 54–60. Scientific Papers 1. Mammoth Site of Hot Springs, South Dakota.

Graham, Russell W., and E. L. Lundelius

1984 Coevolutionary Disequilibrium and Pleistocene Extinctions. In *Quaternary Extinctions: A Prehistoric Revolution*, edited by P. S. Martin and R. G. Klein, pp. 223–249. University of Arizona Press, Tucson.

Graham, Russell W., Ernest L. Lundelius Jr., Mary Ann Graham, Erich K. Schroeder, Rickard S. Toomey III, Elaine Anderson, Anthony D. Barnosky, James A. Burns, Charles S. Churcher, Donald K. Grayson, R. Dale Guthrie, C. R. Harington, George T. Jefferson, Larry D. Martin, H. Gregory McDonald, Richard E. Morlan, Holmes A. Semken Jr., S. David Webb, Lars Werdelin, Michael C. Wilson

1996 Spatial Response of Mammals to Late Quaternary Environmental Fluctuations. *Science* 272:1601–1606.

Graham, Russell W., and Holmes A. Semken Jr.

1976 Paleoecological Significance of the Short-Tailed Shrew (Blarina), with a Systematic Discussion of *Blarina ozarkensis*. *Journal of Mammalogy* 57:433–449.

Gramly, Richard M.

1980 Raw Materials Source Areas and "Curated" Tool Assemblages. *American Antiquity* 45:823–833.

1993 *The Richey Clovis Cache: Earliest Americans along the Columbia River.* Monographs in Archaeology. Persimmon Press, Kenmore, NY.

1998 *The Sugarloaf Site: Palaeo-Americans on the Connecticut River.* Monographs in Archaeology. Persimmon Press, Kenmore, NY.

1999 *The Lamb Site: A Pioneering Clovis Encampment.* Monographs in Archaeology. Persimmon Press, Kenmore, NY.

Grange, Roger T., Jr.

1964 A Cache of Scrapers near Crow Butte, Nebraska. *Plains Anthropologist* 9:197–201.

Graves, Adam C., Leland C. Bement, and Brian J. Carter

2006 The JS Cache: An Early Paleoindian Tool Cache in the Oklahoma Panhandle. *Current Research in the Pleistocene* 23:103–105.

Grayson, Donald K.

1989 The Chronology of North American Late Pleistocene Extinctions. *Journal of Archaeological Science* 16:153–165.

Grayson, Donald K., and David J. Meltzer

2002 Clovis Hunting and Large Mammal Extinction: A Critical Review of the Evidence. *Journal of World Prehistory* 16:313–359.

2003 A Requiem for North American Overkill. *Journal of Archaeological Science* 30:585–593.

Green, F. Earl

1963 The Clovis Blades: An Important Addition to the Llano Complex. *American Antiquity* 29:145–165.

Greiser, Sally T.

1983 A Preliminary Statement About Quarrying Activity at Flattop Mesa. *Southwestern Lore* 49:6–14.

1985 Predictive Models of Hunter-Gatherer Subsistence and Settlement Strategies of the Central High Plains. Memoir 20. *Plains Anthropologist* 30:1–134.

Grenfell, Suzanne E., William N. Ellery, and Michael C. Grenfell

2009 Geomorphology and Dynamics of the Mfolozi River Floodplain, Kwazulu-Natal, South Africa. *Geomorphology* 107:226–240.

Gustavson, Thomas C., and Vance T. Holliday

1999 Eolian Sedimentation and Soil Development on a Semi-arid to Subhumid Grassland, Tertiary Ogallala and Quaternary Blackwater Draw Formations, Texas and New Mexico High Plains. *Journal of Sedimentary Research* 69:622–634.

Guthrie, R. Dale

1968 Paleoecology of the Large Mammal Community in Interior Alaska during the Late Pleistocene. *American Midland Naturalist* 79:346–363.

1980 Bison and Man in North America. *Canadian Journal of Anthropology* 1:55–75.

1982 Mammals of the Mammoth Steppe as Paleoenvironmental Indicators. In *The Paleoecology of Beringia*, edited by D. M. Hopkins, J. V. Matthews, C. E. Schweger, S. B. Young, pp. 307–329. Academic Press, New York.

1984a Mosaics, Allelochemics, and Nutrients: An Ecological Theory of Late Pleistocene Megafaunal Extinctions. In *Quaternary Extinctions: A Prehistoric Revolution*, edited by P. S. Martin and R. G. Klein, pp. 259–298. University of Arizona Press, Tucson.

1984b Alaskan Megabucks, Megabulls, and Megarams: The Issue of Pleistocene Gigantism. In *Contributions in Quaternary Vertebrate Paleontology: A Volume in Memorial to John E. Guilday*, edited by H. H. Genoways and M. R. Dawson, pp. 482–510. Special Publication 8. Carnegie Museum of Natural History, Pittsburgh.

1990a *Frozen Fauna of the Mammoth Steppe: The Story of Blue Babe.* University of Chicago Press, Chicago, IL.

1990b Late Pleistocene Faunal Revolution: A New Perspective on the Extinction Debate. In *Megafauna and Man: Discovery of America's Heartland*, edited by L. D. Agenbroad, J. I. Mead, and L. W. Nelson, pp. 42–53. Scientific Papers 1. Mammoth Site of Hot Springs, South Dakota.

Hall, Christopher T., and Mary Lou Larson

2004 Evaluating Prehistoric Hunter-Gatherer Mobility, Land-Use, and Technological Organizational Strategies Using Minimum Analytical Nodules Analysis. In *Aggregate*

Analysis in Chipped Stone, edited by C. Hall and M. L. Larson, pp. 139–155. University of Utah Press, Salt Lake City.

Hamilton, Marcus J., and Briggs Buchanan

2007 Spatial Gradients in Clovis-Age Radiocarbon Dates Across North America Suggest Rapid Colonization from the North. *Proceedings of the National Academy of Sciences, USA* 104:15629–15634.

Hammatt, Hallett H.

1969 Paleo-Indian Blades from Western Oklahoma. *Bulletin of the Texas Archeological Society* 40:193–198.

1970 A Paleo-Indian Butchering Kit. *American Antiquity* 35:141–152.

Hartwell, William T.

1994 The Ryan's Site Cache: Comparisons to Plainview. *Plains Anthropologist* 40:165–184.

Hassan, Fekri A.

1981 *Demographic Archaeology*. Academic Press, New York.

Hay, Oliver P.

1912 The Pleistocene Mammals of Iowa. *Iowa Geological Survey Annual Report* 23.

Hayden, Brian

1979 *Lithic Use-Wear Analysis*. Academic Press, New York.

Haynes, C. Vance, Jr.

1964 Fluted Points: Their Age and Dispersion. *Science* 145:1408–1413.

1975 Pleistocene and Recent Stratigraphy. In *Late Pleistocene Environments of the Southern High Plains*, edited by F. Wendorf and J. J. Hester, pp. 57–96. Publication No. 9. Fort Burgwin Research Center, Dallas.

1982 Were Clovis Progenitors in Beringia? In *The Paleoecology of Beringia*, edited by D. M. Hopkins, J. V. Matthews Jr., C. E. Schweger, and S. B. Young, pp. 383–398. Academic Press, New York.

1987 Clovis Origin Update. *Kiva* 52:83–93.

1992 Contributions of Radiocarbon Dating to the Geochronology of the Peopling of the New World. In *Radiocarbon After Four Decades*, edited by R. E. Taylor, A. Long, and R. Kra, pp. 355–374. University of Arizona Press, Arizona.

1993 Clovis-Folsom Geochronology and Climate Change. In *From Kostenki to Clovis*, edited by O. Soffer and N. D. Praslov, pp. 219–236. Plenum Press, New York.

1995 Geochronology of Paleoenvironmental Change, Clovis Type Site, Blackwater Draw, New Mexico. *Geoarchaeology* 10:317–388.

2008 Younger Dryas "Black Mats" and the Rancholabrean Termination in North America. *Proceedings of the National Academy of Sciences* 105:6520–6525.

Haynes, C. Vance, Jr., and George A. Agogino

1966 Prehistoric Springs and Geochronology of the Clovis Site, New Mexico. *American Antiquity* 31:812–821.

Haynes, C. Vance, Jr., and Bruce B. Huckell (editors)

2007 *Murray Springs: A Clovis Site with Multiple Activity Areas in the San Pedro Valley, Arizona*. Anthropological Papers No. 71, University of Arizona, Tucson.

Haynes, C. Vance, Jr., and James M. Warnica

2012 *Geology, Archaeology, and Climate Change in Blackwater Draw, NM: F. Earl Green and the Geoarchaeology of the Clovis Type Site*. Contributions in Anthropology, Vol. 15, edited by J. David Kilby. Eastern New Mexico University, Portales.

Haynes, Gary

2002a The Catastrophic Extinction of North American Mammoths and Mastodons. *World Archaeology* 33:391–416.

2002b *The Early Settlement of North America: The Clovis Era*. Cambridge University Press, Cambridge.

Haynes, Gary (editor)

2009 *American Megafaunal Extinctions at the End of the Pleistocene*. Springer, New York.

Haynes, Gary, David G. Anderson, C. Reid Ferring, Stuart J. Fiedel, Donald K. Grayson, C. Vance Haynes Jr., Vance T. Holliday, Bruce B. Huckell, Marcel Kornfeld, David J. Meltzer, Julie Morrow, Todd Surovell, Nicole M. Waguespack, Peter Wigand, and Robert M. Yohe II

2007 Comment on "Redefining the Age of Clovis: Implications for the Peopling of the Americas." *Science* 317:320b. doi:10.1126/science.1141.960.

Helton, Bill

1957 A Second Cache Found Near Satanta. *Kansas Anthropological Association Newsletter* 3:1.

Hemmings, C. Andrew, Michael B. Collins, D. Clark Wernecke, Jon C. Lohse, and M. Samuel Gardner

2006 Clovis Lithic Technology at Gault: Our Evolving View of Technological Organization at the End of the Pleistocene. Poster presented at the 64th Plains Anthropological Conference, Topeka, KS.

Henry, Donald O., C. Vance Haynes Jr., and Bruce A. Bradley

1976 Quantitative Variations in Flaked Stone Debitage. *Plains Anthropologist* 21:57–61.

Hensel, Kenneth C., Daniel S. Amick, Thomas J. Loebel, and Matthew G. Hill

1999 Morrow-Hensel: A New Fluted Point Site in Far Western Wisconsin. *Current Research in the Pleistocene* 16:25–27.

Hester, James J.

1972 *Blackwater Locality No. 1: A Stratified Early Man Site in Eastern New Mexico*. Publication 8. Fort Burgwin Research Center, Southern Methodist University, Taos, NM.

Hibbard, C. W.

1960 An Interpretation of Pliocene and Pleistocene Climates in North America. *Michigan Academy of Sciences Arts and Letters, 62nd Annual Report*.

Hicks, Keri

2002 Local Variability in Paleoindian Lifeways: A Comparison of the Lime Creek and Allen Site Worked Stone Assemblages, Southwest Nebraska. Unpublished master's thesis, Department of Anthropology, University of Colorado, Boulder.

Hill, Kim, and Keith Kintigh

2009 Can Anthropologists Distinguish Good and Poor Hunters?

Implications for Hunting Hypotheses, Sharing Conventions, and Cultural Transmission. *Current Anthropology* 50:369–377.

Hill, Matthew E., Jr.

2007 Causes of Regional and Temporal Variation in Paleoindian Diet in Western North America. Unpublished PhD dissertation, Department of Anthropology, University of Arizona, Tucson.

Hill, Matthew E., Jr., Matthew G. Hill, and Christopher C. Widga

2008 Late Quaternary Bison Diminution on the Great Plains of North America: Evaluating the Role of Human Hunting Versus Climate Change. *Quaternary Science Reviews* 27:1752–1771.

Hill, Matthew G.

1994 Paleoindian Projectile Points from the Vicinity of Silver Mound (47JA21), Jackson County, Wisconsin. *Midcontinental Journal of Archaeology* 19:223–259.

Hoard, Robert J., John R. Bozell, Steven R. Holen, Michael D. Glascock, Hector Neff, and J. Michael Elam

1993 Source Determination of White River Group Silicates from Two Archaeological Sites in the Great Plains. *American Antiquity* 58:698–710.

Hoard, Robert J., Steven R. Holen, Michael D. Glascock, Hector Neff, and J. Michael Elam

1991 Neutron Activation Analysis of Stone from the Chadron Formation and a Clovis Site on the Central Plains. *Journal of Archaeological Science* 19:655–665.

Hofman, Jack L.

1990 Paleoindian Mobility and Utilization of Niobrara or Smoky Hill Jasper on the Southern Plains. *Kansas Anthropologist* 9:1–13.

1991 Folsom Land Use: Projectile Point Variability as a Key to Mobility. In *Raw Material Economy Among Prehistoric Hunter-Gatherers*, edited by A. Montet-White and S. R. Holen, pp. 335–355. Publication in Anthropology 19. University of Kansas, Lawrence.

1992 Recognition and Interpretation of Folsom Technological Variability on the Southern Plains. In *Ice Age Hunters of the Rockies*, edited by Dennis J. Stanford and Jane S. Day, pp. 193–224. University Press of Colorado, Niwot.

1994 Paleoindian Aggregations on the Great Plains. *Journal of Anthropological Archaeology* 13:341–370.

1995 The Busse Cache: A Clovis-Age Find in Northwestern Kansas. *Current Research in the Pleistocene* 12:17–19.

1997 The Busse Cache. In *The Paleoindians of the North American Midcontinent*, edited by A. Montet-White, pp. 32–35. Musée Départemental de Préhistoire de Solutré, France.

1999 Unbounded Hunters: Folsom Bison Hunting on the Southern Plains Circa 10,500 BP, the Lithic Evidence. In *Bison Subsistence Through Time: From Paleolithic to Paleoindian Times*, edited by J. Ph. Brugal, F. David, J. G. Enloe, and J. Jaubert, pp. 383–415. Editions APDCA, Antibes, France.

Hofman, Jack L., and Andrew S. Gottsfield

2010 Clovis Evidence in Kansas. *Current Research in the Pleistocene* 28:96–98.

Hofman, Jack L., and India Hesse

2001 Clovis in Kansas. *TER-QUA Symposium Series*, Vol. 3, edited by W. Dort and L. D. Martin.

Hofman, Jack L., and Donald G. Wyckoff

1991 Clovis Occupation in Oklahoma. *Current Research in the Pleistocene* 8:29–32.

Holen, Steven R.

1983 Lower Loup Lithic Procurement Strategy at the Gray Site, 25CX1. Unpublished master's thesis, Department of Anthropology, University of Nebraska, Lincoln.

1989 *The Smoky Hill Chalk Member of the Niobrara Formation in Kansas: Implications for the Distribution of Smoky Hill Jasper.* Report submitted to the Kansas Historic Preservation Office, Kansas State Historical Society, Topeka.

1991 Bison Hunting Territories and Lithic Acquisition Among the Pawnee: An Ethnohistoric and Archaeological Study. In *Raw Material Economies Among Prehistoric Hunter-Gatherers*, edited by A. Montet-White and S. R. Holen, pp. 399–411. Publications in Anthropology No. 19. University of Kansas, Lawrence.

1998 *The Eckles Site, 14JW4: A Clovis Assemblage from Lovewell Reservoir, Jewell County, Kansas.* Nebraska Archaeological Survey Technical Report 98-103. University of Nebraska State Museum, Lincoln.

2001a Clovis Mobility and Lithic Procurement on the Central Great Plains of North America. Unpublished PhD dissertation, Department of Anthropology, University of Kansas, Lawrence.

2001b The Fuller Biface: A Probable Clovis Bifacial Flake Core from the Central Great Plains. *Current Research in the Pleistocene* 18:26–27.

2002 Edwards Chert Clovis Bifaces from Nebraska. *Current Research in the Pleistocene* 19:37–38.

2003 Clovis Projectile Points and Preforms in Nebraska: Distribution and Lithic Sources. *Current Research in the Pleistocene* 20:31–33.

2006 Taphonomy of Two Last Glacial Maximum Mammoth Sites in the Central Great Plains: A Preliminary Report on La Sena and Lovewell. *Quaternary International* 142–143:30–44.

2007 The Age and Taphonomy of Mammoths at Lovewell Reservoir, Jewell County, Kansas, USA. *Quaternary International* 169–170:51–63.

2010 The Eckles Clovis Site, 14JW4: A Clovis Site in Northern Kansas. *Plains Anthropologist* 55:299–310.

Holen, Steven R., and Mark P. Muñiz

2005 A Flattop Chalcedony Clovis Biface Cache from Northeastern Colorado. *Current Research in the Pleistocene* 22:49–50.

Holliday, Vance T.

1989 The Blackwater Draw Formation (Quaternary): A 1.4 Plus

m.y. Record of Eolian Sedimentation and Soil Formation on the Southern High Plains. *Geological Society of America Bulletin* 101:1598–1607.

1995 *Stratigraphy and Paleoenvironments of the Late Quaternary Valley Fills on the Southern High Plains*. Memoir 186. Geological Society of America, Boulder, CO.

1997 *Paleoindian Geoarchaeology of the Southern High Plains*. University of Texas Press, Austin.

2005 Ice Age Peopling of New Mexico. In *New Mexico's Ice Ages*, edited by S. G. Lucas, G. S. Morgan, and K. E. Zeigler, pp. 263–276. Bulletin 28. New Mexico Museum of Natural History and Science, Albuquerque.

Holliday, Vance T., C. Vance Haynes Jr., Jack L. Hofman, and David J. Meltzer

1994 Geoarchaeology and Geochronology of the Miami (Clovis) Site, Southern High Plains of Texas. *Quaternary Research* 41:234–244.

Holliday, Vance T., and Julie K. Stein

1989 *Variability in Laboratory Procedures and Results in Geoarchaeology*. Geoarchaeology 4:347–358.

Holmes, William H.

1897 Stone Implements of the Potomac-Chesapeake Tidewater Province. *Fifteenth Annual Report, Bureau of American Ethnology, 1893–1894*:13–152.

Howard, Edgar B.

1943 The Finley Site: Discovery of Yuma Points, in situ, near Eden, Wyoming. *American Antiquity* 8:224–234.

Huckell, Bruce B.

1999 Camps, Kills, and Caches: Reconstructing Clovis Lithic Technological Organization in the Western United States. Paper presented at "The Land and the People: Explorations of Late Pleistocene and Early Holocene Human and Environmental History in North America" (papers in Honor of C. Vance Haynes), University of Arizona, Tucson.

2007 Clovis Lithic Technology: A View from the San Pedro Valley. In *Murray Springs: A Clovis Site with Multiple Activity Areas in the San Pedro Valley, Arizona*, edited by C. Vance Haynes Jr. and Bruce B. Huckell, pp. 170–213. Anthropological Papers of the University of Arizona No. 71. University of Arizona Press, Tucson.

Huckell, Bruce B., Bruce A. Bradley, and Peter J. Mehringer Jr.

In review *Clovis on the Columbia River: Flaked Stone artifacts from the East Wenatchee Cache*. Manuscript in review, University of Arizona Press.

Huckell, Bruce B., and J. David Kilby

2002 Folsom Point Production at the Rio Rancho Site, New Mexico. In *Folsom Technology and Lifeways*, edited by J. Clark and M. B. Collins, pp. 11–29. Lithic Technology Special Publication No. 4. University of Tulsa, Tulsa, OK.

2009 Beach: A Clovis Cache in Southwestern North Dakota. *Current Research in the Pleistocene* 26:68–70.

Huckell, Bruce B., J. David Kilby, Mathew Boulanger, and Michael Glascock

2011 Sentinel Butte: Neutron Activation Analysis of White River Group Chert from a Primary Source and Artifacts from a Clovis Cache in North Dakota, USA. *Journal of Archaeological Science* 38:965–976.

Huckell, Bruce, J. David Kilby, Briggs Buchannan, and Lisa W. Huckell

2002 Bifaces to Go: An Experimental Study of the Genesis of Transport Wear. Poster presented at the 67th Annual Meeting of the Society for American Archaeologists. Denver, CO.

Hurst, Stance

2002 Caching Behavior on the Southern Plains. Unpublished master's thesis, Department of Anthropology, University of Oklahoma, Norman.

Ingbar, Eric E.

1994 Lithic Raw Material Selection and Technological Organization. In *The Organization of North American Prehistoric Chipped Stone Tool Technologies*, edited by Philip J. Carr, pp. 45–56. Archaeological Series 7. International Monographs in Prehistory, Ann Arbor, MI.

Ingbar, Eric E., and George C. Frison

1987 The Larson Cache. In *The Horner Site: The Type Site of the Cody Cultural Complex*, edited by G. C. Frison and L. C. Todd, pp. 461–473. Academic Press, New York.

Iverson, Neal

2005 Des Moines River Valley: Late-Wisconsinan History of the Upper Des Moines Lobe. In *Rockin' in the Heartland: The Paleozoic/Quaternary Geology and Hydrogeology of Central Iowa*, pp. 51–57. Proceedings of the 66th Annual Tri-State Geological Field Conference. Iowa State University, Ames.

Jefferson, George T, and Judith L. Goldin

1989 Seasonal Migration of *Bison antiquus* from Rancho La Brea, California. *Quaternary Research* 31:107–112.

Jenkins, Dennis, Loren G. Davis, Thomas W. Stafford Jr., Paula F. Campos, Bryan Hockett, George T. Jones, Linda Scott Cummings, Chad Yost, Thomas J. Connolly, Robert M. Yohe II, Summer C. Gibbons, Maanasa Raghavan, Morten Rasmussen, Johanna L. A. Paijmans, Michael Hofreiter, Brian M. Kemp, Jodi Lynn Barta, Cara Monroe, M. Thomas, P. Gilbert, and Eske Willerslev

2012 Clovis Age Western Stemmed Projectile Points and Human Coprolites at the Paisley Caves. *Science* 337:223–228.

Jennings, Thomas A.

2013 The Hogeye Clovis Cache, Texas: Quantifying Lithic Reduction Signatures. *Journal of Archaeological Science* 40:649–658.

Johnson, Eileen

1991 Late Pleistocene Cultural Occupation on the Southern Plains. In *Clovis Origins and Adaptations*, edited by Robson Bonnichsen and Karen L. Turnmire, pp. 215–236.

Center for the Study of First Americans, Oregon State University, Corvallis.

Jones, Scott, and Robson Bonnichsen
1994 The Anzick Clovis Burial. *Current Research in the Pleistocene* 11:42–43.

Justice, Noel D.
1987 *Stone Age Spear and Arrow Points of the Midcontinental and Eastern United States: A Modern Survey and Reference.* Indiana University Press, Bloomington.

Kay, Marvin, and Richard E. Martens
2004 Clovis Scrapers from the Martens Site. *Missouri Archaeologist* 65:44–67.

Keeley, Lawrence H.
1980 *Microwear Analysis of Stone Tools.* University of Chicago Press, Chicago, IL.
1982 Hafting and Retooling: Effects on the Archaeological Record. *American Antiquity* 47:798–809.

Kelly, Robert L.
1988 The Three Sides of a Biface. *American Antiquity* 53:717–734.
1995 *The Foraging Spectrum: Diversity in Hunter-Gatherer Lifeways.* Smithsonian Institution Press, Washington, D.C.
2003a Maybe We Do Know When People First Came to North America; and What Does It Mean If We Do? *Quaternary International* 109–110:133–145.
2003b Colonization of New Land by Hunter-Gatherers: Expectations and Implications Based on Ethnographic Data. In *Colonization of Unfamiliar Landscapes: The Archaeology of Adaptation*, edited by Marcy Rockman and James Steele, pp. 44–58. Routledge, New York.

Kelly, Robert L., and Lawrence C. Todd
1988 Coming into the Country: Early Paleoindian Hunting and Mobility. *American Antiquity* 53:231–244.

Kent, Susan
1991 The Relationship Between Anticipated Mobility Strategies and Site Structure. In *The Interpretation of Archaeological Spatial Patterning*, edited by E. M. Knoll and T. D. Price, pp. 33–59. Plenum Press, New York.

Kilby, J. David
2008 An Investigation of Clovis Caches: Content, Function, and Technological Organization. Unpublished PhD dissertation, Department of Anthropology, University of New Mexico, Albuquerque.
2011 Les caches Clovis dans le cadre du paléoindien ancien en Amérique du Nord (Clovis caches and the early paleoindian record of North America). In *Peuplements et préhistoire de l'Amérique*, edited by Denis Vialou. Muséum National d'Histoire Naturelle, Paris.
In press A Regional Perspective on Clovis Blades and Blade Caching. In *Clovis: Current Perspectives on Technology, Chronology, and Adaptations*, edited by Tom Jennings and Ashley Smallwood. Center for the Study of the First Americans, Texas A&M University, College Station.

Kilby, J. David, and Bruce B. Huckell
2003 A Comparison of Caches: An Initial Look at Regional Variation in Clovis Caching. Paper presented at the 68th Society for American Archaeology Annual Conference, Milwaukee.
2013 Clovis Caches: Current Perspectives and Future Directions. In *Paleoamerican Odyssey*, edited by Kelly E. Graf, Caroline V. Ketron, and Michael R. Waters, pp. 257–272. Center for the Study of the First Americans, Department of Anthropology, Texas A&M University, College Station.

Kim, Hyung Keun
1986 Late-Glacial and Holocene Environment in Central Iowa: A Comparative Study of Pollen Data from Four Sites. Unpublished PhD dissertation, Department of Geology, University of Iowa, Iowa City.

Knapp, Alan K., John M. Blair, John M. Briggs, Scott L. Collins, David C. Hartnett, Loretta C. Johnson, and E. Gene Towne
1999 The Keystone Role of Bison in North American Tallgrass Prairie? Bison Increase Habitat Heterogeneity and Alter a Broad Array of Plant, Community, and Ecosystem Processes. *BioScience* 49:39–50.

Kneberg, Madeline
1952 The Tennessee area. In *Archeology of Eastern United States*, edited by J. B. Griffin, pp. 190–198. Chicago, IL.

Knudson, Ruthann
1983 *Organizational Variability in Late Paleo-Indian Assemblages.* Reports of Investigations, Washington State University Laboratory of Anthropology, Pullman.

Koch, Amy, James C. Miller, Michael Glascock, and Robert J. Hoard
1996 *Geoarchaeological Investigations at the Lyman Site (25SF53) and Other Cultural Resources Related to Table Mountain Quarry near the Nebraska/Wyoming Border.* Nebraska State Historical Society, Lincoln.

Kohntopp, Steve W.
2010 *The Simon Clovis Cache: One of the Oldest Archaeological Sites in Idaho.* Center for the Study of the First Americans, Department of Anthropology, Texas A&M University, College Station.

Konert, Martin, and Jef Vandenberghe
1997 Comparison of Laser Grain Size Analysis with Pipette and Sieve Analysis: A Solution for the Underestimation of the Clay Fraction. *Sedimentology* 44:523–535.

Kornfeld, Marcel, Kaoru Akoshima, and George C. Frison
1990 Stone Tool Caching on the North American Plains: Implications of the McKean Site Tool Kit. *Journal of Field Archaeology* 17:301–309.

Kuhn, Steven L.
1994 A Formal Approach to the Design and Assembly of Mobile Toolkits. *American Antiquity* 59:426–442.
1996 The Trouble with Ham Steaks: A Reply to Morrow. *American Antiquity* 61:591–595.

Kuhn, Steven L., and Mary C. Stiner
2006 What's a Mother to Do? Division of Labor among Neanderthals and Modern Humans in Eurasia. *Current Anthropology* 47:953–980.

Lahren, Larry A.
2001 The On-Going Odyssey of the Anzick Clovis Burial in Park County, Montana (24PA506): Part I. *Archaeology in Montana* 42:55–59.

Lahren, Larry A., and Robson Bonnichsen
1974 Bone Foreshafts from a Clovis Burial in Southwestern Montana. *Science* 186:147–150.

Larson, Mary Lou
1994 Toward a Holistic Analysis of Chipped Stone Assemblages. In *The Organization of North American Stone Tool Technology*, edited by P. J. Carr, pp. 57–69. Archaeological Series 7. International Monographs in Prehistory, Ann Arbor, MI.

Larson, Mary Lou, and Marcel Kornfeld
1997 Chipped Stone Nodules: Theory, Method, and Examples. *Lithic Technology* 22:4–18.

Leavitt, Steven W., Ronald F. Follett, John M. Kimble, and Elizabeth G. Pruessner
2007 Radiocarbon and $\delta^{13}C$ Depth Profiles of Soil Organic Carbon in the U.S. Great Plains: A Possible Spatial Record of Paleoenvironment and Paleovegetation. *Quaternary International* 162–163:21–34.

Lee, Richard B.
1990 Primitive Communism and the Origin of Social Inequality. In *The Evolution of Political Systems: Sociopolitics in Small-Scale Sedentary Societies*, edited by Steadman Upham, pp. 225–246. Cambridge University Press, New York.

Leonhardy, Frank C.
1966 *Domebo: A Paleo-Indian Mammoth Kill in the Prairie Plains*. Contributions of the Museum of the Great Plains, Lawton, OK.

Lepper, Bradley T., and Robert E. Funk
2006 Paleo-Indian: East. In *Environment, Origins, and Population*, edited by Dennis Stanford, Bruce D. Smith, Douglas H. Ubelaker, and Emoke J. E. Szathmary, pp. 171–193. Handbook of North American Indians, Vol. 3, William C. Sturtevant, general editor, Smithsonian Institution, Washington, D.C.

LeTourneau, Philippe D.
2000 Folsom Toolstone Procurement in the Southwest and Southern Plains. Unpublished PhD dissertation, Department of Anthropology, University of New Mexico, Albuquerque.

Levi-Sala, Irene
1986 Use-Wear and Post-Depositional Surface Modification: A Word of Caution. *Journal of Archaeological Science* 13:229–244.

Levy, Janet E.
1982 *Social and Religious Organization in Bronze Age Denmark: An Analysis of Ritual Hoard Finds*. BAR International Series 124. British Archaeological Reports, Oxford.

Lewis, Thomas M. N., and Madeline Kneberg
1958 *Tribes That Slumber: Indian Times in the Tennessee Region*. University of Tennessee Press, Knoxville.

Lewis, Thomas M. N., and Madeline Kneberg Lewis
1961 *Eva: An Archaic Site*. University of Tennessee Press, Knoxville.

Loebel, Thomas J.
2005 The Organization of Early Paleoindian Economies in the Western Great Lakes. Unpublished PhD dissertation, Department of Anthropology, University of Illinois–Chicago.

Loendorf, Lawrence L., David D. Kuehn, and Nels F. Forsman
1984 Rainy Buttes Silicified Wood: A Source of Lithic Raw Material in Western North Dakota. *Plains Anthropologist* 29:335–338.

Logan, Wilfred D.
1976 *Woodland Complexes in Northeastern Iowa*. Publications in Archaeology 15. U.S. Department of the Interior, National Park Service, Washington, D.C.

Lohse, Jon C.
2010 Evidence for Learning and Skill Transmission in Clovis Blade Production and Core Maintenance. In *Clovis Technology*, edited by Bruce A. Bradley, Michael B. Collins, and C. Andrew Hemmings, pp. 157–177. Archaeological Series 17. International Monographs in Prehistory, Ann Arbor, MI.
2011 Step by Step: The Influence of Reduction Sequence Models on Understanding Learning and Skill Transmission. *Lithic Technology* 36:97–108.

Long, Charles A., and Christopher J. Yahnke
2011 End of the Pleistocene: Elk-Moose (*Cervalces*) and Caribou (*Rangifer*) in Wisconsin. *Journal of Mammalogy* 92:1127–1135.

Lothrop, Jonathan C.
1989 The Organization of Paleoindian Lithic Technology at the Potts Site. In *Eastern Paleoindian Lithic Resource Use*, edited by C. J. Ellis and J. C. Lothrop, pp. 99–137. Westview Press, Boulder, CO.

Lundelius, Ernest L., Jr.
1989 The Implications of Disharmonious Assemblages for Pleistocene Extinctions. *Journal of Archaeological Science* 16:407–417.

Lyman, R. Lee, Michael J. O'Brien, and Virgil Hayes
1998 A Mechanical and Functional Study of Bone Rods from the Richey-Roberts Clovis Cache, Washington, U.S.A. *Journal of Archaeological Science* 25:887–906.

MacDonald, Douglas H.
1999 Subsistence, Sex, and Cultural Transmission in Folsom Culture. *Journal of Anthropological Archaeology* 17:217–239.

MacDonald, George F.
1968 *Debert: A Palaeo-Indian Site in Central Nova Scotia.*

Anthropology Papers No. 16. National Museums of Canada, Ottawa, Ontario.

McDonald, Jerry N.

1981 *North American Bison: Their Classification and Evolution.* University of California Press, Berkeley.

McKee, Richard

1964 Flint Cache Discovery. *Oklahoma Anthropological Society Newsletter* 12:3–4.

Magilligan, Frank J.

1992 Sedimentology of a Fine-Grained Aggrading Floodplain. *Geomorphology* 4:393–408.

Malinowski, Bronislaw

1922 *Argonauts of the Western Pacific.* George Routledge and Sons, London.

Mallouf, Robert J.

1994 Sailor-Helton: A Paleoindian Cache from Northwestern Kansas. *Current Research in the Pleistocene* 11:44–46.

Mandel, Rolfe D.

2008 Buried Paleoindian-Age Landscapes in Stream Valleys of the Central Plains, USA. *Geomorphology* 101:342–361.

Mandel, Rolfe D., Jack L. Hofman, Steven R. Holen, and Jeannette M. Blackmar

2004 Buried Paleo-Indian Landscapes and Sites on the High Plains of Northwestern Kansas. *Geological Society of America Field Guide* 5:69–88.

Marlowe, Frank W.

2010 *The Hadza: Hunter-Gatherers of Tanzania.* University of California Press, Berkeley.

Martin, Larry D., and A. M. Neuner

1978 The End of the Pleistocene in North America. *Transactions of the Nebraska Academy of Sciences* 6:117–125.

Martin, Paul S.

1984 Prehistoric Overkill: The Global Model. In *Quaternary Extinctions: A Prehistoric Revolution*, edited by Paul S. Martin and R. G. Klein, pp. 354–402. University of Arizona Press, Tucson.

Martin, Paul S., Robert S. Thompson, and Austin Long

1985 Shasta Ground Sloth Extinction: A Test of the Blitzkrieg Model. In *Environments and Extinctions: Man in Late Glacial North America*, edited by J. I. Mead and D. J. Meltzer, pp. 5–14. Peopling of the Americas Publication. University of Maine, Orono.

Mason, Joseph A., Xiaodong Miao, Paul R. Hanson, William C. Johnson, Peter M. Jacobs, and Ronald J. Goble

2008 Loess Record of the Pleistocene-Holocene Transition on the Northern and Central Great Plains, USA. *Quaternary Science Reviews* 27:1172–1783.

Mason, Ronald J.

1962 The Paleo-Indian Tradition in Eastern North America. *Current Anthropology* 3:227–278.

May, David W.

2005 Geoarchaeology of the Arikaree River Basin. In *The Arikaree River Survey: Class III Survey of 3500 Acres in Kit Carson, Lincoln, and Yuma Counties, Colorado*, edited by M. P. Muñiz, S. R. Holen, and D. W. May, pp. 93–116. Denver Museum of Nature & Science Technical Report 2005-02.

Mehringer, Peter J., Jr.

1988 Weapons of Ancient Americans. *National Geographic* 174:500–503.

Mehringer, Peter J., Jr., and Franklin F. Foit

1990 Volcanic Ash Dating of the Clovis Cache at East Wenatchee, Washington. *National Geographic Research Reports* 6:495–503.

Meltzer, David J.

1984 On Stone Procurement and Settlement Mobility in Eastern Fluted Point Groups. *North American Archaeologist* 6:1–24.

1989 Was Stone Exchanged Among Eastern North American Paleoindians? In *Eastern Paleoindian Lithic Resource Use*, edited by C. J. Ellis and J. C. Lothrop, pp. 11–39. Westview Press, Boulder, CO.

1993 Is There a Clovis Adaptation? In *From Kostenki to Clovis: Upper Paleolithic—Paleo-Indian Adaptations*, edited by O. Soffer and N. D. Praslov, pp. 293–310. Plenum Press, New York.

2002 What Do You Do When No One's Been There Before? Thoughts on the Exploration and Colonization of New Lands. In *The First Americans: The Pleistocene Colonization of the New World*, edited by Nina G. Jablonski, pp. 27–58. Memoirs No. 27. California Academy of Sciences, San Francisco.

2003a Lessons in Landscape Learning. In *Colonization of Unfamiliar Landscapes: The Archaeology of Adaptation*, edited by Marcy Rockman and James Steele, pp. 222–241. Routledge, New York.

2003b Peopling of North America. *Developments in Quaternary Science* 1:539–563.

2004 Modeling the Initial Colonization of the Americas: Issues of Scale, Demography, and Landscape Learning. In *The Settlement of the American Continents*, edited by C. Michael Barton, Geoffrey A. Clark, David R. Yesner, and Georges A. Pearson, pp. 123–137. University of Arizona Press, Tucson.

2006 *Folsom: New Archaeological Investigations of a Classic Paleoindian Bison Kill.* University of California, Berkeley.

2009 *First Peoples in a New World: Colonizing Ice Age America.* University of California Press, Berkeley.

Meltzer, David J., Donald K. Grayson, Gerardo Ardila, Alex W. Barker, Dena F. Dincauze, C. Vance Haynes Jr., Francisco Mena, Lautaro Nunez, and Dennis J. Stanford

1997 On the Pleistocene Antiquity of Monte Verde, Southern Chile. *American Antiquity* 62:659–663.

Meltzer, David J., and Jim I. Mead

1983 The Timing of Late Pleistocene Extinctions in North America. *Quaternary Research* 19:130–135.

Miller, D. Shane, and Ashley M. Smallwood

2009 Paleoindian Settlement in the American Southeast: A GIS-Based Approach to Identify Potential Aggregation Loci. Paper presented at the 74th Annual Meeting of the Society for American Archaeology, Atlanta.

Miller, James C.

1991 Lithic Resources. In *Prehistoric Hunters of the High Plains*, 2nd ed., edited by G. C. Frison, pp. 449–478. Academic Press, New York.

2010 Lithic Resources. In *Prehistoric Hunter-Gatherers of the High Plains and Rockies*, 3rd ed., edited by Marcel Kornfeld, George C. Frison, and Mary Lou Larson, pp. 553–598. Left Coast Press, Walnut Creek, CA.

Miller, Kevin A.

1993 A Study of Prehistoric Biface Caches from Texas. Unpublished master's thesis, Department of Anthropology, University of Texas, Austin.

Miller, Mark E., Michael D. Stafford, and George W. Brox

1991 The John Gale Site Biface Cache. *Plains Anthropologist* 36:43–56.

Minc, Leah D.

1986 Scarcity and Survival: The Role of Oral Tradition in Mediating Subsistence Crises. *Journal of Anthropological Archaeology* 5:39–113.

Montet-White, Anta

1968 *The Lithic Industries of the Illinois Valley in the Early and Middle Woodland Period.* Anthropological Papers No. 35. Museum of Anthropology, University of Michigan, Ann Arbor.

Montgomery, John, and Joanne Dickenson

1992a Additional Blades from Blackwater Draw Locality No. 1, Portales, New Mexico. *Current Research in the Pleistocene* 9:32–33.

1992b Five More Llano Complex Blades at Blackwater Draw Locality No. 1, Portales, New Mexico. Paper presented at the 50th Annual Plains Anthropological Conference, Lincoln, NE.

Morris, Elizabeth Ann, and Richard C. Blakeslee

1987 Comment on the Paleoindian Occurrence of Spurred End Scrapers as Reported by Rogers. *American Antiquity* 52:830–831.

Morrow, Juliet E., and Toby A. Morrow

1999 Geographic Variation in Fluted Projectile Points: A Hemispheric Perspective. *American Antiquity* 64:215–230.

2002 Rummells-Maske Revisited: A Fluted Point Cache from East Central Iowa. *Plains Anthropologist* 47:307–321.

Morrow, Toby A.

1994 A Key to the Identification of Chipped-Stone Raw Materials Found on Archaeological Sites in Iowa. *Journal of the Iowa Archaeological Society* 41:108–129.

1996 Bigger Is Better: Comments on Kuhn's Formal Approach to Mobile Tool Kits. *American Antiquity* 61:581–590.

Morrow, Toby A., and Juliet E. Morrow

1994 A Preliminary Survey of Iowa Fluted Points. *Current Research in the Pleistocene* 11:47–48.

Morse, Dan F.

1997 *Sloan: A Paleoindian Dalton Cemetery in Arkansas.* Smithsonian Institution Press, Washington, D.C.

Morse, Dan. F., Phyllis A. Morse, Robert C. Mainfort Jr., Jami J. Lockhart, and Glen Akridge

1997 Provenience of the Artifacts. In *Sloan: A Paleoindian Dalton Cemetery in Arkansas*, edited by Dan F. Morse, pp. 72–95. Smithsonian Institution Press, Washington, D.C.

Muñiz, Mark P.

2004 Exploring Technological Organization and Burial Practices at the Paleoindian Gordon Creek Site (5LR99), Colorado. *Plains Anthropologist* 49:253–279.

2005 The Cody Complex Revisited: Landscape Use and Technological Organization on the Northwestern Plains. Unpublished PhD dissertation, Department of Anthropology, University of Colorado, Boulder.

2009 Microwear, Typology, and the Cody Component. In *Hell Gap: A Stratified Paleoindian Camp Site at the Edge of the Rockies*, edited by Mary Lou Larson, Marcel Kornfeld, and George C. Frison, pp. 195–215. University of Utah Press, Salt Lake City.

2013 Managing Risk on the Western Plains During the Cody Complex. In *Paleoindian Lifeways of the Cody Complex*, edited by Edward J. Knell and Mark P. Muñiz, pp. 269–289. University of Utah Press, Salt Lake City.

Muñiz, Mark P., and Steven R. Holen

2005 *The Arikaree River Survey: Class III Survey of 3500 Acres in Kit Carson, Lincoln, and Yuma Counties, Colorado.* Denver Museum of Nature & Science Technical Report 2005-02.

Murray, Andrew S., J. M. Olley, and G. G. Caitcheon

1995 Measurement of Equivalent Doses in Quartz from Contemporary Water-Lain Sediments Using Optically Stimulated Luminescence. *Quaternary Science Reviews* 14:365–371.

Murray, Andrew S., and Ann G. Wintle

2003 The Single Aliquot Regenerative Dose Protocol: Potential for Improvements in Reliability. *Radiation Measurements* 37:377–381.

Muto, Guy R.

1971 A Stage Analysis of the Manufacture of Chipped Stone Implements. In *Great Basin Anthropological Conference 1970: Selected Papers*, edited by C. Melvin Aikens. University of Oregon Anthropological Papers No. 1, Eugene.

Myers, Thomas P.

1987 Preliminary Study of the Distribution of Fluted Points in Nebraska. *Current Research in the Pleistocene* 4:67–68.

Nelson, Margaret C.

1991 The Study of Technological Organization. In *Advances in Archaeological Method and Theory*, Vol. 3, edited by

Michael B. Schiffer, pp. 57–100. University of Arizona Press, Tucson.

Nelson, Richard K.

1969 *Hunters of the Northern Ice.* University of Chicago Press, Chicago, IL.

Newcomer, Mark

1976 Spontaneous Retouch. In Second International Symposium on Flint. *Staringia* 3:62–64.

Nowak, Timothy R., L. Adrian Hannus, John M. Butterbrodt, Edward J. Lueck, and R. Peter Winham

1982 *Survey and Testing at West Horse Creek Quarry Site, 39SH37.* Archaeology Laboratory, Augustana College, Sioux Falls, SD.

1984 *White River Badlands Regional Research Project Report, Volume 2: 1981 and 1982 Survey and Testing at West Horse Creek Quarry, Site 39SH37.* Archaeology Laboratory of the Center for Western Studies, Augustana College, Sioux Falls, South Dakota. Submitted to the Historical Preservation Center, Office of Cultural Preservation, Vermillion, SD.

O'Brien, Patricia J.

1984 The Tim Adrien Site (14NT604): A Hell Gap Quarry Site in Norton County, Kansas. *Plains Anthropologist* 29:41–55.

Odell, George H.

1981 The Morphological Express at Function Junction: Searching for Meaning in Lithic Tool Types. *Journal of Anthropological Research* 37:319–342.

Owsley, Douglas W., and David R. Hunt

2001 Clovis and Early Archaic Crania from the Anzick Site (24PA506), Park County, Montana. *Plains Anthropologist* 46:115–121.

Patten, Bob

n.d. Unpublished Watts Clovis cache report. Electronic document, http://stonedagger.com/SDPcaches.html#Watts, accessed June 18, 2011.

2005 *Peoples of the Flute: A Study in Anthropolithic Forensics.* Stone Dagger Publications, Denver, CO.

Pearson, Georges A., and Joshua W. Ream

2005 Clovis on the Caribbean Coast of Venezuela. *Current Research in the Pleistocene* 22:28–31.

Pelegrin, Jacques

1990 Prehistoric Lithic Technology: Some Aspects of Research. *Archaeological Review Cambridge* 9:116–125.

Pettipas, Leo

2011 "An Environmental and Cultural History of the Central Lake Agassiz Region, with Special Reference to Southwestern Manitoba." Special issue, *Manitoba Archaeological Journal* 21(1 & 2). Manitoba Archaeological Society.

Petraglia, Michael D.

1992 Stone Artifact Refitting and Formation Processes at the Abri Defaure, an Upper Paleolithic Site in Southwest France. In *Piecing Together the Past: Applications of Refitting Studies in Archaeology,* edited by Jack L. Hofman and James G. Enloe, pp. 163–178. BAR International Series 578. British Archaeological Reports, Oxford.

Prasciunas, Mary M.

2008 Clovis First? An Analysis of Space, Time, and Technology. Unpublished PhD dissertation, Department of Anthropology, University of Wyoming, Laramie.

2011 Mapping Clovis: Projectile Points, Behavior and Bias. *American Antiquity* 76:106–126.

Prasciunas, Mary M., and Todd A. Surovell

In press Reevaluating the Duration of Clovis: The Problem of Non-Representative Radiocarbon Dates. In *Clovis: Current Perspectives on Technology, Chronology, and Adaptations,* edited by Ashley Smallwood and Thomas Jennings. Center for the Study of the First Americans and Texas A&M University Press, College Station.

Prescott, John R., and John T. Hutton

1994 Cosmic-Ray Contributions to Dose-Rates for Luminescence and ESR Dating: Large Depths and Long-Term Time Variations. *Radiation Measurements* 23:497–500.

Preston, Douglas

1999 Woody's Dream. *New Yorker.* November 15:80–87.

Prior, Jean C.

1991 *Landforms of Iowa.* University of Iowa Press, Iowa City.

Puseman, Kathryn

2004 *Protein Residue Analysis of a Plainview Projectile Point from Site 34BV177, Oklahoma.* Paleo Research Institute Technical Report 04-23, on file at the Oklahoma Archeological Survey, Norman.

2006 *Protein Residue Analysis of Artifacts from the Bull Creek Cache, Site 34BV180, Oklahoma.* Paleo Research Institute Technical Report 06-23, on file at the Oklahoma Archeological Survey, Norman.

Ray, Jack H.

2007 *Ozarks Chipped-Stone Resources: A Guide to Identification, Distribution, and Prehistoric Use of Cherts and Other Siliceous Raw Material.* Missouri Archaeological Society, Springfield.

Reher, Charles A.

1991 Large Scale Quarries and Regional Transport Systems on the High Plains of Eastern Wyoming: Spanish Diggings Revisited. In *Raw Material Economies Among Prehistoric Hunter-Gatherers,* edited by A. Montet-White and S. R. Holen, pp. 251–284. University of Kansas Publications in Anthropology 19. University of Kansas, Lawrence.

Reid, Kenneth C.

1980 Upper Pennsylvanian Cherts of the Forest City Basin: Missourian Stage. *Plains Anthropologist* 25:121–134.

Reimer, Paula J., Mike G. L. Baillie, Edouard Bard, Alex Bayliss, J. Warren Beck, Chanda J. H. Bertrand, Paul G. Blackwell, Caitlin E. Buck, George S. Burr, Kristen B. Cutler, Paul E. Damon, R. Lawrence Edwards, Richard G. Fairbanks,

Michael Friedrich, Thomas P. Guilderson, Alan G. Hogg, Konrad A. Hughen, Bernd Kromer, Gerry McCormac, Stuart Manning, Christopher Bronk Ramsey, Ron W. Reimer, Sabine Remmele, John R. Southon, Minze Stuiver, Sahra Talamo, F. W. Taylor, Johannes van der Plicht, and Constanze E. Weyhenmeyer

2004 Intcal04 Terrestrial Radiocarbon Age Calibration, 0–26 Cal Kyr BP/UC. *Radiocarbon* 46:1029–1058.

Reynolds, John D.

1990 Ceremonial Bifaces from the Whiteford Archaeological Site, 14SA1. *Kansas Anthropologist* 11:6–20.

Roberts, Frank H. H., Jr.

1942 *Archeological and Geological Investigations in the San Jon District, Eastern New Mexico.* Smithsonian Miscellaneous Collections 103 (4). Smithsonian Institution, Washington, D.C.

Robinson, Brian S., Jennifer C. Ort, William A. Eldridge, Adrian L. Burke, and Bertrand G. Pelletier

2009 Paleoindian Aggregation and Social Context at Bull Brook. *American Antiquity* 74:423–447.

Rogers, Richard A.

1986 Spurred End Scrapers as Diagnostic Paleoindian Artifacts: A Distributional Analysis on Stream Terraces. *American Antiquity* 51:338–341.

Root, Matthew J.

1993 *Site 32DU955A: Folsom Occupation of the Knife River Flint Primary Source Area.* Project Report Number 22. Center for Northwest Anthropology, Department of Anthropology, Washington State University, Pullman.

2000 *The Archaeology of the Bobtail Wolf Site.* Washington State University Press, Pullman.

Root, Matthew J., Jerry D. Williams, Marvin Kay, and Lisa K. Shifrin

1999 Folsom Ultrathin Biface and Radial Break Tools in the Knife River Flint Quarry Area. In *Folsom Lithic Technology: Explorations in Structure and Variation*, edited by Daniel S. Amick, pp. 144–168. Archaeological Series 12. International Monographs in Prehistory, Ann Arbor, MI.

Roper, Donna C.

1991a Comparison of Contexts of Red Ochre Use in Paleoindian and Upper Paleolithic Sites. *North American Archaeologist* 12:289–301.

1999 Identifying Clovis Sites by Blade Technology: A Cautionary Note. *Current Research in the Pleistocene* 16:69–71.

Salisbury, Neil E., James C. Knox, and Richard A. Stephenson

1968 *The Valleys of Iowa—1: Valley Width and Stream Discharge Relationships in the Major Streams.* Iowa State Water Resources Research Institute, Ames.

Sanders, Thomas Nolan

1990 *Adams: The Manufacture of Flaked Stone Tools at a Paleoindian Site in Western Kentucky.* Persimmon Press, Buffalo, NY.

Santarone, Paul

2006 A New Look at the Simon Cache. Paper presented at the 64th Plains Anthropological Conference, Topeka, KS.

2007 The Simon Clovis Cache: History, Technology, Habits and Expert Artisans. Unpublished master's thesis, Department of Anthropology, Idaho State University, Pocatello.

Sargeant, B. L., J. Mann, P. Berggren, and M. Krützen

2005 Specialization and Development of Beach Hunting, a Rare Foraging Behavior, by Wild Bottlenose Dolphins (*Tursiops* sp.). *Canadian Journal of Zoology* 83:1400–1410.

Saucier, Roger T.

1997 Late Quaternary Geologic History of the Western Lowlands. In *Sloan: A Paleoindian Dalton Cemetery in Arkansas*, edited by Dan F. Morse, pp. 96–102. Smithsonian Institution Press, Washington, D.C.

Saunders, Jeffrey J.

1992 Blackwater Draw: Mammoths and Mammoth Hunters in the Terminal Pleistocene. In *Proboscidean and Paleoindian Interactions*, edited by John W. Fox, Calvin B. Smith, and Kenneth T. Wilkins, pp. 123–148. Baylor University Press, Waco, TX.

2007 Processing Marks on Remains of *Mammuthus columbi* from the Dent Site, Colorado, in Light of Those from Clovis, New Mexico: Fresh-Carcass Butchery Versus Scavenging? In *Frontiers in Colorado Paleoindian Archaeology*, edited by R. H. Brunswig and B. L. Pitblado, pp. 155–184. University Press of Colorado, Boulder.

Saunders, Jeffrey J., Eric C. Grimm, Christopher C. Widga, G. Dennis Campbell, B. Brandon Curry, David A. Grimley, Paul R. Hanson, Judd P. McCullum, James S. Oliver, and Janis D. Treworgy

2010 Paradigms and Proboscideans in the Southern Great Lakes Region, USA. *Quaternary International* 217:175–187.

Schaetzl, Randall J., and Steven L. Forman

2008 OSL Ages on Glaciofluvial Sediment in Northern Lower Michigan Constrain Expansion of the Laurentide Ice Sheet. *Quaternary Research* 70:81–90.

Schiffer, Michael B.

1987 *Formation Processes in the Archaeological Record.* University of New Mexico Press, Albuquerque.

Schlanger, Sarah H.

1981 Tool Caching Behavior and the Archaeological Record. Paper presented at the 46th Annual Meeting of the Society for American Archaeology, San Diego.

Schmits, Larry J.

1987 The Diskau Site: A Paleoindian Occupation in Northeast Kansas. *Current Research in the Pleistocene* 4:69–70.

Schmits, Larry J., and Ed J. Kost

1985 The Diskau Site: A Paleo-Indian Clovis Occupation in Northeast Kansas. Paper Presented at the 43rd Plains Anthropological Conference, Iowa City.

Schultz, C. Bertrand, and Larry D. Martin

1970 Quaternary Mammalian Sequence in the Central Great Plains. In *Pleistocene and Recent Environments of the Central Great Plains*, edited by Wakefield Dort Jr. and J. Knox Jones Jr., pp. 341–353. University Press of Kansas, Lawrence.

Seeman, Mark F.

1985 Craft Specialization and Tool Kit Structure: A Systemic Perspective on the Midcontinental Flint Knapper. In *Lithic Resource Procurement: Proceedings from the Second Conference on Prehistoric Chert Exploitation*, edited by Susan C. Vehik, pp. 7–36. Center for Archaeological Investigations, Southern Illinois University, Carbondale.

Sellet, Frédéric

2004 Beyond the Point: Projectile Manufacture and Behavioral Inference. *Journal of Archaeological Science* 31:1553–1566.

2006 Two Steps Forward, One Step Back: The Inference of Mobility Patterns from Stone Tools. In *Archaeology and Ethnoarchaeology of Mobility*, edited by Frédéric Sellet, Russell Greaves, and Pei-Lin Yi, pp. 221–239. University Press of Florida, Tallahassee.

Semken, Holmes A., Jr., and Carl R. Falk

1987 Late Pleistocene/Holocene Mammalian Faunas and Environmental Changes on the Northern Plains of the United States. In *Late Quaternary Mammalian Biogeography and Environments of the Great Plains and Prairies*, edited by Russell W. Graham, Holmes A. Semken Jr., and Martha A. Graham, pp. 176–313. Scientific Papers Vol. 22. Illinois State Museum, Springfield.

Service, Elman R.

1962 *Primitive Social Organization: An Evolutionary Perspective*. Random House, New York.

Shott, Michael J.

1989 Technological Organization in Great Lakes Paleoindian Assemblages. In *Eastern Paleoindian Lithic Resource Use*, edited by C. J. Ellis and J. C. Lothrop, pp. 221–237. Westview Press, Boulder, CO.

1996 Stage Versus Continuum in the Debris Assemblage from Production of a Fluted Biface. *Lithic Technology* 21:6–22.

2002 Sample Bias in the Distribution and Abundance of Midwestern Fluted Bifaces. *Midcontinental Journal of Archaeology* 27:89–123.

Shott, Michael J., and Jesse A. M. Ballenger

2007 Biface Reduction and the Measurement of Dalton Curation: A Southeastern United States Case Study. *American Antiquity* 72:153–175.

Simons, Donald B.

1997 The Gainey and Butler Sites as Focal Points for Caribou and People. In *Caribou and Reindeer Hunters of the Northern Hemisphere*, edited by L. Jackson and P. Thacker, pp. 105–131. Avebury, Aldershot, UK.

Smallwood, Ashley M.

2012 Clovis Technology and Settlement in the American Southeast: Using Biface Analysis to Evaluate Dispersal Models. *American Antiquity* 77:689–713.

Smith, Adam

1970 [1776] *The Wealth of Nations*. Bks. 1–3. Penguin Books, New York.

Smith, Melinda D., and Alan K. Knapp

1999 Exotic Plant Species in a C_4-Dominated Grassland: Invasibility, Disturbance, and Community Structure. *Oecologia* 120:605–612.

Snow, Dean R.

1980 *The Archaeology of New England*. Academic Press, New York.

Soffer, Olga

1985 Patterns of Intensification as Seen from the Upper Paleolithic of the Central Russian Plain. In *Prehistoric Hunter-Gatherers: The Emergence of Cultural Complexity*, edited by T. Douglas Price and James A. Brown, pp. 235–270. Academic Press, New York.

Spiess, Arthur S., and Deborah B. Wilson

1989 Paleoindian Lithic Distribution in the New England-Maritimes Region. In *Eastern Paleoindian Lithic Resource Use*, edited by C. J. Ellis and J. C. Lothrop, pp. 75–97. Westview Press, Boulder, CO.

Spiess, Arthur S., Deborah B. Wilson, and James Bradley

1998 Paleoindian Occupation of the New England-Maritimes Region: Beyond Cultural Ecology. *Archaeology of Eastern North America* 26:201–264.

Stanford, Dennis J.

1979 The Dutton and Selby Sites: Evidence for a Possible Pre-Clovis Occupation on the High Plains. In *Pre-Llano Cultures of the Americas: Paradoxes and Possibilities*, edited by R. L. Humphrey and D. Stanford, pp. 101–123. Anthropological Society of Washington, Washington, D.C.

1991 Clovis Origins and Adaptations: An Introductory Perspective. In *Clovis: Origins and Adaptations*, edited by R. Bonnichsen and K. L. Turnmire, pp. 1–14. Center for the Study of the First Americans, Oregon State University, Corvallis.

1997 The Drake Cache: A Clovis Site from North Central Colorado. In *The Paleoindians of the North American Midcontinent*, edited by A. Montet-White, pp. 36–39. Musée Départemental de Préhistoire de Solutré, France.

1999 Paleoindian Archaeology and Late Pleistocene Environments in the Plains and Southwestern United States. In *Ice Age People of North America: Environments, Origins, and Adaptations*, edited by R. Bonnichsen and K. L. Turnmire, pp. 281–339. Oregon State University Press, Corvallis.

Stanford, Dennis J., and John Albanese

1975 Preliminary Results of the Smithsonian Institution Excavation at the Claypool Site, Washington County, Colorado. *Southwestern Lore* 41:22–28.

Stanford, Dennis J., and Bruce A. Bradley

2002 Oceans and Prairie Paths? Thoughts about Clovis Origins. In *The First Americans: The Pleistocene Colonization of the New World*, edited by Nina G. Jablonski, pp. 255–271.

Memoirs No. 27. California Academy of Sciences, San Francisco.

2004 The North Atlantic Ice-Edge Corridor: A Possible Paleolithic Route to the New World. *World Archaeology* 36:459–478.

2012 *Across Atlantic Ice: The Origin of America's Clovis Culture.* University of California Press, Berkeley.

Stanford, Dennis J., and R. W. Graham

1985 Archaeological Investigations of the Selby and Dutton Mammoth Kill Sites, Yuma, Colorado. *National Geographic Research Reports* 19:519–541.

Stanford, Dennis J., and Margaret A. Jodry

1988 The Drake Clovis Cache. *Current Research in the Pleistocene* 5:21–22.

Steinacher, Terry L., and Gayle F. Carlson

1998 The Central Plains Tradition. In *Archaeology on the Great Plains*, edited by W. R. Wood, pp. 235–268. University Press of Kansas, Lawrence.

Stoltman, James B.

1971 Prismatic Blades from Northern Minnesota. *Plains Anthropologist* 16:105–109.

Storck, Peter L., and Peter H. von Bitter

1989 The Geological Age and Occurrence of Fossil Hill Formation Chert: Implications for Early Paleoindian Settlement Patterns. In *Eastern Paleoindian Lithic Resource Use*, edited by C. J. Ellis and J. C. Lothrop, pp. 165–189. Westview Press, Boulder, CO.

Straus, Lawrence, David J. Meltzer, and Ted Goebel

2005 Ice Age Atlantis: Exploring the Solutrean-Clovis "Connection." *World Archaeology* 37:507–532.

Surovell, Todd A.

2000 Early Paleoindian Women, Children, Mobility, and Fertility. *American Antiquity* 65:493–508.

Surovell, Todd A., and Nicole M. Waguespack

2008 How Many Elephant Kills Are 14? Clovis Mammoth and Mastodon Kills in Context. *Quaternary International* 191:82–97.

Swanson, Earl H., Douglas Bucy, Carla Bucy, and C. Vance Haynes Jr.

n.d. A Geological Association for the Simon Clovis Site Artifacts. Unpublished manuscript on file at the Idaho Museum of Natural History, Pocatello.

Tankersley, Kenneth B.

1989 A Close Look at the Big Picture: Early Paleoindian Lithic Resource Procurement in the Midwestern United States. In *Eastern Paleoindian Lithic Resource Use*, edited by C. J. Ellis and J. C. Lothrop, pp. 259–291. Westview Press, Boulder, CO.

1995 Paleoindian Contexts and Artifact Distribution Patterns at the Bostrom Site, St. Clair County, Illinois. *Midcontinental Journal of Archaeology* 20:40–61.

1998 The Crook County Clovis Cache. *Current Research in the Pleistocene* 15:86–88.

2002 *In Search of Ice Age Americans.* Gibb Smith, Salt Lake City.

Tankersley, Kenneth B., and Juliet E. Morrow

1993 Clovis Procurement and Land Use Patterns in the Confluence Region of the Mississippi, Missouri, and Illinois Rivers. In *Highways to the Past*, edited by T. E. Emerson, A. C. Fortier, and D. L. McElrath, pp. 119–129. Center for American Archaeology, Kampsville, IL.

Taylor, D. C.

1969 The Wilsall Excavations: An Exercise in Frustration. *Proceedings of the Montana Academy of Science* 29:147–150.

Taylor, R. Ervin, C. Vance Haynes Jr., and Minze Stuiver

1996 Clovis and Folsom Age Estimates: Stratigraphic Context and Radiocarbon Calibration. *Antiquity* 70:515–525.

Thomas, David Hurst

1985 *The Archaeology of Hidden Cave, Nevada.* Anthropological Papers 61, pt. 1. American Museum of Natural History, New York.

Tixier, Jacques

1974 *Glossary for the Description of Stone Tools, with Special Reference to the Epipaleolithic of the Maghreb.* Translated by M. H. Newcomer. Newsletter of Lithic Technology Special Publication No. 1.

Todd, Lawrence C., David J. Rapson, and Jack L. Hofman

1996 Dentition Studies of the Mill Iron and Other Early Paleoindian Bison Bonebed Sites. In *The Mill Iron Site*, edited by G. C. Frison, pp. 145–175. University of New Mexico Press, Albuquerque.

Toth, N.

1991 The Material Record. In *The First Americans: Search and Research*, edited by D. J. Meltzer and T. Dillehay, pp. 53–76. CRC Press, Boca Raton, FL.

Tunnell, Curtis

1978 *The Gibson Lithic Cache from West Texas.* Office of the State Archaeologist, Texas Historical Commission, Austin.

Tuohy, Donald R., and L. Kyle Napton

1986 Duck Decoys from Lovelock Cave, Nevada, Dated by C-14 Accelerator Mass-Spectrometry. *American Antiquity* 51:813–816.

Van Nest, Julieann

1985 Patination of Knife River Flint Artifacts. *Plains Anthropologist* 30:325–339.

van Schaik, Carel P., and Gauri R. Pradhan

2003 A Model for Tool-Use Traditions in Primates: Implications for the Coevolution of Culture and Cognition. *Journal of Human Evolution* 44:645–664.

Vaughan, Patrick C.

1985 *Use-Wear Analysis of Flaked Stone Tools.* University of Arizona Press, Tucson.

Vehik, Susan C.

1984 Late Prehistoric Settlement Strategy and Exploitation of Florence-A Chert. In *Lithic Resource Procurement:*

Proceedings from the Second Conference on Prehistoric Chert Exploitation, edited by S. C. Vehik, pp.81–98. Occasional Papers No. 4. Center for Archaeological Investigations, Southern Illinois University, Carbondale.

Waguespack, Nicole M.

2005 The Organization of Male and Female Labor in Foraging Societies: Implications for Early Paleoindian Archaeology. *American Anthropologist* 107:666–676.

2007 Why We're Still Arguing About the Pleistocene Occupation of the Americas. *Evolutionary Anthropology* 16:63–74.

Waguespack, Nicole M., and Todd A. Surovell

2003 Clovis Hunting Strategies, or How to Make Out on Plentiful Resources. *American Antiquity* 68:333–352.

Walthall, John A., and Brad Koldehoff

1998 Hunter-Gatherer Interaction and Alliance Formation: Dalton and the Cult of the Long Blade. *Plains Anthropologist* 43:257–273.

Waters, Michael R., Steven L. Forman, Thomas A. Jennings, Lee C. Nordt, Steven G. Driese, Joshua M. Feinberg, Joshua L. Keene, Jessi Halligan, Anna Lindquist, James Pierson, Charles T. Hallmark, Michael Collins, and J. Wiederhold

2011 The Buttermilk Creek Complex and the Origins of Clovis at the Debra L. Friedkin Site, Texas. *Science* 331:1599–1603.

Waters, Michael R., Steven L. Forman, Thomas W. Stafford, and John Foss

2009 Geoarchaeological Investigations at the Topper and Big Pine Tree Sites, Allendale County, South Carolina. *Journal of Archaeological Science* 36:1300–1311.

Waters, Michael R., and Thomas Jennings

Forthcoming The Hogeye Clovis Cache, Texas. Texas A&M University Press, College Station.

Waters, Michael R., Charlotte D. Pevny, and David L. Carlson

2011 *Clovis Lithic Technology: Investigation of a Stratified Workshop at the Gault Site, Texas.* Texas A&M University Press, College Station.

Waters, Michael R., and Thomas W. Stafford Jr.

2007 Redefining the Age of Clovis: Implications for the Peopling of the New World. *Science* 315:1122–1126.

Waters, Michael R., Thomas W. Stafford Jr., Brian G. Redmond, and Kenneth B. Tankersley

2009 The Age of the Paleoindian Assemblage at Sheriden Cave, Ohio. *American Antiquity* 74:107–111.

Wedel, Waldo R.

1986 *Central Plains Prehistory.* University of Nebraska Press, Lincoln.

Weedman, Kathryn

2002 On the Spur of the Moment: Effects of Age and Experience on Hafted Stone Scraper Morphology. *American Antiquity* 67:731–744.

Wells, Philip V.

1970 Historical Factors Controlling Vegetation Patterns and Floristic Distributions in the Central Plains Region of North America. In *Pleistocene and Recent Environments of the Central Great Plains*, edited by Wakefield Dort Jr. and J. Knox Jones Jr., pp. 211–221. University Press of Kansas, Lawrence.

White, Todd A., Bruce D. Campbell, Peter D. Kemp, and Chris L. Hunt

2001 Impacts of Extreme Climatic Events on Competition During Grassland Invasions. *Global Change Biology* 7:1–13.

Whittaker, John C.

1994 *Flintknapping: Making and Understanding Stone Tools.* University of Texas Press, Austin.

Wiessner, Polly

1996 Leveling the Hunter: Constraints on the Status Quest in Foraging Societies. In *Food and the Status Quest: An Interdisciplinary Perspective*, edited by Polly Wiessner and Wulf Schienfenhövel, pp. 171–192. Berghahn, Providence, RI.

Wilke, Philip J.

2002 Bifacial Flake-Core Reduction Strategies and Related Aspects of Early Paleoindian Lithic Technology. In *Folsom Technology and Lifeways*, edited by J. E. Clark and M. B. Collins, pp. 345–370. Special Publications No. 4. University of Tulsa, Tulsa, OK.

Wilke, Philip J., Gayle Carlson, and John Reynolds

2002 The Late Prehistoric Percussion Blade Industry of the Central Plains. *Central Plains Archaeology* 9:1–24.

Wilke, Philip J., J. Jeffrey Flenniken, and Terry L. Ozbun

1991 Clovis Technology at the Anzick Site, Montana. *Journal of California and Great Basin Archaeology* 13:242–272.

Wilmsen, Edwin N.

1968 Functional Analysis of Flaked Stone Artifacts. *American Antiquity* 33:156–161.

1973 Interaction, Spacing Behavior, and the Organization of Hunting Bands. *Journal of Anthropological Research* 29:1–31.

Wilmsen, Edwin N., and Frank H. H. Roberts Jr.

1978 *Lindenmeier, 1934–1974, Concluding Report on Investigations.* Smithsonian Contributions to Anthropology No. 24. Washington, D.C: Smithsonian Institution.

Winters, Howard D.

1981 Excavating in Museums: Notes on Mississippian Hoes and Middle Woodland Copper Gouges and Celts. *Annals of the New York Academy of Sciences* 376:17–34.

Wiseman, Regge N., Dorothy Griffiths, and James V. Sciscenti

1994 The Loco Hills Bifacial Core Cache from Southeastern New Mexico. *Plains Anthropologist* 39:63–72.

Wittoft, John

1952 A Paleo-Indian Site in Eastern Pennsylvania: An Early Hunting Culture. *Proceedings of the American Philosophical Society* 96:464–495.

Wolman, M. Gordon, and Luna B. Leopold

1957 *River Flood Plains: Some Observations on Their Formation.* Professional Paper 282-C. U.S. Geological Survey, Denver, CO.

Woods, James C., and Gene L. Titmus

1985 A Review of the Simon Clovis Collection. *Idaho Archaeologist* 8:3–8.

Wormington, Marie

1957 Ancient Man in North America. 4th ed. Denver Museum of Natural History, Popular Series No. 4. Peerless Printing, Denver, CO.

Wright, Herbert E., Jr.

1970 Vegetational History of the Central Great Plains. In *Pleistocene and Recent Environments of the Central Great Plains*, edited by W. Dort Jr. and J. K. Jones Jr., pp. 157–172. University Press of Kansas, Lawrence.

1981 Vegetation East of the Rocky Mountains 18,000 Years Ago. *Quaternary Research* 15:113–125.

Wyckoff, Don G.

1993 Gravel Sources of Knappable Alibates Silicified Dolomite. *Geoarchaeology* 8:35–58.

Yahnig, Carl

2004 Lithic Technology of the Little River Clovis Complex, Christian County, Kentucky. In *New Perspectives on the First Americans*, edited by Bradley T. Lepper and Robson Bonnichsen, pp. 111–117. Center for the Study of the First Americans, Texas A&M University, College Station.

Yohe, Robert M., II, and Douglas B. Bamforth

2013 Late Pleistocene Protein Residues from the Mahaffy Cache, Colorado. *Journal of Archaeological Science* 40:2337–2343.

Young, Bill, and Michael B. Collins

1989 A Cache of Blades with Clovis Affinities from Northeastern Texas. *Current Research in the Pleistocene* 6:26–28.

Zar, Jerrold H.

1999 *Biostatistical Analysis*. 4th ed. Prentice Hall, Upper Saddle River, NJ.

Zier, Christian J., Daniel A. Jepson, Michael McFaul, and William Doering

1993 Archaeology and Geomorphology of the Clovis-Age Klein Site near Kersey, Colorado. *Plains Anthropologist* 38:203–210.

Contributors

Douglas B. Bamforth
Department of Anthropology
University of Colorado
Boulder, CO 80309
bamforth@colorado.edu

Leland C. Bement
Oklahoma Archeological Survey
111 E. Chesapeake, Room 102
University of Oklahoma
Norman, OK 73019
lbement@ou.edu

Michael B. Collins
Texas State University
Department of Anthropology
601 University Drive
San Marcos, TX 78666
Mc82@txstate.edu

Peter C. Condon
Geo-Marine, Inc.
4725 Ripley Drive, Suite A
El Paso, TX 79922
pcondon@geo-marine.com

George Crawford
Blackwater Draw Site
Eastern New Mexico University
Portales, NM 88130
george.crawford@enmu.edu

C. Vance Haynes Jr.
Departments of Anthropology and Geosciences
Emil W. Haury Building
University of Arizona
Tucson, AZ 85721

C. Andrew Hemmings
Archaeological Institute
Mercyhurst College
501 East 38th Street
Erie, PA 16546
chemmings@mercyhurst.edu

Matthew G. Hill
Department of Anthropology
Iowa State University
Ames, IA 50011
mghill@istate.edu

Steven R. Holen
Center for American Paleolithic Research
PO Box 452
Erie, CO 80516
sholen@skybeam.com

Vance T. Holliday
Departments of Anthropology and Geosciences
Emil W. Haury Building
University of Arizona
Tucson, AZ 85721
vthollid@email.arizona.edu

Bruce B. Huckell
Maxwell Museum of Anthropology
Department of Anthropology
MSC 01 1050
University of New Mexico
Albuquerque, NM 87131
bhuckell@unm.edu

J. David Kilby
Department of Anthropology and Applied Archaeology
Eastern New Mexico University
Portales, NM 88130
david.kilby@enmu.edu

Thomas J. Loebel
Illinois State Archaeological Survey
Prairie Research Institute
University of Illinois at Urbana–Champaign
Champaign, IL 61820
tjl2@illinois.edu

Jon C. Lohse
Coastal Environments, Inc.
1260 Main St.
Baton Rouge, LA 78401
jonclohse@gmail.com

David W. May
Department of Geography
University of Northern Iowa
Cedar Falls, IA 50614
dave.may@uni.edu

Mark P. Muñiz
Department of Sociology
and Anthropology
720 Fourth Avenue SE
St. Cloud State University
St. Cloud, MN 56301
mpmuniz@stcloudstate.edu

Jill Onken
Department of Geosciences
Gould-Simpson Building
University of Arizona
Tucson, AZ 85721
jonken@email.arizona.edu

Paul Santarone
Department of Anthropology
University of Wyoming
Laramie, WY
psantaro@wyoming.edu

David M. Yelacic
Center for Archaeological Studies
Texas State University–San Marcos
601 University Drive
San Marcos, TX 78666
dyelacic@txstate.edu

Index

Page numbers in italic text indicate illustrations.